Igor Mel'čuk
Ten Studies in Dependency Syntax

Trends in Linguistics
Studies and Monographs

Editor
Chiara Gianollo
Daniël Van Olmen

Editorial Board
Walter Bisang
Tine Breban
Volker Gast
Hans Henrich Hock
Karen Lahousse
Natalia Levshina
Caterina Mauri
Heiko Narrog
Salvador Pons
Niina Ning Zhang
Amir Zeldes

Editor responsible for this volume
Chiara Gianollo

Volume 347

Igor Mel'čuk
Ten Studies in Dependency Syntax

ISBN 978-3-11-110440-9
e-ISBN (PDF) 978-3-11-069476-5
e-ISBN (EPUB) 978-3-11-069481-9

Library of Congress Control Number: 2020941531

Bibliographic information published by the Deutsche Nationalbibliothek
The Deutsche Nationalbibliothek lists this publication in the Deutsche Nationalbibliografie;
detailed bibliographic data are available on the Internet at http://dnb.dnb.de.

© 2022 Walter de Gruyter GmbH, Berlin/Boston
This volume is text- and page-identical with the hardback published in 2021.
Typesetting: raumfisch.de/sign, Berlin
Printing and binding: CPI books GmbH, Leck

www.degruyter.com

Acknowledgments

> This book would not exist if there were not several extraordinary people who have helped me at different stages of my research.

The first to be named is, of course, Lidija Iordanskaja, my Reader in Residence; she read and reread every piece in the volume many times, from the first sketch to the last proofs.

The second to be named is David Beck, without whose advice, suggestions and corrections—over many years!—I could never have reached the results that I present here. He has been a severe critic and an efficient editor of all my texts.

Then come three colleagues and friends, with whom all my texts were discussed and who hunted down many mistakes and ironed out countless inconsistencies: Jasmina Milićević, Alain Polguère and Elena Savvina.

And finally, Margarita Alonso Ramos, Jurij Apresjan, Igor Boguslavskij, Alexander Grosu, Leonid Iomdin, Sylvain Kahane, François Louis, Sébastien Marengo, Simon Mille, Nikolaj Pertsov, Rafaël Poiret, Leo Wanner and Anton Zimmerling went through different chapters of the volume, helping me with their judicious remarks to significantly improve the presentation. Thanks to the several constructive suggestions by the Anonymous Reviewer (of the Publisher) I was able to better organize the volume.

Chiara Gianollo, Frank Junghanns, Barbara Karlson and Birgit Sievert—the de Gruyter team that worked on this book—pulled off a miracle commensurable with the proverbial transformation of water into wine: they turned my uncouth manuscript into this beautiful volume.

Very special thanks are also due to the people who have offered me their consultations and advice concerning various languages:

Acehnese:	Mark Durie
Amele:	John Roberts
Basque:	Georges Rebuschi
Chinese (Mandarin):	Haitao Liu, Jian-Yun Nie, Ruochen Niu, Rafaël Poiret
English:	David Beck
Georgian:	Zurab Baratashvili
Hindi:	Omkar Koul
Korean:	Chai-Song Hong, Mi-Hiyun Kim, Seong-Heon Lee, Geun-Seok Lim, John B. Whitman
Tagalog:	Jean-Michel Fortis
Tongan:	Yoko Otsuka

I did my best to take into account my colleagues' proposals, and I thank them from the depth of my heart. It goes without saying that I am alone responsible for the final product.

Contents

Acknowledgements —— v

Symbols, abbreviations and writing conventions —— ix

Introduction —— 1

Part I: A Brief Overview of the Meaning-Text Model

1 Meaning-Text linguistic model —— 7

Part II: Surface-Syntactic Relations

2 A general inventory of surface-syntactic relations in the world's languages —— 31

3 Syntactic subject: syntactic relations, once again —— 117

4 "Multiple subjects" and "multiple direct objects" in Korean —— 179

5 Genitive adnominal dependents in Russian: surface-syntactic relations in the N→N$_{GEN}$ phrase —— 205

Part III: Some Hard Nuts in Syntax Cracked by Dependency Description

6 Relative clause: a typology —— 235

7 ESLI …, TO … 'if …, then …': syntactic description of binary conjunctions in Russian —— 275

8 The East/Southeast Asian answer to the European passive —— 289

9 Pronominal idioms with a blasphemous noun in Russian and syntactically similar expressions —— 309

Part IV: **Word Order – Linearizing Dependency Structures**

10 Word order in Russian —— 335

11 Linear ordering of genitive adnominal dependents cosubordinated to a noun in Russian —— 369

References —— 387

Index of definitions —— 403

Index of notions and terms, supplied with a glossary —— 406

Index of languages —— 441

Index of semantic and lexical units —— 443

Symbols, abbreviations and writing conventions

All the relevant notions and formalisms cannot be explained here; the reader is kindly invited to consult the Glossary (pp. 406*ff*) and the monograph Mel'čuk 2012–2015.

All interlinear glosses in the examples are literal; two English words that correspond to one foreign form are united by a dot: Rus. *boli* 'of.pain'.

Symbols

| C	condition part of a linguistic rule
L	a particular language
L	a particular lexical unit
«L»	a particular fictitious lexeme (in the deep-syntactic structure)
L('X')	a particular lexical unit L expressing the meaning 'X'
$L_{(x_1, x_2, ..., x_n)}$	$(x_1, x_2, ..., x_n)$ is the syntactics of lexical unit L, $x_1, x_2, ..., x_n$ being syntactic features
⌜$L_1 ... L_n$⌝	a particular idiom $L_1 ... L_n$
L_1–sem→L_2	L_2 directly depends on L_1 semantically
L_1–synt→L_2	L_2 directly depends on L_1 syntactically
L_1–⋯→L_2	L_2 indirectly depends on L_1
L_1◂⋯▸L_2	L_1 and L_2 are co-referential (= L_1 and L_2 have the same referent)
NB	important but tangential (= logically not necessary) information
r	a particular surface-syntactic dependency relation
R	Rheme (communicative value)
R_{DSynt}	deep-syntactic Rheme (communicative value)
R_{Sem}	semantic Rheme (communicative value)
'σ'	a particular semanteme
'<u>σ</u>'	a particular semanteme that is communicatively dominant within the semanteme configuration it belongs to
'σ̃'	a particular configuration of semantemes
T	Theme (communicative value)
T_{DSynt}	deep-syntactic Theme (communicative value)
T_{Sem}	semantic Theme (communicative value)
«they»	the expression «they» represents the indefinite-personal pronoun, such as THEY (in the sentence *In Yorkshire they say "eh" whenever they don't understand something*), Fr. ON, Ger. MAN
$\{x_i\}$	a set of elements x_i
«X»	x, a feature of syntactics of a linguistic sign

x —— Symbols, abbreviations and writing conventions

⟨x, y, ..., z⟩	an ordered set of elements x, y, ..., z
X	a linguistic expression
*X	an ungrammatical linguistic expression
?X	an incorrect or dubious linguistic expression
#X	a pragmatically deficient or semantically anomalous linguistic expression
(X)	an optional X
[X]	1) government pattern
	2) additional explanation
X ⟨Y⟩	Y, a variant of X
X | Y	Y, conditions of use of X
X ⇔ Y	correspondence between linguistic entities X and Y of two adjacent representation levels ⟨= 'X corresponds to Y and vice versa'⟩
X̲	the context X of a linguistic rule
X + Y	Y follows X immediately
X + ... + Y	Y follows X with a possible gap
⟦'X'⟧	a presupposed semantic component 'X'
|, ||, |||	pauses of increasing duration and importance
1, 2, 3	pronominal/verbal person 1, 2, 3
I, II, ..., VI	DSynt-actants **I, II, ..., VI**
Ø	zero sign (= linguistic sign whose signifier is empty)
⊕	operation of linguistic union
■!	directly relevant important information
☞	explanations concerning conventions and notations

Abbreviations

-A	actant
A ⟨= ADJ⟩	adjective (part of speech)
ACC	accusative (grammeme of nominal/adjectival case)
ACT	active (grammeme of verbal voice)
ADV	adverb (part of speech)
AgCo	agentive complement (a clause element)
AOR	aorist (grammeme of verbal tense)
APPEND	the **APPENDITIVE** deep-syntactic relation
ART	article
ATTR	the **ATTRIBUTIVE** deep-syntactic relation
CLAUS	clausative (part of speech)
colloq.	colloquial (stylistic label)

COORD	the **COORDINATIVE** deep-syntactic relation
CONJ	conjunction (part of speech)
CONV	converb (grammeme of verbal finiteness: deverbal adverb)
D	(syntactic) dependent
D-	deep (sublevel of a linguistic representation)
DAT	dative (grammeme of nominal/adjectival case)
DECL	declarative (grammeme of verbal mood)
DEF	definite (grammeme of nominal determination)
DET	determiner (syntactic class of lexemes)
DirO	direct object (a clause element)
DMorphR	deep-morphological representation
DPhonR	deep-phonic (= phonological) representation
DSyntA	deep-syntactic actant
DSynt-AnaphS	deep-syntactic anaphoric structure
DSynt-CommS	deep-syntactic communicative structure
DSynt-ProsS	deep-syntactic prosodic structure
DSyntR	deep-syntactic representation
DSyntRel	deep-syntactic relation
DSyntS	deep-syntactic structure
ECD	*Explanatory Combinatorial Dictionary*
FEM	feminine (grammeme of adjectival/verbal gender)
fem	feminine (gender; a value of the syntactic feature GENDER of a noun)
FUT	future (grammeme of verbal tense)
G	(syntactic) governor
GER	gerund (grammeme of verbal finiteness)
GP	Government Pattern
HON	honorific (grammeme of the category of politeness)
iff	if and only if
impers	impersonal (value of a syntactic feature of a pronoun)
IMPF	imperfective (grammeme of verbal aspect)
IND	indicative (grammeme of verbal mood)
INF	infinitive (grammeme of verbal finiteness)
IndirO	indirect object (a clause element)
INDEF	indefinite (grammeme of nominal determination)
intrans	intransitive (value of the syntactic feature TRANSITIVITY of a verb)
LDOCE	*Longman Dictionary of Contemporary English*
LF	lexical function
LU	lexical unit
lit.	literal

MASC	masculine (grammeme of adjectival/verbal gender)
masc	masculine (gender; value of the syntactic feature GENDER of a noun)
MTM	Meaning-Text model
MTT	Meaning-Text theory
MV	Main Verb
N	noun (part of speech)
NEU	neuter (grammeme of adjectival/verbal gender)
neu	neuter (gender; value of the syntactic feature GENDER of a noun)
neut.	neutral (stylistic label)
NOM	nominative (grammeme of nominal/adjectival case)
NUM	cardinal numeral (part of speech)
OBL	oblique (grammeme of nominal case [Eng. *me, him, her,* ...])
OblO	oblique (≈ prepositional) object (a clause element)
PART	participle (grammeme of verbal finiteness)
PASS	passive (grammeme of verbal voice)
PAST	past (grammeme of verbal tense)
PERF	perfective (grammeme of verbal aspect)
PL	plural (grammeme of nominal/adjectival/verbal number)
PREP	preposition (part of speech)
PRES	present (grammeme of verbal tense)
pron	pronominal (value of a syntactic feature)
-R	representation (linguistic)
RefS	referential structure
RhetS	rhetorical structure
S-	surface (sublevel of a linguistic representation)
-S	structure
SAE	Standard Average European (language)
Sem-	semantic
SemA	semantic actant
Sem-CommS	semantic-communicative structure
SemR	semantic representation
SemS	semantic structure
SG	singular (grammeme of nominal/adjectival/verbal number)
SMorphR	surface-morphological representation
SSyntA	surface-syntactic actant
SSyntR	surface-syntactic representation
SSyntRel	surface-syntactic relation
SSyntS	surface-syntactic structure
SUBJ	subjective (grammeme of nominal case)
Synt-	syntactic

SyntR	syntactic representation
SyntSubj	syntactic subject (a clause element)
trans	transitive (value of the syntactic feature TRANSITIVITY of a verb)
V	verb (part of speech)
V$_{FIN}$	finite verb
vulg.	vulgar (stylistic label)

Writing conventions

Linguistic examples are in *italics*.

Textual glosses are in roman and between 'semantic quotes'.

Lexical units are in SMALL CAPITALS.

Grammemes (= inflectional values) are in UPPER CASE: PAST, PL(URAL), etc.

Derivatemes are in *HELVETICA ITALICS CAPS*: 'ONE WHO [L-s]' (*read+er* from *read*$_L$, *teach+er* from *teach*$_L$).

The names of lexical functions are in `Courier New`: S$_0$, Magn, Oper$_1$, etc.

At their first mention (and sporadically where it is deemed useful), technical terms are in Helvetica in the main text: antonymy, dependency, semanteme, etc.

Introduction

This volume, which you, my dear reader, are (I hope) about to start perusing, presents a number of case studies in dependency syntax carried out within the Meaning-Text approach. The expression "dependency syntax" refers to a type of linguistic description in which the syntactic structure of a sentence is described in terms of syntactic dependencies—hierarchical binary relations between lexical units of the sentence. In point of fact, there is no other, *non-dependency*, syntax. The **syntactic** structure of a sentence cannot be described in any other way—for instance, in terms of constituents, or phrases, as the overwhelming majority of linguists have striven to do over the last half-century. This impossibility is strictly logical: phrases in the sentence under production are themselves a way to express its syntactic structure, and therefore, they cannot simultaneously be part of what they express. Indeed, phrase structure in syntax will someday be seen in the history of science in a similar light to Ptolemy's epicycles in astronomy, phlogiston and the luminiferous ether in physics, or the Scientific Socialism of the Soviet era in social sciences. However, owing to near uncontested reign of the phrase structure perspective in linguistics over the last several decades, it is necessary to emphasize from the start the strictly **dependential nature** of syntax as it is understood in this book, a point that I will return to again and again.

It is impossible to enter here into the intricacies of the appearance and development of dependency representations in syntax. Suffice it to mention the trailblazing book Tesnière 1959 and the first dependency descriptions mentioned in Mel'čuk 2014a; see also Mel'čuk 1988. For main references on dependency syntax, see Chapter 2 below.

Right now, I need to present the overall organization of this volume.

The subsequent discussion will be conducted in terms of what is known as a Meaning-Text model [MTM] of natural language. An MTM is a logical device (= a system of rules) that is intended to represent the functional nature of a language—namely, the transition from a chunk of meaning 'σ' to the text or several synonymous texts $T_i($'σ'$)$ that express 'σ'; indeed, the formula 'σ' $\Leftrightarrow T_i($'σ'$)$ could be taken to be the trademark of the whole Meaning-Text business: 'σ' is the meaning, $T_i($'σ'$)$ are the corresponding texts, and $\Leftrightarrow$ is the Language. A brief sketch of the linguistic Meaning-Text model is offered in Chapter 1.

As far as syntax is concerned, the Meaning-Text approach presupposes three levels of syntactic description for a sentence: 1) the deep-syntactic representation, 2) surface-syntactic representation, and 3) the deep-morphological representation (Chapter 1, Subsection 1.2.2, pp. 11*ff*):

{DSyntRs} $\Leftarrow$ deep syntax $\Rightarrow$ {SSyntRs} $\Leftarrow$ surface syntax $\Rightarrow$ {DMorphRs}

https://doi.org/10.1515/9783110694765-001

This volume considers only the transition between the surface-syntactic representation of the sentence to be produced and its deep-morphological representation. The linguistic rules that ensure said transition constitute the surface-syntactic module of the Meaning-Text model; thus, I will speak exclusively of **surface syntax**.

The full characterization of surface syntax requires three elements:

- the specification of the surface-syntactic representation [SSyntR];
- the specification of the deep-morphological representation [DMorphR];
- the specification of the MTM surface-syntactic module, which maps SSyntRs onto DMorphRs.

A complete presentation of general surface syntax would need several volumes; as a result, my goals have to be limited to just two aspects of syntactic description: surface-syntactic relations and word order rules, which are part of the MTM's surface-syntactic [SSynt-]module. In conformity with this limitation, the book is divided in four thematic parts.

Part I – A brief overview of the Meaning-Text model
This part contains only one chapter—Chapter 1, which exposes the theoretical framework for what follows.

Part II – Surface-syntactic relations
Surface-syntactic relations [SSyntRels] form the surface-syntactic structure [SSyntS] of a sentence, and the SSyntS is the central component of an SSyntR. Strange as it may seem, as of today, no language has a full universally agreed-upon inventory of SSyntRels. Therefore, I feel justified in dedicating Chapters 2 through 5 to the various problems of creating such an inventory. More specifically, these chapters present:

Chapter 2 – a tentative set of SSyntRels found in various languages and grouped according to their syntactic properties: actantial, modifying, attributive, auxiliary, etc. This chapter constitutes the foundation on which rest all other subsequent deliberations.

Chapter 3 – linguistically universal formal definitions of syntactic subject and direct object, the **subjectival** and **direct-objectival** SSyntRels being the basic SSyntRels.

Chapter 4 – a discussion of so-called "multiple subjects and objects" in Korean.

Chapter 5 – an analysis of the syntactic organization of genitive adnominal dependents in Russian; in other words, this chapter proposes several SSyntRels for the description of such dependents.

Part III – Some Hard Nuts in Syntax Cracked by Dependency Description

Here four very different syntactic phenomena are analyzed which constitute a challenge for a coherent linguistic description; this is done in four chapters:

Chapter 6 is dedicated to a typology of relative clauses.

Chapter 7 deals with so-called binary conjunctions (e.g., IF ..., THEN...); the surface-syntactic description of sentences containing these conjunctions is proposed.

Chapter 8 shows that what is sometimes considered a passive construction in Mandarin Chinese is in fact a verb meaning '[to] undergo' that introduces a full-fledged clause; there is no passive in Chinese. As a basis for the definition of passive construction, some requirements on a good linguistic definition are formulated.

Chapter 9 offers a syntactic description of Russian phrasemes that are indefinite pronouns (e.g., ČËRT EGO ZNAET 'devil it/him knows'). This chapter also includes a universal typology of phrasemes.

Part IV – Word order: linearizing dependency structures

Word order is studied in linguistics much better that surface-syntactic relations, although not enough has been done from the angle of dependency structure; Chapters 10 and 11 deal with formal word order rules exactly in a strictly dependency-oriented perspective. More specifically:

Chapter 10 presents a sketch of a general method for linearizing a dependency syntactic structure, introducing the input and output formalisms for linearization rules and detailing major types of these rules. The proposed methodology is developed on the basis of Russian, a language famous for its extremely flexible, but not arbitrary, word order.

Chapter 11 analyzes a particular case of SSyntS linearization—the arrangements of the genitive nouns cosubordinated "in parallel" to a noun in Russian; this arrangement is compared with the ordering of Russian adjectives also cosubordinated to the same noun.

Given the character of the present volume, which includes abundance of formalisms and technical terms, I have also provided a Glossary, where all the terms used in the text are defined and (succinctly) explained; see pp. 406*ff*. On top of this, the volume includes:

- An index of definitions proposed therein, so that the reader can easily compare them.
- An index of languages mentioned and discussed.
- An index of semantemes and lexical units treated in this volume one way or another.

And so with that,

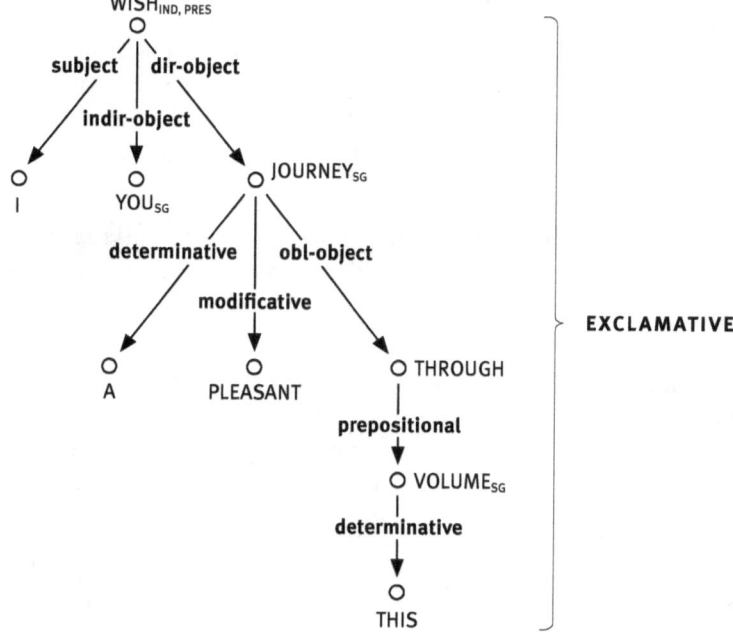

Part I: **A Brief Overview of the Meaning-Text Model**

1 Meaning-Text linguistic model

1.1 Functional models in sciences
1.2 Meaning-Text theory and functional models of natural language: Meaning-Text models
    1.2.1 The Meaning-Text theory's three postulates
    1.2.2 Linguistic representations in a Meaning-Text model
    1.2.3 Linguistic rules in a Meaning-Text model
        1.2.3.1 Semantic Meaning-Text rules
        1.2.3.2 Deep-syntactic Meaning-Text rules
        1.2.3.3 Surface-syntactic Meaning-Text rules
        1.2.3.4 Morphological Meaning-Text rules
    1.2.4 Modeling two important linguistic phenomena: paradigmatic and syntagmatic lexical choices
        1.2.4.1 Paradigmatic lexical choices
        1.2.4.2 Syntagmatic lexical choices
        1.2.4.3 Correlations between the meaning and the collocates of a lexical unit
1.3 The value of functional models in linguistics

> The sciences do not try to explain, they hardly even try to interpret, they mainly make models. By a model is meant a mathematical construct which, with the addition of certain verbal interpretations, describes observed phenomena. The justification of such a mathematical construct is solely and precisely that it is expected to work—that is, correctly to describe phenomena from a reasonably wide area. Furthermore, it must satisfy certain esthetic criteria—that is, in relation to how much it describes, it must be rather simple.
>
>   John von Neumann, in L. Leary (ed.), *The Unity of Knowledge* (1955: 158)

All discussions of syntactic phenomena in this volume are conducted strictly within the formal framework of the Meaning-Text approach. In order to help the reader navigate the technical complexities of the following proposals, a few words have to be said about the Meaning-Text approach in general and about the Meaning-Text linguistic model in particular: this approach and this model essentially underly all the syntactic studies presented below.

1.1 Functional models in sciences

The Meaning-Text approach is based on the idea of functional modeling, so it is natural to start with the notion of functional model.

How do we know what happened a few seconds after the Big Bang? Nobody was there, and no observation device could exist at the moment of the creation of the Universe. However, we know a lot, and this is made possible by abstract cosmological models—systems of equations, which, based on known physical laws

https://doi.org/10.1515/9783110694765-002

and general logic, relate to one another various facts observable ≈ 14 billion years after the Big Bang. From these models, scientists can reach conclusions about the state of the Universe at different stages of its existence.

This is but one example among many that could be cited. In countless cases, a researcher who is in no position to directly observe the internal structure of an object or a phenomenon has recourse to a model. Exaggerating a bit, any hard science is mainly the construction of models. This has been well known at least since Galileo. "There is no scientist who does not reason in terms of models—even if he does not admit this to others or to himself" (Auger 1965: 4).

Linguistics, which has natural language as its object, is in the same position with respect to language as cosmology with respect to the Big Bang. Language, an extremely complex system of rules, is encoded in the brains of its speakers and thus it is inaccessible to direct observation: linguists cannot open the skulls or penetrate the brain with electrodes at their will. The only solution is **the recourse to models**. And this trend—constructing formal models of (fragments of) languages—has already launched.

On the one hand, N. Chomsky's Generative-Transformational Grammar, since 1950s till the beginning of the 21st century, has solidly implanted the idea of modeling in linguistics. Thus, as early as in Nagel et al. (eds.) 1962 we find several articles that discuss the topic of linguistic models.

On the other hand, intensive work in different branches of computational linguistics has heavily contributed to this trend. Today we can take it for granted that modeling is *de facto* fully accepted in linguistics. However, it remains to be established what types of linguistic models are the most promising and to make the notion of model more specific—so that it can be accepted *de jure*. In fact, the term model itself is ambiguous; in order to eliminate confusion, a rigorous definition must be proposed.

Let there be an entity E (an object or a system of objects); E functions in the sense that it receives observable inputs and produces for them corresponding observable outputs. The researcher is interested in the functioning of E rather than in its internal structure (which is in any case not observable). To describe E, he constructs a functional model M of E, that is, M(E).

Definition 1.1 – functional model

> A system of symbolic expressions M(E) created by the researcher to describe the functioning of E is a functional model of E if and only if it associates with the given inputs the same outputs as E does.

The model **M** is functional in two senses: 1) it seeks to represent the **functioning** of **E**, and 2) it does so by using mathematical **functions**, so that **M** is actually a very complex function in the mathematical sense, mapping inputs to outputs.

NB Our term *functional [model]*, having the indicated meaning, should not be confused with *functional* in *functional theories of grammar*, which take the **functionality** of language and its elements to be the key to understanding linguistic processes and structures.

1.2 Meaning-Text theory and functional models of natural language: Meaning-Text models

Meaning-Text theory [MTT] is characterized here in three steps: the postulates that underlie it (1.2.1), the linguistic representations it uses (1.2.2), and some basic types of MTT rules (1.2.3).

1.2.1 The Meaning-Text theory's three postulates

More than 60 years ago, work started on the development of a functional model of Natural Language, the Meaning-Text model [MTM]. The project was begun in Moscow in the 1960s by the present author, together with several colleagues, principally—A. Zholkovsky and Ju. Apresjan (see, e.g., Žolkovskij & Mel'čuk 1967, Mel'čuk 1974, 1988, 2012–2015, 2016). The linguistic theory underlying MTMs is known as Meaning-Text theory; it is based on the following three postulates.

Postulate 1 – Answer to the question "What is natural language?"
> A natural language is a system of rules that are stored in the brains of speakers and describe the correspondence between a denumerable (= infinite, but countable) set of linguistic meanings and a denumerable set of linguistic texts.

Linguistic meanings (in the technical sense of the term) appear as formal symbolic objects called **semantic representations** [SemRs], and texts—as **phonetic representations** [PhonRs]. Postulate 1 can then be expressed in symbolic form as (1):

(1) $\{SemR_i\} \Leftarrow\textbf{language}\Rightarrow \{PhonR_j\} \mid i \neq j,\ 0 < i,\ j \leq \infty$

Logically, the Meaning-Text correspondence (i.e., "$\Leftarrow$**language**$\Rightarrow$") is bidirectional and represents equivalence; yet in linguistics it should be studied and described in the Meaning-to-Text direction: natural language is mainly about speaking, not understanding. Linguistic **synthesis**, or **text production**, is much more important for linguistics than analysis, or text understanding. This is so because text understanding inevitably involves, to a greater or lesser extent, the understanding of the subject matter, i.e., the understanding of the extralinguistic reality, which muddles the picture. Going from a **given** meaning to all the texts that can express it liberates the researcher from huge "non-linguistic" difficulties leaving him face-to-face with the language in its purest state. To this it can be added that any text, before it can be analyzed, has to be synthesized: text synthesis is obviously primary to analysis.

The meaning-to-text orientation of linguistic research and description gives absolute priority to the study of synonymy, in particular—of linguistic paraphrase (Milićević 2007).

Postulate 2 – Answer to the question "What is a description of a language?"

> The Meaning-Text correspondence in (1) is described by a logical device, or system of formal rules, which constitutes a functional model of language: an MTM.

An MTM takes meanings, or SemRs, as its inputs, and produces texts, or PhonRs, as its outputs—in the same way that native speakers do. It is in this sense that an MTM is a mathematical function: $f(SemR) = \{PhonR_j\}$. Applied to a SemR, it produces the set of all (nearly) synonymous PhonRs that correspond to it. (An MTM can also be used in the inverse direction: taking texts as inputs and extracting meanings from them. In this chapter, however, only the Meaning-to-Text direction is considered.)

The Meaning-Text correspondence is many-to-many: one SemR can correspond to an astronomical number of PhonRs (several million; there is incredibly rich synonymy: see, e.g., Mel'čuk 2012–2015: vol. 1, 65–67, 155), and one PhonR can express many SemRs (ambiguity). Because of this, Postulate 3 is needed.

Postulate 3 – Answer to the question "How should an MTM be structured?"

> To successfully describe the complicated Meaning-Text correspondence, two intermediate levels of linguistic representation are needed in an MTM: Synt(actic)R, corresponding to sentences, and Morph(ological)R, corresponding to wordforms.

As a result, an MTM has the following general architecture:

(2) $\{SemR_i\} \iff \{SyntR_k\} \iff \{MorphR_l\} \iff \{PhonR_j\}$
     semantics   syntax   morphology +
                                  phonology

The boldfaced words are the names of MTM's major components, or modules.

Linguistic representations of all levels, except for the semantic level, are each subdivided into deep, or meaning-geared, and surface, or form-geared, sublevels. Including the final—phonic—level, this gives us a total of seven representations.

NB To avoid unnecessary complications, in this book only graphic representations of actual sentences will be used.

1.2.2 Linguistic representations in a Meaning-Text model

To make clearer the basic ideas underlying an MTM, examples of the basic, or main, structures of the linguistic representations of all levels will be supplied (and in the next subsection, a few rules relating them). Due to lack of space, many approximate descriptions will be used and many explanations foregone.

Semantic structure

The semantic structure [SemS] is one of the four components of a SemR—its basic structure. Formally, it is a network whose nodes are labeled with semantemes (meanings of disambiguated lexical units [LUs] of the language in question) and arcs are labeled with numbers used to distinguish the arguments of a predicate.

The other three components of a SemR—the peripheral structures, namely, the semantic-communicative structure [Sem-CommS], the rhetorical structure [RhetS] and the referential structure [RefS]—are not shown.

The SemS in Figure 1.1 (next page) can be verbalized by a huge number of sentences, of which only three are shown in (3):

(3) Three of the sentences that can be obtained from the SemS in Figure 1.1
  a. *Abu-Khalaf has been permitted by Damascus to step up the flow of terrorists into Iraq to 30 a month.*
  b. *The government of Syria let Abu-Khalaf increase the number of terrorists slipping into Iraq up to 30 per month.*
  c. *Abu-Khalaf has the permission of the Syrian government to raise the number of terrorists going to Iraq to 30 each month.*

For the reader's conevenience, all illustrative representations are given for sentence (3a).

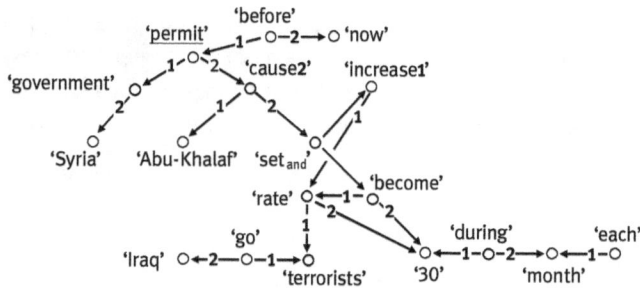

☞ 1. The underscoring of a semanteme (here, 'permit') indicates its communicative-dominant character (Mel'čuk 2001: 29ff). In other words, the whole Sem-network above is about 'permitting'.
2. The semanteme 'set$_{and}$' represents a logical conjunction of elements, in our case—of the semantemes 'increase1' and 'become'. Since all elements of a conjunction are semantically "equal," the branches leading from 'set$_{and}$' to its Sem-dependents are not labeled. The semanteme 'increase1' represents the meaning of the intransitive verb INCREASE1: 'become more intense'.

Figure 1.1 A semantic structure

Deep-syntactic structure

The **deep-syntactic structure** [DSyntS] of a sentence is an unordered labeled dependency tree (the physical disposition of its nodes on the page has no logical relevance).

– Its **nodes** represent only the (semantically) **full lexical units** [LUs] that compose the sentence, including ordinary (i.e. non-auxiliary) lexemes, idioms, fictitious lexemes, lexical functions (see below, 1.3.3), and such complex LUs as compound numerals (such as THREE MILLION TWO HUNDRED THOUSAND THIRTY-FOUR= 3 200 034) and compound proper names (such as ROBERT MALCOLM WARD DIXON). Each node of DSyntS is labeled with the name of one of these LUs. Structural (auxiliary, or grammatical) LUs are not present in a DSyntS. In a language that has inflectional morphology, each LU in a DSyntS is supplied with appropriate **deep**, or semantic, **grammemes** (= grammemes which have their source in the semantic representation, i.e. which carry meaning; such as, for instance, the number and definiteness of nouns and the voice, mood, aspect and tense of verbs). **Surface grammemes**, imposed by government and agreement (such as the case for nouns, the person and number for verbs, the gender, number and case for adjectives), are not shown.
– Its **branches** represent the **DSynt-relations** [DSyntRels] that link the LUs in the sentence and are labeled with the names of 13 universal DSyntRels; see Chapter 2, 2.2.1, pp. 32ff.

The DSyntS of sentence (3a) is presented in Figure 1.2.

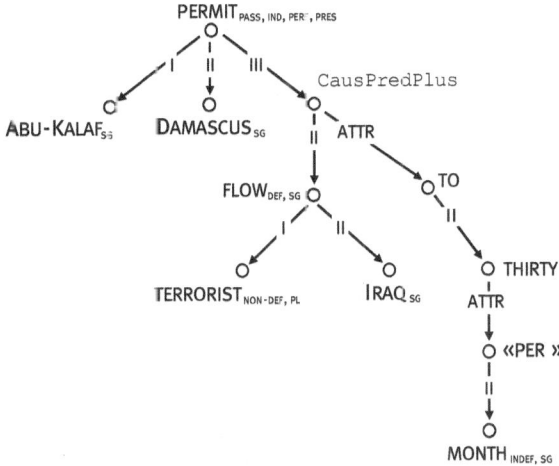

Figure 1.2 The deep-syntactic structure of sentence (3a)

The other three components of a DSyntR—the peripheral structures, namely, the deep-syntactic-communicative structure [DSynt-CommS], the deep-syntactic-anaphorical structure [DSynt-AnaphS] and the deep-syntactic-prosodic structure [DSynt-ProsS]—are not shown.

Surface-syntactic structure
The surface-syntactic structure [SSyntS] of a sentence is also—just like the DSyntS—an unordered labeled dependency tree; however, its composition and, consequently, labeling are different from that of a DSyntS.

- Its nodes represent **all** actual lexemes of the sentence, including all pronouns and structural (= grammatical) words, and are labeled with their names. Each lexeme, just as in the DSynt-structure, is supplied with appropriate deep grammemes. (All the surface grammemes are introduced in the DMorph-structure at the following step—by SSynt-rules.)
- Its branches represent the SSyntRels that link the lexemes and are labeled with the names of language-specific SSynt-relations. Their number seems to be about 60–70 per language. (See Chapter 2, Section 2.5 for a general inventory of SSyntRels in the languages of the world.)

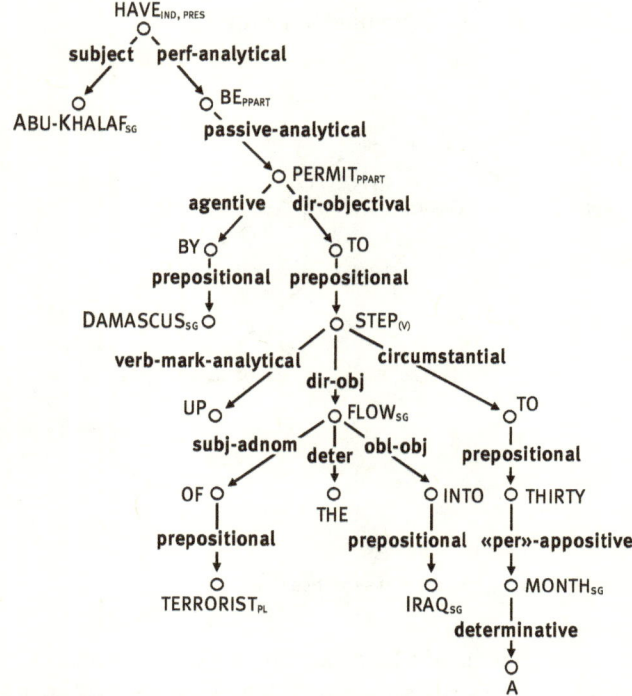

Figure 1.3 The surface-syntactic structure of sentence (3a)

Deep-morphological structure

The **deep-morphological structure** [DMorphS] of a sentence is a string of **all** its lexemes supplied with **all** the values of their inflectional categories, i.e., with all their **grammemes**.

ABU-KHALAF$_{SG}$ | HAVE$_{IND, PRES, 3, SG}$ BE$_{PPART}$ PERMIT$_{PPART}$ BY DAMASCUS$_{SG}$ ||
TO STEP$_{INF}$ UP |
THE FLOW$_{SG}$ OF TERRORIST$_{PL}$ INTO IRAQ$_{SG}$ |
TO THIRTY A MONTH$_{SG}$ |||

☞ The symbols "|," "||" and "|||" stand for pauses of different duration; these pauses are elements of the deep-prosodic structure of the sentence.

Figure 1.4 The deep-morphological structure of sentence (3a)

Surface-morphological structure

The **surface-morphological structure** [SMorphS] of a sentence is a string of morphemes that are fed to the SMorph-module of an MTM, to produce a string of morphs supplied with necessary prosodies.

{ABU-KHALAF}+{SG} |
{HAVE}+{IND.PRES}+{3.SG} {BE}+{PPART} {PERMIT}+{PPART} {BY} {DAMASCUS}+{SG} ||
{TO} {STEP}+{INF} {UP} |
{THE} {FLOW}+{SG} {OF} {TERRORIST}+{PL} { NTO} {IRAQ}+{SG} |
{TO} {THIRTY} {A} {MONTH}+{SG} |||

Figure 1.5 The surface-morphological structure of sentence (3a)

The phonemic and the phonetic structures of sentence (3a) are not shown, since they are irrelevant to the topic of the present monograph.

1.2.3 Linguistic rules in a Meaning-Text model

Linguistic representations of adjacent levels are linked by corresponding linguistic rules, which map a linguistic representation of the level n onto the representation of the level $n+1$ (and vice versa). To simplify the exposition, only rules dealing with the basic structures of representations are considered.

Three major classes of linguistic rules will be illustrated:

- semantic: {SemSs} ⇔ {DSyntSs}
- syntactic: {DSyntSs} ⇔ {SSyntSs} ⇔ {DMorphSs}
- morphological: {DMorphSs} ⇔ {SMorphSs} ⇔ {DPhonSs}

The rules presented below are used in transitions between the structures in Figures 1.1 through 1.5.

1.2.3.1 Semantic Meaning-Text rules

The semantic Meaning-Text rules come in three major types:

- Lexicalization rules map configurations of semantemes (in the starting semantic structure) on deep lexical units, which label the nodes of the deep-syntactic structure of the sentence to be synthesized.
- Morphologization rules map configurations of semantemes on deep grammemes, which are subscripted to the deep lexical units.
- Arborization rules map semantic relations between semantemes on the deep-syntactic relations.

It is impossible to give examples of every type of Sem-rule here; I will limit myself to just three Lexicalization rules.

☞ 1. The expression of the form "L('σ')" stands for lexical unit L that expresses the meaning 'σ'.
  2. Shading marks the context of the rule—that is, elements that are not impacted by the rule, but whose presence in the input structure is necessary for the rule to apply.

Individual lexemic Sem-Rule

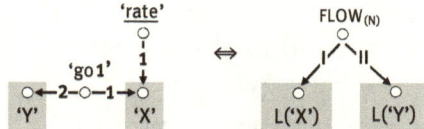

Figure 1.6 The Sem-rule for the lexeme FLOW(N) ('go1' ≈ 'move towards')

The meaning 'rate of Xs that go1 to Y' can be expressed by the lexeme FLOW(N) [*of Xs (in)to Y*] (*daily flow of visitors to the museum*). This is, roughly speaking, a part of the lexicographic entry for the noun FLOW(N) 'movement of X's ...'—namely, its definition.

Individual lexical-functional Sem-Rule

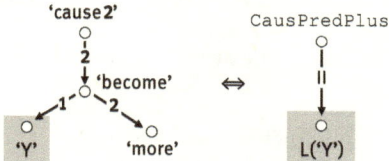

☞ The semanteme 'cause2' represents voluntary, teleological causation, as in *John killed the wolf* ['X is the causer of Y']; 'cause1' stands for non-voluntary, spontaneous causation, as in *The bullet killed the wolf* ['X is the cause of Y'].

Figure 1.7 The Sem-rule for the lexical function CausPredPlus (see 1.2.4.2, p. 22)

The meaning 'cause2 Y to become more [than Y was]' can give rise to the lexical function [LF] CausPredPlus, whose value is specified for its second argument, i.e., its DSynt-actant II, in the dictionary: CausPredPlus(*flow*(N)) = **step up** *the flow*; CausPredPlus(*gap*(N)) = **widen** *the gap*; CausPredPlus(*ties*(N)) = **solidify** *the ties*; etc.

Individual metonymic Sem-rule

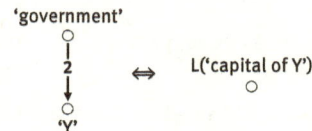

Figure 1.8 The Sem-rule for the metonymy: 'government of country Y' ~ 'capital of country Y'

The meaning 'the government of country Y' can be expressed by the name of the capital of Y ('government of Russia' ⇔ MOSCOW, 'government of USA' ⇔ WASHINGTON, etc., as in *strong ties between Moscow and Riyadh*).

For syntactic rules, it is necessary to present DSynt- and SSynt-rules separately; I will give three rules of each type.

1.2.3.2 Deep-syntactic Meaning-Text rules
DSyntS ⇔ SSyntS rules (deep syntax)
Establishing the value of an LF (*step up* [*the flow*])

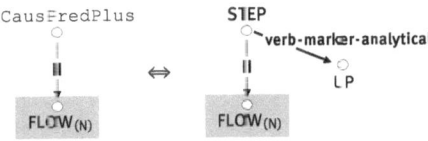

Figure 1.9 The DSynt-rule for the value of LF `Caus PredPlus`

The elements of the value of an LF **f** applied to L are taken from L's lexical entry, in this case L being FLOW$_{(N)}$.

NB For the SSynt-relations whose names appear in the rules, see Chapter 2.

Expressing the agent of a passive verb (*permitted by Damascus*)

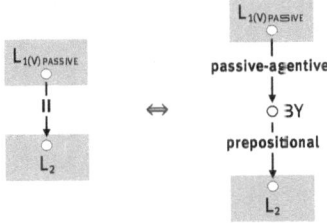

Figure 1.10 The DSynt-rule for the agentive complement

Expressing the *Genitivus Subjectivus* complement of a noun (*flow of terrorists*)

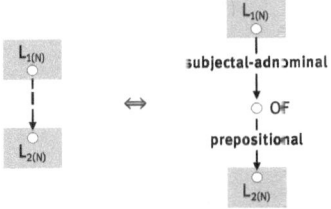

Figure 1.11 The DSynt-rule for the subjectal adnominal complement

1.2.3.3 Surface-syntactic Meaning-Text rules
SSyntS ⇔ DMorphS rules (surface syntax)

☞ 1. The symbol "+" specifies linear order of lexemes, and "...", a possible gap between two lexemes.
   2. The expression "II[N]" in the syntactics of a verb indicates that its DSynt-actant II can be expressed by a prepositionless noun—that is, that this verb is transitive.

Constructing the direct-object phrase (*step up the **flow**; Have you seen (just) **him**?*)

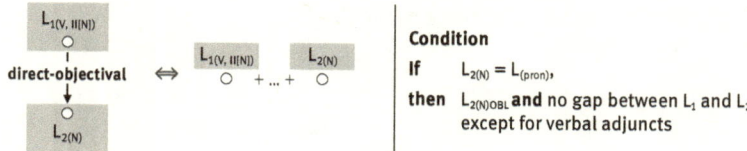

Condition
If $L_{2(N)} = L_{(pron)}$,
then $L_{2(N)OBL}$ **and no gap between** L_1 **and** L_2 **except for verbal adjuncts**

☞ "OBL" stands for 'oblique case of pronouns' (*me, you, him/her, us, them, whom*).

Figure 1.12 The SSynt-rule for a direct object

Constructing the determinative phrase (***the** new computer, **our** president, **these** and other girls*)

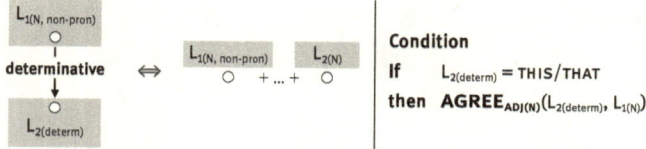

Condition
If $L_{2(determ)}$ = THIS/THAT
then $AGREE_{ADJ(N)}(L_{2(determ)}, L_{1(N)})$

☞ $AGREE_{ADJ(N)}(L', L)$ is an agreement operator (set of rules) that ensures the agreement in number between the demonstrative pronominal adjectives and the governing noun (*this tree* vs. *these trees*).

Figure 1.13 The SSynt-rule for a determiner

Constructing the perfective-analytical phrase (***Having**, as everybody knows, already **written** to Father, ...*)

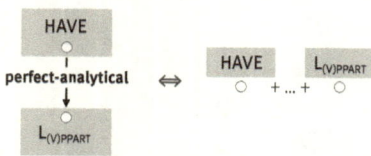

Figure 1.14 The SSynt-rule for a perfect form

1.2.3.4 Morphological Meaning-Text rules
Two DMorph- and two SMorph-rules are given below.

DMorphS ⟺ SMorphS (Deep Morphology)

PL ⟺ {PL} (nominal plural suffixes)
PAST ⟺ $A_{PAST}^{I \to æ}$ (past tense apophony of the *sing ~ sang* type)

SMorphS ⟺ morph string (Surface Morphology)

{PL} ⟺ /z/ | not | /C$_{[-sibilant],\ [+voiced]}$/ __
     ⟺ /s/ | with an N$_{(-ən)}$ | /C$_{[-sibilant],\ [-voiced]}$/ __
     ⟺ /ɪz/ | | /C$_{[+sibilant]}$/ __
     ⟺ /ən/ | with an N$_{(-ən)}$

$A_{PAST}^{I \to æ}$ (/drínk/) ⟺ /drǽnk/

There is no need to enter into the details of Meaning-Text morphology since the interested reader has Mel'čuk 1992–2000 and 2006a at his disposal.

To conclude this section, a general architecture of an MTM is presented in Figure 1.15.

Note that **conceptics** (= the module describing the correspondence between a Conceptual Representation of reality and the SemR of the utterance) and **phonetics** (= the module responsible for the correspondence between the SPhonR and actual articulated sound) remain outside of an MTM. They belong to a more general model of linguistic behavior—a Reality-Speech model.

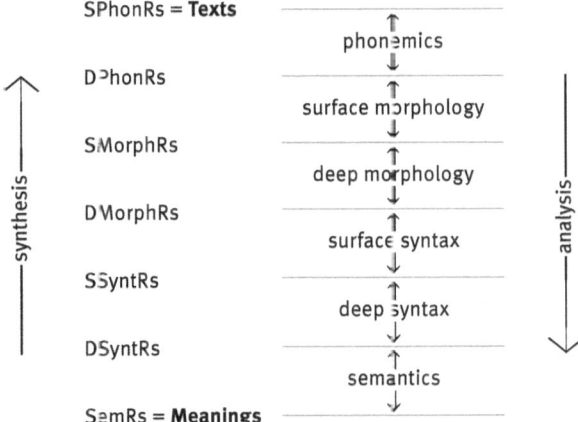

Figure 1.15 General structure of a Meaning-Text linguistic model

1.2.4 Modeling two important linguistic phenomena: paradigmatic and syntagmatic lexical choices

As we have known since F. de Saussure and R. Jakobson, any linguistic activity is carried out by the Speaker along two axes: **paradigmatic**, where the selection of linguistic units happens, and **syntagmatic**, where the units selected are combined to produce utterances. To highlight certain advantages of MTMs, one particular aspect of this activity can be considered: lexical choices.

1.2.4.1 Paradigmatic lexical choices

A choice of a lexical unit [LU] L by the Speaker is called **paradigmatic** if L is selected from the lexical stock of the language more or less independently of its eventual contextual neighbors. Two types of paradigmatic lexical choices are known: **free** choices, where L is selected only for its meaning (and maybe some other specific properties, syntactic and/or morphological); and **restricted** choices, where L is selected instead of another LU L' as function of L'; in the text, L replaces L'. Free choices are modeled by means of **semantic decompositions**, and restricted choices, by means of **semantic derivations**.

Semantic decomposition
The sentences (4a) and (4b) are synonymous:

(4) a. *John is sure that Mary is in town.* ≡
    b. *John does not doubt that Mary is in town.*

This means that they are mutually substitutable in text *salva significatione* ('with complete preservation of the meaning'). Both sentences are not **factive** and therefore both can be continued by *... but this is not true.*

Now, what type of information must a Speaker have in his brain about the lexemes SURE and DOUBT$_{(V)}$ in order to be able to manipulate them as he actually does? We do not know for sure, but we can propose a plausible model.

Following A. Zholkovsky, A. Bogusławski and A. Wierzbicka, MTT proposes that the meanings of these lexemes (like all lexical meanings, i.e., all **sememes**) consist of simpler meanings—in other words, that meanings are decomposable.

NB These simpler meanings are decomposable into even simpler meanings and so forth, until **semantic primitives**, or meaning atoms, are reached (see Mel'čuk 2012–2015: vol. 2, 287).

1.2 Meaning-Text theory and functional models of natural language — 21

Consider the dataset (5):

(5) a. *I think that Alan has come, but I am not sure of this.*
   b. *I am sure that Alan has come, #but I do not think this.*
   c. *I think that Alan has come, #but I doubt this.*
   d. i. *I am sure that Alan has come.*   ≡
      ii. *I don't doubt that Alan has come.*
   e. i. *I am not sure that Alan has come.*   ≅
      ii. *I doubt that Alan has come.*

☛ The symbol "#" indicates a pragmatically unacceptable continuation.

To enable a logical device to construct the sentences in (5) and to establish their acceptability and synonymy, it is sufficient to represent the meanings under consideration as follows:

(6) a. *X is sure that P:* '⟦Thinking that P takes place,⟧
                              X is not prepared to admit that P does not take place'.
   b. *X doubts that P:* '⟦Not thinking that P takes place,⟧
                              X is prepared to admit that P does not take place'.

☛ 1. Special brackets ⟦..⟧ indicate a **presupposition**—the part of the meaning that does not undergo negation or questioning in case of negation or questioning of the whole meaning.
   2. 'X thinks that P' = '⟦Having the statement "P takes place" in X's mind,⟧ X believes that this statement is true'.

With the definitions in (6), one obtains for sentences in (5) the following semantic decompositions:

(7) a. 'I think that A. has come, but⟦, thinking that A. has come,⟧ I am prepared to admit that A. hasn't come'.
   b. '⟦**Thinking that A. has come,**⟧ I am not prepared to admit that A. hasn't come, #but **I do not think that A. has come**' (a contradiction is marked in boldface).
   c. 'I think that A. has come, #but⟦, **not thinking that A. has come,**⟧ I am prepared to admit that A. hasn't come' (a contradiction is marked in boldface).
   d. i. '⟦Thinking that A. has come,⟧ I am not prepared to admit that A. hasn't come'. =
      ii. '⟦Thinking that A. has come,⟧ I am not prepared to admit that A. hasn't come'.

e. i. '⟦Thinking that A. has come,⟧ I am prepared to admit that A. hasn't come'. ≈

ii. '⟦Not thinking that A. has come,⟧ I am prepared to admit that A. hasn't come'.

NB The case of (7d) vs. (7e) requires an additional explanation. (7e) represents a negation of (7d); if (7d-i) and (7d-ii) are equivalent, how can it be that their negations are not equivalent? The answer is the idiomatic character of the negation in (5d): *I don't doubt* is not a simple, "free" negation of *I doubt*, but an antonym meaning 'I am sure'. (Technically, this is manifested by the impact of the negation on the presupposition of '[to] doubt', which should not have happened under a free negation; see Iordanskaja 1986. If, in (5d), instead of *I don't doubt* we have a free negation *It is not true that I doubt*, sentences (5d-i) and (5d-ii) cease to be semantically equivalent.) For (7e), the contrast of the two presuppositions creates the effect of a lesser certainty of the Speaker in (7e-ii) with respect to (7e-i).

Thus, the proposed decompositions allow for a formal and coherent description of the data in (5). Semantic decompositions constitute an important descriptive tool in MTT.

Semantic Derivation
Suppose the Speaker wants to talk about the person who is at the wheel of a car; he needs the lexeme DRIVER. But a person "driving" a locomotive is called an ENGINEER, the one "driving" a plane, a PILOT, and a ship's "driver" is a HELMSMAN. Similarly, a person who manages (= "drives") a farm is a FARMER, and the one managing a shop is a SHOPKEEPER. On the other hand, the client of a restaurant is a CLIENT or PATRON, that of a hospital, a PATIENT, of a prison, a PRISONER or INMATE, of a theater, a SPECTATOR, of a school, a STUDENT, etc. We see that there are regular semantic links of the type CAR ~ DRIVER, LOCOMOTIVE ~ ENGINEER, PLANE ~ PILOT, SHIP ~ HELMSMAN: they remind one of derivation, except that in this case there can be no formal similarity between the members of the pair. For the purposes of formal modeling of text production such lexical relations should be explicitly specified. MTT proposes to do that by means of **lexical functions** [LFs], which are introduced in the next subsection; more precisely, these are **paradigmatic LFs**.

1.2.4.2 Syntagmatic lexical choices
A choice of an LU L by the Speaker is called **syntagmatic** if L is selected as a function of one of its contextual neighbors; such a choice reflects what is known as **restricted lexical cooccurrence**. Thus, English says *MAKE a mistake* but *DO a favor*, *TAKE an action*, but *BE ENGAGED in an activity*, *HOLD influence over N*, but *GIVE N orders*, etc. Similarly, we have *a GREAT achievement*, [a] *DRASTIC action*, [a]

1.2 Meaning-Text theory and functional models of natural language — 23

FIRM believer, SOLID grounds, [a] CATEGORICAL protest, quick AS LIGHTNING, [to] rain HARD, etc.

Restricted lexical cooccurrence is a serious problem for any lexicographic description. MTT proposes to solve it based on the following hypothesis:

> In the majority of cases, restricted (i.e., synchronically arbitrary) lexical cooccurrence manifests itself in the expression of a limited number of very abstract, nearly-grammatical meanings.

Thus, in the first series of examples above, such a meaning is ≈ 'do', and in the second, ≈ 'very/intense'.

The crucial fact here is that such a meaning corresponds to a function **f** (in the mathematical sense): the lexical unit L to which this meaning is applied is the **argument** of this function and the set of appropriate collocates is its **value**. Formally, we have

$$f(L) = \{L_1, L_2, ..., L_n\}.$$

To describe the lexically restricted expressions in the above examples, two such functions are proposed; these are **simple standard lexical functions** (see immediately below):

Support verb Oper_1

$\text{Oper}_1(mistake) = make$ [ART ~] $\text{Oper}_1(favor) = do$ [ART ~]
$\text{Oper}_1(rage) = be$ [in ART ~] $\text{Oper}_1(action) = take$ [ART ~]
$\text{Oper}_1(activity) = be\ engaged$ [in ART ~] $\text{Oper}_1(belief) = hold$ [ART ~]

Intensifier Magn

Magn(*achievement*) = *great*   Magn(*action*) = *drastic*
Magn(*believer*) = *firm*   Magn(*dispute*$_{(V)}$) = *hotly*
Magn(*quick*) = *as lightning*   Magn(*sell*$_{(V,\ intrans)}$) = ⌈*like hot cakes*⌉

The phrases described by these LFs are nothing other than **collocations**: the collocation's **base**, selected independently by the Speaker for its meaning, is the argument of the LF, and the **collocate**, selected as a function of the base, is one of the elements of its value.

Three properties of standard LFs prove to be especially important:

- Standard LFs are not numerous: there are about 60.
- Standard LFs are equally convenient for the description of both paradigmatic and syntagmatic restricted lexical choices. In other words, they allow for a homogeneous and systematic description of semantic derivations as well as collocations.

- Standard LFs are cross-linguistically valid, that is, they are language-universal in the sense that they are more or less sufficient for the description of restricted lexical choices in all languages. (It is certain that some languages lack some of the proposed standard LFs, but it is not very probable for a new language under consideration to require a new standard LF.)

Several examples of LFs will make the notion of LF clearer. (For more on LFs, see Mel'čuk 1974: 78–109, 1982, 2007, 2012–2015: vol. 3, Ch. 14, and Wanner (ed.) 1996.)

Paradigmatic LFs

Action/property noun S_0
$S_0(accept)$ = *acceptance* $S_0(intrude)$ = *intrusion*
$S_0(capable)$ = *capacity* $S_0(angry)$ = *anger*

Patient noun S_2
$S_2(award)$ = *recipient* $S_2(shoot)$ = *target*
$S_2(sell)$ = *merchandise* $S_2(talk [to N])$ = *addressee*

Active possibility adjective Able_1
$\text{Able}_1(harm)$ = *harmful* $\text{Able}_1(rebellion)$ = *restive*
$\text{Able}_1(fight)$ = *bellicose* $\text{Able}_1(afraid)$ = *cowardly*

Syntagmatic LFs

Positive evaluation adjective Bon
$\text{Bon}(contribution)$ = *valuable* $\text{Bon}(service)$ = *quality*
$\text{Bon}(idea)$ = *good, promising* $\text{Bon}(weather)$ = *fine, lovely, nice, ...*

Support verbs Oper, Func and Labor
$\text{Oper}_1(apology)$ = *offer* [ART ~] $\text{Oper}_2(apology)$ = *receive* [ART ~]
$\text{Func}_1(support)$ = *comes* [from N_X] $\text{Func}_2(support)$ = *goes* [to N_Y]
$\text{Labor}_{123}(inheritance)$ = *leave* [N_Y as ~ to N_Z]
$\text{Labor}_{321}(inheritance)$ = *receive* [N_Y as ~ from N_X]

Realization verbs Real, Fact and Labreal
$\text{Real}_1(duty)$ = *discharge* [N_X's ~] $\text{Real}_2(treatment)$ = *respond* [to ART ~]
$\text{Fact}_0(film)$ = *is playing, is in the theaters*
$\text{Fact}_1(river)$ = *empties* [into N_X] $\text{Fact}_2(bomb)$ = *falls* [on N_Y]
$\text{Labreal}_{112}(artillery)$ = *hit* [N_Y with ~]
$\text{Labreal}_{121}(invitation)$ = *take up* [N_X on $A_{(poss)}(N_X)$ ~]

Locative/temporal preposition Loc_{in}
$\text{Loc}_{in}(list)$ = *on* [ART ~] $\text{Loc}_{in}(end)$ = *at* [ART ~] $\text{Loc}_{in}(program)$ = *on* [ART ~]
$\text{Loc}_{in}(holiday)$ = *on* [~] $\text{Loc}_{in}(socialism)$ = *under* [~] $\text{Loc}_{in}(past)$ = *in* [ART ~]

It is impossible to touch here on several interesting aspects of LFs: standard *vs.* non-standard LFs, simple *vs.* complex LFs, configurations of LFs, fused elements of the value of LFs, etc.

1.2.4.3 Correlations between the meaning and the collocates of a lexical unit

The proposed description of lexical meanings and restricted lexical cooccurrence leads to sharpening of lexicographic definitions. Take, for instance, the noun APPLAUSE. In *Longman Dictionary of Contemporary English*, it is defined as 'the sound of many people hitting their hands together and shouting, to show that they have enjoyed something'. This definition would be OK, if it weren't for the LFs Magn/AntiMagn of the noun APPLAUSE: *deafening, rapturous,* ... vs. *thin, scattered,* etc. These adjectives indicate that the applause is gradable: the strength and frequency of hitting hands together is (roughly) proportional to the approval/enjoyment by the applauder. Therefore, the definition of APPLAUSE (and that of the verb APPLAUD) must be corrected:

X applauds Y : 'X claps hands to express X's approval and/or enjoyment of Y, the strength and frequency of clapping being proportional to X's approval/enjoyment'.

In this way, the lexicographic definition of a headword L and L's collocations are buttressing each other (see Iordanskaja & Polguère 2005 and Iordanskaja 2007). Such a link is vital for the description of language, a system 'où tout se tient' [F. de Saussure].

The Explanatory Combinatorial Dictionary

All types of information about an LU L necessary to ensure the correct use of L in any context are stored in a dictionary of a special type: the **Explanatory Combinatorial Dictionary** [ECD]. It is explanatory since each L receives in it a semantic decomposition (L's "explanation"); it is combinatorial because it specifies each L's syntactic and restricted lexical cooccurrence. In the framework of MTT, such a lexicon plays a central role: L's lexical entry contains all the semantic data concerning L and all the combinatorial data that are used by MTM grammatical rules. In this sense, MTT is lexically based.

Since the ECD has been described in detail in numerous publications (Mel'čuk 1974: 110–140, Mel'čuk et al. 1984–1999, Mel'čuk & Zholkovsky 1984[2016], Mel'čuk & Polguère 2007, Mel'čuk 2012–2015: vol. 2, Ch. 11), suffice it here to state its defining properties:

General properties of the ECD
- The ECD is a theoretical lexicon elaborated within the framework of a full-fledged linguistic theory, namely MTT.
- The ECD is a formalized lexicon, written in terms of several predefined lexicographic metalanguages.
- The ECD is exhaustive at the level of each entry.

Specific properties of the ECD
- The ECD is an active dictionary, supplying all the data in the direction Meaning-to-Text.
- The ECD is a semantically based dictionary: the definition (= semantic representation) of the headword L underlies and determines L's entry.
- The ECD fully and systematically covers L's restricted lexical cooccurrence—in terms of LFs.
- The ECD treats lexemes and idioms in the same way: all of them constitute headwords of the corresponding entries.
- Each ECD's entry describes one (monosemous) LU; LUs related to each other by polysemy are united within a superentry, called a **vocable**.

1.3 The value of functional models in linguistics

An MTM of a natural language is speculative by its very nature: analyzing speakers' behavior, the linguist observes the associations between (understood) meanings and (perceived) texts and makes inferences as to the underlying representations and formal rules that relate them. The question naturally arises: How can we validate the model being proposed? At the present time, at least two experimental techniques are available:

- Computerization of linguistic MTMs and the use of the resulting systems in all branches of Natural Language Processing: machine translation, text generation, question-answering, etc.
- Psycholinguistic experimentation, which could shed precious light on the psychological reality of the basic oppositions and descriptive formal objects put forth in MTT. Thus, psycholinguistic experiments may contribute to our knowledge of whether (or to what extent) it is correct to insist, as MTT does, on the following five oppositions:
    1) Linguistic synthesis (i.e. Meaning $\Rightarrow$ Text) *vs.* linguistic analysis (i.e. Text $\Rightarrow$ Meaning).
    2) Static linguistic knowledge *vs.* dynamic procedural knowledge.

(The information of the first type is specified in linguistic rules, which constitute the MTM itself; the information of the second type is embodied in algorithmic rules that manage the application of linguistic rules.)
3) Linguistic representations of various levels *vs.* modules (i.e. rules) of the MTM that relate them.
4) The semantic representation, which targets meaning of sentences, ignoring their "physical" organization, *vs.* the syntactic-morphological-phonic representations, which target the structure of sentences, ignoring their meaning.
5) The lexicon, where all data concerning individual LUs are stored, *vs.* grammar, which present the information about classes of LUs and grammatical signs (affixes, apophonies, morphological conversions and meaningful syntactic constructions).

It seems crucial to know whether the actual behavior of speakers is based on these oppositions. We need to know more (much more!) on the psychological and neurological differences between speakers' encoding and decoding of texts, on the way the strictly linguistic data are stored in the brain in contrast to procedural knowledge, etc.

At the same time, the psychological correlates of MTT's descriptive formal objects are no less interesting:

- The **semantic structure:** Is meaning really represented in the brain by networks similar (isomorphic?) to those of MTT? Do speakers use semantic decompositions? If so, exactly how? Is it true that the production of a sentence begins with the shallowest and quite approximate semantic structure available (as MTT has it)?
- The **syntactic structure:** Is a sentence really represented in the brain by a structure similar (isomorphic?) to a dependency tree of the MTT type?
- The **lexicon:** Is the storage of lexical information in the brain similar (isomorphic?) to what is presupposed by the ECD of MTT? What are neurological differences between encoding the meaning of sentences *vs.* encoding the meaning of LUs in the lexicon? What are the mechanisms allowing a speaker to apply the descriptions of LUs in his brain to the starting SemS in order to produce the DSyntS of the future sentence? How is the interaction between the starting SemS and the sentence under production carried out?

NB What is said about psycholinguistics here is no more than a wish aimed at the science of tomorrow (or even of the day after tomorrow). The present level of research in psycholinguistics seems insufficient for what is needed to validate/invalidate the Meaning-Text approach.

The studies into the acquisition of language by children and adult learners, into aphasic disorders, into diachronic developments, etc. also could contribute their share to the acceptance/rejection of a given functional model.

To sum up: Functional models in linguistics, including MTMs, do not lack ways and means of validation. These models are of high practical utility in at least three technological and social domains: natural language processing; teaching and learning languages; manufacturing reference books, such as dictionaries, pedagogical grammars, and manuals.

The formal character of MTMs and their orientation ('How is such-and-such a thought expressed in such-and-such a language?') are especially valuable in this connection.

The theoretical impact of MTMs appears even more important. Scientific progress until today has been basically addressing the problems of the physical universe: matter and energy. Since *Homo sapiens* started speaking, we have developed new means of transportation (including spacecraft), enhanced our physical strength manifold (remember the H bomb!), improved our organs of perception (electronic microscopes and radio telescopes), widened our communication abilities (electronic media, the Internet), etc. We have penetrated the atom and the depths of the Universe; we know a lot about the origins of our world and the structure of our genes. But we have as yet made no comparable headway in the mastery of information (in the scientific sense)—this evasive "substance," which is so central to life in general and to the life of humans in particular. We do not know enough about the workings of our brain, while the enhancement of the brain remains task number one for today's science. Facing the challenges of the 21st century, the humanity badly needs good models of human thinking and reasoning (and, why not, of human emotions). This seems to be well understood by the international scientific community, and the majority of scientists would probably be in agreement with such a program.

However, strangely enough, people tend to forget—or disregard?—this vital fact:

> The only reliable key to human thinking, in all its complexity, is natural language.

Without a profound understanding of how language is functioning in our psyche, there will be no good understanding of information processing by the human brain. That is why functional models of language, and MTMs in particular, nowadays have acquired quite a special significance. Linguistics must take a place of honor among the "hard" sciences, and functional models, which embody the typical scientific approach to complex phenomena, will make their contribution.

A heavily reworked version of Mel'čuk 2009b.

Part II: **Surface-Syntactic Relations**

2 A general inventory of surface-syntactic relations in the world's languages

2.1 Introductory remarks
2.2 The deep-syntactic structure
  2.2.1 Deep-syntactic relations
  2.2.2 Fictitious lexemes
2.3 The notion of surface-syntactic relation
2.4 Conditions and criteria for establishing surface-syntactic relations in language **L**
2.5 An inventory of surface-syntactic relations found in the world's languages
Appendix A   Alphabetical index of surface-syntactic relations
Appendix B   Index of passive surface-syntactic valences of word classes

2.1 Introductory remarks

This chapter—as this monograph in general—stands upon the following three assumptions concerning the syntactic structure [SyntS] of a sentence:

1. The SyntS is described in terms of **syntactic dependencies**.
2. The SyntS is described on **two levels of representation: deep**-syntactic structure [DSyntS] and **surface**-syntactic structure [SSyntS].
3. The SyntS uses a set of **labeled relations**—deep-syntactic relations [DSyntRels] and surface-syntactic relations [SSyntRels].

Chapter 2 is dedicated to SSyntRels. For more information on linguistic dependency in general, see Mel'čuk 1988 and 2009a; on SSyntRels in particular, see Iordanskaja & Mel'čuk 2009a.

Let it be emphasized lest there be a misunderstanding: the proposed inventory of SSyntRels is not an *a priori* universal construction; it is "universal" only in the most trivial sense—it represents a set-theoretical union of the lists of SSyntRels established empirically for several languages. That is why it is called a **general** inventory (rather than a universal inventory, as is the inventory of deep-syntactic relations, see Section 2.2). It is not claimed that all of the SSyntRels listed in Section 2.5 are encountered in any language. Rather, the set of these SSyntRels is considered sufficient for the description of SSyntSs in the languages that have been studied.

Tentative lists of SSyntRels for particular languages—Russian, English, French, German, Spanish, Arabic, etc.—have been published over the last 60 years (see the references in Iordanskaja & Mel'čuk 2009a: 153). The general inventory of

SSyntRels proposed below is based on a list of Russian SSyntRels (Mel'čuk 1974: 221–235, 2012c: 135–144; Iomdin 2010c), a list of English SSyntRels (Mel'čuk & Pertsov 1987, Mel'čuk 2012–2015: vol. 3, 444–453 [3.4.11] and 2016: 184–194), a list of German SSyntRels (Zangenfeind 2012), and two partial lists of French SSynt-Rels (Iordanskaja & Mel'čuk 2009a, Poiret & Liu 2019); these lists have profited from many previous works, duly indicated in the above titles. The resulting set of SSyntRels underwent numerous corrections and additions, embodying the experience acquired during the last decade. Therefore, any mismatch between the present list and previous publications must be resolved in favor of the former.

NB There is also a universal inventory of SSyntRels based on syntactic dependency tree banks for over 70 languages: "Stanford Universal Dependencies [UD]" (de Marneffe et al. 2014, de Marneffe & Manning 2008/2015), https://universaldependencies.org. Unfortunately, it is impossible to compare the SSyntRel inventory proposed below with Stanford Universal Dependencies: the theoretical framework and the methodology are so different that a comparison would require a serious special study. See Gerdes et al. 2018, which proposes a modification of Stanford UD, making it closer to a linguistically valid inventory of SSyntRels.

The rest of this chapter is organized as follows: Section 2.2 offers a cursory characterization of the DSynt-structure; Section 2.3 contains a few informal remarks on the notion of SSyntRel; Section 2.4 describes the criteria for establishing the inventory of SSyntRels in a given language; finally, Section 2.5 presents the list of SSyntRels known to me today.

2.2 The deep-syntactic structure

To help the reader evaluate the suggested SSyntRels, it is necessary to present the set of DSyntRels and that of fictitious lexemes appearing in DSynt-structures of sentences: the fact is that each SSyntRel in the inventory of Section 2.5 is supplied with the information of its correspondence to DSyntRels and/or fictitious lexemes. (On DSyntS, see Chapter 1, Subsection 1.2.2, p. 12.)

2.2.1 Deep-syntactic relations

In sharp contrast with the SSyntRels, the DSyntRels are **linguistically universal** in the following sense of the term *universal*:

> Used together with fictitious lexemes, the proposed DSyntRels are sufficient to describe the DSyntSs of any language.

There are thirteen DSyntRels, which have been established by theoretical reasoning (based, of course, on linguistic data).

- All syntactic constructions known in the world's languages are divided into two major families: coordinative vs. subordinative constructions.
  The coordinative constructions are described by two DSyntRels: **COORD**(inative) and **PSEUDO-COORD**.

  NB In several previous publications, the **PSEUDO-COORD** DSyntRel (and the corresponding SSyntRel) was called **QUASI-COORDINATIVE**. In order to improve the terminology, it was decided to use the prefix quasi-[X] for an element that is not an X, but—under appropriate conditions—can be treated as an X, i.e., quasi-Xs can be confounded with genuine Xs (for instance, quasi-elementary [sign], quasi-grammeme, quasi-morph). An element that is not an X and can never be confounded with Xs, but resembles X to a sufficient degree will be called pseudo-[X]. This modification concerns also such names of SSyntRels as *quasi-subjectival ⇒ pseudo-subjectival, etc.

- The subordinative constructions are subdivided, in their turn, into weak-subordinative vs. strong-subordinative. The weak-subordinative constructions are described by the DSyntRels **ADDRESS**(ative) and **APPEND**(itive).
- The strong-subordinative constructions fall into two subsets: the modifying DSyntRels vs. the actantial DSyntRels; this division corresponds to the two main syntactic phenomena: modification (or characterization) vs. complementation.
  - The modifying constructions are described by the DSyntRels **ATTR**(ibutive) and **ATTR**$_{\text{descr(iptive)}}$.
  - The actantial constructions are described by the DSyntRels **I, II, ..., VI,** and **II**$_{\text{dir(ect).sp(eech)}}$.

  NB A deep-syntactic actant [DSyntA] of a lexeme L is, as a rule, a syntactic dependent of L that expresses one of L's semantic actants—that is, a DSynt-actant of L is controlled by L's active valence. For instance, in the sentence *Because of this, John reminded Mary about the exam in my presence* the lexemes JOHN, MARY and EXAM are DSyntAs of REMIND, since they are imposed by the meaning of the verb ('X reminds Y of Z'); however, the expressions *because of this* and *in my presence* are not the verb's actants, but freely added circumstantials.

A lexical unit may have up to six DSynt-actants, which gives six actantial DSyntRels. An additional DSyntRel is introduced for Direct Speech, which functions as an object of a communication verb:

[*Mickey*] *shouted*: –II$_{\text{dir.sp}}$→ ***Come*** [*over right away!"*].

Let me sum up. The 13 DSyntRels used in the Meaning-Text approach are as follows:

Two coordinative DSyntRels

- **COORD**, or the **COORDINATIVE** DSyntRel, which represents normal coordination, either without a conjunction or with one:

    MARY-**COORD**→JOHN-**COORD**→OR ANN   ⇔ *Mary, John or Ann*
    [MARY] COME$_{PAST}$,-[JOHN]-**COORD**→LEAVE$_{PAST}$ ⇔ *Mary came, John left.*
    [MARY] COME$_{PAST}$,-**COORD**→AND [JOHN LEAVE$_{PAST}$]   ⇔ *Mary came, and John left.*

- **PSEUDO-COORD**, or the **PSEUDO-COORDINATIVE** DSyntRel, which represents syntactic constructions of elaboration, where, for instance, a prepositional phrase follows—normally without a conjunction—another such phrase:

    IN-[NEW YORK]-**PSEUDO-COORD**→ON-[MANHATTAN]-**PSEUDO-COORD**→AT [JOHN'S]   ⇔ *[I stayed] in New York, on Manhattan, at John's.*

Eleven subordinative DSyntRels

- **APPEND**, or the **APPENDITIVE** DSyntRel, which subordinates such "extrastructural" elements as parentheticals, interjections and prolepses to the syntactic head of the clause:

    SORRY←**APPEND**-[I]-BE$_{IND, PRES, NON-PERF, NON-PROGR}$ [BUSY]   ⇔ *Sorry, I am busy.*
    OK←**APPEND**-[I]-BE$_{IND, PRES, NON-PERF, NON-PROGR}$-**APPEND**→FORTUNATELY [HERE]
    ⇔ *OK, fortunately I am here.*

- **ADDRESS**, or the **ADDRESSATIVE** DSyntRel, which subordinates direct address expressions to the syntactic head of the clause:

    JOHN←**ADDRESS**-[WHERE]-BE$_{IND, PRES, NON-PERF, NON-PROGR}$ [YOU?]
    ⇔ *John, where are you?*
    OK-**ADDRESS**→CAPTAIN   ⇔ *OK, Captain.*

    In contrast to the **APPEND** DSyntRel, the **ADDRESS** DSyntRel is non-repeatable.

Two modifying DSyntRels

- **ATTR**, or the **ATTRIBUTIVE** DSyntRel, which describes all types of **restrictive** modifier constructions (minus descriptive ones, see the next DSyntRel):

    RED←**ATTR**-FLAG   ⇔ *red flag*
    MAN-**ATTR**→OF [GREAT COURAGE]   ⇔ *man of [great courage]*
    VERY←**ATTR**-INTERESTING   ⇔ *very interesting*
    DRIVE$_{(V)}$-**ATTR**→FAST   ⇔ *[John was] driving [very] fast*

    NB The name **ATTR** is in fact an abbreviation for **ATTR**$_{restr}$, that is, it is used for all **restrictive** modifiers. A restrictive modifier restricts, or constrains, the denotation of the lexical expression modified: thus, the LU [a] BOOK denotes any book, but the phrase [a] FRENCH←**ATTR**$_{restr}$-BOOK denotes only a book printed in French. Since most modifiers are restrictive—it is the default case—it is possible to omit the subscript $_{restr}$ for simplicity's sake.

- **ATTR**$_{descr}$, or the **DESCRIPTIVE-ATTRIBUTIVE** DSyntRel, used for descriptive modifiers, which do not restrict the denotation of the expression modified, but simply qualify it:

  MARY,–ATTR$_{descr}$→TIRED [AND HUNGRY, LEFT] ⇔ *Mary, tired [and hungry, left.]*

Seven actantial DSyntRels

- **I**, as in
JOHN←I–READ	⇔ *John is reading.*
MY/JOHN←I–TRIP	⇔ *my trip, John's trip*
TRANSLATION–I→BY [JOHN]	⇔ *translation [of this novel] by John*

- **II**, as in
BOOK←II–READ	⇔ *[John is] reading [a] book.*
JOHN←II–EXPULSION	⇔ *John's expulsion*
FOR–II→JOHN	⇔ *for John*

- **III**, as in
  [BOOK←II–]SEND–III→JOHN ⇔ *[Mary] sends [a] book$_{II}$ to John$_{III}$. / ... sends John$_{III}$ [a] book$_{II}$.*

- **IV–VI**, as in
  [HUNDRED DOLLAR$_{PL}$←II–]LEND–IV→MONTH ⇔ *[Would you] lend me$_{III}$ $$100$_{II}$ for a month$_{IV}$?*

  [ISTANBUL←III–]MISSION–IV→MONTH
  ⎯⎯⎯V→STUDY ⇔ *[a] mission to Istanbul$_{III}$ for a month$_{IV}$ to study$_V$ [Turkish]*

- **II**$_{dir.sp}$, as in
  WHISPER–II$_{dir.sp}$→COME$_{IMPER}$ ⇔ *[John] whispered: "Come [back!"]*

The full inventory of DSyntRels is given in *Table 2.1*, starting with the strongest subordinative dependencies and going towards the weakest coordinative links.

Table 2.1 Universal inventory of deep-syntactic relations

SUBORDINATIVE DSyntRels									COORDINATIVE DSyntRels	
STRONG DSyntRels								WEAK DSyntRels		
Actantial DSyntRels						Attributive DSyntRels				
I	II	III	IV	V	VI	II$_{dir.speech}$	ATTR$_{restr}$	ATTR$_{descr}$	ADDRESS	APPEND	PSEUDO-COORD	COORD
1	2	3	4	5	6	7	8	9	10	11	12	13

2.2.2 Fictitious lexemes

Along with DSyntRels, the DSynt-structure uses **fictitious lexemes**, which carry the lexical-type meanings expressed by meaningful SSynt-constructions (Mel'čuk 2012–2015: vol. 2, 37–42, 2018c). In other words, a fictitious lexeme represents, in the DSyntS, a meaning expressed on the surface by a **meaningful syntactic construction**, that is, a type of two-lexeme phrase where the surface-syntactic relation carries, in addition to the information about the syntactic link itself, also a lexical-like chunk of meaning. Such constructions are quite idiosyncratic and language-specific. In the DSyntS they have to be represented by artificial lexical units—in order to avoid multiplying the set of DSyntRels. Let me give a couple of examples.

Example 1: indirect object of Beneficiary

(1) *John has painted* **me** *a beautiful landscape.*

The wordform **me** is, of course, a surface-syntactic indirect object. But at the DSynt-level it does not correspond to a DSynt-actant of the verb PAINT; semantically, it expresses the person for whose benefit the painting was created. To represent this construction in the DSyntS, if we do not want to introduce another DSyntRel, we have to use a fictitious lexeme: «FOR».

☞ 1. A fictitious lexeme is indicated by angular quotes: « ».
2. On the form of linguistic rules, see Chapter 1, Subsection 1.2.3, pp. 15*ff*.

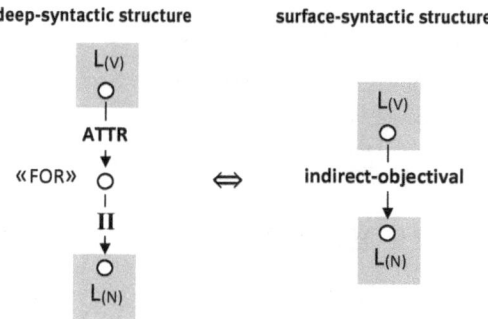

Figure 2.1 Deep-syntactic rule for the fictitious lexeme «FOR», that is, for producing the English construction of the type "*paint me* [something]"

Example 2: "derision" *schm*-noun

(2) *Politics,* **schmolitics!** | *Theory,* **schmeory.** | *Books,* **schmooks.** | *Baby,* **schmaby.**

In English, the so-called *schm*-reduplication of a noun N expresses the Speaker's derision and skepticism about (the referent of) N; the N, *schm*-N phrase means ≈ 'I dismiss N as being ludicrous and worthless'. (*schm*- is the name of the corresponding derivational means, which adds to the derived N the prefix /šm/- and deletes the initial prevocalic cluster, if any.)

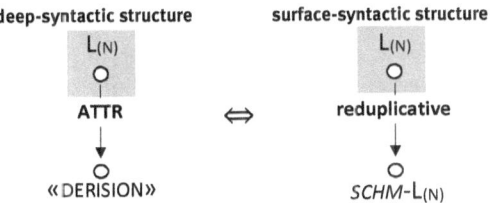

Figure 2.2 Deep-syntactic rule for the fictitious lexeme «DERISION», that is, for producing the English construction "N, *schm*-N"

Note that because of variegated lexical-type meanings attached to the operation of lexeme reduplication in the world's languages, a special **reduplicative** SSyntRel is needed (or even several different **reduplicative** SSyntRels, see Section 2.5, No. 113, p. 108).

Here is an approximate inventory of fictitious lexemes. (It is by no means complete, since it can be established only empirically, by collecting fictitious lexemes found in different languages.)

Table 2.2 Some fictitious lexemes in the world's languages

«AFFECT»	«CONDITION»	«IF»	«REPRESENT»
«AFTER»	«DAT_ETH»	«IF$_{IRR}$»	«RESULT_IN»
«ALTHOUGH»	«DERISION»	«INCLUDE»	«SAY»
«AND_THEN»	«DISTANCE»	«INSTRUMENT»	«SHOULD»
«AS_IF»	«DURING»	«MANNER»	«TERM»
«BE»	«EVERY»	«MAYBE»	«TITLE» (*professor*
«BE_ABLE»	«FOR» (*buy her a dress*)	«MORE»	*Drouin*)
«BE_FROM»	«FROM» (*one from these*)	«MOVE$_{DIR}$»	«VERY»
«BE_LOCATED»	«GOAL»	«NAME»	«WHILE»
«BELONG»	«HAVE»	«PER»	«WILL_BE»
«CAUSE(N)»	«HAVE_TO»	«PRICE»	«WITH»

NB A fictitious lexeme is not a semantic unit; it is only a conventional name for a (possibly, quite complex) configuration of sememes.

2.3 The notion of surface-syntactic relation

A SSyntRel **r** (in the phrase $L_1–r→L_2$) is a linguistic sign of language **L** of the syntactic level—a triplet ⟨signified ; signifier ; syntactics⟩ that describes a family of similar syntactic constructions of **L**.

- The signified of this sign is the name **r** itself; **r** is characterized by a bundle of the deep-syntactic relations to which it corresponds (= which it can express).
- Its signifier is a bundle of formal properties of the phrase $L_1–r→L_2$—namely, word order, prosodic and morphological means applied to L_1 and L_2 in order to express **r** in the sentence.
- Its syntactics is a bundle of combinatorial properties—that is, all indications concerning cooccurrence of **r** with other SSyntRels in an SSynt-structure.

The inventory of SSyntRels of language **L**, just like the inventory of its grammemes or its phonemes, is established based on special criteria of three types: Criteria **A** – **C**, given in Section 2.4.

Each SSyntRel **r** is described by the corresponding surface-syntactic rule; SSynt-rules have the following form:

$$\begin{array}{c} L_1 \\ \circ \\ \big\downarrow r \\ \circ \\ L_2 \end{array} \quad \Leftrightarrow \quad \begin{array}{cc} L_{1m_1} & L_{2m_2} \\ \circ + & \ldots + \circ \end{array} \quad \Big| \quad C$$

The left-hand side of a SSynt-rule is a two-node subtree featuring the SSyntRel linking lexemes L_1 and L_2; its right-hand side is the corresponding linear string of the same lexemes supplied with **syntactic grammemes**, if any (m_1 and m_2); for simplicity's sake, I don't consider prosodies, which mark particular SSyntRels in some tonal languages; C stands for conditions under which this correspondence holds.

SSyntRels are (by definition) language-specific, just as grammatical cases or phonemes. Thus, the **subjectival** SSyntRel in Russian is, of course, not identical to the **subjectival** SSyntRel in Basque or Lezgian, neither semantically nor formally—in the same way as the Russian nominative case is not identical with the nominative in Kurdish or Dargwa, and as the Russian phoneme /t/ is by no means identical with the phoneme /t/ in English, Mandarin Chinese or Hawaiian. These facts, however, do not prevent linguists from compiling general inventories of nominal cases and those of phonemes, based on the **structural** resemblance of the corresponding entities. With all possible distinctions between them, nominatives of different languages are the cases of nomination; and /t/ is everywhere a voiceless dental plosive consonant. Quite similarly, the (syntactic) subject—the dependent element of the **subjectival** SSyntRel—is the most privileged among the surface-syntactic actants of a finite verb in any language, while the direct object— the dependent element of the **direct-objectival** SSyntRel—is the second most privileged among the actants of a transitive verb (see Chapter 3, Subsection 3.8); etc. The idea of a general list of SSyntRels known today suggests itself, and the present chapter picks up the challenge.

Sufficiency of the set of SSyntRels proposed. The SSyntRels on the list have been established based on the following premise:

> The surface-syntactic structure—in combination with the SSynt-communicative and SSynt-anaphoric structures—must be sufficient for determining word order, prosodization and morphologization of the sentence under synthesis.

To put it differently, the SSyntS-to-DMorphS transition should not require information from the preceding levels of representation (the DSyntR or the SemR): whatever information is needed must be contained in the SSyntRels used—plus, of course, the SSynt-communicative and SSynt-anaphoric structures as well as all the necessary lexicographic information about the properties of lexical units involved.

NB This does by no means imply that our present list claims exhaustiveness. It is, of course, not sufficient for the description of SSyntSs of **any** language: to compile such a list for about 7000 languages of the world is an enormous empirical task. But the intention behind this list is exactly being exhaustive. In practical terms, this requires that criticisms leveled at the list should aim at indicating syntactic constructions not covered by it.

Necessity of each SSyntRel on the list. The inventory of SSyntRels proposed below (in Section 2.5) has not been systematically checked for minimality—that is, for the necessity of each SSyntRel included; it is the SSyntRel sufficiency that is pursued in the first place. At the same time, I strive for the maximal clarity, so that I do not collapse two SSyntRels even if this seemed formally possible, but would make the system less transparent. Therefore, some SSyntRels listed below may turn out redundant.

2.4 Conditions and criteria for establishing surface-syntactic relations in language L

Each **r** must meet the following two general conditions (Iordanskaja & Mel'čuk 2009a):

Condition 1. The syntactic constructions described by the SSyntRel **r** resemble each other to a sufficient degree—that is, they share enough linguistic properties. The properties underlying SSyntRels are not linguistically universal in the strict sense of the term: generally speaking, they may be relevant in language **L** under consideration and irrelevant or non-existent in another language. Moreover, the properties relevant for one lexical class (say, for verbs) may be useless or inapplicable to a different class. (For more on relevant linguistic properties, see Chapter 3, 3.2.3, pp. 122*ff*.)

Condition 2. The SSyntRel **r** satisfies the formal requirements of Criteria **A–C**, given below.

There are three groups of criteria for SSyntRels (Mel'čuk 2009a: 27–33, 2012–2015: vol. 3, 411*ff*):

- Criterion **A**   PRESENCE of a SSyntRel between lexemes L_1 and L_2 in an utterance.
- Criteria **B1–B3**   ORIENTATION of the SSyntRel between lexemes L_1 and L_2 in an utterance.
- Criteria **C1–C3**   TYPE of the SSyntRel between lexemes L_1 and L_2 in an utterance.

Criterion A – PRESENCE of a surface-syntactic relation between lexemes L_1 and L_2

For there to be a SSyntRel **r** between lexemes L_1 and L_2 in a given utterance **U**, Criterion **A** requires two things:

- The configuration L_1–**r**–L_2 must be expressible by a prosodic unit, that is, by a phrase of language **L**—not necessarily in the utterance **U** itself, but at least in **L** in general.
- The linear position of one of the lexemes L_1 and L_2 in the utterance **U** must be determined by the other.

2.4 Conditions and criteria for establishing surface-syntactic relations in language L

Prosodic unity and linear arrangement in the configuration L_1-r-L_2
In a given utterance **U** of **L**, the lexemes L_1 and L_2 can have a direct Synt-dependency link, that is, they can form a configuration L_1-r-L_2, if and only if both of Conditions 1 and 2 are simultaneously satisfied:

Condition 1
(a) General case
 L_1-r-L_2 can be implemented by a phrase of language **L**, such as N−V, V−N, ADJ−N, PREP−N, ADV−ADJ, NUM−N, etc.
(b) Special case
 L_1-r-L_2 alone cannot be implemented by a phrase of **L**, but taken together with a convenient configuration of lexemes from the set $\{L_i\}$ appearing in the same utterance it can, such that the following three configurations are implementable by phrases of **L**:

 1) $\overline{L_1-\{L_{1\text{-}1}\}\ L_2}-\{L_{1\text{-}2}\}$, 2) $L_1-\{L_{1\text{-}1}\}$ and 3) $L_2-\{L_{1\text{-}2}\}$.

Condition 2
The linear position of one of the lexemes L_1 and L_2 in the phrase L_1-r-L_2 is specified with respect to the other.

Examples

The Case (b) of Condition 1 covers two types of expressions:

(i) $L_1-L_2-L_{3(N)}$, as in $one_{L1}-of_{L2}-them_{L3}$. Here, *one of is not a phrase, while the utterances of them and one of them are phrases; consequently, the configuration one−of is allowed for.

(ii) $\overline{L_1-\{L_{1\text{-}1}\}\ L_{2(CONJ)}}-\{L_{1\text{-}2}\}$, as in
 $\overline{It\ became_{L1}-\{obvious\}_{\{L1\text{-}1\}}\ that_{L2}}-\{he\ wasn't\ there\}_{\{L1\text{-}2\}}$.

Here, *became that is not a phrase, while became obvious and that he wasn't there are phrases, with became and that as their syntactic heads (see Criteria **B** immediately below); therefore, the configuration became−that is accepted as legitimate.

Criteria B – ORIENTATION of the SSyntRel between lexemes L_1 and L_2

In each configuration of lexemes L_1-r-L_2 in the utterance **U**, one of them syntactically dominates the other, i.e., is its SSynt-governor, or the SSynt-head of the phrase L_1-r-L_2. Informally speaking, the SSynt-head of a phrase is the lexeme that determines—at least, to a greater extent than the other lexeme (its SSynt-dependent)—different properties of the phrase according to Criteria **B1−B3**.
 Let there be a phrase L_1-r-L_2.

Criterion B1 – The passive SSynt-valence of a phrase

> In the phrase L_1–**r**–L_2, the lexeme L_1 is the Synt-governor of L_2 if the following condition is satisfied:
>> The **passive SSynt-valence** of the L_1–**r**–L_2 phrase is determined by the passive SSynt-valence of L_1 to a greater extent than by that of L_2; then we have L_1–**r**→L_2.

To put it differently, the passive SSynt-valence of the phrase L_1–**r**→L_2 is rather that of L_1 than that of L_2; the SSynt-head of a phrase determines more than any other of its elements all the external syntactic links of the phrase.

Criterion B2 – The morphological links between the elements of a phrase and its external context
(in a language that has inflectional morphology)

> If the phrase L_1–**r**–L_2 in which the passive SSynt-valence of its components does not allow one to establish the SSynt-head is such that
>> – L_1 controls the inflection of lexemes external to the phrase
>> – or L_1's inflection is controlled by such lexemes,
>
> then L_1 is the SSynt-head of the phrase: L_1–**r**→L_2.

The morphological "contact point" of the phrase L_1–**r**→L_2 is rather L_1 than L_2; it is the SSynt-head of a phrase that, as a rule, interacts morphologically with its context.

Criterion B3 – The semantic content of a phrase

> If the phrase L_1–**r**–L_2 in which neither the passive SSynt-valence nor the morphology allows one to establish the SSynt-governor means 'a kind/an instance of L_1' rather than 'a kind/an instance of L_2', then L_1 is the SSynt-head of the phrase: L_1–**r**→L_2.

The denotation of the phrase L_1–**r**→L_2 is determined rather by the denotation of its SSynt-head.

For Criteria **B** to be satisfied, at least one of the Criteria **B1** > **B2** > **B3** must be satisfied, such that other Criteria **B** higher in the hierarchy are not operational.

Criteria C1–C3 – TYPE of the syntactic dependency between two lexemes

Criterion C1: presence of semantic contrast (Minimal pair test)
Notation: $w_i(L)$ is a wordform of lexeme L.

> One and the same hypothetical SSyntRel **r** should not describe two phrases
> $w_1(L_1)$-**r**→$w_2(L_2)$ and $w_3(L_1)$-**r**→$w_4(L_2)$
> if Conditions 1 and 2 are simultaneously satisfied:
>
> **Condition 1**
> These phrases contrast semantically, the contrast being manifested either in the form of the phrases themselves or in the syntactic behavior properties of their members.
>
> **Condition 2**
> If these phrases differ in their form, they differ only by some syntactic means of expression—by word order of their elements, syntactic prosody or syntactic grammemes.

If Criterion **C1** is satisfied—that is, if Conditions 1 and 2 are both satisfied, **r** should be split into two different SSyntRels, r_1 and r_2, $r_1 \neq r_2$.

For example, the Russian phrases *žena*-**synt**→*druga*$_{GEN}$ 'wife of.friend' and *žena*-**synt**→*drug*$_{NOM}$ [*žena-drug*] 'wife who is a friend' should be described by two different SSyntRels, since these phrases semantically contrast and formally differ only by the case of DRUG: the genitive case in the first phrase and the same case as that of ŽENA in the second (*žena*-**obj-adnom**→*druga*, Section 2.5, No. 49; *žena*[-]-**qualif-appos**→*drug*, **ibidem**, No. 78).

NB Criterion **C1** is formulated here with an addition, previously absent. Namely, Condition 1 now foresees the possible physical manifestation of the semantic contrast not only in the form of the phrases under analysis, but also "... in the syntactic behavior properties of their members." Syntactic behavior of an LU includes its combinability with other LUs and word order with respect to other phrases). This is an important amendment, which makes Criterion **C1** more sensitive.[1]

---

[1] Here is an example. In Russian, two genitive phrases dependent on the same N are mutually ordered according to their SSyntRel:

(i) *portret neobyčajnoj formy našego otca* lit. 'portrait of.unusual form of.our father'
  — qual-adnom —
  — obj-adnom —
vs. **portret našego otca neobyčajnoj formy*

Two genitive phrases have identical form, but manifest different syntactic behavior of their members—their different linear positions.

Criterion C2 – syntactic substitutability (Substitution test)

> An SSyntRel **r** must have a prototypical dependent that is allowable with any governor.

For example, the Russian phrases *xoču*–**synt**→*vypit'* [*kofe*] 'I.want drink [coffee]' and *mogu*–**synt**→*vypit'* [*kofe*] 'I.can drink [coffee]' should be described by two different SSyntRels—**direct-objectival** and **infinitive-objectival**:

1) The **direct-objectival** SSyntRel has a prototypical dependent, possible with any governor: N_{ACC}; some—but not all—governors accept also V_{INF} and čto/čtoby-clause:

   xoču–**dir-obj**→*kofe*$_{ACC}$ 'I.want coffee'   ~
   xoču–**dir-obj**→*vypit'* [*kofe*]   'I.want to.drink [coffee]'   ~
   xoču–**dir-obj**→*čtoby* [*on pil kofe*]   'I.want that [he drink coffee]'

2) The **infinitive-objectival** SSyntRel also has a prototypical dependent, possible with any governor: V_{INF}; no governor accepts N_{ACC}:

   mogu–**inf-obj**→*vypit'* [*kofe*]   'I.can to.drink [coffee]'   ~
   *mogu–**inf-obj**→*kofe*$_{ACC}$ 'I.can coffee'

If these SSyntRels are not distinguished, the "unified" SSyntRel will have no prototypical dependent.

Criterion C3 – no limited repeatability (Cooccurrence test)

> An SSyntRel **r** must be either unlimitedly repeatable or non-repeatable—that is, it cannot be limitedly repeatable.

The phrases *write*–**synt**→*after lunch*, *write*–**synt**→*in the next room*, *write*–**synt**→*out of frustrastion*, etc. can all be described by the same SSyntRel: **circumstantial**, since the number of such dependents appearing simultaneously with the same governor is theoretically unlimited. On the contrary, the phrases [*They*] *returned*–**synt**→*all* and [*They*] *returned*–**synt**→*drunk* require two different SSyntRels (**floating-copredicative** and **subject-copredicative**), since otherwise the dependent will be repeatable exactly twice (*They returned **all** really **drunk***).

2.5 An inventory of surface-syntactic relations found in the world's languages

And now, to the surface-syntactic relations themselves. But before a general inventory of SSyntRels in various languages is presented, let me illustrate the transition between a DSynt-structure and an SSynt-structure in order to demonstrate the correspondences between DSynt-relations and fictitious lexemes, on the one hand, and the SSynt-relations, on the other hand. This is done for sentence (3):

(3) *Mary washed the floor clean.*

Figure 2.3 Deep-syntactic and surface-syntactic structures of sentence (3)

The SSyntRels in this inventory are not supplied with full systematic explanations and justifications; I limit myself to a minimum of examples and cursory remarks.

It goes without saying that the present proposal is still a sketch that needs to be improved and sharpened in many respects.

For better surveyability, the SSyntRels described here are grouped as follows:

- First, SSyntRels are divided into **subordinative** and **coordinative** relations.
- Second, the subordinative SSyntRels are subdivided into two sets:
  - **Clausal** SSyntRels, which typically hold between the heads of phrases within a clause. These SSyntRels either link the verb to its actants/circumstantials, or are similar to such SSyntRels; certain clausal SSyntRels can also hold between the lexemes within a phrase (for example, **passive-agentive-completive** and **comparative-objectival** SSyntRels).
  - **Phrasal** SSyntRels, which hold only between the lexemes within a phrase, never between heads of phrases within a clause (for example, **determinative** and **modificative** SSyntRels).

- Third, inside of each subdivision of subordinative SSyntRels, the line is drawn between **valence-controlled** SSyntRels, which necessarily embody complementation (e.g., COMPARE→N_1 to N_2), and non-valence-controlled SSyntRels, which can be either modifying (e.g., **SHINING**←MOMENT) or ancillary (= involving structural, or grammatical, LUs; e.g., **HAVE**→WRITTEN).

> An SSyntRel G–r→D is said be valence-controlled if and only if **r** is explicitly mentioned in the government pattern of its syntactic governor G.

NB The terms **modification** and **modifying** are used here in a very broad sense—to refer to any syntactically subordinated element that does not represent complementation and is not an ancillary (structural, or grammatical) element.

The name of an SSyntRel is an adjective derived from the name of its dependent member: subject ~ **subjectival**, direct object ~ **direct-objectival**, etc. The systematic effort to have "self-explanatory," logically derived names for SSyntRels sometimes results in names that are too long and cumbersome; such is, for instance, the **direct-object-comparative-conjunctional-completive** SSyntRel, which subordinates the complement of a comparative conjunction that is semantically correlated with the direct object of the clause (see below, No. 102). For practical use, such names can, of course, be abbreviated at will (in this case, it could be **dir-obj-compar-conj**).

In the examples, the SSynt-dependent of the SSyntRel under examination is boldfaced, and words not participating in the construction illustrated are included in brackets.

First, a synopsis of the inventory of SSynt-relations possible in various languages.

I Subordinative surface-syntactic relations: 1–114
   I.1 Clause-level SSyntRels: 1–46
      I.1.1 Valence-controlled [= actantial, quasi-actantial and actantial-like] SSyntRels: 1–26
      I.1.2 Non-valence-controlled SSyntRels: 27–46
         I.1.2.1 Actantial SSyntRels: 27–28
         I.1.2.2 Copredicative SSyntRels: 29–32
         I.1.2.3 Circumstantial SSyntRels: 33–38
         I.1.2.4 Extra-structural SSyntRels: 39–46
   I.2 Phrase-level SSyntRels: 47–114
      I.2.1 Any type of phrase SSyntRels, non-valence-controlled: 47
      I.2.2 Nominal phrase SSyntRels: 48–83

I.2.2.1 Valence-controlled: 48–59
I.2.2.2 Valence-controlled and non-valence-controlled: 60–64
I.2.2.3 Non-valence-controlled: 65–83
I.2.3 Adpositional phrase SSyntRels, valence-controlled: 84–85
I.2.4 Verbal phrase (= analytical form) SSyntRels, non-valence-controlled: 86–96
I.2.5 Conjunctional phrase SSyntRels, valence-controlled: 97–107
I.2.6 Word-like phrase SSyntRels, non-valence-controlled: 108–114

II Coordinative surface-syntactic relations: 115–122

Each SSyntRel **r** is supplied with the following three types of data:

- **r**'s correspondence with DSyntRels and/or with a fictitious lexeme. If there is no such correspondence (that is, **r** is introduced into the SSynt-structure by DSynt-to-SSynt-structure rules), **r** is not required to have a prototypical dependent.
- **r**'s standard (= most frequent, normal) governor G. Other, more specific governors may be indicated in the examples.
- **r**'s prototypical dependent D.

I Subordinative surface-syntactic relations: 1–114
I.1 Clause-level (= clausal) SSyntRels: 1–46
I.1.1 Valence-controlled SSyntRels: 1–26

Actantial, quasi-actantial and actantial-like SSyntRels (≈ subjects and objects)

It is worth reminding the reader that a SSynt-actant of a lexeme is not necessarily valence-controlled by it (Mel'čuk 2012–2015: vol. 3, 94–99); for instance, the following types of SSynt-actant are non-valence-controlled:

- Beneficiary, as in [He] did–[it]–**oblique-objectival**→ for you
- Price, as in [He] did–[it]–**oblique-objectival**→ for two hundred dollars
- Raised Possessor, as in Fr. [On ne] lui ←**indirect-objectival**–trouve [pas de défauts] lit. 'People don't to.him find of defects'
- Dativus Ethicus, as in Fr. Goûtez–**dat-ethic**→ moi [ça] ! lit. 'Taste on.me this!'

In the DSynt-structure, such actants are introduced by means of fictitious lexemes (in the above examples, «FOR», «PRICE», and «DAT_ETHIC»).

1. **Subjectival** SSyntRel. It expresses the DSyntRel I; the prototypical G is a finite verb V_{FIN}, the prototypical D is a prepositionless N.

The subject is the most privileged dependent element of the clause in the language under consideration (Chapter 3, Section 3.3, Definition 3.1, p. 135).

[*As the*] **reader**←subj–*will* [*see* ...] | *I*←subj–*am* [*fine*.] | *It*←subj–*was* [*dawning*.]

That←subj–[*John left*]–*amazed* [*us*.] | *It*←subj–*amazed* [*us that John left*.]

To←subj–[*mention this point*]–*is* [*important*.]
It←subj–*is* [*important to mention this point*.]

NB In the sentences of the type of *It amazed us that John left* and *It is important to mention this point* the boldfaced phrases are described as pseudo-subjects, see below, No. 6, p. 51.

To←subj–[*read*]–*is* [*to empower,*] *to*←subj–[*empower*]–*is* [*to write*.]

Carrying←subj–[*out attacks*]–*became* [*increasingly difficult*.]

Enough←subj–*has* [*been said on this topic*.]

[*Which*←w*a*̌y] *to*←subj–[*choose*]–*must* [*be decided later*.]
⎿——— dir-obj ———⏌

[*The*] **easiest**←subj–[*of these solutions*]–*turned* [*out to be the last one*.]

— The G = V$_{FIN}$ can be a zero wordform of one of the Russian lexemes ʙʏᴛ' 'be':

Russian

***Ivan*←subj–Ø$^{BYT'}$** [*star*] lit. 'Ivan old'. | ***Ivan*←subj–Ø$^{BYT'}$** [*v Londone*] lit. 'Ivan in London'.

Ja←subj–[*tebe ne*]–Ø$^{BYT'}$ [*mama!*] lit. 'I to.you not mom!' = 'I am not your mom!'

[*Vot*] Ø$^{BYT'}$–[*tebe moja*]–subj→***ruka*** lit. 'Here to.you my hand'. = 'Take my hand'.

The G can be different from a V$_{FIN}$; the following two cases are found.

— The G is an invariable interjection that expresses an instantaneous act and functions as the Main Verb (one of so-called **verbal interjections**):

Russian (a colloquial construction)

Ivan*←subj–*bac [*emu po morde*] lit. 'Ivan «bang» to.him on mug'. = 'Ivan punched him in the face'.

Ivan*←subj–*xvat' [*ego za šivorot*] lit. 'Ivan «grab» him by collar'. = 'Ivan grabbed him by the collar'.

NB The interjection of this type is readily coordinated with a "normal" Main Verb:
  (i) *Ivan* **podbežal** *k Petru i* **bac** *emu po morde*
      'Ivan came.running to Petr and «bang» to.him on mug'.
  (ii) *Ivan* **bac** *Petru po morde i* **ubežal**
      'Ivan «bang» to.Petr on mug and ran.away'.

2.5 An inventory of surface-syntactic relations found in the world's languages — 49

— The G is an invariable adverb (particle?) that introduces Direct Speech:

German

*"Die Reduktion der CO_2-Emissionen war noch nicht so wichtig",]
so–[der]–subj→**Professor*** lit. 'The reduction of CO_2 emissions was still not so important", so [= 'said'] the professor'.

The D can also be different from a prototypical prepositionless noun. Besides quite common subjectival subordinate clauses, infinitives, adverbs, etc., illustrated above, the following cases should be mentioned:

— The D is a zero lexeme—a personal-indefinite pronoun with the meaning of '«they»' (see *Symbols*, p. ix) or a "meteorological" pronoun:

Russian

[*Tam*] $\emptyset^{PEOPLE}_{(3, pl)}$←**subj**–*rabotajut*   lit. 'There «they» are.working'.
  = 'People are working there'.

[*Na dvore*] $\emptyset^{METEO}_{(3, sg, neu)}$←**subj**–*bylo* [*temno*]   lit. 'Outside was dark'. ~
[*Na dvore*] $\emptyset^{METEO}_{(3, sg, neu)}$←**subj**–$\emptyset^{BYT'}$ [*temno*]   lit. 'Outside dark'. = 'Outside is dark'.

Spanish

$\emptyset^{METEO}_{(3, sg)}$←**subj**–*está* [*lloviendo*] 'It is raining'.

On zero lexemes, see Mel'čuk 2006a: 469ff.

— The subject is a dummy (= semantically empty) pronoun introduced by DSynt-to-SSynt-structure rules:

It←**subj**–*is* [*great that you are here.*] | *It*←**subj**–*rained*.

— The subject is a finite verb that is the head of a **pseudo-relative clause** (Chapter 6, Subsection 6.3.2.2):

[*What he* **has**←**subj**–[*written*]–*is* [*interesting.*]
  ⎴ dir-obj ⎴

Note that in some languages, under specific conditions, the subject can be doubled by a **resumptive clitic**:

French

*Le **premier ministre**←subj–considère-t-il que cette conversion n'est pas allée à son terme ?* lit. 'The Prime Minister believes-he that this conversion did not run its course?'

(with dir-obj arrow from *considère* to *que cette conversion...*)

NB 1. The doubling of an actant by a resumptive pronoun—most often, a clitic—does not contradict Criterion **C3** (for establishing surface-syntactic relations), which forbids limited repeatability of a particular type of dependent. The doubling clitic does not represent another dependent: it is a syntax-imposed repetitive marking of the same dependent (among other things, the actant and the doubling clitic are coreferential). Cf. the situation with clitic doubling for objects, No. 14, p. 58.
2. A resumptive clitic cannot be described by a special SSyntRel since this clitic can appear alone in its own right as a subject: *Considère-t-il que cette conversion n'est pas allée à son terme ?*

2. **Consecutive-subjectival** SSyntRel. It expresses the DSyntRel I and the fictitious lexeme «AND_THEN»; the G is an invariable verbal form (a $V_{IMPER, 2, SG}$ or a V_{INF}, with or without preposition) and the prototypical D is a prepositionless N.

— The G is an invariable imperative form in the 2nd person singular:

Russian (a colloquial construction)
***Ivan**←subj–voz'mi$_{IMPER, 2, SG}$ [i skaži$_{IMPER, 2, SG}$ èto vslux]* 'Ivan up and said this aloud'.

— The G is an infinitive or a preposition that introduces an infinitive:

Russian (a colloquial construction)

[A] ***Ivan**←subj–bežat'$_{INF, IMPF}$* lit. 'And Ivan to.run'. = 'And Ivan took immediately to his heels'.

French (a formal narrative construction; see Melis 2000)

[Et] ***moi**←subj–de [répondre$_{INF}$ que je préfère les versions originales]*
lit. 'And me to answer that I prefer the original versions'.

3. **Conditional-subjectival** SSyntRel. It expresses the DSyntRel I and the fictitious lexeme «IF»; the G is a V_{FIN}, and the prototypical D is a prepositionless N.

Russian (mostly colloquial construction)

Znaet–cond-subj→***on***, [*čto ja ego ždu, – xorošo*] lit. 'Knows he that I him am.waiting, is.good'. = 'If he knows that I am waiting for him, this is good'.
Pridëš'–cond-subj→***ty*** [*vo-vremja – vsë budet v porjadke*] lit. 'Will.come you on.time ...' = 'If you come on time, everything will be in order'.
[*O,*] *znal*–[*by*]–cond-subj→***ja***[, *čto tak byvaet!*] lit. ' Oh, would.know I ...' = 'If only I knew that it can be like this!' [B. Pasternak].

NB In the last example the meaning of irrealis is rendered by the conditional-subjunctive form of the verb (marked by the particle **by**), not by the SSyntRel itself.

4. **Irrealis-subjectival** SSyntRel. It expresses the DSyntRel **I** and the fictitious lexeme «IF_{IRR}» (≈ 'if only'); the G is V_{IMPER, 2, SG}, and the D is a prepositionless N.

Russian

(4) *Uznaj*–irr-subj—→***ja*** [*ob ètom, vsë by bylo v porjadke*]
    learn-IMPER.2.SG I-NOM about this everything would be in order
    'Had I learned about this, everything would be in order'.

5. **Debitive-subjectival** SSyntRel. It expresses the DSyntRel **I** and the fictitious lexeme «HAVE_TO»; the G is a V_{IMPER, 2, SG}, and the D is an N.

Russian (a colloquial construction)

(5) [*A*] ***ja***←deb-subj–*rabotaj!*
    and I-NOM   work-IMPERF.IMPER.2.SG
    'And I have to work [when some other people don't]!'

6. **Pseudo-subjectival** SSyntRel. It expresses the DSyntRel **I** or is introduced by DSynt-rules; the G is a V_{FIN}, and its prototypical D varies according to the language (thus, in English it is a THAT-clause or TO-infinitive).

[*It*←subj–]*amazes*–[*us*]–pseudo-subj→***that*** [*John left.*]
[*It*←subj–]*is*–[*vital*]–pseudo-subj→***to*** [*keep accurate records.*]

French

[*Il*←subj–*est*] *venu*–[*trois*]–pseudo-subj→***voisins*** lit. 'It has come three neighbors'.
[*Il*←subj–*est*] *venu*–[*ton*]–pseudo-subj→***frère*** [*et ses enfants*]
lit. 'It has come your brother and his kids'.

— Pseudo-subjects also describe clefts:

[It←subj-]is-[novels that John]-pseudo-subj→***prefers***.
[It←subj-]was-[John who]-pseudo-subj→***reacted*** [first.]
[It←subj-]was-[to John]-pseudo-subj→***that*** [I spoke first.]
[It←subj-]was-[(to) John to whom I]-pseudo-subj→***spoke*** [first.]

French

[C'←subj-]est-[moi qui]-pseudo-subj→***ai*** [ouvert la fenêtre]
lit. 'It is me who have opened the window' [in French, the Main Verb of a relative clause agrees not with the relative pronoun, as in English, but with its antecedent, in this case—with MOI].

NB In the preceding five examples, the lexemes NOVELS, JOHN, TO [John] and MOI depend on the form of the verb 'be' by the **copular-completive** SSyntRel, No. 21, p. 63.

— Pseudo-subjects include a **placeholder** (= a dummy lexical element needed to occupy a particular linear position; the Main Verb does not agree with a placeholder, but agrees with the actual subject):

There←pseudo-subj-exists[-[a]-subj→condition for ...] vs.
There←pseudo-subj-exist[-subj→conditions for ...]
There←pseudo-subj-appear[-[to be better]-subj→rooms.]

German

Es←pseudo-subj-haben[-[einige interessante]-subj→Vorstellungen stattgefunden]
lit. 'It have some interesting shows taken.place'. = 'Some interesting shows have taken place'.

7. **Direct-objectival** SSyntRel. It expresses the DSyntRel **II**; in most cases, the G is a $V_{(trans)}$, and the prototypical D is an N.

The direct object [DirO] is the second most privileged clause element (see Chapter 3, Section 3.8, Definition 3.2, p. 174).

[He wanted to] see-dir-obj→***John***. | [He] knew-dir-obj→***this***.
[He was] given-[the]-dir-obj→***permission*** [to carry out his plans.]
[He] knew-dir-obj→***that*** [Mary was in town.]
[He] knew-[Mary]-dir-obj→***was*** [in town.]
[He] knew-[why Mary]-dir-obj→***was*** [in town.]
[He] knew-[what method]-dir-obj→***to*** [adopt.]

2.5 An inventory of surface-syntactic relations found in the world's languages — 53

[Which] **way**←dir-obj-[to]-choose [must be decided later.]
make-[possible]-dir-obj→**neutralizing** [the consequences]
make-dir-obj→**it** [possible to neutralize the consequences]
NB Cf. make-[it]-object-attributive-completive→possible [to neutralize the consequences], No. 24.

want-dir-obj→**to** [know]; [I] need-dir-obj→**to** [know-[what]-dir-obj→**to** [expect.]]
[This piece of history, the negotiators have] chosen-dir-obj→**to** [ignore.]

— The DirO can be a finite verb—the head of a **pseudo-relative** (= "free relative") clause:

[I] saw-[what John]-dir-obj→**had** [written.]

— The DirO can be a bare infinitive (= infinitive without preposition):

French

[Il] aime-dir-obj→**nager** 'He likes to.swim'.
[Le député] dit-dir-obj→**avoir** [rencontré le patriarche orthodoxe Ignatius]
lit. 'The congressman says have met the orthodox patriarch Ignatius'.

— The DirO can be a pronominal clitic:

French

[Nous] **l'**←dir-obj-avons [perdu] 'We have lost it'.

Serbian

[Mama] **ga**←dir-obj-[je jedva]-naterala [da nosi jaknu]
lit. 'Mom him has barely made that he.wears jacket'. =
'Mom barely made him wear a jacket'.

— The DirO can be a demonstrative nominal pronoun modified by a relative clause (see No. 73, p. 89):

Russian

[Ja] videl-dir-obj→**to**[, čto on napisal] lit. 'I saw that what he had.written'.

French

[J'ai] vu-dir-obj→**ce** [qu'il avait écrit] lit. 'I have seen that what he had written'.

– The DirO can be a dummy pronoun introduced by DSynt-to-SSynt-structure rules:

[*I*] *made*-**dir-obj**→***it*** [*clear that I am serious about tackling the problem.*]

– In some languages, the DirO can be introduced by a preposition (under specific conditions, for instance, if the DirO is animate, definite, etc.):

Spanish

Vi-**dir-obj**→***a*** [*tu amigo*] lit. 'I.saw to your friend'.

Romanian

[*L'am*] *văzut*-**dir-obj**→***pe*** [*prietenul tău*] lit. 'Him I.have seen to friend.the your'.
NB In this sentence we see the doubling of the DirO by a clitic: *l'*[*am*]; see the remark on p. 58.

– The DirO can be a **cognate object** that expresses a Deep-Syntactic manner circumstantial:

[*He*] *died*-[*a terrible*]-**dir-obj**→***death*** ≈ 'He died in a terrible way'.
NB Cf. the description of cognate objects in Russian and Arabic on p. 72.

– The G of a DirO can be an invariable **clausative**:

Russian

Doloj-**dir-obj**→***carja!*** lit. 'Down.with tsar!'
Von-**dir-obj**→***eë*** [*otsjuda!*] lit. 'Off.with her from.here!'

– A special case: an IndirO/OblO masquerading as a DirO (Mel'čuk 2012–2015: vol. 3, 498).

[*It is quite*] *like*-**indir-obj**→***John.*** | [*be*] *worth*-[*a*]-**indir-obj**→***trip***

German

Was$_{ACC}$←**obl-obj**–*fragst* [*Du mich*$_{ACC}$?] lit. 'What ask you me?' =
'About what are you asking me?'

8. **Quasi-direct-objectival-1** SSyntRel. It expresses the DSyntRel **II**; the G is a $V_{(trans)}$ of a particular semantic class, and the prototypical D is a prepositionless N; see Iordanskaja & Mel'čuk 2009a: 190–192.

2.5 An inventory of surface-syntactic relations found in the world's languages — 55

This SSyntRel describes "deficient" DirOs, as those seen below:

[The ticket] cost–[300]–**quasi-dir-obj-1**→*dollars*.
[The table] smells–[the]–**quasi-dir-obj-1**→*herring*.

These DirOs are deficient in the sense that they do not have all the properties of normal DirOs: for instance, they do not passivize.

9. **Quasi-direct-objectival-2** SSyntRel. It expresses the DSyntRel III; the G is a light (= collocative) verb, and the D is a prepositionless N.

This SSyntRel describes, in particular, a V→N collocation that functions syntactically as one transitive verb. In terms of lexical functions, the collocate V is Labor$_{12}$ of the collocation base noun N; see Mel'čuk 2012–2015: vol. 3, 93–94.

(6) a. Korean (see Chapter 4, Section 4.6.2.2, pp. 198–200)

                  —————— dir-obj ——————
              ↓
John+i   enehak +il koŋpu+lil←**quasi-dir-obj-2**–*hay+ss +ta*
SUBJ   linguistics ACC study$_{(N)}$ ACC   do PAST DECL

NB 1. SUBJ is the subjective case, which marks the subject and the pseudo-conjuncts of the subject (No. 122, p. 112), but cannot be used for nomination.

     2. The collocation 'do study$_{(N)}$' functions as a transitive verb '[to] study [something]'; ENEHAK 'linguistics' is a DirO.

b. Persian

Madär Ramin-ra   bedar←**quasi-dir-obj-2**–*kärd*
mother DirO wakening$_{(N)}$ did
'The mother woke Ramin'.

NB The collocation 'do wakening$_{(N)}$' is used as a transitive verb '[to] wake up [someone]'. See Chapter 9, Section 9.2.1.1.2, (13), p. 320.

10. **Pseudo-direct-objectival** SSyntRel. It expresses the DSyntRel II; the G is a V$_{(trans)}$, and the prototypical D is a THAT-clause.

    ⌐ dir-obj ¬
make——[*it clear*]–**pseudo-dir-obj**→*that* [we want to neutralize the consequences.]
            ⌐ dir-obj ¬
[*He*] *doubts*——[*it*]–**pseudo-dir-obj**→*that* [we want to neutralize the consequences.]
[*The rumor*] *has*–[*it*]–**pseudo-dir-obj**→*that* [you are looking for a job.]
make–[*it possible*]–**pseudo-dir-obj**→*to* [neutralize the consequences]
[*Girls*] *like*–[*it very much*]–**pseudo-dir-obj**→*when* [you think of them.]

11. Infinitival-objectival SSyntRel. It expresses the DSyntRel **II**; the G is a $V_{(modal)}$, and the D is a V_{INF}. (In English, it will be a bare infinitive, i.e. without TO.)

can-inf-obj→***read***; *should*-inf-obj→***read***

NB But Fr. [Je] *peux*-dir-obj→*nager* 'I can swim'. ~ [Je] *le*←dir-obj–*peux* lit. 'I can it'.

12. Direct-speech-objectival SSyntRel. It expresses the DSyntRel **II**$_{dir.sp}$; the G is a communication verb/noun, and the D is the head of a Direct Speech expression.

[*Churchill*] *declared*–[*in front of a large audience in Brooklyn:* "*I*]-dir-sp-obj→***am*** [*sure that the great struggle of the future would be between English-speaking nations and communism.*"]

NB Cf. *He whispered,*–"[*Three*]-dir-sp-obj→***words!***" vs. *He whispered*–[*three*]-dir-obj→*words*.

[*Then Edmund Burke uttered his famous*] *sentence*–[*on the wrongs of Ireland:* "*No country, I believe,*]-dir-sp-obj→***suffered*** [*so much on account of religion.*"]

Russian

[*On tol'ko*] *ulybnulsja*–⟨*maxnul*–[*rukoj*]⟩–[: "*Ja vsë*]-dir-sp-obj→*sdelaju!*" '
lit. 'He just smiled ⟨waved with.hand⟩: "I'll do everything!" '

NB Such verbs as ULYBNUT'SJA or MAXNUT' are intransitive and cannot have a DirO. They are not even *bona fide* communication verbs, but they can be used as such to express the fictitious lexeme «SAY». In Russian, Direct Speech can be introduced by a verb denoting its author's gesture (like 'smile'), a brusque change of state (like 'flare up') or a brusque action ('wave his hand'); see Iordanskaja & Mel'čuk 1981.

13. Affected-objectival SSyntRel. It expresses the fictitious lexeme «AFFECT», which represents the meaning of the Mandarin preposition BĂ, in the construction

G–**ATTR**→«AFFECT»–**II**→D

and is the result of Possessor Raising; the G is $V_{(trans)FIN}$, and the D is a BĂ→N phrase (Chapter 8, Section 8.4, p. 304).

Mandarin Chinese

(7) a. [*Wŏ*] ***bă***←aff-obj–[*John*]–*băng* -*le*   [*liăng zhī   jiăo*]
    I   BĂ   tie.up PERF two   CLASS(ifier) foot
    lit. 'I as.for John tied.up two feet'. = 'I tied up John's feet'.

Here, JIĂO 'foot' is a DirO; cf. No. 7, p. 52.

b. [Wǒ] **bǎ**←dir-obj−[wǒ-de qìchē]−mài-le
    lit. 'I BĂ my car sold'. = 'As for my car, I sold it'.

> **NB** The preposition BĂ introduces a special DirO that is a Focalized Given Theme and is anteposed to the Main Verb. This construction is possible only in case of a transitive verb that expresses an action upon the referent of the DirO.

For the affected object in Korean, see Chapter 4, 4.6.2.4, p. 201.

14. **Indirect-objectival** SSyntRel. It either expresses the DSyntRel II or III, or is the result of a raising, or else expresses a fictitious lexeme «FOR»; the G is a $V_{(trans)}$, and the prototypical D is a PREP→N phrase or an N_{DAT}.

The IndirO is the third most privileged clause element (after the Subj and the DirO).

give-indir-obj→***John*** ⟨*him*⟩ [*some money*]
[*France*] *offers*-indir-obj→***Christians*** [*asylum after Mosul threat.*]
give-[*some money*]-indir-obj→***to*** [*John, who needs it*]

French

[*Marie*] ***lui*$_{II}$**←indir-obj−*ressemble* 'Mary resembles-dir-obj→him/her'.

— In French, an IndirO often is a **raised Possessor** of the DirO; the same happens in some other Romance and Slavic languages:

French

[*Le bandit*] ***lui***←indir-obj−*a* [*cassé le bras*] lit. 'The bandit to.him has broken the arm'.
[*Va*] ***te***←indir-obj−*laver* [*les mains*] lit. 'Go to.you wash the hands'.

Spanish

Le←indir-obj−*han* [*robado la cartera*] lit. '[«They»] to.him have stolen the wallet'.

Serbian

Proučavali-[*smo*]-indir-obj→***mu*** [*život*] lit. 'Having.studied we.are to.him life'. = '... his life'.

Russian

[*Ona*] *porvala*-indir-obj→***mne*** [*rubašku*] lit. 'She tore to.me shirt'. = 'She tore my shirt'.
[*Ja*] ***tebe***←indir-obj−[*ne*]−$\emptyset^{BYT'}$ [*mama!*] lit. 'I to.you not mom!' = 'I am not your mom!'

– In many languages, the **indir-objectival** SSyntRel expresses the fictitious lexeme «FOR»:

Mary cooked–indir-obj→***them*** *a good supper.*

Russian

Uberi–indir-obj→***mame*** *komnatu!* 'Clean to.mom room!' = 'Clean mom's room!'

NB Cf. *Postav' èto **mame**←*possessive-[v]*-komnatu!* 'Put this to.mom into room!' = 'Take this to mom's room!' [**Postav' èto mame!*]. See No. 60, p. 84.

In some languages, under specific conditions, the **direct-objectival** and **indirect-objectival** SSyntRels are also repeatable just twice, like the **subjectival** SSyntRel, pp. 49–50. More precisely, an object can or must (depending on the language) be repeated (= "resumed") by the corresponding clitic. As indicated above, this does not contradict Criterion **C3** of syntactic dependency, since the **resumptive clitic** is not another DirO/IndirO, but an additional marker of the same object.

(8) Spanish
    a. (i) ***La***←dir-obj-*veré*-dir-obj→***a*** [*María*]
        lit. 'Her I.will.see to María'.
      (ii) ***Le***←indir-obj-*di*-indir-obj→***a*** [*María el libro*]
        lit. 'To.her I.gave to María the book'.
    Bulgarian
    b. (i) *Knigata **ja***←dir-obj-*četa veče cjal mesec*
        lit. 'The.book it I.read already whole month'.
      (ii) ***I***←indir-obj-*stana*-[*lošo*]-indir-obj→***na*** [*Marija*]
        lit. 'To.her became badly to Maria'. = 'Maria became sick'.

    NB A clitic can of course appear alone—without the noun to resume. This is the reason why it cannot be treated as a different clause element.

In contrast to the DirO, the IndirO can have a noun as its G:

[*John's*] *answer*–indir-obj→***to*** [*Mary*]; [*one of my first*] *gifts*–indir-obj→***to*** [*her*]

Now we come to **oblique-objectival** SSyntRels. Two (or more) **oblique-objectival** SSyntRels are needed for two reasons:

1) In order to control the linear disposition of different OblOs in the absence of communicative indications.

2.5 An inventory of surface-syntactic relations found in the world's languages — 59

2) For languages where different OblOs are marked by different grammatical cases (rather than by prepositions), in order to determine the corresponding case under synthesis.

All OblOs have the same or almost the same syntactic properties; they are distinguished according to their correspondence to DSynt-actants. The G of an OblO can be, as in the case of an IndirO, also a noun.

15. Oblique-objectival-1 SSyntRel. It expresses one of the DSyntRels II–VI; the G is a lexeme with a corresponding government pattern, and the prototypical D is a PREP→N phrase or an N in an oblique case; a completive clause and a TO-infinitive are also possible.

The OblO is the fourth (fifth, sixth, ...) most privileged clause element.

help–[*Mary*]–obl-obj-1→***in*** [*her studies*]; *help*–[*Mary*]–obl-obj-1→***move*** [*to London*]
[*McGuire*] *weighed*–[*in*]–obl-obj-1→***on*** [*what is wrong with our school.*]
[*They*] *proposed*–[*Alan*]–obl-obj-1→***as*** [*director.*]
[*They*] *held*–[*Alan*]–obl-obj-1→***for*** [*a poet.*]
[*old*] *enough*–obl-obj-1→***for*** [*this book*]; [*old*] *enough*–obl-obj-1→***to*** [*understand*]
held–obl-obj-1→***in*** [*contempt by colleagues*]
translate–obl-obj-1→***from*** [*Hungarian into Greek*]
translation–obl-obj-1→***from*** [*Hungarian into Greek*]
sentenced–obl-obj-1→***to*** [*death for his crimes*]
agreement–obl-obj-1→***between*** [*Stalin and Hitler*]
[*with no*] *objections*–obl-obj-1→***from*** [*the Minister*]
NB The synonymous phrases *the Minister's objections* and *objections by the Minister* have different SSyntSs: *the Minister's*←possessive–*objections* and *objections*–subj-adnom→*by* [*the Minister*].

Down–obl-obj-1→***with*** [*the Mullahs!*]
[*It is ten*] ***feet***←obl-obj-1–*high.* | [*fifteen-thousand*]–***foot***←obl-obj-1–*high* [*peak*]
too–[*tired*]–obl-obj-1→***to*** [*go out*]; *too*–[*sweet*]–obl-obj-1→***to*** [*eat*]
[*John was*] *clever*$_{(GP1)}$–obl-obj-1→***to*** [*leave.*] ~ [*To leave was*] *clever*$_{(GP2)}$–obl-obj-1→***of*** [*John.*]
NB These sentences contain the adjective CLEVER with two different government patterns [GPs].

[*travel to several European cities,*] *such*–obl-obj-1→***as*** [*London, Paris and Florence*]

French

[*Il*] ***en***←obl-obj-1–*ressort* [*que les dépenses n'ont pas augmenté*]
lit. 'It from.this follows that the expenses have not risen'. =
'This indicates that expenses ...'.

— Three interesting special cases of oblique object:

- The OblO of a superlative (MOST, LEAST, BEST, HIGHEST, ...); this OblO indicates the scope of the superlative (best in what set?):

[*the*] *most–*[*expensive car*]*-*obl-obj-1→*in* [*France*] ~
[*this car, the*] *most–*[*expensive*]*-*obl-obj-1→*in* [*France*]
NB Cf. [*the*] *most–*[*expensive*]*-*elective→*of* [*French cars*] (see No. 58, p. 83).

[*the*] *best–*[*care*]*-*obl-obj-1→*possible*; [*the*] *highest–*[*energies*]*-*obl-obj-1→*available*
[*the*] *best–*[*care we*]*-*obl-obj-1→*can* [*provide*]

- A completive clause/a TO-infinitive:

[*Mary has*] *such–*[*beautiful eyes*]*-*obl-obj-1→*that* [*she got a job as a make-up model.*]
[*Mary was*] *so–*[*tired*]*-*obl-obj-1→*that* [*she could not eat.*]
[*Mary was*] *too–*[*tired*]*-*obl-obj-1→*to* [*eat.*]

Russian

[*Marija*] *sliškom–*[*ustala,*]*-*obl-obj-1→*čtoby* [*poest'*]
lit. 'Mary too became.tired in.order.to eat'.

- A prepositionless noun

[*Parents*] *named–*[*her*]*-*obl-obj-1→**Mary**
Rus. [*Roditeli*] *nazvali–*[*eë*]*-*obl-obj-1→**Marija**$_{\text{NOM}}$/**Mariej**$_{\text{INSTR}}$ [idem]

16. **Oblique-objectival-2** SSyntRel. It expresses one of the DSyntRels III–VI; the G is a V with a corresponding government pattern, and the prototypical D is a PREP→N phrase or an N in an oblique case.

translate–[*from Hungarian*]*-*obl-obj-2→*into* [*Greek*]
translation–[*from Hungarian*]*-*obl-obj-2→*into* [*Greek*]
sentenced–[*to death*]*-*obl-obj-2→*for* [*his crimes*]

Hungarian

(9) *fordítás–*obl-obj-1→*magyar* +*ról*   *orosz* +*ra*
    translation   Hungarian DEL(ative) Russian SUBL(ative)
    'translation from.Hungarian into.Russian'

17. **Infinitive-oblique-objectival** SSyntRel. It expresses the DSyntRels II or III that correspond to Sem-actants **2** and **3**; the G is a verb with a corresponding government pattern, and the prototypical D is a (PREP→)V_{INF}.

[John] ordered-[his platoon]-inf-obl-obj→***to*** [hide behind growth nearby.]
[John was] forced-inf-obl-obj→***to*** [leave.]
[John] made-[his platoon]-inf-obl-obj→***laugh***.
[John] had-[better]-inf-obl-obj→***leave*** [right away.]

French

[Je me] hâte-inf-obl-obj→***de*** [partir]
lit. 'I myself hurry to leave'. = 'I am in a hurry to leave'.

18. **Infinitive-copredicative-objectival** SSyntRel. It expresses the DSyntRel III that corresponds to a "part" of Sem-actant 2 of the governing verb, the other part being expressed by DSyntRel II; the G is a semantically biactantial transitive verb with a corresponding government pattern, and the prototypical D is a (PREP→)V_{INF}.

This SSyntRel describes the *Accusativus cum infinitivo* construction, which has the following semantic and deep-syntactic structures:[2]

'see-2→waltz-1→people' ⇔ PEOPLE←II−SEE−III→WALTZ

See-[$people_{II}$]-inf-copred-obj→***waltz***$_{III}$, see-[people]-inf-copred-obj→***dance!***
[Ximénez] observed-[the animals]-inf-copred-obj→***to*** [cross waters more than 250 m wide.]
[The test was] determined-[by the UN]-inf-copred-obj→***to*** [be in violation of a UN resolution.]
[I] like-[her]-inf-copred-obj→***to*** [be slim.]
NB Cf. [I] like-[her]-obj-attr-obj→***slim*** (No. 24, p. 65).

Latin

[Ceterum] censeo-[Carthaginem]-inf-copred-obj→***esse*** [delendam]
'Moreover, I.consider Carthago$_{ACC}$ to.be which.must.be.destroyed' [Cato the Elder].

---

2 Accusativus cum infinitivo/participio
The *Accusativus cum Infinitivo/Participio* construction appears with semantically bi-actantial verbs whose SemA 2 is a statement P: 'X knows that P' or 'X says that P'. 'P' itself means 'Y Z-s', so that in the construction under discussion, the lexeme L(Y) becomes a DirO (≈ "accusative") and L(Z) is implemented as an **inf-copred-objectival** SSyntRel ("infinitive") or an **obj-attr-objectival** SSyntRel ("participle"). The particularity of this construction is that, contrary to other actantial infinitives/participles, its Ds do not directly correspond to SemAs of their G, but realize on the surface each a "part" of its SemA 2.

19. Agentive-completive SSyntRel. It expresses the DSyntRel **I**; the G is a non-finite verb form V (an infinitive or a gerund), and the prototypical D is either a FOR→N phrase (in English) or a prepositionless N.

An agentive complement [AgCo] is a transform of a subject with a V_{FIN}.

— The G is an infinitive:

[*His thumb is too sore*] ***for***←agent-compl–[*him*]–*to* [*play next week.*]   ⟨obl-obj-1⟩

[*He asked*] ***for***←agent-compl–[*the British*]–*to* [*stay longer.*]   ⟨obl-obj-1⟩

NB Cf. [*He*] *asked*–[*the*]–dir-obj→***British** to* [*stay longer.*]   ⟨oblique-obj-1⟩

Me←agent-compl–*worry?*

Spanish

[*¿Qué estaba haciendo antes de*] *aparecer*–[*los*]–agent-compl→***problemas****?*
lit. 'What was [s/he] doing before to appear the problems?' = '… before the problems appeared?'

[*Al*] *morir*–[*su*]–agent-compl→***madre*** [*la niña quedó sóla*]
lit. 'At.the to.die [her] mother the girl remained alone'.

— The G is a so-called personal infinitive, which agrees with its agentive complement [AgCo] in person and number:

Portuguese

(10) [*O guarda fez   sinal*] ***para***←agent-compl–[*os motoristas*]–*par+ar +em*
      the guard made signal for   the motorists stop INF 3.PL
      'The guard made the signal for the motorists to stop'.

— The G is a gerund (= a converb):

Spanish

[*Nos casamos hace 50 años*] *estando*–agent-compl→***yo*** [*sin trabajo*]
lit. 'We married 50 years ago being I without work'.

Turkish (c = /ʒ/)

Hasan←agent-compl–*var+inca*$_{\text{CONVERB}}$ [*denize girelim*] ≈ lit. 'Hasan having.arrived, to.sea let's.go'. = 'As soon as Hasan arrives, let's go swimming'.

Kazakh

Kün←agent-compl–*bat+ïp*_{CONVERB}, [*el oringa otirdi*] lit. 'Sun having.set, people on.place sat.down'. = 'When the sun set, people sat.down on their seats'.

More generally, the construction CONVERB–agent-compl→L is found in many Altaic and Uralic languages (Turkish, Mongolic, Tungusic, Finnic), in Nakh-Daghestanian family, in Inuktitut (Eskimo), and elsewhere. Thus, an agentive complement depending on a converb, is also typical of Korean (Chapter 4, Subsection 4.6.1.2, p. 195).

NB The construction *John being sick*, [*we were unable to leave*] is different. Here the noun JOHN is the head of the phrase *John being sick*, and the participle depends on it via the **absolute-modificative** SSyntRel, No. 62, p. 85.

> 20. **Passive-agentive-completive** SSyntRel. It expresses the DSyntRel II; the G is a V_{PASS}, and the prototypical D is a PREP→N phrase or an N in an oblique case.

written–pass-agentive→*by* [*McGuire*]; *baffled*–pass-agentive→*by* [*quantifiers*] [*She was*] *sent*–[*a letter*]–pass-agentive→*by* [*McGuire.*]

French

[*Il a toujours été*] *aimé*–pass-agentive→*des* [*femmes*]
lit. 'He has always been loved of.the [= 'by.the'] women'.

Russian

[*On vsegda byl*] *ljubim*–pass-agentive→*ženščin+ami*_{INSTR}
lit. 'He always was loved by.women'.

The SSyntRels 21–25 describe different copular complements, which appear with verbs of a particular semantic type—namely, **copular verbs**.

NB A copular verb is a copula, i.e. BE and BECOME or a verb whose signified includes the semanteme 'be' not in the dominant position; for instance, SEEM, APPEAR [*as*], LOOK [*nice*], etc.

> 21. **Copular-completive** SSyntRel. It expresses the DSyntRel II; the G is a copula V—'be' or 'become', and the D is an ADJ, which semantically bears on the subject and can agree with it.

NB If the G is a copula that means 'be identical' or 'be an element of the class', the prototypical D is an N:
[*It* ⟨*This person*⟩] *was*–cop-compl→*John*.
[*John*] *is*–cop-compl→*engineer*.

be–cop-compl→***easy***; *become*–cop-compl→***easy***
be–[*a*]–cop-compl→***teacher***; *become*–[*a*]–cop-compl→***teacher***
[*To read*] *is*–cop-compl→***to*** [*empower.*] | [*He has the right to*] *be*–cop-compl→***it***.

— The copula can be a zero wordform:

Russian

[*Ivan*] *Ø*^{BYT'}–cop-compl→***bolen***+*Ø*_{MASC, SG} 'Ivan [is] ill'. ~
[*Ivan*] *byl*—cop-compl→***bolen***+*Ø*_{MASC, SG} 'Ivan was ill'.

    22. Copular-genitive-completive SSyntRel. It expresses the DSyntRel II; the G is a copula V—'be' or 'become', and the D is an N$_{GEN}$ or a PREP→N phrase.

Russian

byl–[*takogo že*]–cop-gen-compl→***tipa*** '[It] was of the same type'.

NB [*Glavnoe prepjatstvie*] *Ø*^{BYT'}–[*ego solidnyj*]–cop-compl→***vozrast***_{NOM}
'The.main obstacle [is] his advanced age'.   vs.
[*On uže*] *Ø*^{BYT'}–[*solidnogo*]–cop-gen-compl→***vozrasta***_{GEN}
'He [is] already of an advanced age'.

    23. Subject-attributive-completive SSyntRel. It expresses the DSyntRels I–III; the G is a copular V, and the prototypical D is an ADJ, which semantically bears on the subject and can agree with it.

[*This task*] *seems*–subj-attr-compl→***easy***. | [*This task was*] *found*–subj-attr-obj→***easy***.
[*This task*] *seems*–subj-attr-compl→***to*** [*be easy.*]
[*This task was*] *found*–subj-attr-compl→***to*** [*be easy.*]

French

[*Le problème*_(masc)] *semble*–subj-attr-compl→***intéressant***+*Ø*_{MASC}
'The problem seems interesting'. ~

[*La tâche*_(fem)] *semble*–subj-attr-compl→***intéressant***+*e*_{FEM}
'The task seems interesting'.

[*Il*] *s'appelle*–subj-attr-compl→***Jean***
lit. 'He calls himself Jean'. = 'His name is Jean'.

Élu–subj-attr-compl→***directeur***_{III}, [*Alain partit en Inde*]
lit. 'Elected director, Alain left for India'.

Élue–subj-attr-compl→***directrice***_{III}, [*Helen partit en Inde*]
lit. 'Elected director, Helen left for India'.

2.5 An inventory of surface-syntactic relations found in the world's languages — 65

24. **Object-attributive-completive** SSyntRel. It expresses the DSyntRel III; the G is a V of a particular semantic class, and the prototypical D is an ADJ or an AS→ADJ phrase, which semantically bears on the DirO (and agrees with it in languages having agreement).

consider−[*him*]-obj-attr-compl→***happy*** ~
consider−[*him*]-obj-attr-compl→***to*** [*be happy*]

consider−[*him a*]-obj-attr-compl→***fool*** ~
consider−[*him*]-obj-attr-compl→***to*** [*be a fool*]

believe−[*him*]-obj-attr-compl→***to*** [*be dumb*] ~
?*believe*−[*him*]-obj-attr-compl→***dumb***

[*John*] *finds*−[*this task*]-obj-attr-compl→***easy***.

make−[*it*]-obj-attr-compl→***possible*** [*to neutralize the consequences*]

judge−[*him*]-obj-attr-compl→***guilty***; [*They*] *want*−[*him*]-obj-attr-compl→***in*** [*jail*.]

identify−[*this element*]-obj-attr-compl→***as*** [*vital / a suffix*]

French

[*Je*] *trouve*−[*le problème*]-obj-attr-compl→***intéressant+Ø***
'I find the problem interesting'. ~

[*Je*] *trouve*−[*la tâche*]-obj-attr-compl→***intéressant+e***
'I find the task interesting'.

— The object-attributive complement D can be a participle in an *Accusativus cum participio* construction, see footnote 2, p. 61):

[*I*] *heard*−[*them*]-obj-attr-compl→***stomping*** [*out of the cabin.*]

Latin

[*Nemo*] *audiebat*−[*eum*$_{SG.ACC}$]-obj-attr-compl→***querentem***$_{SG.ACC}$ ⟨−[*eos*$_{PL.ACC}$]-obj-attr-compl→***querentes***$_{PL.ACC}$⟩ lit. 'Nobody heard him complaining ⟨them complaining⟩'.

Ancient Greek

[*Hē gunḕ*] *eporāi*−[*min*$_{MASC.SG.ACC}$]-obj-attr-compl→***exiónta***$_{MASC.SG.ACC}$
'The woman saw him going.out'.

Finnish

Pekka kuuli−[*junan*$_{SG.GEN}$]-obj-attr-compl→***saapuvan***$_{SG.GEN}$
lit. 'Pekka heard train arriving'.

— The object-attributive complement D can also be a subordinate clause introduced by a relative pronoun (see Chapter 6, Subsection 6.2.2, p. 241, (4c)) :

Italian

    ┌── obj-attr-compl ──┐
Ho visto→Chiara che usciva dal cinema
lit. 'I.have seen Chiara who was.going out of the movie theater'. =
'I saw Chiara go out ⟨going out⟩ of the movie theater'.

   ┌─ obj-attr-compl ─┐
L'ho vista che usciva dal cinema
lit. 'Her I.have seen who was.going out of the movie theater'. =
'I saw her go out ⟨going out⟩ of the movie theater'.

    25. **Predicate-attributive-completive** SSyntRel. It expresses the DSyntRel II or III; the G is a V having a syntactic feature «pred-attr», and the D is an ADJ, which semantically bears on the predicate itself.

smell–**pred-attr-compl**→***good***; *feel*–**pred-attr-compl**→***miserable***
playing–**pred-attr-compl**→***small***; [*to*] *win*–**pred-attr-compl**→***big***

    26. **Comparative-objectival** SSyntRel. It expresses the DSyntRel II; the G is a comparative word, and the prototypical D is a CONJ$_{(compar)}$ (which introduces the object of comparison: the comparand N).

This SSyntRel describes all cases of comparison: 'X is more/less L than Y' and 'X is as L as Y'.

more–[*important*]–**compar-obj**→***than*** [*Peter*]; *older*–**compar-obj**→***than*** [*Peter*]
as–[*important*]–**compar-obj**→***as*** [*Peter*]
[*Beliefs are*] *so*–[*important*]–**compar-obj**→***as*** [*to have people been killed for them.*]
[*John loves Mary*] *more*–**compar-obj**→***than*** [*Peter.*]

Russian

[*byl*] *sil'nee*–**compar-obj**→***Ivana***$_{GEN}$
lit. 'was stronger of.Ivan' [= 'was stronger than Ivan'] ~
[*byl*] *sil'nee*–**compar-obj**→***čem*** [*Ivan*$_{NOM}$] 'was stronger than Ivan' ~
bolee–[*sil'nyj*]–**compar-obj**→***čem*** [*Ivan*$_{NOM}$] lit. 'more strong than Ivan'

I.1.2 Non-valence-controlled SSyntRels: 27–45
I.1.2.1 Actantial SSyntRels: 27–28

The following two SSyntRels represent the situation mentioned above, **I.1.1**, p. 47: SSynt-actants that are not valence-controlled.

    27. **Dative-ethical-objectival** SSyntRel. It expresses the fictitious lexeme «DAT_ETH»; the G is a V, and the D is a PRON$_{(pers)DAT}$—as a rule, of the 1SG or 2SG.

German

Lieb'-dat-eth-obj→*mir* [*nur keinen Hippy!*]
lit. 'Love to.me only no hippie!' = 'Don't you love a hippie on me!'

French

[*Marie*] *te*←[*m'*]-dat-eth-obj–*a* [*donné une de ces gifles !*]
lit. 'Mary to.you to.me has given one of those slaps.in.the.face!' = 'Mary gave me such a bloody slap in the face!'

Bulgarian

[*Ex, da*] *ti*←dat-eth-obj–*pipna* [*az mitnica!*]
lit. 'Oh, that to.you$_{SG}$ I.seize I customs!' = 'Oh, if only I could become the master of the customs!'

— The Ethical Dative can be a clitic form of the masculine substitute pronoun of 3SG:

Bulgarian

[*Ja*] *mu*←dat-eth-obj–*udari*$_{IMPER}$ [*edna rakija!*]
lit. 'It to.him hit one vodka!' = 'Have one vodka!'

NB *Ja* 'she$_{FEM.SG.ACC}$' is a resumptive clitic repeating the DirO *rakija*$_{(fem)}$ 'vodka'.

— Two Ethical Datives are possible in the same clause, at least, in Romanian:

Romanian

⎯⎯⎯⎯⎯⎯⎯ dat-eth-obj ⎯⎯⎯⎯⎯⎯⎯

[*Luând pe băiat de urechi*]   *mi* *ţi*←dat-eth-obj–[*-l*]–*bătea*
lit. 'Grabbing to boy by ears, [he]   me you$_{SG}$ him beat.up'.
These two cooccurring Ethical Datives violate Criterion **C3** of syntactic dependency; is it because of the pragmatically charged character of the Dependents?

28. Modal-objectival SSyntRel. It expresses the fictitious lexeme «SHOULD», «WILL_BE» or «BE_ABLE»; the G is a V$_{INF}$, and the D is an N$_{DAT}$.

Russian

Mne←mod-obj–*ostat'sja*? lit. 'To.me to.stay?' = 'Should I stay?' [«SHOULD»].

Emu←mod-obj–[*by*]–*obratit'sja* [*k vraču*] lit. 'To.him to.turn to doctor'. = 'He should see a doctor' [«SHOULD»].

[*Nu,*] *byt'*-mod-obj→*skandalu!* lit. 'Well, to.be to.a.scandal!' = 'Well, there will be a scandal!' [«WILL_BE»].

Tebe←mod-obj–[*ètogo bylo ne*]–*ponjat'* lit. 'To.you this was not to.understand'. = 'You couldn't understand this' [«BE_ABLE»].

I.1.2.2 Copredicative SSyntRels: 29–32

A copredicative complement is a non-valence-controlled non-actantial dependent of a verb that semantically bears on an actant of this verb.

29. Subject-copredicative SSyntRel. It expresses the fictitious lexeme «BE»:

$$L_1 \leftarrow I - L_{(V)} - \textbf{ATTR} \rightarrow \text{«BE»} - I \rightarrow L_1$$
$$\searrow II \rightarrow L_{2(ADJ)}$$

The G is a V with the corresponding syntactic feature, and the prototypical D is an ADJ, which semantically bears on this V's subject (here, L_1).

[John] returned–**subj-copr**→***rich***. |
[John] returned–**subj-copr**→***in*** [*a new uniform*.]
[John] arrived–**subj-copr**→***third***. |
[Visitors] returned–[fervent]–**subj-copr**→***admirers*** [*of Mao*.]
[They] parted–**subj-copr**→***enemies***.
[The fighting] continued–**subj-copr**→***unabated***.
[John] served–[Mary the salad]–**subj-copr**→***undressed***
['John was undressed'] (Wechsler 1995: 93).

Russian

[Ja] vstretil–[Mariju]–**subj-copr**→***starikom***$_{INSTR}$ 'I [male] met Maria an.old.man'.

30. Object-copredicative SSyntRel. It expresses the fictitious lexeme «BE»:

$$L_1 \leftarrow II - L_{(V)} - \textbf{ATTR} \rightarrow \text{«BE»} - I \rightarrow L_1$$
$$\searrow II \rightarrow L_{2(ADJ)}$$

The G is a V with the corresponding syntactic feature, and the prototypical D is an ADJ, which semantically bears on this V's direct object (here, L_1).

[They] sent–[John home]–**obj-copr**→***rich***. | [They] buried–[Mary]–**obj-copr**→***alive***.
[John] served–[Mary the salad]–**obj-copr**→***undressed*** ['the salad was undressed'] (Wechsler 1995: 93).

Russian

[Ja] vstretil–[Mariju]–**obj-copr**→***staruxoj***$_{INSTR}$ 'I [male] met Maria an.old.woman'.
[Marija] vstretila–[menja]–**obj-copr**→***starikom***$_{INSTR}$ 'Maria met me [male] an.old. man'.

31. **Object-resultative-copredicative** SSyntRel. It expresses the fictitious lexeme
«RESULT_IN»:

$$L_{(V)}\text{–}\mathbf{ATTR}\rightarrow\text{«RESULT\_IN»}\text{–}\mathbf{II}\rightarrow L_{1(\mathrm{ADJ})}$$

The G is a V with the corresponding syntactic feature, and the D is an ADJ, which semantically bears on this V's DirO.[3] (See Goldberg & Jackendoff 2004.)

wash–[the floor]-obj-result-copr→*clean*
wash-obj-result-copr→*clean* [*the inside of the cup*]
hammer–[the box]-obj-result-copr→*flat*
beat–[the prisoner]-obj-result-copr→*dead*
push–[the door]-obj-result-copr→*open*

32. **Floating-copredicative** SSyntRel. It has no correspondent in the DSyntS, but is introduced by DSynt-to-SSynt-structure rules; the G is a V, and the D is a pronominal quantifier adjective such as ALL or EACH.

[*Such sentences*] ***all***←float-copr–*contain* [*a negative word.*]
NB Cf. ***All***←determ–[*such*]–*sentences* [*contain a negative word.*]

[*John and Mary*] ***both***←float-copr–*were* [*expelled.*] ~
[*John and Mary*] *were–[expelled]*-float-copr→***both***.

[*These phonemes*] *have–[two allophones]*-float-copr→***each***.
NB Cf. *Terrier dogs closely resemble*–dir-obj→*each other*; ⌜EACH OTHER⌝ is an idiom (see No. 110, p. 106).

A language that has a rich syntactic morphology may necessitate several **floating-copredicative** SSyntRels, as, for instance, Russian. In this language, a floating quantifier can bear semantically on the SyntSubj, the DirO or the IndirO and agrees with its "antecedent" in gender and case:

Russian

(10) a. [*Rabotnicy*$_{\text{SyntSubj}}$] *javljalis'–[v kontoru]*-subject-float-copr→***každ+aja*** *v svoj den'*
lit. 'Female.workers were.coming to.the.office each on her day'.
b. [*Rabotnic*$_{\text{DirObj}}$] *posylali–[v kontoru]*-dir-object-float-copr→***každ+uju*** *v svoj den'*
lit. 'Female.workers were.coming to.the.office each on her day'.
c. [*Rabotnicam*$_{\text{IndirObj}}$ *velili*] *javit'sja–[v kontoru]*-indir-obj-float-copr→***každ+oj*** *v svoj den'*
lit. 'To.female.workers «they» ordered to.come to.the.office each on her day'.

---

[3] There are cases of **subject-resultative-copredicative** SSyntRel: *He froze **stiff**; The pond froze **solid***. However, I do not know to what extent they are widespread.

I.1.2.3 Circumstantial SSyntRels: 33–38

33. Circumstantial SSyntRel. It expresses the DSyntRel **ATTR** and, in many cases, a fictitious lexeme that expresses the type of the circumstantial (temporal, locative, instrumental, of purpose, etc.); the prototypical G is a V (not necessarily a V_{FIN}); the prototypical D is an ADV, a V_{ING}, a PREP or a CONJ$_{(subord)}$.

Let it be emphasized that a circumstantial can (and often does) depend on a noun, see the remark at the very beginning of **I.2.2.3**, p. 87.

walk–circum→***fast***; *delve*–circum→***deeply***

[*John*] *works*–circum→***there*** ⟨*in* [*this office*]⟩.

[*John*] *works*–circum→***abroad*** ⟨*in* [*Germany*]⟩.

[*Don't*] *waste*–[*time*]–circum→***playing*** [*computer games!*]

Having←circum–[*rushed off, John*]–*forgot* [*his umbrella.*]

[*John*] *works*–circum→***with*** [*several assistants.*]

When←circum–[*summer approaches,*]–*start* [*preparing your car.*]

[*Mary*] *received*–[*John*]–circum→***as*** [*a queen.*]

[*Mary*] *received*–[*John*]–circum→***as*** [*a king.*]

[*Mary*] *sang*–circum→⌜***as if***⌝ [*she knew me.*]

[*Sometimes animals*] *act*–circum→***like*** [*us.*]

[*He will*] *write*–[*next*]–circum→Ø$^{TEMP}_{(prepos)}$ [*week.*]

[*He will*] *write*–circum→***tomorrow***.

[*A new store*] *opened*–[*three*]–circum→***miles***–circum→***West*** [*from here.*]

[*John*] *kissed*–[*Mary three*]–circum→***times***.

Had←circum–[*John been here, he*]–*could* [*have helped us.*]

⌜***Holidays***⌝←circum–[*or no holidays*⌝, *I*]–*have* [*to finish my paper.*]
NB We see here a syntactic idiom ⌜X OR NO X⌝ 'no matter whether there is X or no X'.

French

⌜***Une fois***⌝←circum–[*son travail terminé, Jean*]–*devra* [*retourner à Nice*]
lit. 'Once his work being.over, Jean will.have to.return to Nice'.

[*Jean*] *travaille*–circum→Ø$^{LOC}_{(prepos)}$[*Place de la Nation*] 'John works at Place de la Nation'.
NB The zero preposition Ø$^{LOC}_{(prepos)}$ appears with the names of streets, squares, etc. (Mel'čuk 2018b).

[Jean] mange-circum→***beaucoup*** [*et voracement*] 'Jean eats a lot and greedily'.

NB But [*Jean*] *mange*-dir-obj→***beaucoup*** [*de fruits*] 'Jean eats a lot of fruit'. Cf.:
(i) *On **le** fait manger beaucoup* 'They make him eat a lot'.
vs. (ii) *On **lui** fait manger beaucoup de fruits* 'They make him eat a lot of fruit'.
In the French causative construction FAIRE 'make' + V, the Causee must be a DirO (in the accusative, if a clitic) if V has no DirO, and an IndirO (in the dative, if a clitic) if V has a DirO. The example shows that the adverb *beaucoup* 'a lot' is not a DirO, but a Circumstantial, while the noun phrase *beaucoup de Ns* is a genuine DirO.

— A circumstantial can constitute an absolute construction:

*[John] went-[out, his]-*circum→***gun*** [*in his left hand.*]
With←circum-[*her paper finished, Helen*]-*can* [*afford this trip.*]
[*The sellers*] *offered-[500 tons,]-*circum→***delivery*** [*to be made in October.*]

Latin (Ablativus absolutus)

[*Mortuo*] ***Caesare***_{ABL}←circum-[*bella civilia orta*]-*sunt*
'With Caesar dead, civil wars have started'.

— A circumstantial can be an N marked by a semantically full case (boxed in the examples below) that encodes its role; in the DSynt-structure, the corresponding semanteme is expressed by a fictitious lexeme:

Russian, circumstantial of duration

[*Ivan*] *rabotal-[celuju]-*circum→***nedelju***$_{\text{ACC}}$ 'Ivan worked the whole week'.

Russian, circumstantial of time

[*Ivan*] *rabotal-*circum→***pjatogo***$_{\text{GEN}}$ [*aprelja*] 'Ivan worked on.the.fifth of.April'.
[*Ivan*] *rabotal-[rannim]-*circum→***utrom***$_{\text{INSTR}}$ 'Ivan worked early morning'.

Russian, circumstantial of instrument

[*Ivan*] *rešil-[zadaču obyčnym]-*circum→***metodom***$_{\text{INSTR}}$
'Ivan solved the.problem by.ordinary method'.

Ancient Greek, circumstantial of relation

*Athēnaĩos-[tó]-*circum→***génos***$_{\text{ACC}}$ 'Athenian with. respect.to [= 'by'] birth'
*Kámnō-[toùs]-*circum→***ophtalmoús***$_{\text{ACC}}$ 'I.suffer with.respect.to [= 'from'] the eyes'.

— The circumstantial can be a **cognate object**:

Russian

[*On*] *umer–*[*užasnoj*]*-*circum→***smert'ju***$_{\text{INSTR}}$ lit. 'He died by.a.terrible death$_{\text{[cognate object]}}$'.

NB In the DSyntS, a cognate object corresponds to a circumstantial of manner ('[died] in a terrible way').

Arabic

Dafaʕa–[*al+walad+a*$_{\text{ACC}}$]*-*circum→***dafʕat+a***$_{\overline{\text{ACC}}}$*+n*$_{\text{INDEF}}$ [*kabīrat+a*$_{\text{ACC}}$*+n*$_{\text{INDEF}}$]
lit. 'S/He.pushed the.boy a.push big'. = 'S/He pushed the boy hard'.

— The circumstantial can be a V$_{\text{INF}}$ of purpose (with or without TO):

To←circum–[*simplify the procedure, Dr. Copulatti*]*-has* [*recourse to the following technique.*]

Russian

[*On*] *uexal–*[*v Kanadu*]*-*circum→***učit'sja***$_{\text{INF}}$ 'He went to Canada to.study'.

— The G of a circumstantial can be a noun:

[*Experts share their*] *lessons–*circum→***from*** [*the last year.*]
[*John wants to buy a*] *lodge–*circum→***at*** [*the lake.*]

> 34. **Durative-circumstantial** SSyntRel. It expresses the DSyntRel **ATTR** and the fictitious lexeme «DURING»; the prototypical G is a V (not necessarily a V$_{\text{FIN}}$); the D is a noun that denotes a period of time.

[*John*] *worked–*[*three*]*-*durative-circum→***days***.
[*John*] *worked–*[*the whole*]*-*durative-circum→***year***.

> 35. **Distance-circumstantial** SSyntRel. It expresses the DSyntRel **ATTR** and the fictitious lexeme «DISTANCE»; the G is a V (not necessarily a V$_{\text{FIN}}$) whose meaning includes the component 'directed motion'; the D is a noun that denotes a distance.

[*John*] *walked–*[*three*]*-*dist-circum→***miles***.
[*John*] *walked–*[*four*]*-*dist-circum→***blocks*** [*down High Street.*]

2.5 An inventory of surface-syntactic relations found in the world's languages — 73

The SSyntRels 36–38 are of circumstantial type, but their governor is necessarily a V_{FIN}. Their triple distinction is parallel to the distinction between the three adnominal SSyntRels:

modifier-circumstantial ~ **modificative**
[Amazingly] ***successful***,←mod-circum–[his solution]–became [generally accepted.] ~
[his] ***successful***←modif–solution

apposition-circumstantial ~ **appositive**
[An old] ***man***,←appos-circum–[the officer]–told [us ...] ~
[The] officer,–[an old]–appos→***man***, [told us ...]

attribute-circumstantial ~ **attributive**
Abroad,←attrib-circum–[an American]–is [always preoccupied.] ~
[An] American–attrib→***abroad*** [is always preoccupied.]

36. **Modifier-circumstantial** SSyntRel. It expresses the DSyntRel **ATTR**; the G is a V_{FIN}, and the D is an ADJ/ADV.

[As always] ***elegant***,←mod-circum–[John]–walked [away.]
[As always] ***elegantly***,←mod-circum–[John]–walked [away.]

37. **Apposition-circumstantial** SSyntRel. It expresses the DSyntRel **ATTR**; the G is a V_{FIN}, and the D is an N.

[An old] ***man***,←appos-circum–[John]–works [less.]

38. **Attribute-circumstantial** SSyntRel. It expresses the DSyntRel **ATTR**; the G is a V_{FIN}, and the prototypical D is an ADV or a PREP.

Abroad,← attr-circum–[John]–works [less.]
Without←attr-circum–[his computer, John]–feels [lost.]

I.1.2.4 Extra-structural SSyntRels: 39–46

39. **Parenthetical** SSyntRel. It expresses the DSyntRel **APPEND**; the G is a V_{FIN}, and the D is the head of the parenthetical expression and has the corresponding syntactic feature.

Oddly,←parenth–[John]–works [less.]
[John,] ***oddly***,←parenth–works [less.]

[*John*] *works*–[*less,*]–parenth→***oddly***.

[*John,*] ***naturally***,←parenth–*accepted* [*the offer.*]

[*John*] *accepted*–[*the offer,*]–parenth→***naturally***.

NB Cf. [*John*] *accepted*–[*the offer quite*]–circum→***naturally*** ['in a natural manner']. Here the adverb NATURALLY is subordinated to the Main Verb in the DSyntS by the ATTR DSyntRel.

As←parenth–[*we have known for some time, John*]–*works* [*less.*]

To←parenth–[*give an example, I*]–*will* [*consider nominal suffixes.*]

[*It*] *was,*–parenth→***as*** [*John said, a very hot day.*]

In_general←parenth–[*John*]–*is* [*happy.*] | [*John*]–*is,*–parenth→***in_general***, [*happy.*]

NB The underscoring of a space ("_") between two words means that they form in fact "one word"—that is, in spite of its official spelling as two words, IN_GENERAL is actually one wordform, since its internal structure does not correspond to syntactic rules of English: there is no *PREP→ADJ phrase.

40. **Quasi-parenthetical** SSyntRel. It expresses DSyntRel **APPEND**; the G is the head of a Direct Speech expression, and the D is a V_{FIN}, the head of a Direct-Speech Introductor.

["*Alan*] *will*–[*visit us,*" *John*]–quasi-parenth→***shouted***, ["*next Friday.*"]

["*I*] *am*–[*not going there!*",]–quasi-parenth→***shouted*** [*John.*]

["*I*] *am*–[*not going to kill the project,*" *McGuire*]–quasi-parenth→***declared*** [*in front of cameras.*]

Russian

["*Kak vy*] *smeete!*"–quasi-parenth→***vspyxnula*** [*Elena*] lit. '«How you dare!»—flared.up Elena'.

NB Many verbs that appear as the head of a subordinated parenthetical Direct-Speech Introductor are impossible in the superordinated Direct-Speech Introductor:

French

« *C'est un secret !* », ***élude*** *Isabela Ono* '«This is a secret! », eludes Isabela Ono'.

vs.

*Isabela Ono ***élude***: « *C'est un secret !* » 'Isabella Ono eludes: «This is a secret! »' (see Danlos et al. 2010).

41. **Adjunctive** SSyntRel. It expresses the DSyntRel **APPEND**; the G is a V_{FIN}, and the prototypical D is an interjection.

OK,←adjunct–[*John*]–*will* [*go.*] | ***Wow***,←adjunct–*isn't* [*she stunning!*]

2.5 An inventory of surface-syntactic relations found in the world's languages — 75

42. Proleptive SSyntRel. It expresses the DSyntRel **APPEND**; the G is a V$_{FIN}$, and the D is an N that is, as a rule, the expression of a Focalized Theme or Rheme. (For the proleptive SSyntRel in Russian, see a detailed analysis in Sannikov 2010a.)

[This] **Collins**,←prolept−[we]−hate [him.] | [This] **film**,←prolept−[I]−find [it gorgeous.]

Prolepses are quite typical of French and of many South-East Asian languages.

French

┌─── prolept ───┐
[Ma] **mère**,←prolept−[mes amis, elle les]−adore
lit. 'My mom, my friends, she them adores'.

┌── prolept ──┐
Partir, [c'est] mourir [un peu] lit. 'Leave, it is die a bit'.

Korean

(12) **John**+i←prolept−[k'o + ka] — kil   +ta
     SUBJ   nose SUBJ be.long DECL(arative)
'[It is] John [whose] nose is long'.

43. Addressative SSyntRel. It expresses DSyntRel **ADDRESS**; the G is a V$_{FIN}$, and the D is an N that is the designation of the entity to which the utterance is addressed; quite often, it is a proper name.

Mary,←address−[where]−are [you?]

44. Presentative SSyntRel. It expresses the DSyntRel **APPEND**; the G is a V$_{FIN}$, and the D is the particle ÈTO ≈ 'this, it'.

Russian

Èto←present−[Vanya tam]−sobiraetsja lit. 'This Vanya there is.packing'
[for instance, as an answer to the question What is happening? or What is this?].

NB Cf. **Èto**←restr−Vanya [tam sobiraetsja] lit. 'This [is] Vanya [who] there is.packing' (see No. 47).

Èto←present−stučit [dožd' po kryše] lit. 'This is.drumming rain on roof'.

45. Auxiliary-conjunctive SSyntRel. It expresses the DSyntRel **APPEND**; the G is a V$_{FIN}$, and the D is a coordinating conjunction that marks the beginning of a sentence.

And←auxiliary-conjunct−[everyone]−burst [out laughing.]
But←auxiliary-conjunct−[everyone]−disagreed.

Russian

A ←auxiliary-conjunct–[*zori zdes'*]–Ø^{BYT'} [*tixie*] lit. 'And dawns here [are] quiet'. = 'The dawns here are quiet' [a known 1972 Soviet film].

No ←auxiliary-conjunct–[*esli Ivan ušël, nado*]–*budet* [*ždat' ego vozvraščenija*] lit. 'But if Ivan has.left, necessary will.be wait [for] his return'.

>   **46. Auxiliary** SSyntRel. It does not correspond to any DSynt-relation, but is introduced by DSyntS-to-SSyntS rules in different cases specific to different languages.

Here are two examples.

— In a language with **subordinating binary conjunctions**, when expanding the DSynt-node of a binary conjunction, the **auxiliary** SSyntRel subordinates the second component of the binary conjunction—a specific particle that marks the beginning of the superordinate clause—to the MV of this clause.

⎯⎯⎯⎯⎯⎯⎯ circumstantial ⎯⎯⎯⎯⎯⎯⎯
[*If John gets the job,*] ***then*** ←auxil–[*he*]–*will* [*stay in town.*]

Russian

⎯⎯⎯⎯⎯⎯⎯ circumstantial ⎯⎯⎯⎯⎯⎯⎯
[*Tol'ko ja priotkryl dver',*] ***kak*** ←auxil–*poslyšalsja* [*tixij golos*]
lit. 'As.soon I slightly.opened door as was.heard low voice'.

For binary conjunctions, see Chapter 7, p. 275*ff.*

— In a language that has a lexemic nominalizer, i.e. an "auxiliary" noun that is only used for converting a clause C into a nominal, the auxiliary SSyntRel subordinates C to this noun (underscored in the example):

Korean (see Chapter 6, p. 254, (17b))

(13) *Nay+ka   paŋ+il   č^huŋsoha+nin* ←auxil–<u>*kes*</u>   +*il   towač^wuseyyo*
     I   SUBJ room ACC clean.up   PARTICIPLE «thing» ACC help.IMPER
     lit. 'I room cleaning.up «thing» help!' = 'Help me clean up the room!'

I.2 Phrase-Level SSyntRels: 47–113
I.2.1 Any type of phrase SSyntRel, non-valence-controlled: 47

>   **47. Restrictive** SSyntRel. It expresses the DSyntRel **ATTR**; the G is any lexeme, and the D is a particle.

still←restr-*taller*; [is] *still*←restr-*here*; *not*←restr-*here*; *not*←restr-*me*
so←restr-*rich*; *too*←restr-*tired*; *that*←restr-*far*; *boys*-restr→*only*
not←restr-*only*←restr-*me*
[John] *just*←restr-*arrived*.

Russian

my-restr→*že* ≈ 'but we'/'as for us' (ŽE is a clitic particle that expresses contrast)

French

Ne←restr-[*me*]-*quitte*-restr→*pas* ! [J. Brel] lit. 'No me leave not!'
[*Je*] *ne*←restr-*dors*-restr→*pas* 'I am not sleeping'.
[*Je*] *ne*←restr-*lisais* [*alors*] *que*←restr-[*des*]-*polars* 'I read then only whodunits'.

— In particular, the **restrictive** SSyntRel subordinates the first component of a coordinative binary or repeated conjunction (see Chapter 7, Section 7.3, p. 280):
   [*I liked*] *both*←restrictive-[*the*]-*movie*[-coord→*and*-[*the*]-conj-coord→*play*.]

Russian

[*Ivan ljubit*] *i*←restr-*mjaso*[,-coord→*i*-conj-coord—*rybu*,-coord→*i*-conj-coord→ *ovošči*] lit. 'Ivan likes and meat, and fish, and vegetables'.

NB The linear position of a restrictive particle is controlled either by its syntactic feature («antepos» or «postpos») or by the communicative structure.

I.2.2 Noun phrase SSyntRels: 48–83
I.2.2.1 Valence-controlled SSyntRels: 48–59

For more details on SSyntRels Nos. **48–53**, see Chapter 5, p. 205*ff*.

  48. Subjectival-adnominal-completive SSyntRel. It expresses the DSyntRel I; the G is an N, and the prototypical D is a phrase PREP$_{(subj\text{-}adnom)}$→N or an N in an oblique case (in English, the depending N is in the possessive form).

The subjectival adnominal complement is an adnominal transform of the subject; in a language having case, it is marked on the surface as a rule, by the genitive and is known as *Genitivus Subjectivus*.

[*a*] *translation*-subj-adnom→*by* [*McGuire*]; *objections*-subj-adnom→*by* [*the minister*]
[*a*] *translation*-subj-adnom→*of* [*McGuire*: 'McGuire translated the piece']
McGuire's←subj-adnom-*translation* ['McGuire translated the piece']

arrival–**subj-adnom**→***of*** [*the President*]
shooting–**subj-adnom**→***of*** [*the hunters*: 'the hunters shoot']

NB 1. [*a*] *translation*–**obj-adnom**→***of*** [McGuire: 'Somebody translated a text by McGuire'] is also possible. However, **a translation of Verlaine of McGuire* is ungrammatical; the correct expression is [*a*] *translation of Verlaine by McGuire*.
  2. ***McGuire's***←**possessive**–*translation*; see No. 60, p. 83.

tons–**subj-adnom**→***of*** [*debris*] ('ton-1→debris': a ton of debris is debris)
hundreds–**subj-adnom**→***of*** [*books*] ('hundred-1→books')
walls–**subj-adnom**→***of*** [*the building*] ('walls-1→building')
John's←**subj-adnom**–*heart* ('heart-1→John')

Russian

priezd–**subj-adnom**→***Ivana*** 'arrival of.Ivan'
mečty–**subj-adnom**→***Ivana*** 'dreams of.Ivan'
kuča–**subj-adnom**→***peska*** 'pile of.sand' ('pile-1→sand')
sistema–**subj-adnom**→***padežej*** 'system of.cases' ('system-1→cases')

French

effet–**subj-adnom**→***de*** [*ses actions*] 'effect of his actions'
rien–**subj-adnom**→***d'***[*intéressant*] lit. 'nothing of interesting'

— In some languages the **subj-adnom** SSyntRel describes the phrases of the form "ADV$_{(quantitative)}$ + N":

Rus. *mnogo*–**subj-adnom**→***knig***$_{PL.GEN}$ lit. 'much of.books'
Fr. *beaucoup*–**subj-adnom**→***de*** [*livres*] lit. 'much of books'

    49. **Objectival-adnominal-completive** SSyntRel. It expresses the DSyntRel II; the G is an N, and the D is a PREP$_{(attr)}$→N phrase or an N in an oblique case (in English, the depending N is in the possessive form).

The objectival adnominal complement is, roughly, an adnominal transform of the direct object; in a language having case, it is marked, as a rule, by the genitive and is known as *Genitivus Objectivus*.

shooting–**obj-adnom**→***of*** [*the hunters*: 'the hunters are shot at']
[*John's*] *description*–**obj-adnom**→***of*** [*Alan*] ~
*[*Alan's*] *description*–**obj-adnom**→***of*** [*John*] [in the sense of 'John describes Alan'].
Alan's←**obj-adnom**–*description*[–**subj-adnom**→***by*** *John*]

Spanish

el retrato-obj-adnom→*de Enrique VIII de Holbein del barón Thyssen*
[with brackets: subj-adnom, poss-adnom over the phrase]
'the portrait of Henry VIII by Holbein owned by Baron Thyssen'

Russian

ubijstvo-obj-adnom→*Ivana* 'murder of.Ivan'
priëm-obj-adnom→*Ivana* 'reception of.Ivan' [= 'Ivan is being received']
sposob-obj-adnom→*razdelenija* 'technique of.separation'
('dobyča←1–sposob-2→razdelenie' = 'extraction←1–technique-2→separation')

> **50. Qualificative-adnominal-attributive** SSyntRel. It expresses the DSyntRel
> **ATTR**; the G is an N_1, and the D is a PREP$_{(attr)}$→N_2 phrase or an $N_{2\text{-GEN}}$, where
> N_2 is a predicative noun whose Sem-actant is the G ['$N_2(N_1)$'].

images$_{N1}$-qual-adnom→*of* [*superhuman beauty*$_{N2}$] ('beauty-1→images')
[a] *man*-qual-adnom→*of* [*courage*]; *dress*-qual-adnom→*of* [*a beautiful color*]
[a] *man*$_{N1}$-[*the same*]-qual-adnom→*age*$_{N2}$ ('age-1→man')

Russian

transeja$_{N1}$-[*bol'šoj*]-qual-adnom→*glubiny*$_{N2}$ lit. 'trench of.great depth'

The SSyntRels **subj-adnom, obj-adnom, act-attr** (No. 56, p. 82) and **qual-adnom** are distinguished from the "simple" attributive SSyntRel (No. 63, p. 85) and among themselves because of different placement of their Ds:

Russian

kuča-[*morskogo*]-subj-adnom→*peska* [*ogromnogo*] *razmera* lit. 'pile of.sea sand of.huge size'
[with bracket: qual-adnom spanning to *razmera*]
vs. ?*kuča ogromnogo razmera morskogo peska*

French

pompe-obj-adnom→*à* [*essence*] *du* [*camion*] lit. 'pump to gas of.the truck'
[with bracket: subj-adnom]
vs. **pompe du camion à essence*

moulin-obj-adnom→*à* [*café*] *à* [*piles*] lit. 'grinder for coffee with batteries'
[with bracket: act-attr]
vs. **moulin à piles à café*

51. Possessive-adnominal-attributive SSyntRel. It expresses the DSyntRel **ATTR** and the fictitious lexeme «BELONG»; the G is an N_1, and the D is a $PREP_{(attr)} \rightarrow N_2$ phrase or an $N_{2\text{-GEN}}$.

Russian

sad-**poss-adnom**→***soseda***$_{GEN}$ 'garden of.neighbor'
stadion-**poss-adnom**→***universiteta***$_{GEN}$ 'stadium of.University'

French

jardin-**poss-adnom**→***du*** *voisin* 'garden of.the neighbor'
stade-**poss-adnom**→***de*** *l'Université* 'stadium of the University'
Cf. the **possessive** SSyntRel: No. 60, p. 83.

52. Characterizing-adnominal-attributive SSyntRel. It expresses the DSyntRel **ATTR**; the G is an N_1, and the D is a $PREP_{(attr)} \rightarrow N_2$ phrase or an $N_{2\text{-GEN}}$.

Russian

rukopis'-[*šestnadcatogo*]-**charact-adnom**→***veka***$_{GEN}$ 'manuscript of.sixteenth century'
stol-[*krasnogo*]-**charact-adnom**→***dereva***$_{GEN}$ 'table of.red wood' = 'mahogany table'

53. Metaphorical-adnominal-attributive SSyntRel. It expresses the DSyntRel **ATTR** and the fictitious lexeme «AS_IF»; the G is an N_1, and the D a $PREP_{(attr)} \rightarrow N_2$ phrase or an $N_{2\text{-GEN}}$, N_1 being a metaphor of N_2.

curtain$_{N_1}$-**metaph-adnom**→***of*** [*the night*$_{N_2}$]
[*the bitter*] *bread*-**metaph-adnom**→***of*** [*exile*]

Russian

zerkalo$_{N_1}$-**metaph-adnom**→***ozera***$_{N_2\text{-GEN}}$ 'mirror of.lake'
kolonny-**metaph-adnom**→***sosen***$_{GEN}$ 'columns of.pines'

54. Evaluative-adnominal-attributive SSyntRel. It expresses the DSyntRel **ATTR** and the fictitious lexeme «BE»; the G is an N_1, and the D a $PREP_{(attr)} \rightarrow N_2$ phrase or an $N_{2\text{-GEN}}$, N_1 expressing an "evaluation" of N_2. (See Foolen 2004 and Polguère 2014.)

[*my*] HUSBAND$_{N_2}$-**ATTR**→«BE»–II→IDIOT$_{N_1}$ ⇔ [*my*] *idiot*$_{N_1}$-**eval-adnom**→***of*** [*a husband*$_{N_2}$]
HUSBAND$_{N_2}$←I

[*a*] *bitch*-**eval-adnom**→***of*** [*a problem*]; [*a*] *beast*-**eval-adnom**→***of*** [*a night*]
[*a*] *whale*-**eval-adnom**→***of*** [*a project*]

French

[*votre*] FILS-**ATTR**→«ÊTRE»-II→INGÉNIEUR ⇔ [*votre*] *ingénieur*-**eval-adnom**→*de* [*fils*] lit. 'your engineer of son'

[*ton*] *pharmacien*-**eval-adnom**→*de* [*mari*] 'your pharmacist of husband'

[*ce*] *bijou*-**eval-adnom**→*du* [*lac*] 'this jewel of lake'

German

[*dieser*] *Schuft*-**eval-adnom**→*von* [*einem Hausmeister*] 'this scoundrel of a superintendent'

55. **Modifier-attributive** SSyntRel. It expresses the DSyntRel **ATTR** and the fictitious lexeme «BE»; the G is an ADJ, and the D a PREP$_{(attr)}$→N phrase, ADJ expressing a modification of N.

This construction is rather exotic: contrary to the "normal" case, where a modifying ADJ syntactically depends on the modified N, here the ADJ that semantically subordinates the modified N, syntactically also subordinates it by means of a preposition; that is, a modified noun is implemented in the SSyntS as an attribute of its own semantic modifier. We find this construction in French, although only with four adjectives (CHOUETTE 'nice', DRÔLE 'strange, funny', PUTAIN ≈ 'bloody', and VACHE 'impressive'):[4]

French

(14) | *un* | *drôle*-**modif-attrib**→*de* *garçon* | 'a strange boy'
a-MASC.SG | strange-MASC.SG of boy[MASC]-SG
une | *drôle* | *de voiture* | 'a strange car'
a-FEM.SG | strange-FEM.SG | of car[FEM]-SG
ces | *drôles* | *de garçons* | 'these strange boys'
this-MASC.PL | strange-MASC.PL | of boy[MASC]-PL
ces | *drôles* | *de voitures* | 'these strange cars'
this-FEM.PL | strange-FEM.PL | of car[FEM]-PL

---

4 Here are two more examples (for a detailed analysis of the construction in question, further examples and a bibliography, see Gaatone 1988):

un	*vache*	*de garçon*	'an impressive boy'
a-MASC.SG	impressive-MASC.SG	of boy[MASC]-SG	
une	*vache*	*de voiture*	'an impressive car'
a-FEM.SG	impressive-FEM.SG	of car[FEM]-SG	
ce	*chouette*	*de garçon*	'this nice boy'
this-MASC.SG	nice-MASC.SG	of boy[MASC]-SG	
cette	*chouette*	*de voiture*	'this nice car'
this-FEM.SG	nice-FEM.SG	of car[FEM]-SG	

However, in Sardinian, this construction is fairly productive: it is possible for all prenominal adjectives.

Sardinian (Jones 1993: 76–79)

(15) | unu | bette-**modif-attrib**→ *de* | pittsinnu | 'a big boy'
| a-MASC.SG | big-MASC.SG | of boy[MASC]-SG |
| una | ruja | *de* makkina | 'a red car'
| a-FEM.SG | red-FEM.SG | of car[FEM]-SG |
| sa | manna | *de* ampulla | 'the big bottle'
| the-MASC.SG | big-MASC.SG | of bottle[FEM]-SG |
| | cudda | *de* makkina | 'that car'
| | that-FEM.SG | of car[FEM]-SG |

56. **Actantial-attributive** SSyntRel. It expresses the DSyntRel **I, II, III,** ... whose dependent does not correspond to the subject or the direct object; the G is an N_1, and the D is a $PREP_{(attr)} \rightarrow N_2$ phrase or an $N_{2\text{-GEN}}$.

French

moteur-**act-attr**→*à* [*essence*]   lit. 'engine to gas' = 'gas←**compos**–engine' (see No. 61, p. 84)
gâteau-**act-attr**→*au* [*chocolat*]   lit. 'cake to.the chocolate' = 'chocolate←**compos**–cake'
farine-**act-attr**→*de* [*maïs*]   lit. 'flour from corn'

57. **Actantial-appositive** SSyntRel. It expresses the DSyntRel **II** or **III**; the G is an N, and the prototypical D is an N.

Russian

vesom-[*odna*]-**act-appos**→*tonna*_NOM   lit. '[having] weight one ton'
[*pri*] *vysote*-[*odin*]-**act-appos**→*metr*_NOM   lit. 'with height one meter'
vesom-**act-appos**→*v* [*odnu tonnu*]   lit. '[having] weight in one ton'
[*po*] *cene*-[*tri*]-**act-appos**→*rublja*-**act-appos**→*štuka*_NOM   lit. 'at price three rubles piece'

French

ticket-**act-appos**→*restaurant*   lit. 'ticket restaurant' = 'meal←**compos**–voucher' (see No. 61)
espace-**act-appos**→*enfants*   lit. 'space children'
assurance-**act-appos**→*vie*   lit. 'insurance life'
début-**act-appos**→*mai* 'beginning May'; *mai*-**act-appos**→*2016* 'May of 2016'

58. **Elective** SSyntRel. It expresses the DSyntRel **II**; the G is an ADJ$_{SUPERL}$ or a NUM; the D is a PREP→N phrase.

[*the*] *poorest*-elect→***among*** [*peasants*]; [*the*] *best*-elect→***of*** ⟨***from***⟩ [*these boys*]
[*the*] *most*-[*intelligent*]-elect→***of*** ⟨***from***⟩ [*these boys*]
one-elect→***of*** [*them*]; *five*-elect→***of*** [*these books*]

NB 1. [*the*] *poorest*-elect→*of* [*region's peasants*] vs. [*poorest*-[*peasants*]-obl-obj-1→*in* [*the region*] ~ *these peasants, the poorest*-obl-obj-1→*in the region*
   2. [*the*] *best*-elect→*of* [*national announcers*] vs. *the best national*←modif-*announcer* ~ *the best*-[*announcer*]-obl-obj-1→*of the nation* ~ *this announcer, the best*-obl-obj-1→*of the nation*

59. **Sequential** SSyntRel. It does not express a DSyntRel, but links the SSynt-"reflexes" of DSynt-actants **I–III** of L; the G is an N, and the D is an N.

man-sequent→***machine*** [*interaction*$_L$];[5] *Paris*-sequent→***London*** [*flights*$_L$]
English-sequent→***German*** [*dictionary*$_L$]; *English*-sequent→***to*** [*German translation*$_L$]

I.2.2.2 Valence-controlled and non-valence-controlled SSyntRels: 60–64

60. **Possessive** SSyntRel. It expresses DSyntRel **I, II, III, ATTR** or a fictitious lexeme; the G is an N, and the D is an N in the form that depends on the language.

Semantically, the possessives are quite variegated; syntactically, the **possessive** SSyntRel represents simply the syntactic dependence of a "possessor" on the "possessed" noun, and the numerous particularities of the possessive construction are specific to the corresponding language. Some illustrations are supplied from three languages.

— English has a special possessive form of the noun:

John's←poss-*arrival*; *John's*←poss-*execution*; *John's*←poss-*book*
[*Last*] *year's*←poss-*wishes* [*are this*] *year's*←poss-*apologies*.

---

[5] Government pattern for the noun INTERACTION ('X's interaction with Y')

X ⇔ I	Y ⇔ I
1. N's 2. of N	1. *with* N
3. *between* N$_X$ *and* N$_Y$	
4. –compos→N$_X$–sequent→N$_Y$	

— In Russian we find "possessive" phrases either with the prepositions U 'at' and к 'to' or with N_{DAT}:

[*Stul stoit*] ***u*←poss**-[*Maši v*]-*komnate* lit. 'Chair is at Masha in room'. ≡
[*Stul stoit v*] *komnate*-**poss→*u*** [*Maši*] lit. 'Chair is in room at Masha'. =
'...in Masha's room'.

[*Otnesi stul*] ***k*←poss**-[*Maše v*]-*komnatu!* lit. 'Carry chair to Masha into room!' ≡
[*Otnesi stul v*] *komnatu*-**poss→*k*** [*Maše!*] lit. 'Carry chair into room to Masha!' =
'...into Masha's room'.

[*Otnesi stul*] ***Maše*$_{DAT}$←poss**-[*v*]-*komnatu!* lit. 'Carry chair to.Masha into room!' ≡
[*Otnesi stul v*] *komnatu*-**poss→*Maše!*** lit. 'Carry chair into room to.Masha!' =
'...into Masha's room'.

NB 1. The dative case in this construction expresses the fictitious lexeme «AFFECT», that is, the additional meaning 'N is affected by the action in question'. This means that either we have to consider the dative case to be semantically full in this construction (and mark it in the SSyntS), or to introduce another SSyntRel. For the time being, I am unable to solve this dilemma.
  2. The choice between the prepositions U vs. к is determined by the meaning of the verb on which depends the "possessed" noun: if this verb denotes static localization, then U; if it denotes directed movement, then к or N_{DAT}.
  3. Cf.: (i) [*Ja*] *otnës*–[*stul*]-**indir-obj**→*Maše*$_{DAT}$ ([*v komnatu*])
      'I carried the.chair to.Masha (into the.room)'.
    (ii) [*Stul*] *naxoditsja*-**obl-obj**→*u Maši*
      'The.chair is at Masha's': U N_{GEN} can mean 'at N's'.

— Bulgarian uses for the "Possessor" the clitic dative form of a personal pronoun:

Gradina+ta-**poss→*mi*** ⟨***ti, mu, i***⟩ [*e tam*] 'Garden.the to.me ⟨to.you$_{SG}$, to.him, to.her⟩ is there'. = 'My ⟨your, his, her⟩ garden is there'.

As a clitic should, the possessive dative clitic is linearly positioned after the "possessed" N or after the first wordform of the phrase:

*Prekrasna+ta **mi** gradina e tam* 'Beautiful.the to.me garden is there'.

61. Compositive SSyntRel. It expresses the DSyntRel **I, II** or a fictitious lexeme; the prototypical G is an N, and the D is an N.

man←compos-[-*machine*]-*interaction*; *car*←compos-*repair*
noun←compos-*phrase*

       ┌────── modif ──────┐
[se*c*ure] ***smartphone*←**compos-***shipping*←**compos-*box*

NB A dependent in a compositive phrase [here, *shipping*] that is the governor of another compositive dependent [*smartphone*] can accept an adjectival modifier [*secure*]. This is one of the facts preventing the treatment of compositive phrases in English as compound words, because in this case an internal component (*shipping*) of a presumed compound noun (*smartphone+ shipping+box*) would have its own modifier outside the compound.

fax←compos–*transmission*←compos–*network*←compos–*access*
color←compos–*blind*; *tone*←compos–*deaf*; *tax*←compos–*free*
road←compos–*test* [a car]; *guest*←compos–*conduct* [an orchestra]

62. **Absolute-modificative** SSyntRel. It expresses DSyntRel I (with head-switching and possible omission of the copula verb) or one of the fictitious lexeme «AFTER», «WHILE», «WITH»; the G is an N, and the prototypical D is an ADJ, including participles.

[With the Central] Bank–abs-modif→*refusing* [to budge, there were no ruble buyers.]
[Without] me–abs-modif→*asking* [her, Mary offered me help.]
[John went out, his] anger–abs-modif→*gone*.
John–abs-modif→*being* [sick, we remained with him.]
[His first] attempt–[a]–abs-modif→*failure*, [John decided to try again.]
[He went out, (with) his] gun–abs-modif→*in* [his left hand.]

French

[Le] chat–abs-modif→*étant* [parti, les souris se sont mises à danser]
'The cat having left, the mice started dancing'.

— Ablativus absolutus:

Latin

(16) a. Ciceron+e——abs-modif→*viv* +o   [bellum civile Romae erat.]
       Cicero SG.ABL   alive MASC.SG.ABL   war civil in.Rome was
       'With Cicero alive, there was a civil war in Rome'.
    b. Oppid-is$_{(neu)}$——abs-modif→*incens* +is   [exercitus signa movit.]
       town PL.ABL   set.alight NEU.PL.ABL army standards moved
       'With the towns set on fire, the army marched away'.

63. **Attributive** SSyntRel. It expresses the DSyntRel **ATTR** and a fictitious lexeme: «BE», «HAVE», «DESIGNED_FOR», ...; the G is an N, and the prototypical D is a PREP$_{(attr)}$→N phrase or an N$_{GEN}$.

[a young] man–attr→*from* [Nantucket]; Detroit–attr→*after* [dark]
[every] path–attr→*on* [the island]; life–attr→*abroad*

learners-attr→***with*** [*different backgrounds*]
years-attr→***of*** [*war*]

Russian

rebënok-attr→***s*** [*bol'šim životom*] 'child with big tummy'
čelovek-attr→***bez*** [*očkov*] 'person without glasses'
Ivan-attr→***s*** [*Mašej*] 'Ivan with Masha'

French

carnet-attr→***d'***[*étudiant*] 'student gradebook'   vs.
carnet-subj-adnom→***de*** [*l'étudiant*] 'gradebook of the student'

tronc-attr→***d'***[*arbre*] 'tree trunk'   vs.
tronc-subj-adnom→***de*** [*l'arbre*] 'trunk of the tree'

roue-attr→***de*** [*vélo*] 'bicycle wheel'   vs.
roue-subj-adnom→***d'***[*un vélo*] 'wheel of a bicycle'

robe-attr→***de*** [*mariée*] 'wedding dress'   vs.
robe-subj-adnom→***de*** [*cette mariée*] 'dress of this bride'

NB *un carnet*-attr→*d'étudiant périmé* lit. 'a gradebook of student expired' ~
un carnet-[*périmé*]-subj-adnom→*de l'étudiant* lit. 'a gradebook expired of the student'
vs. **un carnet périmé d'étudiant* lit. 'a gradebook expired of student' ~ **un carnet de l'étudiant périmé* lit. 'a gradebook of the student expired'

course-attr→***à*** [*obstacles*] 'obstacle race'

– The attribute can be an infinitive introduced by a preposition with the meaning 'intended for':

books-attr→***to*** [*read*]

French

[*un*] *appartement*-attr→***à*** [*louer*] 'an apartment to rent'

> **64. Descriptive-attributive** SSyntRel. It expresses the DSyntRel **ATTR**$_{descr}$ and a fictitious lexeme, for instance, «BE_FROM»; the G is an N, and the prototypical D is a PREP$_{(loc)}$→N phrase or an N.

[*Professor*] *Wanner,*-descr-attr→***from*** [*Stuttgart, was also present.*]
[*Professor*] *Wanner,*-descr-attr→***Stuttgart,*** [*was also present.*]
NB Cf. [*A*] *professor*-attr→*from* [*Stuttgart was also present.*]

The semantic contrast between restrictive and non-restrictive (= descriptive, or qualifying) modifiers is well known: a restrictive modifier restricts a set of possible referents of the governor to a narrower subset ('the dogs that are healthy' is a subset of 'dogs'), while a descriptive modifier expresses an additional characterization of the elements of the same set ('these dogs, which are healthy' is the same set as 'these dogs').

It is worthwhile to indicate the following proportionality (Mel'čuk & Pertsov 1987: 152):

modif	:	descr-modif	:	modif-circum	=
attrib	:	descr-attrib	:	attrib-circum	=
appos	:	descr-appos	:	appos-circum	

I.2.2.3 Non-valence-controlled SSyntRels: 65–113

Along with the elements subordinated to the noun by the SSyntRels Nos. 65–113, a noun phrase can contain non-valence-controlled circumstantials of all types— prepositional phrases and adverbs, such as *tower* **on** *Fifth Avenue*, *their meeting yesterday*, etc. They are covered by the **circumstantial** SSyntRel, No. 33, p. 70.

> 65. **Determinative** SSyntRel. It is used in two cases: either it is introduced in the SSyntS to subordinate an article (which implements a deep grammeme) to a G = N; or it expresses the DSyntRel **ATTR**, the G being also an N, and the D a determiner other than an article.

a←determ–*bed*; *those*←determ–*beds*; *my*←determ–*bed*

> 66. **Quantitative** SSyntRel. It expresses the DSyntRel **ATTR**; the G is an N, and the D is a NUM$_{(quant)}$.

three←quant–*beds*; [*three*←num-junct–]*thousand*←quant–*people*
NB Cf. *thousands*–attr→*of*-prepositional→*people* (here THOUSAND is an N).

> 67. **Approximate-quantitative** SSyntRel. It expresses the fictitious lexeme «MAYBE»; the G is an N, and the D is a NUM$_{(quant)}$.

Russian

knig–approx-quant→*dvadcat'* 'maybe twenty books' ~
dvadcat'←quant–*knig* 'twenty books'

knig-[na]-**approx-quant**→***dvadcat'*** 'maybe for twenty books' ~
*[na] **dvadcat'**←***quant*-*knig*** 'for twenty books'

    68. Ordinal SSyntRel. It expresses the DSyntRel **ATTR**; the G is an N, and the D is an ADJ$_{(ordinal)}$.

*[the] **third**←*ordin*-*rank*; [on the hundred forty-]**third**←*ordin*-*day*

    69. Approximate-ordinal SSyntRel. It expresses the DSyntRel **ATTR** and the fictitious lexeme «MAYBE»; the G is an N, and the D is an ADJ$_{(ordinal)}$.

Russian

den'-[na]-**approx-ord**→***šestoj*** lit. 'day on sixth' = 'maybe on the sixth day' ~
*[na] **šestoj**←*ordin*-*den'*** 'on the sixth day'

    70. Modificative SSyntRel. It expresses the DSyntRel **ATTR**; the prototypical G is an N, and the D is an ADJ.

The **modificative** SSyntRel covers the most typical and semantically neutral adjectival modification. The linear position of the ADJ with respect to the N it modifies is controlled by general syntactic rules of the language, the type of the ADJ (anteposed/postposed), the type of the N (e.g., "genuine" N *vs.* nominal pronoun), the phraseological character of the ADJ, etc. However, in some cases, the position of the ADJ expresses a meaning, thus creating a different SSyntRel, which semantically contrasts with the **modificative** SSyntRel: the **special-modificative** SSyntRel (No. 71).

comfortable←modif-*beds*; ***visible***←modif-*stars*; ***French***←modif-*production*
nothing-modif→***interesting***; [*a*] *house*-modif→***ablaze***
secretary-modif→***general***, *notary*-modif→***public***, *God*-modif→***Almighty***,
knight-modif→***errant*** (these examples represent phraseologized expressions, namely collocations).

NB As is the case with the name of DSynt-relation **ATTR** (see Subsection 2.2.1, p. 34), which is a convenient abbreviation of **ATTR**$_{restr}$, the name of SSyntRel **modificative** is an abbreviation for **restrictive-modificative**; it is opposed to **descriptive-modificative**, No. 72 below.

French

dernier←modif-*jour* 'last day'; *message*-modif→***inattendu*** 'unexpected message'
personne-modif→***curieuse1*** 'curious/indiscreet person'
curieuse2←modif-*personne* 'strange/bizarre person'
⌜*Jugement*-modif→***Dernier*⌝** 'Last Judgment'

Russian

papa-modif→***rímskij*** lit. 'Pope Roman'
⌜*Mama*-modif→***ródnaja*** ⌝ [interjection idiom] lit. 'Mom natural!' = 'Goodness!'

— An ADJ can modify another ADJ:

burning←modif-*hot*, ***icy***←modif-*cold*, ***dark***←modif-*green*, ***light***←modif-*green*

Russian

takoj←modif-*milyj* lit. 'such nice' = 'so nice'
⌜***takoj***←[*že*]⌝-modif-*milyj* lit. 'such ŽE nice' = 'equally nice'
⌜***tot***←[*že*]⌝-modif-*samyj* lit. 'that ŽE same' = 'the same'

71. **Special-modificative** SSyntRel. It expresses DSyntRel **ATTR** plus a semantic addition, which depends on the language and is expressed in the DSyntS by a fictitious lexeme; the G is an N, and the D is an ADJ.

[*All*] *stars*-spec-modif→***visible*** [*are named after famous astronomers.*] vs.
[*All*] ***visible***←modif-*stars* [*are named after famous astronomers.*]

[*Every*] *cent*-spec-modif→***available*** [*was put into the project.*] vs.
[*Every*] ***available***←modif-*cent* [*was put into the project.*]

In English, special-modifying adjectives are postposed; they express "ephemeral," temporary properties; in French, special-modifying adjectives (they are anteposed) express subjective, emotional evaluation; in Russian, special-modifying adjectives (postposed) express terminological, rather than qualifying, character of the expression (*tigr sibirskij* lit. 'tiger Siberian'); etc.

72. **Descriptive-modificative** SSyntRel. It expresses the DSyntRel **ATTR**$_{descr}$; the G is an N, and the D is an ADJ.

[*these*] *beds*,-descr-modif→***comfortable*** [*and not expensive*], ...
[*There she met*] *John*,-descr-modif→***tired*** [*of loneliness.*]

73. **Relative** SSyntRel. It expresses the DSyntRel **ATTR**; the prototypical G is an N, and the D is a V$_{FIN}$, the head of a relative clause (see Chapter 6, pp. 235*ff*).

The reasons to have the **relative** SSyntRel different from the general **modificative** SSyntRel is the fact that the **modificative** SSyntRel is unlimitedly repeatable, while the **relative** SSyntRel is non-repeatable.

NB In fact, the name **relative** is an abbreviation for **restrictive-relative**, in the same way and for the same reason as the name of the **modificative** SSyntRel is an abbreviation for **restrictive-modificative**.

[*the*] *paper*-[*that I*]-**rel**→***read*** [*yesterday*]
[*the*] *paper*-[*I*]-**rel**→***read*** [*yesterday*]
[*the*] *girl*-[*who*]-**rel**→***came*** [*first*]
[*the*] *country*-[*where I*]-**rel**→***could*** [*live*]
[*the*] *country*-[*I*]-**rel**→***could*** [*live*-**obl-obj**→*in*]

— The G can be a nominal correlative pronoun:

Russian (the pronoun TOTII.1 'that.one'; for TOTII.2, see below, SSyntRel 112, pp. 107–108)

[*Vernëmsja k*] *tomu*-[, *o čëm my*]-**rel**→***govorili***
lit. 'Let's.return to that about what we.were.talking'.

[*Pogovori s*] *temi*-[, *komu ty*]-**rel**→***posylal*** [*pis'mo*]
lit. 'Talk to those to.whom you have.sent the.letter'.

nastol'ko-[*prošče, naskol'ko èto*]-**rel**→***bylo*** [*vozmožno*]
lit. 'so simpler as.much.as it was possible' = 'simpler to the extent that it was possible'
~ [*prošče*] *nastol'ko*-[, *naskol'ko èto*]-**rel**→***bylo*** [*vozmožno*]

— The G can be an ADJ:

Spanish

[*¡Lo*] *hermosas*-[*que*]-**rel**→***son*** [*esas chicas!*]
lit. 'The beautiful which are these girls!' = 'How beautiful are these girls!'

74. **Descriptive-relative** SSyntRel. It expresses the DSyntRel **ATTR**$_{descr}$; the G is (prototypically) an N, and the D is a V$_{FIN}$.

NB The descriptive-relative clauses that depend not on a noun (= **sentential relative clauses**, Quirk et al. 1991: 1118–1120) are considered by many as a special syntactic construction different for the relative clause proper; this construction is called the **explanatory clause**. In my previous publications (e.g., Mel'čuk 2016: 194) sentential relatives were treated as a subtype of the coordinate clause (they were described as depending on the MV of the superordinate clause by the **explanatory-coordinative** SSyntRel). However, sentential relatives are covered by the definition of relative clause proposed in this volume (Chapter 6, Definition 6.2, p. 240), and I do not see reasons that would force me to change this definition.

[*This*] *paper*-[, *which I*]-**descr-rel**→***read*** [*yesterday, seems interesting.*]
John-[, *who*]-**descr-rel**→***loves*** [*Mary so much, should return.*]
[*Mary*] *gave*-[*me a smile, which*]-**descr-rel**→***was*** [*nice.*]

Russian

[Ivana sčitali] lenivym,-[čto mne]-descr-rel→*kazalos'* [ošibkoj]
lit. 'Ivan was.considered lazy, which to.me seemed a.mistake'.

[Ivana sčitali] lenivym,-[kakovym on, odnako ne]-descr-rel→*byl*
lit. 'Ivan was.considered lazy, which he, however, was not'.

[Ivanu poručili] gotovit',-[čem on]-descr-rel→*ljubil* [zanimat'sja]
lit. 'Ivan was.entrusted with.cooking, which he liked to.do'.

75. **WH-pronominal** SSyntRel. It expresses the DSyntRel **ATTR**; the G is a PRON$_{(\text{rel})}$, and the D is a V$_{\text{FIN}}$ from a small lexical set.

[John disappeared God] **knows**←WH-pronominal-*where*.
[John does you] **will**←WH-pronominal-[never guess]-*what*.

Russian

[Ja budu rabotat'] gde-[vam]-WH-pronominal→*budet* [ugodno]
'I will work where to.you [it] will.be pleasant'.

The **WH-pronominal** SSyntRel describes an open set of expressions equivalent to indefinite pronouns, such as SOMEWHERE or WHATEVER; see Chapter 6, 6.3.2.2, p. 249, and Chapter 9, 9.2.1.1.1. p. 312.

NB Compound indefinite pronouns where the element depending on the L$_{(\text{pron, rel})}$ is not a non-phraseologized clause but a fixed lexical unit from a very limited set—such as Russian ABY←KTO 'no.matter who' or KTO→-TO 'somebody'—are described by the **intraphrasemic** SSyntRel, No. 114, p. 109.

76. **Specifying-appositive** SSyntRel. It expresses the DSyntRel **ATTR** and the fictitious lexeme «BE»: G-**ATTR**→«BE»-**II**→D; the G is an N$_{(\text{prop})}$, and the prototypical D is an ADJ.

Peter-[the]-specif-appos→*Great*; Nicholas-specif-appos→II

Russian

Pëtr-spec-appos→*Pervyj* lit. 'Peter First'

NB Cf. *pervyj*←ordin-*Pëtr* lit. '[the] first Peter', because here the ordinal ADJ denotes one of several Pëtrs who is the first in a series.

77. **Identity-appositive** SSyntRel. It expresses the DSyntRel **ATTR** and the fictitious lexeme «BE»: G–**ATTR**→«BE»–II→D; the G is an N, and the prototypical D is an N.

[the] term–**ident-appos**→*"suffix"*; [the Polish] word–**ident-appos**→*CIASTKO 'pastry'*

78. **Qualifying-appositive** SSyntRel. It expresses the DSyntRel **ATTR** and the fictitious lexeme «BE»: G–**ATTR**→«BE»–II→D; the G is an N$_{(prop)}$, and the prototypical D is an N.

Russian

utës[-]–**qual-appos**→*velikan* lit. 'rock giant'

devuška[-]–**qual-appos**→*počtal'on* lit. 'girl postman'

raketa[-]–**qual-appos**→*nositel'* lit. 'rocket booster'

uragan[-]–**qual-appos**→*ubijca* lit. 'hurricane killer'

79. **Descriptive-appositive** SSyntRel. It expresses the DSyntRel **ATTR**$_{descr}$ and the fictitious lexeme «BE»: G–**ATTR**$_{descr}$→«BE»–II→D; the G is an N, and the D is an N.

[This] term–**descr-appos**→*("suffix") [will be considered later.]*

John,–[a professional–**descr-appos**→*vet*, [came over.]

[You forget about] me,–[your]–**descr-appos**→*mother*.

[The sales totaled] $10,000,–**descr-appos**→*down* [from June.]

80. **Title-appositive** SSyntRel. It expresses DSyntRel **ATTR** and the fictitious lexeme «TITLE»:

G–**ATTR**→«TITLE»–II→D; the G is an N, and the D is an N that denotes a title.

General ←**title-appos**–*Wanner*   vs.
Wanner,–[a]–**descr-appos**→***general*** [in the Catalan army]

Mother ←**title-appos**–*Teresa*   vs.
Teresa,–[your]–**descr-appos**→***mother***

Father ←**title-appos**–*Patrick*; ***Sir*** ←**title-appos**–*Nicholas*

NB Cf. *General*←**title-appos**–*Wanner*,–[the]–**descr-appos**→*commander* [of 32nd Catalan division]

81. **Name-appositive** SSyntRel. It expresses DSyntRel **ATTR** and the fictitious lexeme «NAME»: G–**ATTR**→«NAME»–**II**→D; the G is an N, and the D is an $N_{(prop)}$ or the phrase "$of\ N_{(prop)}$."

[the] ***Gobi***←name-appos–*desert*; *Lake*–name-appos→***Erie***
[the] ***Volga***←name-appos–*river*; [the] *river*–name-appos→***Thames***
[the] ***Vancouver***←name-appos–*island*; [the] *island*–name-appos→***of*** [*Madagascar*]

NB The choice of the linear position for the proper name in cases such as *the **Volga** river* vs. *the river **Thames*** or *the **Vancouver** island* vs. *the island of **Madagascar*** is done according to the syntactic features of the proper name.

[the heavy] *cruiser*–name-appos→***"Saratoga"***; [the] *USS*–name-appos→***Enterprise***
[the] *town*–name-appos→***of*** [*Mount-Royal*]
equation–name-appos→***(23)***; *Section*–name-appos→***B***; [*World*] *War*–name-appos→***II***

NB 1. *Nicholas*-specif-appos→*II* (No. 76), since here "II" is not the name of Nicholas.
2. On the English constructions of the type *the prefix **un-***, *the painting "Seated Woman"*, *the poet **William Blake***, etc., which are described by the SSyntRels Nos. 76, 77, 79 and 81, see Jackendoff 1984.

82. **"Per"-appositive** SSyntRel. It expresses DSyntRel **ATTR** and the fictitious lexeme «PER»: G–**ATTR**→«PER»–**II**→D; the G is a measure noun N_1, and the D is another measure noun N_2, with or without a preposition.

[100] *kilometers–*[*an*]–**"per"**-appos→***hour***; [100] *dollars*–[*a*]–**"per"**-appos→***week***
[100] *kilometers*–**"per"**-appos→***per*** [*hour*]; [100] *dollars*–**"per"**-appos→***per*** [*week*]

Russian

[100] *kilometrov*–**"per"**-appos→***v*** [*čas*] lit. '100 km in hour'
[100] *dollarov*–[*každuju*]–**"per"**-appos→***nedelju*** lit. '100 dollars each week$_{ACC}$'

83. **Adnominal-linking** SSyntRel. It has no correspondent in the DSyntS, but is introduced by DSynt-to-SSynt-structure rules. The G is an N, and the D is a linker—a lexeme that depends on this N and is used to introduce N's postposed modifiers and attributes of various types; as a rule, a linker agrees with its G (= the modified noun) in gender, number, case and definiteness.

(17) Albanian

— The linker introduces an ADJ:

sistem(masc)+∅   +∅–**adnom-link** ⟶ *i*[—— **modif** ⟶ *mirë*]
system   SG.NOM   NON-DEF   MASC.SG.NOM.NON-DEF   good
'a.system **i** good' = 'a good system'

sistem(masc)+*e*   +∅–**adnom-link** ⟶ *të*[—— **modif** ⟶ *mirë*]
system   PL.NOM   NON-DEF   MASC.PL.NOM.NON-DEF   good
'systems **të** good' = 'good systems'

sistem(masc)+∅   +*i*–**adnom-link** ⟶ *i*[—— **modif** ⟶ *mirë*]
system   SG.NOM   DEF   MASC.SG.NOM.DEF   good
'the.system **i** good' = 'the good system'

sistem(masc)+*e*   +*t*–**adnom-link** ⟶ *e*[—— **modif** ⟶ *mirë*]
system   PL.NOM   DEF   MASC.SG.NOM.DEF   good
'the.systems **e** good' = 'the good systems'

— The linker introduces an N_{GEN}:

sistem(masc)+∅   +∅–**adnom-link** ⟶ *i*[—— **subj-adnom** ⟶ *edukim*+*i*   +*t*]
system   SG.NOM   NON-DEF   MASC.SG.NOM.NON-DEF   education SG.GEN DEF
'a.system **i** of.the.education'

sistem(masc)+*e*   +∅–**adnom-link** ⟶ *të*[—— **subj-adnom** ⟶ *edukim*+*i*   +*t*]
system   PL.NOM   NON-DEF   MASC.PL.NOM.NON-DEF   education SG.GEN DEF
'systems **të** of.the.education'

sistem(masc)+∅   +*i*–**adnom-link** ⟶ *i*[—— **subj-adnom** ⟶ *edukim*+*i*   +*t*]
system   SG.NOM   DEF   MASC.SG.NOM.DEF   education SG.GEN DEF
'the.system **i** of.the.education'

sistem(masc)+*e*   +*t*–**adnom-link** ⟶ *e*[—— **subj-adnom** ⟶ *edukim*+*i*   +*t*]
system   PL.NOM   DEF   MASC.PL.NOM.DEF   education SG.GEN DEF
'the.systems **e** of.the.education'

I.2.3 Adpositional phrase SSyntRels, valence-controlled: 84–85

84. Prepositional-completive SSyntRel. It expresses the DSyntRel II; the G is a PREP, and the prototypical D is an N.

in–prepos-compl→*bed*; *without*–[*three hundred*]–prepos-compl→*dollars*

to–prepos-compl→*go to*–prepos-compl→*bed*

Given–[*this*]–prepos-compl→*postulate,* [*what are the values*] *for*–[*the*]–prepos-compl→*velocity?*

NB Here, GIVEN is a preposition.

— The D of the **prepositional-completive** SSyntRel can be a V_{INF}:

[*Do you ever do anything*] *besides*–prepos-compl→*offer* [*your apologies?*]

French

sans–prepos-compl→*parler* 'without to.speak' = 'without speaking'

— The D of the **prepositional-completive** SSyntRel can be a THAT-clause:

[*The iota operator is different*] *in*–prepos-compl→*that* [*its interpretation depends on the context.*]

French

[*Il faut battre le fer*] *pendant*–prepos-compl→*qu'*[*il est chaud*]
lit. 'You have to strike the iron while that it is hot'.

Spanish

[*El hecho*] *de*–prepos-compl→*que* [*"gordo" funciona como un nombre no afecta*] *a*–prepos-compl→*si* [*es fraseologizado*]
lit. 'The fact of that *gordo* functions as a noun does.not affect to whether [it] is phraseologized'.

85. Postpositional-completive SSyntRel. It expresses the DSyntRel II; the G is a postposition, and the D is an N.

[*ten*] *centuries*←postpos-compl–*ago*; [*a few*] *years*←postpos-compl–*back*
[*the whole*] *month*←postpos-compl–*through*
[*The motion passed, our*] *objection*←postpos-compl–*notwithstanding.*

Hungarian

(18) a. *a* ***szobá*+*n***←postpos-compl–*kívül*   'outside the room'
         the room SUPERESS(ive)   outside
     b. ***anya*** +*Ø*←postpos-compl–*szerint*   'according to Mother'
         Mother NOM(inative)   according.to

Hungarian does not have prepositions, only postpositions.

It is necessary to distinguish a **prepositional** and a **postpositional** SSyntRel, since they can coexist in the same language. Thus, English has a **postpositional** SyntRel for such postpositions as AGO, BACK (*three years and a half **back***) and NOTWITHSTANDING; they cannot be lumped together with prepositions, since their behavior is too different.

I.2.4 Verbal phrase (= analytical formation) SSyntRels, non-valence-controlled: 86–94

Analytical SSyntRels are needed to describe two types of phrase:

- **Inflectional** analytical forms, such as *has→written*, *are→writing*, *was→writing*, *was→written*, *have→been→writing* or *more←intelligent*, *most←intelligent*, etc. These are genuine inflectional forms (= lexes) of the corresponding lexemes.
- **Derivational** "analytical formations," such as English **phrasal verbs** ⌜*give→up*⌝ 'abandon, surrender', ⌜*do→in*⌝ 'kill, destroy', ⌜*put→off*⌝ 'postpone', etc. or German verbs with separable prefixes, such as Ger. *X ruft–*[Y]*→an* '[X] phones [Y]' (ANRUFEN '[to] phone'), *X gibt–*[Y]*→auf* '[X] gives Y up' (AUFGEBEN '[to] give up'), *X teilt–*[Y Z$_{DAT}$]*→mit* '[X] communicates Y to Z' (MITTEILEN '[to] communicate'), etc. These are idioms (lexemic or morphemic) split into two parts by particular syntactic rules.

As one sees, there is no sufficient parallelism between these two types of phrase: in an analytical form one of its components expresses a grammeme (or a configuration of grammemes), while the components of a derivational analytical formation have no meaning of their own.

Since at the DSynt-level, an inflectional form of a lexeme as well as an idiom is always represented by one node, the **analytical** SSyntRels do not correspond to any DSyntRel.

An analytical form consists minimally of a lexical part, or a full lexeme (WRITE, INTELLIGENT), and an auxiliary part—that is, grammatical lexemes, which

2.5 An inventory of surface-syntactic relations found in the world's languages — 97

either serve as the markers of the corresponding grammemes (for instance, HAVE expresses PERFECT; BE expresses PROGRESSIVE or PASSIVE; MORE expresses COMPARATIVE; MOST expresses SUPERLATIVE), or represent the separated derivateme marker.

There are two major types of analytical forms:

1) Either the full lexeme is the syntactic governor, while the auxiliary lexeme— the grammeme/derivateme marker—is a (mostly invariable) particle, syntactically depending on it: *more←intelligent* or *stand→up*. Since the dependent component in this type of construction is a grammatical marker, the corresponing SSyntRel can be generally called **marker-analytical**.
2) Or the auxiliary lexeme—the grammeme marker—is the syntactic governor of the full lexeme; in all such cases known to me the auxiliary lexeme is the Main Verb of the clause, while the lexical verb, which depends on it, is in one of its non-finite forms: an infinitive, a participle, a converb, as in *has→written*, *was→writing*, etc. The SSyntRels that describe these analytical forms can be generally called **lexical-analytical**, since their dependent member is a full lexeme (or a preposition/conjunction that introduces a full lexeme, see No. 93, p. 101, the **future-analytical** SSyntRel in Spanish, Russian and Serbian).

Let us now consider the two families of analytical SSyntRels in more detail.

Marker-analytical SSyntRels. If in language **L** analytical markers are used only with lexemes of one part of speech, this construction can be naturally described by one SSyntRel, which will be simply **marker-analytical**. But if **L** uses such markers with two or three parts of speech, for instance, verbs, nouns and adjectives, these constructions do not have a prototypical dependent and different SSyntRels are needed: **verb-marker-analytical**, **noun-marker-analytical** and **adjective-marker-analytical**. The first one links the analytical tense-aspect-voice markers to verbs, the second—the analytical number-case-definiteness markers to nouns, and the third—the analytical degree markers to adjectives. Such a situation obtains in Polynesian languages:

Maori

(19) a. *kei.te*←verb-mark-analyt–*moe*   'be sleeping'
     kua←verb-mark-analyt–*moe*   'have slept'
     i←verb-mark-analyt–*moe*   'slept'

   b. *Kua   moe   te   tamaiti*   'The child has slept'.
      PERF sleep the child

Kua whakareri te tamaiti **i**←noun-mark-analyt–[*te*]–*rama*
PERF prepare the child ACC the torch
'The child has prepared the torch'.

Kua moe +a te tamaiti **e**←noun-mark-analyt–[*te*]–*nanakia*
PERF sleep PASS the child INSTR the monster
lit. 'Has been.slept.with the child by the monster'. =
'The monster has taken the child as wife'.

c. *pai* ~ *pai*-adj-mark-analyt→***atu*** 'better' ~ *pai*--adj-mark-analyt→***rawa*** 'best'
good more most

Thus, in this family we can expect three SSyntRels: 86–88.

86. Verb-marker-analytical SSyntRel.

— The marker of the future tense:

Bulgarian

piša ~ ***šte***←verb-analyt-mark–*piša*; *pišeš* ~ ***šte***←verb-analyt-mark–*pišeš*
I.write will I.write you_SG.write will you_SG.write

— The marker of the conditional-subjunctive mood:

Russian

pisal-verb-analyt-mark→***by*** 'would/should write'
wrote

— The marker of the imperative mood:

Russian

Puskaj/Pust'←verb-analyt-mark–[*on*]–*ujdët!* lit. 'That he goes!' = 'Let him go!'

Hawaiian

E←verb-mark-analyt–*hele* [*'oe i ke kula!*]
lit. 'Let go you to the school!' = 'Go to school!'
E←verb-mark-analyt–*hele* [*kākou i ke kula!*]
lit. 'Let go we to the school!' = 'Let's go to school!'
E←verb-mark-analyt–*hele* [*ia i ke kula!*]
lit. 'Let go he to the school!' = 'Let him go to school!'

— The marker of the reflexive:

French

se←verb-mark-refl-dir-analyt–*laver* lit. 'oneself wash' = 'to wash oneself'
oneself   wash

[*Tu*]   **te**←verb-mark-refl-dir-analyt–*laves* lit. 'You yourself wash' = 'You wash yourself'.
you_SG yourself   wash

[*Nous*] **nous**←verb-mark-refl-dir-analyt–*sommes* [*lavés*] lit. 'We ourselves have washed'.
we   ourselves   are   washed

[*Nous*] **nous**←verb-mark-refl-indir-analyt–*sommes* [*acheté une maison*]
we   ourselves   are   bought a house
'We have bought ourselves a house'.

NB The verb-mark-refl-dir-analyt SSyntRel covers the reflexive as a DirO ('I wash myself') and the verb-mark-refl-indir-analyt SSyntRel covers the reflexive as an IndirO ('I wash the hands to.myself').

— The marker of the "gérondif" (= of the converb):

French

en←verb-mark-analyt–*lavant* ≈ '[while washing'
                                     wash-PRES.PART(iciple)

This SSyntRel is also used to describe the dependence of a separable derivational/inflectional prefix of the German or Hungarian type, as well as that of verbal adjuncts in English phrasal verbs:

— A separable prefix:

German

[*Er*] *will* [*die Tür*] **aufmachen** 'He wants to open the door'.

[*auf-* is a prefix that, added to the verb MACHEN 'make', forms a morphemic idiom with the meaning 'to open'; if a verb with such a prefix appears in an independent clause as the Main Verb, the prefix is separated from the stem and put into the rightmost position].

vs.

[*Er*] *macht*–[*die Tür*]–verb-analyt-mark→***auf*** 'He opens [lit. 'makes up'] the door'.
he   makes   the door   up

Hungarian

Elutazott [Párizsba] '[S/he] travelled to.Paris'.

[*el-* is a prefix of the perfective aspect; such a prefix is separated from the verb under negation and postposed to the verb]

vs.

[*Nem*] *utazott*–verb-analyt-mark→*el Párizsba* '[S/he] did.not travel to.Paris'.

— An idiomatic verbal adjunct (see Jackendoff 2002[2010]):

⌐*put*–verb-mark-analyt→*up*⌐ [*for the night*]; ⌐*bring*–verb-mark-analyt→*down*⌐

NB Free, that is, non-idiomatic, verbal adjuncts are subordinated to the verb by the circumstantial SSyntRel: *climb*–circum→*up*, *run*–circum→*away*, etc. Cf.: *Up he climbed!* vs. **Up he put me!*

The particularities of the syntactic behavior of these elements—in the first place, their linear positioning—can be taken care of thanks to the special indications in their syntactics.

87. Noun-marker-analytical SSyntRel.

Tagalog

— The nominal plural marker MGA /máŋa/:

mga←noun-mark-analyt–*aklat*;	*mga*←noun-mark-analyt–*anak*
PL book	PL child

88. Adjective-marker-analytical SSyntRel.

less←adj-mark-analyt–*intelligent* [*than his brother*]
as←adj-mark-analyt–*intelligent* [*as his brother*]
most←adj-mark-analyt–*frequent*
Rus. *samyj*←adj-mark-analyt–*částyj* 'most frequent'

Lexical-analytical SSyntRels. In this family, the auxiliary verb—in "cooperation" with the inflectional form of the lexical verb—can in principle express all verbal grammemes: voice, aspect, tense, polarity, etc.

89. Passive-analytical SSyntRel. (See Chapter 10, 10.3.2.1, SSynt-rule **I.A**-7, p. 354.)

was–pass-analyt→*written*

2.5 An inventory of surface-syntactic relations found in the world's languages — 101

90. Perfective-analytical SSyntRel.

has–perf-analyt→*written*

Serbian

sam–perf-analyt→*pisao* lit. 'am having.written' = 'I wrote/I was writing'.

Swahili

(20) *Ni   +li   +kuwa*–perf-analyt→*ni   +me   +soma*
     1.SG PAST be   1.SG PERF read
     lit. 'I.was I.have.read'. = 'I had read'.

91. Progressive-analytical SSyntRel.

was–progr-analyt→*writing*

Swahili

(21) *Ni   +li   +kuwa*–progr-analyt→*ni   +ki   +soma*
     1.SG PAST be   1.SG SIMULT read
     lit. 'I.was I.read'. = 'I was reading'.

92. Preterit-analytical SSyntRel.

Catalan (*ig* = /č/, *j* = /ž/, *v* = /b/)

Vaig–pret-analyt→*menjar* lit. 'I.go eat'. = 'I ate'.

93. Future-analytical SSyntRel.

will–fut-analyt→*write*

Spanish

Van–fut-analyt→*a* [*escribir*] 'They.are.going to write'.

Russian

[*Ja*] *budu*–fut-analyt→*pisat'* 'I will write'.

Serbian

(i)   [*Ja*] *ću*–fut-analyt→*pisati* 'I will write'. =
(ii) [*Ja*] *ću*–fut-analyt→*da*[–subord-conj-compl→*pišem*]
      lit. 'I will that I.write'. = 'I will write'.
(iii) *Pisa*←fut-analyt–*ću* (⇐ *pisati ću*) lit. 'Write I.will'.

94. Negative-analytical SSyntRel.

[He] doesn't–**neg-analyt**→***understand***.

Finnish, the verb ANNA- 'give'

(22) anna+Ø +n ~ e +n——**neg-analyt**→***anna*+Ø**
        PRES 1.SG   don't 1.SG   PRES
'I.give'   'I.don't give'.

anno+i +t ~ e +t——**neg-analyt**→***anta*+nut**
        PAST 2.SG   don't 2.SG   PAST.PARTICIPLE
'you.gave'   'you$_{SG}$.didn't give'

anta+isi +Ø ~ e +i——**neg-analyt**→***anta*+isi**
        IRREAL 3.SG   don't 3.SG   IRREALIS
'he.would.give'   'he.wouldn't.give'

95. Interrogative-analytical SSyntRel.

Does–[he]–**interrog-analyt**→***understand***?

96. Assertive-analytical SSyntRel.

[He] does–**interrog-analyt**→***understand***.

I.2.5 Conjunctional-completive Phrase SSyntRels, Valence-controlled: 97–107

97. Subordinative-conjunctional-completive SSyntRel. It expresses DSyntRel II; the G is a CONJ$_{(subord)}$, and the prototypical D is a V$_{FIN}$.

[I'll never be the same] since–[John]–**subord-conj-compl**→***came*** [into my life.]

For empty complementizers such as THAT, Fr. QUE 'that', Rus. ČTO 'that', etc., which do not appear in the DSyntS, the **subord-conj-compl** SSyntRel is postulated by analogy:

[Suppose] that–[John]–**subord-conj-compl**→***comes***.

98. Subordinative-conjunctional-infinitival-completive SSyntRel. It expresses DSyntRel II; the G is a CONJ$_{(subord-inf)}$, and the D is a TO→V$_{INF}$ phrase.

⌜so as⌝–[not]–**subord-conj-inf-compl**→***to*** [irritate Leo]
⌜as if⌝–**subord-conj-inf-compl**→***to*** [show his support]
⌜in order⌝–**subord-conj-inf-compl**→***to*** [avoid irritating Leo]

2.5 An inventory of surface-syntactic relations found in the world's languages — 103

The subordinating conjunctions CONJ$_{(subord\text{-}inf)}$ cannot introduce a completive THAT-clause.

99. **Coordinative-conjunctional-completive** SSyntRel. It expresses DSyntRel II; the G is a CONJ$_{(coord)}$, and the prototypical D is a lexeme of the same part of speech as the G of the CONJ$_{(ccord)}$.

[Alan] and-**coord-conj-compl**→***Helen***; [Alan,] but-[not]-**coord-conj-compl**→***Helen***
[Do you have a place for us] or-[we]-**coord-conj-compl**→***must*** [leave now?]

100. **Comparative-conjunctional-completive** SSyntRel. It expresses DSyntRel II; the G is a CONJ$_{(compar)}$, and the prototypical D is an N.

than-**compar-conj-compl**→***Helen***

— The D can also be a V$_{FIN}$, an ADV or a CONJ$_{(subord)}$:

[more] than-[Vanya]-**compar-conj-compl**→***does***
as-**compar-conj-compl**→***always***
[We are never as unhappy] as-**compar-conj-compl**→***when*** [we lose love.]

In Russian, the morphological case of a nominal comparate (= what the comparand is being compared with) depends on the case of the comparand, while there is no direct syntactic link between the two. As a result, Russian requires five comparative SSyntRels. Each of these results from the ellipsis of a DSynt-configuration where the semantic relations are explicitly reflected. Thus, for No. 101, we have LJUBIT'-**ATTR**→SIL'NYJ$_{COMPAR}$-**II**→LJUBIT'-**I**→VANJA, i.e. 'love more than Vanya loves'. The following five SSyntRels—Nos. 101-105—are needed in the syntax of Russian as well as in that of other languages that have nominal cases: other Slavic languages, German, Hungarian, Finnish, etc.

101. **Subject-comparative-conjunctional-completive** SSyntRel. It expresses DSyntRel I; the G is a CONJ$_{(compar)}$, and the prototypical D is an N.

[Petja$_{NOM}$ ljubit Lenu$_{ACC}$ sil'nee,] čem-**subj-compar-conj-compl**→***Vanja***$_{NOM}$
'Petya loves Lena more than Vanya does'.

[Petja$_{NOM}$ ljubit Lenu$_{ACC}$,] kak-**subj-compar-conj-compl**→***Vanja***$_{NOM}$
'Petya loves Lena like Vanya does'.

102. Direct-object-comparative-conjunctional-completive SSyntRel. It expresses DSyntRel **II**; the G is a CONJ$_{(compar)}$, and the prototypical D is an N.

[Petja$_{NOM}$ ljubit Lenu$_{ACC}$ sil'nee,] čem–**dir-obj-compar-conj-compl**→***Vanju***$_{ACC}$
'Petya loves Lena more than he loves Vanya'.
[Petja$_{NOM}$ ljubit Lenu$_{ACC}$,] kak–**dir-obj-compar-conj-compl**→***Vanju***$_{ACC}$
'Petya loves Lena as he loves Vanya'.

103. Indirect-object-comparative-conjunctional-completive SSyntRel. It expresses DSyntRel **III**; the G is a CONJ$_{(compar)}$, and the prototypical D is an N.

[Lene$_{DAT}$ dostalos' bol'še,] neželi–**indir-obj-compar-conj-compl**→***Vane***$_{DAT}$
lit. 'To.Lena [it] got more than to.Vanya'. = 'Lena was through more [mishaps] than Vanya'.
[Ja tebe$_{DAT}$ verju,] kak–**indir-obj-compar-conj-compl**→***Vane***$_{DAT}$
lit. 'I believe to.you as I believe to.Vanya'.

104. Oblique-object-comparative-conjunctional-completive SSyntRel. It expresses DSyntRel **III**; the G is a CONJ$_{(compar)}$, and the prototypical D is an N.

[Vanja privjazan k Lene bol'še,] neželi–**obl-obj-compar-conj-compl**→***k*** [Maše]
'Vanya is.attached to Lena more than [VANYA IS.ATTACHED] to Masha'.

105. Circumstantial-comparative-conjunctional-completive SSyntRel. It expresses DSyntRel **ATTR**; the G is a CONJ$_{(compar)}$, and the prototypical D is an N.

This SSyntRel is not valence-controlled; it is placed in this subsection by analogy.

[Teper' oni živut lučše,] čem–**circum-compar-conj-compl**→***v*** [Kazani]
'Now they live better than [THEY LIVED] in Kazan'.

106. Absolute-conjunctional-completive SSyntRel. It expresses DSyntRel **II**; the G is a CONJ$_{(subord, abs)}$, and the D is an N.

This SSyntRel subordinates a complete absolute construction—that is, a noun plus an adjectival/an adverbial—introduced by a subordinating conjunction.

French

⌜Une fois⌝–[le]–**abs-conj-compl**→***bateau***[–**abs-modif**→redressé, stabilisez-le]
'Once the boat [is] straightened.up, stabilize it'.

2.5 An inventory of surface-syntactic relations found in the world's languages — 105

107. **Elliptic-absolute-conjunctional-completive** SSyntRel. It expresses DSynt-Rel II; the G is a CONJ$_{(subord, ellipt-abs)}$, and the prototypical D is an ADJ.

This SSyntRel subordinates an incomplete absolute construction—that is, an N, an ADJ or an adverbial—introduced by a subordinating conjunction.

[Obama's voting record] while–ellipt-abs-conj-compl→*senator* [made him the most liberal person in Congress.]
If–[a]–ellipt-abs-conj-compl→*pronoun*[, the grammatical subject may ...]
[even] if–[too]–ellipt-abs-conj-compl→*weak* [to seize power]
[The baby,] if–ellipt-abs-conj-compl→*young* [enough to be easily controlled, need not be regularly dressed.
while–ellipt-abs-conj-compl→*in* [bed]; once–ellipt-abs-conj-compl→*here*

I.2.6 Word-like phrase SSyntRels, non-valence-controlled: 108–114

108. **Numeral-junctive** SSyntRel. It has no correspondent in the DSyntS, where a compound numeral is represented by one node. This SSyntRel is introduced into the SSynt-structure by DSynt-to-SSynt-structure syntactic rules; the G is a NUM/ ADJ$_{(ordin)}$, and the D is a NUM.

two←num-junct–*hundred*←num-junct–*fifty*←num-junct–*three* [= 253]
fifty←num-junct–*third*

— The lexeme AND (and its semantic equivalents in other languages) in compound numerals is not a CONJ$_{(coord)}$:

two←num-junct–*hundred*←num-junct–*and*←num-junct–*three* [= 203]
one←num-junct–*hundred*←num-junct–*and*←num-junct–*third* [= 103rd]

German

drei←num-junct–*und*←num-junct–*vierzigster* [*Band*]
lit. 'three and fortieth volume [of a periodical]' = 'forty-third volume'

NB *three*–pseudo-coord→*and*–[*five*]–coord-conj→*sixths* '3 ⅚' ([*one*] SIXTH, as the names of al fractions, is an N; see SSyntRel No. 122, p. 111).

109. **Name-junctive-1/2/3** SSyntRels. They have no correspondents in the DSyntS, where a compound human name is represented by one node, but are introduced into the SSyntS by DSynt-to-SSynt-structure rules;

the G is an N(prop, hum, first_name), and the D is an N(prop, hum, second_name). These SSyntRels are different in different languages as function of the structure of the proper human names in the language.

Spanish (Vincze & Alonso Ramos 2011; in Spanish, a person has two family names: father's and mother's family names)

Margarita–name-junct-1→***Alonso***–name-junct-2→***Ramos***
⌐────── name-junct-1 ──────↴
José–name-junct-3→***Luis Rodríguez***–name-junct-2→***Zapatero***
José–name-junct-1→***Rodríguez***

The **name-junctive-1** SSyntRel subordinates the first family name to the given name. The **name-junctive-2** SSyntRel subordinates the second family name to the first family name.
The **name-junctive-3** SSyntRel subordinates the second given name to the first given name.

The person officially called *Margarita Luisa Alonso Ramos* can be referred to as *Margarita Alonso Ramos*, *Margarita Alonso*, *Margarita Luisa Alonso*, *Margarita*, *Margarita Luisa*, *Alonso Ramos* and simply *Alonso*. (The second family name alone—in this case, *Ramos*—can be used only for an outstanding and well-known person, preceded by a title: *la presidente/la doctora Ramos*.)

Russian
⌐────── name-junct-1 ──────↴
Igor'–name-junct-2→***Aleksandrovič Mel'čuk***

The **name-junctive-1** SSyntRel subordinates the family name to the given name. The **name-junctive-2** SSyntRel subordinates the patronymic [= a derivative of the father's given name] to the given name.

In Russian the person officially called *Igor' Aleksandrovič Mel'čuk* can also be referred to as *Igor' Mel'čuk*, *Igor' Aleksandrovič*, *Igor'* and simply *Mel'čuk*.

110. **Binary-junctive** SSyntRel. It has no correspondent in the DSyntS, where a "bipartite word" is represented by one node, but is introduced by DSynt-to-SSynt-structure rules.

NB The G is the element that cannot be omitted; if both elements are not omissible, then the G is the element that receives the "external" morphological impact.

each–bin-junct→***other*** [*from*–prepos→*each*–bin-junct→*other*]

2.5 An inventory of surface-syntactic relations found in the world's languages —— 107

French

[*Cette vente fera époque parmi les marchands*] *autant*-bin-junct→*que*[-coord-conj→*parmi les amateurs*] lit. 'This sale will.make history among the merchants as.much among the amateurs'.

The idiom ⌜AUTANT QUE⌝ 'as well as' is a "normal" coordinating conjunction. Consider, however, the following sentence:

[*Cette vente fera époque*] *autant*←restr-*parmi les marchands*-coord→*que*-coord-conj→*parmi les amateurs* lit. 'This sale will.make history as.much among the merchants as among the amateurs'.

This sentence contains another—binary coordinating—conjunction ⌜AUTANT [X] QUE [Y]⌝, also an idiom, but with a different SSynt-structure (for details on binary conjunctions, see Chapter 7, pp. 275*ff*).

Russian

nikto 'nobody' ~ *ni*←bin-junct-[*dlja*]-*kogo* lit. 'not for body' = 'for nobody'
odin←bin-junct-*drugogo*₍masc₎ lit. 'one other', **odin**←bin-junct-[*k*]-*drugomu*₍masc₎ lit. 'one to other' ~ **odna**←bin-junct-*druguju*₍fem₎ lit. 'one other', **odna**←bin-junct-[*k*]-*drugoj*₍fem₎ lit. 'one to other'
drug←bin-junct-*druga* 'each other' ~ **drug**←bin-junct-[*dlja*]-*druga* lit. 'each for other' = 'for each other'

111. **Colligative SSyntRel**. It has no correspondent in the DSyntS, but is introduced by DSynt-to-SSynt-structure rules; the G is a PART$_{PASS}$, and the D is a stranded PREP.

[*The patient is*] *operated*-collig→*upon*.
[*John was*] *done*-[*away*]-collig→*with*.

NB Cf. [*the*] *problem* (*which*) *we deal*-obl-obj→*with in Chapter 7*; here, the complement of the preposition WITH is the relative pronoun WHICH, which can be omitted on the surface.

112. **Correlative SSyntRel**. It has no correspondent in the DSyntS, but is put into SSynt-structure by DSynt-to-SSynt-structure rules; the G is the correlative pronoun Fr. CE, Rus. TOTII.2, etc., and the D is a semantically empty complementizer that introduces a completive clause.[6]

---

6 TOTI is a pronominal adjective meaning 'that [passenger]'
 (*Te passažiry, kotorye sledujut do Moskvy, ...* 'Those passenger who go to Moscow...').
 TOT II.1 is a pronominal correlative noun meaning 'that one'
 (*Tot, kto rabotaet, živët neploxo* 'That.one who works lives well').

The correlative pronoun is used in order to "nominalize" a completive clause—in particular, to fit it into a construction with a preposition or with a verb that requires an oblique case.

French

[*Ne vous attendez pas à*] *ce*-correl→***que*** [*nous vous rappelions de sortir vos ordures*] lit. 'Don't expect this that we remind you to take.out your garbage'.

Russian

[*dlja*] *togo,*-correl→***čtoby*** [*Ivan spal*] lit. 'for this that Ivan sleep' = 'for Ivan to sleep'
[*nedovolen*] *tem,*-correl→***čto*** [*Ivan spal*] lit. 'not.happy with.this that Ivan was.sleeping'

NB Let it be reminded that we see here two correlative pronouns тотII, namely:
(i) тотII.1 governs a pseudo-relative clause turning it into a relative:
Tot,-[*kto*]-rel→*xočet, možet ujti*
lit. 'That who wants, can leave' [SSyntRel No. 73, p. 89].
(ii) тотII.2 governs a completive clause:
Na to,-correl→*čto Ivan spal, možno ne obraščať vnimanija*
lit. 'On this that Ivan was.sleeping, it.is possible not pay attention'.

German

darauf-[*beharren,*]-rel→***daß*** [*wir zu dieser Frage konsultiert werden*]
lit. 'on.this insist that we on this question consulted are' =
'insist that we (should) be consulted on this issue'

> **113. Reduplicative** SSyntRel. It expresses a fictitious lexeme (depending on the language) and subordinates L′—a reduplicate of L—to L.

resolutions$_L$,-redupl→***schmesolutions***$_{L'}$: the fictitious lexeme is «DERISION».

A particular language can require more that one **reduplicative** SSyntRel. Thus, Russian needs several, because of the following contrasts:

Russian (on Russian constructions with repeated wordforms, see Sannikov 2010b)

blizko-redupl-1→***blizko*** lit. 'close, close' = 'close [insistently]': *Prud uže blizko, blizko* 'The.pond [is] already close, close'.
vs.
blizko-redupl-2→***blizko*** lit. 'close-close' = 'very close': *Prud – blizko-blizko* 'The.pond [is] quite close'. | *Nebo bylo sinee-sinee* 'The.sky was very blue'.

gde-**redupl-1**→***gde***
lit. 'where, where = 'where [insistently]': *Gde že on, gde?* 'Where is he, where?'
vs.
gde-**redupl-3**→***gde***
lit. 'where-where' = 'I am not sure about anywhere else': *Gde-gde, a u nas kofe est'* 'I am not sure about anywhere else, but we do carry coffee'.

počitaj-**redupl-1**→***počitaj***
lit. 'read, read' = 'Read! [insistently]': *Počitaj, počitaj, prošu tebja* 'Read, read, [I] beg you'.
vs.
počitaj-**redupl-4**→***počitaj***
lit. 'read-read' = 'Don't you dare to read! [a threat]': *Počitaj-počitaj!* 'Try and read on me!'

NB The four types of Russian reduplicative phrases carry different prosodies.

Hindi needs at least two **reduplicative** SSyntRels:

do-**redupl-1**→***do*** [*laṛke*] lit. 'two two boys' = 'two boys at a time': the fictitious lexeme is «DISTRIBUTIVE».
roz-**redupl-2**→***roz*** lit. 'day day' = 'every day': the fictitious lexeme is «EVERY».

114. **Intraphrasemic** SSyntRel. It has no correspondent in the DSyntS, but is introduced by DSynt-to-SSynt-structure rules; it describes idioms in which each component, except the central one, follows or precedes its governor immediately and is invariable; the linear position of the depending component is marked on it as a syntactic feature.

⌈*kingdom*-**intraphras**→*come*(postoposed)⌉; ⌈*by*-**intraphras**→*far*(postposed)⌉
⌈*as*-**intraphras**→*yet*(postoposed)⌉; ⌈*as*-**intraphras**→*if*(postposed)⌉
⌈*as*-**intraphras**→*of*(postposed) -**intraphras**→*yet*(postoposed)⌉
[*for*] ⌈*each*-**intraphras**→*other*(postposed)⌉

NB But Russian *odin*←**bin-junct**-[*dlja*]-*drugogo* lit. 'one for the other' (No. 110).

— A special case: compound indefinite pronouns

Russian (Chapter 9, 9.2.1.1, pp. 310*ff*)

MALO(anteposed)←**intraphras**–KTO   lit. 'few who' = 'few people'
MALO(anteposed)←**intraphras**–GDE   lit. 'few where' = 'in few places'
MALO(anteposed)_LI←**intraphras**–KTO   lit. 'few whether who' = 'many people'
MALO(anteposed) _LI←**intraphras**–GDE   lit. 'few whether where' = 'in many places'

KTO-**intraphras**→-TO(postposed) 'somebody'
GDE-**intraphras**→-TO(postposed) 'somewhere'
KTO-**intraphras**→BY(postposed)–**intraphras**→TO(postposed)–**intraphras**→NI(postposed)
    –**intraphras**→BYLO(postposed) 'no matter who'
GDE-**intraphras**→BY(postposed)–**intraphras**→TO(postposed)–**intraphras**→NI(postposed)
    –**intraphras**→BYLO(postposed) 'no matter where'

Russian (syntactic idioms with repeated lexemes; see Sannikov 2010b: 200–208)
*Zavtra,-***intraphras**→*tak*-**intraphras**→*zavtra* lit. 'Tomorow, so tomorrow'. = 'Let it be tomorrow'. = 'I don't care whether this is tomorrow or not'.

II Coordinative surface-syntactic relations: 115–122

115. Coordinative SSyntRel. It expresses DSyntRel **COORD**; the G is a lexeme of any part of speech, and the prototypical D is a lexeme of the same part of speech as G.

John,-coord→*Mary,*-coord→*Peter*; *fast,*-coord→*gently,*-coord→*skillfully*
John-coord→*and*[-coord-conj→*Mary*]; *fast,*-coord→*but* [*gently*]
[*for*] *John*-coord→*and* [*Mary*] vs. *for*-[*John*]-coord→*and*[-coord-conj→*for Mary*]
[coordination of prepositions]
[*John*] *was*-[*reading,*]-coord→*and*[-[*Mary patiently*]-coord-conj→*waited*.]
three-coord→*or* [*four times a year*]

116. Elliptic-coordinative SSyntRel. It expresses DSyntRel **COORD**; the G is a lexeme of any part of speech, and the prototypical D is also a lexeme of any part of speech.

[*He*] *works*-[*a lot,*]-ellipt-coord→*but* [*only at night.*]
[*He eats*] *vegetables,*-[*however, not*]-ellipt-coord→*boiled,* [*but fried.*]

Now it is the turn of a special family of SSyntRels introduced to describe what looks like coordination of different syntactic roles. Russian (and several other languages, see Patejuk & Przepiórkowski 2019) has a quirky coordinative construction: if different actants and circumstantials of a verb are all expressed by interrogative, negative or some quantifier-like pronouns, they are conjoined in the most standard way, although they must be in different grammatical cases: Rus. *Kto, kogo, komu i kak poslal?* lit. 'Who$_{NOM}$, whom$_{ACC}$, to.whom$_{DAT}$ and how sent?'; *Nikogo, nikto i ničem ne kormil* lit. 'Nobody$_{ACC}$, nobody$_{NOM}$ and with.nothing$_{INSTR}$ fed'; *Ivan vsegda vsem vsë i pro vsex rasskazyvaet* lit. 'Ivan always to.everybody everything and about everybody tells'. To properly represent the grammatical

2.5 An inventory of surface-syntactic relations found in the world's languages — 111

cases of these actants, Russian needs five more coordinative SSyntRels: 117–121 (at the DSynt-level, this construction is described by actantial DSyntRels linking the Main Verb to each actant and without the conjunction I 'and').

117. Subject-coordinative SSyntRel.

Nikogo,–subj-coord→*nikto*[–obl-obj-coord→*i ničem ne kormil*]
lit. 'Nobody$_{ACC}$, nobody$_{NOM}$ and with.nothing$_{INSTR}$ not fed'. = 'Nobody fed anybody with anything'

118. Direct-object-coordinative SSyntRel.

Kto,–dir-obj-coord→*kogo* [*i komu poslal?*] lit. 'Who, whom and to.whom sent?'

119. Indirect-object-coordinative SSyntRel.

Kto,–indir-obj-coord→*komu* [*i kogo poslal?*] lit. 'Who, to.whom and whom sent?'

120. Oblique-object-coordinative SSyntRel.

Kto,–obl-obj-coord→*čem* [*i kogo kormil?*] lit. 'Who, with.what and whom fed?'

121. Circumstantial-coordinative SSyntRel.

Russian

[*Kto,*–dir-obj-coord→*kogo,*–indir-obj-coord→]*komu*–circum-coord→*i* [*kak poslal?*]
lit. 'Who, whom, to.whom and how sent?'

NB All these "strangely" coordinated SSynt-actants can correspond to DSynt-actants depending on different verbs; cf.:
KTO←I–XOTET'–II→POSLAT'–II→ČTO ⇔
                          ↘III→KTO
Kto,–dir-obj-coord→*čto*–indir-obj-coord→*i komu xočet poslat'?*
lit. 'Who what and to.whom wants to.send?'

This fact does not create any additional problem for the SSynt-representation of the construction under consideration—it is taken care of by DSyntS-to-SSyntS rules.

122. Pseudo-coordinative SSyntRel. It expresses DSyntRel **PSEUDO-COORD**.

The pseudo-coordination resembles normal coordination in its formal aspect only: the D of the **pseudo-coordinative** SSyntRel necessarily follows the G, has the same form, and carries the enumeration prosody. But a coordinating conjunction in this construction is, generally speaking, impossible; and semantically, the **pseudo-coordinative** D adds a more detailed characterization to its G.

in-[Siberia,]-**pseudo-coord**→***on**-[the Ob shore,]*-**pseudo-coord**→***close** [to Novosibirsk]*

[six] dollars,-[80]-**pseudo-coord**→***cents***
[six] dollars,]-**pseudo-coord**→***and** [80 cents]*

tomorrow-**pseudo-coord**→***night**; Monday-[next]*-**pseudo-coord**→***week***

from-[fifty]-**pseudo-coord**→***to** [seventy pounds]*

[Responses ranged] from-[the indifferent,]-**pseudo-coord**→***to**-[the surly,]*-**pseudo-coord**→***to** [the downright obscene.]*

out_of-[political limbo,]-**pseudo-coord**→***towards** [the bright lights of liberty]*

Saturday-**pseudo-coord**→***night,*-**pseudo-coord**→***at** [a quarter to eleven]*

Saturday,-**pseudo-coord**→***at*-[night,]*-**pseudo-coord**→***after*-[dinner,]*-**pseudo-coord**→***at** [a quarter to eleven]*

[He had] everything:-**pseudo-coord**→***family**[, friends, good health.]*

[Such are all voiced] consonants-[, in particular,]-**pseudo-coord**→*/**b**/.*

Pseudo-coordinative dependents, or **pseudo-conjuncts**, are prominent in Korean, where they accompany the subject, the DirO, etc.; see Chapter 4, pp. 179*ff*. (SUBJ stands for the **subjective case,** which marks the subject and the subject's pseudo-conjuncts.)

Korean

(23) a. *Kay+hantey John+i*-**pseudo-coord**→***son** +i   mul+li   +ess +ta*
    dog   DAT   SUBJ   hand SUBJ bite PASS PAST DECLAR(ative)
    lit. 'By.dog John hand was.bitten'. = 'John was bitten by the dog on the hand'.

   b. *Kay+ka   John+il* -**pseudo-coord**→***son** +il   mul+Ø   +ess +ta*
    dog SUBJ   ACC   hand ACC bite ACT PAST DECLAR(ative)
    lit. 'Dog John hand bit'. = 'The dog bit John on the hand'.

An important particular case of the **pseudo-coordinative** SSyntRel is its use to describe the **verb series** (Haspelmath 2016):

(24) a. Ewe

    Ku ———— [*tsi*]–**pseudo-coord**→*klɔ́*   [*ŋkú.me*]
    2.SG.IMPER-scoop water   2.SG.IMPER-wash face
    'Scoop some water and wash your face'.

  b. Paamese

    Ma+kuri   *+ko*–**pseudo-coord**→*lo*   *+va*   *+haa*
    1.SG IMMED-take 2.SG   1.DU.INCL IMMED go
    lit. 'I.will.take.you I.and.you.will. go'. = 'I will take you with me'.

There is an interesting particular case of the verb series: Russian so-called **double verbs** (Vajs 2000), which can also be described by means of the **pseudo-coordinative** SSyntRel:

Russian

[*Ona*] *sidit*-**pseudo-coord**→*xoxočet* lit. '[She] is.sitting is.laughing.uproariously'.

[*Oni*] *xodjat*-**pseudo-coord**→*pobirajutsja* lt. '[They] are.walking.around are.begging'.

Davaj-**pseudo-coord**→*eš'!* lit. 'Give$_{\text{IMPER.2.SG}}$ eat$_{\text{IMPER.2.SG}}$!' [reinforced incitement]

Appendix A

Alphabetical index of surface-syntactic relations

absolute-conjunctional-completive	106	attributive	63
absolute-modificative	62	auxiliary	46
actantial-appositive	57	auxiliary-conjunctive	45
actantial-attributive	56	binary-junctive	110
addressative	43		
adjective-marker-analytical	88	characterizing-adnominal-attributive	52
adjunctive	41	circumstantial	33
adnominal-linking	83	circumstantial-comparative-conjunctional-completive	105
affected-objectival	13		
agentive-completive	19	circumstantial-coordinative	121
apposition-circumstantial	37	colligative	111
approximate-ordinal	69	comparative-conjunctional-completive	100
approximate-quantitative	67		
assertive-analytical	96	comparative-objectival	26
attribute-circumstantial	38	compositive	61

conditional-subjectival	3	metaphorical-adnominal-attributive	53
consecutive-subjectival	2	modal-objectival	28
coordinative-conjunctional-completive	99	modificative	70
coordinative	115	modifier-attributive	55
copular-completive	21	modifier-circumstantial	36
copular-genitive-completive	22		
correlative	112	name-appositive	81
		name-junctive-1/2/3	109
dative-ethical-objectival	27	negative-analytical	94
debitive-subjectival	5	noun-marker-analytical	87
descriptive-appositive	79	numeral-junctive	108
descriptive-attributive	64		
descriptive-modificative	72	object-adnominal-completive	49
descriptive-relative	74	object-attributive-completive	24
determinative	65	object-copredicative	30
direct-object-comparative-conjunctional-completive	102	object-resultative-copredicative	31
direct-object-coordinative	118	oblique-object-comparative-conjunctional-completive	104
direct-objectival	7	oblique-object-coordinative	120
direct-speech-objectival	12	oblique-objectival-1	15
distance-circumstantial	35	oblique-objectival-2	16
durative-circumstantial	34	ordinal	68
elective	58	parenthetical	39
elliptic-absolute-conjunctional-completive	107	passive-agentive-completive	20
elliptic-coordinative	116	passive-analytical	89
evaluative-adnominal-attributive	54	"per"-appositive	82
		perfective-analytical	90
floating-copredicative	32	possessive	60
future-analytical	93	possessive-adnominal-attributive	51
		postpositional-completive	85
identity-appositive	77	predicate-attributive-completive	25
indirect-object-comparative-conjunctional-completive	103	prepositional-completive	84
indirect-object-coordinative	119	presentative	44
indirect-objectival	14	preterit-analytical	92
infinitive-copredicative-objectival	18	progressive-analytical	91
infinitive-objectival	11	proleptive	42
infinitive-oblique-objectival	17	pseudo-coordinative	122
interrogative-analytical	95	pseudo-direct-objectival	10
intraphrasemic	114	pseudo-subjectival	6
irrealis-subjectival	4		
		qualificative-adnominal-attributive	50

qualifying-appositive	78
quantitative	66
quasi-direct-objectival-1	8
quasi-direct-objectival-2	9
quasi-parenthetical	40
reduplicative	113
relative	73
restrictive	47
sequential	59
special-modificative	71
specifying-appositive	76
subjectal-adnominal-completive	48
subject-attributive-completive	23
subject-comparative-conjunctional-completive	101
subject-coordinative	117
subject-copredicative	29
subjectival	1
subordinative-conjunctional-completive	97
subordinative-conjunctional-infinitival-completive	98
title-appositive	80
verb-marker-analytical	86
WH-pronominal	75

Appendix B

Index of passive surface-syntactic valences of word classes
(the numbers identify the SSyntRels of which a lexeme of the given class may be a Dependent)

This index is supposed to help the reader find the SSyntRel that represents a given construction. For instance, what SSyntRels link the elements of the phrases *could resist* and *resist joining* in the sentence *Few writers could resist joining this society*? The wordform *resist* is here a (bare) V_{INF}, so that we have to choose between SSynt-Rels Nos. 7, 11, 17–18, 33, 84, 92, 93; only No. 11 (the **infinitival-objectival** SSyntRel) is good. Similarly, *joining* is a V_{ING}, and the possible choices are SSyntRels Nos. 1, 7, 33, 62 and 91; No. 7 is good—the **direct-objectival** SSyntRel.

N		1–5, 7–9, 14–16, 19–24, 28–30, 33–35, 37, 42–43, 48–57, 59–64, 77–82, 84–85, 99–107, 113
	$N_{(measure)}$	34, 35
	$N_{(pron, pers)}$	27
	$N_{(proper)}$	43, 76, 81, 109
V		
	V_{FIN}	1 [in a pseudo-relative], 7[in a pseudo-relative or an asyndetic completive], 12 [in a Direct Speech clause], 40 [in a Direct Speech clause], 73–75, 91, 97, 100
	V_{INF}	7, 11, 17–18, 33, 84, 92, 93
	V_{ING}	1, 7, 33, 62, 91
	V_{PART}	89–91

ADJ		21, 23–25, 29–31, 36, 62, 70–72, 76, 107
	ADJ(determ)	65
	ADJ(ordinal)	68, 69
	ADJ(pron)	32, 65
LINKER		83
NUM(quant)		66, 67, 108
ADV		1, 33, 36, 38
	ADV(interj)	41
	ADV(adjunct)	86 [go→*down*]
	THERE	6
	Fr. **BEAUCOUP** 'much'	48
	Rus. **MNOGO** 'much'	48
PREP		7 [in some languages], 14–20, 22, 29, 33, 38, 48–56, 63–64, 111
	Chin. **BĂ**	13
	BY	48
	FOR	19
	TO(inf)	1, 6, 7, 10, 98
	Rus. **U**	60
CONJ		
	AND	108
	AS	39
	CONJ(coord)	45, 115–120
	CONJ(subord)	33, 106
	CONJ(compar)	26, 39
	CONJ(complementizer)	1, 6, 7, 84, 93, 106
	THAT[5]	6, 7, 10, 106
PARTICLE		46, 47, 86–88
	Rus. **ÈTO**[1]	47 [*Èto Ivan razbil čašku!* 'It is Ivan who broke the cup!']
	Rus. **ÈTO**[2]	44 [*Èto Ivan tam v mjač igraet* 'This is Ivan who plays ball there'.]
	Rus. **TO**[2]	46 [*Esli X > Y,* **to** *uravnenie ne imeet rešenija* 'If X > Y, then the equation has no solution'.]
DIRECT SPEECH		1, 12

A preliminary version of Chapter 2 was published as Mel'čuk 2015–2016.

3 Syntactic subject: syntactic relations, once again

3.1 The problem stated
3.2 Conceptual preliminaries
    3.2.1 *Grammatical relations ⇒ syntactic relations
    3.2.2 Syntactic relations are syntactic dependency relations
    3.2.3 Syntactic subject as the dependent member of the **subjectival** SSyntRel
    3.2.4 Definitional vs. characterizing parameters of the syntactic subject
        3.2.4.1 Introductory remarks
        3.2.4.2 Definitional parameters of clause elements
        3.2.4.3 Characterizing parameters of clause elements
    3.2.5. Subjecthood properties
    3.2.6. Syntactic subject and ergativity
3.3 Syntactic subject: an attempt at a definition
3.4 Establishing the syntactic subject in a language
    3.4.1 No agreement on the Main Verb
    3.4.2 Monopersonal agreement of the Main Verb
    3.4.3. Polypersonal agreement of the Main Verb
3.5 Syntactic subject problems related to impersonal constructions
3.6 A difficult case: the syntactic subject in Lushootseed
3.7 The syntactic subject: its syntactic role vs. its semantic and communicative roles
3.8 The direct object
3.9 Summing up
    3.9.1 Defining surface-syntactic relations
    3.9.2 Cross-linguistic universality of particular surface-syntactic relations

> **To the fond memory of Sasha Kibrik** (26 Mar 1939 – 31 Oct 2012)
> Linguistics owes him a lot; several languages that he helped to save from oblivion owe him a lot; his students, many of whom are professors now, owe him a lot; I, his friend, owe him a lot. And these debts will never be repaid.

3.1 The problem stated

Syntactic subject (as well as syntactic object) has always been and still is a popular topic in linguistics, especially in typology: it suffices to indicate such studies as Keenan 1976, Foley & Van Valin 1977, Van Valin 1981, Kozinskij 1983, Lazard 1994, Palmer 1994, Givón 1995, Kibrik 1997 and 2001, Testelec 2001: 317–359, Farrell 2005, Falk 2006, Bickel 2011, Siewierska & Bakker 2012, Zimmerling 2012, Handschuh 2014, etc., as well as the collections Li (ed.) 1976, Cole & Sadock (eds.) 1977, Yaguello (ed.) 1994, Burgess et al. (eds.) 1995, Aikhenvald et al. (eds.) 2001, Davies & Dubinsky (eds.) 2001, Bhaskararao & Subbarao (eds.) 2004, and Suihkonen et al. (eds.) 2012. The notions of syntactic subject and syntactic object are known in modern linguistic literature as **grammatical relations**, and they continue to generate controversy, especially, the notion *grammatical subject*—a highly contentious topic since the time the term *subject* appeared in the linguist's toolbox.[1] For instance, some linguistic theories claim that all clauses of all languages must have a grammatical subject, while other theories insist that there is no such category consistent for all languages. As is typical of the science of language, the problem resides in the absence of a rigorously defined notion of subject—that is, for the *n*-th time, we are dealing with a notional/terminological problem. (Thus, in the two-volume collection Bhaskararao & Subbarao (eds.) 2004 we find 28 papers on subjects and subjecthood, but not one definition of syntactic subject or even an attempt at a definition.)

The same things can be said about the direct object; however, this latter notion is, in a sense, "derived" from that of subject, so in what follows I will focus on the subject in order to say a few words about the direct object at the end of the chapter (Section 3.8).

> *The goal of this chapter is to propose rigorous definitions for both above notions, the* syntactic subject *[SyntSubj] and the* direct object *[DirO], and discuss, in sufficient detail, several complex cases involving the SyntSubj.*

The problem of the definition of SyntSubj and DirO is complicated: it involves the representation of the (surface- and deep-) syntactic structure of sentences, the actants, the diathesis and the voice, transitivity, ergativity, agreement and government, zero lexemes, and many other things. As a consequence, I am forced to limit myself to approximate and sketchy characterization of many relevant notions. At the same time, I have to analyze data from languages that I do not sufficiently know, so that factual mistakes are quite probable. This is, however, not that dangerous: the main thrust of this chapter is not in communicating new linguistic facts, but in showing the logical links between facts (independently of whether they are correct or not) and corresponding abstract statements.

---

1 The term *subject* was introduced into scientific literature somewhere in the early Middle Ages, seemingly by Boethius: "In Boethius (5th–6th c.) we find 'subiectum' and 'praedicatum', but these are terms which belong to logic rather than to grammar" (Lepschy 1994: 278). In other words, the term *subject* was originally meant to designate a logical notion. According to Lepschy, its use for the syntactic role of a lexical expression is known only from 18th century; the term *object* is 100 years younger.

3.2 Conceptual preliminaries

3.2.1 *Grammatical relations ⇒ syntactic relations

First things first: language has no such things as *grammatical relations*; the relations that are under discussion are **syntactic**. Generally speaking, the relations between lexical units in a sentence include relations of semantic, syntactic, and morphological dependency; see, e.g., Mel'čuk 1988 105–149 and 2012–2015: vol. 3, Ch. 18. (The relation of coreference is ignored here as being of a completely different nature: coreference is not dependency, but equivalence.) Therefore, the only term allowed in this book for what we are dealing with is **syntactic relations**.

The present discussion is based on the following three postulates:

1. In any language, an utterance is represented at the syntactic level by its **syntactic structure**.
2. The syntactic structure is a **dependency structure**: only this type of structure represents syntactic relations directly and explicitly.
3. There are two sublevels of syntactic structure: the **deep-syntactic** structure and the **surface-syntactic** structure. SyntSubj and DirO belong to the surface-syntactic structure; therefore, in what follows we speak only of surface-syntactic relations [SSyntRels].

As soon as we agree on these postulates, no more discussion is possible as to whether syntactic relations **as such** are universal: of course they are, and that, in the strongest sense possible—namely, syntactic relations are necessarily present in any multilexemic utterance of any language, and they always form a connected structure, since all words of an utterance are syntactically linked. (Strange as it may seem, you can find in the literature statements to the effect that "Grammatical Relations" are not cross-linguistically universal. Would their proponents say that syntactic relations are not cross-linguistically universal? I did not think so and frankly believed that just replacing "grammatical" by "syntactic" would already move us in the right direction. However, I have discovered that some linguists speak quite seriously about languages without syntactic relations...[2] I keep silent, in conformity with L. Wittgenstein's Major Proposition 7.[3])

---

[2] For instance: "Contrary to common assumptions, syntactic relations, especially those of subject and object, are not universal, but are only one of several possibilities of organizing relational clause structure" (Kibrik 1997: 279). See also Gil 1994 (about a language "without syntax"—Riau Indonesian) and Dryer 1997 It is clear that statements of this kind are due to the absence of a rigorous notional apparatus.

[3] "Wovon man nicht sprechen kann, darüber muß man schweigen" ['Whereof one cannot speak, thereof one must be silent'] (Wittgenstein 1922: 162).

Now, from what was just said it does not, of course, follow that **any particular** SSyntRel—in our case, the **subjectival** (and also the **direct-objectival**) SSyntRel—is universal; that is what has to be explored. (The **subjectival** SSyntRel seems to be cross-linguistically universal, as I hope to show. But the **direct-objectival** SSyntRel is not universal: thus, it is absent from ergative languages, see below, Sections 3.2, p. 134 and 3.8, p. 174..)

3.2.2 Syntactic relations are syntactic dependency relations

Our discussion of SyntSubj is based on a dependency representation of the syntactic structure of sentences. It is impossible to present here all the necessary notions, and I will limit myself to three references (Mel'čuk 1988, 2004 and 2009a) concerning the notion of actant, and another reference (Mel'čuk 2006a: 181–262) for the notions of diathesis and (grammatical) voice; the latter two notions have their rigorous definitions in Chapter 8.

A SSyntRel **r** represents a family of two-lexeme syntactic constructions—that is, a set of syntactically similar two-lexeme phrases. Thus, the expression "L_1–r→L_2" describes all phrases (of language **L**) that can be produced out of lexemes L_1 and L_2, if L_2 depends on L_1 via SSyntRel **r**. To illustrate, the descriptions of two SSyntRels will be presented: the **prepositional-completive** SSyntRels of English and the **postpositional-completive** SSyntRel of Hungarian (see Chapter 2, Section 2.4, Nos. 84 and 85, p. 95).

The prepositional SSyntRel of English

The **prepositional-completive** SSynt-relation subordinates a noun L_2 to a preposition L_1 (I ignore here all more complex cases in which the dependent element is not a noun/a pronoun); cf.:

(1) FOR_{L_1}–**prepos**→$JOHN_{L_2}$ (*for John*)
    ON_{L_1}–[*this shaky*]–**prepos**→$BENCH_{L_2}$ (*on this shaky bench*)
    $WITHOUT_{L_1}$–**prepos**→$HE_{L_2\text{-OBL}}$ (*without him*)

What does the name of this SSyntRel—**prepositional–completive**—stand for? It carries three types of information:

- Linear position of L_2 with respect to L_1: 1) L_2 follows L_1; 2) only some types of dependents of L_2 are allowed to be placed between L_2 and L_1 (an exhaustive specification of these dependents is needed, of course).
- Inflection of L_1 (in particular, as a function of L_2, i.e. agreement): none.

- Inflection of L_2 (in particular, as a function of L_1, i.e. government):
  - none, if L_2 is a noun;
  - OBL(ique case), if L_2 is a personal pronoun (*with me*$_{OBL}$) or the interrogative/relative pronoun WHO (*with whom*$_{OBL}$).

The linear position of L_2 with respect to L_1 (plus the specification of lexical units that can appear between L_1 and L_2) and the possible inflection (or the absence thereof) of both L_1 and L_2 are, generally speaking, necessary definitional properties of any SSyntRel (see Subsection 3.2.3).

The postpositional-completive SSyntRel of Hungarian

Hungarian has only postpositions, which play the same syntactic role as English prepositions; a postposition L_1 subordinates its noun L_2 by the **postpositional-completive** SSyntRel, which is specified as follows:

- Linear position of L_2 with respect to L_1: L_2 immediately precedes L_1; only elements coordinated with L_2 are allowed between L_2 and L_1.
- Inflection of L_1 (in particular, as a function of L_2, i.e. agreement):
  - none, if L_2 is a noun different from a personal pronoun;
  - if L_2 is a personal pronoun, L_1 agrees with L_2 in the morphological category of possession, that is, L_1 receives the corresponding possessive form and L_2 itself is deleted (e.g., the meaning 'with you' is expressed literally as 'your.with').
- Inflection of L_2 (in particular, as a function of L_1, i.e. government): L_2 receives the case governed by L_1 (boxed in (2)).

(2) Hungarian

az új	HÁZ	$+\emptyset_{L_2}$←**postpos**–MELLETT$_{L_1}$	⟺	*az új ház mellett*
the new	house	NOM close.to		'close to the new house'

ÉN$_{L_2}$←**postpos**–MELLETT$_{L_1}$	⟹MELLETT$_{L_1}$+*em*	⟺	*mellettem*
I close.to	close.to 1.SG		lit. 'my-close.to' = 'close to me'

az új	HÁZ	$+on_{L_2}$←**postpos**–KIVÜL$_{L_1}$	⟺	*az új házon kivül*
the new	house SUPRESSIVE	outside		'outside the new house'

Examples (1) and (2) illustrate the descriptions of two of the least controversial SSyntRels. In point of fact, these descriptions are rough informal presentations of surface-syntactic rules ({SSyntSs} ⟺ {DMorphSs}) in a Meaning-Text model. An interested reader can see some SSynt-rules of Russian and English in Mel'čuk 1974: 260–300 and Mel'čuk & Pertsov 1987: 178–470.

3.2.3 Syntactic subject as the dependent member of the subjectival SSyntRel

What is being specifically considered in this chapter is the *syntactic subject*—SyntSubj, Rus. *podležaščee*, a purely syntactic entity, that is, a clause element—a lexical expression that is logically independent of semantic and communicative roles it can play (i.e., it is **not** a logical subject and **not** the discourse topic or something of the kind). Thus, talking about SyntSubjs actually means talking about the **subjectival** SSyntRel, of which the SyntSubj is the dependent member.

Since the classic paper Keenan 1976, SyntSubj has been understood as a cluster concept defined inductively. In Keenan's view, the notion of SyntSubj is based on 1) some intuitively clear cases in the simplest sentences possible—canonical SyntSubjs, and 2) a list of cross-linguistically universal **syntactically relevant properties** of clause elements (omissibility/non-omissibility, imposing grammemes on other clause elements, undergoing grammeme imposition, a particular grammatical case, obligatory definiteness, particular linear position, participation in syntactic processes, etc.). Different SSynt-elements are compared to canonical SyntSubjs according to these properties; those SSynt-elements that are similar enough to the canonical SyntSubjs are also recognized as SyntSubjs. Keenan supplied a detailed checklist of syntactically relevant properties—some 30 plus of them. In this chapter, I am using this list, although modified; see, for instance, Iordanskaja & Mel'čuk 2009a, where the syntactic properties of clause elements are discussed for French.

In accordance with Keenan's approach, I will define the SyntSubj as **the most privileged SSynt-actant of the Main Verb**; in other words, the SyntSubj is the most privileged clause element in the given language.

> A clause element CE_1 is more privileged than another clause element CE_2 if and only if CE_1 has more Keenan's properties than CE_2; the most privileged clause element in **L** has more Keenan's properties than any other clause element. (See Comment 2 after Definition 3.1, p. 135.)

However, the word *property* is ambiguous—between 'parameter' (which has several values) and 'a particular value of the parameter'. Thus, in our examples with prepositions in 3.2.2, "linear position of L_2 with respect to L_1" is the name of a parameter, while the indications "L_2 follows L_1, not necessarily immediately" or "L_2 immediately precedes L_1" are ones of its possible values. To avoid confusion, from now on, I will speak of parameters and of their values, using the term *property* only for 'a value of the corresponding parameter'.

3.2.4 Definitional vs. characterizing parameters of the syntactic subject

3.2.4.1 Introductory remarks

Keenan (1976: 324) divided syntactic subjecthood parameters on his checklist into two major classes: **coding** parameters and **behavioral** parameters.

Coding parameters, which I am calling **definitional**, specify the way the given SSyntRel is implemented (= encoded, expressed) in the sentence—roughly, the linear placement and inflection of its members. If and only if these parameters are satisfied to a sufficient degree—that is, if enough of these have the expected positive values for the clause element being tested, this clause element is the SyntSubj. The definitional parameters concern exclusively the governor and the dependent of the SSyntRel **r** under consideration; they do not involve any third, "outside" syntactic element. These parameters are six in number (see below), and they are established by logical reasoning; therefore, they are language-universal, that is, applicable to any language.

Behavioral, or **characterizing**, parameters, in sharp contrast to definitional ones, obligatorily mention an element that is exterior with respect to the expression of the $L_1\text{−r→}L_2$ configuration. For instance, one of the most exploited characterizing subjecthood parameters is the possibility of relativization (the well-known Accessibility Hierarchy of Keenan and Comrie, see Chapter 6, 6.4.3, p. 258): "if some clause element in **L** can be relativized, then the SyntSubj can"; this statement is not about the SyntSubj, but about the relativization, for the possibility of which the fact of being the SyntSubj, DirO, IndirO, etc. serves as a necessary condition. The characterizing parameters are established empirically and, therefore, they are in principle not language-universal. However, some of these are so widespread that they can be called quasi-universal.

Subjecthood behavioral properties are defined for SSynt-elements in surface-syntactic structures; therefore, these elements must themselves be defined prior to and independently from their syntactic behavior. Therefore:

> ❗ Any SSynt-relation—in particular, the **subjectival** SSyntRel—must be defined only by its definitional (= coding), and not by the characterizing (= behavioral), properties (Iordanskaja & Mel'čuk 2009a: 159–160).

Cf. the following relevant remark in Croft 1994: 30: "I wish to invert the usual priority in syntactic theory of behavioral over coding properties of subjects."

The viewpoint proposed here can be illustrated with a simple comparison. What is a woman? The only definitional property of a woman is her gender physiology, allowing for childbirth. Nothing in the physical appearance, social standing or behavior defines a woman as such; no matter whether she looks and dresses like a man, whether she has full civic rights or none whatsoever, she remains a woman: her unique definitional "privilege" is the potential capacity of bringing children into the world. The same can be said about SyntSubjs: a SyntSubj's definitional properties make it what it is, while its behavioral (= characterizing) properties may vary from language to language without changing its fundamental nature.

Once defined, the SyntSubj of language L must, of course, be characterized by its syntactic behavior in larger formations: for instance, its ability to relativize, to control deverbal adverbials and/or reflexives, to control deletions under coreference, etc. This can throw an interesting light on it, as well on some other clause elements—yet this behavior can by no means define the SyntSubj.

It seems that the root of disagreement between linguists with respect to the identification of SyntSubjs lies in the adopted principle for defining them: either solely by their definitional (= coding) properties or by their syntactic behavior—that is, by their participation in syntactic processes, with or without coding properties. In my approach, the choice is clear-cut: any clause element, and the SyntSubj in particular, must be **defined** exclusively by its coding properties and then **characterized** by its syntactic behavior.

3.2.4.2 Definitional parameters of clause elements

A clause element CE is the dependent member of a particular SSyntRel r: L–r→CE. The values of the definitional parameters of r specify the properties of L and CE necessary for the configuration L–r→CE to appear in the surface-syntactic structure of a clause and to be implemented in its deep-morphological structure. If we exclude (for simplicity's sake) the prosody from consideration, there are six such parameters. Since this inventory is established logically, the six parameters are cross-linguistically universal—in the sense that they are sufficient for defining all SSyntRels in all languages. (Some of them, of course, prove irrelevant for some languages—for instance, because of a very flexible word order or the absence of inflection in a given language.)

Table 3.1 Definitional parameters of a surface-syntactic clause element CE (L–r→CE)

1. CE's dependence on the MV as its actant.
2. CE's omissibility from the syntactic structure of the clause.
3. CE's linear position with respect to L.
4. L's form:
   a. L's modification as a function of CE (≈ agreement);
   b. L's valence-changing (voice-like) modification affecting the CE.
5. CE's form as a function of L (≈ government).
6. CE's pronominalization.

NB 1. Although the above definitional parameters are valid for all SSynt-clause elements—that is, for all SSyntRels, I will comment on them using as illustration the SyntSubj, since it is the latter that constitutes my actual target.
2. The names of the parameters are not formulated rigorously: they are meant to refer to sets of properties that have to be sharpened for each specific language.
3. The list of definitional parameters in Table 3.1 features some modifications with respect to the list given in Iordanskaja & Mel'čuk 2009a.

Comments

1. Parameter 1 reflects the assumption that a full-fledged clause contains one and only one Main Verb, as well as one and only one SyntSubj (except for coordination). Thus, the clause element that expresses the Agent of a non-finite verb form—an infinitive or a converb—is not considered to be a SyntSubj. Note that in some languages the syntactic head of a clause can be a unit different from a finite verb—for instance, an infinitive, so that, in point of fact, I am talking here about the dependence on the head of the clause whatever it is (see on the SyntSubj in Russian, Section 3.3 below, pp. 136*ff*).

2. Parameter 2 is aimed at omissibility of a clause element from the syntactic structure of the sentence, not simply from the sentence itself; an omissible element must be omissible from the starting semantic structure and be absent from the SSyntS. Thus, in a Pro-Drop language, the SyntSubj, if it is a pronoun, can or must be absent from the sentence, while it (or its source) is still present in the sentence's syntactic structure; this absence is known as ellipsis. One can see this, for instance, in Spanish: a sentence such as *Desapareció detrás de la esquina* lit. 'Disappeared behind the corner' actually means 'He/She/It disappeared...', where the SyntSubj **él/ella** 'he/she/it' is not present in the sentence itself, but appears of course in the SemS and SyntS of the sentence. Let us consider an example of ellipsis from Navajo.

(3) Navajo (Foley & Van Valin 1977: 300–301)
    a. (i) *'Ashkii 'at'ééd yi+ztał*
          lit. 'Boy girl kicked'. = 'The boy kicked the girl'.
and (ii) *At'ééd yi+ztał*
          lit. '**He/She** girl kicked'. = '**He/She** kicked the girl'.
vs. b. (i) *'At'ééd 'ashkii bi+ztał*
          lit. 'Girl boy was.kicked'. = 'The girl was.kicked by the boy'.
and (ii) *'At'ééd bi+ztał*
          lit. '**He/She** girl was.kicked'. = '**He/She** was.kicked by the girl'.

Here none of the actants of the MV is omissible from the sentence's Synt-structure: its physical absence from the sentence is due to its pronominalization with the subsequent Pro-Dropping. However, in an English sentence such as *The bridge was destroyed* the Synt-actant expressing the Agent is not present in the Sem-structure nor in the Synt-structure: the sentence does not mean '... destroyed by HIM/HER/THEM'. In other words, the Agent of an English passive verb need not be recoverable from discourse (and so it is not amenable to pronominalization); it need not be known or knowable to the Speaker.

NB A SyntSubj can be absent from the sentence while being present in its Synt-structure according to two scenarios.
– In a Pro-Drop language: the SyntSubj is pronominalized and then omitted from the sentence.
– In a language that has the inflectional category of predicativity (see Mel'čuk 1992–2000: vol. 2, 221*ff*), such as Altaic and Samodian languages, as well as Korean: the SyntSubj can be "fused" with the verb 'be' into one wordform, so that it is impossible to distinguish the SyntSubj and the Main Verb; cf.:
(i) Korean
   Pul +i   +ta!   lit. 'Fire.is!' = 'There is fire!'
   fire be DECLAR(ative)
Even if we accept that the SyntSubj is not explicitly present in sentence (i), it is, of course, present in its Synt-structure: it is PUL 'fire'. (See also Chapter 4, 4.5.1, p. 191.)

3. Parameter 3 presupposes a preferred word order in a clause without any communicative effects. Thus, in English, in a simple, communicatively neutral clause the SyntSubj precedes the MV (and all MV's other actants); in Malagasy, the SyntSubj follows the MV (and all its other actants).

4. Parameter 4 covers two cases: 4a and 4b.
Parameter 4a concerns, roughly speaking, the agreement of the L_1 with the CE in question.

No rigorous definition of agreement can be given here (see, e.g., Mel'čuk 2006a: 58*ff*), but an intuitive understanding seems to be sufficient. It must be emphasized that

> "The lexeme L_1 agrees with the lexeme L_2" does not mean that L_1 faithfully copies some features of L_2; this only means that some features of L_2 control the morphological form of L_1.

Thus, the Russian MV agrees with the prepositional phrase PO + NP ≈ 'NP each ...' in the role of SyntSubj by taking the grammemes SG, NEUTER: *Prixodil+o* [NEU.3.SG] ***po** pjat' posetitelej v čas* lit. 'Came **each** five visitors in hour'. = 'Each hour five visitors came'. Similarly, in Arabic, the MV agrees with the SyntSubj, although the rules of this agreement are by no means straightforward. Namely:

- If the SyntSubj denotes humans:
  - If the MV precedes the SyntSubj, then, whatever the number of the SyntSubj:
    - if the SyntSubj denotes male humans, then the MV must be in the singular masculine;
    - if the SyntSubj denotes female humans, then the MV must be in the singular feminine.
  - If the MV follows the SyntSubj, then it has the gender and the number of the SyntSubj.
- If the SyntSubj does not denote humans:
  The MV must be in the singular feminine, whatever the gender and the number of the SyntSubj.

Speaking of MV agreement, two possible complications should be kept in mind.

First, we must make sure that in **L** the agreement of the MV is indeed controlled by a syntactically determined unit rather than by a semantic or communicative factor. Two examples:

- In Awa Pit (Kibrik 2003: 158–160), the MV agrees with the actant higher on the person hierarchy (1 > 2 > 3), whatever its syntactic role:

(4) Awa Pit

    a. (i) **Na**+Ø   pjan+ni +**s**   'I will hit you$_{SG}$/you$_{PL}$/him/them'.
        I   NOM hit   FUT 1.SG

and (ii) **Na**+wa pjan+ni +**s**   'You$_{SG}$/You$_{PL}$/He/They will hit **me**'.
        I   ACC   hit   FUT 1.SG

    b. (i) **Nu** +Ø   /**Us**+Ø   pjan+ni +**zi**   '**You**$_{SG}$/**He** will hit him/them'.
        you$_{SG}$ NOM/he NOM hit   FUT 2/3.SG

and (ii) **Nu** +wa /**Us**+a   pjan+ni +**zi**   'He/They will hit **you**$_{SG}$/**him**'.
        you$_{SG}$ ACC /he ACC hit   FUT 2/3.SG

- In Kinyarwanda (Dalrymple & Nikolaeva 2011) the agreement of the MV is determined by the communicative role of the controller rather than by its syntactic function:

(5) Kinyarwanda (Roman numerals in the glosses indicate noun classes)

    a. *Umu+huûngu **a**+ra +som+a igi+tabo*
       I   boy   I PRES read IND VII book
      'The.boy is.reading the.book'.

vs. b. *Igi+tabo **ki**+ra +som+a umu+huûngu*
VII book **VII** PRES read IND I boy
'It is the boy who is reading the book'.

In (5b), the MV agrees in noun class with its DirO, because the SyntSubj is Rhematic and Focalized.

In a language with semantically or communicatively controlled agreement of the MV, this agreement should not, of course, be considered among definitional properties of the SyntSubj.

Second, the MV often agrees with a zero dummy SyntSubj, as, for instance, in Russian sentence [*Nadkus sdelan, i*] *pal'cem* $\emptyset^{dummy}_{(neu, 3sg)} \emptyset^{BYT'}_{MV}$ ***smjato***$_{NEU, SG}$ lit. '[A.bite is.done, and] with.finger [it] is crumpled' [M. Zoščenko]. When the MV has the "unmarked/neutral/default form" (NEUTER, 3SG) in the absence of an overt SyntSubj, this means that there is a semantically empty zero lexeme SyntSubj $\emptyset^{dummy}_{(neu, 3sg)}$, which imposes this agreement (Mel'čuk 2006a: Ch. 9, especially p. 475). The failure to have recourse to a zero SyntSubj leads to bizarre results, such as treating a normal DirO as a "derived subject." [4]

Parameter 4a foresees not only well-known phenomenon of agreement of the MV with the SyntSubj (in person, number, and gender/noun class), but also more complex situations. For instance, in Dyirbal, only the SyntSubj can be the semantic target of the frequentative verbal suffix **-ḍay**, which expresses a large quantity of referent(s) of the SyntSubj:

---

[4] Consider the example from Biblical Hebrew in Keenan 1976: 325, (26b):

(i) *Bĕ-yorɔl yeḥoleq* **'ɛθ hɔ-'ɔrɛṣ**
by lot divide-PASS.IND.PAST.3.SG.MASC DirO **the land**
lit. 'By lot [it] was.divided the land'.

The phrase 'the land' is not a "derived" SyntSubj; it is a DirO, explicitly marked as such by the corresponding preposition 'ɛθ. The SyntSubj here is a dummy (= empty) zero, corresponding to the English IT; this is an impersonal construction.

Of course, a dummy zero SyntSubj must be postulated with caution:
– It should not be introduced if the MV does not show agreement at all (e.g., Lezgian).
– It should not be introduced for the only reason that the MV is in the least marked form, as, e.g., in the Hindi sentence (ii-a), where the compound MV *dekhā hai* is MASC.3.SG:

(ii) a. *Rītā+ne laṛkī +Ø+ko dekh+Ø +ā hai*
Rita INSTR girl$_{(fem)}$ SG DAT see PERF.PART MASC.SG be-PRES.3.SG
'Rita has seen the girl'.

Here the perfect participle DEKHĀ agrees with LAṚKĪ (recall that agreement does not necessarily mean the identity of features); to see this, it suffices to replace LAṚKĪ with an inanimate noun that appears in the nominative, and the MV reacts to this modification by reflecting the grammatical gender of the DirO (ii-c):

(6) Dyirbal (Dixon 1972: 250)

a. *Bayi+Ø   yaṛa+Ø   ɲinan +ḍa   +ɲu*   '**Many** men sat down'.
   the   NOM man NOM sit.down FREQ PRES/PAST

b. (i) *Balam+Ø   miraɲ   +Ø   ba+ŋgul   yaṛa+ŋgu*
   the   NOM black.bean NOM the INSTR man INSTR
   gundal   +ḍa +n
   get.collected FREQ PRES/PAST
   '**Many** black beans got collected by the man'.

vs. (ii) *Bayi+Ø   yaṛa+Ø   gundal   +ŋa +ḍa +ɲu*
    the   NOM man NOM get.collected PASS FREQ PRES/PAST
    ba +gum   miraɲ   +gu
    the DAT black.bean DAT
    '**Many** men collected black beans'.[5]

---

b. *Rītā+ne   kamr   +ā/e +Ø   dekh+Ø   +ā   /+e hai   /haĩ*
   Rita INSTR room(masc) SG/PL NOM see PERF.PART MASC.SG/PL be-PRES.3.SG/be-PRES.3.PL
   'Rita has seen the room/s'.

c. *Rītā+ne   čiṭṭhī   +Ø/yā+Ø   dekh+Ø   +ī   hai   /haĩ*
   Rita INSTR letter(fem) SG/PL NOM see PERF.PART FEM.SG/PL be-PRES.3.SG/be-PRES.3.PL
   'Rita has seen the letter/s'.

5 The passive in Dyirbal. Dixon 1972: 65–67 speaks simply of the **-ŋay** form and the **-ŋay** construction: 50 years ago, no theoretical tools were available to properly describe the phenomenon. But here are his own examples (the SyntSubj, called "pivot" by Dixon, is boxed):

(i) a. ⌐*Bayi bargan+Ø*⌐$_{X⇔I}$ *baŋgul yaṛa+ŋgu*$_{X⇔II}$ *ḍurga+Ø   +n*
   the wallaby NOM   the man INSTR   spear ACT PRES/PAST
   'The man is spearing the wallaby'.

b. ⌐*Bayi yaṛa+Ø*⌐$_{X⇔I}$ (*baŋun bargan+du*$_{X⇔II}$)   *ḍurga+ŋa +ɲu*
   the man NOM the   wallaby DAT   spear PASS PRES/PAST
   'The man is spearing (at the wallaby)'.

This is an obvious diathesis modification marked on the verb—that is, a voice. True, terminologically it is not OK to call it "passive"—because of semantic connotations of the term *passive*, since in this diathesis the verb acquires an "active" meaning many linguists call it "antipassive." Formally, this voice marks the following diathetic modification:

X	Y
I	II

⇒

X	Y
II	I

It also turns a transitive verb into an intransitive one: in (i-a), the tense suffix **-n** is that of transitive verbs, while in (i-b), its counterpart, **-ɲu**, is used only with intransitives.

This is, of course, a classic passive schema, not some "antipassive." What is "anti-" here is Dyirbal itself: being ergative, it is "anti-nominative," in that all its verbs are semantically oriented in a way that is a mirror image of our verbs. 'X spears Y' corresponds in Dyirbal to 'Y undergoes spearing (by X)'. Since the term *passive* jars as applied to (i-b), the terms *direct voice* and *converse voice* could be used; in nominative languages, direct vs. converse voices appear as *active* vs. *passive*. (For a review of "antipassive" constructions in various language types, see Cooreman 1994.)

To put it differently, in Dyirbal only the SyntSubj can have the multiplicity of its referents to be reflected in the MV. (Dyirbal does not have inflectional nominal number.)

Parameter 4b concerns different valence-changing (= actant-manipulating) inflections of the verbal governor, which may affect the syntactic status of the CE under analysis; such are voices, including reflexives, and voice-like inflectional categories such as (in)transitivization. The stock example is the passive that turns objects into SyntSubjs.

5. Parameter 5 covers, in addition to case government of the SyntSubj by the MV, more "exotic" cases as well. For instance:

- In Ilocano, the noun in the role of SyntSubj can be only definite, so that to express the meaning 'A man can kiss the woman', a passive must be used—in order to demote 'a man' to the agentive complement [AgCo]:

(7) Ilocano (Schwartz 1976)
   a. ***Maka** +bisito **ti** lalaki **iti** babay*   'The man can kiss a woman'.
      can-**ACT** kiss **the** man **a** woman
   b. *****Maka** +bisito **iti** lalaki **ti** babay*   'A man can kiss the woman'.
      can-**ACT** kiss **a** man **the** woman
   c. ***Ma**   +bisito **ti** babay **iti** lalaki*   'The woman can be kissed
      can-**PASS** kiss **the** woman **a** man   by a man'.

The obligatory definiteness is a definitional property of the SyntSubj in Ilocano.[6]

- The syntactic role of the CE under consideration may be marked not only by a grammatical case, but also by a structural lexeme. This happens, for instance, with the direct object in Spanish, Romanian and Hebrew, where it is introduced by a preposition (under particular conditions: the DirO is human, the DirO is definite, etc.):

(8) a. Spanish (human DirO)
       *Saludamos **a** nuestros hermanos* lit. '[We] are.greeting to our brethren'.
    b. Romanian (human and definite DirO)
       *Îi salutăm **pe** fraţii noştri* lit. 'Them [we] are.greeting on our brethren'.
    c. Hebrew (definite DirO)
       *Ani soger **et** ha-dalet* lit. 'I am.closing to the.door'.

---

[6] The same state of affairs is observed in other Malayo-Polynesian languages, for instance, in Malagasy. — It can be the case that the obligatory definiteness is typical not of the SyntSubj, but of the syntactic-communicative Theme, while the Theme can be expressed in these languages only by a SyntSubj. I have no necessary data to solve this problem, but, fortunately, this is not relevant for my general topic here.

6. Parameter 6 requires considering the pronominalization of L, since pronouns often behave differently from nouns (as far as their morphology and linear position are concerned). See, for instance, the Tongan actant clitics, Subsection 3.4.1, (21), p. 146.

Let it be emphasized the a clause element's—and, in particular, the SyntSubj's—definitional parameters must be tested in the simplest clauses of **L**: declarative and communicatively most neutral. The MV must be taken in its least marked form: in the present tense of the indicative, in the imperfective (if **L** has aspects), in the active (if **L** has voices), without negation, etc.

Now, I can switch to characterizing parameters.

3.2.4.3 Characterizing parameters of clause elements

Most of the standard characterizing (= behavioral) parameters of clause element CE have been known for several decades (since Keenan 1976). Here are five of the most frequently mentioned, which are typical of hosts of languages:

- Control of relativization (the capacity of the CE in a relative clause to be coreferential with the modified noun)
- Control of reflexivization (the capacity of the CE to impose reflexivization)
- Control of converbs, in particular, gerunds (the capacity of the CE to be coreferential with the Agent of a converb)
- Control of gapping under coordination (a.k.a. "Equi-NP Deletion"; the capacity of the CE to require the deletion of a coreferential CE in a coordinated clause)
- Control of floating quantifiers (the capacity of the CE to launch a floating quantifier, as in *They arrived* ***all*** *at the same time.*)

In addition to this quasi-universal inventory of characterizing parameters, a language may have its own specific characterizing parameters, which should be, of course, also taken into account. For instance, in Malagasy, the interrogative particle VE, which marks a general question, can be linearly placed only before the SyntSubj:

(9) Malagasy (ao = /o/, c = /u/)
N   +anome vola   an-dRabe **ve**   ianao?
PAST give   money to Rabe   INTERR you$_{SG}$
'Did you give money to Rabe?'

In this language, the control of linear placement of sentence particles is a characterizing parameter of CEs.

As one immediately sees, all characterizing parameters of CEs concern their capacity to control (= to be a necessary condition for) the syntactic behavior of a "third party," that is, of another CE. This is quite an essential property, which should be described in all the details, but not in connection with the definition of the CE that interest us.

From now on, I will concentrate specifically on subjecthood properties.

3.2.5 Subjecthood properties

Definitional properties of clause elements—and, in particular, subjecthood properties
- are language-specific;
- can undergo seeming violations;
- accrue in different degrees to prototypical and to peripheral clause elements.

Subjecthood properties are language-specific. A checklist of definitional parameters for SyntSubj is universal; a checklist of characterizing parameters for SyntSubj is quasi-universal. However, lists of subjecthood definitional and characterizing properties—that is, of concrete values of these parameters—are language-specific; each such list has to be established specifically for language **L**.

Thus, **L** may have no agreement on the MV, it may lack case government of the actants, and its word order may be too flexible to be relevant. Or to take the linear position of the SyntSubj with respect to the MV: In English, one of the definitional subjecthood properties is to be linearly placed before the MV (and before all its other actants, which follow the MV). In Ilocano, (7) above, a definitional property of the SyntSubj is to occupy the closest position after the MV— before all its other actants. And in Malagasy (see (9)), an important Synt-subjecthood privilege is to be placed after the MV and after all its other actants. Similarly, the control of the MV's agreement is in itself an important subjecthood property in English, Russian or French, because in these languages only one clause element can control the personal-number agreement of the MV. But in Acehnese, where both the SyntSubj and the DirO impose agreement on the MV and the only actant of the MV can be either SyntSubj or the DirO (see 3.4.3, Subtype 3b, pp. 163–165), the control of the MV's agreement is not a SyntSubj definitional property. Here, such a property is to impose on the MV the agreement by a prefix, which is obligatory and cannot be linearly separated from the verb, while the agreement suffix is not obligatory and can migrate from the verb to the last word of the verb phrase. Non-omissibility is a subjecthood property in English, French, etc., because only the SyntSubj is not omissible in these languages, but not in Tagalog, where any

actant of the MV is omissible, including the SyntSubj: *May dumating* lit. 'There.is having.arrived'. = 'Someone or something has arrived'.
Therefore:

> ❗ *The list of definitional and characterizing properties (= values of the corresponding parameters) of the SyntSubj in* L *is specific for* L.

"Violation" of subjecthood properties. A definitional property of the SyntSubj valid for L may seem to be violated on several—sometimes even frequent—occasions. Yet if a given violation is triggered by a clearly statable factor (that is, the violation happens only and always in its presence), it is irrelevant. Therefore:

> ❗ *The situation where a definitional property is not satisfied under precisely stated conditions must be ignored—as if it were satisfied.*

Thus, in Finnish, SyntSubj is defined as marked by the nominative; however, if the referent of a non-pronominal SyntSubj is indefinite, the SyntSubj is in the PART(itive):

(10) Finnish

	Lapse+t	*leikk+i*	*+vät*	*ulkona*	'The children played outside'.
	child PL.**NOM**	play	PAST 3.**PL**	outside	
vs.	*Laps+i +a*	*leikk+i*	*+Ø*	*ulkona*	'(Some) children played outside'.
	child PL **PART**	play	PAST 3.**SG**	outside	

This violation—i.e., the SyntSubj in the partitive instead of the nominative—can be safely ignored, since it has an obvious semantic motivation (the SyntSubj's indefiniteness), unrelated to the syntactic role of the SyntSubj.

Prototypical (= canonical) *vs.* non-prototypical (= deviant) SyntSubjs. As foreseen by Keenan (1976) and developed in Iordanskaja & Mel'čuk 2009a (especially, 159*ff*), the whole cluster of a CE's definitional properties does not necessarily apply to all types and varieties of this CE: it can prove valid only for a subset of CEs—namely for prototypical, or canonical, CEs; other CE do not satisfy all definitional properties, but are similar enough to prototypical CEs to be accepted as such. For instance, in Russian the prototypical SyntSubj is a noun in the nominative; however, using syntactic analogy, also an infinitive, a prepositional PO-phrase or a ČTO-clause are also considered SyntSubjs.

3.2.6 Syntactic subject and ergativity

Most cases of problematic SyntSubjs come from languages with ergativity. But what exactly is ergativity? This term is too vague; it does not correspond to a clearly defined notion. If we consider the adjective *ergative*, it is much easier to make its meaning more precise: it is applicable to at least three different nouns—*language*, *construction* and *case*—and has accordingly three different interpretations (Mel'čuk 1988: 251).

- **Ergative language** is a language in which a bi-actantial verb semantically corresponding to a transitive verb in a non-ergative language (for instance, 'build' or 'kill') has as the generic component of its meaning the semantic expression 'X undergoes a change, caused by an action of Y on X' (in a non-ergative language the corresponding meaning is converse: 'Y, by an action on X, causes that X changes'). As a result, a verb in an ergative language cannot, generally speaking, have a DirO; since a transitive verb is a verb that allows a DirO, an ergative language normally does not have "genuine" transitive verbs (it can have such verbs exceptionally, if they are produced by diathetic modifications; see Note 16, p. 154). What is called a *transitive verb* in an ergative language is simply a verb that semantically corresponds to a transitive verb of a non-ergative language.

    Ergative languages include, for instance, Dyirbal, Lezgian, Avar and Archi, see below. This is what could be called **deep**, or **semantic**, **ergativity**. (The current term is **syntactically ergative languages**.)

- **Ergative construction** is a construction SyntSubj←–subj–MV where the SyntSubj is marked by a case other than the nominative, something like 'By. me am.reading a.book'. This construction is found, for instance, in Georgian, Hindi, Chukchi, Inuktitut and Warlpiri; the presence of an ergative construction characterizes **surface**, or **syntactic**, **ergativity**. (The current term is **morphologically ergative languages**.) Note that an ergative language in this sense should not, as a general rule, have an ergative construction, although logically it is not excluded.

- **Ergative case** is a case that exclusively marks either a certain type of SyntSubj—namely, a "transitive," or "active," SyntSubj. The ergative case is found, for instance, in Lezgian (where it marks the agentive complement), Georgian and Basque; two dead languages of Asia Minor, Urartean and Hurrian, also had an ergative case. The ergative case does not imply the existence of an ergative construction, and vice versa: the ergative case can be used outside the ergative construction (when it does not mark the SSynt-subject), and an ergative construction can exist without ergative case. (See the remarks on the necessity of distinguishing ergative construction and ergative case in Tchekhoff 1979: 28–29.) The ergative as a typical case of certain SyntSubjs in certain languages is opposed to the nominative, which is also typical of certain SyntSubjs in certain languages. The nominative, however, is defined not by its syntactic functions, but by the fact that it is the case of nomination: the least marked grammatical case of nouns, appearing, in the first place, when a noun is used to designate an entity (Mel'čuk 1988: 208). For other grammatical cases that mark SyntSubjs in some languages, see Subsection 3.4.1, p. 141.

3.3 Syntactic subject: an attempt at a definition

Here is a universal definition of SyntSubj, applicable to any language.

Definition 3.1 – syntactic subject

> The syntactic subject in a clause of L is the most privileged SSynt-actant of this clause's Main Verb.

Comments

1. What exactly are syntactic privileges in L has to be indicated by a list of specific SyntSubj privileges (= properties) elaborated for L. The syntactic privileges of the SyntSubj in L are, as a general rule, the values of all or at least of some of the six universal definitional parameters, indicated in Table 3.1 above.

2. Definition 3.1 entails the existence of SyntSubj in any L: it is presumed that a language necessarily has the most privileged SSynt-actant. It is logically possible for two actants to share the same syntactic privileges, but the SSynt-actants of the same governor must be distinguishable one way or another, and one of them, most probably, stands out.

3. Definition 3.1 does not entail the existence of SyntSubj in any clause of any L: subjectless clauses are quite common. There are, first, various "degenerate clauses" without a finite MV: *What a beautiful day!*, *Ouch!*, *Never in my life*, etc.; and second, full-blown clauses with a finite MV, but without a SyntSubj—in languages that allow for such a state of affairs, such as Lezgian: for instance, *Čʰimida* lit. 'Is.hot'. = 'It is hot' (the Lezgian verb features no agreement with the SyntSubj, so that there is no justification for a zero dummy subject).

4. Definition 3.1 fully corresponds to the hierarchy of clause element types stated in Keenan & Comrie 1977: SyntSubj > DirO > IndirC > Obl(ique)O . This hierarchy

was based on the diminishing accessibility of noun phrases for relativization; later it was shown that it also covers many other syntactic operations.

Since Definition 3.1 does not mention any particular properties of any particular language, it makes the SyntSubj cross-linguistically universal. However, in a different sense, the SyntSubj is at the same time language-specific in so far as syntactic privileges are different in different languages: thus, in many Indo-European languages the main privilege of a clausal element is to impose agreement on the Main Verb, while in Malagasy it is to occupy the clause-final position.

The general notion of SyntSubj can be well illustrated with Russian data, because in Russian it is straightforward; the same state of affairs is observed in many other languages—Slavic and, more generally, Indo-European languages.

In Russian, the **subjectival** SSyntRel and, consequently, the SyntSubj—boxed in the examples— is defined by the following properties. (For simplicity's sake, I consider only nominal—that is, prototypical, or canonical—SyntSubjs.)

Parameter 1. The SyntSubj L_2 depends only on the head L_1 of the clause, be it a finite verb or any other element (an infinitive, a verbal interjection, a special $V_{\text{IMPER, 2, SG}}$ form, etc.; the syntactic head of the clause—the Synt-predicate—is boldfaced):

(11) Russian

  a. ⟦Ivan⟧ **spit** ⟨**spal**⟩
     'Ivan is.sleeping ⟨was.sleeping⟩'.

  b. A ⟦Ivan⟧ – nu **orat'**$_{\text{INF}}$ i vyskočil iz komnaty
     lit. 'And Ivan—NU to.yell and ran.out of room'. =
     'And Ivan started.yelling and ran out of the room'.

  c. ⟦Ivan⟧ **bac** Petru po morde i vyskočil iz komnaty
     lit. 'Ivan smack! to.Peter on [his] mug [= 'smacked Peter's mug'] and ran.out of room'.

  d. **Pridi** ⟦Ivan⟧ vo-vremja, vsë bylo by v porjadke
     lit. 'Come$_{\text{IMPER, 2, SG}}$ Ivan [= Had Ivan come] on.time, everything would.have been in order'.

Parameter 2. In Russian, the SyntSubj L_2 is non-omissible from the Synt-structure of the clause whose head, i.e., MV, is a finite verb, since the form of this verb is controlled by the SyntSubj (= the finite verb agrees with the SyntSubj). The sentences in (12) include zero subjects —lexemes having empty signifiers and perceptible only due to their syntactics (a dummy $\emptyset^{\text{dummy}}_{\text{(neu, 3, sg)}}$, similar to Eng. IT and Fr. IL;

the indefinite personal $\emptyset^{\text{«PEOPLE»}}_{\text{(3, pl)}}$, similar to Fr. ON and Ger. MAN; and the impersonal $\emptyset^{\text{«ELEMENTS»}}_{\text{(neu, 3, sg)}}$).[7]

(12) Russian
   a. *Menja*_{ACC} $\boxed{\emptyset_{\text{(neu, 3, sg)}}}$ **tošn**+*it*_{3, SG}
      lit. '[It] me nauseates'. ≈ 'I feel nauseated'.
   b. *Mne*_{DAT} $\boxed{\emptyset_{\text{(neu, 3, sg)}}}$ **byl**+*o*_{NEU, SG} *prijatno*
      lit. '[It] to.me was pleasant'. ≈ 'I felt good'.
   c. *Mne*_{DAT} $\boxed{\emptyset_{\text{(neu, 3, sg)}}}$ **povezl**+*o*_{NEU, SG}
      lit. '[It] to.me favored'. ≈ 'I was lucky'.
   d. *Menja*_{ACC} $\boxed{\emptyset^{\text{«PEOPLE»}}_{\text{(3, pl)}}}$ *xorošo* **prinjal**+*i*_{PL}
      lit. '[«They»] me well received'. ≈ 'I was well received'.
   e. (i) *Most*_{ACC} $\boxed{\emptyset^{\text{«PEOPLE»}}_{\text{(3, pl)}}}$ **snesl**+*i*_{PL}
      lit. '[«They»] the.bridge demolished'.
      (ii) *Most*_{ACC} $\boxed{\emptyset^{\text{«ELEMENTS»}}_{\text{(neu, 3, sg)}}}$ **snesl**+*o*_{NEU, SG}
      lit. '[«It»] the.bridge destroyed' [e.g., a flood or a hurricane].

Parameter 3. In a declarative clause, the SyntSubj L_2 normally linearly precedes its governor L_1, although in several cases L_2 may follow L_1 (as determined by a number of particular factors, mainly communicative ones; a list of these is, of course, necessary).

Parameter 4. From a morphological viewpoint, the Synt-head L_1 of the Russian clause agrees (in person, number and gender) with the SyntSubj L_2 and with no other actant (Property 4a) and can undergo passivization, which demotes the SyntSubj and promotes the DirO to the SyntSubj (Property 4b).

NB This holds, of course, only if L_1 is a finite verb capable of agreement: thus, in examples (11b–d), the boldfaced L_1 is invariant and cannot show agreement; in examples (11a–c), L_1 cannot be passivized.

(13) a. Agreement

Ja pokupaj+*u dom*	'I am.buying a.house'.
~ *My pokupaj*+*em dom*	'We are.buying a.house'.
Ty pokupaj+*eš' dom*	'You_{SG} are.buying a.house'.
~ *Vy pokupaj*+*ete dom*	'You_{PL} are.buying a.house'.
On pokupuj+*et dom*	'He is.buying a.house'.
~ *Oni pokupaj*+*ut dom*	'They are.buying a.house'.

---

[7] Recall that a linguistic zero sign is simply a meaningful absence; see Mel'čuk 2006a: 469–516.

b. Passivization

(i) $\boxed{Ivan_{\text{NOM-SyntSubj}}}$ *pokupaet dom*$_{\text{ACC-DirO}}$ 'Ivan is buying the house'.
~ $\boxed{Dom_{\text{NOM-SyntSubj}}}$ *pokupaetsja Ivanom*$_{\text{INSTR-AgCo}}$ 'The house is being bought by Ivan'.
(ii) $\boxed{Ivan_{\text{NOM-SyntSubj}}}$ *kupil dom*$_{\text{ACC-DirO}}$ 'Ivan bought the house'.
~ $\boxed{Dom_{\text{NOM-SyntSubj}}}$ *byl kuplen Ivanom*$_{\text{INSTR-AgCo}}$ 'The house was bought by Ivan'.

Parameter 5. In Russian, the SyntSubj L_2 is marked by the nominative, except for two situations:

- if L_2 is not a nominal and cannot have cases (e.g., the infinitive in (14a), the finite verb as the head of a subordinate subject clause in (14b), and the conjunction čto, also as the head of a subordinate subject clause in (14c));
- if an overriding factor intervenes—for example, if the case of L_2 is controlled by a numeral (14d), or if L_1 is negated (14e–f).

(14) Russian

a. $\boxed{Idti}$ **bylo** *trudno*   'To.walk was difficult'.
b. *Čego on* $\boxed{xočet}$, **bylo** *nejasno*   'What he wanted was unclear'.
c. $\boxed{Čto}$ *on bolen,* **bylo** *očevidno* 'That he [was] sick was obvious'.
d. $\boxed{Ix_{\text{GEN}}}$ **bylo** *pjatero*   'They were five'.
e. $\boxed{Pis'ma_{\text{PL.NOM}}}$ *ne* **prišli**   'The.letters did not arrive'. ~
   $\boxed{Pisem_{\text{PL.GEN}}}$ *ne* **prišlo**   'No letters arrived'.
f. $\boxed{Ivan_{\text{SG.NOM}}}$ *ne* **byl** *na beregu* 'Ivan wasn't on the beach'. ~
   $\boxed{Ivana_{\text{SG.GEN}}}$ *ne* **bylo** *na beregu* 'There was no Ivan on the beach'.

In any language that has grammatical cases the **nominative** is the case of nomination; in other words, when in a language the Speaker names something by a noun, this noun is in the nominative. The nominative is therefore a privileged case, and it is generally expected that the SyntSubj be marked by the nominative.

Parameter 6. Pronominalization does not affect the Russian SyntSubj's properties in any special way.

All the other Synt-subjecthood parameters on the Keenan's checklist—characterizing parameters—concern not so much the syntactically defined clause elements, but some semantic or communicative entities; I will give three examples.

- The control of the coreferential Actor in a phrase of the form ČTOBY + V_{INF} 'in.order.to V' belongs in Russian to the semantic Actor rather than to the SyntSubj (*pace* Kozinskij 1983: 18–19); or, to put it differently, the possibility of using such a phrase depends on the coreference not with the SyntSubj, but with the semantic Actor—the person or body that fired employees in (15):

(15) Russian
Mnogie sotrudniki *byli uvoleny ⟨*lišilis' raboty⟩, čtoby sokratit' štaty*
'Many employees were fired ⟨*lost [their] jobs⟩ in.order.to reduce [the] staff'.

The choice of the ČTOBY + V_{INF} construction happens during the SemS ⇔ DSyntS transition, and it is only natural that the conditions for this choice are semantic (i.e., unrelated specifically to SyntSubj).

– In a similar vein, Nichols et al. 1980: 376–377 demonstrate that, on the one hand, the control of deverbal adverbials in Russian, traditionally ascribed to the SyntSubj, can depend on its Thematicity (= Topicality):

(16) Russian
  a. The SyntSubj is thematic:
  Pereexav v Moskvu, $Ivan_{THEME}$ *ustroilsja na ètot post*
  'Having.moved to Moscow, Ivan obtained this position'.
vs. b. The SyntSubj is the rhematic focus:
  *Pereexav v Moskvu, na ètot post ustroilsja $Ivan_{RHEM.FOCUS}$
  'Having.moved to Moscow, it is Ivan who obtained this position'.

On the other hand, the authors aptly note (pp. 383–384) that the control of deverbal adverbials by a dative IndirObj with psychological predicates (*Uznav ob ètom,* **mne**$_{DAT}$ *zaxotelos' poznakomit'sja s nim* lit. 'Having.learned this, to.me the. desire.came to.meet him') does not constitute an argument in favor of its subjecthood. Its control capacity—to the extent that such sentences are accepted by speakers—is explained by its semantic and communicative roles: it denotes the human Experiencer and is thematic.

– The control of the coreference with the understood "subject" of an infinitive is not an exclusive syntactic property of SyntSubj, either. For instance, in (17), such control belongs to an obvious oblique object *dlja Ivana* 'for Ivan', which is coreferential with the "subject" of the infinitive (it is Ivan who will be going to London):

(17) *Dlja Ivana važno poexat' v London* 'For Ivan [it is] important to.go to London'.

This property accrues to a semantic role (the Experiencer, in this sentence—Ivan, for whom it is important) rather than to a syntactic entity. (For a detailed review of characterizing, or behavioral, properties of the Russian SyntSubj, see Testelec 2001: 317–359.)

Thus, in Russian, the SyntSubj can be defined clearly and robustly since it is specified by the positive values of all definitional parameters of SyntSubjs: it depends only on MV (or, more generally, on the head of the clause); it is non-omissible; in a declarative sentence, it precedes the MV (if communicative factors do not require inversion, which constitutes an explicable "violation"); it is the only actant of the MV that controls the MV's agreement; it is marked by the nominative case; its role is targeted by the passive; and its pronominalization does not affect its status in any way.[8] However, the theoretical debate over SyntSubjs (and DirOs) started not with Russian, but with other languages, where this notion is not so straightforward. Therefore, I will discuss the notion of SyntSubj in some languages considered problematic in this respect.

3.4 Establishing the syntactic subject in a language

The most "material," easily observable properties of the SyntSubj is agreement on the MV and the case marking of the SyntSubj itself; so let us begin with agreement. Based on the agreement properties of the MV, three major different types of languages must be examined: in the sentences of **L**, the MV either does not agree with its actants at all (= no agreement on the MV): 3.4.1; the MV agrees with only one actant (= monopersonal agreement on the MV): 3.4.2; or else the MV agrees with more than one actant (= polypersonal agreement on the MV): 3.4.3.

Recall that agreement must be considered in the simplest clause possible, with the least marked form of the MV (since in a more complex form of the MV the agreement with the SyntSubj might be different).

---

8 Of course, Russian also has some problematic SyntSubjs, for instance:
- In $\boxed{\text{Èto}_{SG}}$ *byli*$_{PL}$ *moi druz'ja*$_{PL}$ 'This were my friends' the copula agrees not with the SyntSubj ÈTO 'this', but with the nominal attribute of the copula.
- The sentence *Mne*$_{DAT}$ *xočetsja pokoj*+*a*$_{GEN}$ ≈ 'I want some peace' = lit. '[It] wants.itself to.me of.peace' does not have an overt SyntSubj, but manifests a dummy zero SyntSubj; the same is true for *Im*$_{DAT}$ *èt*+*ogo*$_{GEN}$ *xvataet* lit. 'To.them of.this [it] suffices'. = 'This is sufficient for them'.
- A number of verbs (usually with the prefix NA-) admit the SyntSubj in the genitive:
   (i) *Naexali sjuda* $\boxed{vsjakie_{NOM}}$
       lit. 'Came here anybodies'. = 'God knows who came here en masse'.
   ~ *Naexalo sjuda* $\boxed{vsjakix_{GEN}}$
       [*idem*, but more colloquial and more depreciative with respect to the Actor].

On the SyntSubj in Russian bi-nominative sentences (of the type *Direktor laboratorii – Ivan* ≈ 'It is Ivan who is the lab director'), see Mel'čuk 2012a.

3.4.1 No agreement on the Main Verb

Language type 1. If in language **L** the MV does not agree with any of its actants, then we have two situations: **L** either has nominal cases, or it does not.

Subtype 1a. In **L** the MV does not agree with its actants, but actants are case-marked for their syntactic role.

The SyntSubj is the actant L that is marked, generally speaking, by one of four cases:
- either 1) by the nominative (= the least marked case, that of nomination);
- or 2) by a special case called the **subjective** (= the case used, in a given language, to mark all SyntSubjs, including the only actant of an intransitive verb; the best known subjective is found in Japanese—the case in **-ga**); 3) by another special case, the **absolutive** (the case used to mark intransitive SyntSubjs and DirOs; we find it, for instance, in Tongan); 4) the SyntSubj can be in a different case, but only exceptionally—with some lexically marked verbs and under special conditions.

A good example of Subtype **1a** language is Lezgian.

Lezgian. The Lezgian verb does not agree with its actants (no person-number or class inflection of the verb); there is no voice and no voice-like categories. The actants of a verb are distinguished solely by case markings: the only actant of a monoactantial MV is in the nominative, as in (18a), while with a biactantial MV the actant that expresses the Agent is in the ergative case in **-di**, and the other one that expresses the Patient is in the nominative, see (18c):

(18) Lezgian (Mel'čuk 1988: 207–249)
  a. $\boxed{Gada+\emptyset/jar+\emptyset}$ χta +na
     boy SG/PL NOM return AOR
     '[The] boy/s returned'.
  b. *χta +na
     return AOR
     'There.was.returning'.
  c. Buba+∅+di $\boxed{gada+\emptyset/jar+\emptyset}$ gat^{h}a+na
     father SG ERG boy SG/PL NOM beat AOR
     'Father beat.up [the] boy/boys'. = lit. 'By.father [the] boy/s got.a.beating'.

d. ‎|Gada+Ø/jar+Ø|‎   gatʰa+na
   boy SG/PL NOM   beat AOR
   '[The] boy/boys got.a.beating'.

e. *Buba+Ø+di   gatʰa+na
   father SG ERG beat AOR
   lit. 'By.father [somebody] got.a.beating'.

f. Buba+Ø+di   Čʰukur+izva
   father SG ERG run   PRES
   lit. 'Father is running'. = 'By.father there.is.running'.

g. Čʰukur+izva
   run   PRES
   'There.is.running'.

h. Gišin +da
   hungry PRES
   'There.is.hunger'.

The actant in the ergative is always omissible, as in (18c) vs. (18d), even if it is the only actant explicitly present in the clause, as in (18f) vs. (18g). The actant in the nominative is, on the contrary, not omissible, cf. (18b) and (18e). Crucially, (18d) is an absolutely normal, context-independent, current type of sentence. If both actants are present with a biactantial MV, the N_{NOM} is positioned closer to the MV. Now, some sentences, such as (18f–g), might give the impression that the nominative actant is absent, yet it is not the case: the verb ČʰUKUR+UN '[to] run' is, in point of fact, a contraction of the phrase ČʰUKUR AV+UN 'running do', so that the noun ČʰUKUR, not used as such in Lezgian anymore, plays the role of SyntSubj and it is in the nominative. Sentences of the type of (18f–g) can be produced only with such "contracted" verbs (which are rather numerous in Lezgian). Genuine subjectless sentences are possible, but just with semantically specific—for instance, meteorological—verbs: Meqʻida '[It] is.cold', Mičʻida '[It] is.dark', etc. The corresponding Indo-European sentences have either an overt dummy SyntSubj—Eng. IT, Fr. IL, Ger. ES —or a zero lexeme SyntSubj $Ø_{(3,\,sg)}$, which imposes the 3.SG or SG.NEU grammemes on the verb (and on the attributive adjective if any): Sp. Hac+$e_{3.SG}$ frío lit. '[It] does cold' or Rus. Byl+$o_{SG.NEU}$ xolodn+$o_{SG.NEU}$ '[It] was cold'. But Lezgian meteorological sentences have no zero dummy SyntSubj, since the Lezgian verb knows no number-person agreement; (18h) is a really subjectless sentence, of the only possible kind in Lezgian.

Without going into more details (see Mel'čuk 1988: 207ff for additional arguments), I conclude that the SyntSubj in Lezgian is the actant marked by the nominative, because it has four out of possible six subjecthood properties (= syntactic privileges):

Parameter 1. The exclusive dependence on the MV.
Parameter 2. Non-omissibility from the syntactic structure.
Parameter 3. The linear position immediately before the MV.
Parameter 5. The nominative marking.

Parameters 4 and 6 are irrelevant: Lezgian has no MV agreement and no voice-like categories, and the pronominalization of the SyntSubj in no way affects it.

Thus, Lezgian does not have an ergative construction, because its SyntSubj is always in the nominative; however, it does have an ergative case: the agentive complement is necessarily in this case, which is not used for anything else. And most importantly, Lezgian is an ergative language —the diathesis of its transitive verbs is inverse with respect to that of the transitive verbs in Standard Average European [SAE] languages (or, for that matter, in Hindi). The English verb 'X beats up Y' corresponds in Lezgian to a verb meaning 'Y gets a beating from X'; 'X sees Y' is in Lezgian 'Y is.visible to X'; etc.[9]

As languages with the SyntSubj marked by the subjective case, I will consider Tagalog and Tongan.

Tagalog. My description of SyntSubj in this language is based on Kroeger 1993.[10]

(19) Tagalog (the marker of the oblique case **ng** is pronounced /naŋ/; voice markers are prefixes, infixes and suffixes, sometimes combined within one wordform; the past—more precisely, the perfective—is expressed by the absence of a reduplication of the radical)

---

9 M. Haspelmath's detailed grammar of Lezgian proposes a different description of Lezgian predicative construction (Haspelmath 1993: 287-298), in which the N_{ERG} is considered the Synt-Subj and the ergativity of Lezgian as a language is rejected; see also Haspelmath 1991.
10 The Tagalog case expressed by the analytical marker **ang** is the subjective, but by no means the nominative (as it is frequently named): it is not used for nomination. The nominative in Tagalog has a zero marker—as a well-behaved nominative should—and is used for nomination, as well as in several syntactic constructions: as the marker of an address (*Oy, lalake*$_{NOM}$! 'Hey, man!'), of a nominal attribute (*Aking apó*$_{NOM}$ *si*$_{SUBJ}$ *Ramon* 'Ramon [is] my grandson'), of the complement of a measure noun (*dakot na bigas*$_{NOM}$ 'handful [of] rice', where **na** is a linker—marker of syntactic dependency, similar to the idafa marker in Persian), of a nominal modifier (*bahay ng mambubukid*$_{NOM}$ 'peasant house', etc., wherever the noun is not referential or indefinite (e.g., *Siyá'y nagsalitáng parang bata*$_{NOM}$ 'He speaks like [a] child' or *May libro*$_{NOM}$ *sa mesa* 'There.is [a] book on [the] table'). The nominative is also used for the SyntSubj—in an alternation with the subjective (under specific conditions): *Kumain na si*$_{SUBJ}$ *nanay* lit. 'Has.eaten already Mother'. ~ *Kumain na nanay*$_{NOM}$; *Napakatamad ang*$_{SUBJ}$ *batang ito* lit. 'Very.lazy.is child this' ~ *Napakatamad batang*$_{NOM}$ *ito* 'This child is very lazy'; *Napakatamad ang*$_{SUBJ}$ *lahat ng anak niya* lit. 'Very.lazy.are all children his'. ~ *Napakatamad lahat*$_{NOM}$ *ng anak niya*'; etc. (My most hearfelt thanks to J.-M. Fortis for his consultations on Tagalog.)

a. *D   +um   +ating* **ang aking apó**   'My grandson came'.
   come...PERF.ACT... come **SUBJ** my grandson
b. *May d   +um   +ating*   'There.is have.come'. =
   exist come... PERF.ACT...come   'Somebody came'.
c. *S +um   +ulat* **ang aking apó**   *ng   liham sa   titser*
   write...PERF.ACT... write **SUBJ** my grandson OBL letter DAT teacher
   'My grandson wrote the teacher the/a letter'.
d. *S +in   +ulat +Ø   ng aking apó*   **ang liham** *sa   titser*
   write...PERF... write PASS-DIR OBL my   grandson **SUBJ** letter DAT teacher
   'The letter was.written by my grandson to the teacher'.
e. *S +in   +ulat +an   ng aking apó   ng liham* **ang titser**
   write...PERF...write PASS-INDIR OBL my   grandson OBL letter **SUBJ** teacher
   lit. 'The teacher was.written.to the/a letter by my grandson'.

Summing up, the SyntSubj's privileges in Tagalog are four:

- Parameter 1. It depends only on the MV.
- Parameter 4a. It imposes optional plural agreement on the MV (Kroeger 1993: 24–25).
- Parameter 4b. It is buttressed by a rich system of passives—among them, a direct and an indirect, or locative, passive, which are shown in (19d–e) and which promote other clause elements to SyntSubj status.[11]
- Parameter 5. It is marked by the subjective case.

The Tagalog SyntSubj is omissible form the Sem- (and Synt-) structures of the clause (Parameter 2), its linear position does not distinguish it from other actants of the MV (Parameter 3), and the pronominalization of its SyntSubj does not affect the latter (Parameter 6).

---

[11] The Tagalog SyntSubj has several typical behavioral characteristics: only the SyntSubj can launch a floating quantifier 'all', only it can relativize, only it controls coreferential deletability, etc. (Kroeger 1993: 19–36). However, the history of ideas surrounding the subjecthood in Tagalog is quite interesting; I learned it from Kroeger 1993: 19–20 and 2007, and I feel it is worth telling here in a few words. The founders of Tagalog studies (beginning with L. Bloomfield in 1917) had no problem with the Tagalog SyntSubj—they identified it exactly as it is done in this chapter. But then in 1958 an eminent American specialist in Austronesian languages, Howard McKaughan, for several false reasons changed the terminology and proposed to call the SyntSubj in Tagalog and structurally similar languages "the Topic." Unfortunately, the idea caught. Later McKaughan realized how wrong he had been and wrote in a 1973 paper: "Please, reader, forgive me for confusing the issue by calling these subjects the 'topic' of the sentence" (a rare example of real scientific honesty and sincerity). However, inexplicably, his incorrect proposal was accepted by acclamation and still persists, while his strong retraction was practically paid no attention at all…

Tongan, genetically related to Tagalog (both belong to the Malayo-Polynesian branch of Austronesian family), is structurally rather different. As in Tagalog, the Tongan verb has no number-personal agreement, and the linear placement of actants with respect to the MV does not give a reliable clue as to their syntactic role, since it is relatively flexible. Again as does Tagalog, Tongan has cases, also expressed analytically, among which I will indicate four: the nominative (unmarked, i.e., having a zero marker **Ø**), the absolutive marked by **'a**,[12] the ergative with the marker **'e** and the dative with the marker **ki**. The SyntSubj is boxed.

(20) Tongan (Tchekhoff 1979, Otsuka 2000 and 2010)
    a. *'Oku 'alu*   ['a   Sione]   'John is leaving'.
        PRES leave   ABS John

    b. *'Oku 'alu*   'He/She [mentioned in the preceding context]
        PRES leave   is leaving'.

Unlike Tagalog, where the SyntSubj is omissible, cf. (19b), in Tongan the SyntSubj is not omissible: in (20b), it is present in the Synt-structure, but is elided from the sentence (although not from its structure!) by a Pro-Drop rule.

    c. *'Oku sio+Ø*   ['a   Sione]
        PRES see NEUTR ABS John
        'John sees'. = 'John is not blind'.

    d. *'Oku sio+Ø*   ['a   Sione] ki   Mele
        PRES see NEUTR ABS John DAT Mary
        'John sees Mary'.

    e. *'Oku sio+'i*   'a   Mele ['e   Sione]
        PRES see TRANS ABS Mary ERG John
        'John stares at Mary'.

    f. *'Oku sio+'i*   'a   Sione
        PRES see TRANS ABS John
        'He/She [mentioned in the preceding text] stares at John'.

    g. *'Oku sio+'i*   ['e   Sione]
        PRES see TRANS ERG John
        'John stares at him/her [mentioned in the preceding text]'.

---

[12] The name of the Tongan absolutive should not be confounded with the name "absolutive" often given to the nominative case in languages with the ergative construction: the Tongan absolutive is formally different from the nominative. Note, however, that this absolutive optionally alternates with the nominative in full referential NPs:

(i) *'Oku 'alu 'a$_{ABS}$ e tamasi.* ~ *'Oku 'alu Ø$_{NOM}$ e tamasi* lit. 'Is leaving the boy'.

For the grammemes NEUTR(al) and TRANS(itivizer), see immediately below.

However, the case marking does not allow us to decide which of the two actants of a transitive MV in (20e) is more privileged. They are both non-omissible (cf. (20f–g)), and, in sharp contrast with Tagalog, Tongan has no voice-like (= actant-shuffling) verbal alternations. Yet there are two phenomena that are helpful: cliticization of the actants and transitivization of the MV with the suffix -'i (20e–g).

Cliticization. Personal pronominal clitics (of the three numbers—singular, dual and plural, of the three persons, and in addition exclusive *vs.* inclusive), which are the only signs[13] allowed between the tense marker and the MV, correspond to the single actant of a $V_{(intrans)}$ and to the ergative-marked actant of a $V_{(trans)}$; the clitics replacing the N_{ABS} and the N_{ERG} are homophonous:

(21) a. *'Oku* ⌐ne̞   /ou⌐ *'alu*
    PRES he-ABS/I-ABS leave
    'He is leaving'./'I am leaving'.

  b. *'Oku* ⌐ne̞   /ou⌐ *sio*+∅
    PRES he-ABS/I-ABS see NEUTR
    'He sees'./'I see'.

  c. *'Oku* ⌐ne̞   /ou⌐ *sio*+'i   *'a Sioné*
    PRES he-ERG/I-ERG see TRANS ABS John
    'He stares at John'./'I stare at John'.

  d. *'Oku* ⌐ne̞   /ou⌐ *sio*+'i
    PRES he-ERG/I-ERG see TRANS
    'He stares at him'./'I stare at him'.

  e. **'Oku ne   /ou ⌐sio+'i⌐   'e Sione*
    PRES he-ABS/I-ABS see TRANS ERG John
    'John stares at him [⇔ *ne*]/me [⇔ *ou*]'.

Examples in (21) show that clitics correspond either to the N_{ABS} with a $V_{(intrans)}$, as in (21a), or to the N_{ERG} with a $V_{(trans)}$, as in (21b–d), but not to the N_{ABS} with a $V_{(trans)}$, as in (21e); one can conclude that an N_{ABS} with a $V_{(intrans)}$ and an N_{ERG} with a $V_{(trans)}$ are SyntSubjs, as shown by the boxes in (21).

Transitivization. The suffix -'i attached to a semantically bi-actantial $V_{(intrans)}$ turns it into a $V_{(trans)}$, without affecting its semantic valence; the verb V+'i requires that its second semantic actant be explicitly expressed syntactically as a

---

[13] With the exception of a handful of adverbs, such as 'often' and 'again'.

DirO—i.e., as an N$_{ABS}$. (NEUTR(al) and TRANS(itivizer) are grammemes of the inflectional category of transitivization, see Note 23, p. 161.) Cf. (21b–d) and (22b), which also identify N$_{ERG}$ as the SyntSubj:

(22) a. *'Oku 'uma+Ø*   ⌐'a   Sione¬ *mo Mele*
  PRES kiss NEUTRAL ABS John and Mary
  lit. 'John kisses with/at Mary'.
 b. *'Oku 'uma+'i*   *'a Mele* ⌐'e   Sione¬
  PRES kiss TRANS ABS Mary ERG John
  'John kisses Mary'.

The three SyntSubj's privileges in Tongan then are as follows:
- Parameter 1. It depends only on the MV.
- Parameter 4b. Its case is affected by transitivization.
- Parameter 6. It is the only clause element expressible by a preverbal pronominal clitic.

Omissibility (Parameter 2) does not distinguish the SyntSubj from the DirO, the word order (Parameter 3) is quite flexible, and the SyntSubj case marking (Parameter 5) is not decisive.

To sum up: unlike Tagalog, Tongan does have an ergative case and an ergative construction, but it is—like Tagalog—a non-ergative language; in this respect it resembles Georgian, Basque and Hindi and contrasts with Lezgian and Archi.

However, the description of Tongan subjectival constructions proposed here faces a problem: the absolutive case. The existence of this case—different from the nominative—in other languages is an open question (as far as I know, other Polynesian languages do not have it), and as such, it weakens my proposal: typological plausibility is required.

Subtype 1b. In **L** the MV does not agree with its actants and the actants are not case-marked for their syntactic role; the MV is not inflected at all.[14]

In such a language, the SyntSubj is the actant L that occupies a special linear position in the sentence. Vietnamese and Mandarin Chinese are good examples: here, the SyntSubj immediately precedes the MV (as before, in the examples the SyntSubj is boxed, and the MV boldfaced).

---

14 In a language without grammatical cases where the verb does not agree with its actants, but has voices, the SyntSubj will be identifiable by the passive permutation (plus, of course, linear position). Such languages are, for instance, Malagasy and Malay/Indonesian.

Vietnamese (Trương 1970)

(23) a. ⟦Tôi/Giáp⟧ **đã về**   lit. 'I/Giap PAST return'. =
                                      'I/Giap returned'.

b. ⟦Tôi/Giáp⟧ **đã đọc** quyển sách   lit. 'I/Giap PAST read book'. =
                                      'I/Giap read [the] book'.

Vietnamese has no voice, so the dependence on the MV and the preverbal linear position are the only privileges of the SyntSubj here. (I do not know about additional definitional properties of the SyntSubj specific to Vietnamese.) However, to prevent possible misunderstandings, let me indicate that the preverbal noun in Vietnamese can also be a prolepsis that expresses the Theme of the sentence:

c. *Giáp,* ⟦*nó*⟧ ***đã đọc*** *quyển sách*
   lit. 'Giap, he PAST read book'. = 'As for Giap, he read [the] book'.

A sentence of the type (23d) shows a DirO turned into a prolepsis (Trương 1970: 105):

d. *Quyển sách,* ***đã đọc***
   lit. 'Book, PAST read'. = 'The book, somebody read it'.

The SyntSubj is absent from the SyntS (and the SemS) of sentence (23d).

In Mandarin Chinese the preverbal noun is also necessarily either a SyntSubj, or a prolepsis, which expresses the Theme of the sentence:

(24) Mandarin Chinese (Li & Thompson 1994: 234–242)

a. ⟦Zéi⟧ kāi -le   mén le   'Thieves opened the door'.
   thief open PERF door CRS [= particle signaling a Currently Relevant State of affairs]

b. ⟦Mén⟧ kāi-le   'The door opened'.
   door open PERF/CRS

c. *Mén,* ‖ ⟦*zéi*⟧ *kāi-le*   lit. 'Door, thieves opened'. =
                                 'The door, the thieves opened it'.

d. *Mén,* ‖ *kāi-le*
   door open PERF/CRS

In (24a–b) we see two different lexemes of the vocable KĀI, just like the English verb OPEN: a transitive and an intransitive one (such verbs are known as *labile*). (24c–d) show MÉN 'door' in the syntactic role of a prolepsis (it is marked by a pause and a mounting contour); in (24c) the DirO of the verb KĀI and in (24d), both the SyntSubj and the DirO are not expressed on the surface.

(24d) shows that in Mandarin the SyntSubj is omissible; here is another couple of examples:

    e. – *Zuò shénme?*   lit. 'Do what?' – *Chī zhe* lit. ≈ 'Eating be'.

This exchange is possible in any circumstances with the question put to somebody about himself or about any third party ('What am/is/are I/he/you/they doing?' – 'I/He/You/They is/am/ are eating'.).

    f. *Diū -le*   *yí*   *kuài*   *biǎo*   lit. '[Somebody] lost a watch'. =
       lose PERF one CLASS watch   'A watch was lost'.

The same state of affairs is characteristic of many other languages that lack inflectional morphology.

3.4.2 Monopersonal agreement of the Main Verb

Language type 2. If in **L** any MV, intransitive or transitive, agrees with only one of its actants, then this actant is the SyntSubj.

This must be true at least for the basic (= least marked) forms of the MV, for instance, the imperfective stem; with the perfective stem, the transitive MV may agree with the DirO.

Enga. The simplest case of Type 2 language known to me is the New Guinea language Enga, which, as far as the SyntSubj is concerned, presents a very clear picture: its MV has strictly monopersonal agreement (in all forms), and this identifies the SyntSubj uniquely.

(25) Enga (Van Valin 1981: 367–371)
     a. $\boxed{Nambá+\emptyset}$ *p+é*   *+ó*   'I went'.
        I   NOM go PAST 1.SG
     b. $\boxed{Namba+mé}$ *mená+∅*   *dóko p +í*   *+ó*   'I hit [= killed] the pig'.
        I   ERG pig   NOM the   hit PAST 1.SG

Like Hindi and Georgian (see below), Enga has the ergative construction, but without split—it is used in all tenses; unlike Hindi, but like Georgian, it has a special ergative case. Enga is, of course, not an ergative language.

Hindi. The situation in Hindi is more complex. Here a perfective transitive MV controls an ergative construction (with the SyntSubj in the instrumental; see (26c)):

(26) Hindi (*ai* = /ɛ/, *aĩ* = /ɛ̃/)

a. |Maĩ| ā   +Ø   +Ø   hū̃   'I [a man] have come'.
   I-NOM [male] come PERF.PART MASC.SG be-PRES.1.SG

   |Maĩ| ā   +Ø   +ī   hū̃   'I [a woman] have come'.
   I-NOM [female] come PERF.PART FEM.SG be-PRES.1.SG

   |Ve| ā   +Ø   +e   haĩ   'They [men] have come'.
   they-NOM [males] come PERF.PART MASC.PL be-PRES.3.PL

   |Ve| ā   +Ø   +ī   haĩ   'They [women] have come'.
   they-NOM [females] come PERF.PART FEM.PL be-PRES.3.PL

b. |Maĩ| čiṭṭʰī +Ø /+yã likʰ+Ø rah +Ø +ā   hū̃
   I-NOM [male] letter₍fem₎ SG.NOM/PL.NOM write CONV remain PERF.PART MASC.SG be-PRES.1.SG
   lit. 'I [a man] letter/s writing remained am'. = 'I am writing a letter/letters'.

   |Ham| čiṭṭʰī +Ø /+yã likʰ+Ø rah +Ø +e   haĩ
   we-NOM [males] letter₍fem₎ SG.NOM/PL.NOM write CONV remain PERF.PART MASC.PL be-PRES.1.PL
   lit. 'We [men] letter/s writing remained are'. = 'We are writing a letter/letters'.

vs. |Tū| čiṭṭʰī +Ø /+yã likʰ+Ø rah +Ø +ī
   you_SG-NOM [female] letter₍fem₎ SG.NOM/PL.NOM write CONV remain PERF.PART FEM.SG
   hai
   be-PRES.2.SG
   lit. 'You [a woman] letter/s writing remained are'. = 'You are writing a letter/letters'.

   |Tum| čiṭṭʰī +Ø /+yã likʰ+Ø rah +Ø +ī
   you_PL-NOM [females] letter₍fem₎ SG.NOM/PL.NOM write CONV remain PERF.PART FEM.PL
   ho
   be-PRES.2.PL
   lit. 'You [women] letter/s writing remained are'. = 'You are writing a letter/letters'.

c. |Maĩ+ne| čiṭṭʰī +Ø /+yã likʰ +Ø +ī
   I INSTR [male] letter₍fem₎ SG.NOM/PL.NOM write PERF.PART FEM.SG/PL
   hai   /haĩ
   be-PRES.3.SG/be-PRES.3.PL
   lit. 'By.me [a man] letter/s written is/are'. = 'I [a man] have written a letter/letters'.

vs. | Tū +ne | čiṭṭʰī +∅ | /+yã | likʰ +∅ | +ī |
yousG INSTR [female] letter₍fem₎ SG.NOM/PL.NOM write PERF.PART FEM.SG/PL
hai /*haĩ*
be-PRES.3.SG/be-PRES.3.PL
lit. 'By.you [a woman] letter/s written is/are'. = 'You [a woman] have written a letter/letters'.

We can be sure, however, that in (26c) the noun čIṭṭʰī(YĀ) 'letter(s)' is a DirO: thanks to the passive, which—as shown in (26d)—promotes this noun to the SyntSubj, demoting the former SyntSubj to an Ag(entive) Co(mplement), which is dispreferred in Hindi (ǯĀ 'go' is the passive auxiliary, here in the form of converb ≈ gerund; RAHĀ 'remain' is the progressive auxiliary, which takes the converb of the lexical verb):[15]

d. | Čiṭṭʰī +∅ | likʰ +∅ | +ī | ǯā+∅ | rah +∅ | +ī |
letter₍fem₎SG.NOM write PERF.PART FEM.SG go CONV remain PERF.PART FEM.SG
hai
be-PRES.3.SG
lit. 'Letter written going remained is'. = 'The letter is being written'.

and | Čiṭṭʰī +yã | likʰ +∅ | +ī | ǯā+∅ | rah +∅ | +ī |
letter₍fem₎ PL.NOM write PERF.PART FEM.PL go CONV remain PERF.PART FEM.PL
haĩ
be-PRES.3.PL
lit. 'Letters written going remained are'. = 'The letters are being written'.

Hindi is thus a non-ergative language: its transitive verb admits a DirO, and the meaning of a Hindi transitive verb typically has '[to] cause' as the generic (= central) component of its definition. Hindi has no special ergative case, either, but it does have an ergative construction—with a transitive MV in a perfective form, where the SyntSubj in the instrumental. With an imperfective MV, Hindi uses a nominative construction, and the verb agrees then with the SyntSubj. (In other words, Hindi manifests what is known as **split ergativity**: the ergative construction appears under special conditions—in this case, with perfective series tense forms; elsewhere we have the nominative construction.) In a perfective form, the MV agrees only with the DirO.

---

15 The AgCo is only used in Hindi either in administrative/legal register (with the postposition DVARA 'through/by') or in non-assertive sentences, which express the ability of the Agent to perform the action (in the ablative in **-se**); see Kachru 2006: 204–205.

Thus, the SyntSubj's privileges in Hindi are the following five (pronominalization being irrelevant):

- Parameter 1. It depends on the MV.
- Parameter 2. It is non-omissible.
- Parameter 3. It occupies the linear position before the MV (and other actants).
- Parameter 4:
    - 4a. It controls the agreement of the MV (but only in an imperfective form).
    - 4b. It is "passivizable" (that is, it is the target of promotion by the passive).
- Parameter 5. It is marked by the nominative case (again, only with an imperfective MV).

Archi. The things are substantially different in Archi, a Daghestanian language. Just like Hindi, Archi has a monopersonal agreement—if the MV is in the one of the least marked synthetic forms, see in (27). But the single actant of the MV that controls its noun-class agreement is—in sharp contrast to Hindi—always in the nominative; it is not omissible and its syntactic position is targeted by an actant-manipulating voice-like transformation (as before, this actant is boxed in the examples; it is the SyntSubj, as will be shown).

(27) Archi (Kibrik 1977, 2003: 332–368; Roman numbers stand for noun classes)

a. $\boxed{Buwa\ \ +\emptyset+\emptyset}$ $da+q\ʻa$ 'Mother came'.
   mother$_{(II)}$ SG NOM II come-PERF

b. *Dija* $+\emptyset+mu$ $\boxed{buwa\ \ +\emptyset+\emptyset}$ χir $a+r+u$
   father$_{(I)}$ SG INSTR mother$_{(II)}$ SG NOM behind do.II.do-PERF
   lit. 'By.father mother behind did' ['BEHIND DO' is an idiom meaning 'bring with oneself']. = 'Father brought mother with him'.

c. *Dija* $+\emptyset+mu$ $\boxed{dos\ \ +\emptyset+\emptyset}$ χir $a+w+u\ [\Rightarrow aw]$
   father$_{(I)}$ SG INSTR friend$_{(I)}$ SG NOM behind do.I.do-PERF
   'Father brought a friend with him'.

d. *Dija* $+\emptyset+mu$ $\boxed{dos\ \ +til+\emptyset}$ χir $a+b+u$
   father$_{(I)}$ SG INSTR friend$_{(I)}$ PL NOM behind do.III.do-PERF
   'Father brought friends with him'.

   All plural Archi nouns belong to the noun class III; the verb AS 'do' shows class III agreement with the plural *dostil* 'friends'.

e. *Dija* $+\emptyset+n$ *buwa* $+\emptyset+ɬu$ $\boxed{anχ\ \ +\emptyset+\emptyset}$ $a+\emptyset+u\ [\Rightarrow aw]$
   father$_{(I)}$ SG GEN mother$_{(II)}$ SG COMIT fight$_{(N,IV)}$ SG NOM do.IV.do-PERF
   lit. 'Father's with.mother fight was.done'. = 'Father fought with mother'.

f. (i) **Ba.ah +∅–∅**   dita +**b**+u   **b** +erχin
trouble₍ₘ₎ SG NOM soon.III.soon III forget-IMPERF
'Trouble gets forgotten quickly'.

(ii) *Arša*   *horōkej* +***b*** +*u*   **iškul +∅+∅**   *da*+***b*** +*l*   +*u*
Archi-INESS long.ago very.III.very school₍ₘ₎ SG NOM open.III.open PERF
'A school opened in Archi very long time ago'.

(iii) ***D*+*ez*   un**   *malgan*
II I-DAT you_{SG(II)}-NOM be.dear
lit. 'To.me you [sg, female] are.dear'. = 'I love you'.

The SyntSubj in Archi has six privileges:

- Parameter 1. It depends only on the MV.
- Parameter 2. The SyntSubj is non-omissible, while all other actants of the MV can be absent from the Synt- and Sem-structure of the sentence; this is true even for causative sentences:

(28) a. (i) *Zari*   **nokƛ' +∅ +∅**   *ek'* +∅+*u*
I-INSTR room₍ᵢᵥ₎ SG NOM sweep.IV.sweep-PERF
lit. 'By.me room underwent.sweeping'. = 'I swept [the] room'.

and (ii) **Nokƛ' +∅ +∅**   *ek'* +∅+*u*
room₍ᵢᵥ₎ SG NOM sweep.IV.sweep-PERF
lit. 'Room underwent.sweeping'.

vs. b. (i) *Dija* +∅ +*mu*   *zari*   **nokƛ' +∅ +∅**   *ek'*   +∅+*a*   +*s*
father₍ᵢ₎ SG INSTR I-INSTR room₍ᵢᵥ₎ SG NOM sweep.IV.sweep INF
a+∅+*w*
do.IV.do-PERF
lit. 'By.Father by.me room to.undergo.sweeping underwent.causation'. = 'Father made me sweep the room'.

and (ii) *Zari*   **nokƛ' +∅ +∅**   *ek'*   +∅+*a*   +*s*   *a*+∅+*w*
I-INSTR room₍ᵢᵥ₎ SG NOM sweep.IV.sweep INF do.IV.do-PERF
lit. 'By.me room to.undergo.sweeping underwent.causation'. = 'I was made to sweep the room'.

and (iii) **nokƛ' +∅+∅**   *ek'*   +∅+*a*   +*s*   *c*+∅+*w*
room₍ᵢᵥ₎ SG NOM sweep.IV.sweep INF do.IV.do-PERF
lit. 'Room to.undergo.sweeping underwent.causation'. = 'The room was made to be swept'.

- Parameter 3. The SyntSubj is positioned immediately before the MV after all other its actants.
- Parameter 4a. The SyntSubj controls—almost exclusively—the noun-class agreement not only of the MV, as seen in (27) – (28), but also of circumstantials and even of certain actants, as in (27f), where the adverb *ditabu* 'soon', the particle *ejbu* 'very' and the actant *dez* 'to.me' agree in noun class with the SyntSubj.
- Parameter 4b. Archi has a "converse" voice[16] that promotes the AgCo to the SyntSubj, while demoting the former SyntSubj to the DirO (and turning the verb into a transitive one):

(29) a. *Buwa* +Ø+*mu* |χʷ*alli* +Ø+Ø| *b* +*a* +*r* +*ši* *b* +*i*
mother₍ₗₗ₎ SG INSTR bread₍ₗₗₗ₎ SG NOM III do IMPF CONV III be-PRES
lit. 'By.mother_AgCo bread_SyntSubj doing is'. = 'Mother is baking bread'.

vs. b. |*Buwa* +Ø+Ø| χʷ*alli* +Ø+Ø *b* +*a* +*r* +*ši* *d*+*i*
mother₍ₗₗ₎ SG NOM bread₍ₗₗₗ₎ SG NOM III do IMPF CONV II be-PRES
lit. 'Mother_SyntSubj bread_DirO doing is'. = 'Mother is baking bread'.

> **NB** The two sentences in (29) contrast: (29a) answers the question "What is happening?", while (29b) constitutes an answer to the question "What about Mother?"; in a sentence of this type, the SyntSubj must be Thematic.

- Parameter 5. The SyntSubj is always marked by the nominative.

As we see, Archi does not have an ergative construction, since its SyntSubj is always in the nominative; it does not have an ergative case, either: its AgCo is in the instrumental. But like Lezgian, Archi is an ergative language.

---

[16] **The "passive" in Archi.** It is to some extent similar to the "passive" of Dyirbal, see Note 5, p. 129. On voice in Archi, see Kibrik 1975 and 2003: 352–354 (however, Kibrik himself does not treat this transformation as voice; he speaks simply of a binominative construction). Testelec 1979 was probably the first to explicitly insist on the voice-like character of this verbal "alternation" in Daghestanian languages and draw a parallel with Dyirbal.
The passive, or converse, voice in Archi has two characteristic properties:
- As in several other Daghestanian languages (Avar, Bezhta, Gunzib, Tsez), this voice is possible only in one of the imperfective aspects: in the durative, the habitual, the progressive and the frequentative.
- In this voice, the Archi MV receives a DirO in the nominative, so that both the SyntSubj and the DirO are in the nominative, which is a kind of anathema for an ergative language. Moreover, the MV agrees with this DirO—along with the SyntSubj, so that the MV becomes bipersonal, and, so to speak, transitive.

3.4.3 Polypersonal agreement of the Main Verb

Language type 3. In language **L**, the MV agrees simultaneously with (at least) two actants, using two sets of agreement markers. In some Type 3 languages, the MV can simultaneously agree with three or even four actants. However, in order to simplify, I consider here the MV's agreement just with two actants—L_1 and L_2, one of which is thus the SyntSubj and the other one, the DirO. This introduces into our inquiry an additional dimension: the necessity to distinguish between SyntSubjs and DirOs.

For a Type 3 language **L**, two situations must be considered: either a monoactantial MV in **L** uses exclusively one set of agreement markers, or it uses alternatively both (as a function of the lexical unit playing the role of MV).

Subtype 3a. In **L** the transitive MV agrees simultaneously with two actants, but an intransitive (≈ monoactantial) MV features only one type of agreement.[17]

In this case, the only actant of an intransitive MV is its SyntSubj, so that the researcher has to decide exclusively between the two actants of a transitive biactantial MV. Such a situation is found in many languages; I select Georgian and Basque for an examination.

Georgian. In contrast to Lezgian and Archi, a transitive Georgian MV agrees—in person and number—simultaneously with two of its actants, which are, therefore, the SyntSubj and the DirO.[18] We have to settle accounts between these two: which one is the boss—i.e. the SyntSubj?

A transitive verb has two sets of agreement markers: Set I and Set II. Only the markers of Set I are exclusively used for the actant of a monoactantial MV, which stands in most cases in the nominative, cf. (30a); as I just said, it is the SyntSubj. But this fact by itself is not sufficient to consider Set I markers as exclusively subject markers, since on a transitive verb they can in principle cross-reference the DirO: precisely this, as we will see, happens in Basque. One has to compare both these actants of a transitive MV as to their case-marking and mutual linear

---

[17] In a given **L**, an intransitive verb V_{intr} can feature one of the two agreement scenarios:
- V_{intr} has the same set of SyntSubj-agreement markers as one of the two agreement marker sets of V_{trans} (e.g., Georgian and Basque, see below);
- V_{intr} has a special set of SyntSubj-agreement markers, as in Yimas, which has three different agreement marker sets: for an intransitive SyntSubj, for a transitive SyntSubj, and for a DirO (Foley 1991). Cf.:

   (i) **Ama** +wa 'I.go'. ~ $P_{\textit{u}}$ +**ka** +tay 'I.see.them'. ~ Pu +**ŋa** +tay 'They.see.me'.
   1.SG$_{SUB}$ go   3.PL$_{OBJ}$ **1.SG**$_{SUB}$ see   3.PL$_{SUB}$ **1.SG**$_{OBJ}$ see

[18] I leave out the agreement with the IndirO (rather than with the DirO), possible with some verbs.

order. In the least marked transitive clause, with the MV in a tense of the present series, the actant cross-referenced by Set I markers is in the nominative and precedes the MV, just as the SyntSubj of an intransitive MV precedes it. The other actant, which is in the dative, in a communicatively neutral sentence either follows the MV, or precedes it, while following the nominative actant. Therefore, the first—nominative—actant is the SyntSubj of the transitive MV, so that Set I markers must be considered to be **subject markers**. As a result, the SyntSubj in a Georgian clause is the element cross-referenced by subject markers; it is boxed in (30), and the subject markers on the MV are boldfaced.

(30) Georgian ("T.E." stands for **thematic element**, a semantically empty suffix used to form a verbal stem in several tenses[19])

a. $\boxed{K'ac+\emptyset+i}$ $\emptyset$ +muša+ob+**s**   '[The] man works'. ~
   man **SG** NOM   3$_{SUB}$ work T.E. PRES.**3.SG**$_{SUB}$
   $\boxed{K'ac+eb+i}$ $\emptyset$ +muša+ob+**en**   '[The] men work'.
   man **PL** NOM   3$_{SUB}$ work T.E. PRES.**3.PL**$_{SUB}$

b. $\boxed{Me}$ **v** +muša+ob+$\emptyset$ 'I work'. ~
   I-NOM 1$_{SUB}$ work T.E. PRES.**SG**$_{SUB}$
   $\boxed{Čven}$ **v** +muša+ob+**t**
   we-NOM 1$_{SUB}$ work T.E. PRES.**PL**$_{SUB}$ 'We work'.

c. $\boxed{K'ac+\emptyset+i}$ m   +xat' +av +**s**   me   ~
   man **SG** NOM 1.SG$_{OBJ}$ draw T.E. PRES.**3.SG**$_{SUB}$ I-DAT
   g+xat'+av+**s** šen   ~ $\emptyset$+xat'+av+**s** mas/mat
   2$_{OBJ}$ you$_{SG}$-DAT   3$_{OBJ}$ he-DAT/they-DAT
   '[The] man draws me ~ you$_{SG}$ ~ him/them'.

d. $\boxed{K'ac+eb+i}$ m   +xat' +av +**en**   me   ~
   man **PL** NOM 1.SG$_{OBJ}$ draw T.E. PRES.**3.PL**$_{SUB}$ I-DAT
   g+xat'+av+**en** šen   ~ $\emptyset$+xat'+av+**en** mas/mat
   2$_{OBJ}$ you$_{SG}$-DAT   3$_{OBJ}$ he-DAT/they-DAT
   '[The] men draw me ~ you$_{SG}$ ~ him/them'.

---

19 As indicated to me by Z. Baratashvili, in Old Georgian the thematic element was linked to the "punctual aspect ~ durative aspect" opposition, being the marker of the durative. — In our Georgian examples all verbs are in the indicative mood; to simplify the presentation, IND is not shown in the glosses.

e. $\boxed{\text{K'ac+}\emptyset\text{+ma}}$ da +m +xat' +a me ~
   man SG ERG PERF 1.SG$_{OBJ}$ draw AOR.3.SG$_{SUB}$ I-NOM
   da+g+xat'+a šen ~ da+$\emptyset$+xat'+a is/isini
   2$_{OBJ}$ you$_{SG}$-NOM 3$_{OBJ}$ he-NOM/they-NOM
   '[The] man drew me ~ you$_{SG}$ ~ him/them'.

f. $\boxed{\text{K'ac+eb+ma}}$ da +m +xat' +es me ~
   man PL ERG PERF 1.SG$_{OBJ}$ draw AOR.3.PL$_{SUB}$ I-NOM
   da+g+xat'+es šen ~ da+$\emptyset$+xat'+es is/isini
   2$_{OBJ}$ you$_{SG}$-NOM 3$_{OBJ}$ he-NOM/they-NOM
   '[The] men drew me ~ you$_{SG}$ ~ him/them'.

g. $\boxed{\text{Me}}$ v +xat' +av +$\emptyset$ mas /mct 'I draw him/them'.
   I-NOM 1$_{SUB}$ draw T.E. PRES.SG$_{SUB}$ he-DAT/they-DAT

h. $\boxed{\text{Me}}$ da +v+xat' +e +$\emptyset$ is /isini 'I drew him/them'.
   I-ERG PERF 1$_{SUB}$ draw AOR.1.SG$_{SUB}$ SG$_{SUB}$ he-NOM/they-NOM

The Georgian SyntSubj has five privileges:

– Parameter 1. It depends only on the MV.
– Parameter 2. It is not omissible.
– Parameter 3. In a communicatively neutral sentence, it precedes the MV and all its other actants.
– Parameter 4:
  a. If the transitive MV is in one of the present series tenses, the SyntSubj is in the nominative: (30a–d); the DirO is in the dative: (30c–d). This is the most common nominative construction, such as seen in SAE and many other languages.

  If the transitive MV is in an aorist series tense, the case marking of the SyntSubj and the DirO changes to, respectively, the ergative and the nominative, as in (30e–h), although their syntactic status does not change. A transitive Georgian MV in an aorist series tense and its two main actants form, of course, an ergative construction. (Just like Hindi, Georgian manifests **split ergativity**: the ergative construction appears only with aorist series tense forms; elsewhere we have the nominative construction.) In accordance with the convention concerning SyntSubj property violations, the appearance of the ergative instead of the "canonical" nominative does not make the definition of the SyntSubj in Georgian any more problematic.
  b. Georgian has a passive (Harris 1981: 103*ff*), which confirms the subjecthood of the ergative SyntSubj:

158 — 3 Syntactic subject: syntactic relations, once again

(31) a. Gogi+**m**   es   stʻatʻia+Ø+Ø   /stʻatʻi+eb+i   da +Ø +cʻer +a
  Gogi ERG this paper SG NOM/paper PL NOM PERF 3$_{SUB}$ write AOR.3.SG
  'Gogi wrote this paper/these papers'.

  b. Es stʻatʻia+Ø+Ø   /stʻatʻi+eb+i   da +cʻer +il   +Ø +i
  this paper SG NOM /paper PL NOM PERF write PASS.PART SG NOM
  Ø +iq+o   Gog +is   **mier**
  3$_{SUB}$ be AOR.3.SG Gogi GEN **by.means.of**
  'This paper/These papers was/were written by Gogi'.

  NB In Georgian, the MV does not reflect the plural of an inanimate SyntSubj; that is why *dacʻerili* 'written' and *iqo* 'was' are in the singular for both SyntSubjs 'paper' and 'papers'.

Thus, Georgian has the ergative construction and the ergative case, but it is not an ergative language.[20]

---

20 Two problematic cases of subjecthood in Georgian. In this connection, the evidential and the affective verbs, known also as "inverse," should be mentioned.
Georgian has a group of verb forms (currently called "perfect forms," or "III series forms"), which carry the meaning 'by hearsay' ≈ 'this being second-hand testimony' ≈ 'apparently' (in the gloss, ALTR stands for the grammeme 'for the other' of the inflectional category of **version**):

(i) a. *Bičʻ+Ø+s*   *gamo+u*   *+gzavni*   *+xar*   *+Ø*   **šen**
  boy SG DAT PERF ALTR send-PASS.PART be-PRES.2$_{SUB}$ SG$_{SUB}$ you$_{SG}$-NOM
  'Apparently, the boy sent you$_{SG}$'.
  b. *Bičʻ+Ø+s*   *gamo+u*   *+gzavni*   *+xar*   *+t*   **tkven**
  boy SG DAT PERF ALTR send-PASS.PART be-PRES.2$_{SUB}$ PL$_{SUB}$ you$_{PL}$-NOM
  'Apparently, the boy sent you$_{PL}$'.
  c. *Bičʻ+Ø+s*   *gamo+u*   *+gzavni*   *+a*   *+Ø*   **gogo+Ø+Ø**
  boy SG DAT PERF ALTR send-PASS.PART be-PRES.3.SG$_{SUB}$ SG$_{SUB}$ girl SG NOM
  'Apparently, the boy sent [a] girl'.
  d. *Bičʻ+Ø+s*   *gamo+u*   *+gzavni*   *+a*   *+Ø*   **gogo+eb+i**
  boy SG DAT PERF ALTR send-PASS.PART be-PRES.3.SG$_{SUB}$ SG$_{SUB}$ girl PL NOM
  'Apparently, the boy sent girls'.
  e. *Bičʻ+eb+s*   *gamo+u*   *+gzavni*   *+a*   *+t*   **gogo+Ø+Ø**
  boy PL DAT PERF ALTR send-PASS.PART be-PRES.3.SG$_{SUB}$ PL$_{OBJ}$ girl SG NOM
  'Apparently, the boys sent [a] girl'.

These forms express an evidential, which requires, as is typologically natural, a perfective form. Traditionally, the noun in the dative is considered to be the SyntSubj. However, judging by agreement, it is the N$_{NOM}$ that is the SyntSubj, the N$_{DAT}$ being an IndirO, which is again typologically quite plausible. But there is a wrinkle: as seen in (i-d) and (i-e), in the evidential, the MV does not agree with the animate SyntSubj of the 3rd person in number as expected, since in (i-d) instead of **gamougzavni+arian*$_{3.PL_{SUB}}$ we have *gamougzavni+a*$_{3.SG_{SUB}}$. This minor irregularity, however, should not change our treatment of the SyntSubj.

Georgian also has a significant class of verbs expressing feelings and attitudes whose basic diathesis is converse with respect to the corresponding English verbs—that is, 'I like you' is in

3.4 Establishing the syntactic subject in a language — 159

Basque. The Basque transitive MV also agrees simultaneously with at least two of its actants.[21] As in Georgian, there are two sets of agreement affixes, the prefixes I_{NOM}, cross-referencing the N_{NOM}, and the affixes II_{ERG}, cross-referencing the N_{ERG}; for the single—nominative—actant of an intransitive MV only the prefixes of set I_{NOM} are used. But here comes the important difference with Georgian: with a transitive MV, one of its two actants is always in the ergative; there is no tense-induced ergative split—that is, no nominative construction that helps us identify the SyntSubj. In Basque, we cannot know which affixes are subjectival. Therefore, in the following examples, the boldfaced agreement affixes are specified by the noun they cross-reference: N_{NOM} vs. N_{ERG}; for instance, "3_{NOM}" as a gloss of a marker **m** means '**m** cross-references the N_{NOM}', etc. (In the examples of (32) the clause element that will be eventually identified as SyntSubj is boxed.)

(32) Basque ($s = /\acute{s}/$, $tx = /\check{c}/$, $z = /s/$)

a. (i) ⟦Gizon+a⟧ +∅+∅   etorri   **d** +∅   +a
       man DEF SG NOM[22] come-PERF.PART 3_{NOM} SG_{NOM} be
       'The man has [lit. 'is'] come'.

  (ii) ⟦Gizon+a⟧ +k+∅   etorri   **d** +**ir** +a
       man DEF PL NOM   come-PERF.PART 3_{NOM} PL_{NOM} be
       'The men have come'.

  (iii) ⟦Ni–∅⟧   etorri   **n** +aiz
       I   NOM   come-PERF.PART 1_{NOM} be
       'I have come'.

Georgian 'You$_{SG}$ are.likable to.me' (verbs similar to the Georgian feeling verbs exist in Russian, French, German etc., where, however, they are rather exceptional):

$mo+m+c'on+xar+\emptyset$ 'You$_{SG}$ are.likable to.me' = 'I like you'.
(**mo-** ⇔ 'towards.me', **m-** ⇔ $1.SG_{OBJ}$, **c'on** ⇔ 'be.likable', **-xar** ⇔ 'you.are', **-∅** ⇔ SG_{SUB});

$m+i+qvar+s$ 'He/They is/are.lovable to.me.' = 'I love him/them'.
(**m-** ⇔ $1.SG_{OBJ}$, **i-** ⇔ IPSE 'for oneself' [grammeme of version], **qvar** ⇔ 'be.lovable', **-s** ⇔ $3.SG_{SUB}$);

$\emptyset+u+qvar+t$ 'He/They is/are.lovable to.them' = 'They love him/them'.
(**∅-** ⇔ 3_{OBJ}, **u-** ⇔ ALTR 'for the other' [grammeme of version], **qvar** ⇔ 'be.lovable', **-t** ⇔ PL_{OBJ});

$v+u+qvar+var$ 'I am.lovable to.him'. = 'He loves me'.
(**v-** ⇔ $1.SG_{SUB}$, **u-** ⇔ ALTR 'for the other', **qvar** ⇔ 'be.lovable', **-var** ⇔ 'I.am');

$g+3ul+t$ 'He/They is/are.hatable to you$_{PL}$'. = 'You$_{PL}$ hate him/them'.
(**g-** ⇔ 2_{OBJ}, **3ul** ⇔ 'be.hatable', **-t** ⇔ PL_{OBJ}).

In traditional view, the SyntSubj is the N_{DAT}. But, as in the case of the evidential, the MV's agreement clearly indicates the N_{NOM} as the SyntSubj (with the same complications).

21 Again, for simplicity's sake, agreement with the IndirO and the so-called allocutive form are not considered.

22 The morphic structure of a Basque nominal wordform is a controversial topic. Here I am using my own description.

b. (i) $\boxed{Gizon+a}$ +Ø +k   kotxe+a +Ø+Ø   saldu
man DEF SG ERG   car   DEF SG NOM   sell-PERF.PART
d +Ø +u +Ø +Ø
$3_{NOM}SG_{NOM}$ have 3_{ERG} SG_{ERG}
'The man has sold the car'.

(ii) $\boxed{Gizon+a}$ +Ø+k   kotxe+a +k+Ø   saldu
man DEF SG ERG   car   DEF PL NOM   sell-PERF.PART
d +*it*   +u +Ø +Ø
3_{NOM} PL_{NOM} have 3_{ERG} SG_{ERG}
'The man has sold the cars'.

(iii) $\boxed{Gizon+e}$ +k   kotxe+a +Ø+Ø   saldu
man PL.DEF ERG   car   DEF SG NOM   sell-PERF.PART
d +Ø   +u   +Ø +te
3_{NOM} SG_{NOM} have 3_{ERG} PL_{ERG}
'The men have sold the car'.

(iv) $\boxed{Gizon+e}$ +k   kotxe+a +k +Ø   saldu
man PL.DEF ERG   car   DEF PL NOM   sell-PERF.PART
d +*it*   +u   +Ø +zte
3_{NOM} PL_{NOM} have 3_{ERG} PL_{ERG}
'The men have sold the cars'.

(v) $\boxed{Ni+k}$ kotxe+a +Ø+Ø   saldu   *d* +Ø   +u   +t
I   ERG   car   DEF SG NOM   sell-PERF.PART 3_{NOM} SG_{NOM} have $1.SG_{ERG}$
'I have sold the car'.

(vi) $\boxed{Ni+k}$ kotxe+a +k+Ø   saldu   *d* +*it*   +u   +t
I   ERG   car   DEF PL NOM   sell-PERF.PART 3_{NOM} PL_{NOM} have $1SG_{ERG}$
'I have sold the cars'.

In Basque, a transitive MV cross-references its DirO by the same markers as an intransitive MV cross-references its SyntSubj. For this reason, in Basque, the existence of actant-shuffling modifications of the verb is crucial. The language has two such modifications (Rebuschi 1978: 76–77, 82–83; Rebuschi 1981: 92, 1982: 299*ff*, 1986; Rebuschi's data are quoted with drastic simplifications): a passive and two detransitivizations, which target the SyntSubj's syntactic position.

Passive: a diathetic permutation "DirO' ⇒ SyntSubj, SyntSubj' ⇒ AgCo" [the prime means 'initial'].

The Basque passive is illustrated in (33), where the sentences semantically correspond to the sentences in (32b):

(33) (i) $\boxed{\textit{Kotxe-a} +\emptyset+\emptyset}$ gizon+a +∅+k saldu +a +∅
    car DEF **SG** NOM man DEF SG ERG sell-PERF.PART DEF SG
    d +∅ +a
    3_{NOM} SG_{NOM} be
    'The car is sold by the man'.

(ii) $\boxed{\textit{Kotxe-a} +\textbf{k}+\emptyset}$ gizon+a +∅+k saldu +a +k
    car DEF **PL** NOM man DEF SG ERG sell-PERF.PART DEF PL
    d +ir +a
    3_{NOM} PL_{NOM} be
    'The cars are sold by the man'.

(iii) $\boxed{\textit{Kotxe-a} +\emptyset+\emptyset}$ gizon+e +k saldu +a +∅
    car DEF **SG** NOM man DEF.PL ERG sell-PERF.PART DEF SG
    d +∅ +a
    3_{NOM} SG_{NOM} be
    'The car is sold by the men'.

(iv) $\boxed{\textit{Kotxe+a} +\textbf{k}+\emptyset}$ gizon+e +∅+k saldu +a +k
    car DEF **PL** NOM man DEF SG ERG sell-PERF.PART DEF PL
    d +ir +a
    3_{NOM} PL_{NOM} be
    'The cars are sold by the men'.

(v) $\boxed{\textit{Kotxe+a} +\emptyset+\emptyset}$ ni+k saldu +a +∅ d +∅ +a
    car DEF SG NOM I ERG sell-PERF.PART DEF SG 3_{NOM} SG_{NOM} be
    'The car is sold by me'.

(vi) $\boxed{\textit{Kotxe+a} +\textbf{k}+\emptyset}$ ni+k saldu +a +k d +ir +a
    car DEF PL NOM I ERG sell-PERF.PART DEF PL 3_{NOM} SG_{NOM} be
    'The cars are sold by me'.

The auxiliary verb 'be' and the participle agree—in definiteness and number—only with the subject.

Detransitivizations: they result in "SyntSubj$_{\text{ERG}}$ ⇒ SyntSubj$_{\text{NOM}}$" [23]

---

23 The category of transitivization. DETRANS(itivizer) is a grammeme of transitivization, an inflectional category of the verb—similar to, but different from, voice. It resembles voice in that it impacts the verb central actants, the SyntSubj and the DirO; it differs from voice in that it does not **permute** the DSyntAs of the verb with the respect to its SemAs, but only modifies their surface realization (see Mel'čuk 2006a: 231ff). This category includes at least three grammemes: NEUTRAL ~ DETRANS ~ TRANS(itivizer). Tongan, examples (21)–(22), features the pair NEUTRAL ~ TRANS. Chukchi has even two detransitivizers: DETRANS-1 and DETRANS-2. DETRANS-1, expressed

Basque has two detransitivizations: a progressive construction and a resultative construction.

– The progressive construction is marked by the adjective ARI 'being in the process of, doing' and uses the auxiliary IZAN 'be' even for transitive verbs, which become *eo ipso* intransitive (since a transitive verb uses as its auxiliary only UKAN 'have'): the SyntSubj, instead of the ergative, takes the nominative, as an intransitive SyntSubj should; the former DirO remains in the nominative, but loses its status as a DirO, since the verb becomes intransitive; the MV agrees only with the SyntSubj:

---

by the prefix **ine-/ena-**, lowers the Synt-rank of the DirO (which becomes an IndirO); DETRANS-2 (the suffix **-tku/-tko**) not only lowers the Synt-rank of the DirO, but it also makes its appearance in the clause undesirable and, at the same time, blocks the expression of all other objects and complements, which are allowed both with the basic form and with the DETRANS-1 form.

(i) Chukchi
    a. *Γəm+nan* *tə*   *+ret*   *+ərkən+Ø*   *kimitʕ+ən*   (*tomy+etə*)
       I   INSTR 1.SG$_{SUB}$ transport PRES 3.SG$_{OBJ}$ load SG.NOM friend SG/PL.DAT
       'I$_{X⇌I}$ transport a.load$_{Y⇌II}$ (to.a.friend/to.friends$_{Z⇌III}$)'.
    b. *Γəm+Ø* *t*   *+ine*   *+ret*   *+ərkən* *kimitʕ+e*   (*tomy+etə*)
       I   NOM 1.SG$_{SUB}$ **DETRANS-1** transport PRES   load SG.INSTR friend SG/PL.DAT
       'I$_{X⇌I}$ transport a.load$_{Y⇌II}$ (to.a.friend/to.friends$_{Z⇌III}$)'.
    c. *Γəm+Ø* *tə*   *+ret*   *+atku* *+rkən* (?*kimitʕ+e*   ?*tomy +etə*)
       I   NOM 1.SG$_{SUB}$ transport **DETRANS-2** PRES load SG.INSTR friend SG/PL.DAT
       'I$_{X⇌I}$ transport (a.load$_{Y⇌II}$) (to.a.friend/to.friends$_{Z⇌III}$)'.

Sentence (i-a) presents an ergative construction, obligatory in Chukchi for any transitive verb: the SyntSubj 'I' is in the instrumental, and the DirO '[a] load', in the nominative. In (i-b), we find a nominative construction, possible only for an intransitive verb: the SyntSubj, which remains 'I', is in the nominative; the DirO '[a] load' has become an OblO in the instrumental, thus losing its salience; the two OblOs are optional. Finally, (i-c) is again a nominative construction: the two OblOs—'load' and 'friends'—are incompatible with each other and even less salient than in the preceding sentence; their omission is preferred.

Roughly, sentence (i-a) answers the question 'What are you transporting and to whom?', (i-b), the question 'What are you doing?', and (i-c), the question 'What is your occupation?'

Degrees of transitivization/detransitivization, related to the degree of the impact of the denoted action upon the object, are not a rarity; here is another example—from Warlpiri (Australia):

(ii) Warlpiri
    a. *Maliki+li* *ka +Ø*   *+Ø*   *ŋarka+Ø* *yaḻki+ṇi*
       dog ERG PRES 3.SG$_{SUB}$.3.SG$_{OBJ}$ NEUTRAL man NOM bite NON-PAST
       'The dog is biting the man'.
    b. *Maliki+li* *ka +la*   *+ʒinta* *ŋarka+ku* *yaḻki+ṇi*
       dog ERG PRES 3.SG$_{SUB}$.3.SG$_{OBJ}$ DETRANS man DAT bite NON-PAST
       'The dog is biting at the man'.

In Warlpiri, DETRANS lowers the transitivity of the verb, turning its DirO into an IndirO; but the verb remains transitive: it still presents an ergative construction, with the SyntSubj in the ergative case.

(34) a. (i) ☐Gizon+a +∅ +∅☐   kotxe+a +∅/k+∅   saltzen ari   d +∅   +a
       man DEF **SG** NOM car DEF SG/PL NOM sell-GER doing $3_{NOM}SG_{NOM}$ be
       'The man is selling the car/s'.
   (ii) ☐Gizon+a +**k** +∅☐ kotxe+a +∅/k+∅   saltzen ari   d +ir   +a
       man DEF **PL** NOM car DEF SG/PL NOM sell-GER doing $3_{NOM}PL_{NOM}$ be
       'The men are selling the car/s'.

– The other detransitivization (called "antipassive" in Rebuschi 1981: 92) produces a resultative construction, in which not only the auxiliary, but also the participle agrees with the SyntSubj (in the nominative) according to definiteness and number; the MV is also intransitive, so that the "former" DirO becomes a Quasi-DirO:

   b. (i) ☐Gizon+a +∅ +∅☐   kotxe+a +∅/k+∅   saldu   –a +∅
       man DEF **SG** NOM car DEF SG/PL NOM sell-PAST.PART DEF **SG**
       d +∅   +a
       3_{NOM} SG_{NOM} be
       'The man is having.sold the car/s'.
   (ii) ☐Gizon+a +**k** +∅☐ kotxe+a +∅/k+∅   saldu   –a +**k**
       man DEF **PL** NOM car DEF SG/PL NOM sell-PAST.PART DEF **PL**
       d +ir   +a
       3_{NOM} PL_{NOM} be
       'The men are having.sold the car/s'.

The four Basque SyntSubj's privileges are as follows:
– Parameter 1. It depends exclusively on the MV.
– Parameter 2. It is non-omissible.
– Parameter 3. It tends to precede the MV and other actants.
– Parameter 4b. Its role is targeted by the passive and is confirmed by detransitivizations.

In conclusion, Basque is a non-ergative language, but it does have an ergative construction (without split) and an ergative case.

Subtype 3b. In **L** the MV can agree simultaneously with two actants, and a monoactantial MV features both types of agreement.

Probably the best-known example here comes from Acehnese (Malayo-Polynesian).

Acehnese (Durie 1985, 1987, 1988). Acehnese has no syntactic processes: no voices, no raisings, no detransitivization, no switch-reference, etc.; word order is extremely flexible. The only reliable syntactic property of actants of the Main Verb that amounts to a privilege is verb agreement—cross-referencing of actants on the MV. The Acehnese MV cross-references two of its actants (only if they are animate): one by a prefixal marker, the other by a suffixal marker. However, in the simplest clauses, which feature a semantically monoactantial verb having just one syntactic actant, both types of agreement occur, which means that in (35a) and (35b), featuring intransitive verbs, we see two different types of actant—one controlling prefix agreement and the other controlling suffix agreement.

(35) Acehnese ($ê$ = /e/, $ô$ = /o/, eu = /ɯ/, $ë$ = /ɤ/, j = /ʒ/)

    a. ***Lôn*+*lôp***   'I enter'.   and   ***Geu*+*lôp***   'He enters'.
        1.SG enter   3.SG enter

    b. ***Rhët*+*lôn***   'I fall'.   and   ***Rhët*+*geuh***   'He falls'.
        fall   1.SG   fall   3.SG

Thus, both these types of actant are privileged in Acehnese, since they, and only they, control the agreement of the MV. Therefore, one of these actants must be the SyntSubj and the other, the DirO. To decide which one of the two is more privileged than the other and thus is the SyntSubj, we need to consider a biactantial verb in a sentence where both types of actant are expressed:

    c. ***Lôn*+*ngieng*+*geuh***   'I see him/her'.
        1.SG see   3.SG
and   ***Geu*+*ngieng*+*lôn***   'He/She sees me'.
        3.SG see   1.SG

Examining sentences with two privileged syntactic actants simultaneously present, we find that:

– The prefixal marker on the verb is obligatory and cannot be linearly separated from the verb (35d-i), while the suffixal marker is not obligatory and can migrate to the outer edge of the verbal phrase (35d-ii):

    d. (i) *Gopnyan* ***lôn*+*ngieng***   'Him I.see'.
           he   1.SG see
and   *Lôn* ***geu*+*ngieng***   'Me he.sees'.
          I   3.SG see

vs.   *Lôn ngieng+**geuh**   'I see.him'.
          I   see   3.SG
and   *Gopnyan ngieng+**lôn**   'He sees.me'.
          he   see   1.SG

     (ii) Ka +leupah+**lôn** u keude baroe. ≡ Ka+leupah u keude baroe+**lôn**.
         PAST reach   1.SG to town yesterday   'I reached the town yesterday'.

–   The imperative requires the prefixal marker and does not allow the suffixal one:

     e. (i) **Neu**+peumeu'ah! 'Forgive me!' ~ *Peumeu'ah! ~ *Neu+peumeu'ah+**lôn**!
          2.SG forgive

     (ii) **Neu**+peujêt   ie   nyoe keu jih! 'Make him drink this water!'
          2.SG make.drink water this to   he

To put it differently, only the prefix-referenced actant can be the Addressee of an imperative utterance.

–   The prefix-referenced actant, and only this actant, can be introduced by the preposition **lê,** when following the Main Verb:

     f. Gopnyan lôn+tët +rumoh **lê** lôn   'I burned down his house'. =
       he   1.SG burn house   I   lit. 'He I.burned.house by I'.

Let me add, as icing on the cake, that only the prefix-referenced actant controls its own obligatory Equi-Deletion with the verb TÊM 'want', no matter whether the governed verb is intransitive or transitive:

     g. (i) ⬚Gopnyan⬚ geu+têm   jak. ~ *Gopnyan geu+têm **geu**+jak 'He wants to go'.
          he   3.SG want go

and   ⬚Gopnyan⬚ geu+têm   taguen bu. ~
          he   3.SG want cook   rice
         *Gopnyan geu+têm **geu**+taguen bu   'He wants to cook rice'.

vs.   (ii) *Gopnyan geu+têm   rhët   'He wants to fall'.
          he   3.SG want fall

        The sentence (35g-ii) is incorrect since the verb RHËT requires the suff x-referencing of its only actant.

Therefore, the prefix-referenced actant is more privileged in Acehnese: it is the SyntSubj. The other one, suffix-referenced, is the DirO. This simply means that in (35b) a literal gloss should be rather '[It.falls me/him'. M. Durie himself does not name these two actants in this way: he calls them Agent and Undergoer, since 35 years ago the notions of SyntSubj and SyntObj were too vague to be of any use; Durie 1985: 190–191 correctly indicates that none of Acehnese clause elements corresponds to the characteristics of the "syntactic pivot," a moot concept used at the time instead of SyntSubj. However, Durie makes it absolutely clear that "Agent" and "Undergoer" are not genuine semantic relations, but clearly syntactic ones (see especially Durie 1987). Therefore, it can be safely concluded that, by calling the prefix-referenced actant the SyntSubj and the suffix-referenced one the DirO, I simply sharpen and, at the same time, generalize the terminology.

What is special about the Acehnese SyntSubj and DirO is their more direct link to semantic roles. In many languages such as English or Russian, a SyntSubj can fulfill various semantic roles: it can express an Agent (***John** beat up Paul.*), a Patient (***John** got a beating.*), a Cause (***John** really worries us.*), an Experiencer (***John** likes boiled potatoes.*), a Property Carrier (***John** is intelligent.*), Time (***The next morning** saw John in Nevada.*), and so on; to a lesser extent, the same is true of the DirO. But in Acehnese, the SyntSubj expresses only the volitional Actor, and the DirO only the non-volitional Undergoer. The semantic opposition of volitionality is extremely important in Acehnese; the language has special derivational means to change the volitionality of a verb (Durie 1988: 7): *jak* 'go, walk' ~ *teu+jak* 'walk without volition' or *seunang* 'be happy' ~ *meu+seunang* 'make oneself happy, enjoy oneself'. However, such an alignment of syntactic relations to semantic roles by no means diminishes the importance of syntactic relations.

With the proposed terminological change, one can draw an interesting parallel between the Acehnese sentences of the (35b) type—that is, sentences with a verb that has a DirO only, but no SyntSubj—and Russian impersonal constructions, in which the only semantic actant of the verb is expressed by a DirO (the verb in these constructions expresses an incontrollable state):

(36) ***Menja*** $_{ACC}$ *tošnit/rvët* lit. '[It] nauseates/vomits me'. = 'I am nauseated/I vomit'.
    Menja $_{ACC}$ *znobit* lit. '[It] chills me'. = 'I have a chill'.
    Menja $_{ACC}$ *trjasët* lit. '[It] shakes me'. = 'I shake'.
    Menja $_{ACC}$ *proneslo* lit. '[It] diarrhea-ed me'. = 'I had diarrhea'.
    Menja $_{ACC}$ *skrjučilo* lit. '[It] completely.bent me'. = 'I was doubled up [in pain]'.
    Menja $_{ACC}$ *razneslo* lit. '[It] expanded me'. = 'I got fat'.

I do not see any substantive difference between Acehnese *Sakêt-lôn* lit. '[It] hurts/sicks me'. = 'I am hurting/sick', which is an impersonal construction, and the Russian impersonal construction of the type *Menja lixoradit* lit. '[It] fevers me'. = 'I have fever'. The difference is quantitative: Russian has a handful of such impersonal verbs, while in Acehnese there are hundreds of them.[24]

3.5 Syntactic subject problems related to impersonal constructions

On several occasions, a dubious treatment of an actant as the SyntSubj is due to the failure to recognize the presence of a zero dummy subject, a lexeme similar to the expletive and meteorological IT of English, but having an empty signifier. Let me consider two cases, in Icelandic and in Amele.

Icelandic (Andrews 2001). Icelandic has a common type of sentences of the form in (37):

(37) Icelandic

a. ***Bát*** +*Ø*   +*inn* /***Bát***+*a*   +*na* rak   á land
   boat SG.ACC DEF /boat PL.ACC DEF drift-PAST.3.SG to shore
   lit. '[It] drifted the.boat/s to shore'. = 'The boat/s drifted to shore'.

b. ***Bát***+*i*   +*num* /***Bát*** +*u*   +*num* hvolf +*di*
   boat SG.DAT DEF /boat PL.DAT DEF capsize PAST.3.SG
   lit. '[It] capsized the.boat/s'. = 'The boat/s capsized'.

c. (i) *Hann*   *kasta*+*ði*   *stein* +*i*   +*num*/*stein*+*u*   +*num*
       he-NOM throw PAST.3.SG stone SG.DAT DEF /stone PL.DAT DEF
       'He threw with.the.stone/s'.

   (ii) ***Stein***+*i*   +*num*/***Stein***+*u*   +*num* var   *kasta*+*ð*
        stone SG.DAT DEF /stone PL.DAT DEF be-PAST.3.SG throw PAST.PART
        'The stone/s were thrown'. lit. '[It] was thrown with.the.stone/s'.

According to Andrews 2001, the boldfaced element in the sentences of (37) is the SyntSubj, since its behavior shows at least 13 features that it shares with the

---

[24] There is also a semantic difference, irrelevant in the present context: in Russian, such verbs denote mostly harmful or at least unpleasant physiological states and processes, while in Acehnese they cover a much larger area of non-volitional properties, states, events, and processes. A formal difference should also be mentioned: the Russian impersonal construction has a dummy zero SyntSubj, which imposes on the verb the agreement in 3.SG.NEU(ter), while Acehnese has no dummy subject (Durie 1985: 180), since the verb does not require automatic subject agreement.

behavior of the "canonical" SyntSubjs of Icelandic: it controls coreference with the "subject" of an infinitive and the choice of the reflexive possessive pronoun *sinni* 'self's' (Rus. *svoj*), it can appear between an auxiliary and the past participle of the lexical verb (where only SyntSubjs are admitted), etc. However, "not only are they not nominative in case, but the verb does not agree with them" (Andrews 2001: 93), while normal SyntSubjs in Icelandic control the agreement of the MV and are marked by the nominative. Therefore, I conclude that these suspicious clause elements are not SyntSubjs—even though they behave in many respects as prototypical SyntSubjs sometimes do under specific conditions. Otherwise, it is not clear what Andrews and many others who share his perspective on this issue understand by a subject: by all means, not a clause element that is the depending member of a particular SSynt-relation.

In reality, the sentences in (37a–b) and (37c-ii) manifest an impersonal construction with a zero subject: in (37a–b), this is the lexeme $\emptyset^{\text{«ELEMENTS»}}_{(3,\,\text{sg})}$, denoting some slightly mysterious natural forces; in (37c-ii), this is the zero dummy subject lexeme $\emptyset_{(3,\,\text{sg})}$, which is semantically empty. These zeroes are equivalent to Eng. IT, Ger. ES and Fr. IL. (Spanish and Russian also have, in such contexts, a zero dummy: for instance, Sp. *Se lee muchas novelas* lit. '[It] itself reads many novels' and Rus. *Zdes' mnoj siženo* 'Here by.me [it is] sat'.) The correct glossing of (37a), (37b) and (37c-ii) would be 'It drifted the boat/s to shore', 'It capsized the boat/s' and 'It was thrown with the stone/s'. That is exactly how all these constructions are described in an elementary manual of Icelandic for non-natives (Glendenning 1983: 49–50).

As for the SyntSubj's coreferential deletion in Icelandic, it does not tell us anything about the subjecthood of the boldfaced clause elements:

(38) Icelandic (Pouplier 2003: 367)

   a. **Þeim**   líkar   maturinn   og   borða   mikið
      they-DAT please-PRES.3.SG food-SG.NOM.DEF and eat-PRES.3.PL much
      lit. 'To.them pleases the food and [they] eat much'. =
      'They like the food and eat much'.

   b. **Okkur** vantaði   peninga   og   vorum   svangir
      we-DAT lack-PAST.3.SG money-PL.ACC and be-PAST.1.PL hungry
      lit. 'To.us [it] lacked money and [we] were hungry'. =
      'We lacked money and were hungry'.

In (38), the deletion of the SyntSubj in the second coordinate clause is controlled by semantic properties of the controlling element (a human Experiencer) rather than by its syntactic nature.

Amele (Roberts 1987, 1988, 2001). In Amele, the MV can simultaneously agree with four types of actant (quadri-personal agreement). Agreement affixes are different for each type of actant; the agreement in the simplest clauses—an intransitive MV and only one actant—allows the researcher to establish the Subject Agreement affix set and thus to identify the SyntSubj without problems: the SyntSubj in an Amele sentence is the noun that imposes the use of these particular agreement affixes.

A problem concerning the SyntSubj in Amele comes from the category of switch-reference: in case a sentence includes two (or more) verbs, the preceding being subordinated to the following ($V^1 \leftarrow$**synt**$-V^2$), a switch-reference grammeme on V^1 is supposed to indicate whether V^2 has a SyntSubj referentially identical to that of V^1. (For instance, in *John came in and sat down* both verbs have the same SyntSubj; in *John came, and I sat down* the verbs have different SyntSubjs.) Cf. (39):

(39) Amele ($j = /ʒ/, q = /\widehat{gb}/$)

   a. |Ija| hu +**f**   +*ig*   *mad* +*ig*   +*en*
      I   come if-**SAME-SUB** 1.SG$_{SUB}$ speak 1.SG$_{SUB}$ FUT
      'If I come, [I] will.speak'.

vs. |Uqa| ho +**o?**   +*b*   *fi* |ija| *mad* +*ig*   +*en*
      he   come if-**DIF-SUB** 3.SG$_{SUB}$ if I speak 1.SG$_{SUB}$ FUT
      'If he comes, I will.speak'.

   b. |Ege| *wen* +Ø +*g*   +*en*
      we hunger give 1.PL$_{OBJ}$ 3.SG$_{SUB}$.REMOTE.PAST
      'We became hungry'. lit. '[It] us hunger gave'.

   c. |Ege| *?o*   +*?ob* +**ob**
      we REAL-GER walk 1.PL$_{SUB}$.**SAME-SUB**
      wen +Ø +*g*   +*en*
      hunger give 1.PL$_{OBJ}$ 3.SG$_{SUB}$.REMOTE.PAST
      lit. 'We walking, [it] us hunger.gave'. = 'As we walked, we became hungry'.[25]

---

[25] Two interesting details about Amele are worth mentioning.
- The semi-auxiliary (≈ light) verb 'give' has a zero stem, so that its observable forms consist solely of suffixes; see Mel'čuk 2006a: 474–475.
- The meaning 'want to Y' is expressed in Amele by means of an impersonal construction with the light verb 'give' and the imperative form of Y; the literal rendering of 'X wants to Y' is 'It gives to.X: «Y!»' (Roberts 2001: 221):

  (i) a. *Ija ma j* +*ag*   +*a*   Ø +*t*   +*ena*   'I want to eat taro'. =
       I taro eat 2.SG$_{SUB}$ IMPER give 1.SG$_{OBJ}$.3.SG$_{SUB}$ PRES   lit. '[It gives] me «Eat$_{SG}$ taro!»'.
     b. *Ege ma j* +*eig*   +*a*   Ø +*g*   +*ena*   'We want to eat taro'. =
       we taro eat 2.PL$_{SUB}$ IMPER give 1.PL$_{OBJ}$.3.SG$_{SUB}$ PRES   lit. '[It gives] us «Eat$_{PL}$ taro!»'.

Both sentences in (i) have a dummy zero subject.

d. *Eu jagel November na* |*uqa*| *odo+ʔo   +b*
this month   in he do **DIF-SUB** 3.SG$_{SUB}$
ʔul   +g   +en
leave 1.PL$_{OBJ}$ 3.SG$_{SUB}$.REMOTE.PAST
lit. 'This in November he had.done, left.[it.]to.us.he'.
[Roberts 1987: 304, (620)]

Now, Amele has an impersonal construction, which expresses physiological and psychological states of a person; the construction has a dummy zero subject $\emptyset_{(3, sg)}$ with which the verb agrees; this is shown by the Subject agreement grammemes 3, SG on the verb: see (39b). The Experiencer appears as DirO (also identified by verb agreement), and the designation of the state itself (a noun or an adjective) is a quasi-object, very much like the quasi-object noun in Persian verbal collocations; it is not cross-referenced on the verb.[26] As a result, what is found in (39b) seems to be an unproblematic construction similar to Russian impersonal constructions of the type *Nas*$_{DirO}$ *trjasët* lit. '[It] shakes us'. = 'We are shaking' or *Nas*$_{DirO}$ *klonit v son* lit. '[It] pushes us into sleep'. = 'We are sleepy', with a dummy zero SyntSubj, cf. above, (12) and (36). So far, so good. But in a two-clause sentence, such as that in (39c), the verb of the first clause, where the SyntSubj is EGE 'we', is marked as having the same SyntSubj as the verb of the second clause, while this latter has a dummy zero subject. This fact makes Roberts remark that, although EGE 'we' in the second clause is a DirO, it has some SyntSubj properties, in the first place—controlling the feature "same/ different subjects" (Roberts 2001: 204). But why do we have to say that the suffix **-ob** indicates the same **SyntSubj** in the next clause? Roberts states himself (1988) that the switch-reference in Amele may track the sequence of Themes ("same Theme/different Theme") rather than that of SyntSubjs. The detailed examples given in Roberts 1987: 292–305 also point to rather semantic character of Amele switch-reference: thus, in (39d), the SyntSubj

---

26 These nominal-verbal collocations are also known as **complex**, or **periphrastic**, **verbs**. Here are a few Persian examples (Samvelian 2012; the quasi-direct-object is in boldface):

(i) *Maryäm otaq+ra*$_{DirO}$ *žaru*   *zäd*
     lit. 'Myriam room broom hit'.   = 'Myriam swept the room'.
(ii) *Maryäm Omid+ra*$_{DirO}$ *šekast däd*
     lit. 'Myriam Omid defeat gave'.   = 'Myriam defeated Omid'.
(iii) *Maryäm Omid+ra*$_{DirO}$ **dust**   *där+äd*
     lit. 'Myriam Omid friend has'.   = 'Myriam loves Omid'.
(iv) *Maryäm Omid+ra*$_{DirO}$ **gušt**   *kärd*
     lit. 'Myriam Omid ear did'.   = 'Myriam listened to Omid'.

The collocations of this type are extremely widespread in Persian: in fact, most verbs of SAE languages correspond to V+N collocations in Persian.

is, of course, the same, but the marker of DIF-SUB signals the change of world setting—a new situation obtains. Therefore, if we accept that switch-reference in Amele marks the preservation/change of Themes (or maybe of situations), the problem disappears: it suffices to replace the names of grammemes SAME-SUB and DIF-SUB in (39c–d) by SAME-THEME and DIF-THEME.

3.6 A difficult case: the syntactic subject in Lushootseed

However, things in general are not as beautiful and well-behaved as the preceding exposition might imply. Let us consider Lushootseed, which has repeatedly been claimed not to have a SyntSubj, but—as Beck 1996 and 2000 convincingly argued—has one after all, although not without a complication.

Lushootseed. Lushootseed is a "kind of" Type 2 language—it features monopersonal agreement, but only for bi-actantial (≈ transitive) verbs: its intransitive verbs do not show agreement with its actant. Therefore, Lushootseed cannot be considered in parallel with genuine monopersonal agreement languages. Here is a relevant dataset for Lushootseed (borrowed from Beck 2000).

(40) Lushootseed (PUNCT stands for 'punctual aspect')

    a. An intransitive verb

        (i) ʔu   +ʔəƛ'   čəd   'I came'.
             PUNCT come   I

        (ii) ʔu   +ʔəƛ'   čəxʷ   'You$_{SG}$ came'.
             PUNCT come   you$_{SG}$

        (iii) ʔu   +ʔəƛ'   ti   č'ač'as   'The child came'.
              PUNCT come   the child

        (iv) ʔu   +ʔəƛ'   Ø$_{(3rd\ person)}$ 'He/She/They came'.
              PUNCT come   he/she/they

The only actant of an intransitive verb is expressed by a second-position pronominal clitic, which is a zero lexeme for the 3rd person (singular and plural).

    b. A transitive verb (LC stands for 'limited control')

        (i) ʔu   +ʔəy'+dxʷ+Ø   čəd ti   č'ač'as
             PUNCT find LC   ACT   I   the child
             'I found the child'.

        (ii) ʔu   +ʔəy'+dxʷ+Ø   čəxʷ ti   č'ač'as
             PUNCT find LC   ACT   you$_{SG}$ the child
             'You$_{SG}$ found the child'.

(iii) ʔu   +ʔəyʼ+dxʷ+Ø   Ø₍3rd person₎   ti   čʼačʼas
     PUNCT find LC ACT   he/she/they   the child
     'He/She/They found the child'.
(iv) ʔu   +ʔəyʼ+du+Ø   +bš   ti   čʼačʼas
     PUNCT find LC ACT 1.SG$_{OBJ}$ the child
     'The child found me'.
(v) ʔu   +ʔəyʼ+du+Ø   +bicid   ti   čʼačʼas
     PUNCT find LC ACT 2.SG$_{OBJ}$ the child
     'The child found you$_{SG}$'.
(vi) ʔu   +ʔəyʼ+du+Ø   +bš   čəxʷ
     PUNCT find LC ACT 1.SG$_{OBJ}$ you$_{SG}$
     'You$_{SG}$ found.me'.
(vii) ʔu   +ʔəyʼ+du+Ø +bicid   čəd
      PUNCT find LC ACT 2.SG$_{OBJ}$ I
      'I found.you$_{SG}$'.
(viii) ʔu   +ʔəyʼ+du+Ø   čəd/čəxʷ   Ø₍3rd person₎
       PUNCT find LC ACT I /you$_{SG}$ he/she/they
       'I/You$_{SG}$ found him/her/them'.

The meaning 'The child/I/You$_{SG}$ found him/her/them' is impossible to express in Lushootseed as is, since there is no physical (= non-zero) pronominal clitic expressing the 3rd person object; and a sentence of the form in (40b-iii) means 'He/She/They found the child'. The only way to verbalize the meaning 'The child found him/her/them' is to turn the Main Verb into the passive:

(ix) ʔu   +ʔəyʼ+du+**b**   Ø₍3rd person₎   ʔə   ti   čʼačʼas
     PUNCT find LC **PASS** he/she/they   by   the child

The SyntSubj in Lushootseed has five syntactic privileges out of six privileges possible (since the language has no cases, case marking—Parameter 4a—is irrelevant):

– Parameter 1. The SyntSubj depends exclusively on the MV.
– Parameter 2. It is non-omissible from the SyntS of the sentence.
– Parameter 3. It follows the MV, preceding another prepositionless actant, which is a DirO.
– Parameter 4b. Its syntactic role is targeted by the passive:

(41) ʔu   +ʔəyʼ+dxʷ+Ø   čəd   ti   čʼačʼas   'I found the child'.
     PUNCT find LC **ACT** I   the child

vs. *ʔu* +*ʔay̓ʿ*+*du*+***b***   *čəd ʔə ti čʿačʿas*   'I was.found by the child'.
     PUNCT find LC **PASS** I   by the child

Parameter 6. It is the only actant that can be expressed by special subject clitics.

However, it is not the SyntSubj that controls the person-number agreement of the Lushootseed bi-actantial (i.e. transitive) MV, but the DirO, and this only if the DirO is of the 1st or 2nd person (cf. Awa Pit, example (4), p. 127). This fact creates an additional difficulty for the declared principle that the MV, if it agrees only with one of its actants, must agree with the SyntSubj, Subsection 3.4.2, p. 149; but otherwise, it does not undermine our approach to the definition of the SyntSubj as a cross-linguistic phenomenon.

3.7 The syntactic subject: its syntactic role vs. its semantic and communicative roles

The problem of defining the SyntSubj has arisen in part as a result of the failure to strictly separate, on the one hand, the purely syntactic properties that define a syntactic element of the clause, and, on the other hand, some semantic and communicative properties characterizing that element. It is true that syntactic clause elements encode—in the ultimate analysis—semantic roles of the corresponding meanings and are tightly controlled by communicative factors. This, however, is not a reason for abandoning syntactic relations; and, by all means, this is impossible. We should simply keep in mind that in some languages the alignment of syntactic relations to semantic roles is very intricate; thus, in English, as illustrated above, a SyntSubj can correspond to a large variety of semantic roles. In other languages such alignment is more straightforward: thus, in a basic clause of Archi the SyntSubj cannot be an Agent, an Experiencer or a Cause. But even if in some cases there is a one-to-one correspondence between syntactic and semantic roles, this should not lead to confusing them (remember that a one-element set is essentially different from an element). In some languages, the correspondence between syntactic, semantic and communicative roles is close to one-to-one. Thus, speaking of Lushootseed, Beck (2000: 310) states "that although there is an unusually close 'fit' between the semantic structure of an utterance and the syntactic role that each participant ... is assigned by the grammar, this fit is not one-hundred percent and so the invocation of a syntactic role ... seems justified." This close fit is not at all astonishing: the SyntSubj as the most privileged syntactic actant tends to express the most privileged semantic role of Agent and the most privileged communicative role available to a nominal—that of the Theme, which in its turn, tends to be Given, referential and definite.

3.8 The direct object

Having dealt with the SyntSubj, I can briefly turn to the DirO—in order to round up my presentation and to show how the proposed parameters work on a larger scale. As the reader was warned, this section is limited to a bare minimum and does not include examples (for good linguistic data concerning the DirO, see Plank, ed. 1984). Without further ado, I will sketch below a universal definition of Direct Object.

Definition 3.2 – direct object
> The **direct object** is the second most privileged SSynt-actant of a transitive verb in a non-ergative **L**; what exactly are syntactic privileges in **L** has to be indicated by a list of specific DirO privileges (= properties) elaborated for **L**.

It is immediately clear that the DirO and, respectively, the **direct-objectival** SSynt-tRel are not cross-linguistically universal: according to our definition of ergative language, they are present only in non-ergative languages (barring some exceptional, derived constructions, such as, for instance, the progressive construction in Archi, p. 154) and only in clauses with a transitive MV. The DirO's syntactic privileges are determined using the same definitional parameters as those of the SyntSubj, but, of course, by different values thereof:

1. The DirO exclusively depends on a verb (the finite form, the infinitive/masdar, the participle, the converb), but not necessarily on the MV.
2. The DirO can be non-omissible from the syntactic structure of the clause.
3. The DirO's linear position is specified with respect to the governing verb and/or with respect to its other actants.
4a. The DirO can have morphological impact on the verb (= agreement L_{DirO}-**morph**→V): in many languages, a transitive verb agrees with its DirO.
4b. The DirO is involved in actant shuffling: as a result of the verb's inflection, the DirO can be promoted to SyntSubj status (the SyntSubj being demoted to Agent Complement or Oblique Object).
5. The verbs can also have morphological impact on the DirO (= government L_{DirO}←**morph**–V); the DirO is quite often marked by a special case: as a rule, the accusative or the nominative (the latter, in an ergative construction).
6. The DirO can pronominalize in a particular way.

3.9 Summing up

The conclusions concern two main aspects of the discussion: establishing and defining particular SSyntRels in particular languages (3.9.1) and their cross-linguistic universality (3.9.2).

3.9.1 Defining surface-syntactic relations

A SSyntRel **r** in the phrase $L_1\text{–}\mathbf{r}{\rightarrow}L$ of language **L** is defined exclusively by a set of parameters concerning the following properties of L_1 and L:

1) the possible syntactic types of L_1;
2) omissibility/non-omissibility of L from the Sem- and Synt-structures;
3) possible linear arrangements of L_1 and L;
4) L's morphological properties;
5) L_1's morphological properties;
6) prosodic properties of the of the $L_1\text{–}\mathbf{r}{\rightarrow}L$ phrase.

In this way, all available linguistic expressive means are taken into account. To put it differently, any SSyntRel **r** is defined strictly by statements necessary to implement the abstract phrase $L_1\text{–}\mathbf{r}{\rightarrow}L$ in an utterance.

A list of parameters necessary for the definition of SyntSubj—that is, of the **subjectival** SSyntRel—is presented in Subsection 3.2.3 above. Each SSyntRel requires, of course, its own set of definitional parameters: thus, prosody is irrelevant for SyntSubj, but it is important for different **appositive** SSyntRels in Russian (*gorod-sad* 'city [which is a] garden' vs. *gorod Sad* 'city [which is named] Sad').

All other properties of a SSyntRel (and of its depending and governing members) are characterizing, or descriptive: they specify the syntactic behavior of the SSyntRel **r** in language **L**, **r** itself being previously established based on its definitional properties.

3.9.2 Cross-linguistic universality of particular surface-syntactic relations

Surface-syntactic relations as a linguistic phenomenon are cross-linguistically universal in the following sense: they are present in all languages, appear in all sentences of a language, and involve all lexical units in a sentence.

The universality of SSyntRels is similar to the universality of parts of speech or phonemes (Dryer 1997: 116–119). Major word classes, known as parts of speech, necessarily exist in any language, but this, of course, does not mean that language L_1 has the same parts of speech as L_2: some languages do not have a class of adverbs, some others lack adverbs and adjectives. Now, all languages seem to have verbs and nouns, but this is simply due to the universalist definitions of 'verb' and 'noun': verbs are lexemes that can, without special modification, fulfill the role of the syntactic head of a clause; nouns are lexemes that can, without special modification, fulfill the role of actants of a verb. Here the similarity between the parts of speech of different languages ends: a semantic equivalent of a noun of L_1 is not necessarily a noun in L_2, since, for instance, L_1 can allow for event and property nouns (such as 'arrival' and 'beauty'), while in L_1 such meanings are implemented exclusively by verbs. The same is true about the verbs, etc. An actual part of speech of L_1 must be defined strictly within L_1, but this does prevent L_2 from having the same part of speech, albeit with different elements! Thus, nouns of L_1 do not always semantically correspond to nouns in L_2 (and vice versa), but there is a heavy overlap, and in both languages a noun can fulfill the same general syntactic role—be an actant of a verb.

Another instructive parallel with a particular SSyntRel is the nominative case. It is the case of nomination, and with such a universalist definition, any language that has cases has a nominative. But the nominatives of two languages are, as a rule, by no means fully equivalent: they can play different syntactic roles; however, for them to be called nominatives it is enough that both are used for nomination. In the same vein, the datives of two languages normally are different in their syntactic behavior (consider the Georgian or Hindi dative, which is used to mark the DirO, with the dative of classical or Slavic languages), yet they are correctly called *datives* because both mark the Receiver actant of the verbs of giving. By the way, the dative is not cross-linguistically universal; even more than that: no other case but the nominative is, since some case languages have only two cases: the nominative and the oblique; such are, for instance, Old French and Kurdish.

It is easy to multiply the examples: the Russian present tense does not have the same senses and the same syntactic uses as the present tense in German or Japanese, but this does not prevent us from calling all the corresponding grammemes PRESENT, since all of them can designate the coincidence with the moment of speech; the singular in Russian and English does not fully correspond to the Hungarian or Turkish singular; etc.

It is in this sense that some SSyntRels are cross-linguistically universal.

NB Deep-syntactic relations (Chapter 2, 2.2.1, pp. 32–35) are not considered here. The set of DSyntRels is postulated deductively for all languages; it is universal in the sense that it is cross-linguistically valid—it is sufficient for the description of deep-syntactic structures in any language (of course, under the condition that we allow for the use of fictitious lexemes: Chapter 2, 2.2.2, pp. 36*ff*). A particular DSyntRel may not appear in all languages. The DSyntRels I, II, II$_{dir.sp}$, III, ATTR, ADDRESS, APPEND and COORD seem to be universal; the DSyntRels IV, V and VI are absent from some languages; I have no solid evidence about ATTR$_{descr}$ and PSEUDO-COORD.

A set of SSyntRels is established empirically for each given language **L** (for a tentative list of SSyntRels of English, see Mel'čuk & Pertsov 1987: 85–156 and Mel'čuk 2016: 184–194). A particular SSyntRel may or may not be cross-linguistically universal. Thus, the **subjectival** SSyntRel, examined in this chapter, is universal, while the Russian **approximate-quantitative** SSyntRel (present in the phrase *knig–*approximate-quantitative→*dvadcat'* lit. 'books twenty' = 'maybe twenty books') is found in Russian, but not in most other languages. The **direct-objectival** SSyntRel is widespread, but not universal: ergative languages do not have it. I don't know whether the **indirect-objective** SSyntRel is universal or not; I have doubts about the **modificative** SSyntRel.

The cross-linguistic universality of the **subjectival** SSyntRel is due, of course, to its universalist definition as the most privileged SSyntRel of **L**.

A corrected version of Mel'čuk 2014b.

4 "Multiple subjects" and "multiple direct objects" in Korean

4.1 Introductory remarks
4.2 The problem stated:
    Is the same-case noun string a sequence of multiple subjects/multiple objects?
4.3 The prolepsis
    4.3.1 The notion of prolepsis
    4.3.2 Prolepses in Korean
4.4 The nominative vs. the subjective case
    4.4.1 The Korean nominative
    4.4.2 The Korean subjective
4.5 What are a syntactic subject and a direct object—in general and in Korean?
    4.5.1 The syntactic subject
    4.5.2 The direct object
4.6 Multiple same-case nouns in a Korean clause
    4.6.1 "Multiple subjects" in a Korean clause
        4.6.1.1 Rhematic prolepsis + subject
        4.6.1.2 Subject + agentive complement/subject of a non-finite verb form
        4.6.1.3 Subject + pseudo-conjunct
    4.6.2 "Multiple direct objects" in a Korean clause
        4.6.2.1 Indirect object + direct object
        4.6.2.2 Direct object + quasi-direct object
        4.6.2.3 Direct object of the Main Verb + direct object of a non-finite form
        4.6.2.4 Affected object + direct object
        4.6.2.5 Direct object + pseudo-conjunct
        4.6.2.6 "Quadruple direct objects"
    4.6.3 Other "multiple objects" in a Korean clause
4.7 Conclusions

4.1 Introductory remarks

For many years I have been fascinated by statements found in numerous reference books and manuals that Korean has multiple subjects [Subjs] and multiple direct objects [DirOs] in one clause; see, for instance, a detailed descriptive grammar Sohn 1994 (e.g., pp. 235 and 237), the paper MacDonald & Welch 2009 or the PhD thesis Cho 2011. It is commonly said that a simple Korean clause—that is, a clause with just one finite verb—can contain several non-coordinated subjects and several non-coordinated DirOs. Here are standard examples, one-clause sentences (1) and (2), in which sequences of "Subjs'" and, respectively, of "DirOs" are shaded (the names of grammatical cases are used in these examples in the traditional way):

(1) *Nay+**ka**   paym+**i**   musep +Ø +ta*
    I   **NOM** snake **NOM** be.fearful PRES DECL(arative)
    lit. 'I snake is.fearful'. = 'I am afraid of the snake'.

(2) *Kay+ka   John+**il**   son +**il**   mul+ess +ta*
    dog NOM   ACC   hand ACC   bite PAST DECL
    lit. 'Dog John hand bit'. = 'The dog bit John on the hand'.

Sentence (1) presents a sequence of two nouns in the case currently called nominative (marked by the suffix **-ka** after a vowel and **-i** after a consonant); both nouns are traditionally considered to be SyntSubjs. Sentence (2) presents two accusative nouns (suffixes **-lil/-il**), both considered to be DirOs.

NB There is no full parallelism between multiple nominative and multiple accusative constructions; they receive different treatments and different descriptions, as we will see in Subsections 4.6.1 and 4.6.2. In particular, sentence (1) is communicatively not neutral—unlike its English gloss; it is translated more precisely as 'It is me who is afraid of the snake' (cf. example (6a) in Subsection 4.3.2).

Longer sequences of nominative and accusative nouns are possible, but, for simplicity's sake, the discussion will be at first limited to sequences of two nominative or accusative nouns.

Transliteration and pronunciation

In this chapter, Yale Romanization of the Korean script is used—with some modifications aimed at a better one-to-one correspondence of our transliteration symbols with letters and digraphs of Korean alphabet (*hankil*). Here are some elementary pronunciation rules for the adopted transliteration:

– An unaspirated lax voiceless consonant is automatically voiced between vowels and semi-voiced in the word-initial position, so that *Maryka* is pronounced as [mæriga], *hata* 'do' as [hada], etc.
– A doubled consonant letter indicates "tenseness": kk = /k̄/, ss = /s̄/, etc. A tense, or strong, consonant is never voiced.
– /l/ has an allophone [r] in an intervocalic position.
– The letter *e* represents [ə] or [ʌ]; the digraphs *ay, ey* and *oy* stand for [ɛ], [e] and [œ].

Sequences of non-coordinated nouns that are in the same grammatical case and are considered to play the same syntactic role ($-\mathbf{r}{\rightarrow}N_{1\text{-CASE-x}} + -\mathbf{r}{\rightarrow}N_{2\text{-CASE-x}} + ...$) are not such a rarity cross-linguistically: a similar situation, although with respect to multiple nominatives only, is observed in Japanese (for instance, Kuno 1973: 34, 62*ff*). Several caseless languages allow for sequences of non-coordinated nouns in the same syntactic role—for instance, Mandarin and quite a few languages across the linguistic board, such as Totonac (Beck 2016) and Kinyarwanda (Kimenyi 1980, Dryer 1983). Multiple N_{CASE-x}s are well known in ancient languages (Ancient Greek, Sanskrit, Biblical Hebrew, Old Church Slavonic): '**The God his voice** entered the room.', 'People admired **the King the face**', 'He was killed **by elephants by their legs**', etc. Here is an actual example of triple accusatives from the "Iliad":

(3) *Idomene +ùs   Oinóma +on   bále   gastér+a   méssē+n*
    Idomeneus NOM Oinomaos ACC struck belly ACC middle ACC
    lit. 'Idomeneus Oinomaos struck belly middle'. =
    'Idomeneus struck Oinomaos in the middle of the belly'.

However, in order to simplify my task, I will leave out any attempt at typological generalizations, limiting myself to Korean.

There is no shortage of studies dedicated to multiple same-case noun sequences in Korean; here I cannot even try a review of the literature.

The goal of this chapter is to establish for Korean some clause elements and their case encodings that would ensure a straightforward transition from a dependency syntactic structure of a Korean sentence to the sentence itself. Therefore, the legitimate question for the examples that are given below is not "Why this expression is described as such and such clause element?"; each example is intended to illustrate the following implication: "**If** this expression is described as such and such clause element, **then** the passage from the syntactic structure to this sentence is simple and consistent with General Syntax." The idea is to put Korean "multiple subjects" and "multiple objects" in the perspective of General Syntax.

Three specific problems with the following discussion

The nature of the present chapter leads to (at least) three complications that a reader has to deal with: the first is related to the character of the Korean language, the second is brought in by the topic itself, and the third one is very general, almost philosophical.

1) Due—at least in part—to the agglutinative character of Korean, the case suffixes can be omitted in various contexts; it is often the case that a given Korean sentence, especially stripped of its spoken prosody, allows for several readings. On the other hand, a given meaning can be expressed by means of different syntactic structures, which results in different, but more or less synonymous sentences. However, these additional options are, as a rule, logically irrelevant for the exposition and can be ignored.

2) The study of multiple clause elements in Korean requires the consideration of the quasi-totality of Korean grammar: the morphology and semantics of grammatical cases, some inflectional categories of the verb (different gerunds), the communicative structure (Rheme ~ Theme, Focus, Contrast, etc.), word order, syntactic intonation and phrasing, and the inventory of the clause elements. It goes without saying that it is impossible to seriously tackle all these outstanding tasks here. I simply have to be less than precise and leave out several details that, with all their importance, are again logically irrelevant for the goals of this chapter.
3) Last, but not least, the proposed description of an interesting syntactic phenomenon of Korean is carried out within the framework of the Meaning-Text perspective, based on general typological considerations, dependency syntactic representation and a formal system of linguistic notions and terms.

4.2 The problem stated: Is the same-case noun string a sequence of multiple subjects/multiple objects?

The tendency to interpret a grammatical case as a marker of a specific syntactic role is quite understandable. In conformity with this tendency, many Koreanists conclude that a sequence of the same-case nouns is a sequence of the same clause elements. As a result, they speak of multiple subjects and multiple direct objects in Korean. However, general linguistics tells us that a given Main Verb in a clause cannot have more than one subject or more than one direct object (without counting, of course, coordinated Subjs and DirOs). The Subj and the DirO are syntactic actants of a lexical unit L; L's syntactic actants correspond to L's semantic actants. But:

> Semantic and main syntactic actants of a lexical unit L—that is, the subject, the direct object and the indirect object—are not repeatable with L. In other words, the Main Verb L of a clause can have just one Synt-actant of each of these three types.

This is so for an obvious semantic reason: each semantic actant saturates a specific semantic slot of L, implementing one of the arguments of the predicate 'L', and a given semantic slot cannot receive, by its very nature, more than one element within a given utterance. Since the three main syntactic actants express semantic actants, the same is true of L's main syntactic slots.

NB The element filling a semantic slot in 'L' can be either **one** semantic entity or **one list** of semantic entities. In the latter case, the corresponding syntactic element (= a phrase) that fills a corresponding syntactic slot of L is a chain of conjoined sentence elements, so that a sentence can actually have several conjoined Subjs or conjoined DirOs (*John, Peter and Mary* arrived or *I saw John, Peter and Mary*). But a given syntactic actant slot can never have a multiple expression by non-coordinated actants.

Therefore, based on general linguistic knowledge, it is possible to state the following:

‖ There cannot be multiple Subjs or multiple DirOs in Korean.

Having said this, I have to solve the contradiction between the most Korean scholars' statements and the corresponding general linguistic statements. In order to do this, I will examine strings of Korean same-case nouns and explain what they are in reality. And for this, I need to answer two questions:

- What is the Subj and the DirO—in general and in Korean?
- What are the elements of a "suspect" Korean same-case noun sequence that are neither subjects nor direct objects?

But before these questions can be attacked, two auxiliary notions absolutely needed for the discussion have to be introduced: **prolepsis** (3) and **nominative case** (4).

4.3 The prolepsis

4.3.1 The notion of prolepsis

A clause element illustrated by the French sentence in (4), which manifests three such (boldfaced) elements, is well-known in linguistics, but strangely has no accepted name:

(4) French
Jacqueline, son père, le frigo*, elle le lui a refilé*
lit. 'Jacqueline, her father, the fridge, she it to him has passed'.

This clause element can be called **prolepsis**. More than 65 years ago, A. Xolodovič (1954: 253–254) described this clause element in Korean, calling it "a complement of a special kind."

Definition 4.1 – prolepsis (Mel'čuk 2001: 130*ff*)

> A lexical unit L (with its syntactic dependents) appearing in a clause is a **prolepsis** if and only if L satisfies simultaneously the following four conditions:
> 1. Syntactically, L is only loosely linked to the rest of the clause: it is neither a syntactic actant of the Main Verb nor one of its circumstantials.
> 2. Linearly, L is positioned clause-initially.
> 3. Prosodically, L is "insulated" from the clause by a pause, a stress and a special intonation contour.
> 4. Morphologically (in a language with cases), L is most often—but not exclusively!—in the nominative, the least marked case. (In Korean, a prolepsis can be marked also by the subjective case, see Subsection 4.4.2.)

A prolepsis L normally serves to express a communicative value assigned to the meaning 'L'—more precisely, the Rheme or the Theme of the clause.

The **Rheme** (also known as *comment*) is the part of the clause that states what the Speaker wants the clause to communicate; the **Theme** (*topic*) is the part of the clause about which the Rheme is stated (e.g., Mel'čuk 2001 and 2012–2015: vol. 1, 306*ff*). In a number of languages, a meaning selected by the Speaker to be presented as the Rheme or the Theme can or must be implemented as a prolepsis.

NB The communicative organization of a clause is quite complicated and cannot be properly dealt with here. However, it is useful to indicate its two following properties.
– The Comm-organization is essentially **semantic**, that is, the distribution of Rhemes and Themes concerns primarily the **meaning** of the clause; the marking of Comm-organization on the syntactic level (and in the clause itself) reflects its surface implementation, which does not stand in one-to-one correspondence with its semantic source.
– The Comm-organization is **recursive**, that is, a thematic or rhematic area can have within it another Rheme ~ Theme division of a lower level.

Thus, the sentence in (6a) has the following Comm-organization on the semantic level:

'[[what is long]$_{Theme^2}$ [is the trunk]$_{Rheme^2}$]$_{Theme^1}$ [at the elephant]$_{Rheme^1}$'

Prolepses, which are widespread in colloquial French, are also possible in English, albeit used rather sparingly: ***John***, *he is a nice guy*. But South-East Asian languages abound in prolepses, and Korean is no exception.

4.3.2 Prolepses in Korean

Korean prolepses are characterized by the following four features:

1. A rhematic prolepsis is marked by the subjective case (**-ka/-i**), see Subsection 4.4.2 below. A thematic prolepsis carries a special Theme marker **-nin/-in**,

4.3 The prolepsis — 185

which is most frequently added to a bare noun stem—that is, to the nominative form; however, the **-nin/-in** marker can also attach to a non-nominative case form, an adverb and a converb:

(5) a. *Seoul+ey*$_{DAT}$*+nin salam+Ø manhta*
   lit. 'In.Seoul$_{THEME}$ person be.many'. = 'In Seoul there are many people'.
   b. *Usen+in nay+ka sakwa+lil mekessta*
   lit. 'First$_{THEME}$, I apple ate'.
   c. *Nay+ka sakwa+lil mek+ko+nin siptta*
   lit. '[I apple eating]$_{THEME}$, [I] want'. = 'To eat an apple, I want it'.

   NB Note an interesting asymmetry in that rhematicity is expressed by a grammatical case, while thematicity has a special marker **-nin/-in**, which can combine with the marker of a case form. For more on the meaning and use of **-nin/-nin**, see Lee & Ramsey 2000: 163–166.

2. Prolepses can be multiple, so that a clause can have several thematic and/or rhematic prolepses (Sohn 1994: 203; Chang 1996: 200); for simplicity's sake, I limit the examples to two prolepses (shaded):

(6) a. [*K^{h}okkili+ka*]$_{Rheme}$ [*k^{h}o +ka*]$_{Rheme}$ *kil +Ø +ta*
   elephant SUBJ   trunk SUBJ   be.long PRES DECL(arative)
   'It is the elephant [such that] it is [his] trunk [that] is long'.
   b. [*K^{h}okkili+Ø +nin*]$_{Theme}$ [*k^{h}o +Ø +nin*]$_{Theme}$ *kil +Ø +ta*
   elephant NOM TH   trunk NOM TH   be.long PRES DECL
   'As for the elephant, as for [its] trunk, [it] is long'.
   c. [*K^{h}o +Ø +nin*]$_{Theme}$ [*k^{h}okkili +ka*]$_{Rheme}$ *kil +Ø +ta*
   trunk NOM TH   elephant SUBJ   be.long PRES DECL
   'As for trunk, it is the elephant [whose trunk] is long'.
   d. [*K^{h}okkili+Ø +nin*]$_{Theme}$ [*k^{h}o +ka*]$_{Rheme}$ *kil +Ø +ta*
   elephant NOM TH   trunk SUBJ   be.long PRES DECL
   'As for the elephant, it is trunk [that] is long'.

   NB Korean is a strong Pro-Drop language; no pronouns coreferential with prolepses can appear in the clause in the roles of SyntSubj, DirO, Possessor, etc.

3. Thematic and rhematic prolepses appear mainly in Theme – Rheme linear order, as seen in (6c–d).

4. A Korean prolepsis can follow a regular clause element, which is fronted for communicative purposes (boxed; SUBJ is the subjective case, see next section):

(7) [Kay+hantey] [John+in]_Theme son +i   mul+li   +ess +ko
    dog DAT   TH   hand SUBJ bite PASS PAST CONV(erb)
    [Mary+nin]_Theme tali+ka   mul+li   +ess +ta
        TH   leg SUBJ   bite PASS PAST DECL
    lit. 'By.dog John hand being.bitten Mary leg was.bitten'. =
    'It is by the dog that John had his hand bitten and Mary, her leg'.

In (7), the thematic prolepses *Johnin* and *Marynin* follow the Agent Complement *kayhantey* 'by.dog'.

NB Korean has over 50 converbs—non-finite verbal forms used as modifiers of the Main Verb. These converbs express various meanings: manner, purpose, intention, reason, result, concomitance, etc. However, since this is irrelevant for the present discussion, the type of the converb will not be indicated.

4.4 The nominative vs. the subjective case

Now an important correction has to be introduced: it concerns the name of what is traditionally called the *nominative case* in Korean grammar.

4.4.1 The Korean nominative

The case in **-ka/-i** is systematically called the *nominative* in Korean grammar, since it is used to mark the syntactic subject (as in Latin!). However, this use of the term is incorrect.

Definition 4.2 – nominative case (Mel'čuk 1988: 208, 255–256, 2006a: 110*ff*, especially 152–153)

‖ The **nominative** is the case of the form of the noun used for nomination.

The genuine nominative case exists, of course, in Korean and has the zero marker **-Ø**, which is quite typical of the nominative in languages of the world: *na+Ø* 'I', *kay+Ø* 'dog', *namu+Ø* 'tree', *salam+Ø* 'person'; Korean grammarians refer to it as the "basic form" of a noun or—as in Xolodovič 1954: 54—the "basic case." The nominative is used in Korean dictionaries as the lexicographic form, as it should be; it appears in texts in various syntactic roles:

(8) Possible syntactic roles of a nominative noun form

Subject	*John+Ø kanta* 'John goes (somewhere)'.
DirO	*Na+Ø John+Ø ponta* 'I John see'.
IndirO	*Ne+Ø John+Ø kike ču+ess+ni?* 'You John this gave?'
Copular attribute	*Na+Ø sensayŋ+Ø ita* 'I teacher am'.
Adnominal attribute	*salam+Ø moksoli* 'person voice' = 'human voice'
Direction circumstantial	*Seoul+Ø kanta* '[I/You/He/... to] Seoul go/goes'.
Address	*Sensayŋnim+Ø, ili osipsio!* 'Respected teacher, come here!'
Thematic prolepsis	*Na+Ø+nin kanta* 'I [= As for me] [I] go'.

NB 1. As one can see, the Theme marker **-nin/-in** is added to the form of the nominative, which is the expected grammatical case of a prolepsis. (This was clearly stated in Xolodovič 1954: 57.)
2. The zero marked nominative can replace the subjective in **-ka/-i** (see immediately below), the accusative in **-lil/-il** and the genitive in **-iy** without affecting the meaning (especially, in colloquial speech).

Therefore, the case in **-ka/-i** is not a nominative. Since it is used to mark all types of SyntSubj, it can be called the *subjective*.

4.4.2 The Korean subjective

Definition 4.3 – subjective case (Mel'čuk 1988: 263, 2006a: 153)

> The **subjective** is the case used first and foremost for marking the syntactic subject of any type, but which cannot serve for nomination.

The Korean subjective marks, of course, the SyntSubj, this being its main, but not only, function. It also marks at least the following three secondary syntactic roles:

1. The <u>attribute of the copula</u> or of a copula-like verb, as in (9):

(9) a. *John+i   sensayŋ+i   ani   +ta*   'John is not a teacher'.
        SUBJ   teacher SUBJ   be.not DECL

   b. *John+i   sensayŋ+i   toy   +ess +ta*   'John became a teacher'.
        SUBJ   teacher SUBJ   become PAST DECL

2. The <u>agentive complement</u> [AgCo] of a nominalized, adjectivalized or adverbialized verb (≈ converb) in (at least) two constructions.

– First, the subjective case marks the AgCo of the manner converb in an analytical causative construction «V_{CONV(erb)} + HATA 'make'»; this AgCo semantically is the Causee Actor, as in (10):

(10) a. *John+i   Mary+ka* ←agent-compl-[*čʰayk+il*]—*ilk +ke   hay +ss +ta*
         SUBJ   **SUBJ**   book ACC read CONV make PAST DECL
    lit. 'John made Mary reading book', where *Mary* is an AgCo of the converb *ilkke* 'reading'.

This causative construction has two further "case frames"—with different cases of the Causee Actor noun:

   b. *John+i   Mary+lil   čʰayk+il   ilk +ke   hay +ss +ta*
         SUBJ   **ACC**   book ACC   read CONV make PAST DECL
   c. *John+i   Mary+eykey   čʰayk+il   ilk +ke   hay +ss +ta*
         SUBJ   **DAT**   book ACC   read CONV make PAST DECL

The subjective on the Causee Actor = agentive complement (here, MARY) alternates with the accusative and the dative (the dative indicates voluntary agentivity of the Causee Actor). The use of an N_{SUBJ} as an AgCo with a manner converb in Korean is similar to the use of an N_{NOM} as an AgCo of an infinitive in Portuguese (as in **Ter eu**$_{NOM}$ *saúde é bom* lit. '**To.have I** health is good'. = 'It is good that I have health'.) or of a gerund in Spanish (as in *Nos casamos hace 50 años* **estando yo** *sin trabajo* lit. 'We married 50 years ago, being I without work'.)

– Second, the subjective case marks the AgCo of a nominalized or adjectivalized verb in what corresponds to a completive or a relative clause in an SAE language, as in:

(11) a. ⟦*John+i*⟧   *čʰayk+il   ssu +m*
         SUBJ   book ACC   write **NOMIN**(alizer)
    'John book write.fact' = 'that John wrote a book'
   b. ⟦*John+i*⟧   *ssu +n*   *čʰayk*
         SUBJ   write **ADJ**(ectivalizer)   book
    'John written book' = 'book that John wrote'

3. The <u>oblique object</u> of a parametric verb ('weigh', 'be.long', 'cost'), as in (12):

(12) *I   čʰayk+i   paek   ⟦kram+i⟧   naka +n +ta*
     this book SUBJ   hundred   gram **SUBJ** weigh PRES DECL
    'This book weighs 100 grams'.

4.4 The nominative vs. the subjective case

The most important property of the Korean subjective, which it shares with the Japanese subjective case in **-ga**, is its use to mark the Rheme (or the Rhematic Focus) of the clause (Chang 1996: 200); two cases have to be distinguished.

In the simplest case, we have a rhematic subject in the subjective case (boxed):

(13) [$K^h okkili + \emptyset \quad +nin$]$_{\text{Theme}}$ $\boxed{k^h o \quad +ka}_{\text{Rheme}}$ $kil \quad +\emptyset \quad +ta$
  elephant NOM TH   trunk SUBJ   be.long PRES DECL
  'As for the elephant, it is his trunk that is long'. ≈
  'With elephants, what is long is their trunk'.

Sentence (13) is good as an answer to the question *As for elephants, what is long with them?* The N$_{\text{SUBJ}}$ is syntactically the SyntSubj, and communicatively the Rheme.

A more complex situation obtains when the subjective marks a rhematic prolepsis (boxed):

(14) $\boxed{Nay+ka}$ John+i   čoh   +ta
  I **SUBJ**   SUBJ be.likable DECL
  'I like John'. = lit. '[It is] I [to whom] John is.likable'.

— Korean allows for an even more complex picture: the subjective case can mark as rhematic a clause element that is different from the SyntSubj, is not a prolepsis and is already marked by another case; the result is what is known as "case stacking" (boxed; Schütze 2001: 194):

(15) $\boxed{Na+eykey+ka}$ paym+i   musep +∅   +ta
  I DAT **SUBJ**   snake SUBJ   be.fearful PRES DECL
  'I am afraid of snakes'. = lit. '[It is] to.me [that] snake is.fearful', where *naeykey* 'to.me' is an IndirO.

The phenomenon of case stacking led some researchers to say that **-ka** and **-i** suffixes are homophonous: each marks either the subjective case or the Rheme (see, for instance, Schütze 2001). However, the subjective has still another suffix— namely, **-kkeyse**, which is honorific; it also can be stacked in a corresponding situation. Thus, not only **-ka** and **-i**, but **-kkeyse** as well should be considered homophonous, which is jarring. In addition, the accusative suffix **-lil/-il** is also used to express the Rheme, thus again producing case stacking (Sohn 1994: 184):

(16) *John+in Mary+eykey+lil ka+ss+ta* 'As for John, it is to Mary that he went'.

Should we see the homophony "accusative *vs.* rhematization" in this suffix, too?

On the one hand, the use of grammatical cases for the expression of communicative values and referentiality is well-known cross-linguistically (Tibetan, Yukaghir, Daghestanian languages); on the other, the Korean subjective and accusative carry the nuance of focusing (emphasis, contrast) even when used in their genuine syntactic function. Therefore, I prefer to consider the corresponding markers to be case suffixes, allowing for rhematizing behavior.

Fortunately (for me), the solution of this additional problem is irrelevant to my topic here.

Summing up, the "suspect" same-case noun strings are not $N_{1\text{-NOM}}$ $N_{2\text{-NOM}}$ ... $N_{n\text{-NOM}}$, but $N_{1\text{-SUBJ}}$ $N_{2\text{-SUBJ}}$ ... $N_{n\text{-SUBJ}}$. This correction does not, however, affect the essence of the problem considered here—namely, the question whether such a string is a string of surface-syntactic subjects. It was implied above and will be shown below that it is not.

NB Some Korean grammarians speak of the use of the subjective to mark a direct object (e.g., Sohn 1994: 237; the boxing is mine—IM):
  (i) *Nay+ka* ⟦*kohyaŋ+i*⟧ *kɨlip+ess+ta*
    lit. 'As.for.me, hometown lacked'. = 'I missed [my] hometown'.
  (ii) *Nay+ka* ⟦*sensayŋnim+i*⟧ *musep+ess+ta*
    lit. 'As.for.me, respected.teacher was.frightening'. = 'I was.afraid of [the] respected.teacher'.

The boxed N_{SUBJ}s are described in Sohn 1994 as DirOs. This is, however, a simple misunderstanding provoked by the English translation. Korean KɨLIP means 'X lacks to Y' rather than 'Y misses X'; in this respect, Korean is like French: *Ma ville natale me manque* lit. 'My hometown to.me lacks'. Analogously, MUSEPTA means 'X is fearful for Y' rather than 'Y is afraid of X'. The boxed nouns are quite regular Subjects.

4.5 What are a syntactic subject and a direct object—in general and in Korean?

4.5.1 The syntactic subject

Definition 4.4 – syntactic subject (Chapter 3, Definition 3.1, p. 135)

|| The **syntactic subject** [SyntSubj] is the most privileged surface-syntactic actant in of the Main Verb language **L**.

Although the definition of SyntSubj is language-universal, its privileges must be specified for each language. Based on the list of universal definitional parameters of a SSynt-clause element (Chapter 3, Table 3.1, p. 124), it is possible to formulate the five privileges of the SSynt-subject in Korean:

1) The SyntSubj can depend only on the Main Verb [MV], which is a genuine finite verb or a predicative adjective (definitional parameter 1 in Chapter 3, Table 3.1).

A clause that underwent adjectivalization or nominalization of its Main Verb ceases to be a clause and cannot have a SyntSubj; the main SSynt-actant of an adjectivalized or nominalized verb is its agentive complement.

2) The SyntSubj cannot be omitted from the SSyntS of the sentence (definitional parameter 2 in Chapter 3, Table 3.1). In a one-word sentence of the type *John+i+ta* 'There is John' the noun JOHN appears in the predicative form (lit. 'John is'), and it is difficult to call it Synt-subject; but it is an obvious SyntSubj in the SSyntS of this sentence (cf. Chapter 3, 3.2.4.2, **NB** in Comment 2, p. 126).

3) The SyntSubj linearly precedes all other MV's actants—with the exception of rhematic elements, which can be fronted; this corresponds to the definitional parameter 3 in Chapter 3, Table 3.1. (The thematically-loaded clause elements that can precede the SyntSubj are **prolepses** and, therefore, not actants.)

4) The SyntSubj is affected by the valence-changing inflection of the MV. Namely, it expresses the "endpoint" of passivization of the MV: the DirO of the active form of the MV becomes the SyntSubj of its passive (definitional parameter 4b in Chapter 3, Table 3.1).[1]

---

1 Clause elements mistakenly taken for SyntSubjects in Korean

1. Sometimes the dative IndirO of a verb or of an adjective of affection/possession is called SyntSubj (Kim & Sells 2010: 609):

   (i) Sensayŋ+nim+kkey   čʰayk+i   manh   +ta
        teacher HON DAT.HON   book SUBJ   be.many DECL
        lit. 'To.respected.teacher books are many'. = 'The teacher has many books'.

   However, the boxed clause element is the subject only in English translation. It is a typical IndirO fronted for communicative and pragmatic reasons. Note that it does not obligatorily impose honorification on the MV (although the honorific form *manh+si+ta* makes the sentence more acceptable).

2. A noun in the locative is not the subject in (ii), either (although some consider it to be a subject):

   (ii) *Hoysa +eyse Ø   na+Ø   hantʰey   pʰosaŋkim+il   ču +ess +ta*
        company LOC   «they» I NOM   to   award   ACC   give PAST DECL
        lit. 'In company, «they» gave to me an award'.

   The SyntSubj here is a zero lexeme, meaning 'indefinite people'—in conformity with Han's (2004, 2006) proposal: $\emptyset_{(pl)}^{«people»}$. It corresponds nicely to the Rus. zero pronoun $\emptyset_{(3, pl)}^{«people»}$ (*V kompanii mne dali premiju* 'In company, «they» gave me award'.) and to the Fr. and Ger. non-zero pronouns ON and MAN. This zero lexeme has a clearly human reference (as it is to be expected):

   (iii) a. *Toŋmulwen+eyse $\emptyset_{(pl)}^{«people»}$ halu+ey   tu +kki   meki +lil   ču +n   +ta*
           zoo   LOC   «they»   day DAT two times   fodder ACC   give PRES DECL
           'In the zoo, «they» give fodder [to animals] twice a day'.
   vs. b. **Toŋmulwen+eyse $\emptyset_{(pl)}^{«people»}$ halu+ey   tu +kki   meki +lil   mek+nin +ta*
           zoo   LOC   «they»   day DAT two times   fodder ACC   eat PRES DECL
           'In the zoo, *«they» [= animals] eat fodder twice a day'.

(17) *Koyaŋi+ka   čwi   +lil   mek+Ø   +ess +ta*
    cat   SUBJ mouse ACC eat ACT PAST DECL
    'The cat ate the mouse'.

vs. *Čwi   +ka   koyaŋi+hantey   mek+hi   +ess +ta*
    mouse SUBJ cat   DAT   eat   PASS PAST DECL
    'The mouse was.eaten by the cat'.

5) The SyntSubj is the only MV's actant that accepts the honorific suffix **-kkeyse** ≈ 'highly respected' of the subject-marking subjective case (definitional parameter 5 in Chapter 3, Table 3.1):[2]

(18) *Eme   +nim+**kkeyse**   ka+si   +ess +ta*
    mother HON **SUBJ**   go HON PAST DECL

    'Mother went (somewhere)'.

---

2 Honorification in Korean

Honorification imposed on the MV by an actant is sometimes considered to be another privilege of the Korean SyntSubj. This is, however, incorrect:

– On the one hand, a SyntSubj does not impose honorification on some verbs (O'Grady 1991: 102):

(i) *John+eykey   sensayŋ+**nim**+i   *p^{h}ilyoha +**si**   +ta*   [the correct form is *p^{h}ilyoha+ta*]
    DAT   teacher HON SUBJ   be.needed HON DECL
    lit. 'To.John the.respected.teacher is.needed'. = 'John needs a respected teacher'.

– On the other hand, other actants of the MV (or even their Possessors) and prolepses can impose honorification on it (Gerdts & Youn 1989: 3 and Jang 1997: 36):

(ii) *Sensayŋ+**nim**+iy   elkul+ey   paykmuk+i   mut   +**isi**   +ess +ta*
    teacher HON GEN   face DAT   chalk   SUBJ smudge HON PASS DECL
    'The chalk respectfully.smudged the respected.teacher's face'.

(iii) *Sensayŋ+**nim**+kkeyse   son +i   čaku+**si**   +ta*
    teacher HON SUBJ.HON   hand SUBJ small HON DECL
    lit. 'It is the respected.teacher whose hands are respectfully.small'. =
    'The respected.teacher has small hands'.

(iv) *John+i   sensayŋ+**nim**+il   ap^{h}u+**si**   +ta +ko   mit   +ess +ta*
    SUBJ   teacher HON ACC   sick HON DECL CONV believe PAST DECL
    'John believes the respected.teacher to be respectfully.sick'.

In (ii), honorification is imposed on the Main Verb by the Possessor of an OblO, in (iii) by a rhematic prolepsis, and in (iv), the DirO of the MV imposes honorification on a converb!

Honorification (as well as reflexivization) is controlled in Korean by the semantic role of the corresponding sentence elements. Cf.: "Phenomena such as reflexive interpretation and honorific agreement are sensitive to the most 'prominent' of a verb's **semantic** arguments" (O'Grady 1991: 105; emphasis added—IM).

4.5.2 The direct object

Definition 4.5 – direct object (Chapter 3); this is a simplified version of Definition 3.2 (p. 174).

> The direct object is the second most privileged surface-syntactic actant in a non-ergative language **L**.

The DirO exists only in non-ergative languages (Chapter 3, Subsection 3.2.6, p. 134); its definition is language-universal, but its privileges must be specified for each language individually. In Korean, the privileges of a DirO are:

1) The DirO tends to linearly follow all other MV's actants—that is, to be placed immediately before the MV (barring a Quasi-DirO).

   NB A quasi-direct object (and a pseudo-subject) are clause elements different from the DirO and the SyntSubj; on the **quasi-direct-objectival-2** surface-syntactic relation in Persian, see Chapter 2, Section 2.4, No. 9, p. 55, and Mel'čuk 2012–2015: vol. 3, 431; on the **pseudo-subjectival** surface-syntactic relation in English, see Chapter 2, Section 2.4, No. 6, p. 51, and Mel'čuk 2012–2015: vol. 3, 445.

2) The DirO is the only MV's actant that accepts the accusative case which does not alternate with any other case except for the nominative.

3) The DirO is the only MV's actant that can be promoted to SyntSubj status by MV's passivization.

   NB The IndirO is defined in the same way: it is the third most privileged actant, whose privileges have to be specified for each individual language; etc.

4.6 Multiple same-case nouns in a Korean clause

After lengthy and fairly cumbersome preparations, the ground is ready for answering the main question of this chapter (Section 4.2, p. 182):

> What actually are, from a syntactic viewpoint, sequences of same-case nouns in Korean?

Several linguists in the past took steps towards a correct analysis of $N_{1\text{-CASE}} N_{2\text{-CASE}} \ldots N_{n\text{-CASE}}$ sequences in Korean. Thus, O'Grady 1991: 235–242 proposes a fine analysis of the N_{ACC} that is in a collocational link with the verb HATA 'make', insisting on its special syntactic role (which I propose to call quasi-direct object). In a similar way, Sohn 1994: 204 explicitly says that in sentence (19) "the predicate is directly related to the last NP which is its subject [boxing is added—IM]. The other preceding ... NPs are best considered topics."

(19) Nay+ka   čʰa+ka   tʰaie+ka   kumeŋ+i   na   +ss   +ta
     I SUBJ   car SUBJ   tire SUBJ   hole SUBJ   occur   PAST   DECL
lit. 'I car tire hole occurred'. = 'I have a hole in a tire of my car'.

However, I don't know of a systematic overview and formal description of same-case noun sequences in Korean. I undertake such overview here, beginning with so-called "multiple subjects" (4.6.1), then considering "multiple direct objects" (4.6.2), and finishing with a few remarks about "other multiple objects" (4.6.3).

4.6.1 "Multiple subjects" in a Korean clause

A Korean clause can contain several consecutive nouns in the subjective case, but only one of them is the surface-syntactic subject of the clause's Main Verb. Let us consider two consecutive N_{SUBJ}s; three situations are to be examined.

1) **$N_{1\text{-}SUBJ}$ and $N_{2\text{-}SUBJ}$ are syntactically not linked**

   a) $N_{1\text{-}SUBJ}$ and $N_{2\text{-}SUBJ}$ depend in parallel on the Main Verb: $N_{1\text{-}SUBJ}$ is a rhematic prolepsis and $N_{2\text{-}SUBJ}$ is the subject (4.6.1.1).
   b) $N_{1\text{-}SUBJ}$ is the SyntSubj of the Main Verb, and $N_{2\text{-}SUBJ}$ is the AgCo (or the SyntSubj?) of a non-finite verbal form, i.e., of a converb (4.6.1.2).

2) **$N_{1\text{-}SUBJ}$ and $N_{2\text{-}SUBJ}$ are syntactically linked**

   c) $N_{2\text{-}SUBJ}$ is a pseudo-conjunct of $N_{1\text{-}SUBJ}$, this latter being the SyntSubj of the Main Verb (4.6.1.3).

4.6.1.1 Rhematic prolepsis + subject

The $N_{2\text{-}SUBJ}$ is the SyntSubj, the $N_{1\text{-}SUBJ}$ being syntactically a prolepsis that expresses the Rheme of the clause. This description was explicitly proposed in O'Grady 1991: 121*ff.* Lee & Ramsey 2000: 144 say that $N_{1\text{-}SUBJ}$ is, so to speak, a "subject" of the whole following clause rather than that of its MV; see also Kim & Sells 2010: 607, where several important references are given that buttress the treatment of $N_{1\text{-}SUBJ}$ as a prolepsis, although they do not use this term.

The N_{SUBJ}s that compose the string under consideration have the following important semantic property: the $N_{2\text{-}SUBJ}$ and the $N_{1\text{-}SUBJ}$ are linked by a metonymic semantic relation. For instance, '$N_{2\text{-}SUBJ}$ is a part of $N_{1\text{-}SUBJ}$', or '$N_{2\text{-}SUBJ}$ is located in/on $N_{1\text{-}SUBJ}$', or else '$N_{2\text{-}SUBJ}$ happens during $N_{1\text{-}SUBJ}$':

(20) a. *John+i* |kʰo +**ka**| kil +∅ +ta
     SUBJ   nose SUBJ   be.long PRES DECL
     '[It is] John [whose] nose is long'.
  b. *Tʰakča+**ka*** |čʰayk+**i**| manh +ta
     table SUBJ   book SUBJ   be.many DECL
     '[It is the] table [where] books are many'.
  c. *Pom +i* |kkočʰ +**i**| manh +ta
     spring SUBJ flower SUBJ be.many DECL
     '[It is the] spring [when] flowers are many'.

The $N_{2\text{-SUBJ}}$ can also represent a rhematic prolepsis; cf. (21), where the nominal clause elements have the same forms as in (13):

(21) [*Kʰokkili+∅ +nin*]$_{\text{Theme}}$ [*kʰo +**ka***]$_{\text{Rheme}}$ *kil* +∅ +*ta*
     elephant NOM TH   trunk SUBJ   be.long PRES DECL
     'As for the elephant, it is his trunk, [it] is long'.

In (21), the SyntSubj is a pronominal lexeme 'it', which does not appear in the sentence.

In (22), the first two N_{SUBJ}s are rhematic prolepses, the last one being the SyntSubj:

(22) *John+i* *enehak +i* |*koŋpu +**ka***| *toy* +*ess* +*ta*
     SUBJ   linguistics SUBJ study$_{(N)}$ SUBJ be.made PAST DECL
     lit. '[It is] John [and] linguistics [that] study was.made'. =
     'A study was done of linguistics by John'.

> **NB** Sentence (22) can be also obtained from a different SSyntS. Namely, JOHN is a rhematic prolepsis; ENEHAK 'linguistics' is the SyntSubj; and KOŊPU 'study$_{(N)}$' is the PseudoSubj of the light verb TOYTA, parallel to the Quasi-DirO of the light verb HATA (4.6.2.2): '[It is by] John [that] linguistics was study done'.

4.6.1.2 Subject + agentive complement/subject of a non-finite verb form

This situation is found in a phrasal causative construction with the verb HATA 'make' and the converb (= gerund) in **-ke** of the lexical verb, see (10a), repeated here as (23a), as well as in constructions with other non-finite forms, see (23b):

(23) a. |*John+i*| *Mary+**ka*** *čʰayk+il* *ilk +ke* *hay +ss +ta*
        SUBJ   SUBJ   book ACC   read CONV make PAST DECL
        'John made Mary read a book'.

b. <u>John+i</u>   Mary+ka   čʰayk+il   ilk +in +ta +ko   mit +nin +ta
   SUBJ   SUBJ book ACC read PRES DECL CONV believe PRES DECL
'John believes Mary is.reading a book'.

In both sentences, *John$_i$* is the SyntSubj of the Main Verb, and *Mary$_{ka}$* is the AgCo (or the SyntSubj) of the gerund (*ilkke* and *ilkintako*).

NB The agentive complement can probably be considered to be the syntactic subject of a non-finite verb form; based on available data, I cannot solve this dilemma. However, it is irrelevant to my point, since whatever the answer, there will be no multiple subjects of the Main Verb.

4.6.1.3 Subject + pseudo-conjunct

The $N_{1\text{-SUBJ}}$ is the SyntSubj, the $N_{2\text{-SUBJ}}$ being a pseudo-conjunct dependent element.

Definition 4.6 – pseudo-conjunct (Chapter 2, Section 2.4, No. 122, p. 111)

> L_2 is a **pseudo-coordinate dependent**, or a **pseudo-conjunct**, of L_1, iff L_2 follows L_1 immediately and can play the same surface-syntactic role as L_1, but does not allow for a coordinating conjunction linking L_2 to L_1.

The semantic load of a pseudo-conjunct L_2 of L_1 is to express an elaboration of L_1: 'L_1, more precisely L_2'; for instance:

(24) *Leo lives in Spain,*–**pseudo-coord**→*in Barcelona,*–**pseudo-coord**→*on 4th May Street,*–**pseudo-coord**→*in a big building,*–**pseudo-coord**→*on the fifth floor.*

Thus, take sentence (25), which is the passive version of sentence (2):

(25) *Kay+hantey* <u>*John+i*</u>   *son +i*   *mul+li +ess +ta*
   dog DAT   SUBJ hand SUBJ bite PASS PAST DECL
lit. 'By.dog John hand was.bitten'.

JOHN is the SyntSubj, and the SON 'hand' is its pseudo-conjunct: 'John, more precisely [his] hand, was bitten by the dog'.

Sentence (25) formally corresponds also to two further syntactic structures:

- JOHN is a rhematic prolepsis, while SON 'hand' is the SSynt-subject: 'It was John whose hand was bitten by the dog' (see 4.6.1.1).
- Both JOHN and SON are rhematic prolepses: 'It was John and his hand, it was bitten by the dog'. This is possible because, as indicated above, Korean is a Pro-Drop language, and the resumptive pronouns such as 'it' or 'his' do not appear in the sentence.

In sentence (26), both nouns in the subjective—MARY and JOHN—can be considered rhematic prolepses: 'It was Mary and John, she put him to sleep' (4.6.1.1).

(26) *Mary+**ka*** *John+i*   *ča* +*ke*   *hay* +*ss* +*ta*
      SUBJ   SUBJ sleep CONV make PAST DECL

Additional interpretations of (26) are also possible: JOHN can be the AgCo/the SyntSubj of the converb *čake*, while MARY can be the SyntSubj of HATA 'make' (4.6.1.2) or a rhematic prolepsis.

A string of consecutive N$_{SUBJ}$s containing more than two components is easily described in proposed terms: one of these N$_{SUBJ}$s can be the SyntSubj of the Main Verb, one can be the CoAg of a non-finite verb form (= of a converb), and all the others are rhematic prolepses.

4.6.2 "Multiple direct objects" in a Korean clause

The situation with strings of accusative nouns is slightly more complex. If we consider a sequence of two N$_{ACC}$s, the following five (rather than three, as for the N$_{SUBJ}$) cases have to be distinguished.

N$_{1\text{-}ACC}$ and N$_{2\text{-}ACC}$ are syntactically not linked

a)   N$_{1\text{-}ACC}$ and N$_{2\text{-}ACC}$ depend in parallel on a ditransitive Main Verb: N$_{1\text{-}ACC}$ is an IndirO, and N$_{2\text{-}ACC}$ the DirO (4.6.2.1).
b)   N$_{1\text{-}ACC}$ and N$_{2\text{-}ACC}$ depend in parallel on a light Main Verb: N$_{1\text{-}ACC}$ is its DirO, and N$_{2\text{-}ACC}$ is its Quasi-DirO (4.6.2.2).
c)   N$_{1\text{-}ACC}$ is the DirO of the Main Verb, and N$_{2\text{-}ACC}$ is the DirO of the gerund in a phrasal (= analytical) causative (4.6.2.3).
d)   N$_{2\text{-}ACC}$ is the DirO of the Main Verb, and N$_{1\text{-}ACC}$ is the affected object of the same verb (4.6.2.4).

N$_{1\text{-}ACC}$ and N$_{2\text{-}ACC}$ are syntactically linked

e)   N$_{2\text{-}ACC}$ is a pseudo-conjunct to N$_{1\text{-}ACC}$ (4.6.2.5).

4.6.2.1 Indirect object + direct object

(27) a. *Mary+ka*   *John+il*   *čʰayk+il*   *ču* +Ø +*ess* +*ta*
       SUBJ   ACC   book ACC   give ACT PAST DECL
      'Mary gave John a book'.

On $N_{1\text{-ACC}}$, but not on $N_{2\text{-ACC}}$, the accusative freely alternates with the dative (without changing its syntactic role):

    b. *Mary+ka   John+**eykey**   čʰayk+**il**   ču +Ø +ess +ta*
        SUBJ   **DAT**   book **ACC** give ACT PAST DECL
        'Mary gave John a book'.

$N_{1\text{-ACC}}$ does not passivize, while $N_{2\text{-ACC}}$ does:

    c. **John+i*   *Mary+ey*   *iyhay*   *čʰayk+il*   *ču +eči +ess +ta*
        SUBJ   DAT   by   book ACC   give PASS PAST DECL
        'John was given a book by Mary'.

vs.   *Čʰayk+i*   *Mary+ey*   *iyhay*   *John+eykey*   *ču +eči +ess +ta*
        book SUBJ   DAT   by   DAT   give PASS PAST DECL
        'The book was given by Mary to John'.

In this respect, Korean is different from English and Japanese, which both have indirect passives.

Another example of the same construction, where $N_{1\text{-ACC}}$ implements an IndirO:

(28) *Mary+ka   loboti+**lil**   pʰal+**il**   ta +Ø +ass +ta*
      SUBJ   robot **ACC**   arm **ACC** attach ACT PAST DECL
      'Mary attached the arm to the robot'.

In Latin, Serbian and German, $N_{1\text{-ACC}}$ turns out to be an IndirO or OblO, while $N_{2\text{-ACC}}$ is a genuine DirO. Consider also Ger. **Was**_ACC_ *fragt er* **mich**_ACC_ ? lit. 'What asks he me?', where WAS 'what' is an OblO: this WAS alternates with WORÜBER 'about what'; only WAS and DAS 'this' are possible in the accusative in this position, while any semantically convenient noun can replace *mich*.

NB On multiple accusatives in various languages, see Mel'čuk 2009a: 96, endnote [3].

4.6.2.2 Direct object + quasi-direct object (O'Grady 1991: 236, 1992)

(29) a. *John+i*   *enehak +**il***   *koŋpu +**lil***   *hay +ss +ta*
       SUBJ linguistics **ACC** study$_{(N)}$ **ACC** make PAST DECL
       lit. 'John makes [a] study linguistics'. = 'John studies linguistics'.

     b. *John+i*   *enehak +iy*   *koŋpu +**lil***   *hay +ss +ta*
        SUBJ linguistics **GEN** study$_{(N)}$ **ACC** make PAST DECL
       'John does a study of linguistics'.

c. *John+i   enehak   +Ø |koŋpu +lil| hay +ss +ta*
   SUBJ linguistics NOM study$_{(N)}$ ACC make PAST DECL
   'John does a linguistics study'

Sentence (29a) presents a well-known phenomenon—a so-called transitive "periphrastic (= compound, or complex) verb." This is a collocation whose base is a predicative noun N_{predic} (KOŊPU '[a] study'), and the collocate is a support verb $V_{support}$ (HATA 'make'); as a whole, the collocation "$N_{predic} V_{support}$" is syntactically equivalent to a transitive verb having a regular DirO N (here, ENEHAK 'linguistics'), something like "$make_{Vsupport}$ [a] $study_{Npredic}]_{Vtrans}$ linguistics$_{N=D.rO}$" ≈ "study linguistics". Inside this collocation, the N_{predic} must be encoded as a Quasi-DirO-2 of the $V_{support}$ HATA, since the latter cannot have two DirOs:

ENEHAK 'linguistics'←dir-obj–HATA 'make'–quasi-dir-obj-2→KOŊPU 'study'
'make [a] study linguistics' = 'study linguistics'

Passivization of (29a) produces (22), in which KOŊPU 'study' can be considered as a pseudo-subject (4.5.2).

The same meaning can be expressed by different syntactic structures, where KOŊPU is a regular DirO of the verb HATA, and it takes ENEHAK as its adnominal attribute (in the genitive or the nominative), see (29b–c).

The **quasi-dir-objectival-2** surface-syntactic relation is necessary for many languages. The best-known among these is, perhaps, Persian, where the role of a transitive verb is played, most of the time, by a phrase "support verb $V_{support}$ + deverbal noun S_0" ("[N-ra]" stands for the DirO, -ra being a postposition that obligatorily marks a definite DirO):

(30) Persian

'[to] end [N]'	= tämäm	kärdän	[N-ra] lit. 'ending	do	[N]'
'[to] begin [N]'	= aġaz	kärdän	[N-ra] lit. 'beginning	do	[N]'
'[to] light up [N]'	= ateš	kärdän	[N-ra] lit. 'fire	do	[N]'
'[to] beat [N]'	= kotak	zädän	[N-ra] lit. 'beating	hit	[N]'
'[to] show [N]'	= nešän	dadän	[N-ra] lit. 'sign	give	[N]'
'[to] learn [N]'	= yad	gereftän	[N-ra] lit. 'memory	take	[N]'
'[to] congratulate [N]'	= tabrik	goftän	[N-ra] lit. 'congratulation	say	[N]'

Since the **quasi-direct-objectival-2** SyntRel is not commonly accepted, it seems worthwhile to indicate four properties of the Quasi-DirO-2 in Korean that illustrate its status.

(31) a. A Quasi-DirO-2 does not accept an adjectival modifier:
 Johni enehakïl *simtoissnin koŋpulïl hayssta lit. 'John linguistics_ACC **deep** study did'.
 b. A Quasi-DirO-2 cannot be pronominalized with KUKES 'that thing':
 Johni enehakïl koŋpulïl hayko, Maryka suhakïl *kukesïl hayssta
 lit. 'John linguistics_ACC study having.done, Mary mathematics_ACC the.same did'.
 c. A Quasi-DirO-2 should not be linearly separated from the verb HATA (otherwise, the sentence is judged awkward by some speakers):
 ?Johni koŋpulïl enehakïl hayssta.
 d. A Quasi-DirO-2 cannot undergo relativization:
 Johni ha+nïn koŋpu 'by.John made study' vs.
 *Johni enehakïl ha+nïn koŋpu 'by.John [of] linguistics made study'.

A Quasi-DirO-2 is more constrained than a regular DirO; it seems to "coalesce" with HATA.

4.6.2.3 Direct object of the Main Verb + direct object of a non-finite verb form

The sentence in (10b), reproduced here as (32), contains two DirOs (boxed), which depend on two different clause elements: *Marylïl* is the DirO of the MV HATA 'make', while *čʰaykïl* is the DirO of the converb *ilkke* 'reading'; cf. (32):

(32) a. *John+i*   Mary+lïl   čʰayk+ïl   *ilk +ke   hay +ss +ta*
  SUBJ   ACC   book ACC   read CONV make PAST DECL
 'John made Mary read a book'.

As is normal for the DirO of an MV, MARY can be promoted to the SyntSubj in a periphrastic passive construction (similar to the English GET-passive):

 b. *Mary+ka   John+ey   iyhay   čʰayk+ïl   ilk +ke   toy   +ess +ta*
  SUBJ   DAT   by   book ACC   read CONV become PAST DECL
 'Mary was made by John to read a book'.

This situation obtains with the phrasal (= analytical) causative construction.

4.6.2.4 Affected object + direct object

(33) a. *Mary+ka   John+il   sačin+il   ččič   +ess +ta*
         SUBJ   ACC   picture ACC tear.up PAST DECL
    'Mary tore up John's picture'.

It is the picture that Mary tore up, not John: SAČIN 'picture, photo' is the DirO of the Main Verb. And what about JOHN? This clause element is known as an **affected object**, referring to the entity affected by the event. The meaning is roughly like this: "What Mary did to John was tear up his picture." In Mandarin Chinese, the affected object is introduced by the preposition BĂ and is called "retained object" (Li & Thompson 1981: 470–471; see Chapter 2, Section 2.5, SSyntRel No. 13, p. 56, and also Chapter 8, Section 8.4, p. 305):

> b. *Mali bǎ Juhen bǎng-le   liǎngzhi jiǎo*
>   Mary John tie.up PERF   two   foot
>   'Mary tied up John's feet'.

> **NB** "Affected object" is simply the name of a surface-syntactic clause element; it should not be construed as a semantic characterization. In this technical sense, WOLF in *John killed the wolf* is not an affected object, but simply a DirO.

4.6.2.5 Direct object + pseudo-conjunct

(34) a. *Kay+ka   John-il   son +il   mul+ess +ta*
         dog SUBJ   ACC   hand ACC   bite PAST DECL
    'The dog bit John on the hand'. (O'Grady 1991: 3)

$N_{1\text{-ACC}}$ is the DirO, and each of the following $N_{i\text{-ACC}}$s is a pseudo-coordinate conjunct of the preceding N_{ACC}. $N_{i\text{-ACC}}$ do not easily allow permutation—(34b-i), but can be omitted without affecting the grammaticality of the sentence—(34b-ii):

> b. (i) ?/**Kay+ka son+il John+il mulessta.*
>   (ii) *Kay+ka John+il mulessta*
>   'The dog bit John'.

This is exactly what is to be expected from a pseudo-conjunct since it expresses an elaboration of the preceding element.

> **NB** The meaning of sentence (34a) can be also expressed by a different sentence with a different syntactic structure, in which SON 'hand' is a DirO and JOHN is a possessor attribute in the genitive:
> *Kay+ka John+uy son+il mulessta* 'The dog bit John's hand'.

4.6.2.6 "Quadruple direct objects"

Sentence (35) features four consecutive N_{ACC}s (O'Grady 1991: 77):

(35) John+i   ki   mune+lil   tali+lil   kkit pupun+il   čokim+il   čal+ass+ta
     SUBJ   the octopus ACC leg ACC   end part   ACC   bit   ACC   cut PAST DECL

lit. 'John the octopus leg end part bit cut'. =
'John cut a bit from the end part of a leg of the octopus'.

The first N_{ACC} MUNE 'octopus' is the DirO, and the following N_{ACC}s are pseudoconjuncts:

ČALİTA 'cut'–**dir-obj**→MUNE–**pseudo-coord**→TALI–**pseudo-coord**→KKİT+PUPUN–**pseudo-coord**→ČOKİM

The situation is, however, furthermore complicated by the fact that (roughly) the same semantic content can be expressed by different syntactic structures, which determine different distributions of case suffixes. Thus, we can have sentences in which the noun MUNE remains in the accusative, but some of other nouns obtain the nominative (these are boldfaced):

(36) a. John+i   ki   mune+lil   tali+lil   **kkit pupun+Ø**   čokim+il   čal+ass+ta
        SUBJ   the octopus ACC leg ACC   **end part**   **NOM**   bit   ACC   cut PAST DECL

     b. John+i   ki   mune+lil   **tali+Ø**   kkit pupun+il   čokim+il   čal+ass+ta
        SUBJ   the octopus ACC **leg NOM**   end part   ACC   bit   ACC   cut PAST DECL

     c. John+i   ki   mune+lil   **tali+Ø**   **kkit pupun+Ø**   čokim+il   čal+ass+ta
        SUBJ   the octopus ACC **leg NOM** end part   **NOM**   bit   ACC   cut PAST DECL

In sentences (36) an N_{NOM} is an adnominal complement/attribute of the following N; all N_{ACC}s keep their syntactic role. Formally:

KKİT+PUPUN$_{NOM}$←**subj-adnom**–ČOKİM   'end.part bit',
TALI$_{NOM}$←**subj-adnom**–KKİT+PUPUN   'leg end.part', etc.

(For the **subj-adnom** SSyntRel, see Chapter 5, 5.3.1/2, p. 211*ff*.) An adnominal dependent can also be in the genitive (the suffix **-iy**): *kkit+pupun+iy čokim+il* 'bit of end.part' or *tali+iy kkit+pupun+il* 'end.part of the leg'.

Due to optional "subjective ~ nominative" and "accusative ~ nominative" alternations, Korean allows for sequences of N_{NOM}s:

(37) John+∅   ki mune+∅   tali+∅   kkit pupun+∅   čokim+∅   čalassta
     NOM   NOM   NOM   NOM   NOM
   lit. 'John the octopus leg end part bit cut'.

However, such a sequence does not present new problems. The wordform sequence in (37) implements one of the two syntactic structures:

- Either JOHN is the SyntSubj and MUNE 'octopus' is the DirO; each of the following N_{NOM}s is a pseudo-conjunct to the preceding noun ('John cut the octopus, on the leg, the end part, a bit').
- Or JOHN is the SyntSubj and ČOKIM 'bit' is the DirO; each of the N_{NOM}s that precede ČOKIM is an adnominal attribute to the following N ('John cut a bit of the end part of the leg of the octopus').

The syntactic ambiguity of sequence (37), as well as of all such sequences, is in fact resolved by prosody, which is not considered in this chapter.

4.6.3 Other "multiple objects" in a Korean clause

As it can be expected, Korean allows for other "multiple cases"; thus, it has sequences of N_{DAT}s (Maling & Kim 1992):

(38) a. Nay+ka   Mary–eykey   kwi+ey   pimil –il   soksaki+ess +ta
        I SUBJ   DAT   ear DAT   secret ACC   whisper PAST DECL
      lit. 'I to.Mary to.ear secret whispered'. =
      'I whispered the secret into Mary's ear'.

   b. Koŋčaŋ+ey   cʰaŋko +ey   pul+i   na +ss +ta
      factory DAT storeroom DAT fire SUBJ occur PAST DECL
      lit. 'In.factory in.storeroom fire occurred'. =
      'A fire broke out in the factory's storeroom'.

Such examples do not add anything new to the discussion: the first N_{DAT} is an IndirO or a circumstantial, and the second is its pseudo-conjunct.

4.7 Conclusions

1. Korean has neither "multiple subjects" nor "multiple direct objects": what is theoretically not possible is impossible in any of the possible worlds (≈ in

any language). Korean does have, however, multiple subjective case nouns and multiple accusative case nouns—that is, strings of N_{SUBJ}s and N_{ACC}s in one clause.
2. The noun form commonly called "nominative" in Korean grammar is in fact the subjective case (in **-ka/-i/-kkeyse**); the nominative exists as well and is marked by a zero suffix: **-Ø**.
3. The Korean subjective marks the syntactic subject, the attribute of a copula-like verb, the agent complement of a non-finite verb form, a rhematic prolepsis, and the oblique object of a parametric verb.
4. A string of N_{SUBJ}s represents one of three syntactic possibilities:
   – either the last N_{SUBJ} is the SyntSubj, all the preceding ones being rhematic prolepses;
   – or the $N_{1\text{-}SUBJ}$ is the SyntSubj and the $N_{2\text{-}SUBJ}$ is an AgCo (or the SyntSubj) of a non-finite verb form;
   – or else the $N_{1\text{-}SUBJ}$ is the SyntSubj, each of the following N_{SUBJ}s being a pseudo-conjunct to the previous N_{SUBJ}.
5. A string of N_{ACC}s corresponds to four syntactic possibilities:
   – either the $N_{1\text{-}ACC}$ is the indirect object, the $N_{2\text{-}ACC}$ being the direct object;
   – or the $N_{1\text{-}ACC}$ is the direct object, the $N_{2\text{-}ACC}$ being a quasi-direct object with a light verb;
   – or the $N_{1\text{-}ACC}$ is the direct object of the Main Verb, while the $N_{2\text{-}ACC}$ is the direct object of the lexical converb in the periphrastic causative;
   – or else the $N_{1\text{-}ACC}$ is the direct object, each of the following N_{ACC}s being a pseudo-conjunct to the previous N_{ACC}.

A corrected version of Mel'čuk 2015b.

5 Genitive adnominal dependents in Russian: surface-syntactic relations in the N→N$_{GEN}$ phrase

5.1 The problem stated
5.2 Criteria for distinguishing surface-syntactic relations within N→N$_{GEN}$ phrases
5.3 The problem solved
    5.3.1/2 Genitivus Subjectivus vs. Genitivus Objectivus: the **subjective-adnominal-completive** and **objective-adnominal-completive** SSyntRels
    5.3.3   Genitivus Qualitatis: the **qualificative-adnominal-attributive** SSyntRel
    5.3.4   Genitivus Possessivus: the **possessive-adnominal-attributive** SSyntRel
    5.3.5   Genitivus Attributivus: the **characterizing-adnominal-attributive** SSyntRel
    5.3.6   Genitivus Metaphoricus: the **metaphorical-adnominal-attributive** SSyntRel
    5.3.7   Genitivus Phrasemicus: no special SSyntRel
5.4 Overview of the six SSyntRels proposed
5.5 Closing remarks: N$_{GEN}$ cannot be a personal pronoun
5.6 Conclusions

5.1 The problem stated

Russian has several types of N→N$_{GEN}$ phrases: a noun N and its syntactic nominal dependent N$_{GEN}$ in the genitive case without preposition (*smert' Ivana*$_{GEN}$ 'death of.Ivan', *prosmotr fil'mov*$_{GEN}$ 'watching of.films', *čelovek udivitel'noj sud'by*$_{GEN}$ 'man of.amazing destiny'). For the convenience of an overview, the N$_{GEN}$ dependents in these phrases can be grouped according to the type of the semantic relation between N and N$_{GEN}$. (By "semantic relation" is meant here the relation between the meanings 'N' and 'N$_{GEN}$'—that is, between the sources of N and N$_{GEN}$ in the underlying semantic structure; 'X' stands for "meaning of a linguistic entity X.") Four major cases are logically possible:

- N$_{GEN}$ implements one of N's semantic actants,
    N expressing a semantic predicate (or quasi-predicate)   'N(N$_{GEN}$)'
- N$_{GEN}$ expresses a semantic predicate,
    N implementing one of N$_{GEN}$'s semantic actants   'N$_{GEN}$(N)'
- N$_{GEN}$ is semantically linked to N by a predicate
    (or a configuration of predicates) 'σ'   'σ(N, N$_{GEN}$)'

> **NB** The predicate 'σ' typically has no segmental (= phonemic) expression in the sentence; the corresponding meaning is either carried by the surface-syntactic relation that links N and N$_{GEN}$ or remains unexpressed, to be accessed by the Addressee through the context. (One exception, leading to a semantic-syntactic mismatch, is presented below, in Subsection 5.3.5.)

https://doi.org/10.1515/9783110694765-006

- N_{GEN} and N are semantically not linked, since neither N_{GEN} nor N have separate semantic sources: they form together a semantic unit; in other words, the N→N_{GEN} phrase is a non-compositional phraseme, that is, an **idiom** or a **nomineme** (Mel'čuk 2012–2015: vol. 3, 293–362)[1] 'N_N_{GEN}'

All these cases are represented among Russian N→N_{GEN} phrases; the respective examples follow. For the ease of reference, each group of examples is given a conventional Latin name; all glosses are literal.

(1) 'N(N_{GEN})'
   a. **Genitivus Subjectivus**: $N_{GEN\text{-subj}}$ expresses DSynt-actant [DSyntA] I of N, e. g.:
      zasedanie komiteta$_I$ 'meeting of.committee'
      otsutstvie [neskol'kix] lic$_I$ 'absence of.several persons'
      steny tualeta$_I$ 'walls of.bathroom'
   b. **Genitivus Objectivus**: $N_{GEN\text{-obj}}$ expresses DSyntA II of N (or, in some rather infrequent cases, N's DSyntA III, see Raxilina 2010: 253), e. g.:
      sozdanie komiteta$_{II}$ 'creation of.committee'
      arest [neskol'kix] lic$_{II}$ 'arrest of.several people'
      pokupatel' ryby$_{II}$ 'buyer of.fish' ~
      pokupatel' Fedi$_{III}$ 'buyer of.Fedya' = 'buyer from.Fedya'

   NB $N_{GEN\text{-obj-II}}$ and $N_{GEN\text{-obj-III}}$ do not cooccur with the same syntactic governor (**pokupatel' ryby*$_{II}$ *Fedi*$_{III}$ vs. *pokupatel' ryby*$_{II}$ *u Fedi*$_{III}$ 'buyer of.fish from Fedya'), which allows us to not distinguish them at the surface-syntactic [SSynt-]level — that is, to use the same SSynt-relation for both.

(2) 'N_{GEN}(N)'
   Genitivus Qualitatis, e.g.:
      ploščadka [nebol'šogo] razmera 'area [of.small] size'
      čelovek [redkogo] uma 'man [of.rare] intelligence'
      suščestvitel'noe [množestvennogo] čisla 'noun [of.plural] number'
      devuška [moej] mečty 'girl [of.my] dream'

(3) 'σ(N, N_{GEN})'
   a. 'N←1–σ–2→N_{GEN}': the noun N is semantic actant [SemA] 1 of the predicate 'σ'

---

[1] The components of a compositional phraseme—a collocation or a cliché—have their independent semantic sources; N_{GEN} in these phrasemes is subordinated to N by the **charact-adnom** SSyntRel: see Section 5.4, Item 5, p. 228.

i. *Genitivus Possessivus*:
'N←1–belong–2→N_GEN' ['belong' = 'be owned'], e.g.:
igruški Miši 'toys of.Misha', *fabrika otca* 'factory of.father'
al'bom Anny 'album of.Anna'

ii. *Genitivus Characteristicus*:
'N←1–σ–2→N_GEN', e.g.:
vozdux Pariža 'air of.Paris' = 'air **existing.in** Paris'
ženy [šaxskogo] garema 'wives [of.Shah's] harem'
= 'wives **being.elements.of** the Shah's harem'
putešestvija prošlogo veka 'travels of.past century'
= 'travels **that.took.place.in** the past century'
Mefistofel' Šaljapina 'Mephisto of.Shalyapin'
= 'Mephisto **as.interpreted.by** Shalyapin'
Saskija Rembrandta 'Saskia of.Rembrandt'
= 'Saskia **as.painted.by** Rembrandt'
kontinent l'vov i žirafov 'continent of.lions and of.giraffes'
= 'continent **inhabited.by** lions and giraffes'

b. 'N←2–σ–1→N_GEN': the noun N is SemA 2 of the predicate 'σ'
Genitivus Metaphoricus:
'N←2–similar–1→N_GEN' ['N_GEN is similar to N' = 'as if N_GEN were N'], e.g.:
sutany dyma 'soutanes of.smoke', *okean tajgi* 'ocean of.taiga'
čaša utra 'cup of.morning' (F. García Lorca in M. Cvetaeva's translation)
raduga [jarkostrekočuščix] kryl 'rainbow [of.brightly.chirping] wings'
[the title of an article about a congress of entomology]

(4) 'N_N_GEN'
Genitivus Phrasemicus: no semantic link between N and N_GEN, both forming together a semantic unit (the phrase N→N_GEN is a non-compositional phraseme: an idiom or a nomineme); N and N_GEN-phras have no separate semantic sources in the underlying semantic structure.

a. N_GEN-phras in an idiom (the top corners ⌜...⌝ enclose idioms), e.g.:
⌜*džentel'men udači*⌝ 'gentleman of.fortune' ≈ 'bandit'
⌜*trubka mira*⌝ 'pipe of.peace', ⌜*čaška Petri*⌝ 'cup of.Petri' = 'Petri dish'
⌜*kapli [datskogo] korolja*⌝ 'drops [of.Danish] king' = 'expectorant cough syrup'

b. N_GEN-phras in a nomineme, e.g.:
Ostrova [Zelënogo] Mysa 'Islands [of.Green] Cape'
Mys [Dobroj] Naděždy 'Cape [of.Good] Hope'
ploščad' Puškina 'Square of.Pushkin'
korifej [vsex] vremën i narodov 'corypheus [of.all] times and peoples'
[Comrade Stalin]

The first two N_{GEN}s—*Genitivus Subjectivus* and *Genitivus Objectivus*—are adnominal complements; the following five types of N_{GEN}—*Genitivus Qualitatis, Genitivus Possessivus, Genitivus Characteristicus, Genitivus Metaphoricus,* and *Genitivus Phrasemicus*—are adnominal attributes.

As far as I know, there is no in-depth description of SSyntRels linking an N_{GEN} to its syntactic governor N in Russian. In Mel'čuk 1974: 224, all Russian N→N_{GEN} phrases (and a host of others) were described by three SSyntRels:

- the **agentive** SSyntRel (*priezd ministra* 'arrival of.minister'), corresponding to deep-syntactic relation [DSyntRel] I;
- the **1ˢᵗ completive** SSyntRel (*provody ministra* 'send-off of.minister'), corresponding to DSyntRel II or III; and
- the **attributive** SSyntRel (*mal'čik [vysokogo] rosta* 'boy [of.tall] height')—with the admission that the **attributive** SSyntRel is a "dump ground" for all non-agreeing postmodifiers of a Russian noun N that do not correspond to N's DSynt-actants.

This tripartite division—two actantial and one "general-attributive" N_{GEN}s— was retained in Iomdin 2010c: 26–43 and then in Mel'čuk 2012b: 137–140 (different names of SSyntRels being used). But today I think that the time is ripe for a substantive linguistic analysis of Russian N→N_{GEN} phrases, which must allow me to better determine their SSynt-description.

The question asked in this chapter is straightforward:

> How many different surface-syntactic relations—and, of course, which ones— are needed to describe N→N_{GEN} phrases in Russian?

The problem of acceptability—that is, of linguistic correctness—of particular N→N_{GEN} phrases is left out of consideration (see Raxilina 2010 and Borščëv & Parti 2011, as well as many other studies mentioned in these titles). Only correct N→N_{GEN} phrases are considered here.

5.2 Distinguishing surface-syntactic relations within N→N_{GEN} phrases

To establish an inventory of SSyntRels in a language the linguist has to observe two types of requirements (Iordanskaja & Mel'čuk 2009a).

- Linguistic requirements: all dependents of an SSyntRel must exhibit identical (or quite similar) syntactic properties relevant in the given language.
- Formal requirements: an SSyntRel must satisfy formal Criteria **A**–**C** of the definition of SSyntRel (Chapter 2, Section 2.4, pp. 40*ff*).

In our particular case—that is, the Russian N→N$_{GEN}$ phrases—the linguistic requirements are satisfied trivially: all phrases considered are of the same structure, and all dependent N$_{GEN}$s have the same syntactic properties except for their mutual ordering; this latter property is used for distinguishing the SSyntRels involved. As far as Criteria **A**–**C** are concerned, Criteria **A** (presence of a syntactic dependency relation between two lexemes in an utterance) and **B** (orientation of the syntactic dependency relation between two lexemes in an utterance) are irrelevant for the present discussion. Only Criteria **C1** and **C3** need to be used for the definition of SSyntRels within Russian N→N$_{GEN}$ phrases; for the reader's convenience, these criteria are reproduced here. (Criterion **C2**, that of syntactic substitutability, is not relevant, either: it is satisfied for all N→N$_{GEN}$ phrases.)

Criterion C1 (presence of semantic contrast)
    Notation: $w_i(L)$ is a wordform of lexeme L.

> One and the same hypothetical SSyntRel **r** should not describe two phrases $w_1(L_1)$-**r**→$w_2(L_2)$ and $w_3(L_1)$-**r**→$w_4(L_2)$
> if Conditions 1 and 2 are simultaneously satisfied:
>
> **Condition 1**
> These phrases contrast semantically, the contrast being manifested either in the form of the phrases themselves or in the syntactic behavior properties of their members.
>
> **Condition 2**
> If these phrases differ in their form, they differ only by some syntactic means of expression—by word order of their elements, syntactic prosody, or syntactic grammemes.

If Criterion **C1** is satisfied—that is, if Conditions 1 and 2 are both satisfied, **r** should be split into two different SSyntRels, r_1 and r_2, $r_1 \neq r_2$.

Since this chapter only deals with the phrases of the same form (namely, N→N$_{GEN}$), Condition 2 of Criterion **C1** is irrelevant (just like Criterion **C2**), because it is always satisfied. Our reasoning is thus based on a semantic contrast that manifests itself "outside" the phrase in question; and in this case, the semantic contrast can manifest itself only by its syntactic behavior with respect to cosubordinated other N→N$_{GEN}$ phrases—in particular, in their mutual ordering.

Criterion C3 (no limited repeatability)

> An SSyntRel **r** must be either unlimitedly repeatable or non-repeatable—that is, it cannot be limitedly repeatable.

Criterion **C3** is actively exploited in the following reasoning.

Now we are fully equipped to take on the problem formulated in Section 5.1: What are the SSyntRel r_i in a Russian phrase of the N–r_i→N$_{GEN}$ form?

5.3 The problem solved

Following the indications of Criteria **C1** (Condition 1) and **C3**, the description of the N→N$_{GEN}$ phrases requires six SSyntRels, which will be introduced below.

Each pair of N→N$_{GEN}$ phrases being contrasted must be compared strictly under the "everything else being equal" condition, the latter understood in the following sense:

1) The cosubordinated noun phrases being mutually ordered are of the same **weight**—roughly, of the same number of stressed syllables and of the same syntactic complexity. As is known (see, for instance, Wasow & Arnold 2003), in a string of cosubordinated phrases postposed to their governor, heavier phrases tend to follow lighter ones. Thus, the dubious expression ?*perevod Bunina "Gajjavaty"* 'translation of.Bunin of.Hiawatha' becomes perfect with a heavier N$_{GEN\text{-}obj}$ phrase: *perevod Bunina zamečatel'noj poèmy Longfello* 'translation of.Bunin of.brilliant poem of.Longfellow'.
2) No communicative factors intervene (such as topicalization, focalization, emphasis, etc.). This means, among other things, that all the examples are considered under neutral prosody; emphatic intonation can make acceptable otherwise ungrammatical expressions.
3) All cosubordinated noun phrases considered below are **restrictive** modifiers, since **descriptive** modifiers, characterized by special prosody, can violate the standard ordering: *kovry **nebol'šogo razmera** ètogo perioda* 'carpets of.small size of.this period' ~ **kovry ètogo perioda **nebol'šogo razmera*** [restrictive modifier], but *kovry ètogo perioda, **nebol'šogo razmera**, ...* [descriptive modifier].
4) No ambiguity is created by the given linear arrangement.

5.3.1/2 *Genitivus Subjectivus* vs. *Genitivus Objectivus*:
The subjective-adnominal-completive and objective-adnominal-completive SSyntRels

Criterion **C1**, Condition 1:

(5) a. Semantic contrast between N$_{GEN\text{-}subj}$ and N$_{GEN\text{-}obj}$
 perevod Bunina 'translation of.Bunin':
 either Bunin translated somebody/something, or somebody translated Bunin.
 b. Different syntactic behavior of N$_{GEN\text{-}subj}$ and N$_{GEN\text{-}obj}$
 i. *perevod "Gajavaty"*$_{N_{GEN\text{-}obj}}$ *Bunina*$_{N_{GEN\text{-}subj}}$
 'translation of.*Hiawatha* of.Bunin' vs.
 ?*perevod Bunina "Gajavaty"*
 ii. *portret devočki*$_{N_{GEN\text{-}obj}}$ *Serova*$_{N_{GEN\text{-}subj}}$ 'portrait of.young.girl of.Serov' vs.
 ?*portret Serova devočki*

N$_{GEN\text{-}subj}$ (*Genitivus Subjectivus*) that corresponds to N's SemA 1 and N$_{GEN\text{-}obj}$ (*Genitivus Objectivus*) that corresponds to N's SemA 2 semantically contrast, see (5a). Everything else being equal, N$_{GEN\text{-}obj}$ precedes N$_{GEN\text{-}subj}$, that is, it is positioned closer to their common governor N than N$_{GEN\text{-}subj}$, see (5b). The word order difference in these phrases' syntactic behavior is the manifestation of their semantic contrast.

The semantic contrast of N$_{GEN\text{-}subj}$ and N$_{GEN\text{-}obj}$ is rather limited in scope—it is possible only in the context of a handful of governing nouns. However, in typological perspective it is important. On the one hand, the same contrast is found in Russian modificative adjectives: *repinskie ženskie portrety* 'Repin women's portraits' ~ ??*ženskie repinskie portrety*, where the "objectival" adjective must be closer to the governor than the "subjectival" one. On the other hand, the linear precedence of N$_{GEN\text{-}obj}$ with respect to N$_{GEN\text{-}subj}$ in Russian N→N$_{GEN}$ phrases corresponds to a universal typological feature of natural languages: the direct object manifests closer semantic ties to its governor than the subject. Two well-known examples suffice to illustrate this point:

- The wide-spread ergative construction, where the DirO is marked by the nominative case and controls the agreement of the Main Verb, while the Subject is in oblique case and—in some languages and/or some contexts—does not affect the form of the Main Verb.
- V–dir-obj→N collocations, whose base N is the direct object of the support verb, like *launch an* ATTACK or *pay* ATTENTION, are the most frequent among verbal collocations.

Following Criterion **C1**, Condition 1 (the N$_{GEN\text{-}subj}$ and N$_{GEN\text{-}obj}$ phrases do not differ in their form, but show a semantic contrast manifested in different syntactic behavior—namely, different word order), N$_{GEN\text{-}subj}$ and N$_{GEN\text{-}obj}$ must be subordinated to their governor N by two different SSyntRels: **subjectival-adnominal(-completive)** and **objectival-adnominal(-completive)**. (The names **subjectival** and **objectival** are meant strictly as conventional labels, without any semantic load. Thus, in the phrases *stakan*–**subj-adnom**→*moloka* 'glass of.milk', *člen*–**subj-adnom**→*partii* 'member of.party', *serdce*–**subj-adnom**→*materi* 'heart of.mother' or *pjatoe*–**subj-adnom**→*janvarja* '[the] fifth of.January' the **subj-adnom** SSyntRel shows only that the N$_{GEN\text{-}subj}$ expresses DSyntA I of N, whatever its semantic role.)

Criterion **C3** confirms the proposed solution: the **subj-adnom** and **obj-adnom** SSyntRels are both non-repeatable; if **subj-adnom** and **obj-adnom** SSyntRels are not distinguished, the dependent N$_{GEN}$ will be repeatable exactly twice, which is forbidden by Criterion **C3**.

In traditional descriptions of Russian, the proper semantic representation of predicate nouns is, as a rule, lacking. Thus, the genitive *peska* 'of.sand' in *kuča peska* 'pile of.sand' is treated as *Genitivus Quantitatis*, while *brat Ivana* 'brother of.Ivan' is said to manifest *Genitivus Possessivus*. In point of fact, PESOK 'sand' expresses SemA 1 (DSyntA I) of KUČA (our *Genitivus Subjectivus*), and IVAN, SemA 2 (DSyntA II) of BRAT (our *Genitivus Objectivus*). The overwhelming majority of Russian adnominal genitives turn out to be *Genitivus Subjectivus* or *Objectivus*.[2] (For more on semantic predicates and semantic/deep-syntactic actants, see Mel'čuk 2012–2015: vol. 1, 215*ff*; vol. 3, 4*ff*.)

The **subj-adnom** SSyntRel describes only N→N$_{GEN}$ phrases; semantically close phrases with the instrumental case or with a preposition are represented in the SSynt-structure in a different way: by the **agentive** SSyntRel (*rassmotrenie*–**agentive**→*komitetom* 'study by.committee'; *dogovor*–**agentive**→*meždu stranami* 'treaty between countries').

The **obj-adnom** SSyntRel also describes only N→N$_{GEN}$ phrases; the N$_i$ that depends on N and is not in the genitive is subordinated to N by the **indir-objectival** or **oblique-objectival** SSyntRel (*podarok*–**indir-objectival**→*Ivanu*$_{DAT}$ 'gift to.Ivan';

---

[2] Mel'čuk 2016 proposes a slightly different syntactic description of Russian N→N$_{GEN\text{-}subj}$ and N→N$_{GEN\text{-}obj}$ phrases. Namely: 1) The present **subj-adnom** SSyntRel was called **agentive-attributive**; this **agentive-attributive** SSyntRel covered also N→N$_{INSTR}$ phrases, for which I reserve now the **agentive** SSyntRel. 2) The present **obj-adnom** SSyntRel was called **patientive-attributive**. 3) There was the **actantial-attributive** SSyntRel, designed to describe the N→N$_{GEN}$ phrases in which N$_{GEN}$ expresses N's DSyntA I or II not corresponding to the syntactic subject or the direct object. Now I believe that this description is too semantic and replace it.

zanjatija–oblique-objectival→*matematikoj*$_{\text{INSTR}}$ lit. 'doing with.mathematics' = 'studying/working in mathematics').

5.3.3 *Genitivus Qualitatis*: the qualificative-adnominal-attributive SSyntRel

Criterion **C1**, Condition 1:

(6) a. Semantic contrast between $N_{\text{GEN-qual}}$ and $N_{\text{GEN-subj}}/N_{\text{GEN-obj}}$
portret neobyčnoj formy 'portrait of.extraordinary form':
either the form of the portrait is extraordinary ($N_{\text{GEN-qual}}$), or
the portrait was painted by somebody called "Extraordinary Form"
($N_{\text{GEN-qual}}$), or
else the portrait represents somebody/something called "Extraordinary Form" ($N_{\text{GEN-obj}}$).
b. Different syntactic behavior of $N_{\text{GEN-qual}}$ with respect to both $N_{\text{GEN-subj}}$ and $N_{\text{GEN-obj}}$
i. *portret **neobyčnoj formy**$_{N_{\text{GEN-qual}}}$ Adeli Blox$_{N_{\text{GEN-obj}}}$ blestjaščego Klimta$_{N_{\text{GEN-subj}}}$*
'portrait of. extraordinary form of.Adel Bloch of.brilliant Klimt'
***neobyčnoj formy** portret Adeli Blox blestjaščego Klimta* and
vs. **portret Adeli Blox blestjaščego Klimta **neobyčnoj formy***
??*portret Adeli Blox **neobyčnoj formy** blestjaščego Klimta* and
ii. *tovary **vysšego sorta**$_{N_{\text{GEN-qual}}}$ našego magazina$_{N_{\text{GEN-obj}}}$*
'products of.highest class of.our store'
vs. **tovary našego magazina$_{N_{\text{GEN-obj}}}$ **vysšego sorta**$_{N_{\text{GEN-qual}}}$*

As in the preceding case, the semantic contrast in (6a) is manifested through different syntactic behavior of $N_{\text{GEN-qual}}$ with respect to $N_{\text{GEN-subj}}/N_{\text{GEN-obj}}$, see (6b): everything else being equal, $N_{\text{GEN-qual}}$ precedes $N_{\text{GEN-subj}}$ and $N_{\text{GEN-obj}}$. Similarly:

(7) *statuja **ogromnogo razmera** Aleksandra Tret'ego Paolo Trubeckogo*
'statue of.huge size of.Alexander III of.Paolo Trubetzkoy' and
***ogromnogo razmera** statuja Aleksandra Tret'ego Paolo Trubeckogo*
vs. ??*statuja Aleksandra Tret'ego Paolo Trubeckogo **ogromnogo razmera*** and
statuja Aleksandra Tret'ego **ogromnogo razmera Paolo Trubeckogo*

Deviation from the standard ordering $N_{\text{GEN-qual}} + N_{\text{GEN-subj}}$
If N denotes a set or a quantity that measures the denotation of $N_{\text{GEN-subj}}$, then $N_{\text{GEN-subj}}$ precedes $N_{\text{GEN-qual}}$, see (8).

(8) a. *kuča morskogo peska **ogromnogo razmera*** 'pile of.sea sand of.huge size'
   vs. ??*kuča **ogromnogo razmera** morskogo peska*
   b. *tolpa studentov-fizikov **ogromnogo razmera***
       'crowd of.students physicists of.huge size'
   vs. ??*tolpa **ogromnogo razmera** studentov-fizikov*

In what follows, we will see other cases where the meaning of N or of N_{GEN} plays a role in determining the mutual ordering of different N_{GEN}s, see Subsection 5.3.5, p. 220.

The indicated standard ordering can be violated, for instance, by the weight of the phrase under consideration:

(9) a. *statuja Friny Praksitelja **neobyčajnogo izjaščestva***
       'statue of.Phryne of Praxiteles of.extraordinary elegance'
   vs. **statuja **neobyčajnogo izjaščestva** Friny Praksitelja*
   b. *fragmenty DNK **fiksirovannogo razmera*** 'fragments of.DNA of.fixed size'
   vs. *fragmenty **fiksirovannogo razmera** različnyx dezoksiribonukleinovyx kislot*
       'fragments of.fixed size of.various desoxyribonucleic acids'

In this construction, N typically expresses N_{GEN}'s SemA 1: '$N \leftarrow 1-N_{GEN}$', as, e.g., in *portret$_N$ neobyčajnoj krasoty$_{N_{GEN}}$* 'portrait of.extraordinary beauty'; less frequently, N can implement SemA 2 of N_{GEN}: '$N \leftarrow 2-N_{GEN}$', as, e. g., in *devuška moej mečty* 'girl of.my dream' [= 'a girl of whom I dream'], *losos' xolodnogo kopčenija* 'salmon of.cold smoking' [= 'salmon that has been smoked cold'] or *sumka ručnoj raboty* 'bag of.handiwork' [= 'the bag that has been manufactured manually'].

Criterion **C3**:

$N_{GEN\text{-}qual}$ is repeatable; we can have, for instance, three cosubordinated $N_{GEN\text{-}qual}$s: *neobyčajnoj krasoty$_{N_{GEN\text{-}qual}}$ šarfik jarkogolubogo cveta$_{N_{GEN\text{-}qual}}$ nebol'šogo razmera$_{N\ GEN\text{-}qual}$*
'of.extraordinary beauty little.scarf of.bright.light.blue color of.small size'

Note that the problem of mutual ordering of different cosubordinated N_{GEN}s is not considered in this chapter; however, since the main tool for establishing different SSyntRels in $N \rightarrow N_{GEN}$ phrases is exactly their mutual ordering, this problem cannot be completely avoided. Thus, the repeatability of the **qualificative-adnominal** SSyntRel raises the following question. Suppose a noun N has two or more **qual-adnom** dependents; what should be their mutual linear arrangement? How do we specify it, since a particular order may be preferable? Thus, *sumka krasnogo cveta sovremennogo dizajna* 'handbag of.red color of.modern design' is OK, while ??*sumka sovremennogo dizajna krasnogo cveta* 'handbag of.modern design of.red color' is not. Shouldn't this force us to distinguish the SSyntRel subordinating CVET 'color' from the SSyntRel subordinating DIZAJN 'design':

N–r_1→CVET and N–r_2→DIZAJN, where $r_1 \neq r_2$?

The answer is no, and the reason is as follows:

> The linear position of a **qual-adnom** dependent N_{GEN-1} with respect to another **qual-adnom** dependent N_{GEN-2} is determined by the meaning of these dependent N_{GEN}s: an N_{GEN} that denotes the color (of N's denotation) tends to precede an N_{GEN} denoting its design, etc.

The situation is identical to what holds for many codependent (= cosubordinated) adjectives modifying the same noun: as shown in Iordanskaja 2000 for Russian and in Iordanskaja & Mel'čuk 2017: 221–237 for French (based on the classic work Vendler 1968), a string of anteposed codependent adjectives is linearized according to their meanings;[3] roughly:

"SUBJECTIVE ESTIMATE" > "SIZE" > "SPACIAL POSITION" > "FORM" > "COLOR" > "MATERIAL" > "KIND" N
(*udivitel'naja ogromnaja vnešnjaja kruglaja krasnaja kirpičnaja protivolavinnaja stena*
'amazing   enormous   external   round   red   brick   anti-avalanche   wall')

NB Note that the order of anteposed modifiers is (roughly) a mirror image of that of postposed modifiers. In point of fact, we deal here with the **proximity** of different modifiers to the noun modified.

The mutual ordering of codependent N_{GEN}s in Russian is considered in Chapter 11, pp. 381*ff*.

Different **qual-adnom** N_{GEN}s are linearly ordered between themselves based on the same principle, *viz.* according to their meanings. It must, however, be emphasized that this rule works, of course, only under the condition "everything else being equal"—that is, if the cosubordinated genitive-noun phrases being mutually ordered are of the same weight, etc.

Genitivus Qualitatis in Russian has at least three relevant particularities:

– $N_{GEN-qual}$ requires a modifying adjective: **portret krasoty* 'portrait of.beauty'; some $N_{GEN-qual}$s (lexically marked) allow – instead of an adjective – a modifying

---

3 English has so-called Royal Order of Adjectives; see, for instance,
https://theeditorsblog.net/2014/04/08/keeping-adjectives-in-line/ or
https://www.ucl.ac.uk/internet-grammar/adjectiv/ordering.htm

genitive noun or an apposition: *statuètka raboty*_{NGEN-qual} *Čellini*_{GEN} 'statuette of.work of.Cellini', *traktor zavoda "Krasnyj Molot"* 'tractor of.plant «Red Hammer»'. $N_{GEN\text{-}qual}$ can also be modified by an idiom: *gostinica ⸢srednej ruki⸣* 'hotel of.middle hand' = 'hotel of mediocre quality' ~ *⸢srednej ruki⸣ gostinica*.
- $N_{GEN\text{-}qual}$ can be anteposed with respect to N under certain conditions (see Chapter 11, Section 11.1, p. 371).
- Not every noun can appear as $N_{GEN\text{-}qual}$:
  *devuška neobyčajnoj **sud'by*** 'girl of.extraordinary destiny'   vs.
  devuška neobyčajnoj **učasti* 'girl of.extraordinary fate'.

This constraint seems to be lexical (rather than semantic); therefore, all nouns that can be $N_{GEN\text{-}qual}$ (or those that cannot?) must be supplied with a special syntactic feature.

The same considerations as in Subsection 5.3.2 (based on Criteria **C1** and **C3**) allow for postulating the third SSyntRel for Russian N→N_{GEN} phrases: **qualificative-adnominal(-attributive)**.

The **qual-adnom** SSyntRel describes not only the N→N_{GEN} phrases, but also three other constructions:

- N→[$N_{1(parameter)INSTR}$ + v 'in' + NUM←$N_{2(measure)ACC}$]; for instance:
  most$_N$–**qual-adnom**→*širinoj*$_{N1\text{-}INSTR}$ *v 10 metrov*$_{N2}$ 'bridge by.width in 10 meters'
- N→[$N_{1(parameter)INSTR}$ + NUM←$N_{2(measure)NOM}$]; for instance:
  most$_N$–**qual-adnom**→*širinoj*$_{N1\text{-}INSTR}$ *10 metrov*$_{N2}$ 'bridge by.width 10 meters';
- N→[NUM←$N_{2(measure)NOM}$] + v 'in' + $N_{1(parameter)ACC}$; for instance:
  most$_N$–[*10 metrov*]–**qual-adnom**→*v širinu*$_{N1\text{-}ACC}$ 'bridge 10 meters into width'.

In the perspective of text synthesis, the choice between these constructions and –**qual-adnom**→$N_{GEN\text{-}qual}$ is done according to the dependent of $N_{1(parameter)}$: if $N_{1(parameter)}$ has a dependent of the form –**qual-adnom**→$N_{2(measure)}$→NUM (= expressing a numerical value), then $N_{1(parameter)}$ has the instrumental case or is introduced by the preposition v 'in' and cannot be anteposed; otherwise, $N_{1(parameter)}$ is in the genitive and can be anteposed. Cf.:

*most širin+**oj** (v) 10 metrov* ~ **širin+**oj** (v) 10 metrov most*   vs.
*most neobyčajnoj širin+**y*** 'bridge of.extraordinary width' ~
*neobyčajnoj širin+**y** most*.

In all the remaining types of the N→N_{GEN} phrase, 'N_{GEN}' is semantically not linked to 'N' directly by a predicate-argument relation: either 'N_{GEN}' and 'N' are linked indirectly—via an additional predicate (or a configuration of predicates), or they are semantically not linked at all, forming a non-compositional phraseme.

5.3.4 *Genitivus Possessivus*: the possessive-adnominal-attributive SSyntRel

$N_{GEN\text{-poss}}$ and N are semantically linked indirectly—via the predicate 'belong.to' [= 'be.owned.by']:

(10) *sad otca* 'garden of.Father'
= 'garden **belonging.to** Father'

derev'ja soseda 'trees of.neighbor'
= 'trees **belonging.to** the neighbor'

stadion universiteta 'stadium of.University'
= 'stadium **belonging.to** the University'

bol'nica ministerstva 'hospital of.ministry'
= 'hospital **belonging.to** the ministry'

[*zamorskie*] *territorii Francii* '[overseas] territories of.France'
= 'territories **belonging.to** France'

Consequently, $N_{GEN\text{-poss}}$ denotes a person in the broadest sense: an individual, an organization, a country, etc., and N, an entity that can be owned. This means that 'N' can be only a semantic name or a quasi-predicate, so that the possibility of a semantic contrast between $N_{GEN\text{-poss}}$ and $N_{GEN\text{-subj/obj}}$ is limited, although not excluded.

Criterion **C1**, Condition 1:

(11) a. Semantic contrast between $N_{GEN\text{-poss}}$ and $N_{GEN\text{-subj}}/N_{GEN\text{-obj}}$
skul'ptura Nikolaeva 'sculpture of.Nikolaev':

either *skul'ptura Nikolaeva*$_{N_{GEN\text{-poss}}}$ 'sculpture belonging to Nikolaev';
or *skul'ptura Nikolaeva*$_{N_{GEN\text{-subj}}}$ 'sculpture created by Nikolaev';
or else *skul'ptura Nikolaeva*$_{N_{GEN\text{-obj}}}$ 'sculpture representing Nikolaev'.

b. Different syntactic behavior of $N_{GEN\text{-poss}}$ with respect to $N_{GEN\text{-subj}}/N_{GEN\text{-subj}}$ and $N_{GEN\text{-qual}}$

i. *skul'ptury Nikolaeva*$_{N_{GEN\text{-subj}}}$ [*Omskogo*] ***muzeja***$_{N_{GEN\text{-poss}}}$
'sculptures created by Nikolaev belonging to Omsk Museum' ~
*skul'ptury [*Omskogo*] ***muzeja*** *Nikolaeva*

ii. *fabriki* [*kuxonnoj*] *mebeli*$_{N_{GEN\text{-obj}}}$ [*našego*] ***goroda***$_{N_{GEN\text{-poss}}}$
'factories of kitchen furniture belonging to our town' ~
*fabriki [*našego*] ***goroda*** [*kuxonnoj*] *mebeli*

iii. *park [ogromnogo] razmera*$_{\text{NGEN-qual}}$ *[našego]* **goroda**$_{\text{NGEN-poss}}$
'park [of.huge] size [of.our] town' ~
park [našego]* **goroda *[ogromnogo] razmera* (for the meaning 'huge-size park')

As far as linear ordering is concerned, N$_{\text{GEN-poss}}$ follows all other N$_{\text{GEN}}$s.

Since N$_{\text{GEN-poss}}$ expresses the semanteme 'belong.to', it is quite natural to introduce the corresponding SSyntRel: **possessive-adnominal-attributive**.[4]

Criterion **C3**:

The **poss-adnom** SSyntRel is non-repeatable, just as the **subj-adnom** and **obj-adnom** SSyntRels.

At the DSynt-level, the N$_{\text{GEN-poss}}$ is marked by the fictitious lexeme «PRINADLEŽAT'»
[= «BELONG»].

The "possessive" syntactic relation—interpreting "possession" in the most liberal way possible— occupies a place of honor in linguistic typology (see, e. g., Aikhenvald 2013). On the one hand, all actual uses of the genitive case developed out of its possessive use (in the strict sense of ownership); on the other hand, languages manifest a multitude of formal means to express "possession." This is a weighty argument in favor of introducing the **genitive-possessive** SSyntRel.

The **possessive-adnominal** SSyntRel describes exclusively N→N$_{\text{GEN}}$ phrases.

5.3.5 *Genitivus Attributivus*: the characterizing-adnominal-attributive SSyntRel

N$_{\text{GEN-attr}}$ and N are semantically linked by an "additional" predicate 'σ':

'$\underline{N}$←i–σ–j→N$_{\text{GEN-attr}}$'.

This can be almost any general binary predicate, as is seen in (12):[5]

---

[4] The **possessive** SSyntRel was proposed for English (Mel'čuk & Pertsov 1987: 139–140; Mel'čuk 2016: 97) to describe N's←N phrases (***Dad's arrival**, a whole **month's work***).
[5] "Almost" is necessary since some constraints do exist. First, this 'σ' is different from 'belong.to' (the **possessive** SSyntRel) and 'similar.to' (the **metaphorical** SSyntRel). Second, as Raxilina (2010: 253) noted, the predicative semanteme 'X prednaznačen dlja Y-a' ≈ 'X is for Y' cannot be expressed by N$_{\text{GEN}}$ but requires an explicit expression: 'book that is.for Pete' ⇔ *kniga dlja Peti*/*kniga Peti. And, of course, there can be other such cases.

(12) *vozdux gor* 'air of.mountains'
= 'air that **exists.in** the mountains'

životnye savanny 'animals of.savannah'
= 'animals that **live.in** the savannah'

filosofija dvadcatogo veka 'philosophy of.twentieth century'
= 'philosophy **practiced.in** 20th century

strana l'vov 'country of.lions'
= 'country that **is.inhabited.by** lions'

dela [minuvšix] dnej [Puškin] 'events [of.past] days'
= 'events that **took.place.in** the past'

krik boli 'cry of.pain'
= 'cry **caused.by** pain'

[dva] časa dnja/noči '[two] o'clock of.day [PM] / of.night [AM]'
= 'two o'clock **during** the day/the night'

KADEŠ [drevneegipetskix] xronik 'KADESH [of.ancient.Egyptian] chronicles'
= 'KADESH that **is.mentioned.in** ancient Egyptian chronicles'

Criterion **C1**, Condition 1:

(13) a. Semantic contrast between $N_{\text{GEN-attr}}$ and $N_{\text{GEN-subj}}$
  i. *lob borca*$_{N_{\text{GEN-attr}}}$ 'forehead of.wrestler' [A. Žolkovskij]
      = 'forehead **typical.for** a wrestler' vs.
  ii. *lob [étogo] borca*$_{N_{\text{GEN-subj}}}$ forehead [of.this] wrestler'
  iii. *polovina [18-go] veka*$_{N_{\text{GEN-attr}}}$ 'half of.18th century'
      = 'a half [of an artifact] **manufactured.in** the 18th century'
      (while the other half was manufactured in a different century) vs.
  iv. *polovina [18-go] veka*$_{N_{\text{GEN-subj}}}$ '[one] half of.18th century'

  b. Different syntactic behavior of $N_{\text{GEN-attr}}$ with respect to $N_{\text{GEN-subj}}$/ $N_{\text{GEN-obj}}$, $N_{\text{GEN-qual}}$ and $N_{\text{GEN-poss}}$
  i. *lob borca*$_{N_{\text{GEN-attr}}}$ *[našego] polkovnika*$_{N_{\text{GEN-subj}}}$ 'forehead of.wrestler [of.our] colonel' ~ **lob [našego] polkovnika borca*
  ii. *bjust karrarskogo mramora*$_{N_{\text{GEN-attr}}}$ *molodoj ženščiny*$_{N_{\text{GEN-obj}}}$ 'bust of.Carrara marble of.young woman' = 'bust **made.of** Carrara marble' ~ *?bjust molodoj ženščiny karrarskogo mramora*

NB The construction in (13b-ii) is quite similar to the constructions described by the **qual-adnom** SSyntRel, see Subsection 5.3.3. However, in spite of this similarity, there are two essential differences:

- Semantic difference: N$_{GEN-qual}$ expresses a predicate denoting a property and takes N as its Sem-actant, while N$_{GEN-attr}$ in (13b-ii) denotes a substance—material of which the denotation of N is made.
- Syntactic difference: N$_{GEN-qual}$ can precede N, but N$_{GEN-attr}$ cannot: *neobyčajnoj krasoty bjust molodoj ženščiny* 'of.extraordinary beauty bust of.young woman' vs. **karrarskogo mramora bjust molodoj ženščiny*.

  iii. *vozdux [neobyčajnoj] čistoty*$_{NGEN-qual}$ [***gimalajskix***] ***vysot***$_{NGEN-attr}$
   'air [of.extraordinary] purity [of.Himalayan] heights' [= 'air **existing in** Himalayan heights'] ~
   ?*vozdux **gimalajskix vysot** neobyčajnoj čistoty*

  iv. *mašina [moskovskogo]* ***avtozavoda***$_{NGEN-attr}$ *ètogo] general-majora*$_{NGEN-poss}$
   'car [of.Moscow] automaker [of.this] major-general' [= 'car **manufatured.by** the Moscow automaker **belonging.to** this major-general'] ~
   mašina ètogo general-majora moskovskogo **avtozavoda*

Deviations from the standard ordering N$_{GEN-attr}$ + N$_{GEN-obj}$ and N$_{GEN-qual}$ + N$_{GEN-attr}$

1. If N$_{GEN-attr}$ denotes localization (of N), it follows the cosubordinated N$_{GEN-obj}$, see (14a).
2. If N$_{GEN-attr}$ denotes material or kind (of N), it precedes a cosubordinated N$_{GEN-qual}$, see (14b–c).

(14) a. *fabriki obuvi*$_{NGEN-obj}$ ***Italii***$_{NGEN-attr}$ 'factories of.shoes of.Italy' = 'factories **situated.in** Italy' ~   **fabriki **Italii** obuvi*
   b. *stol **krasnogo dereva***$_{NGEN-attr}$ *ogromnyx razmerov*N$_{GEN-qual}$
   'table of.red wood of.huge dimensions' ~
   stol ogromnyx razmerov*$_{NGEN-qual}$ ***krasnogo dereva*$_{NGEN-attr}$

The versatility of the predicate 'σ', which semantically underlies the N→N$_{GEN-attr}$ phrase, reminds one of nominal compounds, e. g. in English. The attempts at describing semantic relations between the members of an English nominal compound—that is a phrase of the N$_1$ + N$_2$ type—are numerous; suffice it to indicate, for instance, the classic Hatcher 1960 and Levi 1978, as well as more recent Weiskopf 2007 ones. The researchers specify a couple dozen meanings, insisting, however, that their inventory is not and cannot be exhaustive. That is what I think as well; but in this chapter I will not try to circumscribe more precisely the range of possible 'σ' in the Russian semanteme configuration 'N←i–σ–j→N$_{GEN-attr}$'.

The N→N$_{GEN-attr}$ phrase is described by the **characterizing-adnominal-attributive** SSyntRel.

The **charact-adnom** SSyntRel is opposed to the **subj-adnom, obj-adnom, qual-adnom,** and **poss-adnom** SSyntRel.

Criterion **C3**:

Since 'σ' is so variegated, the $N_{GEN\text{-}attr}$ is repeatable:

(15) *kol'co [dutogo] zolota*$_{NGEN\text{-}attr}$ *[šestnadcatogo] veka*$_{NGEN\text{-}attr}$[6]
'ring [of.filled] gold [of.sixteenth] century'

The description of the $N \rightarrow N_{GEN\text{-}attr}$ phrase requires two additional remarks.

– Not every N_{GEN} semantically fit for the $N \rightarrow N_{GEN\text{-}attr}$ construction can be freely used in it. First, several $N_{GEN\text{-}attr}$s are subject to **semantic** constraints (Raxilina 2010); for instance, in the $N \rightarrow N_{GEN\text{-}attr}$ phrase with the underlying predicate 'be.in' the noun N must be used generically: *devuški Moskvy* or *každaja devuška Moskvy*, but not **èta devuška Moskvy*. Second, there are also **lexical** constraints: thus, *mebel' [krasnogo] dereva* 'furniture [of.red] wood' = 'of mahogany' is perfectly OK, while **mebel' [karel'skoj] sosny* 'furniture [of. Karelian] pine' is impossible (the correct expression is *mebel' iz* ['from'] *karel'skoj sosny*). Similarly, *kolonny [čërnogo] mramora* 'columns [of.black] marble' vs **kolonny [zolotistogo] pesčanika* 'columns [of.golden] sandstone' (the correct expression is *kolonny iz [zolotistogo] pesčanika*). Therefore, the nouns that can be used as dependents of the **qual-adnom** SSyntRel must be lexically marked—that is, they must be supplied with a special syntactic feature. This applies at least to the names of materials.
– Since the **charact-adnominal** SSyntRel is so "loose," it can cover cases of semantic-syntactic mismatches in which an N_{GEN} participates; here is one such case, linked to particular lexical units (or classes of lexical units).

The semantic-syntactic mismatch linked to lexical units of LJUBIMYJ 'favorite' type:

'X←1–ljubimyj–2→Y' ⇔ LJUBIMYJ←ATTR–L('X')–ATTR→L('Y') ⇔
LJUBIMYJ←**modif**–L('X')–**charact-adnom**→L('Y') ⇔
ljubimyj šokolad$_X$ *Peti*$_Y$ 'favored chocolate of.Petya'

The noun N_Y, which semantically depends on 'ljubimyj' (it is its Sem-actant 2), depends syntactically (as an $N_{GEN\text{-}attr}$) on the noun N_X, modified by LJUBIMYJ. (Cf. Partee & Borschev 2000 on the similar behavior of the English adjective FAVORITE.)

The adjective RODNOJ 'native' [= 'where someone was born'] behaves in the same way:

---

[6] $N_{GEN\text{-}attr}$ denoting material requires an adjectival modifier: **kol'co zolota*$_{NGEN\text{-}attr}$ 'ring of.gold'.

'X←1-rodnoj-2→Y' ⇔ RODNOJ←ATTR-L('X')-ATTR→L('Y') ⇔
RODNOJ←**modif**-L('X')-**charact-adnom**→L('Y') ⇔
rodnoj gorod$_X$ *Peti*$_Y$ 'native town of.Petya'

To this we have to add all superlatives:

'X←1-samyj.znamenityj-2→Y' ⇔ ZNAMENITYJ$_{SUPERL}$←ATTR-L('X')-ATTR→L('Y')
samyj znamenityj xokkeist$_X$ *Kanady*$_Y$ 'the.most famous hockey-player of.Canada'

The corresponding representations are given in Section 5.4. This mismatch is due to the fact that the predicate 'σ' linking N and N$_{GEN}$ is, in this case, expressed by a lexeme that does not accept N$_{GEN}$ as syntactic dependent.

Along with the N→N$_{GEN}$-$_{attr}$ phrases, the **charact-adnom** SSyntRel describes as well all PREP→N phrases functioning as adnominal attributes:

(16) a. *knigi   s   poželtevšimi stranicami v kožanyx pereplëtax*
       books with yellowish   pages   in leather bindings
    b. *prestuplenija kommunizma* **protiv** *čelovestva v točnom smysle*
       crimes   of.Communism against humanity in proper meaning
       slova
       of.the.word

5.3.6 *Genitivus Metaphoricus*: the **metaphorical-adnominal-attributive** SSyntRel

N$_{GEN\text{-metaph}}$ and N are semantically linked indirectly — via the predicate 'be.similar. to', but with what is known as head-switching:

'X←1-similar-2→Y' ⇔ L('Y')-ATTR→«PREDSTAVLJAT'»-II→L('X')
zvëzdy, poxožie na iskry 'stars similar to sparks' ⇒ *iskry zvëzd* 'sparks of.stars'

This construction is marked in the DSynt-structure by the fictitious lexeme «PREDSTAVLJAT'» [= «REPRESENT»], which marks the expression as metaphoric.

N$_{GEN\text{-metaph}}$ expresses the basis of a metaphoric transfer to N. Suppose that the Speaker wants to compare the Moon—the basis of a metaphoric transfer—to a cold eye, which is the metaphor: the Moon is similar to a cold eye; and he says [*xolodnyj*] *glaz luny* '[cold] eye of.moon' (see, for instance, Mixeev 2000).

(17) *iskry zvëzd* 'sparks of.stars'; *sutany dyma* 'soutanes of.smoke'
    lenta dorogi 'ribbon of.road'; *bacilly straxa* 'bacilli of.fear'
    poluxleb ploti 'halfbread of.flesh' [O. Mandelštam]
    [*opozdavšie*] *pticy gazet* [R. Roždestvenskij] '[belated] birds of.newspapers'

bljudečki-očki [spasatel'nyx] krugov [V. Majakovskij] 'saucers-eyeglasses of.life.buoys'

Criterion **C1**, Condition 1:

(18) a. Semantic contrast between $N_{GEN\text{-}metaph}$ and $N_{GEN\text{-}subj}/N_{GEN\text{-}obj}/N_{GEN\text{-}qual}/N_{GEN\text{-}attr}/N_{GEN\text{-}poss}$
  i. *kolesnica solnca* 'chariot of.Sun':
  kolesnica solnca$_{N_{GEN\text{-}metaph}}$ 'Sun as if it were a chariot'   vs.
  kolesnica Solnca$_{N_{GEN\text{-}subj}/N_{GEN\text{-}poss}}$
  'chariot of somebody [e. g., a god] called Sun'
  ii. *pytka ljubvi* 'torture of.love':
  pytka ljubvi$_{N_{GEN\text{-}metaph}}$ 'love as if it were a torture'   vs.
  pytka ljubvi$_{N_{GEN\text{-}obj}/N_{GEN\text{-}attr}}$ 'torture applied to love/induced by love'
  iii. *požar cvetov* 'fire of.colors':
  požar cvetov$_{N_{GEN\text{-}metaph}}$ 'colors as if they were a fire'   vs.
  požar [raznyx] cvetov$_{N_{GEN\text{-}qual}}$ 'fire [of.different] colors'

  b. Different syntactic behavior of $N_{GEN\text{-}metaph}$ with respect to $N_{GEN\text{-}qual}$ and $N_{GEN\text{-}attr}$ (with all other N_{GEN}s, $N_{GEN\text{-}metaph}$ cannot cooccur for semantic reasons)
  i. *iskry [neobyčajnoj] jarkosti*$_{N_{GEN\text{-}qual}}$ *[takix dalëkix]* **zvëzd**$_{N_{GEN\text{-}metaph}}$ ~
  'sparks [of.extraordinary] brightness [of.so faraway] stars'
  iskry [takix dalëkix]* **zvëzd *neobyčajnoj jarkosti*
  [for the meaning 'sparks are extraordinarily bright']
  ii. *poluxleb* **ploti**$_{N_{GEN\text{-}metaph}}$ *Mandel'štama*$_{N_{GEN\text{-}attr}}$
  'half-bread of.flesh of.Mandelstam'
  [= 'expression "half-bread of flesh" used by Mandelstam'] ~
  poluxleb Mandel'štama* **ploti

The SSyntRel for $N_{GEN\text{-}metaph}$ can be called **metaphorical-adnominal-attributive**.

Criterion **C3**:

The **metaphorical-adnominal** SSyntRel is non-repeatable.
  Note that the **metaph-adnom** SSyntRel is used in the collocations with the LF Figur:[7]

---

[7] Lexical function Figur returns for a lexical unit L the lexical unit L' that expresses the standard metaphor for L:
Figur(*tuman* 'fog') = *pelena [tumana]* 'curtain of.fog'   or
Figur(*gnev* 'anger') = *plamja [gneva]* 'flame of.anger'.

stena-**metaph-adnom**→*doždja*
'wall of.rain'

plamja-**metaph-adnom**→*strasti*
'flame of.passion'

červ'-**metaph-adnom**→*somnenija*
'worm of.doubt'

luč-**metaph-adnom**→*nadeždy*
'ray of.hope'

grad-**metaph-adnom**→*pul'*
'hail of.bullets'

znamja-**metaph-adnom**→*bor'by*
'banner of.fight'

The **metaph-adnom** SSyntRel describes only N→N$_{GEN}$ phrases.

5.3.7 *Genitivus Phrasemicus*: no special SSyntRel

N$_{GEN\text{-}phras}$s appear within phrasemes and come in two major types: an N$_{GEN\text{-}phras}$ being part of a compositional phraseme (a collocation or a termeme) and an N$_{GEN\text{-}phras}$ being part of a non-compositional phraseme (an idiom or a nomineme). This difference is relevant since in the deep-syntactic structure, a compositional phraseme is represented by its complete subtree (so that the N$_{GEN}$ must be present already at this level), while a non-compositional phraseme appears as a single node (and the N$_{GEN}$ enters the scene only in the surface-syntactic structure).

(19) a. Collocations
    i. *čelovek dela* ⟨*dolga, slova, česti*⟩
       'man of.business ⟨of.duty, of.word, of.honor⟩'
       dom [našix] grëz 'house [of.our] dreams'
       roman veka 'novel of.century'
    ii. *gvardii seržant* 'of.Guards sergeant'
       ordena [Lenina] zavod «Molot» 'of.Order [of.Lenin] factory «Hammer»' = '«Hammer» factory decorated with the Order of Lenin'

  b. Termemes
    dvigatel' [vnutrennego] sgoranija 'engine [of.internal] combustion'
    zakon Oma 'law of.Ohm'; *bolezn' Al'cgejmera* 'disease of.Alzheimer'

(20) a. Idioms
    ⌜*čaška Petri*⌝ 'cup of.Petri' = 'Petri dish'
    ⌜*koktejl' Molotova*⌝ 'cocktail of.Molotov' = 'Molotov cocktail'
    ⌜*roza vetrov*⌝ 'rose of.winds' = 'compass rose'
    ⌜*krik duši*⌝ 'scream of.soul' = 'verbal expression of very strong emotions'
    ⌜*pojas vernosti*⌝ 'belt of.fidelity' = 'chastity belt'
    ⌜*dama serdca*⌝ 'lady of.heart' = 'beloved woman'

⌜*pir Valtasara*⌝ 'feast of.Belshazzar'
⌜*lico* [*kavkazskoj*] *nacional'nosti*⌝ 'person [of.Caucasian] ethnicity' =
'[a] native of the Caucasus region'
b. Nominemes
More Laptevyx 'Sea of.Laptevs'
sozvezdie Gončix Psov 'Constellation of.Greyhounds'
Ostrova Zelënogo Mysa 'Islands [of.Green] Cape'

An $N_{GEN\text{-phras}}$ is special only in that it is an element of a phraseme, since from a purely syntactic viewpoint it is like any other, not phraseologized N_{GEN}. However, exactly because of its phraseological nature, it linearly precedes all other N_{GEN}s and, in some cases (specified lexically), it can or must be anteposed to its N. These particularities of an $N_{GEN\text{-phras}}$ can be indicated in the surface-syntactic structure in one of two ways: either by a special SSyntRel or by special syntactic features of the $N_{GEN\text{-phras}}$. Postulating for $N_{GEN\text{-phras}}$s a geni**t**ive-phrasemic-adnom SSyntRel seems, at first blush, an easy solution, but, unfortunately, it cannot be accepted. The reason is simple: There are lots of phraseologized clause elements that show unusual word order and other "deviations." Thus:

- Phraseologized modifiers, with obligatory postposition of the modifying adjective, e. g.: *papa*–modificative→*Rimskij* 'Pope **Roman**' or *xmyr'*–modificative→*bolotnyj* 'douche.bag swampy' ≈ 'insignificant, despicable man'.
- Phraseologized subjects, with obligatory anteposition/postposition of the subject, e. g., the idioms ⌜*Čërt*←subjectival-[*ego*]-*poberi!*⌝ '**Devil** him take!' = 'Let the devil take him!', with obligatory anteposition of the subject, vs. ⌜*Ne daj*–subjectival→*Bog!*⌝ 'Not allow **God**!' = 'God forbid!', with obligatory postposition of the subject.
- Phraseologized direct objects with obligatory anteposition of the DirO, e. g., the idioms ⌜***pal'čiki***←dir-obj-*oblížeš*⌝ 'fingers you.will.lick' = 'this is very tasty' or ⌜***sobaku***←dir-obj-*s″est*⌝ 'dog [to] eat' = 'be very experienced'.
- Phraseologized circumstantials, with obligatory anteposition of the circumstantial (and of the DirO), e. g., the idioms

```
                  ┌─────── direct-obj ───────┐
```
Moju ustalost' ⌜***kak***←circumstantial-[*rukoj*]-*snjalo*⌝
'My tiredness **as** with.hand [it] took.away'. = 'My tiredness vanished in a trice'.

```
              ┌────── direct-obj ──────┐
```
Ivana ⌜***kak***←circumstantial-[*vetrom*]-*sdulo*⌝
'Ivan **as** by.wind [it] blew away'. = 'Ivan disappeared in a trice'.

- Phraseologized preposition complements, with obligatory postposition of the PREP, e. g., the idiom ⌜*ne korysti*←**prepositional**-*radi*⌝ 'not gain **for**' = 'not for gain'.

If we systematically apply this solution—that is, if we introduce special *X*-phrasemic SSyntRels, we will have to double all SSyntRels whose dependents can be phraseologized and as a result acquire "exotic" syntactic properties within phrasemes. Therefore, we are forced to accept the opposite solution: a lexeme that manifests deviant behavior because it is part of a phraseme must receive the corresponding syntactic features at the moment where the node of this phraseme is expanded into its subtree. The conclusion: there is no special **phrasemic-adnom** SSyntRel; an $N_{GEN\text{-}phras}$ is subordinated to its governing N by the **charact-adnom** SSyntRel. For instance:

koktejl'–**charact-adnom**→*Molotova* 'cocktail of.Molotov' = 'incendiary weapon—a glass bottle with flammable liquid ...'

5.4 Overview of the six SSyntRels proposed

Six SSyntRels are proposed for the description of the Russian $N{\rightarrow}N_{GEN}$ phrases:

1) **subjectival-adnominal-completive**
2) **objectival-adnominal-completive**
3) **qualificative-adnominal-attributive**
4) **possessive-adnominal-attributive**
5) **characterizing-adnominal-attributive**
6) **metaphorical-adnominal-attributive**

For each of these six SSyntRels the corresponding formal representations are given: the semantic subnetwork—its semantic source, the deep-syntactic subtree, the surface-syntactic subtree, as well as an example.

1) Subjectival-adnominal-completive SSyntRel

Sem	'$\underline{Y}$–1→X' [8]
DSynt	L('Y')$_{(N)}$–I→L('X')$_{(N)}$
SSynt	L('Y')$_{(N)}$–subj-adnom→L('X')$_{(N)}$
Example	'$\underline{spat'}_{'Y'}$–1→Ivan$_{'X'}$' [= 'Ivan <u>sleeps</u>'] SON–I→IVAN 'Ivan's sleep' SON–subj-adnom→IVAN: *son Ivana*

---

[8] A reminder: underscoring of a semanteme '$\underline{\sigma}$' in a semantic structure 'S' shows its communicatively dominant status: '$\underline{\sigma}$' is a minimal paraphrase of the whole 'S', such that 'S' can be reduced to '$\underline{\sigma}$' with loss, but without distortion, of information. Thus, 'dog←1–$\underline{sleeps}$' represent *A/The dog sleeps*, and '$\underline{dog}$←1–sleeps' underlies *a/the sleeping dog* and *a/the dog that is sleeping*.

2) Objectival-adnominal-completive SSyntRel

Sem	'Y–2→X'
DSynt	L('Y')$_{(N)}$–II→L('X')$_{(N)}$
SSynt	L('Y')$_{(N)}$–obj-adnom→L('X')$_{(N)}$
Example	'nagradit'$_{Y'}$–2→Ivan$_{X'}$' [= '[Somebody] decorates Ivan [with a medal]'] NAGRAŽDENIE–II→IVAN 'decorating of Ivan' NAGRAŽDENIE–ob-adnom→IVAN: *nagraždenie Ivana*

3) Qualifying-adnominal-attributive SSyntRel

Sem	'X←1–Y←1–Z'
DSynt	L('X')$_{(N)}$–ATTR→L('Y')$_{(N)}$–ATTR→L('Z')$_{(ADJ)}$
SSynt	L('X')$_{(N)}$–qual-adnom→L('Y')$_{(N)}$–modif→L('Z')$_{(ADJ)}$
Example	'dom'$_{X'}$←1–krasivyj'$_{Y'}$←1–očen'–očen'$_{Z'}$' [= 'an extraordinarily beautiful house'] DOM–ATTR→KRASOTA–ATTR→Magn [Magn ⇒ NEOBYČAJNYJ 'extraordinary'] 'house of extraordinary beauty' DOM–qual-adnom→KRASOTA–modificative→NEOBYČAJNYJ: *dom neobyčajnoj krasoty / neobyčajnoj krasoty dom*

Only the case where N implements SemA 1 of N$_{GEN}$ is presented. Similarly:

(21) a. 'čelovek←1–duša←1–kristal'nejšij' ⇔
'human.being←1–soul←1–crystal.purest'
ČELOVEK–ATTR→DUŠA–ATTR→KRISTAL'NEJŠIJ ⇔
ČELOVEK–attr-adnom→DUŠA–modif→KRISTAL'NEJŠIJ ⇔
Kristal'nejšej duši čelovek! 'Of.crystal.purest soul human.being!'
[V. I. Lenin about his wife, N. K. Krupskaja, in a risqué political joke]

4) Possessive-adnominal-attributive SSyntRel

Sem	'X←1–prinadležat'–2→Y' [= 'X←1–belong–2→Y']
DSynt	L(X)$_{(N)}$–ATTR→«PRINADLEŽAT'»–II→L(Y)$_{(N)}$ [«PRINADLEŽAT'» 'belong' is a fictitious lexeme marking the possessive relationship]
SSynt	L(X)$_{(N)}$–possessive-adnom→L(Y)$_{(N)}$
Example	'dom'$_{X'}$←1–prinadležat'–2→ministr$_{Y'}$' [= 'house that belongs to the minister'] DOM–ATTR→«PRINADLEŽAT'»–II→MINSTR 'house of.minister' DOM–possessive-adnom→MINISTR: *dom ministra*

5) Characterizing-adnominal-attributive SSyntRel

Sem	'X←1–naxodit'sja–2→Y' [= 'X←1–be.located–2→Y']
DSynt	L('X')₍ₙ₎–ATTR→«NAXODIT'SJA»–II→L('Y')₍ₙ₎
	[«NAXODIT'SJA» 'be.located' is a fictitious lexeme marking the localization relationship]
SSynt	L('X')₍ₙ₎–charact-adnom→L('Y')₍ₙ₎
Example	'<u>mosty</u>.ₓ,←1–naxodit'sja–2→Pariž.ᵧ,' [= 'bridges that are in Paris']
	MOST_PL–ATTR→«NAXODIT'SJA»–II→PARIŽ 'bridges of.Paris'
	MOST_PL–charact-adnom→PARIŽ: *mosty Pariža*

Only the case where 'σ' = 'be.located' is presented. Similarly:

(22) a. '<u>putešestvija</u>←1–proisxodit'←1–vremja–2→vek←1–vosemnadcatyj' ⇔
'travels←1–happen←1–time–2→century←1–eighteenth'
PUTEŠESTVIE_PL–ATTR→«PROISXODIT'»–II→VEK–ATTR→VOSEMNADCATYJ ⇔
PUTEŠESTVIE_PL–charact-adnom→VEK–modif→*vosemnadcatyj* ⇔
putešestvija vosemnadcatogo veka 'travels of the 18th century'

b. '<u>opyt</u>←1–[priobretënnyj]–v_tečenie–2→nedelja←1–ètot' ⇔
'experience←1–[acquired]–during–2→week←1–this'
OPYT–ATTR→«V_TEČENIE»–II→NEDELJA–ATTR→ÈTOT ⇔
OPYT–charact-adnom→NEDELJA–modificative→ÈTOT ⇔
opyt ètoj nedeli 'experience of this week'

Special Cases of N_GEN-attr

The semantic-syntactic mismatch caused by the adjective LJUBIMYJ 'favorite' (Section 5.3.5)

Sem	'X←1–ljubimyj–2→Y' [= 'X←1–favorite–2→Y']
DSynt	LJUBIMYJ←ATTR–L('X')₍ₙ₎–ATTR→L('Y')₍ₙ₎
SSynt	LJUBIMYJ←modificative–L('X')₍ₙ₎–charact-adnom→L('Y')₍ₙ₎
Example	'<u>fil'm</u>←1–ljubimyj–2→Petja' [= 'film that is favorite of Petya']
	LJUBIMYJ ←ATTR–FIL'M–ATTR→PETJA 'favorite film of.Petya'
	LJUBIMYJ←modificative–FIL'M–charact-adnom→PETJA: *ljubimyj fil'm Peti*

5.4 Overview of the six SSyntRels proposed — 229

$N_{GEN-attr}$ in a non-standard collocation

Sem	'$\underline{X}$←1–Y'
	The meaning 'Y' corresponds to a non-standard collocational LF Ψ in the lexical entry for L('X')
DSynt	L('X')$_{(N)}$–ATTR→ –$_{phras, synt1, ...}$
	[The DSynt-structure contains the lexeme L, which is the value of the non-standard LF Ψ(L('X')); L is taken, together with additional syntactic features, from the lexical entry for L('X').]
SSynt	L('X')–**r**→L$_{(phras, synt1, ...)}$
	[The SSyntRel **r** is also taken from the lexical entry for L('X') — together with L.]
Example	'seržant←1–služit'–2→gvardija' [= 'sergeant that serves in the Guards']
	SERŽANT$_{L('X')}$–ATTR→GVARDIJA$_{(phras, antepcs)SG-L('Y')}$ 'sergeant of.Guards'
	SERŽANT–charact-adnom→GVARDIJA$_{(phras, antepos)SG}$: *gvardii seržant* 'of.Guards sergeant'

$N_{GEN-attr}$ in a termeme

Sem	'$\underline{X}$←1–Y' | The meaning 'Y' corresponds to a non-standard termemic LF Ψ in the lexical entry for L('X')
DSynt	L(X)$_{(N)}$–ATTR→«TERMIN»–II→L
	[The lexeme L, which is the value of Ψ(L('X')) is taken, together with additional syntactic features, from the lexical entry for L('X'); the fictitious lexeme «TERMIN» means 'term'.]
SSynt	L(X)$_{(N)}$–**r**→L
	[The SSyntRel **r** is also taken from the lexical entry for L('X')$_{(N)}$—together with L.]
Example	'bolezn'←1–affecting the brain of older people...' [= 'Alzheimer's disease']
	BOLEZN'$_{L('X')}$–ATTR→«TERMIN»–II→AL'CGEJMER$_L$ 'disease of.Alzheimer'
	BOLEZN'–charact-adnom→AL'CGEJMER: *bolezn' Al'cgejmera*

$N_{GEN-attr}$ in an idiom

Sem	'X'
DSynt	⌐L$_1$_L$_2$...¬ [one node]
SSynt	L$_1$–**r**→L$_{2(phraseological)}$
	[The SSyntRel **r** is specified in the lexical entry for the idiom ⌐L$_1$_L$_2$...¬ — in its SSynt-tree.]
Example	'ničtožnaja ličnost'' [= 'totally unimportant person', 'a nobody']
	⌐OTSTAVNOJ$_{L_3}$ KOZY$_{L_2}$ BARABANŠČIK$_{L_1}$¬ [one node] 'retired goat's drummer'
	BARABANŠČIK–charact-adnominal→KOZA$_{(phras, antepos)SG}$: *otstavnoj kozy barabanščik*

N_{GEN-attr} in a nomineme	
Sem	'X'
DSynt	L₁_L₂_... [one node]
SSynt	L₁–r→L₂(phraseological)
Example	'Zemlja_Franca-Iosifa' [a polar archipelago] [= 'Franz-Joseph Land'] ZEMLJA_FRANC-IOSIF [one node] 'Land of.Franz-Joseph' ZEMLJA $_{SG_{L_1}}$–charact-adnominal→FRANC$_{L_2}$–name-junctive-3→IOSIF: *Zemlja Franca-Iosifa*

6) Metaphorical-adnominal SSyntRel	
Sem	'$\underline{X}$←1–poxožij–2→Y' [= '$\underline{X}$←1–similar–2→Y']
DSynt	L('Y')$_{(N)}$–ATTR→«PREDSTAVLJAT'»–II→L('X')$_{(N)}$ [«PREDSTAVLJAT'» 'represent' (a fictitious lexeme) marks a metaphoric relationship.]
SSynt	L('Y')$_{(N)}$–metaph-adnom→L('X')$_{(N)}$
Example	'*zvëzdy*←1–poxožij–2→iskry' [= 'stars similar to sparks'] ISKRA$_{PL}$–ATTR→«PREDSTAVLJAT'»–II→ZVEZDA$_{PL}$ 'sparks of.stars' ISKRA$_{PL}$–metaph-adnom→ZVEZDA$_{PL}$: *iskry zvëzd*

5.5 Closing remarks: NGEN cannot be a personal pronoun

The SSyntRels proposed above for the description of the Russian N→N$_{GEN}$ phrases have the following syntactic property: their dependent, i. e. N$_{GEN}$, cannot be a nominal personal pronoun (JA 'I', TY 'you$_{SG}$', ON 'he', ...). For the **qualif-adnom** SSyntRel this is obvious, since the N$_{GEN\text{-}qual}$ must have a dependent adjective, and this is impossible for a personal pronoun. The other five adnominal SSyntRels could in principle allow for N$_{GEN}$ being a pronoun, but they do not (with one exception, to be mentioned right away):

(23) *son*–**subj-adnom**→*Ivana*   'sleep of.Ivan'   vs.
     *son–**subj-adnom**→***menja***   'sleep of.me'

   portret–**obj-adnom**→*Ivana*   'portrait of.Ivan'   vs.
   *portret–**obj-adnom**→***menja*** 'portrait of.me'

   dom–**poss-adnom**→*Ivana*   'house of.Ivan'   vs.
   *dom–**poss-adnom**→***menja***   'house of.me'

   mosty–**charact-adnom**→*Pariža*   'bridges of.Paris'   vs.
   *mosty–**charact-adnom**→***menja*** 'bridges of.me'
   [Paris is speaking, e.g. in a fantastic tale]

iskry-**metaph-adnom**→*zvëzd*   'sparks of.stars'   vs.
*iskry-**metaph-adnom**→*nas*   'sparks of.us'
[stars are speaking, e.g. in a fantastic tale]

At the same time, the replacement of N_{GEN} by a pronominal possessive adjective remains possible: ***moj*** *son* 'my sleep', ***moj*** *portret* 'my portrait', ***moj*** *dom* 'my house', ***moi*** *mosty* 'my bridges', ***naši*** *iskry* 'our sparks'.[9] Therefore, the impossibilities in (23) have to be blocked by the following general rule of Russian:

> A nominal personal pronoun in the genitive case cannot syntactically depend on a noun; the corresponding adjectival possessive pronoun must be used instead.

There is, however, an interesting exception: with some governors an **obj-adnom** N_{GEN} can be pronominalized by a nominal personal pronoun in the genitive, cf.:

(24) *vključenie*-**obj-adnom**→***menja*** *v sostav komiteta*
'inclusion of.me in body of.committee'
presledovanie-**obj-adnom**→***menja*** *policiej*   'persecution of.me by.police'
otpravka-**obj-adnom**→***menja*** *obratno*   'sending of.me back'

These expressions are highly constrained—both semantically (process-denoting nouns accept personal pronouns in the genitive more easily) and/or lexically (the capacity of having a genitive actant pronominalized has to be specified in the Government Pattern of the corresponding nouns.[10] (See relevant remarks in Apresjan 2010: 12–14.)

5.6 Conclusions

Three important conclusions can be drawn from the above discussion.

1. The six adnominal SSyntRels proposed for the SSynt-description of the Russian N→N_{GEN} phrases are necessary (barring my possible mistakes), but not sufficient for this task—not because more SSyntRels are needed, but simply because establishing the necessary SSyntRels for a particular type of

---

[9] The pronominal possessive adjectives are used here in the 1st person because in the 3rd person the forms of the nominal personal pronoun in the genitive and those of the corresponding possessive pronominal adjective are homophonous: EGO 'of.him/ his', EË 'of.her/her', IX 'of.them/their'.
[10] Once again, we see the special nature of direct objects which was mentioned in Subsection 5.3.1/2, p. 211.

phrase is but a very first step. To ensure a proper treatment of Russian N$_{GEN}$s, and in the first place, their correct linear ordering (with respect to other N$_{GEN}$s as well as to different dependents of the modified noun) we need a set of syntactic features for nouns that allow/disallow their appearance in particular construction of the N→N$_{GEN}$ type. As the next step, the following three sets of rules must be elaborated:

- The SSynt-rules for the N→N$_{GEN}$ phrases; these rules stipulate how the actual phrases (strictly speaking, their deep-morphological representations) are obtained from their SSynt-representations and positioned with respect to their governor and other cosubordinated N$_{GEN}$ phrases. These rules need a thorough description of linear ordering of Russian cosubordinated N$_{GEN}$s; such a description is presented in Chapter 11, pp. 369ff.
- The DSynt-rules for the N→N$_{GEN}$ phrases; these rules stipulate how their SSynt-representations are obtained from their DSynt-representations.
- The Sem-rules for the N→N$_{GEN}$ phrases; these rules stipulate how their DSynt-representations are obtained from their Sem-representations.

2. Linear ordering of cosubordinated N$_{GEN}$ phrases must be studied within a much broader frame of mutual ordering of all types of cosubordinated modifiers, in the first place—cosubordinated adjectives. Various semantic, referential, communicative, and phonological factors play a role and must be taken into account.

3. Since this chapter aims at a linguistically and typologically valid justification for the SSyntRels proposed, it is necessary to widen its linguistic base—that is, to compare our solution to adnominal dependents in other languages.

Previously published as Mel'čuk 2018a.

Part III: Hard Nuts in Syntax – Cracked by Dependency Description

6 Relative clause: a typology

6.1 The problem stated
6.2 What is a relative clause
    6.2.1 Some basic terms
    6.2.2 The notion of relative clause
    6.2.3 Restrictive vs. descriptive relative clauses
6.3 What is not a relative clause: constructions often confused with relative clauses
    6.3.1 Constructions isofunctional with relative clauses: non-clausal modifiers
        6.3.1.1 Modifying construction headed by a verb adjectivalization
                [= participial phrase]
        6.3.1.2 Modifying construction headed by a verb nominalization
                [= appositional phrase]
        6.3.1.3 Clause introduced by an expression meaning 'such that'
    6.3.2 Constructions isostructural with relative clauses: clausal non-modifiers
        6.3.2.1 Introductory remarks
        6.3.2.2 Pseudo-relative clauses
        6.3.2.3 Indirect-interrogative clauses
        6.3.2.4 Cleft clauses
        6.3.2.5 Nominalized clauses [= "internally-headed relative clauses"]
6.4 Typology of the restrictive relative clause
    6.4.1 Relative clauses at the semantic, deep-syntactic and surface-syntactic levels
    6.4.2 Deep- and surface-syntactic relations subordinating a relative clause
    6.4.3 Syntactic constraints on relative clauses
    6.4.4 Syntactic parameters characterizing a relative clause construction
    6.4.5 Illustrations of different types of RC constructions (L→RC)
        6.4.5.1 The RC's governor is a non-pronominal noun (L(N, non-pron)→RC)
        6.4.5.2 The RC's governor is a nominal pronoun (L(N, pron)→RC)
    6.4.6 Deep-morphological parameters characterizing the implementation of an RC
        6.4.6.1 Word order parameters characterizing an RC
        6.4.6.2 Inflectional parameters characterizing an RC

The present chapter has been conceived under the impact of the trail-blazing paper Zaliznjak & Padučeva 1975: I wanted to take the next step and bring the typology of relative clause to the modern level, 45 years later. However, many obstacles stood in my way—most then anything, the lack of many necessary notions and formalisms. As a result, my journey took years... Finally, in 2017 I was close to completion and looking forward to submitting my modest contribution to the evaluation and criticism of the two close friends, Andrej Zaliznjak and Elena Padučeva, who had introduced me to the domain. And then the tragedy struck: on 24th December 2017 Andrej Zaliznjak passed away, and on July 16th 2019 Elena Padučeva left us.

I dedicate this text to the loving memory of these two extraordinary human beings.

> Confusion is worse than error.
> Francis Bacon (1561–1626)

6.1 The problem stated

The relative clause [RC] is a hot topic in today's linguistics: Google offers hundreds of thousands of titles dealing with the RC, one way or another. It is absolutely out of the question to offer even a cursory overview of the relevant literature; I will limit myself to indicating just some major publications from which I took the data and some ideas for my own study: Benveniste 1957–58, Peranteau et al. (eds.) 1972, Zaliznjak & Padučeva 1975[2002], Keenan & Comrie 1977, Comrie & Keenan 1979, Lehmann 1984, Keenan 1985, Givón 1990: 645–698, Alexiadou et al. (eds.) 2000, Andrews 2007, Comrie & Estrada-Fernández (eds.) 2012, Xolodilova 2014, Matsumoto et al. (eds.) 2017; to this one has to add Dixon 2010: 313–369, a detailed typological study of relative clauses and similar constructions in the world's languages. In this connection, I can only repeat the famous statement by Newton: "If I have seen further, it is by standing on the shoulders of Giants."

The RC fully deserves this heightened attention: it is a very special type of subordinate clause. It is unique in that, as will be shown (6.4.4, p. 263), in the world's languages, RCs come in 36 syntactic types, each featuring a different syntactic structure and allowing—in principle—15 deep-morphological (= linear/inflectional) realizations. And all this without taking in consideration innumerable minor particularities found in RCs of various languages.

The task of this chapter is twofold:

1. To propose a rigorous definition of the RC.
2. To propose a rigorous typology of the RC—that is, a deductively organized calculus of its logically possible major types.

At the same time, the corresponding terminology must be stabilized and refined, where needed. However, no new linguistic facts are introduced: my account is 100% based on data already available.

NB I take linguistic facts and their analyses as they are presented in the original source; the relatively full bibliography on the RC is found in De Vries 2018.

In the present context, what matters most is the logic of the discussion. This chapter is, in the first place, an exercise in elaborating and perfecting the conceptual apparatus of linguistics.

6.2 What is a relative clause

6.2.1 Some basic terms

The first step must be sketching out, if only in broad lines, what exactly will be defined. (On principles for formulating linguistic definitions, see Chapter 8, Subsection 8.2.1, pp. 291*ff*.)

|| The relative clause is treated here as a **lexeme-modifying subordinate clause**.

Thus, the RC is considered strictly as a **syntactic phenomenon** with a well-defined **semantic function**, and therefore it receives a **combined semantic-syntactic definition**: it is a particular syntactic construction implementing a particular subclass of modifiers.

NB I do not follow the path blazed in Keenan & Comrie 1977: "It is necessary to have a largely **syntax-free way** of identifying RCs in an arbitrary language. Our solution to this problem is to use an essentially **semantically based** definition of RC" (p. 63; emphasis added—IM).

Definition 6.1 – modifier

$\tilde{L}$ stands for a lexical expression (= a phrase).

|| $\tilde{L}$ is a modifier of L in utterance **U** if and only if in the semantic structure of **U**, L depends on $\tilde{L}$ semantically (= 'L' is a semantic actant of '$\tilde{L}$'), and, in the deep-syntactic structure of **U**, $\tilde{L}$ directly depends on L syntactically:

$$\tilde{L} \underset{\leftarrow\text{synt}-}{\overset{-\text{sem}\rightarrow}{}} L$$

This happens if in **U** the expression '$\tilde{L}$' semantically governs 'L', but communicatively '$\tilde{L}$' is dominated by 'L', which is shown by the underscoring of L: '$\tilde{L}$-**sem**→L'; see 6.2.2, p. 242, Figure 6.1). As is obvious, **communicative dominance** plays a crucial role in specification of syntactic modifiers.

NB Definition 6.1 uses two shorthand formulations:
1. "L depends on $\tilde{L}$ semantically" means "L semantically depends on a lexeme L' in $\tilde{L}$"—that is, 'L' is a semantic actant of 'L'".
2. "$\tilde{L}$ directly depends on L syntactically" means "$\tilde{L}$'s top node L'—that is, $\tilde{L}$'s head—syntactically directly depends on L."

The second step is sharpening the terminology: giving more precise meanings to the terms *clause* and *relative*, while banning the misleading, but frequently appearing terms *head/top node of the relative clause* and *antecedent of the relative clause*.

Clause. In the current literature on RCs, the noun *clause* is applied to different types of phrase, provided the phrase is formed and controlled by a semantically predicative word—a finite or non-finite verb form (***reading*** *a fascinating book*; ... [*agreement*] ***obtained*** *from Mazda after long negotiations*), an adjective with its actants (***equal*** *to the previous group*) or even a noun with its actants (*the* ***march*** *of military units along Pennsylvania Avenue*). In this monograph only the finite-verb phrases are considered as clauses: the expression **non-finite clause* is not allowed.

Relative. This term needs two refinements: what it is applied to and what it denotes.
- In the literature, the adjective *relative* is applied to the names of three different syntactic units:
  – to a subordinate clause that functions as a modifier, marked in (1) as **A**;
  – to the noun phrase formed by a noun and a subordinate clause that modifies it, marked as **B**;[1]
  – to the whole sentence that contains an RC: **relative sentence*, marked as **C**.[2]

(1) *Intellectuals* [**who had mastered higher mathematics**] *wanted to apply their knowledge.*

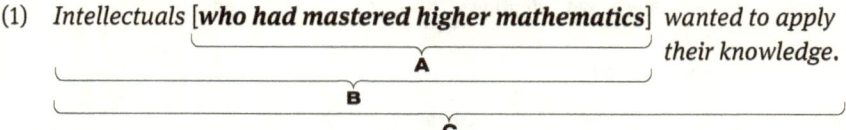

In this chapter, only the usage **A** is allowed: the term *relative clause* will denote a particular type of subordinate clause in the strict sense, without inclusion of the lexeme L it modifies. For **B**, following Lehmann (1984 and 1986: 664), a more convenient term will be used: **relative construction**, that is L–synt→RC. The usage **C** is banned altogether.

- In the literature, the term *relative clause* is often used to denote a clause having a specific internal structure (in particular, containing a **WH-word**) no matter what its external semantic and syntactic functions in the sentence are; as a result, one can see in linguistic texts such terminological monstrosities as **object relative clause* (as in [*John brought*] **what Mary had cooked**.) or **independent relative clause* (as in Fr. **Qui ne dit mot** [*consent*] 'Who does not say word agrees': Sandfeld 1965: 85*ff*). For me, an RC can only be a modifier; it would be logical to drop the use of the adjective *relative* and speak of *modifier (subordinate) clauses*—as we do about subject, object, circumstantial, etc. subordinate clauses. This is not done here simply in order to avoid a clash with the universally accepted term of *relative clause*, extremely frequent and well rooted in practice.

---

[1] "The term *RC* is used to apply to the collocation of the head NP and the restricting clause" (Keenan & Comrie 1977: 64).
[2] The search for the phrase "relative sentence" returned over 27,000 hits on Google (2021-02-23).

Head. In the current literature, the name *head/top node* is often applied to the lexeme—mostly a noun—modified by an RC; thus, in *the book that John is reading* the noun *book* is called *"the head of the relative clause *that John is reading*." This usage is banned: the syntactic head of a phrase (= its top node) is an element of the phrase—that is, it is structurally inside the phrase (in the case of an RC, it is its Main Verb); the external lexical unit that syntactically subordinates the phrase is its syntactic governor, not its head. Thus, **bcd** is a phrase whose head is **c**, while **a** is its governor:

As a consequence, the term **headless relative clause* is absurd: no clause (and no phrase, for this matter) can be headless.

Antecedent. The lexeme L modified by an RC is often called its *antecedent*, that is, 'the antecedent of the relative clause,' which is quite infelicitous. This term is normally used for the noun whose repeated occurrence is replaced by a substitute (= anaphoric) pronoun, as in (2a), where the noun COUNTRY is the antecedent of the pronoun IT, or (2b), where the noun BOMBINGS is the antecedent of the relative pronoun THAT[3], but not of the relative clause *that kill both police and civilians*:

(2) a. The COUNTRY must behave as **it** has behaved in the past.
    b. They carry out BOMBINGS **that** kill both police and civilians.

    NB To avoid confusion, here are different lexemes of the vocable THAT.

    THAT[1] demonstrative adjectival pronoun (***that** decision*, ***those** decisions*)
    THAT[2] demonstrative nominal (= substitute) pronoun (***Those** who want to go must sign up tomorrow.*)
    THAT[3] relative nominal pronoun (*a decision **that** was made in a hurry*)
    THAT[4] degree adverb (*not **that** intelligent*)
    THAT[5] empty subordinating conjunction (*He wrote **that** he would be absent.*)

In this chapter, a lexeme modified by an RC is called simply *the lexeme modified by the RC* or *the RC's (syntactic) governor*.

6.2.2 The notion of relative clause

An RC must be defined by two conditions:

1) Its semantic function, which specifies the closest superset—the set of all modifiers; it corresponds to *genus proximum*, or the closest kind, in an Aristotelian definition.

2) Its syntactic organization, which specifies the necessary subset—that of modifiers of a particular clausal type; this is Aristotle's *differentiae specificae*.

Definition 6.2 – relative clause

C is a full-fledged clause.

|| A subordinate clause C is called **relative** iff C is a modifier of an LU L.

C is a **subordinate clause**, C' being its **superordinate** (= matrix) **clause**; L is C's syntactic governor.

– If 'C' does not semantically bear on 'L' (= 'L' is not a Sem-actant of 'C'), then C is not a relative, but a completive clause (it semantically depends on L and expresses one of L's Sem-actants):

(3) a. *the case*$_L$ [*where/when a definition introduces a technical term*]$_C$
  the fact$_L$ [*that/*which Johnson was able to succeed*]$_C$

  b. *the reason*$_L$ [*why Johnson was unable to succeed*]$_C$
  the requirement$_L$ [*that airline advertising be more transparent*]$_C$
  the fear$_L$ [*that his life was in danger*]$_C$

In (3), C is a completive subordinate clause that expresses a Sem-actant of L and is L's DSynt-actant [DSyntA] rather than its modifier: in (3a), C is L's DSynt-actant I, and in (3b), L's DSynt-actant II.[3] (Cf. *the case of a definition introducing a technical term* and *the fact of Johnson being able to succeed*, where the actants of CASE and FACT are expressed by OF-phrases.)

– If, however, 'C' semantically bears on 'L', but C does not syntactically depend on L, then C is not a relative, but an **direct-object clause** or an **object-attributive-completive clause** (see Chapter 2, Section 2.5, Nos. 7 and 24):

(4) a. *John says→about life*$_L$ [*that it is not easy*]$_C$.
     ⌜——— dir-obj ———⌝

  NB (4a) is perceived by some speakers as not natural, even if grammatical; but its Russian equivalent, (4b), is perfectly OK:

  b. *Džon govorit→pro žizn'*$_L$[, *čto ona nelegka*]$_C$.
     ⌜——— dir-obj ———⌝

---

3 A completive clause of this type can be synonymous with an RC, which we see in (i) and (ii):
(i) *the* CASE [*in* WHICH **a definition introduces a technical term**] or
(ii) *the* REQUIREMENT [*according to* WHICH **airline advertisement must be more transparent**]
This should not, of course, prevent us from formally distinguishing them.

c. Fr. *Je le*$_L$←*vois* [*qui*←⎯obj-attr-compl⎯↓ *traverse la rue*]$_C$
   lit. 'I him see who is.crossing the street'.

In (4), the clause C is not a modifier. In (4a–b), it is a direct-object clause that semantically and syntactically depends on the verb SAY/GOVORIT'—it expresses its Sem-actant **2**; in (4c), 'C' semantically bears on the source of the pronoun LE 'him' (in a way quite similar to *Je le vois endormi* 'I him see asleep' or *Je le vois traverser la rue* 'I him see cross the street'), while syntactically, C depends on the verb VOIR 'see' and is an object-attributive clause (see Sandfeld 1965: 139–159 and van der Auwera 1985).

NB Sentences such as (4c) are typical of Romance languages; see a detailed review in Graffi 2017. The subordinate clause such sentences contain is commonly called pseudo-relative, a terminological usage I cannot accept: I reserve the term pseudo-relative for a completely different type of clause: see Subsect on 6.3.2.2, pp. 249*ff*.

Note that the governor of an RC is not necessarily a noun; it can be a lexical unit of any part of speech: see below, Subsection 6.2.3, (8), p. 244.

I do not know of an expression that intuitively is not an RC, but would be accepted by Definition 6.2.

The diagrams in Figure 6.1 below present the schematic structures of a prototypical relative construction, that is, an RC together with its syntactic governor, as seen in (5):

(5) *Husby put on the book a* BINDING$_{L\text{-RC's governor}}$ [THAT *was designed to be easily taken apart*]$_{RC}$.

These structures are given at three levels of representation: semantic [Sem-], deep-syntactic [DSynt-], and the surface-syntactic [SSynt-]; they are abstract in that they are formulated regardless of any specific language.

❗ The general schema of the RC construction's syntactic structures foresees the image of the governor (boxed in cells b, c-i and c-ii of Figure 6.1), while it is known that in many languages the governor's image cannot physically appear in the RC at the morphological surface (see 6.4.4, Item 4, p. 263). However, at a syntactic level, the presence of the governor's image in the RC's structure is necessary: it is its surface-syntactic role that decides whether, in the given language, the relativization of the given phrase is possible or not. Thus, in a language that only allows for relativization of the SSynt-subject (like Malagasy), the configuration $-\mathbf{i}\rightarrow \boxed{L(`X')}$, where $\mathbf{i} \neq$ **subjectival**, in the SSyntS of the sentence to be synthesized blocks the production of an RC. This is one of filter rules mentioned in 6.4.3 below, p. 258.

At the SSynt-level, the governor's image undergoes obligatory **pronominalization** in a broad sense: 1) either it remains as is—as a duplicate of the governor (zero pronominalization); 2) or it is elided (= deleted, or gapped); 3) or else it is replaced by a pronoun—personal or relative.

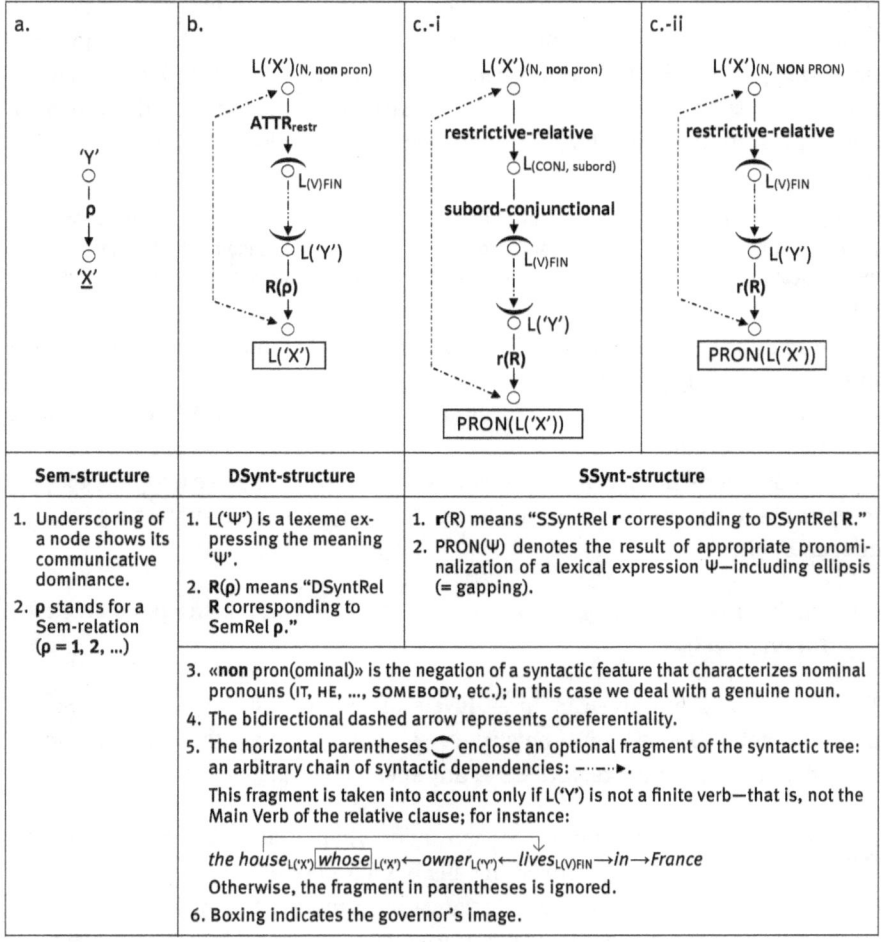

Figure 6.1 Schematic structures of a prototypical relative clause

    The diagrams in (b–c) show:
    – The lexeme L('X') modified by the RC; L('X') is the RC's governor.
    – The lexeme L('X')—a duplicate—within the RC which is coreferential with the governor; this is the image of the RC's governor.
    – The chain of syntactic links between the two occurrences of L('X').

The diagram in (c-i) represents an RC with an explicit subordinator—$L_{(CONJ, subord)}$, while that in (c-ii) an RC without an explicit subordinator.

6.2 What is a relative clause — 243

(6) Illustrations of Figure 6.1

   a. An RC with a subordinator

   Hebrew

   HA+YELED$_L$ [še   ani←dibarti→ ALAV [⇐ al+hu]]
   the boy   that I   talked   about.him
   'the boy about whom I talked' [the subordinator is the conjunction ŠE 'that']

   b. An RC without a subordinator

   the sea-level INCREASE$_L$ [to→ WHICH the climate system is→committed]

- At the **semantic level**, the L→RC construction has the same structure as any modificative construction of any language (including the adjective←noun construction). More specifically, it has a communicatively dominating meaning 'X'$_L$ semantically dominated by meaning 'Y'$_C$: 'Y–sem→X'. This schema is a linguistically universal semantic description of any modifier Y of X.

   NB Our semantic characterization of the RC does not include the requirement of narrowing the reference of its governor; this property distinguishes two subclasses of RCs—restrictive vs. descriptive RCs, see the next subsection.

- At the **deep-syntactic level**, an RC construction has quite a specific structure: all and only RC constructions have this form, which is valid cross-linguistically. To put it differently, in any language, any RC construction has this DSynt-form, and any construction having this DSynt-form is an RC construction. The DSynt-form of an RC construction is specified by the following two properties:

   – The dependency of the DSynt-head of the RC on L (= its governor) is direct.
   – The RC contains an image L of its governor L, this image being anaphorically related to L (Padučeva 1974: 130–133).

The DSynt-relation [DSyntRel] subordinating the RC—more precisely, the RC's head—to its governor L is **ATTR**$_{restr}$ (i.e., restrictive-attributive; a descriptive RC is subordinated to its governor by **ATTR**$_{descr}$, see 6.2.3).

- At the **surface-syntactic level**, an RC construction has one of two possible structures, depending on the language—with or without an explicit subordinator, that is, a marker of the subordinate character of the clause. Schema (c-i) in Figure 6.1 covers Persian-type RCs, see (18), p. 256; schema (c-ii) describes more familiar RCs of European types.

- The behavior of an RC at the **deep-morphological level** of sentence representation is irrelevant for its definition: the linear ordering of the elements of the RC and of the RC itself with respect to its governor in the superordinate clause, as well as concomitant morphological markings, characterize the **surface implementation** of an RC in a particular language, rather than the RC itself.

❗ The schemata in Figure 6.1 do not cover all possible types of RC: they describe only the RC whose governor is a genuine noun, while there are RCs with pronominal governors, see below, 6.4.5.2.

6.2.3 Restrictive vs. descriptive relative clauses

As is well known, RCs—like all syntactic modifiers of nouns or pronouns—fall into two major classes according to their impact on the reference of the lexeme modified:

(7) a. *He approved a LAW$_L$ [THAT strips parliamentarians of their legal immunity].*
   b. *He approved this LAW$_L$, [WHICH ⟨?that⟩ strips parliamentarians of their legal immunity].*

– In (7a), a **restrictive** [= defining] RC "enriches" the meaning of L—that is, more precisely, it narrows its reference: the sentence talks about a particular law such that it strips parliamentarians of immunity; this RC ensures the identification of the law for the Addressee.
– In (7b), a **descriptive** [= qualifying] RC does not impact the reference of L, but adds some additional information about the law that is already known to the Addressee ("this law").

Restrictive and descriptive RCs show many differences, the best known being that in English the descriptive RC requires the relative pronoun WHICH rather than THAT[3] (see Carlson 1977 and Platzak 2000, where other differences are discussed; however, according to D. Beck, the prohibition against THAT[3] in descriptive RCs is dying out in contemporary English).

NB Not all languages make a distinction between restrictive and descriptive RCs. Thus, it does not exist in Japanese (Kuno 1973: 235).

An RC modifying a verb or a non-pronominal adjective can be only descriptive, cf. (8):

(8) *But Johnson objected$_L$,*   *[which amazed everybody]$_C$.*
   Johnson asked to be released$_L$,   *[to which everyone agreed]$_C$.*
   Johnson called our friend Peter lazy$_L$, *[which he is not]$_C$.*

(This type of RC is what is called in Quirk et al. 1991: 1118–1120 sentential relative clause, opposed to phrasal relative clause.)

In this chapter, descriptive RCs are left out of consideration.[4]

6.3 What is not a relative clause: constructions often confused with relative clauses

The description of RCs in modern linguistics is often impeded by the confusion between RCs and other complex constructions that are either **isofunctional** with RCs, playing the same semantic and syntactic role as an RC (being semantic and syntactic modifiers; 6.3.1), or **isostructural** with RCs, having the same—or, at least, similar—syntactic structure (among other things, containing relative or similar pronouns; 6.3.2). To ensure a rigorous treatment of RCs, it is necessary to specify the syntactic formations that are not RCs, but tend to be perceived as RCs.

6.3.1 Constructions isofunctional with relative clauses: non-clausal modifiers

According to the part of speech of the syntactic head (= top node) of a noun-modifying construction, three types of this construction are possible: 1) finite-verb headed constructions—that is, our RCs; 2) adjectivalized-verb headed constructions; and 3) nominalized-verb headed constructions. The constructions of types 2 and 3 can fulfill the same semantic and syntactic roles as an RC: they can modify a lexical unit both semantically and syntactically; however, they are not relative clauses—because they are not clauses in the strict sense of the term (see 6.3.1.1 and 6.3.1.2).

6.3.1.1 Modifying construction headed by a verb adjectivalization [= participial phrase]

English stock examples of noun-modifying non-clausal constructions are [*passengers*] *wanting to go to Glasgow* and [*the General Assembly*] *immobilized in those troubled days*.

---

[4] On the descriptive relatives that depend on a lexeme different from a noun, see Chapter 2, No. 74, p. 90. — Some researchers propose to distinguish another class of RC: "relative clauses of the third kind" (Carlson 1977 and Grosu & Landman 1998), of the type of *I took the three books **(that) there were on the table***.

Since "non-finite clauses" are not clauses, noun-modifying constructions headed by an adjectival form of a verb—that is, by a participle—are not RCs.[5]

(9) a. Russian

čitajušč+ego knig+u mal'čik+a ~
reading MASC.SG.GEN book SG.ACC boy₍masc₎ SG.GEN
'[of] reading book boy'

mal'čik+a, **čitajušč+ego knig+u**
'of [a] boy reading book'

udivlënn+ye podark+om devočk+i ~
amazed PL.NOM gift SG.INSTR girl₍fem₎ PL.NOM
'amazed by.gift girls'

devočk+i, **udivlënn+ye podark+om**
'girls amazed by.gift'

b. Kolyma Yukaghir (Maslova 2003: 418)

purk+in šoromo lē+je šoromo
seven ATTR person eat ATTR person
'seven people having.eaten person' = 'person who ate seven people'

c. Turkish (ğ is not pronounced; ş = /š/)

Ada +Ø+da gör+düğ +üm kişi +Ø+Ø
island SG LOC see PAST_PART 1.SG person SG NOM
lit. 'on.island my.having.seen person' = 'person whom I saw on the island'

The bold-faced expressions in (9) are typical participial phrases, not clauses.[6]

---

[5] "English also has nonfinite participial relative clauses, as in *the man reading the book*. Nonfinite relative clauses are sometimes not considered as relative clauses; however, since there are many languages where relative clauses are all nonfinite and since these constructions mean the same thing as finite relative clauses in English, such participial constructions are considered as relative clauses" (Dryer 2013, after (8)). Curiously, it is exactly for this reason that I do not want to consider participial constructions to be RCs.

[6] Participial phrases have an interesting variety, infelicitously called "Possessive Relative" (Ackermann & Nikolaeva 2013):

(i) Western Khanty
xans+əm nēpək+ēm lit. 'written my.book' = 'book written by me'
write PARTICIPLE book 1SG

In such a construction, the Agent of the participle is marked not on the participle (as, for instance, in Turkish: (9c)), but on the modified noun.

6.3.1.2 Modifying construction headed by a verb nominalization [= appositional phrase]

Actual English examples are unavailable, since this construction does not exist in that language. artificial examples could be as follows:

*passengers **to-go-to-Liverpool wanters***
'passengers wanting to go to Liverpool'

*boy **my yesterday meetee***
'boy whom I met yesterday'

NB In spite of the fact that the Patient noun suffix **-ee** is not fully productive in English, it will be used in the glosses here and further. so that **meetee** means 'that whom [somebody] meets/met'.

(10) a. Seri (Marlett 2012; *c, qu* = /k/, *cö* = /kʷ/, *j* = /χ/, *x* = /x/)

*hapxa **cö** +**c** +aasitim quij* 'rabbit **his/her.deceiver** the' =
rabbit 3.SG SUBJ.NOMINAL deceive the 'the rabbit who deceived him/her'

*hapxa **h** +**oco** +aasitim quij* 'rabbit **my.deceivee** the' =
rabbit 1.SG OBJ.NOMINAL deceive the 'the rabbit whom I deceived'

As can be seen from (10a), Seri has two prefixal nominalizers, the subjectival **c-** [≈ Eng. **-er**] and the objectival **oco-** [≈ Eng. **-ee**] (underscored); they correspond to the meanings of the lexical functions S_1 (≈ Agent noun) and S_2 (≈ Patient noun) and turn the verb into an agent or patient noun.

 b. Yaqui (Álvarez González 2012; *ch* = /č/, *j* = /χ/)

*Joan uka chu'u+ta **Maria-ta ke'e+ka +m** +ta*
Juan the-ACC dog ACC Maria ACC bite PERF SUBJ.NOMINALIZER ACC
me'a+k
kill PERF
'Juan the dog **Maria biter**$_N$ killed'. = 'Juan killed the dog that bit Maria'.

*Joan uka bachi+ta **em jinu-ka +'u** +ta*
Juan the-ACC corn ACC you$_{SG}$-GEN buy PERF OBJ.NOMINALIZER ACC
bwa'a+k
eat PERF
lit. 'Juan the corn **your buy**$_N$ ate'. = 'Juan ate the corn that you bought'.

*Joan uka kari +ta **em tomte +ka +'apo***
Juan the-ACC house ACC you$_{SG}$-GEN be_borne PERF LOC.NOMINALIZER
jinu+k
buy PERF
lit. 'Juan the house **your birthplace**$_N$ bought'. =
'Juan bought the house where you were born'.

Like Seri, Yaqui also has clausal nominalizers, but they differ from those of Seri in that, first, they are suffixal and, second, there are three of them. (Several interesting details are omitted: thus, the Seri objectival nominalizer **oco-** is used only for a DirO, while Yaqui objectival nominalizer **-'u** can be used for all types of object—direct, indirect and oblique; etc.)

The picture presented for Seri and Yaqui is typical of many other American Indian languages: they do not have an RC, but use a nominal apposition in the same semantic role—as a modifier.

6.3.1.3 Clause introduced by an expression meaning 'such that'
Subordinate clauses introduced by an adjective with the meaning of 'such ... that ...' are semantically very close to RCs:

(11) a. *... and with brutality*$_L$ ***such that the rest of the world cannot stand idly by***.
b. *It was **such** a cold afternoon*$_L$ ***that we stopped playing***.
c. *It is a differential operator*$_L$ ***such that its restriction on T vanishes***.

A SUCH.THAT-clause bears semantically on the governor (= modified) noun L, just like an RC, and sometimes it alternates freely with an RC; thus, (11c) is synonymous with a sentence containing an RC: *It is a differential* OPERATOR$_L$ [WHOSE ***restriction on T vanishes***]. However, in a SUCH.THAT-clause, the THAT-introduced clause C syntactically depends on SUCH and is its DSyntA II: L–ATTR→SUCH–II→C. Therefore, Definition 6.2 is violated (C does not directly depend on L), and therefore C is not an RC. Moreover, in SUCH.THAT-clauses we have the subordinate conjunction THAT[5] rather than a relative pronoun THAT[3] (see 6.2.1 above, p. 239). SUCH.THAT-clauses should not be considered in a discussion of RCs.[7]

6.3.2 Constructions isostructural with relative clauses: clausal non-modifiers

6.3.2.1 Introductory remarks
Two major types of isostructurality with RCs can be distinguished: internal and external isostructurality.

---

[7] In French, a noun-modifying clause introduced by the conjunction COMME 'as' constitutes a special case similar to SUCH.THAT-clauses:

(i) *gâteaux*–**modif**→*comme* [*je les aime*] 'cakes as I like them'

The comparative conjunction COMME is semantically full and appears in the DSyntS; therefore, the subordinate clause proper (in this case, *je les aime*) does not depend on GÂTEAU directly, and thus Definition 6.2 is violated.

- Internal isostructurality consists in the presence of a WH-pronoun. In practically all European languages an RC normally includes a WH-pronoun: in English it is WHICH, WHO, WHERE, ..., and THAT[3] (seen, e.g., in *moving screens that bob up and down*); this pronoun constitutes the image of the RC's governor. WH-pronouns feature many semantic and syntactic particularities that have always attracted, and still attract, linguists' attention; unfortunately, there exists a clear tendency to identify the set of relative clauses and that of subordinate clauses including WH-pronouns [WH-clauses]. However, this is an unwarranted step:
  - On the one hand, a large number of the world's languages do not have relative pronouns at all, while having RCs—that is, they have RCs without relative WH-pronouns (we will see this in 6.4.3 below).
  - On the other hand, there are various types of WH-clause that are by no means RCs.

Therefore, we have to accept the following statement:

> The set of relative clauses and the set of WH-clauses have a large intersection—there are RCs that are also WH-clauses (for instance, in familiar European languages), but there are RCs that are not WH-clauses and there are WH-clauses that are not RCs.

NB At least four subclasses of WH-pronouns have to be distinguished:
  - interrogative (*What/Who is this?*)
  - indirect-interrogative (*I know who is this boy.*)
  - relative (*The person who brought the letter is here.*)
  - pseudo-relative (*What* [= 'that.thing.which'] *he did is a crime.*)

It would be unwise to undertake here an overview of possible WH-clauses; I will limit myself to three most common types: pseudo-relative clauses (6.3.2.2), indirect-interrogative clauses (6.3.2.3) and cleft clauses (6.3.2.4); cf. also object-attributive subordinate clauses, illustrated in 6.2.2, (4c), p. 241.

- External isostructurality of a clause with RCs consists in its role in the sentence: semantically it is a modifier while being, at the syntactic level, not a modifier, but an actant of the Main Verb. This is the notorious "internally-headed RC" (6.3.2.5).

6.3.2.2 Pseudo-relative clauses

In (12), a particular type of subordinate WH-clause is illustrated that is commonly called *free/ headless relative*:

(12) a. *You can buy*~Y~ [*what these people sell*~Z~]~C~.
   b. *I like*~Y~ [*how she dances*~Z~]~C~.
   c. *His decision*~Y~ *depends on* [*where Mary is*~Z~ *now*]~C~.

However, the term *free/headless relative* cannot be accepted:

- What is called a *free/headless relative clause* is in no sense relative—syntactically it does not modify anything, but is an actant or a circumstantial.
- It is not free—syntactically it necessarily depends on something, being a subordinate clause.
- It is not headless—as all clauses, it necessarily has a syntactic head (its Main Verb).[8]
- The lexeme WHAT seen in (12a) is not a relative pronoun: a relative pronoun is semantically empty (= has no source in the Sem-structure), while this WHAT has a meaning, although very general—'that.something'. Moreover, WHAT cannot be used as a relative pronoun in a genuine RC: **the house what we bought*. Pronouns of this type could be called **demonstrative-relative**, or **pseudo-relative**.

Therefore, the clauses *what these people sell*, *who she loves* and *where Mary is now* in (12) are not RCs. Since, however, they are superficially similar to RCs, they can be called **pseudo-relative clauses** [pseudo-RCs].

NB In linguistic literature, the term *pseudo-relative clause* is often used in several different senses. Among other things, object-attributive clauses in Romance languages are regularly called pseudo-relatives; see Subsection 6.2.2 above, example (4c), p. 241.

A pseudo-RC is syntactically equivalent to a noun phrase, is used as an SSynt-actant or an SSynt-circumstantial and is subordinated to its governor by the **subjectival, direct-objectival, ..., prepositional** or **circumstantial** SSyntRels. While a genuine RC modifies a noun, a pseudo-RC "incorporates" the meaning it seems to modify: in (12a), the pronoun WHAT actually means 'that.thing.which'.[9] We can indicate this by ascribing to this WHAT the syntactic feature «pseudo-rel(ative)».

Figure 6.2 (next page) presents the structures of typical pseudo-RCs at the three levels.

The Sem-, the DSynt- and the SSynt-structures of the sentences of the type (12b) and (12c) are the same, with 'the.way.that' and 'the.place.where' instead of 'something' and, respectively, HOW and WHERE instead of WHAT.

---

[8] Already in Kručinina 1968 such clauses were called *antecedentless*, which is by far more logical.
[9] A similar description of this WHAT was already proposed in 1960s (Kuroda 1968: 246). Pseudo-relatives were treated as noun phrases in Mel'čuk & Pertsov 1987: 486–487.

A particular type of pseudo-RCs are pseudo-RCs that form compound indefinite pronouns of the type boldfaced in sentences such as *I met yesterday **you will never guess whom*** or *John lives **where he wants*** (Chapter 9, Subsection 9.2.1.1.1, p. 312; see also Chapter 2, Section 2.5, No. 75, p. 91).

Pseudo-RCs can easily be and often are confused with RCs whose governor is a pronoun.

NB For more on pseudo-RCs, see, among others, Horvath & Grosu 1987 and Caponigro et al. 2013.

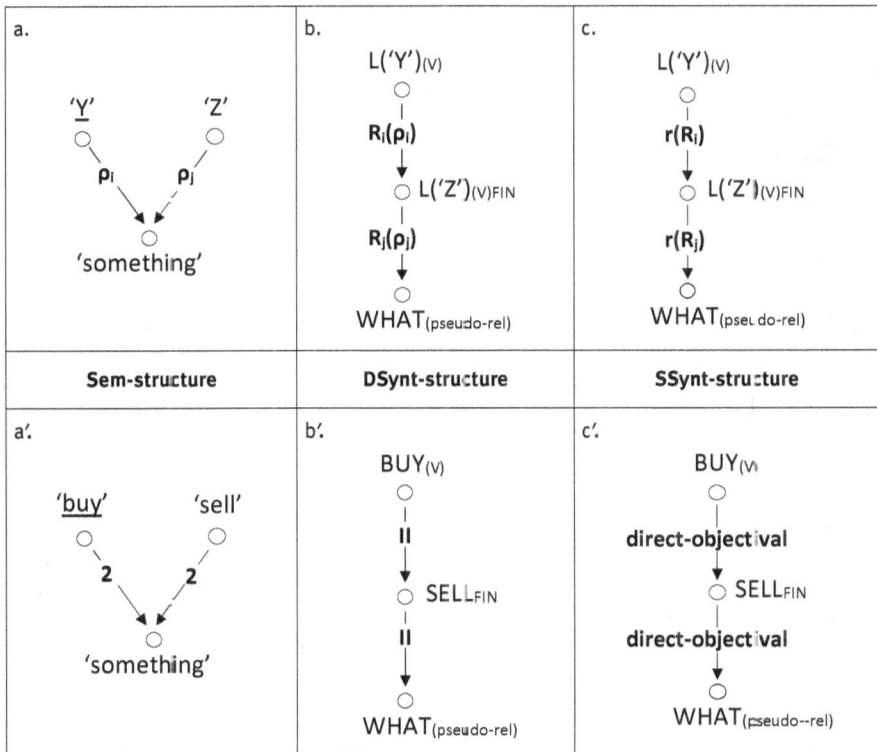

Figure 6.2 Schematic semantic, deep-syntactic and surface-syntactic structure of sentences with a prototypical pseudo-relative clause of (12a) type

Here are a couple of slightly more complex pseudo-relatives, where the interrogative-relative pronoun is adjectival.

(13) a. Russian, highly colloquial or archaic

[*Kotor+uju*   KNIG +U   *najd*   *+ëš',*]
which FEM.SG.ACC book$_{(fem)}$ SG.ACC find-PERF.FUT 2.SG

        čitaj+Ø   tut že
        read IMPER.2.SG right.away
        lit. '[**Which book you.will.find**,] read (it) right away'.

   b. Latin (Caesar)
        Sabin+us   [*qu*   +*os*   TRIBUN +OS
        Sabin SG.NOM which MASC.PL.ACC tribune(masc) PL.ACC
        habe*+*ba +*t*]   *se*   *sequi*   *iube* +Ø +*t*
        have IMPF 3.SG himself follow-INF order(v) PRES 3.SG
        lit. 'Sabin, [**which tribunes he.had**,] himself follow [them] orders'. =
        'Sabin orders the tribunes he had to follow him'.

6.3.2.3 Indirect-interrogative clauses

(14) *I know [who/where this boy is ⟨when this boy arrived⟩].*

The subordinate clauses in (14) are indirect questions; they do not modify anything and are DSyntAs (in this case, II) of the verb KNOW. They contain an interrogative WH-pronoun and thereby differ from pseudo-RCs (with their pseudo-relative WH-pronoun).

    Interestingly, in a particular language, an indirect-interrogative clause (15a) can contrast semantically with a genuine RC having a pronominal governor, i.e. a correlative TO [a form of TOT II.1] as in (15b):

(15) Russian
   a. *Menja interesuet*, [*čto Ivan pišet*]_{INDIR-INTERR}
      lit. 'I am interested in.what Ivan is writing'. =
      'I don't know what Ivan is writing, and I am interested to know it'.
   b. *Menja interesuet TO*, [ČTO ***Ivan pišet***]_{RC}
      'I am.interested.in the.stuff that Ivan is writing'. =
      'I know what Ivan is writing something, and I am interested in it'.

6.3.2.4 Cleft clauses

A cleft sentence contains a subordinate WH-clause:

(16) *It is me [who pushed John].*

However, this WH-clause does not modify anything: it is a pseudo-subject of the verb BE, as seen in Figure 6.3. (On pseudo-subjects, see Chapter 2, Section 2.5, SSyntRel No. 6, p. 51.)

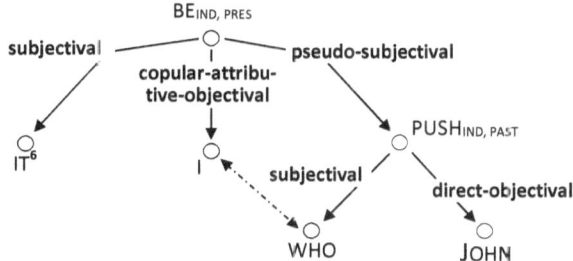

Figure 6.3 The surface-syntactic structure of sentence (16). — IT⁶ stands for the empty—dummy—IT.

Therefore, this WH-clause is not an RC: it is a cleft.

6.3.2.5 Nominalized clauses [= "internally-headed relative clauses"]
A special case was already mentioned above: a phrase that is formed by a clause nominalized as a whole (which is, of course, different from a phrase formed by a nominalized verb) and is used as a bizarre hybrid: a semantic modifier, but a syntactic actant.

> **NB** When only the Main Verb of a clause is nominalized, all its syntactic dependents change their form, adapting it to the nominal governor, as in *John reads the book* ⇒ *John's reading of the book*; but under the nominalization of the whole clause all dependents of the Main Verb remain as they are—a nominalizer is added to the clause and nothing else changes:
>
> *John reads the book* ⇒ *[John reads the book]*+NOMINALIZER.

Clause nominalizations of this kind are known as *internally headed relative clauses* (see Xolodovič 1971, Grosu 2002, 2012 and Hiraiwa et al. 2017, with a vast bibliography). The most discussed type of this clause nominalization is found in Japanese and Korean; Lakhota supplies a different variety.

(17) a. Japanese
  Keikan +wa   dorobō+ga   ginkō+kara
  policeman THEME robber   SUBJ bank   ABL
  deteki +ta   +no +o   tukamae+ta
  come.out PAST «fact» ACC arrest₍ᵥ₎ PAST
  lit. 'Policeman robber from.bank came.out «fact» arrested'.
  = 'The policeman arrested the robber who came out from the bank'.¹⁰

---

10 For a detailed discussion of Japanese nominalized clauses, see Grosu & Hoshi 2009, where it is shown, among other things, that a **-no**-clause can be 4-way ambiguous.

b. Korean

Kyoŋčʰal +*in*   *kaŋto*+*ka*   *unhaŋy*+*eye nao*   +*nin*
policeman THEME robber SUBJ bank   ABL come.out PARTICIPLE
<u>*kes*</u> +*il*   *čap*   +*ass* +*ta*
«fact» ACC arrest₍ᵥ₎ PAST DECLAR(ative)
lit. 'Policeman robber from.bank coming.out «fact» arrested'. =
'The policeman arrested the robber who came out from the bank'.

c. Lakhota (Williamson 1987)

Mary owiza wã kaġe <u>ki</u>   he   ophewalthu
Mary quilt   a   make the that.one I.buy.it
lit. 'Mary quilt a make the that.one I bought'.
= 'I bought the quilt that Mary had made'.

> **NB** Japanese and Korean both have special markers on the lexical item that expresses the semantic-communicative Theme of the main clause, the suffixes **-wa** and **-in**, respectively. SUBJ(ective) stands for the subjective case, which marks the syntactic subject (and is different from the nominative, the case of nomination, having the **-Ø** suffix).

All the three languages use overt clause nominalizers (underscored):

- Japanese has a morphological clause nominalizer—the suffix **-no**. It is added to the last lexeme of the clause, but since in Japanese the Main Verb is obligatorily clause-final, **-no** attaches to it and turns the clause into a noun phrase that accepts case suffixes required by its external context. All dependents of the Main Verb retain their case marking and remain verbal dependents: *Dorobōga ginkōkara detekita* lit. 'Robber from.bank came.out' is a complete finite clause that can be used as such.
- Korean recurs to a lexical clause nominalizer—the auxiliary noun KES, which is used either with a determiner in the sense of 'thing', or—as in (17b)—as an empty nominalizer governing a participial phrase. Both **-no** and KES can be approximately glossed as 'fact'.
- In Lakhota, the clause is nominalized by the definite article KI 'the'.

In (17a) and (17c), the bold-faced clause is not an RC since it is not a modifier; in (17b), the bold-faced expression is not even a (finite) clause.

Sentences in (17) illustrate Case 9 in the general calculus of possible combinations of semantic, syntactic and morphological dependencies between two lexemes in an utterance (Mel'čuk 1988: 123–124 and 2012–2015: vol. 3, 457–458, 480): a case of **head-switching**, or reversal of semantic *vs.* syntactic dependencies. Syntactically, Japanese and Korean say that the policeman "arrested the coming_out–**synt**→[of the robber]," but semantically, this means, of course, that he arrested the robber who was coming out of the bank. Similarly, in the Lakhota example, I bought not the Mary's making–synt→[of a quilt], but the quilt that was made by Mary.

The bold-faced phrases in (17) are currently called *relative clauses* only because they are used as (approximate) equivalents of European RCs. However, they have a completely different syntactic structures: in the first place, they do not syntactically modify a lexical unit L and they do not feature L's image. They should not be called *relative*. A possible term could be *nominalized clauses*.

NB For a detailed discussion of nominalized clauses, see, for instance, Grosu 2012.

Figure 6.4 below gives the schematic structures of prototypical nominalized clauses at the three representation levels.

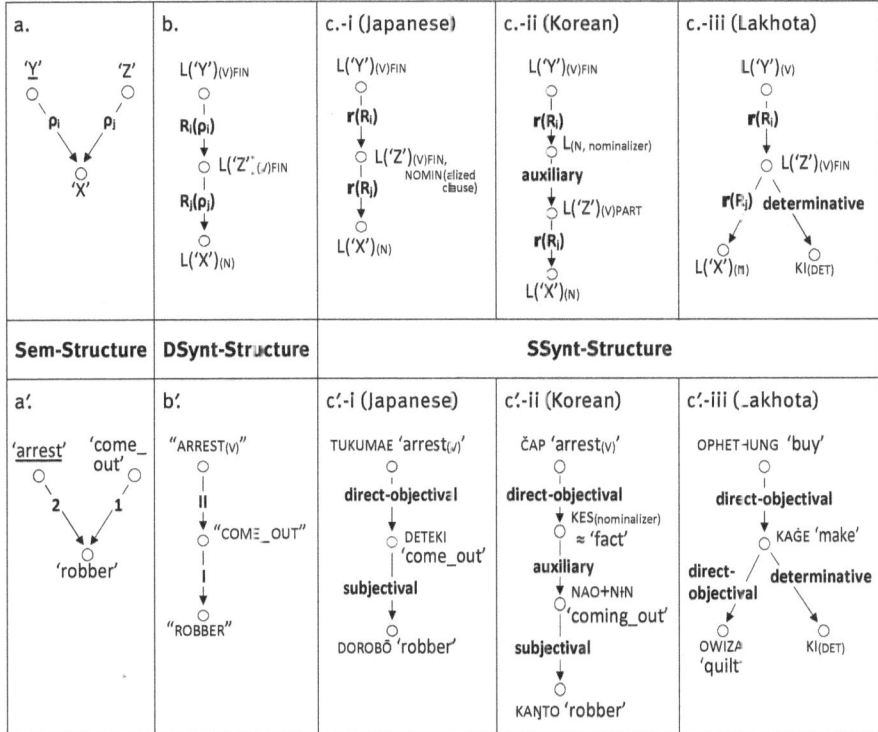

Figure 6.4 Partial semantic, deep-syntactic and surface-syntactic structures of a nominalized clause. — The DSyntSs of the sentences (17a–b) are strictly isomorphic and can be presented as three versions: with a morphological nominalizer (Japanese-style, c′.-i) and with a lexical nominalizer (Korean-style, c′.-ii; and Lakhota-style, c′.-iii).

6.4 Typology of the restrictive relative clause

The typology of RCs will be sketched in six steps: a couple of prototypical RCs with their semantic and syntactic structures (6.4.1); the DSyntRel and the SSynt-Rel subordinating an RC (6.4.2); syntactic constraints on RCs (6.4.3); parameters that specify structural types of RC (6.4.4); illustrations of different types of RCs (6.4.5); and deep-morphological parameters that specify possible linearizations and morphologizations of RCs (6.4.6).

6.4.1 Relative clauses at the semantic, deep-syntactic and surface-syntactic levels

To add some linguistic flesh to our abstract RC skeleton, here are RC-construction structures at the three levels, in Persian and in Russian.

(18) Persian

pesär+i   [*ke* *be* U   *ketab*+Ø+*ra*   *dad*   +*änd*]
boy   DEF   that   to   s/he   book   SG   DirO   give-PAST   3.PL
lit. 'the boy that **to him a book** [«they»] **gave**'
= 'the boy to whom they gave a book'

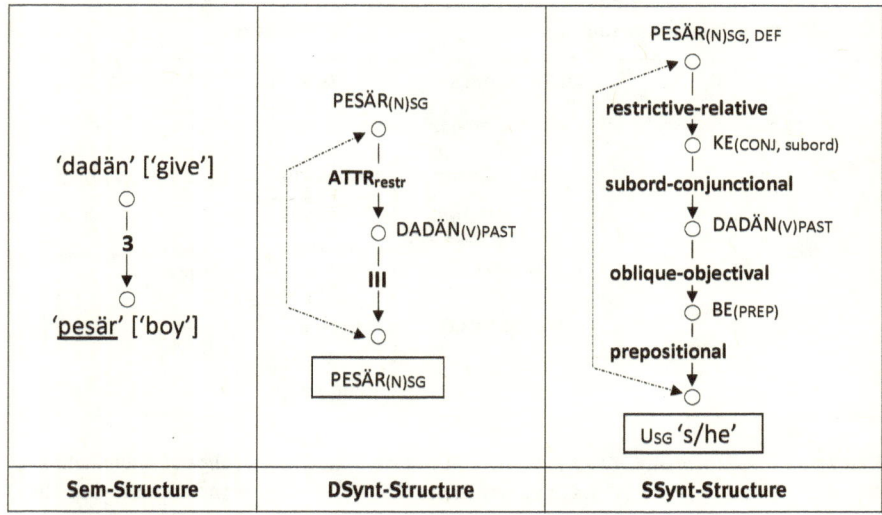

Figure 6.5 Partial semantic, deep-syntactic and surface-syntactic structures of the Persian phrase (18)

(19) Russian

MAL'ČIK₍masc₎+∅,   [KOTOR+OMU]   da +l +i   knig+u]
boy   SG.NOM   which MASC.SG.DAT give PAST PL book SG.ACC
'boy **to.whom [«they»] gave a book**'

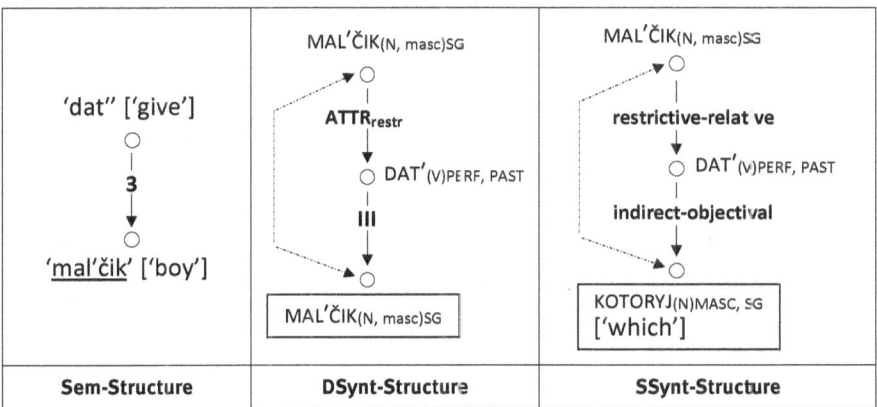

Figure 6.6 Partial semantic, deep-syntactic and surface-syntactic structures of the Russian phrase (19)

6.4.2 Deep- and surface-syntactic relations subordinating a relative clause

The situation with the DSyntRel that subordinates a restrictive RC is unproblematic: it is **ATTR**ᵣₑₛₜᵣ, as is the case with all restrictive modifiers. However, as far as the corresponding SSyntRel is concerned, the situation becomes more complicated. In the first place, it is different in different languages, so that what is said below describes, strictly speaking, English and perhaps some other structurally similar languages. The following question arises: Is a special SSyntRel to subordinate RC—the **relative** SSyntRel,[11] as proposed, e.g., in Iomdin 2010c: 33 and Mel'čuk 2016: 190—needed or one can do simply with the **modificative** SSyntRel, the same as for adjectival modifiers? In all other cases the SSyntRels do not distinguish between LUs and clauses as their dependents: thus, the **subjectival** and **direct-objectival** SSyntRels subordinate an LU and a clause the same way; probably, we should not make the distinction for modifiers, either? However, such a conclusion would be wrong: in English (and other European languages), the

---

[11] "Relative" means by default "restrictive-relative"; a descriptive RC is subordinated to its governor by the **descriptive-relative** SSyntRel.

modificative SSyntRel is repeatable (a noun can have a theoretically unlimited number of cosubordinated—not coordinated!—adjectives, as in *large expensive square black table*), while the **relative** SSyntRel is not repeatable: normally, a noun can have only one restrictive RC.[12] To unify these two SSyntRels—the **relative** and the **modificative**—would mean violating Criterion **C3** for postulating SSyntRels, see p. 44.

6.4.3 Syntactic constraints on relative clauses

Languages differ as to their ability to relativize particular elements of the clause. In other words, the possibility of constructing an RC in a given language is sensitive to the SSynt-role to be played by the image of the RC's governor within the RC itself. This fact was established by Keenan and Comrie (Keenan & Comrie 1977, Comrie & Keenan 1979) and formulated as the fundamental **Keenan-Comrie Accessibility Hierarchy:**[13]

Subject > DirO > IndirO > OblO > Gen(itival)Co(mplement) > Compar(ative)Co(mplement)

This hierarchy stipulates that, if the language under consideration allows for RCs where the SSynt-image of the RC's governor is, say, an IndirO, then in this language an RC can contain the governor's image in any SSynt-role placed higher in the hierarchy—in this case, in the role of DirO and Subject.

This means that the DSynt-rules of a language must include a **filter rule** that checks the SSyntS of each RC under synthesis and rejects those that violate the options allowed for the governor's image in this language. For an example of such a filter rule, see the ■ remark after (5), p. 241.

---

12 Interestingly, a restrictive RC and a descriptive RC can cooccur with the same governor:

(i) *The* BOOK [***THAT** you hold now*]_{restrictive} [, ***WHICH** belongs to John,*]_{descriptive} *is precious*.

In fact, even two restrictive RCs can exceptionally cooccur (in a very particular context):

(ii) Fr. *la seule* FEMME [***QUE** je connaisse*] [***QUI** ne croit pas en Dieu*]
  'the only woman whom I know who does not believe in God' (Sandfeld 1965: 216).

13 The Keenan-Comrie hierarchy was proposed with an eye to relativization, but it turned out to be valid in regard to other properties of clause elements. In particular, this hierarchy manifests itself in the ability of a clause element to control reflexive and reciprocal anaphora (Pollard & Sag 1992: 266) and to allow extraction (Abeillé 1997: 23). Cf. also an over-all hierarchy of the syntactic privileges of clausal elements in French obtained by using a set of relevant syntactic properties (Iordanskaja & Mel'čuk 2009a).

6.4.4 Syntactic parameters characterizing a relative clause construction

The surface-syntactic structure of an RC construction is specified by the following five logically independent parameters:

- Syntactic class of the RC's governor
- Presence (in the RC) of a subordinator
- Presence (in the RC) of a relative pronoun
- Presence and form of the RC's governor's image
- Form of the RC's governor

Systematic illustration of different types of RC is offered below, in Subsection 6.4.5.

1) Syntactic class of the RC's governor
This parameter has two possible values:

the RC's governor is a genuine noun — the RC's governor is a pronoun

(20) Russian

A Russian pronoun that can function as an RC's governor is a nominal or adverbial pronoun of one of the following four types:

- Demonstrative—of the type TOT 'that.somebody', TAM 'in that place', TOGDA 'at that time', ...; see below, (23d).
- Indeterminate—of the type NEKTO 'somebody', NEČTO 'something', KOE-KTO ≈ 'somebody', KTO-TO ≈ 'somebody', KTO-NIBUD' 'anybody', GDE-NIBUD' 'anywhere', KOE-KOGDA ≈ 'some time', ...
- Negative—of the type NIKTO 'nobody', NIČTO 'nothing', NIGDE 'nowhere', NIKOGDA 'never', ...
- Quantifier-like—of the type VSE 'everybody', LJUBOJ 'anybody', KAŽDYJ 'each', VSJUDU 'everywhere', VSEGDA 'always', ...

(21) a. English

The CCUNTRY [THAT *controls the sea*] controls the land.   vs.
HE [WHO *controls the sea*] controls the land.

b. German

Nur DER   verdient sich Freiheit wie   das Leben,
only that.person deserves oneself freedom as.well.as the life
[DER täglich sie   erobern muß]
who daily   these conquer must

'He only earns both freedom and existence / Who must reconquer them each day' [W. Goethe].

> **NB** Note the homonymy of the two **der**: the first (the RC's governor), a wordform of DER[1], is a nominal demonstrative pronoun meaning 'that person', while the second (the governor's image), a wordform of DER[2], is a relative pronoun 'which/who'.

RCs whose governor is a pronoun were formally introduced into the discussion of RC typology by Zaliznjak & Padučeva 1975 [2002: 663], to be later analyzed by Lehmann 1984: 299–304 and Citko 2004; this type of RC is widespread in Slavic and Romance languages. A stock example is given in (22a):

(22) Polish (Citko 2004; c = /c/, cz = /č/, $ż$ = /ž/, $ó$ = /u/, $ą$ = /õ/, $ę$ = /ẽ/, y = /ɨ/)
    a. *Jan czyta* TO,   [CO   *Maria czyta*]
       Jan reads that$_{(N)ACC}$ what$_{ACC}$ Maria reads
       'Jan reads that **what Maria reads**'.
    b. *Jan czyta* KSIĄŻK +Ę,   [KTÓRĘ   *Maria czyta*]
       Jan reads book$_{(fem)}$ SG.ACC that$_{FEM.SG.ACC}$ Maria reads
       'Jan reads the book **that Maria reads**'.

Citko wittily called such RCs "light-headed relatives," since the demonstrative pronoun TO 'that.something$_{(N)}$' is semantically almost empty (= "light") in comparison with, e.g., KSIĄŻKA 'book'. However, RCs with a pronominal governor cannot be "light-headed," since TO is the governor of the RC, but by no means its head. However, it is true that such RCs are special in many respects.

Let me indicate some prominent facts about RCs with a pronominal governor in Russian: examples (23a–d).

(23) Russian: RCs where the governor is a correlative
    a. These RCs are synthesized from pseudo-RCs (underscored). Special syntactic rules introduce into the SSyntS of a pseudo-relative clause the semantically empty pronoun TO, called **correlative**,—in order to ensure the grammatical and/or stylistic correction of the sentence (with the correlative the RC becomes more formal):
       Kto xočet poexat' na èkskursiju$_{pseudo-RC}$, *dolžen zapisat'sja zdes'*. ~
       who wants to.go   for excursion,   must sign.up   here
       TOT, [KTO *xočet poexat' na èkskursiju,*]$_{RC}$ *dolžen zapisat'sja zdes'*.
    b. For the same reason, the correlative TOT can also be introduced in the superordinate clause, which gives two more versions of the sentence being synthesized:

Kto xočet poexat' na èkskursiju~pseudo-RC~, TOT dolžen zapisat'sja zdes'. ~
who wants to.go for excursion, must sign.up here
TOT, [KTO *xočet poexat' na èkskursiju,*]~RC~ TOT dolžen zapisat'sja zdes'.

The last sentence features a double expression of the subject: by the RC with TOT and by another TOT. However, the duplication of a clause element by an empty pronoun is known in several Slavic and Romance languages, as well in Modern Greek and Albanian.

c. A syntactically introduced "duplicating" TOT can be easily mistaken for the governor of the pseudo-relative; thus, in the following sentence *togo* is not the governor of the pseudo-relative:

Čem serdce bednoe polno, togo ne vyrazjat slova
with.what heart poor is.full that.thing not will.express words
'Words cannot express what fills [my] poor heart'. [D. Merežkovskij]

The syntactically primary form of this sentence is *Čem serdce bednoe polno, ne vyrazjat slova.*

d. An RC with a pronominal governor does not use the "regular" relative pronoun KOTORYJ 'that/which', but uses instead a special relative pronoun corresponding to the pronominal governor. As a result, there are the following pairs:

built on the T-stem	built on the K-stem
TO 'that.somehing'	~ ČTO 'what'
TOT 'that.somebody'	~ KTO 'who'
TOGDA 'then'	~ KOGDA 'when'
TAK 'this.way'	~ KAK 'how'
TAM 'there'	~ GDE 'where'
TUDA 'to.there'	~ KUDA 'to.where'
OTTUDA 'from.there'	~ OTKUDA 'from.where'
Etc.	

2) Presence of a subordinator
This parameter has two possible values:

> the subordinator is present — the subordinator is absent

A subordinator (a.k.a. complementizer, or—in our case—a relativizer), either invariable or morphologically agreeing with the RC's governor, is part of the RC—it constitutes its syntactic head. It can be either a lexeme—a subordinating conjunction, as in (24a); or a morphological marker—an affix, as in (24b); or else a specific prosody, as in (24c–d). In the examples the subordinator is underscored:

(24) a. Hebrew

HA+IŠA [še Roni natan LA   et   ha+sefer]
the woman that Roni gave to.her DirO the book
lit. 'the.woman **that Roni gave to.her the.book**'
= 'the woman to whom **Roni gave the book**'

b. Swahili (ch = /č/, j = /ǯ/; Roman numerals in the glosses stand for noun classes)

Ni   +li   +nunua ki+tabu jana   'I.bought [a] book yesterday'. ~
1.SG$_{subj}$ PAST buy VII book yesterday

KI+TABU [ni+li+ch+o+nunua jana]   '[the] book **I.bought yesterday**'

NB The subordinator prefix **o-** marks the clause as subordinated; the prefix
ch- [⇐ ki- |_/Vowel/]
shows the agreement in noun class (VII) with the governor, KITABU.

c. Chichewa (Downing & Mtenje 2011; th = /tʰ/, the acute accent indicates the high tone)

M+BALÁ i   +ná +bá   n+dalámá z+àángá 'A.thief stole my money'. ~
IX thief IX$_{subj}$ PAST steal X money X my

M+BALÁ [í   +ná +bá   n+dalámá z+àángá] i   +ku +tháawa
IX thief IX$_{subj}$-REL PAST steal X money X my   IX$_{subj}$ PRES run.away
'The thief who stole my money is running away'.

NB In (24c), the subordinator is expressed by the high tone on the subject prefix **i-** of the Main Verb of the RC. This tonal subordinator of an RC can cooccur with the suffixal subordinator **-o** and with the relative pronoun MÉNÉ 'which':

d. Chichewa

M+BALÁ [I   +MÉNÉ í   +ná +bá n+dalámá z+angáa+y+o]
IX thief IX$_{subj}$ which IX$_{subj}$-REL PAST steal X money X my   IX REL
i   +ku +tháawa
IX$_{subj}$ PRES run.away
'The thief who stole my money is running away'.

If the subordinator is a lexeme, in the SSyntS this lexeme is the syntactic governor of the RC's Main Verb, i.e. the head of the RC. It can, but need not, cooccur with the RC's governor's image. Schematically (an artificial English example):

the MAN→[that WHOM I←met yesterday...]

3) Presence of a relative pronoun
This parameter has three values:

the relative pronoun is present (in the RC)	—
the relative pronoun is present (in the RC) and a correlative pronoun is present (in the superordinate clause)	—
the relative pronoun is absent (from the RC)	

A relative pronoun present in the RC may require a correlative demonstrative pronoun in the superordinate clause (underscored in (25)); this correlative pronoun syntactically depends on the RC's governor.

(25) Hindi

mužhe <u>vah</u> ĀDMĪ [žo   Sītā+ko aččʰā lagtā   hɛ] pasand nahĩ hɛ ~
I-DAT that man   which Sita DAT nice   seeming is   likable not is
lit. 'To me that man which to.Sita nice seeming is likable not is'.
= 'I don't like the man who seems nice to Sita'.

[žo   Sītā+ko aččʰā lagtā   hɛ] mužhe <u>vah</u> ĀDMĪ pasand nahĩ hɛ
which Sita DAT nice   seeming is   I-DAT that man likable not is
lit. 'Which to.Sita nice seeming is, to.me that man likable not is'.
= 'I don't like the man who seems nice to Sita'.

Hindi has fairly complex rules that allow/require the introduction of the correlative demonstrative, as well as the use of the correlative instead of the governor or its image (Mahajan 2000); these rules do not concern us here.

4) Presence and form of the governor's image
This parameter has three possible values:

the governor's image is a duplicate of the governor	—
the governor's image is elided (= gapped)	—
the governor's image is replaced with a pronoun	

NB In a more detailed study, the type of the replacing pronoun—relative or personal—should be taken into account. Interestingly, relative pronominalization characteristic of European languages is, according to Comrie 1998, a typological rarity.

See examples (27)–(32) below.

Combining the values of Parameters 1–4 ($2 \times 2 \times 3 \times 3$) produces 36 logically possible syntactic types of restrictive RC. As will be shown, deep morphology—word order and inflection—multiplies this number by 15; as a result, we have 540 types all in all. Small wonder, then, that the description of RC is so difficult! Of course, not all logically possible combinations are actually allowed in all languages, but there still are too many possible syntactic-morphological types of RC, which defies their systematic exhaustive overview in this chapter. Consequently, only some types of RC are illustrated in Subsection 6.4.5.

6.4.5 Illustrations of different types of RC constructions (L→RC)

The RC and its gloss are boldfaced and put in square brackets; the RC's governor is printed in italic CAPS; the governor's image is also printed in boldfaced italic caps and BOXED.

6.4.5.1 The RC's governor is a non-pronominal noun ($L_{(N,\ non\text{-}pron)}$→RC)

A subordinator is absent; a relative pronoun is absent; the governor's image is a duplicate of the governor

(26) Vietnamese

a. *Đứa*   CON   [*đứa* CON   *trễ*]   khóc
   CLASS child CLASS child be.late cry
   lit. 'The child [**the child is.late**] is.crying'. = 'The child who is late is crying'.

b. *Đứa*   CON   [*đứa* CON   khóc] *trễ*
   CLASS child CLASS child cry   be.late
   lit. 'The child [**the child is.crying**] is.late. = 'The child who is crying is late'.

A subordinator is absent; a relative pronoun is absent; the governor's image is elided

(27) a. Japanese (Kuno 1973: 249, (12a))

[***sin*+*da* +*no***   +*de*   **minna**   +***ga*   *kanasin*   +*da***]   HITO
die PAST NOMINALIZER LOC everybody SUBJ be.saddened PAST person
lit. '[**died.fact.because.of everybody saddened.was**] person'
= 'person because of whose death everybody was saddened'.

Japanese allows for relativization of **any** clause elements and does not require explicit expression of the semantic relation between the RC and its governor:

atama+ga yoku naru hon
lit. 'head good becomes [because of it] book'
= 'a book that makes you smart'

toire+ni ikenai komāsyaru
lit. 'to.toilet do.not.go [because of it] commercial'
= 'a commercial that won't let you go to the bathroom'

hon+o katta oturi
lit. 'book$_{ACC}$ have.bought change' = 'change from buying the book'

(See Shibatani 2009: 167–168 on the obligatory ellipsis of the governor's image as one of the means of marking the subordinate character of the RC in Japanese; the other one is word order: Japanese being a strict verb-final language, the linear position of a finite verb before a noun marks this verb as the Main Verb of an RC.)

    b. Ancash Quechua (Cole 1987)

    [***Nuna*+Ø**   ***ranti+shqa*+n**] BESTYA+Ø   alli   ka+rqo +n
    man   NOM buy   PERF 3   horse   NOM good be PAST 3
    lit. '[**Man bought**] horse good was'. = 'The horse the man bought was good'.

    c. Mohave (Lehmann 1984: 111)
    ʔaqʷaq+nʸ   ʔ   +akʸā+k   +e   ʔUTIS [***m* +*ūmač*]+nʸ +m**
    deer   DEF 1.SG shoot REAL EMPH.3 gun   2.SG find   DEF with
    lit. 'Deer.the I.did.shoot gun [**you.find.the.with**]'.
    = 'I did shoot the deer with the gun you had found'.

<u>A subordinator is absent; a relative pronoun is absent; the governor's image is present—as a personal pronoun</u>

(28) Arabic, with an indefinite governor
    KITAB   +ĀNI   [*a* +*qraʔ*+*u*   =$\boxed{HUMĀ}$]   hunā
    book$_{(masc)}$ DUAL.NOM 1.SG read 1.SG   they-MASC.DUAL.ACC here
    lit. 'Two.books [**I.read.them.two**] [are] here'. = 'Two books that I read are here'.

NB 1. The equality sign (=) shows the adjunction of a clitic rather than that of an affix.
    2. If the RC 's governor is definite, the subordinator is necessary; cf. (32b).

<u>A subordinator is absent; a relative pronoun is present; the governor's image is present—as this relative pronoun</u>

(29) Russian
    KNIG   +A,   [$\boxed{KOTOR+UJU}$ *ja*   *čitaj*+*u*,]   *naxoditsja zdes'*
    book$_{(fem)}$ SG.NOM which FEM.SG.ACC I-NOM read PRES.1.SG is   here
    lit. 'Book [**which I am.reading**] is here'.

A subordinator is absent; a relative pronoun is present; the governor's image is present—as the governor's duplicate subordinating this relative pronoun

(30) a. Latin (Livius)

[*Qu +ibus*   DIE +BUS   *Cum +ae*
which MASC.PL.ABL day(masc) PL.ABL Cumae PL.NOM
liberat +ae   sunt,] i +s   +dem DIE +BUS
liberated FEM.PL.NOM are   this MASC.PL.ABL same day(masc) PL.ABL
Semproni +us   prospere   pugna+Ø +t
Sempronius SG.NOM successfully fight PRES 3.SG
lit. '[**Which days Cumae are liberated,**] the.same days Sempronius successfully fights'. = 'The same days that Cumae are liberated, Sempronius fights successfully'.

b. Burushaski (Tiffou & Patry 1995: 371, (76))

[*Ámen* HÍRA   *xat   čía,]   khéne* HÍRE
which man-SG.DAT letter-SG.NOM I.to.him.gave this man-SG.ERG
sía   aúlum   bái
read-INF unable is
lit. '[**Which to.man letter I sent,**] this man read [it] unable is'.

A subordinator is present; a relative pronoun is absent; the governor's image is elided

(31) Basque: the suffixal subordinator (more precisely, a relativizer) **-n** is invariable

[*gizon+a +k   libur+a +Ø   eman dio+n*]   EMAKUME+A +Ø
man   the ERG book the NOM given has RELATIVIZER woman   the NOM
lit. '[**the man the book given has.REL**] the woman'
= 'the woman to whom the man has given the book'

A subordinator is present; a relative pronoun is absent; the governor's image is present—as a personal pronoun

(32) a. Persian: the lexemic subordinator KE ≈ 'that' (a subordinating conjunction) is invariable[14]

KETAB+E   *xub +i*   [*ke* AN+RA *mi +xan+äm*] *inǰast*
book   IZAFET good DEF that it DirO PRES read 1.SG here.is
lit. 'Book good [**that it I.am.reading**] here.is'.
= 'The good book that I am reading is here'.

---

[14] If the governor's image is the SSynt-subject in the RC it is obligatorily elided:
(i) *ketab+i ke inǰast* 'the.book that is.here' vs. **ketab+i ke u inǰast* 'the.book that **it** is.here'

b. Arabic, with a definite governor: the lexemic subordinator ALLAÐ- ≈ 'such that...' (an adjective) agrees with the governor in gender, number and case

AL+KITĀB   +ĀNĪ   [allað +āni   a   +qraʔ+u
the book₍ₘₐₛc₎ DUAL.NOM which MASC.DUAL.NOM   1.SG read 1.SG
= HUMĀ]   hunā
they-MASC.DUAL.ACC   here

lit. 'The.two.books [two.which I.read them.two] [are] here'.
= 'The two books that I am reading are here'.

NB If the RC's governor is indefinite, the subordinator is absent; cf. (28).

6.4.5.2 The RC's governor is a nominal pronoun (L₍N, pron₎→RC)

A subordinator is absent; a relative pronoun is present; the governor's image is present—as this relative pronoun

(33) Russian; the governor is a correlative pronoun

a. Without duplication of the governor

TOT,   [KTO   išč +et,]   vsegda najd   +ët ~
that.person-MASC.SG.NOM who-NOM seek PRES.3.SG always find-FUT 3.SG

lit. 'That.person [= 'he'] **who seeks** always will.find'.
= 'One who seeks finds' [*The Gospel of Matthew*].

b. With duplication of the governor

TOT,   [KTO   išč +et,]
that.person-MASC.SG.NOM who-NOM seek PRES.3.SG
tot   vsegda najd   +ët
that.person-MASC.SG.NOM always find-FUT 3.SG

lit. 'That [= 'he'] [**who seeks,**] that.person always will.find'.

(34) Latin (Cicero; Zaliznjak & Padučeva 1975 [2002: 670])

ILL +O   iugul   +e   +t   [qu   +em   tradidit
this SG.ABL jugulate SUBJUNCT.PRES 3.SG which MASC.SG.ACC transferred
ENS   +EM]_pseudo-RC
sword₍ₘₐₛc₎ SG.ACC

lit. 'With.this let.him.jugulate [**which he.transferred sword**]'.
= 'Let him jugulate [somebody] with the sword that he transferred'.

> Let it be emphasized that sentences like the following one do not contain an RC:
> [KTO išč +et,]   (tot)   vsegda najd +ët
> who-NOM seek PRES.3.SG (that.person-MASC.SG.NOM) always find-FUT 3.SG
> lit. '**Who seeks**, (that.person [= 'he']) always will.find'.

The boldfaced clause in brackets is not an RC, but a pseudo-RC, which is the subject of the verb *najdët* 'will.find'. The optional correlative TOT in the matrix clause is a resumptive pronoun duplicate of the subject expressed by the pseudo-relative.

An identical situation obtains with any other correlative pronoun as the RC's governor, for instance:

(35) Russian
 a. Without duplication of the governor
    OTTUDA,   [OTKUDA   **on prišël**,] k nam   dobiraj+utsja   mašinoj
    from.there from.where he came   to us   reach PRES.3.PL by.car
    lit. 'From.there [**from.where he came**] [people] reach us by car'.
 b. With duplication of the governor
    OTTUDA,   [OTKUDA   **on prišël**,] ottuda   k nam
    from.there from.where he came   from.there   to us
    dobiraj+utsja   mašinoj
    reach PRES.3.PL   by.car
    lit. 'From.there **from.where he came** from.there [people] reach us by car'.

However, in the sentence [OTKUDA **on prišël**,] (*ottuda*) *k nam dobirajutsja mašinoj* the clause *otkuda on prišël* is not an RC, but a pseudo-RC. (Cf. 6.4.4, (23), p. 260.) Here is another example of pseudo-RCs of the same kind:

(36) Old Russian (Zaliznjak & Padučeva 1975 [2002: 652])
   [A   čto   brat +ъ   tvoi dějalъ   NASILI   +E
   and   which   brother SG.NOM your was.doing   violence(neu) SG.ACC
   na Nověgorodě] a   t   +ogo   sja   otstupi
   in Novgorod   and that.one NEU.SG.GEN REFL   renounce-IMPER
   lit. 'And [**which violence [your] brother committed in Novgorod**,] and from.that renounce!' = 'The violence_ACC that your brother committed in Novgorod, renounce that_GEN!'

   NB 1. The conjunction A ≈ 'and' at the beginning of each clause is irrelevant for our illustration. Such a conjunction is a typical means to mark the beginning of a clause in many languages.
   2. In (36), the pseudo-RC functions syntactically as a prolepsis.

6.4.6 Deep-morphological parameters characterizing the implementation of an RC

The deep-morphological representation [DMorphR] of a clause is a linear sequence, i.e. a string, of the DMorphRs of all its lexemes; this string is supplied with the information on phrasing (pauses, stresses, intonation contours). This subsection is concerned with word order (6.4.6.1) and morphological marking (6.4.6.2) in and around an RC.

6.4.6.1 Word order parameters characterizing an RC

1) **Linear position of the RC (with respect to its superordinate clause)**
   The RC can occupy one of the five possible linear positions with respect to its superordinate clause (Lehmann 1984: 49ff; Dryer 2013):

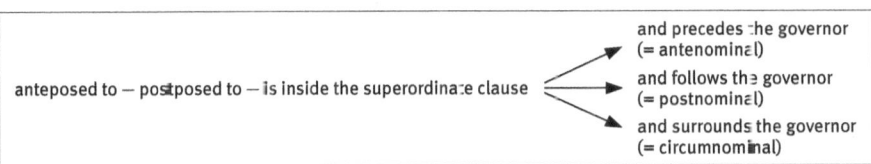

NB If the RC is ante- or post-posed to its superordinate clause, it can linearly not be in contact with the governor (and its dependents). This is what is known as an **extraposed** RC.

(37) a. The RC is anteposed to its superordinate clause
   Latin (Ovidius; Zaliznjak & Padučeva 1975[2002: 678], with a slight modification of the word order)
   [QU +AE   *praeteriit,*] nec   *iterum revocabitur*
   which FEM.SG.NOM passed   and.not back will.be.called.back
   UND +A
   wave(fem) SG.NOM
   lit. '[**Which flowed.past,**] and.not back will.brought the.wave .

   b. The RC is postposed to its superordinate clause
      An aeroelastic SYSTEM is considered [THAT *includes the cubic stiffness*].

   c. The RC is inside its superordinate clause and precedes its governor
      Latin (Ovidius; Zaliznjak & Padučeva 1975 [2002: 673])
      Alter +a,   [QU +AS   *orien*+s   *hab*+u   +*it*],
      another FEM.SG.NOM which FEM.PL.ACC East SG.NOM have PERF 3.SG
      prelat +a   PUELL+IS
      preferred FEM.SG.NOM   girl   PL.DAT
      lit. 'Another, [**which East had,**] preferred to.girls'. = 'Another [girl is] preferred to the girls East had'.

d. The RC is inside its superordinate clause and follows its governor
   Reviews of this BOOK, [**which was published last year,**] *are mostly positive.*
e. The RC is inside its superordinate clause and surrounds its governor (in other words, a discontinuous RC is wrapped around its governor)
   (i) Hittite (Lehmann 1986: 6)
   [*KASKAL* +*z*   +*a* $\boxed{K^w \;\; +IT}$]...   *ASSU*   +∅
   campaign SG.ABL and which NEU.SG.ACC goods$_{(neu)}$ SG.NOM
   ... [*utaḫḫun*]   *n* +*at*   *apedanda halissiyanun*
   brought-1.SG and it-ACC this-INSTR decorated-1.SG
   lit. '[**And.from.campaign which**] GOODS [**I.brought,**] and.it with.this I.decorated'. = 'And the booty which I brought from the campaign, I decorated it [something mentioned before] with this'.

   (ii) Bambara (Keenan & Comrie 1977: 65)
   Cὲ   *ye*   [*ye*]... *so* ... [$\boxed{MIN}$ *ye*] *san*
   man PAST PAST horse which see buy
   lit. 'Man has [I have]... horse ...[which seen] bought'. = 'The man bought the horse which I had seen'.
   NB The discontinuous RC [*n ye ... min ye*] 'I have ... which seen' = 'which I have seen' is "wrapped" around its governor **so** 'horse'.

   (iii) Kabiyé (Hiraiwa et al. 2017: 24, (88))[15]
   [*Ɛso tɪ* *ya*]...   *MANGU* ... [*ŋgʊ*   *yɔ*] *kɪ* +*we ḍeu*
   Eso not bought mango   which the 3.SG be good
   lit. '[**Eso not bought**] mango [**which the**] is good'.
   = 'The mango which Eso did not buy is good'.

Tagalog allows for all the three linear positions of the RC with respect to its governor:

(38) Tagalog (the oblique case marker **ng** is pronounced /naŋ/)
   a. The RC precedes the governor
      [*nagbigay ng bigas sa bata*] *na*   LALAKI
      gave   OBL rice DAT child LINKER man
      lit. '[**gave rice to.child**] LINKER man' = 'the man who gave rice to the child'
      NB The **linker** is an auxiliary (= structural) lexeme that marks an expression as a modifier to the following or to the preceding noun; thus, *X na Y*$_{(N)}$ and *Y*$_{(N)}$ *na X* both mean 'Y which is X'.

---

[15] The proposed syntactic description of this Kabiyé sentence is buttressed by the possibility of sentence (i), absolutely synonymous with it, but showing a different word order:
(i) *Mangu* **ŋgʊ** *Ɛso tɪ ya yɔ kiwe ḍeu* lit. 'Mango which Eso not bought the is good'.

b. The RC follows the governor

LALAKI na   [nagbigay ng bigas sa bata]
man   LINKER gave   OBL rice DAT child
lit. 'man LINKER [gave rice to.child]'
= 'the man who gave rice to the child'

c. The RC surrounds the governor

[nagbigay]... na   LALAKI ...[ng bigas sa bata]
gave   LINKER man   OBL rice DAT child
lit. '[gave] LINKER man [rice to.child]'
= 'the man who gave rice to the child'

2) Linear position of the relative pronoun (inside the RC)
The relative pronoun can occupy one of the following three linear positions:

> the first — the last — in situ (that is, where it is required by the syntactic structure of the RC)

Deep-morphological parameters 1 and 2 specify 5 × 3 = 15 major morphological types of RC, of which the following six are illustrated in (39).

(39) Hindi (Koul 2008: 187–194)

Hindi features much flexibility in linear placement of the RC and of the relative pronoun within it. The sentences meaning 'The boy who lives in Delhi is my brother' can be implemented as follows:

a. (i) [ʒo   dillī +mẽ rahtā   hɛ] vah LAṚKĀ+Ø
       which-SG Delhi in live-PRES_PART.SG.MASC is   that boy   NOM
       merā bhāī +Ø   hɛ
       my   brother NOM is
       lit. '[Which in.Delhi living is] that boy my brother is'.

   (ii) [dillī+mẽ ʒo rahtā hɛ] vah LAṚKĀ+Ø merā bhāī+Ø hɛ

b. (i) vah LAṚKĀ+Ø   merā bhāī   +Ø   hɛ [ʒo   dillī +mẽ
       that boy NOM my   brother NOM is   which-SG Delhi in
       rahtā   hɛ]
       live-PRES_PART.SG.MASC is
       lit. 'That boy my brother is [which in Delhi living is]'.

   (ii) vah LAṚKĀ+Ø merā bhāī+Ø hɛ [dillī+mẽ ʒo rahtā hɛ]

c. (i) vah LAṚKĀ+Ø [ǰo dillī +mẽ rahtā   hɛ]
       that boy NOM which-SG Delhi in live-PRES_PART.SG.MASC is
       merā bhāī +Ø hɛ
       my brother NOM is
       lit. 'That boy [**which in Delhi living is**] my brother is'.

(ii) vah LAṚKĀ+Ø [dillī+mẽ ǰo rahtā hɛ] merā bhāī+Ø hɛ

6.4.6.2 Inflectional parameters characterizing an RC

Inflectional parameters specific to RCs are 1) the inflection of the subordinator, 2) the "relative" inflection of the RC's Main Verb (that is, the inflection characterizing the Main Verb as part of an RC), and 3) the inflection of the RC's governor and the governor's image. Only the RC-related inflection of the governor and its image will be considered here.

1) Inflection of the governor's image: progressive case attraction

The expression "progressive case attraction" refers to the deviant grammatical case of the governor's image due to the impact of the governor's case; cf. regressive case attraction in (42).

(40) a. Latin (Horatius; Bianchi 2000: 58)

   notant +e   IUDIC +E   [QU +O   nost +ī]
   judging MASC.SG.ABL judge₍masc₎ SG.ABL who MASC.SG.ABL know 2.SG
   lit. 'judging judge [**by.which you_SG.know**]'
   = 'while the judge you know was judging'

b. Ancient Greek (Xenophon; Grimm 2007: 140)

   ándr+es   áksio +i   t +ēs   ELEPHTERÍ+ĀS
   man PL.NOM worthy PL.NOM the FEM.SG.GEN freedom₍fem₎ SG.GEN
   [H +ēs   kektḗ +sthe]
   which FEM.SG.GEN possess PRES.2.PL
   lit. 'men worthy of.the freedom [**of.which you_PL.possess**]'
   = 'men worthy of the freedom which you possess'

In (40a), the expected case of the relative pronoun QUIS 'which, who' is the accusative *qu+em* 'MASC.SG.**ACC**', required by the transitive verb 'know'; the deviation—i.e., the ablative *qu+o*—is caused by the ablative case of the governor, the noun IUDEX 'judge' in the Ablativus Absolutus construction. In (40b), the genitive of the governor noun, ELEPHTERÍA 'freedom', is the cause of the deviant genitive *h+ēs* of the relative pronoun HOS 'who, which', instead of the "legitimate" accusative *h+ēn*.

2) Inflection of RC's governor

a. Definiteness of the governor

Persian requires an RC-modified N (= the governor of the RC) to have an obligatory definiteness marker, the suffix **-i**:

(41) Persian

ZÄN   +I   [ke   män U   +RA   dust   dar+äm]   inžast
woman DEF   that I   s/he DirO friend have 1.SG here.is
('DUST DAR' is an idiom meaning '[to] love')
lit. 'The.woman [that I her love] here.is'.

b. Regressive case attraction

"Regressive case attraction" (also known as inverse attraction) refers to the deviant grammatical case of the governor due to the impact of the governor image's case; cf. progressive case attraction above, (40).

(42) a. Latin (Vergilius; Bianchi 2000: 59)

URB +EM |QU   +AM| statu+o]
city(fem) SG.ACC which FEM.SG.ACC found IND.PRES.1.SG
vestr+a   est
yours FEM.SG.NOM   is
'The city_ACC [which_ACC I found] is yours'.

b. Ancient Greek (Sophocles; Grimm 2007: 140)

T +on   ANDR +ÓN   [H   +ON|
the MASC.SG.ACC   man(masc) SG.ACC which MASC.SG.ACC
pálai   zêt   +eis]   éstin entháde
for.long.time   look.for PRES.2.SG is   here
lit. 'The man_ACC [which_ACC you_SG look.for for.a.long.time] is here'.

The case of the noun URBS 'city', which is the subject of the sentence (42a), should be the nominative: *urb+s*; the deviation is caused by the influence of the accusative of the governor's image *quam*. Similarly, in (42b) the subject noun ANÉR 'man' must be in the nominative, but receives the accusative by "assimilating" its own case to the accusative of the relative pronoun.

c. Ingrian (= Izhorian); Kholodilova 2013)

IHMIS+TÄ [*KE +TÄ* *siä* *nä+i* *+t*] *ja* *miu+n*
man SG.PART who SG.PART you.NOM see PAST 2SG and I GEN
veiko *+in* *o +vat* *üstäv +i +ä*
brother.NOM 1SG be PRES.3PL friend PL PART
'The man whom you saw and my brother are friends'.

The head of the subject phrase of the matrix clause, IHMINE 'man', is supposed to be in the nominative case; but it can get the partitive case under the impact of the relative pronoun KE, which obtains its partitive as the direct object of the verb NÄ- 'see'.

7 ESLI ..., TO ... 'if ..., then ...'
Syntax of binary conjunctions in Russian

7.1 The problem stated: the binary conjunction ESLI ..., TO ... 'if ..., then ...'
    in the syntactic structure of a sentence
7.2 The problem solved
7.3 Conjunctions: a small typology
7.4 Binary conjunctions in Russian
7.5 Phraseological nature of binary conjunctions

7.1 The problem stated: the binary conjunction ESLI ..., TO ... 'if ..., then ...' in the syntactic structure of a sentence

The object of this chapter is the set of binary conjunctions (Rus. *parnye sojuzy*), subordinating and coordinating; they are also known in the English-language literature as correlative subordinators/coordinators (Quirk et al. 1991: 935–941, 999–1001). A typical example can be the Russian binary subordinating conjunction ESLI ..., TO ... 'if ..., then ...'; and the question asked is as follows:

> What is the syntactic structure of a complex sentence including this conjunction?

For instance:

(1) Rus. *Esli ty—somnevaeš'sja,* **to** *ja←mogu→proverit'*
    'If you doubt, then I can verify'.

All syntactic links in sentence (1) are obvious, except for the particle TO², the second component of the binary conjunction under analysis.[1] The problem with TO² stems from the fact that this lexeme cannot be used alone—i.e. without ESLI 'if' (unlike the English THEN in the English binary conjunction IF ..., THEN ...). As a result, the first idea that comes to mind is to make TO² syntactically dependent on ESLI: ESLI–r→TO²; all the more so, because TO² is linearly positioned with respect to ESLI, namely, necessarily after it (see immediately below, Criterion **A** for the presence of a syntactic link, Condition 2). Then the binary conjunction ESLI ...,

---

[1] TO¹ is a component of three Russian repeated conjunctions TO¹ ..., TO¹ ..., TO¹ ... 'now ..., now ..., now ...', ⌈TO¹ LI⌉..., ⌈TO¹ LI⌉..., ⌈TO¹ LI⌉ ... 'whether..., or..., or...' and ⌈NE TO¹⌉..., ⌈NE TO¹⌉..., ⌈NE TO¹⌉ ... 'maybe ..., or ..., or ...'.

https://doi.org/10.1515/9783110694765-008

то² ... can be stored in the lexicon exactly in the form of this syntactic subtree. Such a description—launched, probably, by myself—has been tacitly accepted and applied for almost half a century:

- In Mel'čuk 1974: 231, No. 31, (e), the surface-syntactic relation [SSyntRel] r between ESLI and TO² was called **"1ˢᵗ auxiliary."**
- In Mel'čuk & Pertsov 1987: 331, No. 19.1, it was rebaptized **"binary-junctive."**
- In Iomdin 2010c: 43, 1.2.4.5, it appears under the name of **"correlative."**
- In Mel'čuk 2012b: 143, No. 51, it is **"correlative-auxiliary."**

The name of this SSyntRel is, of course, not important: what really matters is the syntactic dependency of TO² on ESLI.

However, the syntactic description of the conjunction under analysis as ESLI–r→TO² contradicts the definition of syntactic dependency! More precisely, I am referring to the definition of surface-syntactic relation that was advanced in Mel'čuk 1988: 130–144 and has been used as such since (Mel'čuk 2009a: 25–40 and 2012–2015: vol. 3, 411–433). For the ease of reading, I will reproduce here the first part of this definition: Criterion A of the presence of a syntactic dependency between two lexemes in a sentence. (Criteria B and C are not relevant to the following discussion.)

Criterion A: Presence of a surface-syntactic relation between lexemes L_1 and L_2 (Chapter 2, Section 2.4, p. 40)

> **Prosodic unity and linear arrangement in the configuration L_1–r–L_2**
> In a given utterance U of L, the lexemes L_1 and L_2 can have a direct Synt-dependency link, that is, they can form a configuration L_1–r–L_2, if and only if both of Conditions 1 and 2 are simultaneously satisfied:
>
> **Condition 1**
> (a) General case
> L_1–r–L_2 can be implemented by a phrase of language L, such as N—V, V—N, ADJ—N, PREP—N, ADV—ADJ, NUM—N, etc.
> (b) Special case
> L_1–r–L_2 alone cannot be implemented by a phrase of L, but taken together with a convenient configuration of lexemes from the set $\{L_i\}$ appearing in the same utterance it can, such that the following three configurations are implementable by phrases of L:
>
> 1) $\overline{L_1-\{L_{i\cdot 1}\}\ L_2}-\{L_{i\cdot 2}\}$, 2) $L_1-\{L_{i\cdot 1}\}$ and 3) $L_2-\{L_{i\cdot 2}\}$.
>
> **Condition 2**
> The linear position of one of the lexemes L_1 and L_2 in the phrase L_1–r–L_2 is specified with respect to the other.

Examples

The Special case (b) of Condition 1 covers two types of expressions:
(i) L_1–L_2–$L_{3(N)}$, as in one_{L_1}–of_{L_2}–$them_{L_3}$. Here, *one of is not a phrase, while the utterances of them and one of them are phrases; consequently, the configuration one—of is allowed for.
(ii) L_1–{L_{i-1}} $L_{2(CONJ)}$–L_{i-2}},

as in It $became_{L_1}$–{$obvious$}$_{\{L_{i-1}\}}$ $that_{L_2}$–{$he\ wasn't\ there$}$_{\{L_{i-2}\}}$.

Here, *became that is not a phrase, while became obvious and that he wasn't there are phrases, with became and that as their heads; therefore, the configuration became—that is accepted as legitimate.

7.2 The problem solved

Rus. $ESLI_{L_2}$ Y, $TO^2_{L_1}$ X 'if Y, then X' (a binary subordinating conjunction):
- The expression *esli to is not a phrase; Condition 1 does not allow for the configuration *ESLI—TO².
- $ESLI_{L_2}$ is a subordinating conjunction; it forms a phrase with the subordinate clause $Y_{\{L_{i-2}\}}$ it introduces. The particle $TO^2_{L_1}$ forms a phrase with the superordinate clause $X_{\{L_{i-1}\}}$.
- $ESLI_{L_2}$ syntactically subordinates the Main Verb of Y and is itself subordinated to the Main Verb of X: $MV(X)_{\{L_{i-1}\}} \rightarrow ESLI_{L_2} \rightarrow MV(Y)_{\{L_{i-2}\}}$.
- $TO^2_{L_1}$ syntactically depends on the Main Verb of X.[2]

As a result, we have the following SSynt-structure: $esli \rightarrow Y, to^2 \leftarrow X$. The second component of a binary conjunction—in this case, the particle TO²—is subordinated to the MV of the superordinate clause by the **auxiliary** SSyntRel (Chapter 2, Section 2.5, SSyntRel No. 46, p. 76).

For readers acquainted with the dependency syntactic descriptions in the Meaning-Text framework the proposed updating must seem quite natural. What is surprising is the fact that it took so long to see the problem. I am correcting here a mistake that has been being perpetrated for many years; it concerns all the binary conjunctions and a motley set of expressions similar to them.

---

[2] TO² changes the syntactic combinability of the clause C it introduces: a TO²-clause C can be used only if it has a subordinate clause C′ introduced by the conjunction ESLI. This, however, is a feature of the active SSynt-valence of the clause, not of its passive valence, which remains unchanged.

7.3 Conjunctions: a small typology

Before an inventory of Russian binary conjunctions can be offered, I need to sketch a general typology of conjunctions—in order to give the discussion a certain depth.

- According to their meaning/function, conjunctions are divided in two major families: **subordinating** vs. **coordinating**.
- According to their form, conjunctions are classified along two independent axes:
  - the number of components: **single** (just one component) vs. **binary** (two components) vs. **repeated** (built by a theoretically unlimited repetition of the first component);
  - the structure of components: **simple** (all its components are monolexemic) vs. **compound** (at least one component is plurilexemic).

A binary or repeated conjunction is necessarily discontinuous: its components cannot be in linear contact within an utterance.

Since repeated conjunctions can be only coordinating, there are 10 logically possible classes of conjunctions, exemplified with Russian conjunctions in the following table (KĂK and TĂK stand for unstressed particles), see Table 7.1, next page.

Comments

1. Consider the expressions of the form *v svjazi s tem, čto...* lit. 'in connection with the.fact that ...' (cf. *v svjazi s ètim rebënkom* 'in connection with this child'), *vsledstvie togo, čto...* lit. 'as.consequence of.the.fact that ...' (cf. *vsledstvie ètogo rešenija* 'as.consequence of.this decision'), *v silu togo, čto...* lit. 'in virtue of.the.fact that ...' (cf. *v silu ètoj teoremy* 'in virtue of.this theorem'), etc. In spite of often repeated statements, such an expression is not a compound conjunction, although syntactically it is equivalent to one. An expression of this type consists of a preposition that syntactically subordinates a nominal correlative pronoun: either TOTII.1 ≈ 'this. one' or TOTII.2 ≈ 'the.fact'; this, in turn, leads to one of the following two specific cases:

— TOTII.1 subordinates a relative clause introduced by the relative nominal pronoun ČTO² 'what'; both are seen in sentence (2a), whose SSyntS is given in (2b):

(2) a. *Oni pošli tuda nesmotrja na to, čto im skazala mat'*
    'They went there, despite of this what to.them had.said Mother'.

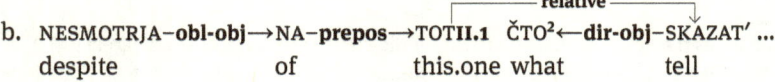

   b. NESMOTRJA-**obl-obj**→NA-**prepos**→TOTII.1 ČTO²←**dir-obj**–SKAZAT' ...
      despite   of   this.one what   tell

Table 7.1 Universal types of conjunctions

	simple: monolexemic components		compound: plurilexemic components	
	subordinating	coordinating	subordinating	coordinating
single	1	2	3	4
	EDVA 'as soon as'	I 'and', A '≈ and'	⌈KAK TOL'KO⌉ 'as soon as'	⌈TO ES⌉ 'that is'
	ESLI 'if', RAZ '≈ if'	ILI 'or', LIBO 'or [exclusive]'	⌈POTOMU ČTO⌉ 'because'	⌈A TAKŽE⌉ 'as well as'
	KOGDA 'when'	NO 'but'	⌈TAK KAK⌉ 'since'	
	XOTJA 'although'		⌈V TO VREMJA KAK⌉ 'in the time as'	
binary	5	6	7	8
	ESLI …, (TO²) … 'if …, then …'	I …, I … 'and …, and …'	⌈KAK TOL'KO⌉ …, (TAK) … 'as soon as …'	⌈KAK .. , TAK I⌉ … 'both …, and …'
	EDVA …, (KAK) … 'no sooner …, than …'	ILI …, ILI … 'or…, or…'	⌈NE TAK (on xoroš), KAK⌉ (my v něm nuždaemsja) 'not so much he [is] good, as we need him'	⌈NE STOL'KO (slyšimye), SKOL'KO⌉ (ugadyvaemye) 'not so much (heard), but rather guessed'
	TOL'KO …, (KAK) … 'as soon …, then …'	NI …, NI … 'nor …, nor …'		
	XOTJA …, (NO) … 'although …, but …'			
repeated		9		10
	—	I …, I …, I … 'and …, and …, and …'	—	⌈TO¹ LI⌉…, ⌈TO¹ LI⌉…, ⌈TO¹ LI⌉ … 'whether…, or…, or…'
		TO¹ …, TO¹ …, TO¹ … 'now …, now …, now …'		⌈NE TO¹⌉…, ⌈NE TO¹⌉…, ⌈NE TO¹⌉… 'maybe …, or …, or …'
		LIBO…, LIBO…, LIBO… 'either …, or…, or…'		

TOTII.1 and ČTO² are declined independently, each one in conformity with the government by its own syntactic governor: *vopreki **tomu**, o **čëm** im govorila mat'* lit. 'despite this about what to.them was saying Mother'. TOTII.1 accepts VES' 'all' as modifier: *nesmotrja na **vsë** to, čto im skazala mat'* lit. 'despite of **all** this what to.them had.said Mother'.

— The pronoun TOTII.2, which has the surface forms only in neuter singular, subordinates the invariable semantically empty complementizer (subordinating conjunction) ČTO¹ 'that⁵', which introduces a completive clause. Thus, sentence (3a) has the SSyntS, (partially) shown in (3b):

(3) a. *Oni pošli tuda nesmotrja na to, čto mat' zapretila im èto*
   'They went there despite of this that Mother had.forbidden them this'.
   b. POJTI–circum→NESMOTRJA–obl-obj→NA–prepos→TOTII.2–correl
      go   despite   of   the.fact
      →ČTO¹–subord-conjunct→ZAPRETIT' ...
      that⁵₍CONJ₎   forbid

TOTII.2 does not, of course, accept any modifier.

2. The parentheses around the second component of a binary conjunction indicate that this component is optional, which means that the given conjunction is but an "expanded" version of the basic—single—conjunction. Thus, ESLI ..., (TO²) ... is an optional expansion of ESLI, and so forth.

NB The omissibility of the optional component of a binary conjunction is not absolute, but depends on contextual conditions. Thus, in the Russian sentence *Edva ja vstal*, **kak** *upal snova* 'No.sooner I stood.up than [I] fell again' the component KAK cannot be left out. On the other hand, the optional component of a binary conjunction can be excluded in a particular context: see Section 7.5, the lexical entry for ESLI 'if', p. 285.

3. All plurilexemic components of compound conjunctions are idioms, which is shown, as always, by top corners: ⌈POTOMU ČTO⌉ 'because', ⌈KAK TOL′KO⌉ ..., (TĂK) ... 'as soon as ..., ...', etc.

4. The initial component of a binary or repeated coordinating conjunction—shown in (4) in boldface—behaves not as a conjunction, but as a particle syntactically subordinated to the head of the first coordinated phrase by the **restrictive** SSyntRel:

(4) a. *Ja ne xoču **ni**←restr–est',–coordinative→ni–coord-conjunct→pit'*
      'I don't want neither eat nor drink'.
   b. *Ja xoču **to_li**←restr–est',–coordinative→to_li–coord-conjunct→pit'*
      'I want or.maybe eat or.maybe drink'.

Similarly, the second component of a binary subordinating conjunction is not a conjunction, either, but also a particle:

(5) a. Edva ja priotkryl dver', (**kak**) kot vyskočil na ploščadku
    ⎿───── circumstantial ─────⎾─ auxil ─⏋
    'No.sooner I had.slightly.opened the.door than the.cat jumped onto the. landing'.

   b. Esli ja uedu, (**to**) kto budet polivat' cvety?
    ⎿──── circumstantial ────⎾─ auxil ─⏋
    'If I leave, (then) who will water the.plants?'

NB The **auxiliary** SSyntRel links the second component of a binary subordinating conjunction—in this case, KAK and TO²—to the syntactic head of the superordinate clause.

5. Russian has syntactic constructions that express the conjunction-like meaning 'as soon as…'/'no sooner…, than…' and play the role of binary conjunctions:

– STÓIT/STÓILO X-u Y$_{INF, PERF}$, KAK…   ***Stoilo*** *mne pojavit'sja,* ***kak*** *Ivan uxodil* 'As soon as I appeared, Ivan would leave'.
– NE USPEL$_{ASPECT}$ X Y$_{INF, PERF}$, KAK… MV$_{ASPECT}$ ***Ne uspela***$_{PERF}$ *ja pojavit'sja,* ***kak*** *Ivan ušël*$_{PERF}$ 'As soon as I [female] appeared, Ivan left'. ~ ***Ne uspevala***$_{IMPF}$ *ja pojavit'sja,* ***kak*** *Ivan uxodil*$_{IMPF}$ 'As soon as I [female] was appearing, Ivan would be leaving'.

For simplicity's sake, these constructions are ignored here, since they do not add any theoretical difficulty.

7.4 Binary conjunctions in Russian

Here is an illustrative inventory of Russian binary conjunctions (probably, incomplete):

1. ⌈ČEM – TEM⌉   'the A$_{1COMPAR}$ …, the A$_{2COMPAR}$ …'
2. EDVA – (KĂK)   'no sooner …, than …'
3. ESLI – (TO²)/(TĂK)   'if …, then …'
4. EŽELI – (TO²)/(TĂK)   'if …, then …'
5. ⌈KAK – TAK I⌉¹   'both … and …'
6. ⌈KAK – TAK I⌉² ≈   'from the moment that …, then …'
7. KOGDA – (TO²)   'when …, then …'

8. ⌜KOL' SKORO⌝ – (TO²)   'if ..., then ...'
9. ⌜LIŠ' TOL'KO⌝ – (KĂK)   'as soon ..., then ...'
10. ⌜NE STOL'KO – SKOL'KO⌝   'not so.much ..., but.rather ...'
11. ⌜NE TAK – KAK⌝   'not so.much ..., as ...'
12. NE TOL'KO – NO I   'not only ..., but also ...'
13. RAZ – (TO)/(TĂK) ≈   'if ..., then ...'
14. ⌜TAK KAK⌝ – (TO²)   'since ..., then ...'
15. TOL'KO – (KĂK)   'as soon ..., then ...'
16. XOTJA – (NO)   'although ..., but ...'

Interestingly, a half of these conjunctions are expanded versions of the corresponding single conjunctions.

A couple of examples will be helpful.

(6) ⌜ČEM – TEM⌝ 'the ..., the ...' (binary subordinating conjunction; an idiom)

a. *Čem bol'še my uglubljaemsja v prošloe, tem*←**restr**–*žëstče*←*stanovitsja granica mužskogo i ženskogo mirov*
'The more we go.deeper into past, the rigider becomes the.border [between] male and female worlds'.

It is worthwhile to show the same SSyntS for this sentence, but with a different ordering of the superordinate and subordinate clauses:

b. *Granica mužskogo i ženskogo mirov stanovitsja tem*←**restr**–*žëstče,*–**compar**→*čem bol'še my uglubljaemsja v prošloe*
'The.border [between] male and female worlds becomes the rigider the more we go.deeper into past'.

Unlike other Russian binary conjunctions, ⌜ČEM – TEM⌝ allows for both the anteposition and the postposition of the subordinate clause.

(7) ⌜NE STOL'KO – SKOL'KO⌝ 'not so.much ..., but.rather ...'
(coordinating binary conjunction; an idiom)

a. *On ne stol'ko*←**restr**–*sražalsja,*–**coord**→*skol'ko*–**coord-conjunct**→*byl sražaem*
'He not so.much was.battling, but.rather was being.battled'.

Here the second component, which corresponds to the interrogative-relative pronominal adverb SKOL'KO 'how much', is a coordinating conjunction, to similar to A/NO 'but'; cf.:

b. *On ne*←**restr**-*sražalsja*,-**coord**→*a/no*-**coord**-**conjunctive**→*byl sražaem*
   'He not was.battling, but was being.battled'.

Several expressions are sometimes listed among binary conjunctions, while in fact they are not. For instance, ⌜NE_TO ⟨NE_TAK, NE_SKAZAT'⟩_ČTOBY⌝ lit. 'not this ⟨not so, not to.say⟩ that' – A ⟨NO⟩ 'but' is not a binary conjunction, because it is not a conjunction at all. Its first component is an idiom ⌜NE_TO⟨NE_TAK, NE_SKAZAT'⟩_ČTOBY⌝ ≈ 'not quite', which is a kind of adverb that can appear alone—without the second component A ⟨NO⟩ 'but'; while the second component is a simple coordinating conjunction, which can also appear alone, without the first component:

(8) a. *Ne_to_čtoby ja ustal,*→*a prosto vremja isteklo*
    'Not this that I got.tired, but simply time ran.out'.
   b. *Ja ne ustal,*→*a prosto vremja isteklo*
    'I am not tired, but simply time ran.out'.

7.5 Phraseological nature of binary conjunctions

A binary conjunction is by its very nature a plurilexemic expression that is not free: it is a **phraseme** (Mel'čuk 2012d, 2012–2015: vol. 3, 263–362, 2015a). However, it is quite an uncommon phraseme: its components are not syntactically linked in a direct way. As far as I know, such syntactically discontinuous phrasemes have not been considered before. Indeed, a phraseme is "a phrase that...," while ESLI – TO² or EDVA – KAK are obviously not phrases of Russian. The solution to this difficulty is simple: one has to consider these expressions together with their actantial variables: ESLI Y, TO² X and EDVA Y, KAK X are *bona fide* phrases. It is under this form that they must be stored in a dictionary.

Now, if binary conjunctions are phrasemes, what type of phraseme are they?

- Eight of 16 Russian binary conjunctions are **idioms**, since they are non-compositional (for the idioms ⌜KAK Y, TAK I X⌝¹/², see Mel'čuk 2017):

⌜ČEM Y, TEM X⌝	'the Y, the X'
⌜KAK X, TAK I Y⌝¹	'both X and Y'
⌜KAK Y, TAK I X⌝² ≈	'from the moment that Y, then X'
⌜KOL' SKORO Y⌝, ⟨TO²⟩ X	'if Y, then X'
⌜LIŠ' TOL'KO Y⌝ – ⟨KAK⟩ X	'as soon ..., then ...'
⌜NE TAK Y, KAK X⌝	'not so.much X, as Y'
⌜NE STOL'KO X, SKOL'KO Y⌝	'not so.much X, but.rather Y'
⌜TAK KAK⌝ – ⟨TO²⟩	'since ..., then ...'

- One coordinating binary conjunction—NE TOL'KO – NO I 'not only ..., but also ...' (*Dlja ètogo važny ne tol'ko finansy, no i političeskaja volja* lit. 'For this [are] important not only finances, but also political will'.)—is a **formuleme** (a subclass of clichés; see Mel'čuk 2015a), since it is compositional, but fixed: there is no **ne liš' – a takže*, where each component is substituted by its synonym.
- The remaining seven Russian binary conjunctions are **collocations**, although of an unusual type: there is no direct syntactic link between the base and the collocate. The base is the first component, which controls the use of the second component (collocate); the latter is semantically empty, optional, must follow the base and occupies the initial linear position in the superordinate clause.

It seems worthwhile to show how Russian binary conjunctions could be presented in a lexicon of the ECD type (our illustrations are, of course, rough and incomplete sketches of lexical entries.

A binary conjunction that is an idiom is lexicographically described in a separate lexical entry as follows.

⌜ČEM Y, TEM X⌝ 'the Y, the X', idiom; conjunction, binary, subordinating

Definition

⌜*Čem*–subord-conj→MV(Y), *tem*←restr–A_{COMPAR}/ADV_{COMPAR}←⋯–MV(X)⌝: ≈ 'X is a function of Y'

Government pattern

Y ⟺ II
1. V_{FIN} | V_{FIN} –⋯→ A'_{COMPAR}/ADV'_{COMPAR}

Čem bol'še ljudej budet$_{MV(Y)}$ *učastvovat', tem vyše budet*$_{MV(X)}$ *verojatnost' uspexa* 'The more people will participate, the higher will.be probability of.success'.

Syntactic properties

The clause Y precedes or follows the clause X.

The conjunction ⌜ČEM – TEM⌝ has as DSynt-actant II a V_{FIN}—the Main Verb of the subordinate clause; this V_{FIN} has as its (maybe indirect) dependent an adjective/an adverb of comparative degree. The conjunction depends itself on the an adjective/an adverb of comparative degree in the superordinate clause.

⌜**NE STOL'KO X, SKOL'KO Y**⌝ 'not so.much X, but.rather Y', idiom; conjunction, binary, coordinating

Definition
⌜*ne*←**restr**-*stol'ko*←**restr**-X,-**coord**→*skol'ko*-**coord-conj**→Y⌝: 'not so.much X, but rather Y'

Government pattern

Y ⟺ II	
1. L	L stands here for a lexical unit of any part of speech

Takoe videnie buduščego javljaetasja ne stol'ko vozvyšennym$_X$, skol'ko spravedlivym$_Y$
'Such a.vision of.future is not so.much noble, but.rather just'.

On sidel ne stol'ko za$_X$ stolom, skol'ko na$_Y$ stole
'He was.sitting not so.much at.the.table, but.rather on.the.table'.

Syntactic properties
The clause Y follows the clause X.

A binary conjunction that is a formuleme appears in the lexical entry of its lexical anchor (see the Glossary); it is described by means of a non-standard lexical function. In NE TOL'KO – NO I 'not only ..., but also ...' the lexical anchor is NO 'but'.

NO 'but', conjunction, coordinating

Definition
X, *no* Y: 'X, but Y'.
...

Lexical Functions
...
«not only X, but also Y» : ne←**restr**-tol'ko—**restr**-X,-**coord**→⌜coord-conj⌝→no i←**restr**-Y

Finally, a binary conjunction that is a collocation of the basic (single) conjunction is lexicographically described in the entry for its base also by a non-standard LF. In ESLI – TO² 'if ..., then ...', the base is ESLI.

ESLI 'if', conjunction, subordinating

Definition
Esli Y, X: 'if Y, X'.

Government Pattern

Y ⟺ II
1. V$_{FIN}$

Esli bol'še ljudej učastvuet, verojatnost' uspexa vyše
'If more people participate, the probability of success [is] higher'.

Lexical Functions

...

to introduce the superordinate clause Y: TO² ←restr–MV(Y)	1) ESLI + ... + TO²; 2) **not** *tol'ko/liš'*←*esli* (*Esli Ivan pridët, to ja ujdu* 'If Ivan comes, I'll leave'; *Tol'ko esli Ivan pridët, (*to) ja ujdu.*); 3) **not** Y₁ + *esli* + ...+ TO² + Y₁ (*Ivan, esli ty pridëš'*, (**to*) *pokažet tebe vsë* 'Ivan, if you come, will.show you everything'; see Testelec 2001: 263)

As for a repeated conjunction, only its initial component shows any specificity (see Section 7.3 above, Comment 4): it is not a conjunction, but a particle depending on the syntactic head of the first coordinated phrase and indicating the beginning of a repeated conjunction. Thus:

(9)   ⸢restrictive⸣   ⸢coord-conj⸣   ⸢coord-conj⸣
razrabotat' **ili** *nadëžnyj fil'tr*,–coord→*ili novuju krasku,*–coord→*ili xorošee ograždenie*
'develop either a reliable filter, or a new paint, or a good fence'

The second component of a repeated conjunction forms a collocation with the first one; the second component is the base, the first being its collocate, while the third, the fourth, etc. components are free repetitions of the second one.

Binary conjunctions are characterized by their "discontinuous" character: they form phrases only together with their actants, since their own components are syntactically not directly linked. In this, they are unlike almost all other phrasemes. However, they share this feature with a few idioms, which I would like to quote here:

Rus. ⸢POKA I.2b NE←X⸣
'before X [takes place]' (Iordanskaja & Mel'čuk 2009b): *Poka on* **ne** *ušël*$_x$, ...
'Before he leaves, ...', with an expletive NE 'not', which is obligatory and does not negate.

7.5 Phraseological nature of binary conjunctions — 287

Rus. ⌐PRI VSËM←X-e⌐

'despite X' (V. Apresjan 2014):

pri vsëm ego talante$_X$ 'despite [lit. with all] his talent'

Rus. ⌐TO_LI EŠČË←X$_{(V)}$⌐

'I signal that X$_{(V)}$ will take place with an extraordinary (very bad or very good) actant r': *To li ty togda eščë uvidiš'*$_X$!

    'This whether you then still will.see!' =

    'I signal that you will then see something very bad'.

Rus. ⌐ČTO ZA←X⌐? ≈

'What kind of X?': *Čto Ivan za čelovek*? 'What kind of human being is Ivan?'

Eng. ⌐NOTHING→IF NOT←X$_{(ADJ)}$⌐ ≈

'extremely X': *Barbara was nothing if not feminine*$_X$.

Fr. ⌐EN TOUT←X$_{(N)}$⌐

'while being completely ADJ(X)': *Tu le feras en toute liberté*$_X$ lit. 'You this will. do in all freedom'. = 'You will do this while being fully free' (Anscombre 2001).

An expanded and corrected English version of Mel'čuk 2017.

8 The East/Southeast Asian answer to the European passive

8.1 The problem stated
8.2 The passive voice
   8.2.1 Requirements on a scientific definition
      8.2.1.1 Substantive requirements on a scientific definition
      8.2.1.2 Formal requirements on a scientific definition
   8.2.2 Prototypical passives
   8.2.3 Diathesis
   8.2.4 Grammatical voice
   8.2.5 Passive
8.3 Chinese "passive construction"
8.4 Affected-subject construction in Chinese
8.5 Affected-subject constructions in Southeast Asian languages
8.6 The problem solved

To Vitja Xrakovskij
Kak vse my znaem, on takovskij,
Naš slavnyj Viktor Ès Xrakovskij!
Svoj nežnyj šlju emu privet,
Želaju žit' sto dvadcat' let!¹

8.1 The problem stated

This chapter tries to answer a seemingly simple question:

> *Is there a passive voice in Mandarin Chinese?*

---

1 'As we all know, he's like that, / Our glorious Viktor Es. Khrakovskij! / I am sending him my tender greetings, / And wishing that he live hundred twenty years!' — However, while formulating this desire, I feel slightly embarrassed. The fact is that way back, in 1948, the Soviet Union was celebrating the 70-th anniversary of the Greatest Leader of all times and peoples, the Most Famous General and the Most Beloved Father of scientists and athletes, as well as the First Linguist and the First Gynecologist, Comrade Joseph V. Stalin. In the middle of the festivities, students of the Moscow Foreign Languages "Maurice Thorez" Institute prepared, as was the custom, a handwritten wall newspaper dedicated to the event. It featured a poem created by a local Homer, in which the author wished that "the Great Stalin might live hundred thousand years." Everything seemed perfect, when, suddenly, the school's Communist Party Bureau ordered the paper removed from the wall and destroyed. The editor got a Party reprimand. "Why should we limit our greatest Leader's longevity?", he was told. Many years later, I have my doubts: Maybe the Party Bureau was right after all? Maybe we really should not limit?

A number of descriptive grammars, reference books, manuals and special studies speak about the passive voice in Chinese, indicating, however, its particularities with respect to what is called *passive* in many European languages. I will start with presenting my blunt answer:

> ‖ No, there is no such a thing as passive voice in Mandarin Chinese.

The goal that "our" languages achieve by using the passive is reached in Chinese—and several Southeast Asian languages—in quite a different way. The rest of the chapter demonstrates what exactly this way is.

What is needed to establish whether there is or is not the passive voice in Chinese? I will try to answer by following the example of a Soviet-era military medical cadet of the last century, who was asked at the final examination at his Academy: "What do you need to give an enema?" He became famous for his prompt answer: "First, you need an enema; second, you need an anus; third, you need to apply the first to the second." In the same vein, I need, first, a definition of the passive voice; second, a precise description of the relevant Chinese facts; third, I have to apply the first to the second—and bingo!

Consequently, the chapter is organized in an obvious way: Section 8.2 presents a definition of the passive voice; Section 8.3 describes the construction called *passive* in Chinese; Section 8.4 applies the definition of the passive to the Chinese facts in order to achieve and buttress the conclusion that what we see is not the passive voice, but an essentially different phenomenon; Section 8.5 sketches the situation in a couple of Southeast Asian languages facing a similar problem; and Section 8.6 presents the conclusion.

It is not by chance that the first version of this text was written as a contribution for Viktor Xrakovskij's *Festschrift*: Xrakovskij is one of those scholars who pioneered intensive and extensive investigations into the problems of voice in many languages. He also published several important and influential studies in the domain: Xrakovskij 1974, 1975, 1981, to name but a few (they were republished, with corrections and additions, in Xrakovskij 1999); see also Xrakovskij (ed.) 1981 and the "summing-up" paper Xrakovskij 2004. Therefore, this chapter is a tribute to his long-standing and fruitful work in the domain.

8.2 The passive voice

To propose a rigorous definition of the passive voice, we need to formulate the principles on which such a definition must be based (8.2.1) and then give the definitions of diathesis (8.2.2), of voice (8.2.3), and of the passive (8.2.4).

8.2.1 Requirements on a scientific definition

Since this chapter is essentially based on the definitions of the concepts used, it is worthwhile to dwell on the concept of scientific definition itself. I will consider definitions of linguistic concepts, although what is said might well apply in other fields (see Mel'čuk 2006b).

8.2.1.1 Substantive requirements on a scientific definition
A scientific definition of a concept X must satisfy the following three substantive requirements related to the question "What exactly is to be defined?"

1) A definition of the phenomenon X one wants to define must be oriented towards **prototypical cases** of X; "deviant" cases are to be covered by additional special conditions.
2) The phenomenon X must be defined as **a particular case**, or a subclass, of a more general phenomenon Y. In other words, a definition must be strictly deductive—that is, to be an Aristotelian/Boetian analytical definition of the form "X is a Y that is Z," where Y and Z have been defined previously.
3) Specific differences Z—properties that define X as a subclass of Y—must be reduced to the **simplest[2] defining features possible**, so that they ensure a systematic hierarchical class inclusion.

For instance, consider a commonly used definition of ergative construction (which does not satisfy one of the above requirements and will be shown to be incorrect):

Definition *8.1 – *ergative construction
> Ergative construction [= X] is a transitive verb predicative construction of the form
> $$\text{Subj} - \text{Verb} - \text{DirO} \; [= Y]$$
> such that [= Z]:
> (i) its direct object is marked in the same way as the subject of an intransitive verb in this language;
> (ii) its direct object is marked by the nominative case;
> (iii) its subject is marked by a special case different from the nominative.

---

[2] 'Simplest' is to be construed liberally enough: simplest, but such that allows for a sensible classification.

This definition satisfies our first and second substantive requirements above, but fails the third one: its Z is not the simplest possible—it consists of three independent properties each of which can be absent. Taking out one of them produces a new definition that defines ... what? Something for which there is no name and which does not belong to a previously defined subclass. What is indeed a transitive verb predicative construction for which Condition (i) is not satisfied—its direct object is **not** marked (under specific circumstances) in the same way as the subject of an intransitive verb, but Conditions (ii) and (iii) are satisfied? Such a situation is found, for instance, in Motu (Lister-Turner & Clark 1931: 28–30), in common sentences of type (1b):

(1) a. *Sisia+**na***   vada   e   +*la*
        dog   PATH   PERF   3.SG$_{SUB}$ go
        'The dog has gone'.
   b. *Sisia+**ese*** *boroma+Ø*   vada   e   +*kori+a*
        dog   ERG   pig   NOM   PERF   3.SG$_{SUB}$ bite   3.SG$_{OBJ}$
        'The dog has bitten the pig'.
   c. *Sisia+**ese*** *mero+**na***   vada   e   +*kori+a*
        dog   ERG   boy   PATH   PERF   3.SG$_{SUB}$ bite   3.SG$_{OBJ}$
        'The dog has bitten the boy'.

> **NB** In Motu, the DirO is marked by the nominative, except for human nouns: with them, it is marked by the **pathetive** case (a special case found also in some Malayo-Polynesian and Australian languages, see Mel'čuk 1988: 180–181). The intransitive subject in Motu is marked by the pathetive (≠ nominative!), and the transitive subject, by the ergative case.

According to the letter of Definition *8.1, (1b) is not an ergative construction because its DirO is not marked the same way as an intransitive subject. But what is it? This type of construction clearly belongs to a subclass of transitive verbal constructions that also includes the ergative construction in the sense of Definition *8.1; however, this subclass has no definition and no name. The construction in (1c), which is very close to (1b), belongs nevertheless to a different subclass (of transitive verbal constructions), to which we even cannot refer: it does not have a name, either. Worse, these two subclasses do not form a common subclass within the class of transitive constructions. In order to avoid such violations of step-wise consistent hierarchical classification, I propose to define first the most general subclass of verbal predicative constructions that includes the Definition *8.1 ergative construction as a particular case (see Mel'čuk 1988: 182, 251, 258*ff*; Mel'čuk 2006a: 269*ff*).

Definition 8.1 – ergative construction

> Ergative construction [= X] is a verbal predicative construction [= Y] whose SSynt-subject is marked by a case different from the nominative [= Z].

Proceeding from Definition 8.1, one would say that in (1a) we have an intransitive ergative construction, in (1b) a transitive ergative construction with a nominative DirO (the most current type), and in (1c) a transitive ergative construction with a non-nominative DirO. The ergative construction in the sense of Definition *8.1 is then a transitive ergative construction with a nominative DirO that coincides with the intransitive nominative Subject—a very particular case.

The proposed way of defining guarantees a systematic inclusion of concepts in the corresponding subclasses, without missing important intermediate classes.

8.2.1.2 Formal requirements on a scientific definition

A definition must also be formally correct in the three respects, related to the question "How do we define what we define?":

4) A definition must be **formal**—that is, it should be applicable verbatim (= mechanically).
5) A definition must be **rigorous**—that is, it should contain only concepts which either have been defined prior to it or else are indefinable (and previously enumerated as such).
6) A definition must be **adequate**—that is, sufficient and necessary, covering all the phenomena that are perceived as subsumable under the corresponding notion, and nothing but such phenomena.

In this chapter these six requirements on scientific definitions are accepted as postulates.

8.2.2 Prototypical passives

As prototypical cases of passives, I take the passive in Latin, Armenian and Swahili:

(2) a. Latin
    (i) *Serv+i*   *reg+em*   *porta+Ø*   *+nt +Ø*
        slave PL.NOM king SG.ACC carry PRES.IND 3.PL ACT
        'The slaves are carrying the king'.
    (ii) *Rex*   (*a*) *serv+is*   *porta+Ø*   *+t +ur*
        king-SG.NOM by slave PL.ABL carry PRES.IND 3.SG PASS
        'The king is being carried by the slaves'.
b. Armenian
    (i) *Ašot+Ø+Ø* *+ə*   *namak+er+Ø* *+ə*   *gr +Ø +ec +Ø*
        Ashot SG NOM DEF letter   PL NOM DEF   write ACT AOR IND.3.SG
        'Ashot wrote the letters'.[3]
    (ii) *Namak+er+Ø* *+ə*   *gr +v +ec +in*   *Ašot +Ø +i +Ø*
        letter   PL NOM DEF write PASS AOR IND.3.PL Ashot SG DAT NON-DEF
        koymic
        from.side
        'The letters were written by Ashot'.
c. Swahili (Roman numerals stand for noun classes)
    (i) *Wa+tanzania* *wa+na* *+sem +Ø*   *+a*   *Ki+swahili*
        II   Tanzania II   PRES speak ACT DECLAR VII Swahili
        'Tanzanians speak Swahili'.
    (ii) *Ki+swahili*   *ki+na*   *+sem +w* *+a*   *na*   *Wa+tanzania*
        VII Swahili VII PRES speak PASS DECLAR with/by II   Tanzania
        'Swahili is spoken by Tanzanians'.

Here is what can be stated about these prototypical passives:

- There is no **propositional semantic difference** between sentences (i) and (ii). They show, of course, a communicative semantic difference: in sentence (i), the Actor is the Sem-Theme (= topic) of the sentence, while in sentence (ii), the Patient is. The passive is used to express communicative information.

---

[3] Note the following particularity of the nominal case system in Modern Armenian: it does not have an accusative, so that the subject and the DirO are both marked by the nominative. A similar situation is found in other languages, for instance, in Romanian and Nivkh. Here, the DirO is case-marked the same way as the subject of an intransitive verb. However, the transitive predicative construction of these languages is never called ergative!

- The crucial **syntactic difference** between sentences (i) and (ii) is as follows:
  – In sentence (i), the Actor is expressed as the deep-syntactic actant **I**/the surface-syntactic subject, and the Patient, as the DSyntA **II**/the direct object.
  – In Sentence (ii), the Actor is expressed as the deep-syntactic actant **II**/the surface-syntactic agent complement, and the Patient, as the DSyntA **I**/the SSynt-subject.
- The crucial **morphological difference** between sentences (i) and (ii) consists in the difference between the forms of the Main Verb: in sentence (ii) it has a special suffix (opposed to a zero suffix in sentence (i)), which marks the communicative and syntactic modification, stated above; this suffix is the marker of the passive. As a result, we obtain the opposition of active *vs.* passive forms. All other morphological differences observed in the verb and the actantial nouns are automatic consequences of that difference.

Based on the active ~ passive opposition observed in prototypical cases, we must call *passive* such verbal forms that are semantically (= propositionally) identical to active forms, but syntactically entail the transformation characterized above and are formally marked for this. To describe this transformation, the concept of diathesis is needed.

8.2.3 Diathesis

Each lexeme that expresses a predicative meaning has actants at the three levels: SemAs, DSyntAs and SSyntAs. What interests us here is the correspondence between the SemAs and DSyntAs of a lexeme. For instance, the noun JOY (X's *joy over* Y) has two SemAs: 'X', who experiences the feeling, and 'Y', which is the cause and the object of that feeling; JOY also has two DSyntAs: DSyntA **I** (implemented on the surface by a possessive form or by a phrase with OF), which expresses 'X', and DSyntA **II** (implemented by a prepositional phrase with OVER), which denotes 'Y'.[4]

Definition 8.2 – diathesis

> The diathesis of a lexeme L is the correspondence between L's SemAs and DSyntAs.

---

[4] There is a huge literature on the concepts of diathesis and voice, which I cannot survey even cursorily. I base this exposition on my own work—in particular, Mel'čuk 2004 and 2006a: 181–262.

The noun JOY has the following diathesis: X ⇔ I, Y ⇔ II; it can also be written as

X	Y
I	II

In many languages, a verbal lexeme (e.g., a transitive verb) can have more than one diathesis: such is exactly the case in Latin, Armenian, and Swahili. One of the diatheses corresponds to the basic, lexicographic form of the verb, while the other one corresponds to the passive—that is, a form "derived" from the basic form by the corresponding affix. This other diathesis can be written as X ⇔ II, Y ⇔ I, or as

X	Y
II	I

Now we can say that passivization is the following modification of the basic diathesis:

X	Y		X	Y
I	II	⇔	II	I

Three operations are possible on diatheses—**permutation** of DSyntAs with respect to SemAs, **suppression** of DSyntAs, and **referential identification** of SemAs (with violation of the correspondence between SemAs and DSyntAs in the basic form). These operations produce, for a binary basic diathesis, 12 possible distinct modifications, including the zero one (see, e.g., Mel'čuk 2006a: 184–191, 2006b: 194–209). The zero modification of the basic diathesis corresponds to the active, and the simplest permutation produces the diathesis that corresponds to the passive.

8.2.4 Grammatical voice

At this juncture, the definition of grammatical voice seems straightforward.

Definition 8.3 – grammatical voice

> Grammatical voice is an inflectional verbal category whose grammemes (= particular voices) mark the modification of the basic diathesis of the verb and are themselves formally marked on the verb.

Note that *formally marked on the verb* does not necessarily mean 'marked on the verb by an affix': a modification of the basic diathesis can be marked by a structural word such as an auxiliary verb, as in (3a), or an invariable particle, as in (3b).

(3) a. English/French, German
*The letter **was written** by John.* ≡
*La lettre **a été écrite** par Jean*
'The letter has been written par Jean'. ≡
*Das Brief **wurde** von Hans **geschrieben***
'The letter became by Hans written'.

b. Albanian, the forms of the aorist indicative ($ë = /ə/$)

Active		vs.	Passive	
'I opened'	*hapa*	~	'I was opened'	*u hapa*
'You$_{SG}$ opened'	*hape*	~	'You$_{SG}$ were opened'	*u hape*
'He opened'	*hapi*	~	'He was opened'	*u hap*
'We opened'	*hapëm*	~	'We were opened'	*u hapëm*
'You$_{PL}$ opened'	*hapët*	~	'You$_{PL}$ were opened'	*u hapët*
'They opened'	*hapën*	~	'They were opened'	*u hapën*

Thus, voices can have analytical forms, just like any other inflectional category.

But can there be a change of the basic diathesis that is not marked on the verb, but on one of its actants? Yes, such a situation is logically possible, and it exists, for instance, in Ancient Chinese (Jaxontov 1965: 47, 1974: 201):

(4) a. *Sha ren* '[He] killed [a] man'. ~ *Sha **yu** ren* '[He] was.killed by [a] man'.

b. *Cheng bao min, de bao cheng*
city.walls protect people virtue protect city.walls
'City walls protect people, the virtue protects city walls'. ~

*Min bao **yu** cheng, cheng bao **yu** de*
people be.protected **by** city.walls city.walls be.protected **by** virtue
'People are protected by city walls, city walls are protected by virtue'.

The diathesis of the verbs SHA 'kill' and BAO 'protect' in the first members of the pairs of sentences in (4) changes in their occurrences in the second members of these pairs. However, since this change of the basic diathesis is not marked on the verb, second sentences of the pairs in (4) do not represent grammatical voice. These sentences manifest the **pseudo-passive construction**; a genuine passive construction needs a passive verbal form.

8.2.5 Passive

Based on Definitions 8.2 and 8.3, passive voice can be now defined.

Definition 8.4 – passive voice

> Passive is a (grammatical) voice that marks a modification of the basic diathesis such that it involves the permutation of DSyntA I.

In other words, a passive voice necessarily entails demotion of DSyntA I.
Summing up:

> The passive voice of verb V is a synthetic or analytical form of the lexeme V that expresses a modification of the basic diathesis of V such that consists in permuting at least V's DSyntA I.

We have the first piece of our puzzle. Let's move to the second one.

8.3 Chinese "passive construction"

Unfortunately (for me), I do not know Chinese, and in what follows I proceed strictly from the data available in printed sources. In the first place, these are Li & Thompson 1981, Hashimoto 1988, Ren 1993, Paris 1998, Huang 1999, and Huang et al. 2008, from which I take my examples; see also Liu 2016, where a rich bibliography of the question is found. (I modified these examples a bit, to make them easier to understand; among other things, I replaced the Chinese human names by English ones.) Here is a typical example of what is currently called *passive sentence/passive construction* in Chinese:

(5) *Mary **bèi tǔfěi shā-le bàba***
           bandits kill PERF father
'Mary BÈI bandits killed father'. = 'Mary lost her father to bandits'.
(The lexeme BÈI cannot be properly glossed before its meaning and syntactic function are clarified.)

Huang 1999, following in some respects Hashimoto 1988, demonstrates that the lexeme BÈI, commonly called "the passive marker," is in fact an auxiliary verb with a very vague meaning ≈ '[to] undergo [that ...]' or '[to] be affected by ...', and a rather syntactic function. Generally speaking, what follows BÈI is a normal full clause with its own syntactic subject. As a result, sentence (5) is best literally translated as 'Mary «underwent.that» bandits killed father'. Here are Huang's four arguments for this description (again, I slightly reformulated and rearranged them).

1) BÈI is not a preposition. In spite of many traditional approaches that classify BÈI as a preposition (e.g., Alleton 1973: 121–122, Li & Thompson 1981: 365, Ren 1993: 127*ff*),[5] the presumed passive marker BÈI is by no means a preposition introducing an agent noun complement. Consider, for instance, (6a), a very common type of sentence containing the lexeme BÈI:

(6) a. *Mary zuótiān* **bèi** *John dǎ-le*
yesterday underwent hit PERF
'Mary was hit by John yesterday'.

One cannot say that here BÈI forms a prepositional phrase with JOHN, for at least three reasons:

– The presumed prepositional phrase **bèi John* cannot be positioned in any other slot in the sentence, while normal prepositional phrases can appear in all these slots—except for the position between BÈI and the subject of the subordinate clause, see (6b) *vs.* (6c):

(6) b. **Bèi John Mary zuótiān dǎ-le.*
*Mary bèi John zuótiān dǎ-le.
*Mary zuótiān dǎ-le bèi John.
*Mary bèi John dǎ-le zài jiālǐ.
c. *Zài jiālǐ Mary bèi John dǎ-le.*
at home
Mary zài jiālǐ bèi John dǎ-le.
Mary bèi John zài jiālǐ dǎ-le.

NB But not **Mary bèi zài jiālǐ John dǎ-le*; see below, before (14), on the particularities of the clause introduced by BÈI.

– Very often (actually, more often than not) BÈI is not followed by a noun, but by the subjectless verb:

(6) d. *Mary bèi dǎ-le* 'Mary was beaten'.

---

5 M.-C. Paris (1998: 363, footnote 7) says that she considers BÈI to be a verb; however, she calls it "Agent Marker" and describes it as forming a phrase with the Agent noun, that is, technically treats it as a genuine preposition. – Let me emphasize that, as far back as more than half a century ago, Solnceva 1962: 66–67 clearly stated that BÈI cannot be considered a preposition, but rather represents a defective verbal form.

In this case, it is customary to speak of an ellipsis of the noun; however, the ellipsis of a noun between a preposition and a verb would be an exceptional situation in Chinese. Moreover, this is not a contextual ellipsis: the missing indication of the agent is absent from the syntactic (and the semantic) structure of the sentence: it cannot be "restored" from previous context.

- BÈI normally is not repeated in coordination, although this repetition is near-obligatory for prepositions in Chinese (Hashimoto 1988: 331–332):

(7) a. *Mary **bèi** qīnrén huáiyí wàirén zhǐzé*
     relative suspect stranger criticize
    'Mary is suspected by relatives [and] criticized by strangers'.
  b. *Mary **zài** xuéxiào xuéxí, **zài** jiālǐ xiūxi*
     in school study in home rest
  vs. ?*Mary **zài** xuéxiào xuéxí jiālǐ xiūxi.*

2) Syncategorematic (= subject-oriented) lexemes in the BÈI-governed clause. If BÈI is not a preposition, it is a verb, and the phrase following it is a subordinate clause—an object of BÈI. Let us see what type of clause it is.

- The BÈI-governed clause can contain the adverb GÙYÌ 'intentionally', as in (8):

(8) *Mary **bèi** John gùyì dǎ-le*
     intentionally hit PERF
    'Mary underwent.that John intentionally hit [her]'.

Since GÙYÌ can semantically bear only on the syntactic subject and in (8) it bears on JOHN, the use of GÙYÌ shows that JOHN is the syntactic subject in the BÈI-governed clause (BÈI-clause for short).

- The BÈI-clause can also contain the reflexive pronoun zìjǐ ≈ '(one)self', which can be coreferential only with the syntactic subject:

(9) *Zhè fēng xìn **bèi** John dàihuí **zìjǐ-de** jiā qù-le*
    this CLASS letter   bring.back self's home go PERF
    'This letter was brought back by John$_i$ to **his**$_i$ house'.

This gives another indication to the effect that JOHN is the subject of the BÈI-clause (rather than the complement of the "preposition" BÈI).

3) Syntactic phenomena characteristic of normal clauses. A BÈI-clause can feature various constructions that show it to be a normal clause, with a subject, a Main Verb, and even—if its MV is transitive—with a DirO:

- Coordination with gapping, illustrated by (10):

(10) *Mary **bèi** John mà -le liǎng-cì, Peter dǎ-le sān-xià*
　　　　　　scold PERF two times　　hit PERF three times
'Mary was scolded twice by John and hit three times by Peter'.

- So-called "long-distance dependencies," where the element coreferential with the subject of the BÈI-clause syntactically depends on the Main Verb of this clause not directly, but through a string of subsequent dependencies:

(11) *Mary **bèi** zhèngfǔ pài jǐngchá zhuāzǒu-le*
　　　　　　government send police arrest PERF
'Mary underwent.that government sent police have.arrested'. =
'Mary was arrested by the police on government's orders'.

As one can see, the understood (but not expressed) DirO 'her' in the BÈI-clause depends on 'arrest', which in its turn depends on the MV 'send'.

- The verb in a BÈI-clause can have its own DirO (Chappell 1986: 274 and 277, where the conditions imposed on this DirO are specified):

(12) a. *Tā **bèi** dírén dǎshāng -le tuǐ*
　　　　he enemy hit.wound PERF leg
'He underwent.that enemy hit.wounded leg'. =
'He had his leg wounded by the enemy's fire'.

　b. *Tā **bèi** péngyou kāi -le yī ge wánxiào*
　　　　he friend play PERF a CLASS joke
'He underwent.that friends played a joke'. =
'He had a joke played on him by his friends'.

　c. *Yīfu **bèi** shāo-le yī ge dòng*
　　　cloths burn PERF a CLASS hole
'Cloths underwent.that [fire] burnt a hole'. =
'The fire burnt a hole in his cloths'.

4) Resumptive pronoun in the BÈI-clause. A BÈI-clause can contain a resumptive pronoun fulfilling the role of its DirO and coreferential with the subject of the sentence—in at least two types of context:

- If the resumptive pronoun is not sentence-final, but is followed by a lexical expression, as in (13a):

(13) a. *Mary **bèi** John dǎ-le tā **sān-xià***
　　　　　　hit PERF she three times
'Mary underwent.that John hit her three times'. =
'Mary was hit by John three times'.

- If the resumptive pronoun is turned into an affected object, introduced by the preposition BĂ and preceding the Main Verb, see (13b):

(13) b. *Mary bèi John **bă tā** dă-le*
      she hit PERF
      'Mary underwent.that John her hit'. = 'Mary was hit by John'.

This would not be possible if the Main Verb of the BÈI-clause were (in any sense) passive.⁶

Taking all this into consideration, we have to accept Hashimoto's and Huang's proposal, summarizing it in the following two points:

- Syntactically, BÈI is the Main Verb of the whole sentence; it is a bivalent auxiliary verb and roughly means something like 'undergo that ...' = 'be affected by ...'.
- The BÈI-clause is a normal active clause with its own Main Verb. However, this clause has a few special properties: it can lack an overt subject not in a contextual controlled ellipsis; if its MV is transitive, its own DirO most often—although by no means always!—semantically corresponds to the subject of BÈI; if this DirO occupies the last linear position in the sentence, it cannot be expressed by a resumptive pronoun, but otherwise it can; its subject cannot be preceded by a prepositional phrase, which otherwise is quite common, cf. (6c) above; etc.⁷

Therefore, a Chinese "passive" sentence is, if literally glossed, something like this:

(14) a. *Mary **bèi** dă-le*
     'Mary underwent.that [some.people] hit [her]'.
   b. *Mary **bèi** John dă-le*
     'Mary underwent.that John hit [her]'.
   c. *Mary **bèi** John dă-le tā sān-xià*
     'Mary underwent.that John hit her three.times'.

---

6 A resumptive pronoun cannot appear in a BÈI-clause as a DirO (coreferential with the subject of the sentence) if this pronoun turns out to be clause-final element:
  (i) *Mary **bèi** John dă-le *tā* lit. 'Mary BÈI John hit her'. = 'Mary was hit by John'.
There is still another argument supplied by Hashimoto 1988: 335 against the sentences with the BÈI-sentence being "passive" constructions: the possible absence of the "active" counterpart. Thus, for (ii) there is no correspondent sentence without BÈI:
  (ii) *Kānshŏu bèi fànrén păo-le*
     '[The] jailer underwent [= suffered because of] [the] criminal's escape'.
This argument is, however, invalid: "passives without actives" are not a rarity at all. Recall the Japanese passive, let alone *verba deponentia* of Classical languages.
7 Huang 1999: 11:
  (i) *John bèi Mary **zài xuéxiào** dă-le* 'John was hit by Mary at school'.
vs. (ii) **John bèi **zài xuéxiào** Mary dă-le* 'John was hit at school by Mary'.

BÈI is the MV of the whole sentence;[8] the SSynt-structure of (14c) is as follows:

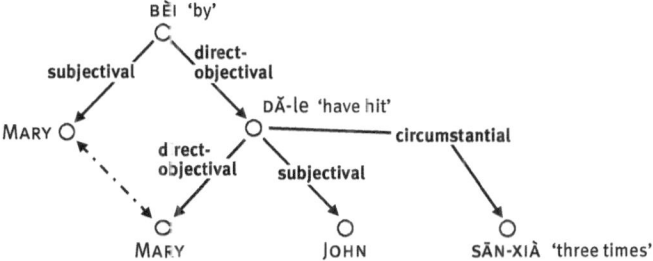

Figure 8.1 Surface-syntactic structure of sentence (14c)[9] (The BÈI-clause is subordinated to BÈI by the **direct-objectival** SSyntRel.)

---

[8] It is true that BÈI does not have several properties of normal Chinese verbs: thus, it does not accept aspect suffixes **-le, -guo, -zhe**, etc. But then, several Chinese lexemes that are traditionally accepted as auxiliary verbs—for instance, SHǏ 'let', NÉNG 'can' or YÀO 'want'—do not have these properties, either (Li & Thompson 1981: 172ff; Hashimoto 1988: 339–340). Also BÈI alternates with genuine verbs GĚI 'give', JIÀO 'be called' and RÀNG 'let, allow' (Li & Thompson 1981: 506):
(i) *Wǒ gěi/jiào/ràng tā tōu -le   liǎng kuài jīn*
    I   got   he steal PERF two   dollar money
    'I underwent/allowed that he stole two dollars [from me]'.
On the other hand, Hashimoto 1988: 340 indicates that the continuous aspect suffix **-zhe** is found on BÈI in texts, even if rarely.
   It is interesting to mention a linguistic phenomenon happening in Chinese now: BÈI begins to be increasingly used to introduce such verbs as ZÌSHĀ 'commit suicide' or ZÌYUÀN 'volunteer', for instance, *Tā bèi zìshā* lit. 'He underwent committing.suicide', to mean that he was murdered, the murder disguised as a suicide; *Tā bèi zìyuàn* lit. 'He underwent volunteering'—that is, he was forced to volunteer. No matter how sporadic such usages, they show that BÈI is not perceived by speakers as a preposition.
[9] The SSyntS presented in Figure 8.1 needs two additional comments.
 - If BÈI is not recognized as the MV of the sentence, but is considered to be a passive-agent marking preposition, the SSyntS of (14c) appears as follows:

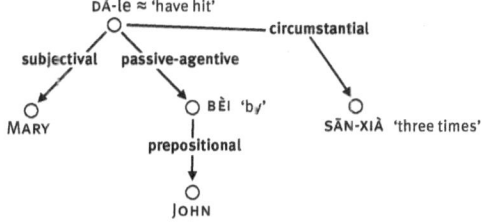

The alternative SSyntS of (14c)—with BÈI as an agentive preposition

In this structure, the MV DǍ-*le* has to be interpreted as 'have been hit', i.e., as having an "inverted" diathesis without any overt marking.
 - As indicated to me by R. Niu (p. c.), some Chinese linguists—for instance, Dexi Zhu, *Yufa*

The discussion in Section 8.3 gives us the second piece of the puzzle: the BÈI-construction is not passive; it is a normal "active" clause introduced by the auxiliary verb BÈI, which has very little semantic content in Modern Chinese and is used mostly for syntactic and communicative purposes. The schematic form of a BÈI-clause is as follows:

'X undergoes.that Y Z-s (X)' ⟺ X BÈI Y Z$_{(V)}$ (X)

Now I have to apply the first piece of the puzzle to the second one. If something does not walk like a duck and does not quack like a duck, why call it duck? Perhaps simply because it reminds us of a duck (for instance, a small goose). Yet this is not a compelling reason. The BÈI-construction is not passive at all: it is built around the transitive verb BÈI that does not change its only diathesis and, quite naturally, has no marking of a diathesis change; nor does it somehow change the diathesis of its subordinate verb Z$_{(V)}$. But it does resemble a passive construction in some essential respects, which will be presented in the next subsection.

8.4 Affected-subject construction in Chinese

The BÈI-construction is used when the Speaker wants to speak about X and say about X that Z done by Y happened to X or at least somehow affected X. Suppose that Y Z-ed (e.g., offended) X, and the Speaker chooses to communicate this while talking about X; since in Chinese, as a general rule, the syntactic subject must express the Sem-Theme of the sentence, he has to say *X bèi Y Z*. In this way, the BÈI-construction does two things with one blow: communicatively, it turns 'X' into the Sem-Theme; syntactically, it turns L('X') into an affected subject. This is what makes this construction similar to the passive of many languages: both the BÈI-construction and the passive construction fulfill (almost) the same communicative and syntactic roles. However, the similarity, even identity, of roles fulfilled by two linguistic phenomena does not entail the similarity, let alone identity, of the phenomena themselves. Should we consider English prepositions to be case markers simply because they often play the same role as cases (marking syntactic dependencies)?

The Chinese construction in question should by no means be called passive; I would suggest for it the straightforward name of **affected-subject construction**. In

---

jiangyi [*Lectures on grammar*], 1982, Beijing: Commercial Press, while considering BÈI as a verb, propose to describe it as trivalent rather than bivalent: thus, BÈI in (14c) would have as its DSyntA I the noun MARY, as its DSyntA II, the noun JOHN, and as its DSyntA III, the verb DĂ-*le*. However, for the present discussion this distinction is irrelevant.

addition to its being explicit and clear, this term has another advantage: it forms a pair with the name of another Chinese construction, described, e.g., in Li & Thompson 1981: 463*ff*: the BĂ-construction, or affected object construction. Let us start with an example:

(15) Wǒ **bǎ** chábēi nòngpò-le
 I **as.for** tea.cup break PERF
 'I as.for tea.cup broke'. = 'I broke the tea cup'.

If a nominal expression N (here, CHÁBĒI 'tea cup') is intended to be the direct object, it must follow the Main Verb (here, NÒNGPÒ 'break'), as all DirOs do. But, if supplied with the preposition BĂ ≈ 'as for', it ceases to be a DirO and must precede the verb. (The BĂ-construction must satisfy several constraints: the verb in this construction must express an action that really affects the referent of N; N itself must be definite or generic, but not indefinite specific; etc. This, however, is not relevant for my purposes here.) The sentence element implemented by BĂ + N cannot be considered a DirO: first, it is difficult to call a nominal introduced by a preposition a direct object;[10] and second, more importantly, a sentence with the BĂ-construction can contain a genuine DirO (boxed in (16)):

(16) a. Wǒ **bǎ** júzi bō -le pí
 I tangerine remove PERF skin
 'I as.for tangerine removed skin'. = 'I removed the skin from the tangerine'.
 b. Wǒ **bǎ** John bǎng-le liǎngzhī jiǎo
 I tie.up PERF two foot
 'I as.for John tied up two feet'. = 'I tied up John's feet'.

Therefore, from a syntactic angle, the BĂ + N phrase must be given a special name; it is known as **affected object**. The surface-syntactic relation that links it to the Main Verb also cannot be called **direct-objectival**; I propose **affected-objectival** (see Chapter 2, Section 2.5, No. 13, p. 56).

The affected-object construction also thematizes the nominal expression involved, just as the affected-subject construction does; this enhances its similarity with the latter. Huang et al. 2008: 155–162 emphasizes the parallelism of

---

10 A few cases where a preposition marks a DirO are known. Such is, for instance, the preposition ET in Hebrew, which marks exclusively definite DirOs and does nothing else; the preposition z- 'as' marking the DirO in Classical Armenian; or the prepositions A in Spanish and PE in Romanian, which are necessary for animate DirOs under particular conditions of referentiality and specificity. However, in none of these cases is the preposition-marked DirO compatible within the clause with another DirO.

both constructions in several respects. But of course this parallelism is not complete: to begin with, BĂ in the BĂ-construction is a preposition, while BÈI in the BÈI-construction is a verb; BĂ does not carry any propositional meaning, and BÈI does (even if not much); there are other differences as well. But this is beyond the limits of our discussion.

8.5 Affected-subject constructions in Southeast Asian languages

To drive the nail home, I will consider what is called "passive" in Vietnamese, based on Truong 1970 and Tam 1976. Here are examples borrowed from Tam 1976:

(17) a. *Nga đánh Nam* 'Nga beat Nam'. ~
  Nam bị[11] Nga đánh 'Nam was beaten by Nga'.
 b. *Nga khen Nam* 'Nga congratulated Nam'. ~
  Nam được Nga khen 'Nam was congratulated by Nga'.

BỊ and ĐƯỢC are auxiliary verbs with meanings, respectively, 'undergo, suffer' and 'receive, benefit from'; accordingly, they produce sentences with adversative or beneficial/neutral meaning.

The same situation obtains in Lao, Khmer and Thai (Tam 1976: 442):

(18) a. Lao
  Khacaw khaa muu khoi 'They killed my friend'. ~
  they killed friend I
  Muu khoi thyyk khacaw khaa 'My friend was killed by them'.
  friend I **undergo** they killed
 b. Khmer
  Kee bɔmbaek kbaal kñom 'They broke my head'. ~
  they break head I
  Kñom trəw kee bɔmbaek kbaal (kñom) 'I got my head broken by them'.
  I **undergo** they break head I
 c. Thai
  Dek tii maa 'The child hit the dog'. ~
  child hit dog
  Maa thuuk dek tii 'The dog was hit by the child'.
  dog **undergo** child hit

---

11 The auxiliary verb BỊ stems from the Chinese BÈI, borrowed into Vietnamese.

A similar situation is observed in Burmese:

(19) *Cuŋdɔ yaʔ+ði*   *ðu+go*   'I hit him'. ~
    I   hit DECLAR   he DirO
    Ɖu cuŋdɔi əyaiʻ+gɔ **khang**   **+ya**   +ði
    he my   blow DirO **experience receive** DECLAR
    'He experience.received my blow'. = 'He was hit by me'.

The difference with the preceding three languages is that what corresponds to the BÈI-clause is nominalized in Burmese: 'I hit' ⇒ 'my blow'; however, in the present context this is irrelevant.

8.6 The problem solved

Summing up, the Chinese construction with the lexeme BÈI is not passive; the category of voice does not exist in Chinese. BÈI is a verb, and the BÈI-construction can be called the affected-subject construction. The same recommendation applies to similar constructions in Vietnamese, Thai, Lao, Khmer, and Burmese.

A corrected version of Mel'čuk 2014c.

9 Pronominal idioms with a blasphemous noun in Russian and syntactically similar expressions

9.1 The problem stated
9.2 K-expressions: their surface-syntactic structure and lexicographic description
    9.2.1 Ξ+K-expressions
        9.2.1.1 Phraseologized Ξ+K-expressions
            9.2.1.1.1 ⌐Ξ←K⌐-expressions: idioms with a blasphemous noun (*Tam živët ⌐čërt znaet kto*⌐ 'There lives devil knows who')
            9.2.1.1.2 Ξ-···→K-expressions: collocations governing an indirect-interrogative clause (*Čërt znaet, kto on takoj* 'Devil knows who he [is]')
        9.2.1.2 Free Ξ←K-expressions
    9.2.2 K+Ξ-expressions
        9.2.2.1 Phraseologized K→Ξ-expressions: collocations (*Maša poedet kuda→ugodno* 'Masha will.go to.where pleasant')
        9.2.2.2 Free K←···-Ξ-expressions (*Maša poedet kuda ty zaxočeš'* 'Masha will go to.where you$_{SG}$ will.want')
9.3 Blasphemous idioms are not syntactic phrasemes

9.1 The problem stated

The object of this chapter is the set of Russian expressions such as [*Ona poexala*] *čërt znaet kuda* lit. 'She went devil knows to.where' vs. [*Ona poexala*] *kuda eë otpravili* lit. 'She went to.where [«they»] her had.sent' vs. *Čërt (eë/ego) znaet, kuda* [*ona poexala*] lit. 'Devil (her/it) knows to.where [she went]'. The characteristic component of such an expression is an interrogative-relative pronoun, or a K-word (to use an Isačenko-Apresjan-Iomdin term, analogous to WH-word): KUDA 'to.where', KTO 'who', KAK 'how', SKOL′KO 'how much/many', ... These expressions will be called **K-expressions** and represented by means of the symbols K (for the K-word itself) and Ξ (for the remaining part of the expression).

In connection with Russian K-expressions two important questions have to be asked:

- What is the surface-syntactic structure of a K-expression and what must be its lexicographic description? The answer is given in Section 9.2.
- K-expressions are often called *syntactic phrasemes*, but I think that this is conceptually incorrect. Section 9.3 considers the notion of syntactic phraseme and characterizes K-expressions from the standpoint of their phraseological status.

The proposed description of Russian K-expression is based on the data presented and analyzed in several studies by L. Iomdin: Iomdin 2005, 2007 and 2010a,b.

All glosses supplied to Russian examples below are literal.

9.2 K-expressions: their surface-syntactic structure and lexicographic description

Russian K-expressions are divided (Iomdin 2010b: 148–149) into two major classes:

- those that end with a K-word, that is, Ξ+K, e.g., [*Zdes' možno vstretit'*] *čërt znaet kogo* 'Here [is] possible to.meet devil knows whom';
- those that begin with a K-word, that is, K+Ξ, e.g., [*Zdes' možno vstretit'*] *kogo tol'ko xočeš'* 'Here [is] possible to.meet whom only you.want'.

The mutual linear position of K and Ξ is invariable in each of these classes.

I follow Iomdin's division: Ξ+K-expressions are considered in Subsection 9.2.1, and K+Ξ-expressions, in Subsection 9.2.2.

9.2.1 Ξ+K-expressions

Ξ+K-expressions come in two types: phraseologized, i.e., containing a phraseologized part Ξ (9.2.1.1), and free, i.e., where Ξ is not phraseologized (9.2.1.2).

9.2.1.1 Phraseologized Ξ+K-expressions

A phraseologized Ξ+K-expression consists of two major components: a collocation Ξ, and an interrogative-relative pronoun—a K-word, which can be introduced by a preposition. (On collocations, see Chapter 1, Section 1.2.4.2, p. 23; see also below, Section 9.3.)

In its turn, the collocation Ξ has:

- As its base, the verb ZNAT' 'know' in the present indicative.
- As its collocate, a noun $N_{(devil)}$, which is the SyntSubj of the verb ZNAT'.

The noun $N_{(devil)}$ belongs to a set that was called by the Russian linguist Aaron Dolgopolsky (1930–2012) about 50 years ago *imja čertyxatel'noe* (more than approximately, 'blasphemous/swearing noun').[1] This set includes the names of:

---

[1] The adjective ČERTYXATEL'NYJ, invented by Dolgopolsky, is derived from the verb ČERTYXAT'SJA '[to] swear uttering the name of Devil (= ČËRT)' = '[to] blaspheme'.

1) unholy power (ČERT 'devil', BES ≈ 'demon', D'JAVOL 'devil', LEŠIJ 'wood goblin', old LJAD ≈ 'devil');
2) holy power (BOG 'God', ALLAX 'Allah');
3) a plant (XREN 'horseradish'; actually, a euphemism for "penis");
4) an animal (PËS 'male dog');
5) a human (KTO 'who', ŠUT 'buffoon');
6) a gesture (FIG 'fig sign', ŠIŠ 'fig sign'; also a euphemism for "penis");
7) the old Russian letter "x" (XER; another euphemism for "penis"); and
8) the penis (X-- [extremely vulgar and therefore offensive]).[2]

As one sees, the set of blasphemous nouns is a syntactic rather than a semantic class: it includes such a semantically neutral (pro)noun as KTO 'who' and such divine nouns as BOG 'God' and ALLAX 'Allah'.

---

2 Here are some diagnostic contexts for a blasphemous noun $N_{(devil)}$ (note that not every $N_{(devil)}$ can appear in all of these contexts):

1) $N_{(devil)}$ *znaet* 'knows', ... (*Čërt znaet, gde ona sejčas!* 'Devil knows where she [is] now!')
2) *Na koj* 'For what' $N_{(devil)}$ *X i-u?* (*Na koj ljad èto mne?* 'For what hell this [is needed] to.me?')
3) *Na* 'For' $N_{(devil)}$-*á Y-u X?* (*Na xrená koze bajan?* 'For [what] horseradish to.a goat an.accordeon?')
4) *Kakogo* 'Of.what' $N_{(devil)}$-*a ...?* (*Kakogo čerta on prišël?* 'Of.what devil [= What for] did he come?')
5) *Ná* 'To' $N_{(devil)}$ *Y!* (*Ná fig ètu drjan'!* 'To fig.sign [= Down with] this shit!')
6) *do* 'up.to' $N_{(devil)}$-*á X-a* (*Piva/Deneg u nix do figá* 'Of.beer/Of.money at them [is] up.to fig.sign [= very much]'.)
7) *Ni* 'No' $N_{(devil)}$-*á* (*Ni figá emu ne sdelaetsja* 'No fig.sign [= Nothing] to.him will. happen'.)
8) $N_{(devil)}$ *X-u!* (*Šiš/Xren emu!* 'A.fig.sign/Horseradish [= Nothing] to.him!')
9) $N_{(devil)}$ *s* 'with' *X-om* (*Bog/Allax s nim...* 'God/Allah with him...' ≈ 'I don't care about him'.)
10) *K* 'To' $N_{(devil)}$-*u Y!* (*K čërtu vse zaboty!* 'To devil [= Down with] all problems!')

An expression of this form belongs to one of the following three families of linguistic units:

• **Idioms**, for instance, ⌐DO ČERTÁ⌐ [X-a/-ov] 'very much X/very many Xs', ⌐NA ČERTÁ⌐ [Y-u_DAT X_NOM]/ ⌐NA KOJ ČERT⌐ [Y-u_DAT X_NOM] 'Y does not need X at all' and ⌐NA FIG⌐/⌐K ČERTU⌐ [Y-a_ACC]⌐ ≈ 'I wish Y to cease to be in my personal domain' [a very rude rejection]. For a detailed description of these idioms, see Iomdin 2010b: 174–190.

• **Collocations**, for instance *A čërt eë znaet, gde Maša živët* 'But devil her knows where Masha lives'. = 'I don't know where Masha lives, and I don't want to know' [the utterance expresses a strongly negative attitude of the Speaker toward Masha].

• **Lexemes** (namely, clausatives), for instance, interjections such as ČERT [*s Y-om*]! 'Devil with Y!' ≈ 'I don't care what happens with Y, who annoys me', FIG [*Y-u_DAT*]! 'Fig.sign to Y!' ≈ 'Y won't get anything!', etc.

In a Ξ+K-expression the blasphemous noun N$_{(devil)}$ appears always in the singular as the syntactic subject of the verb ZNAT' 'know'.

The Russian Ξ+K expressions are of two subtypes according to their syntactic structure: either the collocation Ξ depends directly on the K-word, forming with it an idiom (⌜Ξ←K⌝; 2.1.1.1), or the K-word indirectly depends on (the head of) the collocation Ξ (Ξ–⋯→K; 2.1.1.2).

NB Russian has other similar Ξ+K expressions, for instance: *odnomu bogu izvestno kto/kogda/skol'ko/...* 'to.only God is.known who/when/how.many/...'; *jasnoe delo kto/kogda/skol'ko/...* 'obvious thing who/when/how.many/...'; *malo (li) kto ...* 'few (whether) who ...'; etc. These expressions will not be considered in order not to encumber the presentation, since whatever is said below applies, *mutatis mutandis*, to them as well.

9.2.1.1.1 ⌜Ξ←K⌝-expressions: idioms with a blasphemous noun (*Tam živët ⌜čërt znaet kto⌝* 'There lives devil knows who')

> *A kogda noč'ju svetit mesjac,*
> *To on svetit čërt znaet kak...*
> 'And when at.night shines the.moon,
> Then it shines devil knows how...'
> S. Esenin

⌜Ξ←K⌝-expressions can be illustrated by the sentences in (1):

(1) a. [*Sjuda prixodit*] ⌜*čërt znaet kto*⌝
   'To.here comes devil knows who'.

   b. [*On otpravilsja tuda*] ⌜*bog znaet začem*⌝
   'He went there God knows for.what'.

   c. ⌜*Xren znaet skol'ko*⌝ [*on spal*]
   'Horseradish knows [for] how.long he slept'.

   d. ⌜*Pës znaet kuda*⌝ [*my idëm*]
   'Dog knows to.where [we are.walking]'.

   e. [*Do goroda my dojdëm*] ⌜*fig znaet kogda*⌝
   'To city we will.arrive fig.sign knows when'.

The ⌜Ξ←K⌝-expression in each of (1) sentences is an idiom—a non-compositional multiword lexical unit that needs to be entered in a lexicon as a whole (for a definition of idiom, see Section 9.3; idioms are indicated by top corners: ⌜...⌝).

Semantically, all idioms in (1) are quite similar—up to the degree of expressivity and the language register: they express negative evaluation of the situation by the author of the utterance.[3] But they are not synonymous: each one of these ⌜Ξ←K⌝ idioms has its own meaning. However, since what interests us here is the syntactic structure of these idioms (rather than their meaning), I limit myself to a lexicographic description of only three of these.

⌜**ČERT ZNAET KTO**⌝ 'devil knows who', **colloquial**, idiom, N, pronominal
⌜*čërt znaet kto*⌝: 'person whom the author of the utterance evaluates very negatively'

> **NB** In the surface realization of the construction PREP→⌜ČËRT ZNAET KTO⌝ the preposition is placed before KTO or (less frequently) before ČËRT ZNAET: *On pišet čërt znaet **dlja** kogo* 'He writes devil knows for whom'. ~ *On pišet **dlja** čërt znaet kogo* 'He writes for devil knows whom'.

Na ètom sajte čërt znaet kto registriruetsja 'On this site devil knows who is.registered'. | *Opasenija bol'nogo popast' v ruki čërt znaet k komu ne bezosnovatel'ny* 'The patient's apprehensions to.find.himself in the.hands of devil knows who [are] not groundless'. | *Ja obedal čërt znaet s kem vo frake* 'I was.dining devil knows with whom in tails' [I. Brodskij]. | *On izvestnyj pevec, a Džastin Timberlejk prosto čërt znaet kto* 'He [is] a well.known singer, but Justin Timberlake [is] simply devil knows who'.

⌜**ČERT ZNAET GDE**⌝ 'devil knows where', **colloquial**, idiom, ADV, pronominal
⌜*čërt znaet gde*⌝: 'in a very faraway or wrong place'

... esli by ne odin strannyj čelovek, živšij čërt znaet gde, a točnee – v gorode Ure Xaldejskom '... if it weren't for one strange person, who lived devil knows where, and more.precisely—in the.city of Ur of.Chaldees' [I. Guberman & A. Okun']. | *No čto delat', esli ty sam živëš' čërt znaet gde?* 'But what to.do if you yourself live devil knows where?'

⌜**ČERT ZNAET SKOL'KO**⌝ 'devil knows how.much/many', **colloquial**, idiom, ADV, pronominal, (+ $N_{X\text{-GEN}}$)
⌜*čërt znaet skol'ko*⌝: 'a very large quantity [of Ξ]'

Kopajus' čërt znaet skol'ko vremeni i nikak ne mogu najti ošibku 'I am.looking. into.this [for] devil knows how.much time and still [I] cannot find [the] error'. | *Vy uže čërt znaet skol'ko drug s drugom znakomy, začem tratit' vremja na preljudii?* 'You already devil knows how.much.time with each other [are] acquainted, why waste time on preludes?' | *Za period trenirovok ja probežal čërt znaet*

---

[3] The author of the utterance **U** is either the Speaker or a person to whom the Speaker ascribes **U**. Consider the utterance U_1 = *Puškin writes that there is no happiness in the world*; U_1's author is me Igor Mel'čuk, that is, the Speaker. But the utterance U_2 = *there is no happiness in the world* was produced by Puškin, U_2's author. In other words, the Speaker is the author of the primary utterance. (On the contrast "the Speaker *vs.* author of the utterance," see, in particular, Iordanskaja & Mel'čuk 1995.)

skol'ko kilometrov krossov 'During the training period I have.run devil knows how.many kilometers of.cross-country races'. | *Da ja tam uže čërt znaet skol'ko raz byval!* 'But I there already devil knows how.many times have.been!'

All ⌜Ξ←K⌝ idioms can include an expletive personal pronoun of 3sg ON 'he/she/it' in the accusative: *Ona pišet čërt* **eë/ego**←*znaet čto* 'She writes devil her/it knows what'; this phenomenon is described below, in Subsection 9.2.1.1.2.

An ⌜Ξ←K⌝ idiom can contain only some of the blaspemous nouns: *On živët* *kto[4] 〈*šiš, *bes, *ljad〉 *znaet gde*. At the same time, some $N_{(devil)}$s can alternate in these idioms, with a more or less significant semantic and/or stylistic difference: *čërt/bog/xren/fig/... znaet gde* 'devil/God/ horseradish/fig.sign/... knows where'. However, even in case where two such idioms are semantically and syntactically fully equivalent, each one of them is a separate linguistic sign, that is, a separate lexical unit.

The surface-syntactic structure of an ⌜Ξ←K⌝ idiom is obvious: its surface-syntactic head is the K-word (an interrogative-relative pronoun $L_{(pron,\ interr\text{-}rel)}$): the phrase ⌜ČËRT←ZNAET←KTO⌝ is syntactically similar to KOE-←KTO ≈ 'someone', ABY←KTO 'no.matter who' or KTO→-NIBUD' ≈ 'somebody' (**koe-kto, koe-gde; aby kto, aby** *gde*; *kto-nibud'*, *gde-nibud'*). In an ⌜Ξ←K⌝ idiom the pronoun K satisfies all three Criteria **B1** – **B3**, which determine the SSynt-head of a phrase (Chapter 2, Section 2.4).

For the convenience of the reader, here are these criteria.

Criteria B – SSynt-dominance

Criterion B1 – The passive SSynt-valence of a phrase

> In the phrase L_1–r–L_2, the lexeme L_1 is the Synt-governor of L_2 if the following condition is satisfied:
> The passive SSynt-valence of the L_1–r–L_2 phrase is determined by the passive SSynt-valence of L_1 to a greater extent than by that of L_2; then we have L_1–r→L_2.

Criterion B2 – The morphological links between an element of a phrase and its external context (in a language that has inflectional morphology)

> If the phrase L_1–r–L_2 in which the passive SSynt-valence of its components does not allow one to establish the SSynt-head is such that
> —either L_1 controls the inflection of lexemes external to the phrase
> —or L_1's inflection is controlled by such lexemes,
> then L_1 is the SSynt-head of the phrase: L_1–r→L_2.

---

[4] Cf. *He lives* **who** *knows where*, which is quite normal in English.

Criterion B3 – The semantic content of a phrase

If the phrase L_1–r–L_2 in which neither the passive SSynt-valence nor the morphology allows one to establish the SSynt-governor means 'a kind/an instance of L_1' rather than 'a kind/an instance of L_2', then L_1 is the SSynt-head of the phrase: L_1–r→L_2.

In conformity with these criteria, the SSynt-head of an idiom of the ⌈ČËRT←ZNAET ←KTO⌉ type is the K-word:

- Syntactically, the K-word determines the passive syntactic valency of a ⌈Ξ←K⌉ idiom: the idiom appears in all surface-syntactic slots where the K-word can appear; thus, *pisat' komu* 'to.write to.whom' ~ *pisat' čert znaet komu* 'to.write devil knows to.whom'; *exat' v kakoj gorod* 'to.go to what city' ~ *exat' čert znaet v kakoj gorod* 'to.go devil knows to what city'; *poterjat' gde* 'to.lose where' ~ *poterjat' čert znaet gde* 'to.lose devil knows where').

    NB Strictly speaking, Criterion B1 being satisfied is already sufficient to recognize the K-word as the syntactic head of a ⌈Ξ←K⌉ idiom. But the two other criteria, B2 and B3, buttress this result; and even if their indications are redundant, it seems interesting to consider them, too.

- Morphologically, the K-word is the morphological contact point of a ⌈Ξ←K⌉ idiom: it is the K-word that is declined in conformity with the syntactic context; thus, *On est čert znaet čto*$_{ACC}$ 'He eats devil knows what'. ~ *On pišet čert znaet komu*$_{DAT}$ 'He writes devil knows to.whom'. ~ *On zanimaetsja čert znaet čem*$_{INSTR}$ 'He is.busy devil knows with.what'.
- Semantically, the K-word expresses the generic notion in the meaning of the whole ⌈Ξ←K⌉ idiom: KTO ⇔ 'a person', GDE ⇔ 'in a place', SKOL'KO ⇔ 'a quantity', etc.

At the SSynt-level, (the head of) the Ξ component ($Ξ = N_{(devil)}$←subjectival–ZNAT'$_{PRES}$), that is, the verb ZNAT', is subordinated to K-word by means of the **WH-pronominal** SSyntRel (Chapter 2, Section 2.5, SSyntRel No. 75, p. 91): the Ξ component is an incomplete clause depending on the K-word. For instance:

On est čert znaet←WH-pronominal–*čto* 'He eats devil knows what'.

At the deep-syntactic level, the ⌈Ξ←K⌉ idiom is represented, as any idiom, by one node.

The technique of joining to a K-word a dependent collocation engenders in Russian an open class of syntactically formed indefinite pronouns: the whole ⌈Ξ←K⌉ expression is syntactically equivalent to a "compound" indefinite pronoun, of the same type as KTO-NIBUD' ≈ 'anybody', KTO BY TO NI BYL(O) 'whoever', MALO KTO 'few who' = 'few people', KOE-KTO ≈ 'somebody', ABY KTO ≈ 'no matter who'. (For a detailed description of this class of indefinites in Russian, see Testelets & Bylinina 2005.)

This phenomenon is well known in many other languages. M. Haspelmath (1997) indicates four major types of such pronouns in more than hundred structurally very different languages:

1. 'Dunno' type: *On rabotaet **bog znaet gde***
   'He works God knows where'.
2. 'No matter' type: *On rabotaet **dlja nas nevažno gde***
   'He works for us irrelevant where'.
3. 'Pleases' type: *On rabotaet **gde xočet***
   'He works where [he] wants'.
4. 'Maybe' type: *On rabotaet **gde emu predlagajut***
   'He works where to.him [«they»] propose'.

Ξ+K-expressions, discussed in Subsection 9.2.1, are of the first and the second type, and K+Ξ-expressions (Subsection 9.2.2), of the third and the fourth.

The DSynt- and SSynt-structures of a sentence containing an ⌜Ξ←K⌝ idiom are as follows:

(2) a. *On žil **čërt znaet gde*** 'He lived devil knows where'.
   b. The DSyntS of (2a):
      ⌜ČËRT_ZNAET_GDE⌝←II–ŽIT′$_{PAST}$–I→ON
   c. The SSyntS of (2a):
      ČËRT$_{SG}$←subj–ZNAT′$_{PRES}$←WH-pronominal–GDE←circumstantial–ŽIT′$_{PAST}$–subj→ON

9.2.1.1.2 Ξ–⋯→K-expressions: collocations governing an indirect-interrogative clause (*Čërt znaet, kto on takoj* 'Devil knows who he [is]')

> *I kto ego znaet, čego on morgaet?*
> 'And who him knows why he is.blinking?'
> [M. Isakovskij; a popular Soviet song].

Typical examples of Ξ–⋯→K-expressions are given in (3):

(3) a. *Čërt znaet, kto [sjuda xodit]*
   'Devil knows who to.here comes'.

9.2 K-expressions: their surface-syntactic structure and lexicographic description — 317

b. ***Bog znaet, za čem*** [*on otpravilsja*]
   'God knows for what he went'.
c. ***Xren znaet, skol´ko*** [*on spal*]
   'Horseradish knows [for] how.much.time he slept'.
d. ***Pës znaet, kuda*** [*nam idti*]
   'Dog knows to.where we must.go'.
e. ***Šut znaet, kakogo*** [*goda èta krepost´*]
   'Buffoon knows of.which year [is] this fortress'.
f. ***Fig znaet, kogda*** [*my dojdëm do goroda*]
   'Fig.sign knows when we will.reach [the] town'.

Here, the component Ξ, as stated above, is a collocation of the verb ZNAT' 'know', which governs a completive clause that contains a K-word. The SSynt-structure of this completive clause is quite normal: it depends, via its top Main Verb [MV], on ZNAT' (being its DirO), for instance:

(4) a. ***Čërt znaet, gde*** [*on žil*] 'Devil knows where he was.living'.
   b. DSyntS of (4a): ČËRT$_{SG}$←I–ZNAT'$_{PRES}$–II→ŽIT'$_{PAST}$–I→ON
                                                        ╲─II→GDE
   c. SSyntS of (4a): ČËRT$_{SG}$←**subj**–ZNAT'$_{PRES}$–**dir-obj**→ ŽIT'$_{PAST}$–**subj**──→ON
                                                              ╲─**circum**→GDE

The collocation of the verb ZNAT' with N$_{(devil)}$ is described by means of a non-standard lexical function «I don't [know] ...», which means 'the Speaker signals that he does not know the answer to the question "Ψ?" about a situation P(X, ..., Ψ), to which he is indifferent or which he evaluates negatively' (for lexical functions, see Chapter 1, Subsection 1.2.4.2, p. 23). Ψ stands for an indefinite pronoun that means 'somebody', 'something', 'somewhere', etc., and Ψ? denotes the corresponding interrogative pronoun: 'who?', 'what?', 'where?'.

Let it be emphasized that the meaning of this type of collocation includes the semanteme 'the Speaker' (i.e., 'I') and 'signaling' (in the communicative sense): in this way is reflected the fact of "insubordinability," or "non-quotability," of this collocation, see immediately below.[5]

An idiom of the ⌜ČËRT ZNAET GDE⌝ type and a collocation of the ČËRT ZNAET [, GDE ...] type, both containing a blasphemous noun, differ in several aspects.

---

[5] On 'signaling' vs. 'communicating', see Mel'čuk 2001: 242–260.

- Semantically, a ⌜Ξ←K⌝ idiom expresses a negative attitude of the utterance's author toward the referent of the meaning "⌜Ξ←K⌝" (5a); however, the corresponding collocation simply states his ignorance of the information 'K' (plus indifference or perhaps annoyance of the utterance's author), cf. (5b):

(5) a. *Ivan zivët čërt znaet gde – v Kryžopole!*
    'Ivan lives devil knows where—in Kryzhopol!'
    [The author knows where Ivan lives, but condemns his place of residence: the town of Kryzhopol.]
  b. *– Gde zivët Ivan?*
    'Where does Ivan live?' – ***Čërt (ego) znaet*** 'Devil (him/it) knows'.
    [The author does not know where Ivan lives and does not want to know.]

- Communicatively, a ⌜Ξ←K⌝ idiom is a descriptive expression (although it is expressive), while a Ξ—···→K expression is a **signalative** (Mel'čuk 2001: 354). Therefore, only a ⌜Ξ←K⌝ idiom can be subordinated to the verb of a superordinate clause, and a Ξ—···→K collocation, as is typical of signalatives, cannot:

(6) a. *Ivan zajavil, čto Maša zanimaetsja čërt znaet čem*
    'Ivan declared that Masha was.doing devil knows what'.
  b. *Ivan zajavil, čto *čërt znaet, čem Maša zanimaetsja*
    'Ivan declared that devil knows what Masha was.doing'.

- Syntactically, a ⌜Ξ←K⌝ idiom includes the K-word; the string *čërt znaet kto* 'devil knows who' is a phrase. In a Ξ—···→K expression only the collocation Ξ—that is, *čërt znaet, ...*—is a phrase; the K-word (= кто 'who', ČEM 'with. what', GDE 'where', ...) is part of the completive clause governed by the collocation. This K-word depends directly on the MV of the completive clause via one of the ...-**obj** or **circum** SSyntRels, and indirectly on the verb ZNAT′, the head of the Ξ collocation: *čërt znaet,—···→kto*. The completive clause that contains the K-word is an indirect question and, therefore, allows for the interrogative particle LI 'whether' and the conjunction ILI 'or', which is excluded in the case of the idiom:

(7) a. *Čërt znaet, priexala **li** ona* 'Devil knows whether she arrived'.
  b. *Čërt znaet, priexala ona **ili** net* 'Devil knows [whether] she arrived or not'.

With a Ξ collocation, the completive clause can be omitted altogether in an answer:

(8) [*– A čem ona zanimaetsja?* 'And what [is] she doing?']
    – Čërt (eë) znaet (čem) 'Devil (her) knows (what)'.

- Prosodically, the idiom carries a continuous intonation contour, while the collocation can have a pause after ZNAT'.
- Lexically, the idiom allows for the replacement of ČĖRT ZNAET by the expression ČĖRT-TE (where -te is possibly a reduction of *tebe* 'to.you', a Dativus Ethicus; cf. POLNOTE ≈ 'enough, stop it' ⇐ *polno tebe* 'enough to.you'), but the collocation does not (" | " stands for a minor pause):

(9) a. *Ona zanimaetsja | čërt-te čem*
   'She does devil-TE what'. ~ *Čërt-te čem | ona zanimaetsja*.
   b. **Čërt-te, | čem ona zanimaetsja*.

Both phrasemes of the Ξ+K type, that is, the idiom and the collocation, can include the expletive personal pronoun of 3rd person ON 'he/she/it' in the accusative, depending on *znaet* 'knows'. Two constructions, semantically equivalent, are possible:

- Either ON is used non-referentially, in the neuter singular form *ego* 'it': (10a, b) and (11a, b).
- Or ON is coreferential to the SSynt-subject of the superordinate clause, which contains the idiom, or to the SSynt-subject of the completive subordinate clause, which depends on the collocations; in this case, ON agrees with this SyntSubj in gender and number: (10c, d) and (11c, d).

(10) a. ***Maša*** *zanimaetsja čërt **ego** znaet čem*
   'Masha does devil it knows what'.
   b. ***Deti*** *zanimajutsja čërt **ego** znaet čem*
   'Children do devil it knows what'.
   c. ***Maša*** *zanimaetsja čërt **eë** znaet čem*
   'Masha does devil her knows what'.
   d. ***Deti*** *zanimajutsja čërt **ix** znaet čem*
   'Children do devil them knows what'.

(11) a. *Čërt **ego** znaet, čem **Maša** zanimaetsja*
   'Devil it knows what Masha does'.
   b. *Čërt **ego** znaet, čem **deti** zanimajutsja*
   'Devil it knows what children do'.
   c. *Čërt **eë** znaet, čem **Maša** zanimaetsja*
   'Devil her knows what Masha does'.
   d. *Čërt **ix** znaet, čem **deti** zanimajutsja*
   'Devil them knows what children do'.

There are no semantic differences between (a, b) and (c, d) variants; the ON pronoun reinforces the colloquial character of both expressions, but does not impact their meaning. Nevertheless, the idiom and the collocation differ in the frequency of the expletive ON: ON is more typical of the collocation, where, in some specific contexts, it becomes nearly obligatory, cf. (12):

(12) [– *Čem že ona zanimaetsja?* 'What is she doing?']
– *A čërt ego/eë znaet!* 'But devil her/him knows!' ⟨??*A cërt znaet!*⟩

The addition of the expletive ON$_{ACC}$ raises the question of the syntactic role of this pronoun inside the idiom/collocation. Its accusative points at a DirO; but the collocation under analysis has already a DirO: the completive clause subordinated to ZNAT'. Moreover, the expletive ON 'it' carries no meaning and is optional. This allows us to consider it as a **quasi-direct object**. A stock example of Quasi-DirO is the noun in the Persian verb-noun collocations and idioms that are transitive verbal expression—that is, as a rule, they have a genuine DirO:

(13) a. *Reza bäčče-ra* **tänbih** *kärd*
Reza child DirO punishment did
'Reza punished the.child'.
b. *Reza bäčče-ra* **färib** *dad*
Reza child DirO deception gave
'Reza deceived the.child'.
c. *Reza bäčče-ra* **dust** *dašt*
Reza child DirO friend got
'Reza befriended the.child'.

The noun in boldface is the Quasi-DirO-2 of the verb. In the SSyntS, it is subordinated to the verb by the **quasi-direct-objectival-2** SSyntRel, see Chapter 2, Section 2.5, SSyntRel No. 9, p. 55.

Now, let us see a lexicographic description of collocations of the «I don't [know]» type in the lexical entry for the verb ZNAT' 'know'.

9.2 K-expressions: their surface-syntactic structure and lexicographic description — 321

ZNAT' 'know'
...
«I don't [know]»: $N_{(devil)}$←subjectival–ZNAT'$_{PRES}$ (coll. –quasi-dir-objectival-2→ON 'he') (|)

Conditions
1) ZNAT' 'know'–direct-objectival→Δ_{CLAUSE} | L←subject–L_2–···→$L_{1(pronoun, interr-rel)}$.
2) $N_{(devil)}$ = {BOG 'God', coll. ČERT 'devil', substandard FIG 'fig sign', KTO 'who', substandard PËS 'dog', substandard ŠUT 'buffoon', vulg. XREN 'horseradish'}.
3) ON 'he': either ON$_{SG, NEU}$, or [g, n](ON) ⇐ [g, n](L); C N$_{SG, NEU}$ must be positioned immediately after $N_{(devil)}$.

☞ 1. (|) is an optional minor pause; ' represents a very strong stress.
2. Δ_{CLAUSE} stands for the SSynt-tree of a completive clause that depends on the verb ZNAT' 'know' in conformity with the government pattern of this verb; this clause has the SSynt-structure of the form: L←subject–L_2–···→$L_{1(pronoun, interr-rel)}$.
3. g and n stand, respectively, for "gender" and "number."

Russian also has other phraseologized Ξ+K-expressions, for instance, MALO/REDKO KTO 'few/rare [are] who' [*Malo kto èto čitaet* 'Few [are] who read this'] or ABY KTO ≈ 'no.matter who' [*Ja ne pojdu aby k komu* 'I will.not visit no.matter whom']. These are as well non-standard collocations of some (by no means all) pronouns $L_{(pron, interr-rel)}$. An example:

KTO
...
«few»   MALO$_{(antepos)}$←intraphrasemic–KTO   'few [are] who',
             REDKO$_{(antepos)}$←intraphrasemic–KTO   'rare [are] who'
«no matter» ABY$_{(antepos)}$←intraphrasemic–KTO   'no.matter who',
             ČERT-TE$_{(antepos)}$←intraphrasemic–KTO 'no.matter who'

The particles/adverbs MALO, REDKO, ABY and ČERT-TE are subordinated to the interrogative-relative pronoun by the **intraphrasemic** SSyntRel, which links a dependent component of a "quasi-compound word," including, in particular, the particle KOE-, to its central component—the relative pronoun. (In the inventory of Russian SSyntRels in Mel'čuk 1974: 221–235 this SSyntRel—№ 31, p. 231—was called **1st auxiliary**.)

9.2.1.2 Free Ξ←K-expressions

(14) a. *Maša zanimaetsja* **ne pripomnju**←wh-pronominal–***čem***
         ⎿————oblique-objectival————⏋
   'Masha does I.don't remember what'.
   b. *Maša zanimaetsja* **nikto v Moskve ne znaet čem**
   'Masha does nobody in Moscow doesn't know what'.

c. *Maša zanimaetsja **vse v Moskve znajut čem***
   'Masha does everybody in Moscow knows what'.
d. *Maša zanimaetsja **mat' Petra daže predpoložit' ne možet čem***
   'Masha does mother of.Peter even presume cannot what'.
e. *Maša zanimaetsja **ty nikogda ne ugadaeš' čem***
   'Masha does you never won't guess what'.

This type of expressions in English was studied in depth in Lakoff 1974.[6]

Free Ξ←K-expressions do not contain a blasphemous noun, but, syntactically, they are similar to phraseologized Ξ+K-expressions, which contain one. Namely, the SSyntS of a free Ξ+K-expression is the same as that of its phraseologized counterpart: the SSynt-head is an L$_{(pron, interr-rel)}$ (i.e. K-word), which subordinates—by the **WH-pronominal** SSyntRel—the top node MV of the rest.

Let us consider in more detail the production of sentence (14e). Its (simplified) SemS, DSyntS and SSyntS are presented in Figure 9.1 ['what?' represents the meaning of the interrogative pronoun čto?]:

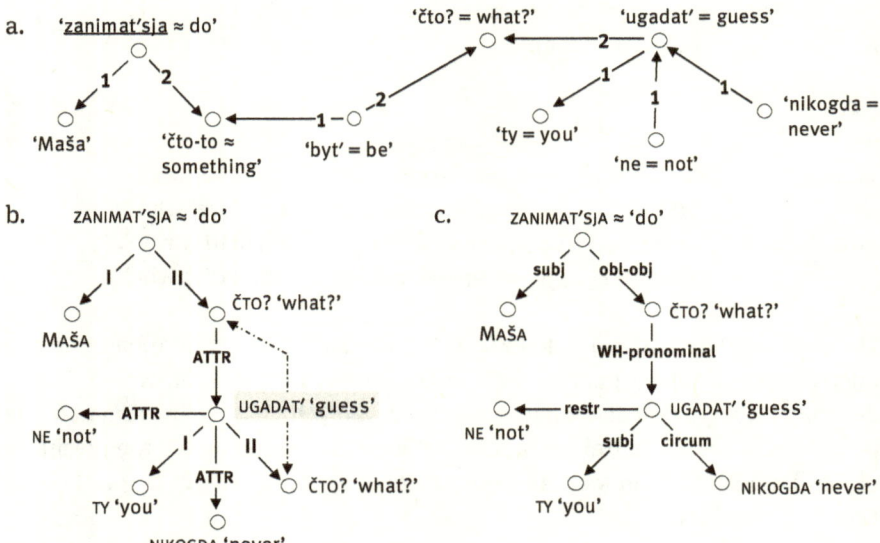

Figure 9.1 Semantic, deep-syntactic and surface-syntactic structures of sentence (14e)

---

6 Here is one of Lakoff's examples (p. 322):
(i) *John invited you'll never guess how many people to you can imagine what kind of a party at it should be obvious where with God only knows what purpose in mind, despite you can guess what pressure.*

The SemS in Figure 9.1(a) can be implemented more or less literally:

(15) a. *Maša zanimaetsja čem-to, i ty nikogda ne ugadaeš', čtó èto*
'Masha does something, and you will never guess, what is this'.
b. *Maša zanimaetsja čem-to, i ty nikogda ne ugadaeš', čem* (*imenno*) (*ona zanimaetsja*)
'Masha does something, and you will never guess, what (exactly) (she does)'.

The sentences (15a, b) are produced from the SemS in Figure 9.1(a) according to standard Sem-, Synt- and Morph-rules. However, free Ξ+K-expressions, in particular, that in (14e), have quite specific deep- and surface-SyntSs; consequently, a special Sem-rule—or, more precisely, a schema for an open set of Sem-rules—is needed:

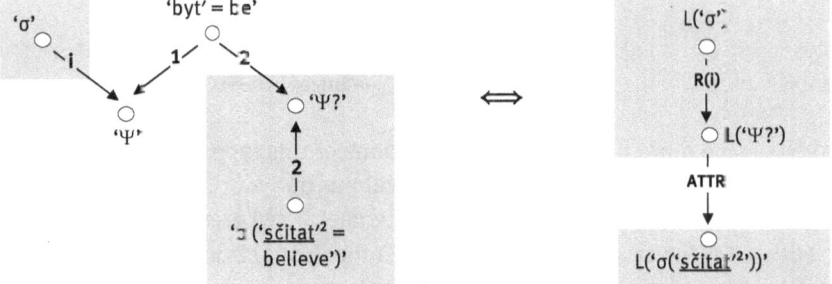

Conditions

1) 'Ψ' :   'čto-to'   'gde-to'   'kuda-to'   'kogda-to'   kak-to'   'začem-to'   'počemu-to'   'skol'ko-to'
             'something'   'somewhere'   'to.somewhere'   'some-time'   'somehow'   'for some purpose' 'for some reason'   'some.how.many'

   'Ψ?':   ČTO?   GDE?   KUDA?   KOGDA?   KAK?   ZAČEM?   POČEMU?   SKOL'KO?

   The inventory of LUs that can appear in this Sem-rule is only illustrative, that is, not exhaustive.

2) Sem-actant 1 of the predicate 'σ('*sčitat'*² = believe')' is:
   'ja = I', 'ty = you_SG', 'nikto = nobody', 'vse = everybody' or 'even←N'.

3) The verb L('σ('*sčitat'²*')') is either in the imperfective present, or in the perfective future, or else in the conditional-subjunctive.

Notations

L('σ') stands for an LU L that has the meaning 'σ';
'σ('*sčitat'²* = believe')' is a meaning whose central component is '*sčitat'²* = believe'; for instance:
'σ' = 'znat' = know'   'X believes that Y holds, and this is true';
'σ' = 'dogadat'sja = have guessed'   'caused1 by X's intuition, X began to believe that Y holds, and this is true';
'σ' = 'predpolagat' = presume'   'caused1 by X's logical reasoning, X believes that Y holds'.

Figure 9.2 Sem-rule 'Ψ←1–be–2→' ⇔ –ATTR→ (so to speak, a semantic ellipsis)

9.2.2 K+Ξ-expressions

The K+Ξ-expressions, just like the Ξ+K-expressions, are also of two types: phraseologized, in which Ξ is a lexeme or an idiom (9.2.2.1), and free (9.2.2.2).

9.2.2.1 Phraseologized K→Ξ-expressions: collocations (*Maša poedet kuda→ugodno* 'Masha will.go to.where wanted')

Interrogative-relative pronouns form a series of collocations. Thus, čto 'what' has two non-standard collocations of the K→Ξ-type, where čto is the base: in the one the collocate is the idiom ⌐BOG POSLAL/POŠLËT⌐ 'God has.sent/will.send', which constitutes an incomplete clause depending on the pronoun); in the second the collocate is the adverb UGODNO lit. 'pleasant' ≈ 'any':

ČTO 'what'
...
«what is available»: ⌐BOG POSLAL/POŠLËT⌐₍postposed₎←**intraphrasemic**–ČTO
«anything»   : UGODNO₍postposed₎←**intraphrasemic**–ČTO

ČTO has some more non-standard collocations of this type, the collocates being the idioms ⌐BOG NA DUŠU POLOŽIT⌐ 'God will.put on [your] soul' ≈ 'whatever' or ⌐PÓD RUKU POPADËTSJA⌐ 'under.hand will.come' ≈ 'whatever' and the adverbs NI_POPADJA ≈ '-ever' or POPALO ≈ '-ever'. In the SSynt-structure these collocates are subordinated to the K-word by the **intraphrasemic** SSyntRel.

Other interrogative-relative pronouns—KTO 'who', KUDA 'to.where', GDE 'where', KOGDA 'when', ZAČEM 'what.for', etc.—also have these collocates, which gives a few dozens of K→Ξ-collocations.

9.2.2.2 Free K←⋯–Ξ-expressions (*Maša poedet kuda ty zaxočeš'* 'Masha will go to.where you₍SG₎ will.want')

Examples (16) and (17) present free K←⋯–Ξ-expressions.

⌐ subjectival ⌐
(16) a. *Maša vsegda xorošo ispol'zuet **čto k nej popadët v ruki***
       'Masha always uses well what to her falls into hands'.
   b. *Maša poedet **kuda eë pošljut***
       'Masha will.go to.where [«they»] her will.send'.

⌐———— oblique-objectival ————⌐
(17) a. *Maša zanimalas' **čem Vanja xotel**[, čtoby ona zanimalas']*
       'Masha was.doing what Vanya wanted [that she were.doing]'.

b. *Maša vstretitsja* **s kem vam budet ugodno**[, čtoby ona vstretilas']
'Masha will.meet with whom to.you will.be pleasant [that she were. meeting]'.

☞ The struck-through fragment in (17a–b) is a part of the sentence that is present in the surface-syntactic structure, but can be (and most often is) elided in the sentence itself.

The free K+Ξ-expressions in the sentences of (16) and (17) are **pseudo-relative clauses** (the current name being **headless/free relatives**: see, for instance, Bresnan & Grimshaw 1978; this type of clause is analyzed in Chapter 6, Section 6.3.2.2). Such a clause can always be "reconstructed" to become a genuine relative clause by adding to it the correlate pronoun TOT/TO 'this', TUDA 'to.there', TOGDA 'then', etc.: *kto javitsja k nej* 'who comes to her' ≡ *tot, kto javitsja k nej* 'the.person who comes to her' or *kuda eë pošljut* 'to.where [«they»] her will.send' ≡ *tuda, kuda eë pošljut* 'to.there to.where [«they»] her will.send'.

The SSynt-structure of a pseudo-relative clause must be the same as that of a genuine relative clause and as that of its independent equivalent—that is, of an interrogative clause. Namely, the K-word, i.e. the L$_{(pron, rel)}$, of the pseudo-relative clause is an object or a circumstantial of the MV of this clause, and the MV itself depends, also as the subject, an object or as a circumstantial, on the MV of the superordinate clause, see (16).

In a pseudo-relative clause, the L$_{(pron, rel)}$ pronoun plays, metaphorically speaking, a double role: from the angle of its meaning it appears to be simultaneously an element of the two clauses—that is, of both the pseudo-relative and its superordinate. Syntactically, this is, of course, impossible; but the pressure from the meaning is so high that, for instance, in Russian the surface (= morphological) form of L$_{(pron, rel)}$ must satisfy the government pattern of the MVs of both these clauses—otherwise, the result is ungrammatical. (In the sentences of the (17) type, by "MV of the pseudo-relative clause" is meant the elided verb shown in square brackets.) Let it be emphasized that just a formal coincidence of the signifiers is required: thus, in (16a), the wordform *čto* 'what' corresponds to two different DMorphSs, i.e. to different cases—ČTO$_{ACC}$ (in the superordinate clause) and ČTO$_{NOM}$ (in the pseudo-relative).[7]

---

[7] This constraint is known in many languages. Thus, in German the K-word can "combine" two different cases, but only if both these cases have identical signifiers (Dalrymple & Kaplan 2000: 759, (2) *ff*; I slightly modified the examples for better clarity):
(ii) a. *Ich habe gewaschen* **was** *übrig blieb* 'I have washed what extra remained'.
vs. b. **Ich habe gewaschen* **wen/wer** *übrig blieb* 'I have washed whom/who extra remained'.
Both superordinate clauses in (ii) must have a K-word in the accusative, and both corresponding pseudo-relatives require a K-word in the nominative. However, the pronoun WAS 'what' has

The SemS, the DSyntS and the SSyntS of sentence (17a) are presented, respectively, in Figure 9.3:

a.
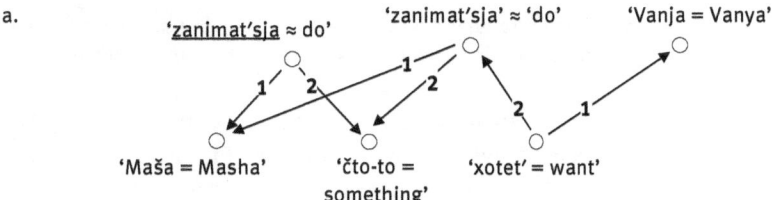

b.
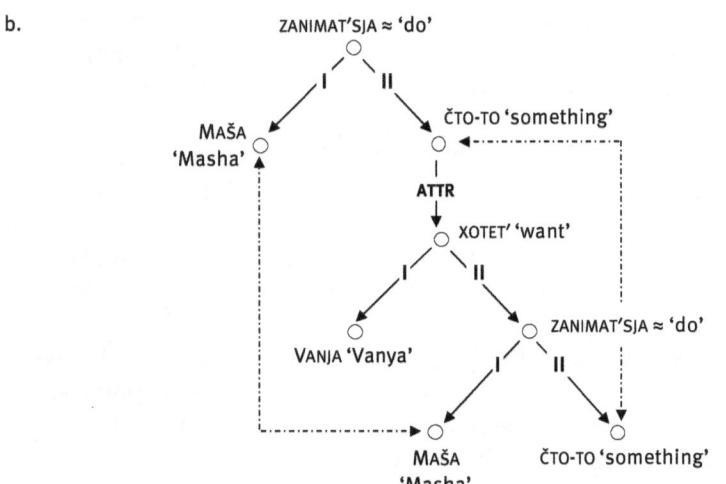

---

identical forms of the accusative and the nominative, while the forms of the accusative and the nominative of the pronoun WER 'who' are different; therefore, sentence (ii-a) is correct, and sentence (ii-b) is not.

Spanish allows for the following construction (Suñer 1984):

(iii) *Escribí **a quien** viste ayer* 'I.wrote to whom you.saw yesterday'.

In the superordinate clause, the preposition A introduces DSyntA III of the verb ESCRIBIR 'write' (i.e. it corresponds to the dative), and in the subordinate clause it introduces its DSyntA II (i.e. it corresponds to the accusative).

The question of the presence and the nature of constraints on government patterns of the MVs of the superordinate and the subordinate clauses in the case of pseudo-relatives used to be very popular in linguistics; see, for instance, Grosu 1988.

9.2 K-expressions: their surface-syntactic structure and lexicographic description — 327

c.
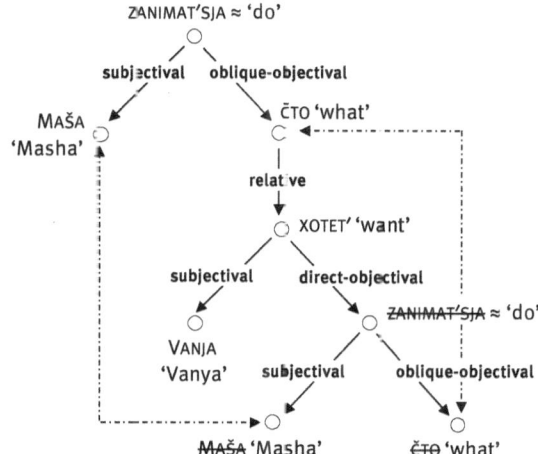

Figure 9.3 Semantic, deep-syntactic and surface-syntactic structures of sentence (17a).

☞ The struck-through lexemes in the SSyntS in Figure 9.3(c) represent the clause elements to be elided: they do not appear in the DMorphS of the sentence.

The semantic rule (SemS ⇔ DSyntS) that ensures the transition between the structures in (a) and (b) of Figure 9.3 looks as follows:

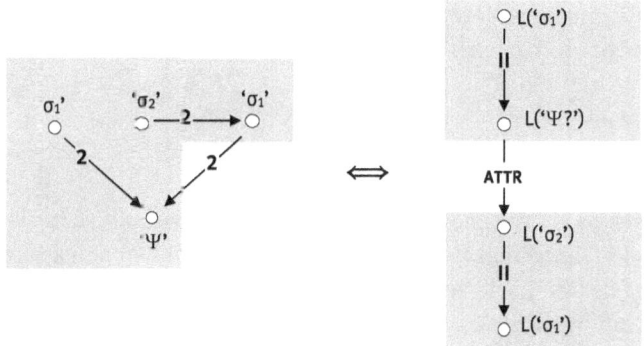

Figure 9.4 Sem-rule '–2→' ⇔ –ATTR→

☞ 'Ψ' and 'Ψ?' have here the same meaning as in Sem-rule of Figure 9.2 above: 'Ψ' represents the meaning of an indefinite pronoun ('čto-to ≈ something'), and 'Ψ?' is the meaning of the corresponding interrogative pronoun ('čto? = what?').

The Sem-rule in Figure 9.4 describes the "translation" of Sem-relation **2** by DSynt-relation **ATTR** in the given—quite specific!—context; this translation presupposes head-switching: DSynt-dependencies are inverted with respect of the corresponding Sem-dependencies.

The transition between the structures in (b) and (c) of Figure 9.3 is specified by a DSynt-rule that includes the following condition on the resulting SSynt-tree:

$$\| \ \text{form}(GP_{[r]}(L_1)) = \text{form}(GP_{[r]}(L_2)), \ \& \ L_1\text{-}r{\rightarrow}L(\text{'}\Psi?\text{'}), L_2\text{-}r{\rightarrow}L(\text{'}\Psi?\text{'}), L(\text{'}\Psi?\text{'}) \dashleftarrow L(\text{'}\Psi?\text{'})$$

("Line **r** of the government patterns of lexemes L_1 and L_2, which directly syntactically govern, via SSyntRel r, coreferential occurrences of lexeme $L_{(\text{pron, rel})}$, i.e. $L(\text{'}\Psi?\text{'})$, specifies the identical inflectional forms of lexeme $L_{(\text{pron, interr-rel})}$.")

This conditions is the notorious "matching constraint" on both coreferential occurrences of the **K**-word that appear in the DSynt-structure. Our formulation is, of course, incomplete: we also need an inventory of all specific cases where the given language allows for grammatical non-identity of the coreferential occurrences of the **K**-word under the condition of identity of their signifiers.

9.3 Blasphemous idioms are not syntactic phrasemes

Blasphemous idioms of the type ⌜ČËRT ZNAET KTO⌝ 'devil knows who' are syntactically quite particular, which has lead to them being often called "**syntactic phrasemes,**" or "**syntactic** idioms." I do not think that this is a felicitous usage, and I will try here to put some order into the linguist's notional system in what concerns phrasemes (see Mel'čuk 2012-2015: vol. 3, 293–386).

Syntactic phrasemes are, of course, a subclass of phrasemes; it is natural to see them as opposed to lexemic and morphemic phrasemes. But first of all, what is a phraseme *tout court*?

Definition 9.1 – phraseme

> A phraseme is a complex linguistic sign (= a configuration of no less than two linguistic signs) that is not free—that is, it is such that at least one sign in it cannot be freely selected by the Speaker
> 1) according to this sign's meaning and particular combinatorial properties,
> 2) following general rules of the language, and
> 3) independently of all other individual signs being part of the complex sign under consideration.
>
> **NB** In this definition, the term (*linguistic*) *sign* is used as a shorthand for 'sign or appropriate -emic set of signs'. Lexemes and morphemes making up phrasemes are not signs but sets of signs; the term *phraseme* can itself apply both to an actual sign ([*They*] *kill two birds with one stone, killed two birds with one stone, killing two birds with one stone*, etc.) and to a set of signs ⌜KILL TWO BIRDS WITH ONE STONE⌝.

The best known type of phrasemes are lexemic phrasemes (for more, see Mel'čuk 2012d and 2015a).

Definition 9.2 – lexemic phraseme

‖ A **lexemic phraseme** is a phraseme consisting of no less than two lexemes.

In other words, a lexemic phraseme consists of several (two or more) minimal lexical units, i.e. lexemes.
There are three major classes of lexemic phrasemes.

- Non-compositional fully constrained phrasemes:
    1) **Idioms**, such as ⌜DO ČERTÁ⌝ lit. 'up to devil' = 'a lot of'; ⌜KOT NAPLAKAL⌝ lit. 'tomcat cried' = 'very little of'; ⌜DAT' PO ŠAPKE⌝ lit. 'give on hat' = 'fire [an employee]'.
- Compositional phrasemes:
    A. Half constrained, where one component is selected freely according to its meaning and corresponding linguistic rules, while the second is selected as a function of the first one:
    2) **Collocations**, such as *zakljatyj* vrag 'sworn enemy', *nanesti* udar 'deal a blow', *sdat'* èkzamen 'pass an exam', where the collocate (boldfaced) is selected as a function of the base.
    B. Fully constrained:
    3) **Clichés**, such as *Menja zovut ...* lit. '[«They»] call me ...' = 'My name is ...'; *Skol'ko vam let?* lit. 'How.many to.you years?' = 'How old are you?'; *Naskol'ko ja mogu sudit',* ... lit. 'As.far.as I can judge, ...'

The borderlines between these three classes of lexemic phrasemes are determined exclusively on the basis of their internal properties (compositionality and constrained character) and are absolute: intermediate cases are logically impossible.

Morphemic phrasemes are defined in an analogous way (Mel'čuk 1964 and 1992–2000: vol. 4, 398–403; Beck & Mel'čuk 2011).

Definition 9.3 – morphemic phraseme

> A morphemic phraseme is a phraseme consisting of morphemes inside one wordform—that is, either a phraseologized complex stem, or a phraseologized complex affix, or else a phraseologized combination of a stem with an affix.

A morphemic phraseme also consists of minimal morphological units.

Morphemic phrasemes fall in the same three major classes as lexemic phrasemes:

1) Morphemic idioms:
    KON+ËK   lit. 'horse+DIMINUTIVE'   = 'hobby-horse'
                     [⌐sest' na svoego kon'ka⌐ 'get on one's hobby-horse']
    NA+KAZ(-at')   lit. '[to] up+show'   = '[to] punish'
    O+GROM(-nyj)   lit. 'about+thunder(-ous)'   = 'enormous'
2) Morphemic collocations (the collocates are boldfaced):
    TUL+**JAK**   lit. 'Tul(-a)+-er'   = 'inhabitant of Tula'
    vs. MOSKV+**IČ**   lit. 'Moskv(-a)+-er'   = 'inhabitant of Moscow'
    vs. KALUŽ+**ANIN**   lit. 'Kalug(-a)+-er'   = 'inhabitant of Kaluga'
3) Morphemic cliché:
    From POMOGAT' '[to] help'   POMOŠČ+NIK 'helper'   ~ *POMOG+ATEL'
    From RAZBIRAT' '[to] dismantle' RAZBOR+K(A) 'dismantling' ~ *RAZBIR+ANI(E)

A syntactic phraseme must be defined in the same way—as a phraseme consisting of minimal syntactic units. A minimal syntactic unit is a minimal syntactic structure L_1–r→L_2, where L_1 and L_2 are lexemic variables, r being a surface-syntactic relation [SSyntRel].

Definition 9.4 – syntactic phraseme (Mel'čuk 1987)[8]

> A syntactic phraseme is a phraseologized complex linguistic sign that consists of at least two minimal syntactic trees such that its signifier is non-segmental, that is, contains prosody or a bound lexemic variable, e.g., L(X), symbolizing the operation of duplication of the phraseme's actant X.

---

[8] In Mel'čuk 2012-2015: vol. 3, Ch. 16 syntactic phrasemes are called *constructional phrasemes*.

The signifier of a lexemic phraseme is segmental: a lexemic phraseme contains only lexemes of the language, but no special prosody and no bound lexemic variables; the opposition "lexemic phrasemes ~ syntactic phrasemes" is obvious.

All syntactic phrasemes are idioms—i.e., they are non-compositional. Stock examples of syntactic idioms are, for instance (like lexemic idioms, syntactic idioms are also indicated by top corners ⌐ ¬):

SLON ⌐(*byl*) KAK SLON¬
lit. 'elephant (was) as elephant' = 'It is/was quite an ordinary elephant'.

NOS ⌐(*byl*) KAK NOS¬
lit. 'nose (was) as nose' = 'It is/was quite an ordinary nose'.

VOJNA ⌐(*byla*) KAK VOJNA¬
lit. 'war (was) as war' = 'It is/was quite an ordinary war'.

The semantic and deep-syntactic rules for this syntactic idiom are as follows:

'quite' ○–1→○–1→○ 'X' ⟺ X ○←I—○—II→○ ⌐QUITE ORDINARY¬ ⟺
        'ordinary'   BYT' 'be'

X ○←subjectival–○–copular-completive→○–comparative-conjunctional→○ L$_X$
     BYT' 'be'   KAK 'as'

☛ X stands for «a lexical unit that expresses the meaning 'X'»; L$_X$ means «a duplicate of the lexical unit X».

The meaning 'quite ordinary' is expressed by a whole SSynt-subtree and cannot be expressed piecemeal.

Here are a few more examples of Russian syntactic idioms (expressions in square brackets are actants of the idiom; the lexemic variable L$_X$ stands for a duplicate of X).

[Y$_{DAT}$] ⌐I [X$_{NOM}$] BYT' NE V $_{X-ACC}$¬
lit. 'To.Y even X is not as X' = 'X is even unable to enjoy Y'
Maše$_Y$ *i prazdnik*$_X$ *ne v prazdnik*$_X$
lit. 'To.Masha even feast [is] not as feast'. = 'Masha even cannot enjoy the feast'.

⌐[X$_{NOM}$ U Y$_{GEN}$ DO-Z-*itsja*]¬
lit. 'X at Y will.up-Z' = 'X will suffer at the hands of Y because of X's excessive Z-ing'
Maša$_X$ *u nego*$_Y$ *dokritikuetsja*$_Z$!
lit. ≈ 'Masha at him will.suffer.from.criticizing'. = 'Masha will suffer at his hands for criticizing too much'.

⌈[X$_{NOM}$ U Y$_{GEN}$ Z$_{FUT}$]⌉
lit. 'X at Y will.Z' = 'X will suffer at the hands of Y because of X's Z-ing'
    Ty$_X$ u nego$_Y$ poguljaeš'$_Z$!
    lit. 'You at him will.go.for.a.walk!' = 'Don't even try to go for a walk on him!'

[X$_{INF}$] ⌈TAK L$_{X\text{-}INF}$⌉!
lit. 'X so X!' = 'If we must X, let's do X intensely!'
    Spat'$_X$ tak spat'$_X$!
    lit. 'Sleep so sleep!' = 'If I must sleep now, let me do it with gusto!'

[X$_{NOM}$] ⌈EST' L$_{X\text{-}NOM}$⌉
lit. 'X is X'
    Ženščina$_X$ est' ženščina$_X$
    lit. 'A woman is a woman'. = 'The person in question is a woman and behaves as a typical woman does'. (On reduplicative syntactic idioms in several languages, see Wierzbicka 1991: 391–452.)

Auxiliary, or structural, lexemes that appear in syntactic phrasemes are the copula BYT' 'be', the particles I ≈ 'also' and NE 'no', the indefinite adverb (unaccented) TĂK 'so', the relative pronoun ČTO 'what', prepositions and conjunctions.

The expressions ⌈KAKOGO ČĚRTA?⌉, ⌈NA KOJ ČĚRT?⌉, ⌈ČĚRTA S DVA!⌉ etc. should not be called syntactic phrasemes: they are quite regular lexemic idioms, since they include at least two specific lexemes. Neither are syntactic phrasemes the expressions of the type ČĚRT ZNAET[, *čto*/*gde*/*začem*...], discussed above, in 9.2.1.1.2: these are normal non-standard lexemic collocations, since the verb ZNAT' 'know' retains in them its full meaning. And, finally, the expressions of the form *Čěrt s X-om* lit. 'Devil with X' = 'I don't care at all about X' are not phrasemes at all: they contain one of the lexemes of the vocable ČĚRT—an interjection (a clausative) with its governed complement [*s* 'with' N$_{INSTR}$] (such as **Doloj** *terroristov!* 'Down with terrorists' or ***T'fu*** *na tebja!* 'I spit on you!').

A reworked English version of Mel'čuk 2012d.

Part IV: **Word Order – Linearizing Dependency Structures**

10 Word order in Russian

10.1 The problem stated
10.2 The input and output for linearization rules
10.3 Linearization rules (illustrated with Russian data)
    10.3.1 Three major types of linearization rules
    10.3.2 Linearization rules for Russian
        10.3.2.1 Type I: Syntactic linearization (+ morphologization) rules
        10.3.2.2 Type II: Adjusting linearization rules
        10.3.2.3 Type III: Filtering linearization rules
10.4 Conclusions
Appendix: Communicative differences that determine the six word arrangements in Motto 2

To Jura Apresjan, with admiration.
1. *Ju. Apresjan – kak mnogo v ètom zvuke!*
lit. 'Ju. Apresjan, how much there is in this sound!'
2. 'I love you!' in Russian:
Ja tebja ljublju!
Ja ljublju tebja!
Ljublju ja tebja!
Ljublju tebja ja!
Tebja ja ljublju!
Tebja ljublju ja!

10.1 The problem stated

The words in a sentence necessarily follow each other in a particular order—speech has a strictly linear character, which is physiologically determined. But meaning expressed by a sentence is not organized linearly. Therefore, at some point in the process of sentence production, the Speaker (or a model of the Speaker's language—for instance, an automatic device) has to **linearize** the lexical units that are selected to construct the sentence. Therefore, linearization of a structure built from lexical units is actually **the** operation to examine while discussing word order. At least since Tesnière 1959: 17–20, linearization is recognized as one of the main linguistic operations, cross-linguistically universal: the expression of non-linear meaning by linear sentences.

The description of linearization in language **L** can be broken down into three steps:

1) Define the **input and output representations**, i.e., specify the two sets of structures: the structures of the first set (these are non-linear, i.e. arborescent,

input structures) must be processed by linearization rules, and the structures of the other set (these are linear output structures) must be arrived at.
2) Define the **relevant linguistic factors**, i.e., determine the types of linguistic phenomena of **L** that affect linearization and have to be accounted for in linearization rules.
3) Define the **set of linearization rules** such that any valid input is properly matched by them to some valid output.

The present chapter addresses only two of these steps: it describes (partially) the input and output representations needed for linearization in Russian and sketches out the major classes of linearization rules, their form and their interaction. An in-depth discussion of linguistic factors affecting word order in Russian is left out, although such factors are used in the rules proposed.

Due to its importance in the process of speech and its universality, linearization occupies a place of honor in linguistics. One certainly cannot complain about the scarcity of publications dealing with word order in the most diverse languages; if anything, they are too numerous to be reviewed.

Apology No. 1 Since even a short list of selected references would be impossibly long, I abstain from giving any general references concerning word order as such or word order in Russian in particular.

In spite of this overwhelming wealth of texts on word order, there are, to the best of my knowledge, no word order studies in which the input syntactic structure is defined in terms of dependencies and the linearization rules are formally presented. Only two exceptions are known to me:

– My own sketch of linearization rules for Russian (Mel'čuk 1965 and 1974: 260–290; see also the book Mel'čuk & Pertsov 1987, which presents local rules for word order in English), based on a dependency syntactic structure and the **step-by-step strategy** of linearization (see Section 10.3). Published more than 50 years ago, this proposal produced no echo in general or Russian linguistics; therefore, it seems permissible to take these rules up, using newer knowledge and newer skills, and present them in an improved form. That is what will be done in this chapter.[1]
– The work of Kim Gerdes, Sylvain Kahane and their collaborators on word order (Gerdes & Kahane 2001, 2004, 2007; Gerdes 2002; El-Kassas & Kahane

---

[1] Within the framework of a pilot project on the automatic rephrasing the claim sentences in patents, S. Mille and L. Wanner (2008) developed some linearization rules for English (drawing upon the rules implemented by F. Lareau in the scope of the MARQUIS Project).

2004; Bohnet 2007). It is also based on a dependency syntactic structure but uses an essentially different technique of linearization: the strategy of **predefined full-sentence pattern** (Subsection 10.3.1, p. 343), also known as "topological model." Therefore, I cannot build directly on their findings and will limit myself to this brief remark.

NB There is, however, a special case that needs to be mentioned. The last decade has seen a series of computer programs that are "trained," by using statistical methods, to linearize dependency structures: the program is given a set of dependency structures, each with a corresponding sentence, and by trial and error method it finds the patterns of correspondences—the typical linearization for a given configuration of depencencies. A good example of such a program for Chinese (a language where linear order is almost a unique means for expressing the dependencies in the sentence) is found in He et al. 2009. But these programs, no matter how well they carry out the linearization, do not give us the linguistic rules describing word order, while it is exactly such rules that interest us here. See also Filippova & Strube 2009.

The description of word order in this chapter proceeds in the Meaning-to-Text, i.e. **linguistic synthesis**, direction and appears as a set of rules for linearization of a starting non-linearized dependency structure.

Although the dominant philosophy in linguistics has been and still is to analyze texts and represent the results of the analysis, word order has always been studied by linguists in the synthesis direction.

Russian is chosen as the object language of the description not only because it is my mother tongue, but also because it is ideal as the target of a word order study. There are at least two reasons for this.

On the one hand, word order in Russian is extremely flexible in two senses.

- First, almost every permutation of words—or, more precisely, of "saturated" phrases—in a Russian sentence is grammatical, see Motto 2. However, these different word arrangements are not optional or arbitrary: they are controlled by subtle, but strict communicative conditions, so that actually they are not anarchically free, but well regulated (see Appendix, p. 366).
- Second, the syntactic structure of a Russian sentence is highly independent of its communicative structure: in Russian almost any element of the clause can play almost any communicative role. Because of that Russian is rich in variegated and complex word order phenomena. In sharp contrast, English requires, for instance, that, as a general rule, the Synt-Theme of a sentence be expressed by the Synt-Subject; to achieve this, English often has recourse to the passive:

Rus. ***Stat'ju***$_\text{ACC-Synt-T, DirO}$ *popravil Leo*$_\text{NOM}$ lit. 'The article$_\text{ACC}$ has.corrected Leo$_\text{NOM}$'.
vs. Eng. ***The paper***$_\text{Synt-T, Subj}$ *was corrected by Leo.*

On the other hand, word order in Russian is well studied (although rather informally), enabling the researcher to draw data from many sources; unfortunately, only few main references can be mentioned here: Sirotinina 1965, Kovtunova 1976, 1980, and Yokoyama 1985, 1986: 171*ff.*

Apology No. 2 The description of linearization rules, no matter how sketchy and approximate, requires a huge number of concepts and formalisms from surface syntax. To explain all these would amount to writing a thick volume. Therefore, I use in this chapter what I need without warning; I ask my readers for forgiveness and hope that examples and minimal explanations will prove sufficient.

Apology No. 3 Linearization is intimately linked to prosodization of the deep-morphological structure obtained: the word groups that undergo linearization must feature an appropriate prosody; in fact they do not exist without this prosody (see Yokoyama 1985, Gerdes & Kahane 2007 and Zimmerling 2008 for well-justified insistence on this relationship). However, in order to simplify my task, I omit everything concerning prosodization.

> *The main goal of the present chapter is to outline, in a very rough way, the linearization rules for a natural language, stated on the basis of Russian data, but in a relatively general form.*

In Russian, as well as in other languages where inflectional morphology is used along word order to express syntactic dependencies, linearization rules are intimately related to morphologization. (In syntax, **morphologization** is an operation that computes the **syntactic, or surface, grammemes**, or syntactically-conditioned morphological values, such as the grammatical case of the noun, the person and number of the finite verb, the gender, number and the case of the adjective—based on the information contained in the surface-syntactic structure.) Although I am interested in linearization only, it is convenient to include in the picture relevant data on morphologization, since this does not require special effort.

Formally speaking, linearization rules proper should be kept distinct from morphologization rules. However, two factors interfere with such an approach, a theoretical and a practical one.

- Theoretically, in many cases morphologization is inextricably intertwined with linearization: thus, languages (for instance, Arabic) often have different type of agreement of the Main Verb with the SyntSubj depending on the linear position of the latter with respect to the verb. This is quite understandable:

morphological markers constitute, together with linear arrangement of words, **one** complex signifier for a surface-syntactic relation in a given context.
— Practically, mixed linearization + morphologization rules are more familiar for a not-too-formally minded reader and, therefore, easier to grasp. In what follows word order rules are presented in this mixed form, together with the indication of corresponding syntactic grammemes they impose on the members of a SSynt-dependency relation.

The remainder of the chapter is naturally divided into three sections: Section 10.2 describes the input and output for word order rules, while Section 10.3 presents a fragment of surface-syntactic rules—linearization + morphologization rules—for Russian; Section 10.4 contains some conclusions.

10.2 The input to and output of linearization rules

Two linguistic entities are generally assumed to be the main sources of information that determines the linear arrangement of words in sentences: the syntactic structure [SyntS] and the syntactic-communicative structure [Synt-CommS] of the sentence to be produced. Here, the two are considered to be the necessary and sufficient input to the linearization rules. They will be introduced in very general terms as postulates, without detailed explanations or justifications.

The rules for linearization of the lexemes of sentence S, or linearization rules, have as their input two structures of S's surface-syntactic representation: the surface-syntactic structure [SSyntS] and the surface-syntactic-communicative structure [SSynt-CommS]. They produce, as their output, the deep-morphological structure [DMorphS] of S, which, generally speaking, must be supplied with deep-morphological prosodic structure [DMorph-ProsS]; however, in conformity with the convention adopted (see **Apology No. 3** above), the latter is not considered.

The input to linearization rules

Definition 10.1 – the surface-syntactic structure of a sentence

|| The SSyntS of sentence S is an unordered dependency tree where each lexeme of S is represented by a node (of which this lexeme is the label) and whose branches represent language-specific surface-syntactic relations [SSyntRels], which link these lexemes; the names of the SSyntRels are labels on the branches.

(On SSyntRels, see Chapter 2.)

Definition 10.2 – the surface-syntactic-communicative structure of a sentence

> The SSynt-CommS of sentence *S* is a division of *S*'s SSyntS into communicative areas (= subtrees) such that each has its Comm-dominant node specified and is labeled with a value of a Synt-Comm-opposition.

(On Comm-Dominance and Comm-oppositions, see Mel'čuk 2001.)

The SSynt-CommS (as well as the DSynt-CommS) uses fewer communicative oppositions than the semantic-communicative structure [Sem-CommS], namely— the following five:

1. SSynt-Thematicity
2. SSynt-Givenness (not relevant for linearization in article languages)
3. SSynt-Focalization (not relevant for linearization in languages with lexical expression of Focalization)
4. SSynt-Perspective
5. SSynt-Emphasis

The remaining Sem-Comm-oppositions—those of Assertivity, Unitariness and Locutionality—are fully transcoded at the syntactic level into lexical units, grammemes and syntactic constructions; they, so to speak, disappear from the scene. Moreover, the **Synt**-Comm-oppositions are different with respect to their **Sem**-Comm-sources (Mel'čuk 2001: 64-66). In this chapter, only the Synt-Comm-opposition of Thematicity is taken into account. This reduces, of course, the power of the proposed description, which misses several word arrangements that are possible in Russian for the expression of Focalization, Perspective, and Emphasis; yet this simplifies the presentation a great deal.

Output of linearization (+ morphologization) rules

Definition 10.3 – the deep-morphological structure of a sentence

> The **DMorphS** of sentence *S* is the linear sequence of all *S*'s lexemes supplied with all relevant grammemes.

As a basic example, let me consider Russian sentence (1), its SSyntS with the superposed partial SSynt-CommS in Figure 10.1, and its DMorphS in Figure 10.2.

(1) *Metodom gravitacionnoj razvedki byla otkryta neft' v Kazaxstane*
lit. 'By.method of.gravitational exploration was discovered oil in Kazakhstan'. ≈
'The method of gravitational exploration led to the discovery of oil in Kazakhstan'.

This sentence comes from an elementary physics manual, where the preceding paragraph is dedicated to the characterization of gravitational technology in geophysical explorations; the sentence corresponds to the underlying question *What else about gravitational exploration?* In the diagram, **T**_SSynt_ stands for the surface-syntactic Theme (= topic), and **R**_SSynt_, for the surface-syntactic Rheme (= comment).

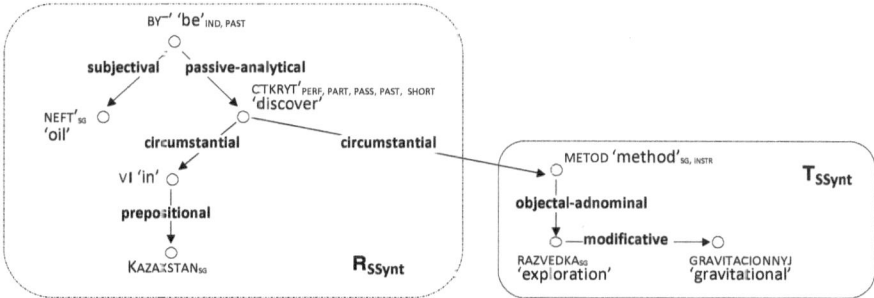

Figure 10.1 Partial surface-syntactic representation of sentence (1)

The corresponding deep-morphological structure of sentence (1) is shown in Figure 10.2:

METOD$_{SG, INSTR}$ GRAVITACIONNYJ$_{SG, FEM, GEN}$ RAZVEDKA$_{SG, GEN}$
BYT'$_{PAST, SG, FEM}$ OTKRYT'$_{PERF, PART, PASS, PAST, SHORT, SG, FEM}$
NEFT'$_{SG, NOM}$ V KAZAXSTAN$_{SG, LOC}$

Figure 10.2 Deep-morphological structure of sentence (1)

Word order rules—that is, linearization + morphologization rules, schematically represented in (2),—are responsible for producing the linear arrangement of fully inflected lexemes, that is, the DMorphS of the sentence (without prosodic organization, as stated above). Linearization and morphologization rules constitute a submodule of the SSynt-module of the Meaning-Text model (this module also includes rules for Prosodization, omitted here):

(2) $\left\{ \begin{array}{c} \text{SSyntS} \\ \text{SSynt-CommS} \end{array} \right\} \Leftarrow \left\{ \begin{array}{c} \text{Morphologization} \\ \text{Linearization} \end{array} \right\}$ rules $\Rightarrow$ DMorphS

SSyntS and SSynt-CommS, which essentially determine linearization, are represented as input structures for word order rules.

There are, to be sure, other factors that affect linearization:

- Semantic factors: e.g., semantically different circumstantials may be positioned differently; the position of a circumstantial can depend on its semantic scope; etc.
- Rhetorical factors: e.g., a particular arrangement may be highly colloquial or poetic.
- Stylistic factors: e.g., longer word groups preferably follow shorter ones in postposition to the common governor; some languages encourage the word order that produces chaining dependencies rather than embedded ones:

$a{\to}b{\to}c{\to}d$ is preferred over $a\ \ c{\to}d\ \ b$

- Lexical factors: e.g., the adverb *enough* is exceptional in that it is placed after its adjectival governor; pronouns may be positioned with respect to their governor differently than the corresponding non-pronominal lexemes.
- The clarity of the text produced: e.g., a particular word arrangement can be chosen to avoid ambiguity or else to reduce the number of embedded dependencies.

Word order rules must in principle account for all these factors.

10.3 Linearization rules (illustrated with Russian data)

Linearization rules are presented here in general form, but are illustrated with specific Russian examples. The rules given are sufficient to carry out the transition from the SSyntS of Figure 10.1 to the DMorphS of Figure 10.2: they describe word order in the Russian sentence (1).

Apology No. 4 My characterization of word order in Russian concerns but a small fragment of the possible arrangements in written texts of a scientific-official nature—that is, the most neutral word arrangements, whatever that means.

10.3.1 Three major types of linearization rules

The general architecture of the linearization submodule of the SSynt-module of a Meaning-Text linguistic model depends on the researcher's choice of the overall linearization strategy; there are two basic possibilities.

The first linearization strategy is top-down: it uses a **Predefined Full-Sentence Pattern** [PFSP]. First, the researcher constructs a general pattern (or patterns) of whole sentences in language **L**—a sequence of hierarchically embedded slots, which represent linear positions of sentence elements. The sentence word-order pattern is divided into fields, each of which is filled by boxes, themselves divided into fields, and so on; a box is provided for a particular element of the sentence. Under the PFSP-strategy, linearization rules compute for each element of the starting dependency structure its place in the PFSP and the box it opens, with appropriate fields for its dependents. In the course of this operation, all other word-order factors, such as communicative structure, special lexical properties, etc. are equally taken into account. Such an approach seems to be especially good for German—see the above-mentioned work by Gerdes & Kahane and Bohnet.

The second linearization strategy is **step-by-step**, or bottom-up: linearization rules compute, by stages, the mutual disposition of the elements of the starting dependency SSyntS; they first build (≈ linearize) simple phrases, then unite them in complete phrases, then build clauses out of complete phrases, and, finally, unite clauses to produce the sentence. Here, again, two approaches are possible: a one-stage or multiple-stage approach.

– One-stage approach would be to formulate the rules for each SSynt-relation, supplying every rule with all the conditions necessary for a correct placement of its dependent member. For instance, a rule for the direct object [DirO] would say that a DirO follows the governing verb and precedes its other Synt-actants, if 1) this DirO is not part of the Synt-Theme, 2) it is not part of Synt-Rheme-focus, 3) it is not a pronoun, 4) it is not a very long ("heavy") word group followed by another shorter group, which is another Synt-actant of the same verb, etc.

– The other approach, which I favor, stipulates that all such conditions are formulated separately (from purely syntactic rules) in very general terms: Synt-communicative linearization rules, Pronoun linearization rules, Word-group heaviness-based linearization rules, etc. This is possible to do since these rules are logically and linguistically (at least in Russian!) independent from syntactic rules. Such a presentation allows for a more compact and better organized set of rules, avoiding unnecessary repetitions of the same conditions in several rules. But the price to be paid for this advantage is to separate the linearization process into stages: first you do approximate linearization, according only to general syntactic rules; then you reshuffle the preliminary arrangement thus obtained, pressing into service all additional rules; finally, you check the result for inadmissible sequences and reshuffle once more to avoid these. It is this—step-by-step—strategy that is adopted here.

> ❗ *Let me emphasize, lest confusion arises, that I do not mean here a real procedure separated into three consecutive stages. I am talking only about a **way of representing** things that better agrees with a linguist's intuition. All the constraints introduced in different blocks of rules below can in fact be applied together. This problem, however, exceeds the limits of the present chapter.*

In accordance with the above strategy, linearization—that is, roughly speaking, the transition from an SSyntS to the corresponding DMorphS—is performed using three major types of rules:

I. **Syntactic** linearization + morphologization rules, which are responsible for Stage 1. Based exclusively on the SSyntS, they produce the preliminary "frame" of the linearized sentence —an arrangement of wordforms that may be good if it weren't for the impact of other factors, see immediately below. This is the most neutral, unmarked word order, or the default case.

II. **Adjusting** linearization rules, which, at Stage 2, apply to the output of syntactic linearization rules—that is, to the preliminary frame of the sentence— and alter it to reflect all additional factors: requirements of the SSynt-Comm-structure, obligatory extractions (WH-words) and inversions (**Is he** busy?), pronominalization (especially cliticization, where it exists), reshuffling of word groups according to their heaviness, etc. These rules lead to serious modifications of the neutral word order.

III. **Filtering** linearization rules work at Stage 3 and apply to the output of Stage 2. They constitute, in fact, a list of undesirable word sequences. Each "bad" sequence is assigned a "fine," which is an empirically established negative number; the sentence-to-be receives a cumulative fine and is processed— that is, undergoes possible permutations of word groups—in such a way as to reduce to zero or at least to minimize the overall fine "slapped on" the arrangement under consideration.

It is assumed that these three major types of linearization rules are sufficient for the description of word order in many (if not most) languages.[2]

Although the types of linearization rules are presented in sequence, one type after another, this is only a manner of speaking: these rules are not externally

---

[2] Some languages feature additional factors perturbing neutral word order. However, I think that any such additional difficulty can be treated as a new subtype of Adjusting rules. Thus, for instance, languages featuring **second-position** clitics, such as Serbian/Croatian, need special rules to position the clitic cluster—after all other elements of the sentence are linearly arranged (Milićević 2009). These rules are part of our Type 2 rules.

ordered—that is, there are no special indications concerning the order of their application. Each rule is formulated in such a way that it effectively applies only when this application produces a correct result. The linguistic model can try to apply them in any order, in parallel and/or repeatedly; I assume that this will never lead to incorrect linearization.

10.3.2 Linearization rules for Russian

Some illustrative linearization rules for Russian are presented below in three subsections corresponding to the three above types.

10.3.2.1 Type I: Syntactic linearization + morphologization rules
Syntactic linearization rules fall into five groups: I.A – I.E.

I.A: SSyntS ⇔ DMorphS correspondences

These rules do two things:

- they establish the preliminary, or the most unmarked, arrangement of word-forms in the sentence, according only to the SSyntRels that link them;
- they produce the necessary syntactic grammemes, i.e., they carry out morphologization.

A rule stating an SSyntS ⇔ DMorphS correspondence has the general form

$$L_{1\xi}\text{-}r\rightarrow L_{2\zeta} \Leftrightarrow 1)\ L_{1\xi'} +(...+) L_{2\zeta'}\ |\ C_1$$
$$\Leftrightarrow 2)\ L_{2\zeta'} +(...+) L_{1\xi'}\ |\ C_2$$

Here:
- The left-hand side contains a minimal SSynt-subtree with the SSyntRel **r**; L_1 and L_2 are lexemes, ξ and ζ being the sets of appropriate semantic (= deep) grammemes.
- The right-hand side contains one or two possible strings made up of the same lexemes, with ξ' and ζ' being ξ and ζ with addition of all necessary syntactic grammemes.
- "+" indicates the linear sequence, while "..." shows a possible gap between lexemes L_1 and L_2, that is, the presence of other lexemes separating L_1 and L_2 in the sentence; parentheses mark optionality.
- C is the set of conditions that are essentially constraints on L_1 and L_2; among other things, they describe the context in which the particular subrule applies

and thus determine different linear arrangements of L_1 and L_2. C also may include additional indications concerning the placement of L_1 and L_2 into particular positions in **linearization patterns**; see below.

Such a rule specifies the linear—and, when needed, morphological—expression of the SSyntRel **r**. (Stating that the dependent element of **r** can be positioned both after or before its governor also constitutes an indication of the linear expression of **r**.)

From the viewpoint of linearization, there are three types of SSyntRels: **local, semi-local**, and **non-local**.

1) **Local SSyntRels** control linearization within rigidly organized **minimal word groups** [MWGs], such as a nominal minimal word group [MWG_N], an adjectival minimal word group [MWG_A], etc.; see MWG linearizing patterns below, pp. 355–356. An MWG represents a sequence of wordforms with a completely fixed order (within the framework adopted in this chapter—neutral academic-register texts—no element of a MWG can change position).

A local SSyntRel **r** has the following three properties:

- **r** specifies the only possible linear disposition for its members. (Within MWGs there are no options for different word arrangements, and neither the Synt-CommS nor other factors have significant impact here.)

- **r** is unique, or not repeatable: **r**'s governor can have only one immediate **r**-dependent.

    An important exception
    The **modificative** SSyntRel allows for several parallel adjectival modifiers depending on the same governor, as in the phrase

    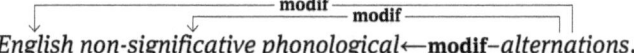
    *English non-significative phonological←**modif**–alternations*.

    Such adjectives have to be ordered in a unique position in the linearizing pattern according to special rules such as those discussed in Vendler 1968 and Iordanskaja 2000.[3]

- The mutual disposition of all local co-dependents is fixed: they are assigned pre-established positions in the corresponding linearizing pattern.

---

[3] Rules that are referred to here as special do not fall into any of major rule types introduced in the present chapter; they are really special. Special rules are organized in blocks; such a block is attached to one or several "normal" rules.

Local SSyntRels include cross-linguistically the **prepositional** SSyntRel (PREP→N), the **determinative** SSyntRel (DET←N), the **quantitative** SSyntRel (NUM←N), the **modificative** SSyntRel (A←N), the **coordinative-conjunctional** SSyntRel (CONJ$_{(coord)}$→Ψ), etc. One important local SSyntRel is **coordinative** (Y→X): its dependent always follows the governor, as in

John–**coord**→*and Mary* or
attacked,–**coord**→*advanced*–**coord**→*and captured*, etc.

An MWG corresponds to a "very compact" phrase, which practically cannot be torn apart by any factors and is moved around as a whole.

2) **Semi-local SSyntRels** control linearization of MWGs within complete word groups [CWGs], that is, linearly ordered word sequences that roughly correspond to complete clause elements: the subject CWG, the direct-object CWG, the duration-circumstantial CWG, etc. Within CWGs, word order is more flexible than within MWGs, yet it still remains rather constrained: the co-dependent MWGs can be arranged differently among themselves, but all of them are allowed to occupy only one position with respect to their governor: all of them either precede the governor or all of them follow it. Note that:

- the dependencies between MWGs are, of course, those between their heads;
- semi-local SSyntRels also control the linear disposition of clauses within the sentence.

The properties of a semi-local SSyntRel **r** are:

- **r** also specifies just one linear disposition for its members.
- **r** is also near-unique: **r**'s governor can have, in most cases, only one immediate **r**-dependent.
- The mutual disposition of semi-local co-dependents is not fixed, and special rules are needed to compute the arrangement into one CWG of several MWGs that "semi-locally" depend in parallel on the same governor.

Semi-local SSyntRels include several **adnominal-completive/attributive** (N$_1$→N$_{2\text{-GEN}}$) SSyntRels, the **relative** and **descriptive-relative** SSyntRels (N→CLAUSE$_{rel}$), the **circumstantial** SSyntRel (N→PREP), etc.; see Chapter 2, Section 2.5, Nos. 48–56, Nos. 73–74 and No. 83. (Note that with a verb the **circumstantial** SSyntRel is non-local, see immediately below.)

A CWG represents a phrase that traditionally corresponds to an element of the clause: the subject, the direct object, a circumstantial, etc. Such a phrase is also relatively compact, but less so than a phrase corresponding to an MWG: it can be cut in two parts that exchange their linear positions following the requirements of the Synt-CommS.

3) **Non-local**, or **global**, SSyntRels, responsible for the mutual arrangement of CWGs within a clause, link the top node of the clause SSyntS, that is, the finite verb (in Standard Average European type languages), to its immediate dependents (i.e., actants and circumstantials). A non-local SSyntRel **r** is opposed to local and semi-local SSyntRels:

- A non-local **r** normally does not specify a unique order of its members. Even in languages with a rather rigid word order various inversions and/or permutations are possible between the Main Verb and the SyntSubj, the Main Verb and the DirO, etc.
- A non-local **r** is not necessarily unique: **r**'s governor can have several immediate **r**-dependents (several oblique objects or several circumstantials).
- The mutual disposition of non-local dependents is not fixed; it depends on numerous, very complex and sometimes even contradictory factors.

An SSyntRel can simultaneously be of more than one type as a function of its governor. Thus, all **circumstantial** SSyntRels are non-local if their governor is a finite verb, but semi-local otherwise.

In accordance with the three types of SSyntRels, four further groups of linearization rules are needed:

I.B—for local SSyntRels (= for the construction of MWGs by means of linearizing patterns);
I.C—for semi-local SSyntRels (= for the construction of CWGs);
I.D—for non-local SSyntRels (= for the construction of clauses);
I.E—for arranging the clauses within the sentence.

Remark

The moment seems ripe for a short theoretical digression: **dependency** vs. **constituency** (see, e.g., Mel'čuk 2009a: 89–95). As is well known, in modern linguistic literature the dependency description of the syntactic structure of a sentence is opposed to the phrase-structure, or constituent, description. The dependency approach categorically rejects constituents as a **means for representing the syntactic structure** of a sentence. This is due to the fact that a syntactic structure written in terms of constituents combines—or, if we do not mince our words, confuses—two very different relations between lexical units: **syntactic dependency** (governor ~ dependent) and **linear order** (precedes ~ follows), a distinction that cannot be ignored following Tesnière 1959. Linear order is the most important means that natural languages use for expressing (= marking) syntactic relations. In languages without inflectional morphology (like Chinese or Vietnamese) it is the only means (plus, of course, prosody); in languages like English it is the central and most exploited means; and even in Russian, where on many occasions the word order seems irrelevant (cf. Motto 2), it still plays a leading role: for a number of constructions it remains the basic marker of syntactic relations. Therefore, constituency logically cannot be used as a formal means to represent the syntactic structure of a sentence. It's not necessary to have long discussions about two ways of representing syntactic structure: constituency in syntactic structures is a logical absurdity. However, **constituents**, or **phrases**, do of course exist in language and have to be modeled in any linguistic description. But their legitimate place is 1) in the DMorphS of the sentence, where they appear as prosodic phrases, and 2) in the linearization rules, where they serve as building blocks in the process of the linearization of the SSyntS. These two types of constituents do not stand in one-to-one correspondence with each other. The above-mentioned MWGs and CWGs are nothing but constituents of the second kind; each represents a projection of the corresponding subtree. These constituents change during linearization: they can be united, cut in two, have their parts moved around separately, etc., and finally they emerge as phonological phrases, or constituents of the first kind (which can be different from projections of the corresponding subtrees). And now, back to linearization rules.

Since the SyntS of sentence (1) contains 7 different SSyntRels, at least 7 SSyntrules for Russian must be presented. The following symbols and conventions are used:

- **AGREE**$_{V(N)}$ ("Verb-Noun agreement operator") is a set of rules that describe agreement of the Main Verb [MV] with the noun that in most cases is its subject; **AGREE**$_{A(N)}$ ("Adjective-Noun agreement operator") is a set of rules that describe agreement of a modifying adjective with the modified noun.
- $_{(«\Sigma»)}$ is a feature of the syntactics of a lexeme; e.g.: the feature $_{(«subj\text{-}gen»)}$ marks in the lexicon a verb that requires its subject to be in the genitive, like XVATAT' 'be sufficient': *Gorjučego*$_{GEN}$ *xvatit* 'Fuel will.be.sufficient'.
- "L ⇒ No.r(MWG$_X$)" means that the lexeme L must go into the n-th position in the corresponding linearizing pattern (these patterns for MWGs are described below, **I.B**, p. 356).
- "g(L)" stands for the syntactic word group of the lexeme L (the "projection" of the full subtree having L as the top node); units of g(L) type do not appear at any representation level: they are used only in syntactic rules.
- In order to save space, the syntactics of the elements in the left-hand side of the rule are not repeated in the right-hand side. (The syntactics, which are elements of the lexicon, actually constitute the context of the application of the rule and could have been indicated in the Condition part.)
- Shading indicates the context—that is, the elements that are not affected by the rule, but whose presence is necessary for the rule to apply.

The SSyntS ⇔ DMorphS rules for Russian presented below are approximate; their conditions are simply hinted at. In fact, each of these rules is just a placeholder for a serious study of all contextual factors.

Actantial dependency rules

SSynt-rule I.A-1: SSynt-subject [a non-local SSyntRel]

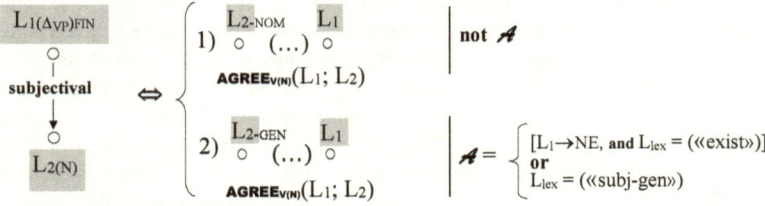

☞ Δ_{VP} stands for 'verbal standard subtree' (on standard subtrees, see Mel'čuk & Pertsov 1987: 485ff): a chain of subsequently dependent lexemes of the form $L_{1\text{-FIN}} \rightarrow L_{i\text{-}1} \rightarrow L_{i\text{-}2} \rightarrow ... \rightarrow L_{lex}$, where possible L_i have to be specified by a list (for instance, *could*$_{L1\text{-FIN}}$ *have*$_{Li\text{-}1}$ *begun*$_{Li\text{-}2}$ *to*$_{Li\text{-}3}$ *separate*$_{Llex}$; L_{lex} is the lexical verb whose combinatorial properties concerning the subject percolate to the top node of this standard subtree. This is what was called the **verbal nucleus** by S. Kahane (Kahane 1997 and 2001, Kahane & Mel'čuk 1999). Δ_{VP} is used only in the formulation of syntactic rules and does not appear as such in the SSyntS of a sentence. The notation "$L_{(\Delta VP)}$" means 'lexeme L that is the syntactic head of Δ_{VP}.'

Comments

1. Rule **I.A**-1 does not uniquely specify the linear position of the subject with respect to the MV, since, generally speaking, both positions are possible; the appropriate one must be established by rules **I.DI**, see below, p. 358.
2. The condition 𝓐 is intended to capture the use of the genitive on the subject with some verbs marked "$_{(\text{«exist»})}$" that are negated and with other verbs that always have the subject in the genitive and are marked "$_{(\text{«subj-gen»})}$".
3. Rule **I.A**-1 ignores the following two frequent cases of the implementation of the subjectival SSyntRel:
   - Agreement of the copula MV. If the subject is ÈTO 'this', the copula agrees with its complement (rather than with the subject): *Èto byl*$_{\text{MASC}}$ *Ivan*$_{(\text{masc})}$ 'This was Ivan'. ~ *Èto byla*$_{\text{FEM}}$ *Marija*$_{(\text{fem})}$ 'This was Mary'.
   - Agreement of the MV if the subject is an infinitive or a subordinate ČTO-clause; the MV must be in the 3SG, NEU: *Učit'sja*$_{\text{INF}}$ *mne* **nravilos'**$_{\text{SG.NEU}}$ lit. 'To.study me pleased'; *Čto Ivan otsutstvuet,* **udivljaet**$_{\text{3.SG}}$ *vsex* lit. 'That Ivan is.absent amazes everyone'.

   Such cases require additional SSynt-rules.

Examples (the glosses here and below are literal)

mogla$_{L1}$ *byt' obnaružena* **neft'**$_{L2}$ 'could be discovered oil'
~ **neft'**$_{L2}$ *mogla*$_{L1}$ *byt' obnaružena*   'oil could be discovered'

10.3 Linearization rules (illustrated with Russian data) — 351

    ***My*_{L2}, *kak uže jasno*, *možem*_{L1} *sčitat'*...**   'We, as [it is] already clear, can believe ...'
~ ***Možem*_{L1} *li my*_{L2} *sčitat'*...**   'Can whether we believe ...'

    Nikakix novyx ***ulik*_{L2} *ne pojavilos'*_{L1 = L_{lex} = («exist»)}**
    'Of.no new evidence not appeared'.

    Ètoj ***nefti*_{L2}.GEN *xvatilo*_{L1= L_{lex} = («subj-gen»)}**   'Of.this oil was.sufficient'.
~ *Ètoj* ***nefti*_{L2}.GEN *ne xvatilo*_{L1}**   'Of.this oil was.not sufficient'.

SSynt-rule **I.A**-2: Complement of a preposition [a local SSyntRel]

Notation: "L_(II[case])" means 'DSyntA II of L is expressed by the grammatical case **case**.'

$$L_{1(Prep,\ II[case])} \;\longrightarrow\; prepositional \;\longrightarrow\; L_{2(N)} \quad\Leftrightarrow\quad L_1 \underset{\circ}{+} (\ldots +) \underset{\circ}{L_2\text{-CASE}} \quad \text{and } L_1 \Rightarrow \text{No.3(MWG}_N), \; L_2 \Rightarrow \text{No.10(MWG}_N)$$

Examples

    ***v*_{L1} *našem rasporjaženii*_{L2}; *vo*_{L1} *vsex nix*_{L2}; *dlja*_{L1} *togo*_{L2}, *čtoby*...;**
    at our   disposal'   in all   them for this   that...
    ni ***s*_{L1} *kem*_{L2}**
    no with body = 'with nobody'

Comments

There are several complications in the use of Russian prepositions, not covered by this rule; for instance:

- Some prepositions can or must be postposed to the nouns they introduce: *Boga radi'* 'God's sake!', *rassudku vopreki* 'to.reason in.spite', *mesjac tomu nazad/spustja* 'month ago/back'. For such prepositions/postpositions, another SSynt-rule of type **I.A** is needed.
- A preposition is always postposed in approximate-quantitative and approximate-ordinal constructions: *dnja na tri* 'days for three' = 'for approximately three days', *den' na tretij* 'day on third' = 'approximately on the third day'. This linear arrangement is ensured by the SSynt-rules for **approximate-quantitative** and **approximate-ordinal** SSyntRels (Chapter 2, Section 2.5, Nos. 67 and 69, p. 87*f*).
- Some special choices have to be made: the choice of the vocalic form of a consonantal primary preposition (*vo* instead of *v*, *ko* instead of *k*, etc.); the

choice of the **n**-form of a substitute pronoun governed by the preposition (*nix* instead of *ix*, *nemu* instead of *emu*, etc.); the choice of the split form of such negative pronouns as NIKTO, NIČTO, etc. (*s nikem ⇒ *ni s kem*, etc.). These and similar complications are taken care of by deep-morphological rules that realize the corresponding radical morpheme of the preposition, of the substitute pronoun and of the negative pronoun.

<u>Adjunctial dependency rules</u>

SSynt-rule **I.A**-3: Instrumental circumstantial
[a non-local SSyntRel, if L_1 is a finite verb; semi-local otherwise]

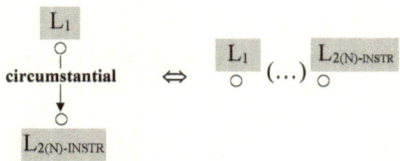

Examples

> ***Polučajut*** $_{L1}$ sok sledujuščim ***obrazom*** $_{L2}$
> '[«They»] obtain juice in.following way'.

> *Tekst byl* ***sostavlen*** $_{L1}$ *izvestnym* ***metodom*** $_{L2}$
> 'Text was constructed by.known method'.

SSynt-rule **I.A**-4: Adjectival modifier
[a local SSyntRel, if L_2 is a single ADJ; semi-local otherwise][4]

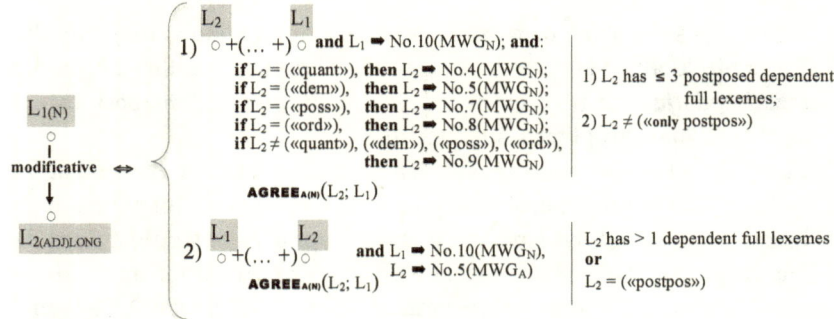

---

[4] The position of a complex adjectival modifier depends in fact on many subtle and closely intertwined factors; see Sannikov 1963.

L_2 can be only a long-form adjective—i.e., an adjective bearing the grammeme LONG.[5]

Examples

važnaja$_{L2}$ *ocenka*$_{L1}$; *èta*$_{L2'}$ *isključitel'no*   *važnaja*$_{L2''}$ *ocenka*$_{L1}$;
important estimate   this   extraordinarily important estimate

važnaja$_{L2}$ *dlja vsex nas ocenka*$_{L1}$ ≡ *ocenka*$_{L1}$, *važnaja*$_{L2}$ *dlja vsex nas*, ...
important for   all   us   estimate

ocenka$_{L1}$, *važnaja*$_{L2}$ *dlja vsex nas v svjazi   s   processom*
estimate important for   all   us in connection with process
formirovanija novyx grupp,   ...
of.formation of.new groups

polnyj$_{L2}$ *tragizma   period*$_{L1}$ ≡ *period*$_{L1}$, *polnyj*$_{L2}$ *tragizma*
full   of.tragic.events period

papa$_{L1}$ *rimskij*$_{L2}$ = («only postpos») 'Pope Roman' ~ *rimskij$_{L2}$ *papa*$_{L1}$

SSynt-rule **I.A-5**: Adnominal complement/attribute [a semi-local SSyntRel]

$$L_{1(N)} \atop \text{o} \atop |\atop \text{...-adnominal-...}\atop \downarrow \atop \text{o} \atop L_{2(N)} \quad \Leftrightarrow \quad L_1 \quad L_{2\text{-GEN}} \atop \text{o} + (... +) \text{o}$$

This rule processes several adnominal SSyntRels: see Chapter 2, Nos. 48–53, p. 77*ff*.

Examples

razdača$_{L1}$ *bogatstv*$_{L2}$; *važnost'*$_{L1}$ *ètoj   zadači*$_{L2}$; *granicy*$_{L1}$
distribution of.wealth   importance of.this problem   borders
evropejskix stran$_{L2}$
of.European countries

---

5 The Russian adjective has the inflectional category of PREDICATIVITY: as a general rule, a qualitative adjective has a long, or attributive, form and a short, or predicative, form: e.g., the adjective VYSOKIJ 'high' has a set of 48 long forms (*vysokij, vysokogo, ..., vysokaja, vysokoj, ..., vysokoe, ..., vysokie, ...*) and a set of 4 short forms (*vysok, vysoka, vysoko, vysoki*). An adjective in the long form is used in all syntactic roles possible for an adjective—as a modifier and as the attributive complement of a copula verb; an adjective in the short form is used in Contemporary Russian only as the attributive complement of a copula verb.

židkost′ $_{L1}$ ***golubogo   cveta*** $_{L2}$; ***kollekcii*** $_{L1}$ ***ètogo millionera*** $_{L2}$
liquid   of.light-blue color   collections of.this millionaire

SSynt-rule I.A-6: Prepositional/Adverbial circumstantial of Time or Location
[a non-local SSyntRel, if L_1 is a finite verb; a semi-local SSyntRel otherwise]

$$\begin{array}{c} L_1 \\ \circ \\ \text{circumstantial} \\ \downarrow \\ \circ \\ L_{2(\Delta\text{PREP})/\text{ADV}} \end{array} \quad \Leftrightarrow \quad \begin{array}{cc} L_1 & L_2 \\ \circ & (\ldots) \circ \end{array} \quad \Big| \quad L_2 = (\text{«temporal»/«local»})$$

Examples

polučennoe $_{L1}$ ***v*** $_{L2}$ ***Moskve*** *pis′mo*; ***V*** $_{L2-1}$ ***1989 godu*** *Ivan* ***rabotal*** $_{L1}$ ***v*** $_{L2-2}$ ***Moskve***.
received   in Moscow letter   in 1989 year Ivan worked   in   Moscow
Včera $_{L2}$ ***šël*** $_{L1}$ *dožd′* 'Yesterday was.falling rain'.

Ancillary dependency rules

SSynt-rule I.A-7: The analytical form of the passive [a non-local SSyntRel]

$$\begin{array}{c} L_3 \quad\quad L_{1(\text{BYT}')} \\ \circ \leftarrow \cdots - \text{subjectival} - \circ \\ \quad\quad\quad \text{passive-analytical} \downarrow \\ \quad\quad\quad \circ \\ \quad\quad\quad L_2 \end{array} \quad \Leftrightarrow \quad \left\{ \begin{array}{c} L_3 \quad\quad L_1 \quad\quad L_2\text{-PASS.PART, PERF, PAST, SHORT} \\ \circ \leftarrow \cdots - \text{subjectival} - \circ \quad (\ldots) \circ \\ \textbf{AGREE}_{A(N)}(L_2; L_3) \end{array} \right.$$

Comment

The **passive-analitycal** SSyntRel is introduced as a special SSyntRel because both members of the **passive-analytical** SSyntRel are fixed. In contrast, for instance, to the **copular-completive** SSyntRel, it admits as its governor only the verb BYT′ 'be', but no other copula; and as its dependent, only a short perfective passive past participle:

(3) a. **Passive-analytical SSyntRel**
  byl $_{L1}$ *polučen* $_{L2}$ 'was received' ~ **okazalsja polučen* 'proved received',
                                       *stal polučen 'became received',
                                       *kažetsja polučen 'seems received'

b. **Copular-completive SSyntRel**
 byl cernym 'was valuable' ~ *okazalsja cennym* 'proved valuable',
          stal cennym 'became valuable',
         kažetsja cennym 'seems valuable'
 byl vračom 'was a.doctor' ~ *okazalsja vračom* 'proved a doctor',
          stal vračom 'became a.doctor',
         kažetsja vračom 'seems a.doctor'

Examples

Ocenka$_{L3}$ *byla*$_{L1}$ by nemedlenno **polučena**$_{L2}$. | *Ivan*$_{L3}$ $Ø^{BYT'}{}_{L1}$ **uvolen**$_{L2}$.
Estimate would have.been immediately obtained Ivan is fired
Buduči$_{L1}$ **prinjaty**$_{L2}$, èti *studenty*$_{L3}$ *polučajut stipendiju*.
Being admitted these students receive scholarship

I.B: linearization patterns for MWGs

The linearization of the dependents of a local SSyntRel is done by means of linearizing patterns [LPs], describing the word order in MWGs. An LP is a rigid sequence of positions, each of which admits one syntactic element L; these positions correspond to local SSyntRels.

Exception Position No. 9 for the **modificative** SSyntRel admits several co-dependent adjectives; their mutual order is established by special rules attached to this position. (For a sketch of such rules, based on semantic and syntactic properties of Russian adjectives modifying the same noun, see Iordanskaja 2000 and 2003.)

If an L that is meant to occupy a position in a linearizing pattern LP1 has its own dependents, L is not put into the MWG under construction: another linearizing pattern LP2 ensures the construction of L's own MWG, which, at the next stage, is united with the MWG specified by LP1. Thus, if a NUM(eral), which is supposed to go into Position No. 6 of a nominal MWG [MWG$_N$], is a compound NUM (e.g., *tri milliona šest'sot sorok sem' tysjač dvesti tridcat' odin* '3 647 231'), then a numeral MWG [MWG$_{NUM}$] is first built, and it is embedded into MWG$_N$ as a whole at the stage of uniting MWGs into CWGs (see example below).

There are several MWG linearizing patterns for a language; they correspond to MWGs of different word classes: for instance, MWG$_N$, MWG$_{ADJ}$, MWG$_{NUM}$, MWG$_{ADV}$, MWG$_{V-INF}$ and MWG$_{V-FIN}$ in Russian. A SSyntS ⇔ DMorphS rule indicates for both members of the SSyntRel described the positions in the corresponding pattern. Not all of the positions in a linearizing pattern have to be filled: the pattern represents a maximal possible string associated with an MWG, i.e., a potential minimal phrase.

Two linearizing patterns of MWGs are cited here for Russian: MWG_N and MWG_A.

Pattern of a minimal nominal word group
(in a broad sense: including the prepositional groups)

1	2	3	4	5	6	7	8	9	10	11
CONJ$_{(coord)}$	PARTICLE	PREP	A$_{(quant)}$	A$_{(dem)}$	NUM	A$_{(poss)}$	A$_{(ord)}$	A	N	Ψ$_{invar}$
no 'but'	*liš'* 'only'	*dlja* 'for'	*vsex* 'all'	*ètix* 'these'	*semi* 'seven'	*našix* 'our'	*vtoryx* 'second'	*važnyx* 'important'	*čisel* 'numbers'	l$_i$

☞ Ψ$_{invar}$ stands for any non-Russian expression: a technical symbol, a number, a formula, a foreign-lan-guage word/phrase, etc.

Pattern of a minimal adjectival word group

1	2	3	4	5
CONJ$_{(coord)}$	PARTICLE	ADJ$_{(pron)}$	ADV	ADJ
ili 'or'	*tol'ko* 'only'	*takoj* 'such'	*očen'* 'very'	*tëmnyj* 'dark'

For better readability, both patterns are simplified. Thus, the position for the negative particle NE 'not' is not shown (NE can precede practically any element of a pattern, except for the first one), nor is the position for a contrastive particle such as ŽE ≈ 'as for' (*Natural'nye čisla že rassmatrivat'sja ne mogut* ≈ 'As for natural numbers, they cannot be considered'.) or UŽ ≈ 'very' (*ne takoj už tëmnyj* 'not so very dark'). Such particles are "squeezed" into MWGs by the corresponding linearization rules of type **I.A**.

The MWG$_N$ admits the embedding of the MWG$_{ADJ}$ and MWG$_{NUM}$: for instance, MWG$_{NUM}$ *pjat' tysjač šest'sot sorok sem'* 'five thousand six.hundred forty seven' and MWG$_A$ *ne nastol'ko už važnyx* ≈ 'not so very important' can be introduced as wholes into positions Nos. 6 and 9 of an MWG$_N$, respectively. In a similar way, practically all positions admit embedding of coordinated WGs: for instance, *ètix ili tex* 'these or those' must be embedded in position No. 5, or *vtoroj, četvërtyj i desjatyj* '[the] second, fourth and tenth', in position No. 8, etc. This type of embedding is carried out by rules of **I.C** group.

Let me emphasize the following interesting fact: what is known in the Russian grammatical tradition as a "complex verbal predicate" (auxiliary BYT'$_{FUT}$ 'be' + the infinitive; auxiliary BYT' + passive past participle; copula BYT' 'be' + attributive noun/adjective; etc.) does not correspond to an MWG or even to a CWG. From the viewpoint of linearization, the complements/attributives of auxiliary and copular verbs behave like any other SSynt-actants: they are non-local dependents and are ordered at the stage of linearizing CWGs inside the clause.

For the SSyntS of Figure 10.1, Rules **I.B** (= linearizing patterns) produce six MWGs, listed in alphabetical order:

1. *byla*; 2. *gravitacionnoj razvedki*; 3. *metodom*; 4. *neft'*; 5. *otkryta*; 6. *v Kazaxstane*.

I.C: Arranging word groups within a complete word group

I.CI: Positioning of the dependent word group Ψ with respect to the governing word group Ξ

In these rules, the following writing convention is used: the dependency shown between two word groups [WGs] represents the dependency between their top nodes. The WGs that form a **complete** WG can be themselves both minimal and complete.

- r = coord:
  I.CI-1. $\Xi\text{-coord}\to\Psi$ $\quad\Leftrightarrow\quad$ $\Xi + (...+) \Psi$

- r ≠ coord:
  I.CI-2. $WG_N' \to WG_N$ * $\quad\Leftrightarrow\quad$ $WG_N' + (...+) WG_N$
  I.CI-3. $WG_N \to WG_{ADJ}$ ** $\quad\Leftrightarrow\quad$ 1) $WG_N + (...+) WG_{ADJ}$
  $\quad\Leftrightarrow\quad$ 2) $WG_{ADJ} \Rightarrow$ No. 9 (WG_N)
  I.CI-4. $WG_N \to WG_{INF}$ $\quad\Leftrightarrow\quad$ $WG_N + (...+) WG_{INF}$
  I.CI-5. $WG_N \to WG_{ADV}$ $\quad\Leftrightarrow\quad$ $WG_N + (...+) WG_{ADV}$
  I.CI-6. $WG_A \to WG_N$ $\quad\Leftrightarrow\quad$ $WG_{ADJ} + (...+) WG_N$
  I.CI-7. $WG_{ADJ} \to WG_{ADV}$ ** $\quad\Leftrightarrow\quad$ 1) $WG_{ADJ} + (...+) WG_{ADV}$
  $\quad\Leftrightarrow\quad$ 2) $WG_{ADV} + (...+) WG_{ADJ}$

  * **Exception:** NP of the form *takogo roda* 'of such a type' can be anteposed—by another rule of I.CI type not given here.
  ** The choice between the two subrules is made according to Conditions not specified here.

Examples

I.CI-2 [*maksimal'naja verojatnost'*]$_{WG-N'}$ [*vsex podobnyx raspredelenij*]$_{WG-N}$
maximal probability of.all such distributions

I.CI-3(1) [*ili veličina*]$_{WG-N}$ [*ne polnost'ju opredelënnaja*]$_{WG-ADJ}$
'or [a] magnitude not fully determined'

I.CI-3(2) [*ili* [*ne polnost'ju opredelënnaja*]$_{WG-ADJ}$ *veličina*]$_{WG-N}$
'or [a] not fully determined magnitude'

I.CI-4   [*ego udivitel'naja sposobnost'*]$_{\text{WG-N}}$ [*spat'*]$_{\text{WG-Inf}}$
'his amazing ability to.sleep'

I.CI-5   [*vse simvoly*]$_{\text{WG-N}}$ [*sleva*]$_{\text{WG-ADV}}$
'all symbols on.the.left'

I.CI-6   [*polnost'ju lišeny*]$_{\text{WG-ADJ}}$ [*neobxodimyx sredstv*]$_{\text{WG-N}}$
'[are] fully deprived of.necessary means'

I.CI-7(1)   [*vstrečajuščiesja*]$_{\text{WG-ADJ}}$ [*liš' izredka*]$_{\text{WG-ADV}}$
'encountered only rarely'

I.CI-7(2)   [*liš' izredka*]$_{\text{WG-ADV}}$ [*vstrečajuščiesja*]$_{\text{WG-ADJ}}$
'only rarely encountered'

I.CII: Mutual arrangement of codependent word groups Ψ

either Ξ + WG$_{\text{agent}}$ + WG$_{\text{adnom.compl}}$ + WG$_{\text{adnom.compl}}$ + WG$_{\text{Circ, non-manner}}$ + WG$_{\text{obl-obj}}$ + WG$_{\text{obl-obj}}$
+ WG$_{\text{Circ-manner}}$

or Ξ + WG$_{\text{Circ-manner}}$ + WG$_{\text{adnom.compl}}$ + WG$_{\text{agent}}$ + WG$_{\text{Circ-manner}}$

In our test sentence, Rule **I.CII** unites MWGs 2 and 3, which gives us five CWGs:

| 1. *byla*, 2. *metodom gravitacionnoj razvedki*, 3. *neft'*, 4. *otkryta*, 5. *v Kazaxstane* |

I.D: Arranging complete word groups within a clause

The arrangements proposed here are valid only without taking into account the SSynt-Comm-structure and other "perturbing" factors—that is, for the word order traditionally called neutral. The neutral word order obtains in cases where the SSyntS and the SSynt-CommS are not in conflict (the subject is (in) the SSynt-Theme, there is no Focalization, etc.). Rules **I.D** perform three operations:

I.DI   linearizing the elements of the verbal nucleus (referred to below as $\widetilde{\text{MV}}$, MV being the lexical verb, the last element of the nucleus)
I.DII   linearizing the actants with respect to $\widetilde{\text{MV}}$
I.DIII   linearizing the circumstantials with respect to $\widetilde{\text{MV}}$ and the actants

I.DI: Building the verbal nucleus

Within an $\widetilde{\text{MV}}$, with a neutral word order, a dependent follows its governor: $\Xi \rightarrow \Psi \Leftrightarrow \Xi + \Psi$. In our case, Rule **I.D**I gives [*byla* + *otkryta*]$_{\widetilde{\text{MV}}}$.

I.D II: Linearizing the actants

The SSynt-actants are numbered: A_1 is the subject; A_2 is the DirO, the strongest OblO with an intransitive verb or the complement of a copula; A_3 is the IndirO or an OblO; and A_4 is another OblO. Different arrangements of the actants A_i with respect to the MV are mostly determined by the nature of the MV: the MV is a copula, the MV is an existence verb, or the MV is neither. An additional case is a non-finite verb that governs actants.

Governor = MV

MV = («copula»)

	additional conditions	arrangement	examples
1.	$A_1 \neq V_{INF}$ or $A_2 = V_{INF}$	$A_1 +...+ \widetilde{MV} +...+ A_2$	$Saša_{A_1}$ —$_{MV}$ $naš$ $vožd'_{A_2}$ 'Sasha [is] our leader'. $Saša_{A_1}$ byl_{MV} $našim$ $voždëm_{A_2}$ 'Sasha was our leader'. $Saša_{A_1}$ $(budet)$ $dovolen_{A_2}$ 'Sasha (will be) happy'. Ves_{A_1} $okazalsja$ $ravnym_{A_2}$ $1,008$ kg 'The.weight turned.out.to.be equal [to] 1.008 kg'. $Postupit'_{A_1}$ tak $označalo$ by $poterjat'_{A_2}$ $kontrol'$ nad $situaciej$ 'To.act like.this would.mean lose control over the.situation'.
2.	$A_1 = V_{INF}/CONJ_{(\text{«subord»})}$ and $A_2 = ADJ/ADV_{(\text{«pred-inf»})}$	$A_2(A_2) +...+ \widetilde{MV} +... + A_2 +...+ A_1$ ["$A_2(A_2)$" means 'The second actant of the second actant']	$\emptyset_{BYT'\text{-}MV}$ $neobxodimo/Budet_{MV}$ $neobxodimo_{A_2}$ $učest'_{A_1}$ vse $faktory$ '[It is/will.be] necessary to.account.for.all factors'. $Vam_{A_2(A_2)}$ $budet_{MV}$ $nado_{A_2}$ $učest'_{A_1}$ vse $faktory$ 'To.you [it] will.be necessary to.account.for.all factors'. $Osobenno$ $važno_{A_2}$ $čto_{A_1}$ $učteny$ vse $faktory$ '[It is] especially important that [are] accounted.for all factors'.

MV = («exist»)

	additional conditions	arrangement	examples
3.	—	$A_2 +...+ \widetilde{MV} +...+ A_1$	$Šël$ $sil'nyj$ $dožd'$ '[It was.falling [a] heavy rain'. Na $doroge$ $pojavilsja$ $vsadnik$ 'On road [it] appeared [a] rider'. U nas $imeetsja$ $veličina_{A_1}$ $c > 0$, $zavisjaščaja$ ot P At us, [there] is magnitude $c > 0$, depending on P'.

MV ≠ («copula»), ≠ («exist»)

	additional conditions	arrangement	examples
4.	MV ≠ («pred-inf»), ≠ («aux»)	$A_1 -...+ \widetilde{MV} +...+ A_2 +...+ A_3 +...+ A_4 +...+ A_5 +...+ A_6$	$Ètot$ $operator$ $sopostavljaet$ $čislo$ A $čislu$ B s $pomoščju$ $funckcii$ f 'This operator associates number A to number B by using function f'.
5.	MV = («pred-inf»)	$A_2 -...+ A_1$	Mne_{A_2} $xočetsja$ $žit'_{A_1}$ lit. 'To.me is.desire to.live'.

6.	MV = («aux»), A_2 = PART, PASS and $A_2(A_2)$ = —	$\widetilde{MV}$ +...+ A_1 [A_2(MV) is inside $\widetilde{MV}$]	V Avstralii byl predotvraščën$_{A2}$ krupnyj terakt$_{A1}$ 'In Australia, was thwarted [a] serious act.of.terror'.

Governor ≠ MV

Governor = (V)$_{\text{NON-FIN}}$

	additional conditions	arrangement	examples
7.	—	Governor + A_2 + A_3 + A_4	svesti$_G$ zadaču$_{A2}$ k$_{A3}$ predyduščej 'to.reduce [the] problem to.the previos [one]'; svjazyvavšix$_G$ indejcev$_{A2}$ s$_{A3}$ francuzskimi perekupščikami 'that.were.connecting Indians with French merchants'

The application of Rule **I.D**II-4 results in the following arrangement of actantial groups:

[byla + otkryta]$_{\widetilde{MV}}$ + neft'$_{A1}$

I.DIII: Linearizing the circumstantials

Linear disposition of circumstantials is controlled mainly by their semantic nature. Thus, Time and Location circumstantials tend to occupy the left edge of the clause, while Direction circumstantials mostly follow the $\widetilde{MV}$; manner circumstantials behave differently—as a function of their own structure: a simple adverb precedes the $\widetilde{MV}$, while a prepositional phrase follows $\widetilde{MV}$. Therefore, the rules for circumstantial linearization need a list of all circumstantial types (in the rules below only 8 such types are given). The semantic type of a Circum is identified:

- Either by the subordinating SSyntRel, such as **durative-circumstantial** (Rus. *Ivan spal*–[*dva*]–**dur-circum**→*časa* lit. 'Ivan slept two hours'.), Chapter 2, Section 2.5, No. 34, p. 72.
- Or by the lexicographic features, semantic and syntactic; for instance, "L = Circum$_{\text{time}}$" means that L is an L$_{(\text{«temporal»})}$, as, e.g., LATE, WEEK, AFTER, etc.
- Or by the full (= semantic) case of L; thus, "L = Circum$_{\text{INSTR}}$" means that L is an L$_{(N)\text{INSTR}}$, etc.

In the table below, numbers attached to an arrangement indicate mutual order of two codependents; negative numbers specify the distance from the governor to the left, and positive numbers specify the distance from it to the right. The number after the indication "leftmost" is to be understood as follows: 0—the very first element of a clause (a conjunction), +1—the second element (a non-conjunctional connector: $\angle_0$, *sledovatel'no*$_{+1}$, ... 'And, consequently, ...'), etc. Thus, Rules **I.D**III-4/5 stipulate that Circum$_{manner}$ is positioned closer to the verb than the Circum$_{quant}$.

	the type of Circum	arrangement	examples
1.	Circum$_{time}$	left of [MV, A$_i$], −3	*V 1932 godu on pereexal v Moskvu* 'In year 1932 he moved to Moscow'.
2.	Circum$_{loc}$	left of [MV, A$_i$], −3	*V Moskve on rabotal nad knigoj* 'In Moscow he worked on [the] book'.
3.	Circum$_{dur}$	right of [MV, A$_i$], +2	*On rabotal nad knigoj vsju nedelju* 'He worked on [the] book [the] whole week'.
4.	Circum$_{manner}$	left of G, −1 and right of A$_1$	*On mog by tščatel'no proverit'*$_{MV}$ *zamk.* 'He could.have carefully checked [the] locks'.
5.	Circum$_{quant}$	left of G, −2 and right of A$_1$	*On tri raza tščatel'no proveril zamki* 'He three times carefully checked [the] locks'.
6.	Circum$_{way}$, Circum$_{instr}$, Circum$_{comit}$	right of [MV, A$_i$], +1	*On pereskočil čerez lužu odnim pryžkom* 'He jumped over [the] puddle in.one leap'. *On poexal v Moskvu s dvumja druz'jami* 'He went to Moscow with two friends'.
7.	Circum$_{parenth}$	left of MV	*Kak izvestno, on poexal v Moskvu s dvumja druz'jami* 'As [is] known, he went to Moscow with two friends'. ~ *On, kak izvestno, poexal v Moskvu s dvumja druz'jami* 'He, as [is] known, went to Moscow with two friends'.
8.	Circum$_{connect}$	leftmost, +1	*Sledovatel'no, my dokazali naše predpoloženie* 'Therefore, we have.proven our assumption'.

According to Rules **I.D**III-2 and **I.D**III-6, the locative circumstantial *v Kazaxstane* and the instrumental circumstantial *metodom gravitacionnoj razvedki* are positioned as follows:

[*V + Kazaxstane*]$_{C-loc}$ + [*byla + otkryta*]$_{\overline{MV}}$ + [*neft'*]$_{A1}$ + [*metodom gravitacionnoj razvedki*]$_{C-instr}$

I.E: Arranging clauses within a sentence
[for more details, see Iordanskaja & Mel'čuk 2015]

The linear position of a subordinate clause inside the sentence depends on the type of the clause (that is, on the SSyntRel that subordinates its top node) and on the conjunction that introduces it, being its top node.

☛ TN stands for the top node of a clause; "clause(L)*" means 'the clause headed by L minus the clause headed by TN'.

I.E-1.   L–subject→TN   ⟺ 1) clause(TN) + clause(L)* | L = (V)
                              ⟺ 2) clause(L)* + clause(TN) | L = (A/ADV)
I.E-2.   L–object→TN   ⟺   clause(L)* + clause(TN)
I.E-3.   L–circum→TN   ⟺ 1) clause(TN) + clause(L)* | TN = ESLI, KOGDA
                              ⟺ 2) clause(L)* + clause(TN) | TN = ČTOBY
I.E-4.   L–relative→TN ⟺ L + clause(TN) | clause(TN) becomes part
                                                                  of CWG(L)

The linear arrangements indicated here are valid only for neutral word order and may be changed by communicative and other factors.

Examples

I.E-1(1)   *Čto*$_{TN}$ *on ušël, nikogo ne udivilo*$_L$ 'That he left nobody not astonished'.
I.E-1(2)   *Bylo očevidno*$_L$, *čto*$_{TN}$ *on ušël*   '[It] was obvious that he left'.
I.E-2   *Ja znaju*$_L$, *čto*$_{TN}$ *on ušël*   'I know that he left'.
I.E-3(1)   *Esli*$_{TN}$ *on pridët, ja ujdu*$_L$ 'If he comes I will.leave'.
I.E-3(2)   *On pridët*$_L$, *čtoby*$_{TN}$ *ja mog ujti*   'He will.come that I could leave'.
I.E-4   *professor*$_L$, *k kotoromu ja prišël*$_{TN}$ 'professor to whom I came'

The output sentence (1) consists of just one clause, so that Rules **I.E** do not apply.

10.3.2.2 Type II: Adjusting linearization rules

Adjusting rules account for special linear arrangements determined by such factors as Synt-Comm-organization, WH-words, pronouns and similar phenomena; these rules can be thought of as transformations defined over established preliminary arrangements.

> ☞ The number associated in a rule with a word group manipulated by the rule characterizes the mutual arrangement of elements claiming the same position. Thus, in Rule **II.1**-2, number +3 associated with the group Ψ means that Ψ may be preceded only by the elements with numbers 0 (conjunctions), +1 (WH-words), and +2 (Comm-Specifiers); these numbers are associated with conjunctions and WH-words in the corresponding rules for their positioning.

II.1.   Expressing Synt-Comm-organization

II.1-1. If Ψ ⊆ **Rheme** in a declarative clause, then Ψ must be rightmost in the clause.

II.1-2. If Ψ ⊆ **Theme** in a declarative clause, then Ψ must be leftmost in the clause, that is, Ψ: +3.

The presentation of rules **II.1** is approximate: other Synt-Comm-rules are needed that ensure the expression of **Focalization** and **Emphasis**; all Synt-Comm-rules must also take care of the corresponding prosody, etc. (Eight linear-prosodic transformations of Russian presented in Zimmerling 2008: 560 correspond to our Type **II.1** rules.)

II.2. Extractions

WG($\Xi_{(wh)}$) stands for a word group consisting of a WH-word (a relative or interrogative pronoun) and the string of its successive governors—up to, but with the exclusion of, the MV. This is what is called *nominal nucleus* in Kahane 1997 and 2001.

WG($\Xi_{(wh)}$) must be second leftmost in the clause—it can be preceded only by a conjunction; WG($\Xi_{(wh)}$): +1.

*i ja prišël k kotoromu 'and I came to which' ⇒
i [k kotoromu]$_{WG(\Xi_{(wh)})}$ ja prišël 'and [to which] I came'

II.3. Nominal pronouns

V + A$_{2(N, pronominal)}$ ⇒ A$_{2(N, pronominal)}$ + V

Èto udivilo$_V$ vsex issledovatelej$_{A_2}$ ⇒ Èto **vsex**$_{A2(N, pron)}$ udivilo$_V$
'This astonished all researchers'.   'This all [= everybody] astonished'.

Maša možet ljubit'$_V$ Ivana$_{A_2}$ ⇒ Maša možet **ego**$_{A_2}$ ljubit'$_V$
'Masha may love   Ivan'.   'Masha may him love'.

II.4. Interrogative inversion

A$_1$ + MV ⇒ MV + A$_1$ | in a general question

Since in our test example the CWG$_1$ [= Circum$_{instr}$] expresses the SSynt-**T**, everything else belonging to the Synt-**R**, SSynt-Comm-Rules **II.1**-1 and **II.1**-2 give the prefinal arrangement (4):

(4) Prefinal arrangement:

[metodom gravitacionnoj razvedki]$_{C\text{-instr}}$ + [v + Kazaxstane]$_{C\text{-loc}}$ + [byla + otkryta]$_{MV}$ + [neft']$_{A_1}$

10.3.2.3 Type III: Filtering linearization rules

These rules identify bad word sequences in the sentence under construction and slap on them numerical "fines." Then a special mechanism carries out permutations of CWGs in order to minimize the cumulative fine of the sentence. Such permutations should not be applied to the elements that belong to the SSynt-Theme and the Rhematic Focus.

Table 10.1 Filtering linearization rules
Notation: $l(X)$ stands for 'length of the word group X in terms of the number of stressed wordforms.'

	situation to avoid	"fine"	examples
1.	**Relative heaviness of adjacent CWGs**[6]		
	$CWG_1 + CWG_2 \mid CWG_2 \not\subset$ **Rheme**: $l(CWG_1) - l(CWG_2) > 0$ and ≤ 3	−2	?*On peredal [knigu v krasnom pereplëte]$_{CWG1}$ Ivanu $_{CWG2}$* 'He passed [the book in a red binding] to.Ivan'.
	>3 and ≤ 6	−6	??*On peredal [ètu tolstuju knigu v krasnom pereplëte i obe tetradi]$_{CWG1}$ Ivanu$_{CWG2}$* 'He passed [this thick book in a red binding and both notebooks] to.Ivan'.
	> 6	−15	???*On peredal [ètu tolstuju knigu v krasnom pereplëte i obe tetradi, kotorye byli najdeny našimi sotrudnikami,]$_{CWG1}$ Ivanu$_{CWG2}$* 'He passed [this thick book in a red binding and both notebooks that were found by.our collaborators] to.Ivan'.
2.	**Unbalanced distribution of CWGs around MV**		
	On one side of MṼ there are ≥ 2 CWGs **and** on the other side there is none	−10	??*[V Moskve]$_{SSynt\sim T,\ CWG1}$ [sem'ja Ivana]$_{CWG2}$ živët$_{MV}$* 'In Moscow Ivan's family lives'. ??*Budet$_{MV}$ [možno]$_{CWG1}$ [svesti]$_{CWG2}$ [priznaki fonem]$_{CWG3}$ [k dvoičnym]$_{CWG4}$* '[It] will.be possible to.reduce features of.phonemes to binary [ones]'.
3.	**Misplacement of a non-manner circumstantial**		
	MṼ + $C_{non\text{-}manner}$ + A_1	−3	??*Ètu knigu$_{A2}$ pročël$_{MV}$ v$_C$ 2005 godu Ivan$_{A1}$* 'This book read in year 2005 Ivan'.
4.	$C_{non\text{-}manner}$ + MṼ ǀ C ≠ a SSynt-**Specifier**[7]	−2	?*Kolumbom v$_C$ 1492 godu byla$_{MV}$ otkryta Amerika* 'By.Columbus in year 1942 was discovered America'.
5.	**Misplacement of the agent of a passive verb**		
	$A_2 + A_1$ + MVPASS	−3	??*Kolumbom Amerika byla otkryta v 1492 godu posle dolgogo plavanija* 'By.Columbus America was discovered in year 1942 after [a] long sea.voyage'.

---

[6] On the role of relative heaviness of word groups to be linearized (and other interesting factors), see Abeillé & Godard 2000.

[7] A Comm-Specifier is a part of a Sem-CommS/Synt-CommS that is outside of its Communicative Core (= Rheme + Theme) and semantically bears on this core, specifying some details about it; Comm-Specifiers are divided in Comm-circumstantials, Comm-characterizers and Comm-connectors (Mel'čuk 2001: 96–100).

Another bad arrangement is typical of article languages: thus, in French (Abeillé & Godard 2000) a phraseologized complement that has no determiner cannot be separated from its verb by another complement:

(5) a. *Cela donne à Marie **faim**
    lit. 'This gives to Mary hunger'. ~ Cela donne **faim** à Marie.
   b. Cela donne à Marie une grande faim
    lit. 'This gives to Mary a big hunger'. ~
    Cela donne une grande faim à Marie
    lit. 'This gives a big hunger to Mary'.
   c. Jean donne à Marie une pomme 'John gives to Mary an apple'. ~
    Jean donne une pomme à Marie 'John gives an apple to Mary'.

However, in Russian such a situation is impossible because of the absence of determiners. But being part of a collocation or an idiom may impact the linear position of a clause element.

In our example, the prefinal arrangement in (4) gets the fine of −2 (by Rule III-4: the Circum$_{loc}$ v Kazaxstane is not marked as a **Specifier**: it is part of the SSynt-**R**. To reduce the fine to zero the following permutation can be used (the permuted element is boxed):

$$\text{Circum}_{instr} + \boxed{\text{Circum}_{loc}} + \tilde{\text{MV}} + A_1 \implies \text{Circum}_{instr} + \tilde{\text{MV}} + A_1 + \boxed{\text{Circum}_{loc}}$$

The result is a good linear arrangement:

(6) Metodom gravitacionnoj razvedki byla otkryta neft' v Kazaxstane.

Sentence (6) coincides with our test sentence (1).

10.4 Conclusions

This chapter presents a rough sketch of how linearization (+ morphologization) of the surface-syntactic structure of a sentence can be captured for Russian, a language with extremely flexible word order, within the framework of the Meaning-Text approach. The overview presented here partially defines the input and output representations needed for linearization in general and sketched out the major classes of linearization rules, their form and their interaction. One example Russian sentence has been worked through in some detail, showing how these linearization + morphologization rules function to yield a good linear arrangement of words inside a sentence.

The next step seems to be obvious: to elaborate a more or less exhaustive set of word order rules for Russian. In the process, the researchers must consider and describe systematically prosodic aspects of linearization.

Appendix: Communicative differences that determine the six word arrangements in Motto 2

First, two important remarks.

- Each of the linear arrangements of words in (i) – (vi) can be associated with a particular intonation contour that expresses the communicative organization of the utterance (see Yokoyama 1985, where the importance of the relationship between word order and intonation—especially in Russian—is properly emphasized). These contours are shown here in an approximate way.
- Each of the arrangement of words (i) – (vi) admits several other patterns of prosodization expressing different communicative structures, of which only one is chosen to illustrate my point.

(i) *Ja tebja ljublju*,

uttered with neutral, or level (i.e., unmarked) intonation, is a simple declarative utterance—a logical, non-emotional statement of fact; the whole utterance is Rhematic.

(ii) *Ja ljubljú tebja*

is an emphatic utterance, with strong stress on the verb and uninterrupted falling contour; JA is the Synt-**T**, and the rest, the Synt-**R**.

(iii) *Ljubljú ja tebja*

is also an emphatic utterance, as well with strong stress on the verb and uninterrupted falling contour; the whole utterance is Rhematic and much more colloquial than (ii).

(iv) *Ljubljú tebja ja*

is the same as (iii).

(v) *Tebja* | *jÁ ljublju*

has TY as the Synt-**T**, everything else being the Synt-**R**—with JA as Rhematic Focus (contrasting with another candidate, understood, but not named: 'but not ...!').

(vi) *Tebja ljubiju jÁ* is the same as (v).

Chapter 10 is an expanded and corrected version of Mel'Čuk 2011.

11 Linear ordering of genitive adnominal dependents cosubordinated to a noun in Russian

11.1 The problem stated
11.2 Rules for ordering cosubordinated N_{GEN}s
11.3 Illustrations of N_{GEN} ordering rules
11.4 Ordering of cosubordinated N_{GEN}s vs. ordering of cosubordinated ADJs
   11.4.1 Ordering of cosubordinated ADJs
   11.4.2 Comparison of both orderings: similarities and differences

> To Anna Wierzbicka, a closest friend for 55 years
> *Przyjaźń jest rzeczą diabelnie trudną* 'Friendship is a devilishly difficult thing' (Wierzbicka 1971: 83). Yes, Anna, generally speaking, this is so; but **with you** friendship is the easiest thing!

11.1 The problem stated

This chapter constitutes a natural continuation of Chapter 5 (pp. 205*ff*), where six surface-syntactic relations [SSyntRels] that are necessary for the description of N→N_{GEN} phrases in Russian are proposed: it considers the linear ordering of genitive nouns $N_{1\text{-}GEN}$, $N_{2\text{-}GEN}$, $N_{3\text{-}GEN}$, ... cosubordinated to the same noun N in Russian.

NB In fact what is being ordered are the whole phrases headed by these N_{GEN}s.

Example (1) shows that this order is not free:

(1) a. *glagoly*$_N$ *napravlennogo dviženija*$_{N1\text{-}GEN}$ *soveršennogo vida*$_{N2\text{-}GEN}$ *russkogo*
    verbs   of.directed movement   of.perfective aspect   of.Russian
    jazyka$_{N3\text{-}GEN}$
    language
  b. **glagoly*$_N$ *soveršennogo vida*$_{N2\text{-}GEN}$ *russkogo jazyka*$_{N3\text{-}GEN}$ *napravlennogo*
    dviženija$_{N1\text{-}GEN}$

Therefore, the object of this chapter is, schematically, correspondence (2):

(2) **Surface-syntactic structure**   **Deep-morphological structure**

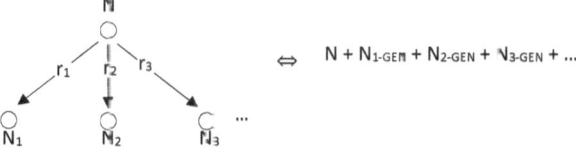

$\Leftrightarrow$ N + $N_{1\text{-}GEN}$ + $N_{2\text{-}GEN}$ + $N_{3\text{-}GEN}$ + ...

https://doi.org/10.1515/9783110694765-012

More specifically, I will present some surface-syntactic [SSynt-]rules that establish the correspondence between a SSynt-subtree and the deep-morphological [DMorph-]string implementing it. The SSynt-subtree under consideration has the following three properties:

(i) It is headed by a noun N on which syntactically depend several nouns N_1, N_2, N_3, ... (each with its own dependents, if any).

(ii) The SSynt-relations r_i that subordinate these N_is to N impose on them the genitive case (in the DMorph-string). These SSynt-relations are six in number (Chapter 5, pp. 226–230):

N—subjectival-adnominal-completive→$N_{GEN-subj}$
priezd—**subj-adnom**→*otca* 'coming of.Father'
stakan—**subj-adnom**→*vody* 'glass of.water'
$N_{GEN-subj}$ expresses N's deep-syntactic [DSynt-]actant **I**.

N—objectival-adnominal-completive→$N_{GEN-obj}$
osvoboždenie—**obj-adnom**→*otca* 'liberation of.Father'
portret—**obj-adnom**→*rebënka* 'portrait of.child'
$N_{GEN-obj}$ expresses N's DSynt-actant **II**.

N—qualificative-adnominal-attributive→$N_{GEN-qual}$
balka—[*nedostatočnoj*]—**qual-adnom**→*dliny* 'beam [of.insufficient] length'
$N_{GEN-qual}$ denotes a predicate whose Sem-actant **1** or **2** is expressed by N ('dlina/ length—1→balka/ beam': *balka dvuxmetrovoj dliny* 'beam of.two.meter length'; 'mečta/dream—2→devuška/girl': *devuška moej mečty* 'girl of.my dream'). In Russian, an $N_{GEN-qual}$ must necessarily have a syntactic dependent, normally an adjective.

N—characterizing-adnominal-attributive→$N_{GEN-charact}$
krik—**charact-adnom**→*boli* 'scream of.pain'
živopis'—**charact-adnom**→*Vozroždenija* 'painting of.Renaissance'
$N_{GEN-charact}$ and N are semantically related not as a predicate and its argument, but by means of an "additional" predicate 'σ', which is not explicitly expressed in the sentence: 'krik, **vyražajuščij**$_{'\sigma'}$ bol''/'scream **expressing**$_{'\sigma'}$ pain' or 'živopis' **vo.vremja**$_{'\sigma'}$ Vozroždenija'/'painting **during**$_{'\sigma'}$ Renaissance'.

N—possessive-adnominal-attributive→$N_{GEN-poss}$
stadion—**poss-adnom**→*universiteta* 'stadium of.University'
$N_{GEN-poss}$ and N are semantically related by means of the predicate 'σ' = 'belong': 'stadion, **prinadležaščij**$_{'\sigma'}$ universitetu/stadium **belonging.to**$_{'\sigma'}$ the University'.

N—metaphorical-adnominal-attributive→N$_{\text{GEN-metaph}}$
lenta—metaph-adnom→*dorogi* 'ribbon of.road'
N$_{\text{GEN-metaph}}$ is the lexeme whose metaphor is N: *lenta*$_\text{N}$ 'ribbon' is the metaphor of *doroga*$_{\text{N}_{\text{GEN-metaph}}}$ 'road'.

(iii) The six SSyntRels in question require the postposition of their dependent N$_{\text{GEN}}$s with respect to the modified N, with one exception: the **qual-adnom** SSyntRel allows the anteposition of its N$_{\text{GEN-qual}}$, if this N$_{\text{GEN-qual}}$ 1) has N as its Sem-actant **1**, 2) does not have itself a depending noun phrase and 3) is lexically marked as allowing for anteposition;[1] for instance:

pojas golubogo cveta 'belt of.light.blue color' ~ *golubogo cveta pojas*

The anteposition of N$_{\text{GEN-qual}}$ is left out of consideration in this chapter.

❗ *The basic order of postposed cosubordinated N$_{\text{GEN}}$s is determined* **syntactically**—*by the above SSyntRels: for each pair of these SSyntRels the mutual order of their dependent N$_{\text{GEN}}$s is indicated. As a result, we obtain a general six-position template (Table 11.1 in Section 11.2 below) that specifies the correct position for each type of N$_{\text{GEN}}$.*

Such a template is possible because of the following essential fact:

> *Generally speaking, a dependent N$_{\text{GEN-i}}$ can occupy different linear positions with respect to its governing N as a function of the SSyntRel r$_i$ in the N—r$_i$→N$_{\text{GEN-i}}$ phrase.*

---

1 The three cases of impossibility of N$_{\text{GEN-qual}}$'s anteposition can be illustrated by the following examples:
1) ***moego razmera** tufli* 'of.my size shoes' ('razmer—**1**→tufli')   vs.
   ****moej mečty** devuška* 'of.my dream girl' ('mečta—**2**→devuška')
2) ***golubogo cveta** lenta* 'of.light.blue color ribbon'   vs.
   *cveta morskoj volny lenta 'of.color of.sea wave ribbon' = 'aquamarine ribbon'; the correct expression: *ler ta **cveta morskoj volny***
3) ***neobyčajnoj krasoty** portret* 'of.extraordinary beauty portrait'   vs.
   *prošedšego vremeni glagol 'of.past tense verb' (VREMJA 'tense' is not lexically marked as allowing for anteposition)

In cases 1) and 2) the anteposition of an N$_{\text{GEN-qual}}$ can be possible under additional communicative and/or syntactic conditions.

Thus:

(3) a. For the meaning 'statue representing Athena and carved by Phidias':
statuja Afiny$_{\text{NGEN}}$ *Fidija*$_{\text{NGEN}}$ 'statue of.Athena of.Phidias' ⟨**statuja Fidija Afiny*⟩;
but for the meaning 'statue representing Phidias and carved by Athena':
statuja Fidija$_{\text{NGEN}}$ *Afiny*$_{\text{NGEN}}$ 'statue of.Phidias of.Athena' ⟨*statuja Afiny Fidija*⟩

b. For the meaning 'poet's soul of this philosopher':
duša poèta$_{\text{NGEN}}$ *ètogo filosofa*$_{\text{NGEN}}$ 'soul of.poet of.this philosopher' ⟨*duša ètogo filosofa poèta*⟩;
but for the meaning 'philosopher's soul of this poet':
duša filosofa$_{\text{NGEN}}$ *ètogo poèta*$_{\text{NGEN}}$ 'soul of.philosopher of.this poet' ⟨*duša ètogo poèta filosofa*⟩

There are 15 logically possible pairs of N_{GEN}s (the number of combinations from 6 by 2 without repetitions): $N_{\text{GEN-subj}}$ – $N_{\text{GEN-obj}}$, $N_{\text{GEN-subj}}$ – $N_{\text{GEN-qual}}$, etc. Three of these pairs are semantically impossible: $N_{\text{GEN-metaph}}$ does not combine with $N_{\text{GEN-obj}}$, $N_{\text{GEN-subj}}$ and $N_{\text{GEN-poss}}$ (it is difficult to imagine a metaphorically used noun that has a subject/object actant or a possessor). As a result, there appear 12 SSyntRel pairs. On the other hand, the **qual-adnom** and **charact-adnom** SSyntRels are repeatable, so that we end up with 14 SSyntRel pairs to consider.

However, the use of SSyntRels alone for the linear ordering of cosubordinated N_{GEN}s is not sufficient: for some SSyntRel pairs, the order of N_{GEN}s depends also on the meaning of N and/or on that of N_{GEN}s. Thus, in the phrase *krik boli*$_{\text{NGEN-charact}}$ *Peti*$_{\text{NGEN-subj}}$ 'scream of.pain of.Pete' the $N_{\text{GEN-charact}}$ can only precede the $N_{\text{GEN-subj}}$ (**krik Peti boli*), but in *proizvedenija vos'midesjatyx godov*$_{\text{NGEN-charact}}$ *L'va Tolstogo*$_{\text{NGEN-subj}}$ 'works of.1880s of.Leo Tolstoy' ~ *proizvedenija L'va Tolstogo vos'midesjatyx godov* the $N_{\text{GEN-charact}}$ can both precede or follow the $N_{\text{GEN-subj}}$—if the $N_{\text{GEN-charact}}$ denotes the temporal coordinate of the fact denoted by the governor N. As a consequence, the proposed rules have to account for semantic factors as well.

Before proceeding to the formulation of N_{GEN}-ordering rules, the following principle has to be stated:

‖ Each of the rules is valid only **everything else being equal.**

This means that the two cosubordinated N_{GEN}s being compared and ordered are of the same weight (the corresponding phrases contain the same number of syllables and are of the same syntactic complexity) and there are no discourse factors intervening.

The expression "discourse factors" should be understood very broadly. It covers communicative and referential phenomena that can disturb the word order observed in discourse-neutral contexts. The following discussion ignores:

- The impact of the communicative structure. For instance, contrastive emphasis on one of cosubordinated N_{GEN}s can change their habitual linear order. Thus, the neutral order is $N + N_{GEN«MATERIAL»} + N_{GEN«COLOR»}$:[2] *stol krasnogo dereva bol'šogo razmera* 'table of.mahogany of.big size' ~ ?*stol bol'šogo razmera krasnogo dereva*; however, under emphasis, the dispreferred order is quite normal:

(4) *Ja išču stol bol'šogo razmera* KRASNOGO DEREVA, *a ne iz karel'skoj berëzy*
    'I am.looking.for a.table of.big size OF.MAHOGANY, and not of Karelian birch'.

- The impact of the referential structure.
  - A modifier either specifies a subclass of possible referents of the modified lexeme L (a **restrictive** modifier) or characterizes L's referents without specifying a subclass of these (a **qualifying** modifier). In what follows we consider only restrictive modifiers. Thus, we exclude from our description the situation where one of the cosubordinated N_{GEN}s is used as a qualifying modifier (in dashes):

(5) *Stoly malogo razmera – krasnogo dereva – u nas imejutsja v bol'šom količestve*
    'We have tables of.small size—of.mahogany—in a large quantity'.

  - A restrictive modifier specifies a subclass of possible referents of the modified lexeme L; cosubordinated restrictive modifiers specify subsequent subclasses of L's possible referents. In a discourse neutral context, the order of isolating these subclasses is irrelevant for the Speaker—different characteristics of the L's referents are, so to speak, informationally equal for him. In this case, the linear order of cosubordinated modifiers is determined by their own properties—syntactic and/or semantic. This is the situation studied in the present chapter. However, we exclude the situation where the Speaker **first** selects a particular subclass of L's referents and **then** introduces a subclass of this subclass. For instance, the dispreferred order ?*stol malogo razmera krasnogo dereva* is quite OK if one speaks about tables of small size and specifies a subclass of these from the viewpoint of their material; sentence (6) is absolutely correct because of the referential and communicative effects:

(6) *Stoly malogo razmera krasnogo dereva u nas imejutsja v bol'šem količestve, čem takie že stoly iz karel'skoj berëzy* 'We have tables of.small size of.mahogany in a larger quantity than such tables of Karelian birch'.

---

[2] Here and below an expression in small caps in « » quotes stands for a semantic label, whose formal status is left vague.

11.2 Rules for ordering cosubordinated N_{GEN}s

The linear order of cosubordinated N_{GEN}s postposed with respect to their common governor N is described by rules of three types:

1) Rule for the standard linear order of different-type N_{GEN}s, represented by their maximal template (Table 11.1 below).

By "**standard** linear order" is meant here the order conditioned exclusively by surface-syntactic relations that subordinate N_{GEN}s to their governor N, without recourse to the semantic properties of the nouns involved. These properties are taken into account by Rules **2**.

2) Rules specifying semantic factors that affect standard linear order of different-type N_{GEN}s.

Rules **2** are, in a sense, stronger than Rule **1**: they impose deviations from the standard order of N_{GEN}s determined by Rule **1**.

3) Rule for the linear order of same-type N_{GEN}s, represented by their semantically-conditioned hierarchy (Table 11.2).

Rules **1–3** are part of word order, or linearization, rules for Russian (Chapter 10); more precisely, they are a subset of the quasi-local word order rules.

1) Standard linear order of different-type N_{GEN}s

Table 11.1 Linear order of different-type postposed cosubordinated N_{GEN}s in Russian

1	2	3	4	5	6
–qual-adnom→N	–metaph-adnom→N	–obj-adnom→N	–charact-adnom→N	–subj-adnom→N	–poss-adnom→N

2) Semantic factors of the linear ordering of different-type cosubordinated N_{GEN}s

Semantic properties of N_{GEN}

1. If N_{GEN} denotes a **kind** of N (rather than characterizing an individual N), then this N_{GEN} precedes all other cosubordinated N_{GEN}s.[3]

2. If N_{GEN} denotes the **material** of which N is made, then this N_{GEN} precedes all other cosubordinated N_{GEN}s except for N_{GEN} denoting **kind**.

---

[3] Fairly often, the kind of N is expressed by an actant of N: *zavod* **boepripasov** 'ammunition plant', *škola* **tancev** 'dancing school', **detskaja** *bol'nica* 'children's hospital'; see Section 11.3, (9b), p. 377.

3. If $N_{GEN\text{-}charact}$ denotes the **time** of N,
   then $N_{GEN\text{-}charact}$ precedes or follows another $N_{GEN\text{-}charact}$, $N_{GEN\text{-}subj}$, $N_{GEN\text{-}obj}$ and $N_{GEN\text{-}poss}$.

4. If $N_{GEN\text{-}charact}$ denotes the **causer** of N,
   then this $N_{GEN\text{-}charact}$ precedes or follows $N_{GEN\text{-}poss}$.

   Semantic properties of N

5. If N denotes the **quantity** of N_{GEN} or a **set** of N_{CEN}s,
   then this N_{GEN} precedes all other cosubordinated N_{GEN}s.

3) **Linear order of the same-type cosubordinated N_{GEN}s**

Several same-type cosubordinated N_{GEN}s are possible only for two repeatable SSyntRels: **qual-adnom** and **charact-adnom**. The mutual order of same-type N_{GEN}s is determined by the following semantic hierarchy:

Table 11.2 Semantic hierarchy of same-type N_{GEN}s*

N < «KIND» < «MATERIAL» < «COLOR» < «SHAPE» < «SIZE»/«WEIGHT»/«ORIGIN» < external characteristics < «(subjective) EVALUATION»

* An **internal** property of a real-world entity is its inherent property, inseparable from it: e.g., kind, material, color, form, texture, size, weight, etc. An **external** property of an entity is its position in space and time, characteristics related to its functioning, its social role, etc.

This hierarchy, based on Vendler 1968: 128,[4] is underlain by the Inherence principle:

> *The modifiers of an N cosubordinated to this N by the same SSyntRel are linearly arranged according to the degree of their semantic "inherence" with respect to the N: a more inherent characterization stands closer to the N.*

The "degree of semantic inherence" of modifiers cannot be formally defined, but one may think that the proposed hierarchy reflects this degree quite well. Thus, the "objective" characteristics are more inherent than the "subjective" ones, the internal properties are more inherent than the external ones, and «KIND» is the most inherent characteristic.

Let it be emphasized that, although this hierarchy is introduced for the same-type N_{GEN}s, it is partially valid also for the different-type N_{GEN}s. More precisely,

---

[4] Vendler's study (1968), following, as he indicates, Ziff 1960, considers English anteposed cosubordinated adjectives with respect to their mutual linear ordering.

Rules 2 are based on the same Inherence principle: thus, the N_{GEN} expressing «KIND» precedes all other N_{GEN}s, etc.

11.3 Illustrations of N_{GEN} ordering rules

The above rules will be illustrated proceeding as follows.
- The SSyntRels are considered pairwise, one after the other, from left to right (in conformity with the template in Table 11.1).
- Each pair of SSyntRels is illustrated by phrases featuring the standard order of the two N_{GEN} nouns.
- Each deviation from this standard order is explicitly indicated.
- Each of the two repeatable SSyntRels—that is, **qual-adnom** and **charact-adnom**— is also considered in combination with itself.
- More than three co-subordinated N_{GEN}s are practically unacceptable.

The rules in question specify the best ordering possible. Deviations from it can be characterized by different degrees of ill-formedness, of which three are distinguished: ungrammatical (*), hardly acceptable (??), jarring (?). We are aware that our judgments of grammaticality can be challenged; however, for the purposes of this chapter it is sufficient to perceive a difference in the degree of correctness.

$\boxed{-\textbf{qual-adnom} \rightarrow \textbf{N}}$

This SSyntRel is repeatable.

With —**qual-adnom**→**N**

(7) a. *tort domašnego prigotovlenija gigantskogo razmera*
 cake of.domestic preparation«ORIGIN» of.giant size«SIZE» and
 tort gigantskogo razmera domašnego prigotovlenija

  b. *kovër pëstryx cvetov nebol'šogo razmera neobyčajnoj*
 carpet of.different colors«COLOR» of.small size«SIZE» of.extraordinary
 krasoty
 beauty«EVALUATION»

 vs. ?*kovër nebol'šogo razmera pëstryx cvetov neobyčajnoj krasoty* and
 **kovër neobyčajnoj krasoty pëstryx cvetov nebol'šogo razmera*

The order of $N_{GEN\text{-}qual}$s in (7b) corresponds to the semantic hierarchy in Table 11.2.

With —metaph→N: $N_{GEN\text{-}qual}$ precedes $N_{GEN\text{-}metaph}$

(8) minarety strel'čatoj formy$_{N_{GEN\text{-}qual}}$ zavodskix trub$_{N_{GEN\text{-}metaph}}$
    minarets cf.arrow shape   of.mill   chimneys
    vs. *minarety zavodskix trub$_{N_{GEN\text{-}metaph}}$ strel'čatoj formy$_{N_{GEN\text{-}qual}}$

With —obj-adnom→N: $N_{GEN\text{-}qual}$ precedes $N_{GEN\text{-}obj}$

(9) a. portret nebol'šogo razmera$_{N_{GEN\text{-}qual}}$ molodoj zenščiny$_{N_{GEN\text{-}obj}}$
       portrait of.small size   of.young woman
       vs. ?portret molodoj zenščiny$_{N_{GEN\text{-}obj}}$ nebol'šogo razmera$_{N_{GEN\text{-}qual}}$

    b. sistema raspredelenija$_{N_{GEN\text{-}obj}}$ toka   vysokoj nadëžnosti$_{N_{GEN\text{-}qual}}$
       system of.distribution«KIND» of.current of.high reliability
       vs. *sistema vysokoj nadëžnosti raspredelenija toka

The N_{GEN} raspredelenija [toka] is an $N_{GEN\text{-}obj}$ (being DSynt-actant II of the noun SISTEMA); according to the standard template (Table 11.1), it should follow an $N_{GEN\text{-}qual}$—as in (9a). However, a semantic factor perturbs the standard order: this $N_{GEN\text{-}obj}$ identifies a **kind** of system (≈ a particular device), not an individual system, so that in conformity with Rule **2.1** it must precede the $N_{GEN\text{-}qual}$.

With —charact-adnom→N: $N_{GEN\text{-}qual}$ precedes $N_{GEN\text{-}charact}$

(10) a. voda kristal'noj čistoty$_{N_{GEN\text{-}qual}}$ ètogo ozera$_{N_{GEN\text{-}charact}}$
        water of.crystal purity   of.this lake
        vs. *voda ètogo ozera$_{N_{GEN\text{-}charact}}$ kristal'noj čistoty$_{N_{GEN\text{-}qual}}$

     b. stol krasnogo dereva$_{N_{GEN\text{-}charact}}$ ogromnyx razmerov$_{N_{GEN\text{-}qual}}$
        table cf.red wood«MATERIAL» of.huge dimensions
        vs. ??stol ogromnyx razmerov$_{N_{GEN\text{-}qual}}$ krasnogo dereva$_{N_{GEN\text{-}charact}}$

(10b) demonstrates again the impact of a semantic factor: according to Rule **2.2** the N_{GEN} denoting material precedes all other N_{GEN}s (except the one denoting kind).

With —subj-adnom→N: $N_{GEN\text{-}qual}$ precedes $N_{GEN\text{-}subj}$

(11) a. kartina nebol'šogo razmera$_{N_{GEN\text{-}qual}}$ neizvestnogo xudožnika$_{N_{GEN\text{-}subj}}$
        painting of.small size   unknown   artist
        vs. ?kartina neizvestnogo xudožnika$_{N_{GEN\text{-}subj}}$ nebol'šogo razmera$_{N_{GEN\text{-}qual}}$

     b. kuča   morskogo peska$_{N_{GEN\text{-}subj}}$ bol'šogo razmera$_{N_{GEN\text{-}qual}}$
        pile«QUANTITY» of.sea sand   of.big size
        vs. ??kuča bol'šogo razmera$_{N_{GEN\text{-}qual}}$ morskogo peska$_{N_{GEN\text{-}subj}}$

c. rjumka   krasnogo vina pričudlivoj formy
   wine.glass$_{\text{«QUANTITY»}}$ of.red   wine of.bizarre shape
vs. *rjumka pričudlivoj formy krasnogo vina⁵

The deviation from the standard order in (11b–c) is imposed by Rule **2.5**.

With **−gen-poss→N**: N$_{\text{GEN-qual}}$ precedes N$_{\text{GEN-poss}}$

(12) kartiny   nebol'šogo razmera$_{\text{N}_{\text{GEN-qual}}}$ ètogo kollekcionera$_{\text{N}_{\text{GEN-qual}}}$
     paintings of.small   size   of.this collector
vs. *kartiny ètogo kollekcionera$_{\text{N}_{\text{GEN-poss}}}$ nebol'šogo razmera$_{\text{N}_{\text{GEN-qual}}}$

$\boxed{\textbf{−metaph-adnom→N}}$

This SSyntRel is non-repeatable and combines only with an N$_{\text{GEN-qual}}$ (see above) and with an N$_{\text{GEN-charact}}$.

(13) minarety zavodskix trub$_{\text{N}_{\text{GEN-metaph}}}$ Leonida   Solov'ëva$_{\text{N}_{\text{GEN-charact}}}$
     minarets of.mill   chimneys   of.Leonid Solovyov
vs. *minarety Leonida Solov'ëva$_{\text{N}_{\text{GEN-charact}}}$ zavodskix trub$_{\text{N}_{\text{GEN-metaph}}}$

$\boxed{\textbf{−obj-adnom→N}}$

This SSyntRel is non-repeatable.

With **−charact-adnom→N**: N$_{\text{GEN-obj}}$ precedes N$_{\text{GEN-charact}}$

(14) a. zavody boepripasov$_{\text{N}_{\text{GEN-obj}}}$ Urala$_{\text{N}_{\text{GEN-charact}}}$
        plants of.ammunition of.the.Urals
   vs. *zavody Urala$_{\text{N}_{\text{GEN-charact}}}$ boepripasov$_{\text{N}_{\text{GEN-obj}}}$

   b. issledovanija dvux   poslednix let$_{\text{N}_{\text{GEN-charact}}}$ processov$_{\text{N}_{\text{GEN-obj}}}$ aromatizacii
      studies   of.two last   years$_{\text{«TIME»}}$ of.processes   of.aromatization
      and
      issledovanija processov$_{\text{N}_{\text{GEN-obj}}}$ aromatizacii dvux poslednix let$_{\text{N}_{\text{GEN-charact}}}$

---

5 This is an interesting case, since it represents a "superposition" of two lexemes: RJUMKA1a 'wine glass with a thin stem...' (rjumka pričudlivoj formy 'wine glass of bizarre shape') and RJUMKA1b 'quantity of liquid...' (rjumka vina 'glass of wine'): Xozjajka postavila peredo mnoj rjumku krasnogo vina pričudlivoj formy 'The hostess put in front of me a glass of red wine of a bizarre shape'. However, this superposition is not possible in all contexts: *On vypil rjumku krasnogo vina pričudlivoj formy 'He drank a glass of wine of bizarre shape'.

The variation of the placement of the N$_{GEN\text{-}charact}$ denoting **time** is allowed by Rule **2.3**.

With —subj-adnom→N: N$_{GEN\text{-}obj}$ precedes N$_{GEN\text{-}subj}$

(15) a. *portret devočki*$_{NGEN\text{-}obj}$ *Serova*$_{NGEN\text{-}subj}$ vs. ?*portret Serova*$_{NGEN\text{-}subj}$ *devočki*$_{NGEN\text{-}obj}$
portrait of.girl of.Serov

b. *talant ljubvi*$_{NGEN\text{-}obj}$ *poèta*$_{NGEN\text{-}subj}$ vs. *talant poèta$_{NGEN\text{-}subj}$ *ljubvi*$_{NGEN\text{-}obj}$
talent of.love«KIND» of.poet

> **NB** The violation of the standard order in (15b) is worse than that in (15a) because of Rule **2.1**: N$_{GEN\text{-}obj}$ in (15b) denotes a **kind** of talent. In other words, if (15a) violates only a syntactic rule, (15b) violates both a syntactic rule and a semantic constraint.

With —gen-poss→N: N$_{GEN\text{-}obj}$ precedes N$_{GEN\text{-}poss}$

(16) *portret devočki*$_{NGEN\text{-}obj}$ *s ser'goj amsterdamskogo muzeja*$_{NGEN\text{-}poss}$
portrait of.girl with earring of.Amsterdam museum
vs. **portret amsterdamskogo muzeja*$_{NGEN\text{-}poss}$ *devočki*$_{NGEN\text{-}obj}$ *s ser'goj*

—charact-adnom→N

This SSyntRel is repeatable.

With —charact-adnom→N

(17) a. *pisateli Vostočnoj Evropy*$_{NGEN\text{-}charact}$ *devjatnadcatogo veka*$_{NGEN\text{-}charact}$
writers of.Eastern Europe«LOCATION» of.19th century«TIME» and
pisateli devjatnadcatogo veka$_{NGEN\text{-}charact}$ *Vostočnoj Evropy*$_{NGEN\text{-}charact}$

The freedom of the placement of the N$_{GEN\text{-}charact}$ denoting **time** is ensured by Rule **2.3**.

(17) b. *klinok damasskoj stali*$_{NGEN\text{-}charact}$ *semnadcatogo veka*$_{NGEN\text{-}charact}$
blade of.Damascus steele«MATERIAL» of.17th century«TIME»
izvestnogo Abu-Vaxba$_{NGEN\text{-}charact}$
of.known Abu-Wahb«CAUSER» and
klinok damasskoj stali$_{NGEN\text{-}charact}$ *izvestnogo Abu-Vaxba*$_{NGEN\text{-}charact}$ *semnadcatogo veka*$_{NGEN\text{-}charact}$
vs. **klinok izvestnogo Abu-Vaxba*$_{NGEN\text{-}charact}$ *damasskoj stali*$_{NGEN\text{-}charact}$ *semnadcatogo veka*$_{NGEN\text{-}charact}$

The impossibility of the last phrase is also determined by semantic hierarchy: the N$_{GEN\text{-}charact}$ denoting «MATERIAL» should precede other N$_{GEN}$s (except «KIND»).

With —subj-adnom→N: N$_{GEN\text{-}charact}$ precedes N$_{GEN\text{-}subj}$

(18) a. *krik   užasa*$_{N_{GEN\text{-}charact}}$ *rebënka*$_{N_{GEN\text{-}subj}}$ vs. **kri̇k rebënka*$_{N_{GEN\text{-}subj}}$ *užasa*$_{N_{GEN\text{-}charact}}$
scream of.horror   of.child

b. *grud' myslitelja*$_{N_{GEN\text{-}charact}}$ *moego druga*$_{N_{GEN\text{-}subj}}$
chest of.thinker   of.my friend
vs. **grud' moego druga myslitelja* [ungrammatical in the intended meaning]

c. *bjust karrarskogo mramora*$_{N_{GEN\text{-}charact}}$ *velikogo Mikelandželo*$_{N_{GEN\text{-}subj}}$
bust of.Carrara   marble   of.great Michelangelo
vs. **bjust velikogo Mikelandželo*$_{N_{GEN\text{-}subj}}$ *karrarskogo mramora*$_{N_{GEN\text{-}charact}}$

d. *rasskazy   vos'midesjatyx godov*$_{N_{GEN\text{-}charact}}$ *Antona Pavloviča   Čexova*$_{N_{GEN\text{-}subj}}$
short.stories of.1880s   of.Anton Pavlovitch Chekhov
and
rasskazy Antona Pavloviča Čexova$_{N_{GEN\text{-}subj}}$ *vos'midesjatyx godov*$_{N_{GEN\text{-}charact}}$

The freedom of placement of the N$_{GEN\text{-}charact}$ that denotes time corresponds to Rule **2.3**.

With —gen-poss→N: N$_{GEN\text{-}charact}$ precedes N$_{GEN\text{-}poss}$

(19) a. *kulinarnye knigi   srednevekovoj Italii*$_{N_{GEN\text{-}charact}}$ *našej   biblioteki*$_{N_{GEN\text{-}poss}}$
cook   books of.medieval Italy   of.our library
vs. **kulinarnye knigi našej biblioteki*$_{N_{GEN\text{-}poss}}$ *srednevekovoj Italii*$_{N_{GEN\text{-}charact}}$

b. *knigi vosemnadcatogo veka*$_{N_{GEN\text{-}charact}}$ *našej biblioteki*$_{N_{GEN\text{-}poss}}$
books of.18th   century   of.our library   and
knigi našej biblioteki$_{N_{GEN\text{-}poss}}$ *vosemnadcatogo veka*$_{N_{GEN\text{-}charact}}$

c. *knigi izdatel'stva*$_{N_{GEN\text{-}charact}}$ *Muton našej biblioteki*$_{N_{GEN\text{-}poss}}$
books of.publisher   Mouton of.our library   and
knigi našej biblioteki$_{N_{GEN\text{-}poss}}$ *izdatel'stva*$_{N_{GEN\text{-}charact}}$ *Muton*

The freedom of placement of the N$_{GEN\text{-}charact}$ that denotes time, as in (19b), or the causer, as in (19c), corresponds, respectively, to Rules **2.3** and **2.4**.

―subj-adnom→N

This SSyntRel is non-repeatable.

With —**gen-poss**→**N**: $N_{\text{GEN-subj}}$ precedes $N_{\text{GEN-poss}}$

(20)   bjust Mikelandželo$_{N_{\text{GEN-subj}}}$ Èrmitaža$_{N_{\text{GEN-poss}}}$
       bust of.Michelangelo   of.Hermitage.museum
vs.   *bjust Èrmitaža$_{N_{\text{GEN-poss}}}$ Mikelandželo$_{N_{\text{GEN-subj}}}$

To demonstrate how the rules proposed can be applied, let us return to example (1), repeated here as (21):

(21)   glagoly napravlennogo dviženija$_{N_{\text{GEN-charact}}}$ soveršennogo vida$_{N_{\text{GEN-qual}}}$
       verbs   of.directed   movement   of.perfective aspect
       russkogo   jazyka$_{N_{\text{GEN-subj}}}$
       of.Russian language

- First, the mutual arrangement of cosubordinated N_{GEN}s is specified by the standard template (Table 11.1) for different-type N_{GEN}s: $N_{\text{GEN-qual}}$ precedes $N_{\text{GEN-subj}}$. The phrase russkogo jazyka 'of.Russian language' is an $N_{\text{GEN-subj}}$ that expresses DSyntA I of glagoly 'verbs', which are elements of the set 'Russian language'; according to the N_{GEN} order template, it must follow the phrase soveršennogo vida 'of.perfective aspect' (an $N_{\text{GEN-qual}}$).
- Second, the mutual arrangement of $N_{\text{GEN-charact}}$ and $N_{\text{GEN-qual}}$ is specified by Rule 2.1: in the standard case (= according to the template), $N_{\text{GEN qual}}$ precedes; but if $N_{\text{GEN-chatact}}$ denotes the kind of N, then $N_{\text{GEN-qual}}$ follows. And in (21), the phrase napravlennogo dviženija denotes a particular kind of verbs.

11.4 Ordering of cosubordinated N$_{\text{GEN}}$s vs. ordering of cosubordinated ADJs

It is interesting to compare the ordering of Russian postposed cosubordinated N_{GEN}s with the ordering of Russian anteposed cosubordinated adjectives. As is to be expected, N_{GEN}s and adjectives, both being noun modifiers and on multiple occasions synonymous, show significant parallelism in their ordering. First the rules for the ordering of cosubordinated adjectives are presented (11.4.1) and then they are compared with the corresponding rules for N_{GEN}s (11.4.2).

11.4.1 Ordering of cosubordinated ADJs

The papers Iordanskaja 2000 and 2003 propose a hierarchical semantic classification of Russian adjectives that determines their mutual linear ordering—more precisely, their relative closeness to the modified noun.[6] Table 11.3 below presents this classification. The higher in the table an adjective semantic class is (i.e., the higher its rank), the closer its instance must be to the modified noun. This is so since an adjective's rank corresponds to the degree of inherence of the characteristic the adjective expresses: the more inherent the characteristic, the closer to the noun is the adjective.

Table 11.3 Hierarchical semantic classification of adjectives (Iordanskaja 2003: 161–162)

I	Objective characteristics: properties			
	A	Qualitative (non-measurable) properties		
		1.	Permanent properties	
			1)	Internal properties
				a) Kind (*kofejnaja* [*čaška*] 'coffee [cup]') b) Material (*farforovaja* [*čaška*] 'china [cup]') c) Color (*golubaja* [*čaška*] 'light blue [cup]') d) Shape (*vytjanutaja* [*čaška*] 'elongated [cup]') e) Other internal properties (*prozračnaja* [*čaška*] 'transparent [cup]')
			2)	External properties (*deševaja* [*čaška*] 'cheap [cup]') a) Functioning/using characteristics (*udobnaja* [*čaška*] 'convenient [cup]')
		2.	Temporary properties (*čistaja* [*čaška*] 'clean [cup]')	
	B	Quantitative (measurable) properties (*kroxotnaja* [*čaška*] 'tiny [cup]')		
II	Subjective characteristics: evaluation (*zamečatel'naja* [*čaška*] 'remarkable [cup]')			

And now some examples.

- Adjectives that express an objective characteristic are closer to the modified noun than adjectives expressing a subjective characteristic:

(22) *zamečatel'naja vysokaja ëlka* vs. ?*vysokaja zamečatel'naja ëlka*
 remarkable tall fur.tree

---

[6] On the topic of ordering cosubordinated adjectives, see Svenonius 2008.

11.4 Ordering of cosubordinated N$_{GEN}$s vs. ordering of cosubordinated ADJs

- Adjectives that express a qualitative characteristic are closer to the modified noun than than adjectives expressing a quantitative characteristic:

(23) *malen'kaja srednevekovaja bašnja* vs. ?*srednevekovaja malen'kaja bašnja*
 small medieval tower

- Adjectives that express a permanent characteristic are closer to the modified noun than adjectives expressing a temporary characteristic:

(24) *razbitoe uglovoe okno* vs. ?*uglovoe razbitoe okno*
 broken corner window

- Adjectives that express an internal property are closer to the modified noun than adjectives expressing an external property:

(25) *dešëvye gorjačie bubliki* vs. ?*gorjačie dešëvye bubliki*
 cheap hot bagels

- Hierarchy of internal property adjectives: for instance, «material» adjectives are closer to the modified noun than «color» adjectives; «kind» adjectives are closer to the modified noun than any other adjectives; etc.

(26) a. *krasnyj aljuminievyj čajnik* vs. ?*aluminievyj krasnyj čajnik*
 read aluminum teapot
 b. *farforovaja kofejnaja čaška* vs. ??*kofejnaja farforovaja čaška*
 china coffee cup

To sum up: The linear ordering of cosubordinated adjectives is determined **semantically**, i.e., by their meaning—of course, everything else being equal, the same as with N$_{GEN}$s (see the end of Section 11.1): that is, the weight of the N$_{GEN}$'s phrase and discourse factors.

However, this is not true for Russian possessive adjectives, such as MAMIN 'Mom's' or PETIN 'Pete's': their mutual linear arrangement is determined by their syntactic role, cf.:

(27) a. *Petin*$_{[subj]/[poss]}$ *mamin*$_{[obj]}$ *portret*
 'Mom's portrait by Pete'/'Mom's portrait belonging to Pete'
 b. *mamin*$_{[subj]/[poss]}$ *Petin*$_{[obj]}$ *portret*
 'Pete's portrait by Mom'/'Pete's portrait belonging to Mom'

(28) a. *Petin*$_{[poss]}$ *mamin*$_{[subj]}$ *portret devočki*
 'a girl's portrait by Mom belonging to Pete'
 b. *mamin*$_{[poss]}$ *Petin*$_{[subj]}$ *portret devočki*
 'a girl's portrait by Pete belonging to Mom'

To account for this fact, in addition to the **modificative** SSyntRel, three more SSyntRels for possessive adjectives in Russian are needed: **possessive-modificative, subjectival-modificative,** and **objectival-modificative**. As can be seen from (27)–(28), the order of possessive adjectives with respect to the modified N is as follows:

ADJ←**poss-modif**– + ADJ←**subj-modif**– + ADJ←**obj-modif**– + N.

For instance:

Petin repinskij mamin portret lit. 'Pete's Repin's Mom's portrait' = 'Mom's portrait by Repin owned by Pete'

NB The cooccurrence of two or more possessive adjectives is rare, so that, generally speaking, it could be ignored. However, this case is interesting from a theoretical viewpoint.

The cooccurrence of possessive adjectives with "normal" ones is determined by two general enough rules:

1) The **possessive-modificative** ADJ precedes all "normal" ADJs

(29) *maminy*$_{[poss]}$ *dovoennye*$_{[external]}$ *požëltevšie*$_{[color]}$ *semejnye*$_{[kind]}$ *fotografii*
    Mom's   pre-war   yellowed   family   photographs

2) The **subjectival-modificative** and **objectival-modificative** ADJs follow all "normal" ADJs

(30) a. *dovoennye*$_{[external]}$ *požëltevšie*$_{[color]}$ *maminy*$_{[subj]}$ *fotografii*   *našego doma*
       pre-war   yellowed   Mom's   photographs of.our house
    b. *dovoennye*$_{[external]}$ *požëltevšie*$_{[color]}$ *maminy*$_{[obj]}$ *fotografii,*   *sdelannye Petej*
       pre-war   yellowed   Mom's   photographs taken   by.Pete

11.4.2 Comparison of both orderings: similarities and differences

Recall that cosubordinated N$_{GEN}$s follow the governing N, while cosubordinated ADJs precede it. Therefore, the order of N$_{GEN}$s is a mirror image of that of ADJs. This means that comparing both orders we speak in fact of the degree of closeness of an N$_{GEN}$ or an ADJ to its governor N.

The ordering of cosubordinated N$_{GEN}$s and that of cosubordinated ADJs in Russian are similar in the following two respects:

– The mutual ordering of Russian possessive ADJs (ADJ←**poss-modif**– + ADJ ←**subj-modif**– + ADJ←**obj-modif**– + N) is the same (of course, mirror-wise) as the mutual ordering of the corresponding N$_{GEN}$s (that is, N + –**obj-adnom**→

N_{GEN}+ —**subj-adnom**→N_{GEN} + —**poss-adnom**→N_{GEN}; Table 11.1). The possessive adjectival modifier is the outermost, and the objectival adjectival modifier is closer to the modified noun than the subjectival one. This is only natural, since possessive ADJs are simply adjectivalizations of N_{GEN}s.
- The mutual ordering of repeatable N_{GEN}s (that is, **qual-adnom** and **charact-adnom** N_{GEN}s) is the same as the mutual ordering of non-possessive ADJs, since it is determined by the same hierarchical semantic classification of the corresponding lexical units. This is also natural, since the closeness of a modifier to its governor N is determined by the degree of semantic inherence of the characteristic expressed: a more inherent characterization stands closer to N.

The ordering of cosubordinated N_{GEN}s and that of cosubordinated ADJs in Russian are different in the following respects:

- The cosubordinated N_{GEN}s are ordered syntactically—according to different SSyntRels that link them to the governor, with several semantic "corrections" imposed by their meaning.
- The cosubordinated ADJs are ordered semantically—according to their meaning, with several syntactic "corrections" concerning possessive ADJs, which are positioned in conformity with the governing SSyntRels.

Chapter 11 is a slightly modified version of Iordanskaja & Mel'čuk 2019.

References

Abeillé, Anne. 1997. Fonction ou position objet ? *Au gré des langues* 11. 8–29.
Abeillé, Anne & Danièle Godard. 2000. French word order and lexical weight. In Robert Borsley (ed.), *The nature and function of syntactic categories* [Syntax and Semantics 32], 325–360.
Ackerman, Farrell & Irina Nikolaeva. 2013. *Descriptive typology and linguistic theory: the study in the morphosyntax of relative clauses*. Stanford, CA: CSLI Publications.
Aikhenvald, Alexandra. 2013. Possession and ownership: a cross-linguistic perspective. In Alexandra Aikhenvald & Robert M. W. Dixon (eds.), *Possession and ownership: A cross-linguistic typology* 1–64. Oxford: Oxford University Press.
Aikhenvald, Alexandra, Robert M. W. Dixon & Masayuki Onishi (eds.). 2001. *Non-canonical marking of subjects and objects*. Amsterdam/Philadelphia: John Benjamins.
Alexiadou, Artemis, Paul Law, André Meinunger & Chris Wilder (eds.). 2000. *The syntax of relative clauses*. Amsterdam/Philadelphia: John Benjamins.
Alleton, Viviane. 1973. *Grammaire du chinois*. Paris: Presses Universitaires de France.
Álvarez Gonzales, Albert. 2012. Relative clauses and nominalizations in Yaqui. In Comrie & Estrada-Fernández (eds.), *Relative clauses in languages of the Americas. A typological overview*, 67–95. Amsterdam/Philadelphia: John Benjamins.
Andrews, Avery. 2001. Noncanonical A/S marking in Icelandic. In Aikhenvald et al. (eds.), *Non-canonical marking of subjects and objects*, 85–111. Amsterdam/Philadelphia: John Benjamins.
Andrews, Avery. 2007. Relative clauses. In Timothy Shopen (ed.), *Language typology and syntactic description, Vol. 2: Complex construction*, 206–236. Cambridge: Cambride University Press.
Anscombre, Jean-Claude. 2001. L'analyse de la construction *En tout N* par D. Leeman : quelques remarques. *Travaux de linguistique* 42–43. 183–197.
Apresjan, Jurij. 2010. Vvedenie [Introduction]. In Apresjan et al., *Teoretičeskie problemy russkogo sintaksisa. Vzaimodejstvie grammatiki i slovarja*, 11–20. Moskva: Jazyki slavjanskix kul'tur.
Apresjan, Jurij, Igor' Boguslavskij, Leonid Iomdin & Vladimir Sannikov. 2010. *Teoretičeskie problemy russkogo sintaksisa. Vzaimodejstvie grammatiki i slovarja* [Theoretical problems of Russian syntax. Interaction between grammar and lexicon]. Moskva: Jazyki slavjanskix kul'tur.
Apresjan, Valentina. 2014. Syntactic idioms across languages: corpus evidence from Russian and English. *Russian Linguistics* 38 (2). 187–203.
Auger, Pierre. 1965. Les modèles dans la science. *Diogène* 52. 3–15.
Beck, David. 1996. Subjecthood, agency, and topicality in Lushootseed. *Toronto Working Papers in Linguistics* 15 (1). 1–29.
Beck, David. 2000. Semantic agents, syntactic subjects, and discourse topics: how to locate Lushootseed sentences in space and time. *Studies in Language* 24 (2). 277–317.
Beck, David. 2016. Uniqueness and grammatical relations in Upper Necaxa Totonac. *Linguistics* 54 (1). 59–118.
Beck, David & Igor Mel'čuk. 2011. Morphological phrasemes and Totonacan verbal morphology. *Linguistics* 49 (1). 175–228.
Benveniste, Émile. 1957–58. La phrase relative, problème de syntaxe générale. *Bulletin de la Société de Linguistique de Paris* 53(1). 39–53. [Reprinted In Benveniste, Émile. 1966. *Problèmes de linguistique générale*, Paris: Gallimard, 208–222.]

Bhaskararao, Peri & Venkata Subbarao (eds.). 2004. *Non-nominative subjects*, vols. 1–2. Amsterdam/Philadelphia: John Benjamins.

Bianchi, Valentina. 2000. Some issues in the syntax of relative determiners. In Artemis Alexiadou, Paul Law, André Meinunger & Chris Wilder (eds.), *The syntax of relative clauses*, 53–81. Amsterdam/Philadelphia: John Benjamins.

Bickel, Balthasar. 2011. Grammatical relations typology. In Jae Jung Song (ed.), *The Oxford handbook of linguistic typology*, 399–444. Oxford: Oxford University Press.

Bohnet, Bernd. 2007. The induction and evaluation of word order rules using corpora based on the two concepts of topological models. In *Language Generation and Machine Translation [UCNLG+MT] workshop at MT Summit XI*, Copenhagen, 38–45.

Borščëv, Vladimir & Barbara Partì. 2011. Genitiv mery v russkom jazyke, tipy i sorta [The genitive of measure in Russian: types and sorts]. In Igor' Boguslavskij, Leonid Iomdin & Leonid Krysin (eds.), *Slovo i jazyk. Sbornik statej k 80-letiju akademika Ju. D. Apresjana*, 95–137. Moscow: Jazyki slavjanskix kul'tur.

Bresnan, Joan & Jane Grimshaw. 1978. The syntax of free relatives in English. *Linguistic Inquiry* 9 (3). 333–391.

Burgess, Clifford, Katarzyna Dziwirek & Donna Gerdts (eds.). 1995. *Grammatical relations: theoretical approaches to empirical questions*. Stanford, CA: CSLI Publications.

Caponigro, Ivano, Harold Torrence & Carlos Cisneros. 2013. Free relative clauses in two Mixtec languages. *International Journal of American Linguistics* 79 (1). 41–96.

Carlson, Gregory. 1977. Amount relatives. *Language* 53 (3). 520–542.

Chang, Suk-Jin. 1996. *Korean*. Amsterdam/Philadelphia: John Benjamins.

Chappell, Hilary. 1986. The passive of bodily effect in Chinese. *Studies in Language* 10 (1). 271–296.

Cho, Yongjoon. 2011. *Multiple nominative construction in Korean and its second language acquisition by adult English speakers*. PhD Thesis. Los Angeles, CA: University of Southern California.

Citko, Barbara. 2004. On headed, headless, and light-headed relatives. *Natural Language & Linguistic Theory* 22 (1). 95–126.

Cole, Peter. 1987. The structure of internally headed relative clauses. *Natural Language and Linguistic Theory* 5 (2). 277–302.

Cole, Peter & Jerrold Sadock (eds.). 1977. *Grammatical relations [Syntax and Semantics 8]*. New York et al.: Academic Press.

Comrie, Bernard. 1998. Rethinking the typology of relative clauses. *Language Design* 1. 59–86.

Comrie, Bernard & Zarina Estrada-Fernández (eds.). 2012. *Relative clauses in languages of the Americas. A typological overview*. Amsterdam/Philadelphia: John Benjamins.

Comrie, Bernard & Edward Keenan. 1979. Noun phrase accessibility revisited. *Language* 55 (3). 649–664.

Cooreman, Ann. 1994. A functional typology of antipassives. In Barbara Fox & Paul Hopper (eds.), *Voice: form and function*, 49–87. Amsterdam/Philadelphia: John Benjamins.

Croft, William. 1994. The semantics of subjecthood. In Marina Yaguello (ed.), *Subjecthood and subjectivity*, 29–75. Paris: Ophrys/Institut français du Royaume-Uni.

Dalrymple, Mary & Ronald Kaplan. 2000. Feature indeterminacy and feature resolution. *Language* 76 (4). 759–798.

Dalrymple, Mary & Irina Nikolaeva. 2011. *Objects and information structure*. Cambridge: Cambridge University Press.

Danlos, Laurence, Benoît Sagot & Rosa Stern. 2010. Analyse discursive des incises de citation. In Franck Neveu, Valelia Muni Toke, Jacques Durand, Thomas Klingler, Lorenza Mondada &

Sophie Prévost (eds.), *Congrès Mondial de Linguistique Française – CMLF2010*, 2237–2254. Paris: Institut de linguistique française. See also: https://www.youtube.com/watch?v=JOHw7lX3Gu4

Davies, William & Stanley Dubinsky (eds.). 2001. *Objects and other subjects. Grammatical functions, functional categories and configurationality.* Dordrecht et al.: Kluwer.

De Vries, Mark. 2018. Relative clauses. In *Oxford Bibliographies in Linguistics*, Oxford University Press.

Dixon, Robert M. W. 1972. *The Dyirbal language of North Queensland.* Cambridge Cambridge University Press.

Dixon, Robert M. W. 2010. *Basic linguistic theory, Vol. 2. Grammatical topics.* New York: Oxford University Press.

Downing, Laura & Al Mtenje. 2011. Prosodic phrasing of Chichewa relative clauses. *Journal of African Languages and Linguistics* 32. 65–112.

Dryer, Matthew. 1983. Indirect objects in Kinyarwanda revisited. In David Perlmutter (ed.), *Relational grammar 1*, 129–140. Chicago/London: The University of Chicago Press.

Dryer, Matthew. 1997. Are grammatical relations universal? In Joan Bybee, John Haiman & Sandra Thompson (eds.), *Essays on language function and language type (dedicated to T. Givón)*, 115–143. Amsterdam/Philadelphia: John Benjamins.

Dryer, Matthew. 2013. Order of relative clause and noun. In Matthew Dryer & Martin Haspelmath (eds.), *The world atlas of language structures online.* Leipzig: Max Planck Institute for Evolutionary Anthropology. See also http://wals.info/chapter/90.

Durie, Mark. 1985. *A grammar of Acehnese on the basis of a dialect of North Aceh* Dordrecht/Cinnaminson: Foris.

Durie, Mark. 1987. Grammatical relations in Acehnese. *Studies in Language* 11(2) 365–399.

Durie, Mark. 1988. Preferred argument structure in an active language. *Lingua* 74 1–25.

El Kassas, Dina & Sylvain Kahane. 2004. Modélisation de l'ordre des mots en arabe standard. In *JEP-TALN 2004*, Fès.

Falk, Yehuda. 2006. *Subjects and Universal Grammar.* Cambridge: Cambridge University Press.

Farrell, Patrick. 2005. *Grammatical relations.* Oxford/New York: Oxford University Press.

Filippova, Katja & Michael Strube. 2009. Tree linearization in English: improving language model based approaches. In *Proceedings of NAACL and HLT 2009*, 225–228. Boulder, CO: Association for Computational Linguistics.

Foley, William. 1991. *The Yimas language of New Guinea.* Stanford, CA: Stanford University Press.

Foley, William & Robert Van Valin. 1977. On the viability of the notion of subject in Universal Grammar. In *Proceedings of the Third Annual Meeting of the Berkeley Linguistics Society* [BLS 3], 293–320.

Foolen, Ad. 2004 Expressive binominal NPs in Germanic and Romance languages. In Günter Radden & Klaus-Uwe Panther (eds.), *Studies in Linguistic Motivation*, 75–100. Berlin/New York: Mouton de Gruyter.

Gaatone, David. 1988. Cette coquine de construction : remarques sur trois structures affectives du français. *Travaux de linguistique* 17. 159–176.

Gerdes, Kim. 2002. *Topologie et grammaires formelles de l'allemand.* PhD Thesis. Paris: Paris-7 University.

Gerdes, Kim, Bruno Guillaume, Sylvain Kahane & Guy Perrier. 2018. *SUD or Surface-Syntactic Universal Dependencies: An annotation scheme near-isomorphic to UD.* Universal Dependencies Workshop 2018, Brussels.

Gerdes, Kim & Sylvain Kahane. 2001. Word order in German: a formal dependency grammar using a topological hierarchy. In *Actes d'ACL 2001*, Toulouse.

Gerdes, Kim & Sylvain Kahane. 2006. L'amas verbal au cœur d'une modélisation topologique de l'ordre des mots. In Kim Gerdes & Claude Muller (eds.), *Ordre des mots et topologie de la phrase française* [= *Linguisticæ Investigationes*] 29 (1). 75–89.

Gerdes, Kim & Sylvain Kahane. 2007. Phrasing it differently. In Leo Wanner (ed.), *Selected lexical and grammatical issues in the Meaning-Text theory*, 297–335. Amsterdam/Philadelphia: John Benjamins.

Gerdts, Donna & Cheong Youn. 1989. Non-nominative subjects in Korean. In Susumu Kuno et al. (eds.), *Harvard studies in Korean linguistics III: Proceedings of the 1989 Workshop on Korean linguistics*, 235–248. Seoul: Hanshin Publishing Company. See also:http://www.sfu.ca/~gerdts/papers/GerdtsYounNonNominativeSubjects.pdf

Gil, David. 1994. The structure of Riau Indonesian. *Nordic Journal of Linguistics* 17. 179–200.

Givón, Talmy. 1990. *Syntax. A functional typological introduction. Vol. II*. Amsterdam/Philadelphia: John Benjamins.

Givón, Talmy. 2012. Toward a diachronic typology of relative clause. In Bernard Comrie & Zarina Estrada-Fernández (eds.), *Relative clauses in languages of the Americas. A typological overview*, 3–25. Amsterdam/Philadelphia: John Benjamins.

Glendenning, Peter Josef. 1983. *Icelandic*. London: Hodder and Stoughton.

Goldberg, Adele & Ray Jackendoff. 2004. The English resultative as a family of constructions. *Language* 80 (3). 532–568.

Graffi, Giorgio. 2017. What are 'Pseudo-Relatives'? In Roberta D'Alessandro, Gabriele Iannàccaro, Diana Passino, Anna M. Thornton (eds.), *Di tutti i colori. Studi linguistici per Maria Grossmann*, 115–131. Utrecht: Utrecht University Repository.

Grimm, Scott. 2007. Case attraction in Ancient Greek. In Balder Ten Cate & Henk Zeevat (eds.), *Logic, Language, and Computation. 6th International Tbilisi Symposium on Logic, Language, and Computation* [TbiLLC 2005], 139–153. Berlin/Heidelberg: Springer.

Grosu, Alexander. 1988. Pied Piping and the matching parameter. *The Linguistic Review* 6. 41–58.

Grosu, Alexander. 2002. Strange relatives at the interface of two millennia. *GLOT International* 6 (6). 145–167.

Grosu, Alexander. 2012. Towards a more articulated typology of internally headed relative constructions: the semantics connection. *Language and Linguistics Compass* 6 (7). 447–476.

Grosu, Alexander & Koji Hoshi. 2016. Japanese internally headed relatives: their distinctness from potentially homophonous constructions. *Glossa: A Journal of General Linguistics* 1 (1). 1–31.

Grosu, Alexander & Fred Landman. 1998. Strange relatives of the third kind. *Natural Language Semantics* 6. 125–170.

Han, Na-Rae. 2004. Korean null pronouns: classification and annotation. In *Proceedings of the ACL 2004 Workshop on Discourse* Annotation, 33–50.

Han, Na-Rae. 2006. *Korean zero pronouns: analysis and resolution*. PhD Thesis. Philadelphia, PA: University of Pennsylvania. See also: http://citeseerx.ist.psu.edu/viewdoc/download?doi=10.1.1.126.3973&rep=rep1&type=pdf

Handschuh, Corinna. 2014. *The typology of marked-S languages*. Berlin: Language Science Press.

Harris, Alice. 1981. *Georgian syntax. A study in relational grammar*. Cambridge et al.: Cambridge University Press.

Hashimoto, Mantaro. 1988. The structure and typology of the Chinese passive construction. In Masayoshi Shibatani (ed.), *Passive and voice*, 329–354. Amsterdam/ Philadelphia: John Benjamins.

Haspelmath, Martin. 1991. On the questions of deep ergativity: the evidence from Lezgian. *Papiere zur Linguistik* 44/45 (1/2). 5–27.
Haspelmath, Martin. 1993. *A grammar of Lezgian*. Berlin/New York: Mouton de Gruyter.
Haspelmath, Martin. 1997. *Indefinite pronouns*. Clarendon Press: Oxford.
Haspelmath, Martin. 2016. The serial verb construction: comparative concept and cross-linguistic generalizations. *Language and Linguistics* 17 (3). 291–319.
Hatcher, Anna. 1960. An introduction to an analysis of English noun compounds. *Word* 16 (3). 356–373.
He, Wei, Haifeng Wang, Yuqin Guo & Ting Liu. 2009. Dependency based Chinese sentence realization. In *Joint Conference of the 47th Annual Meeting of the Association for Computational Linguistics and 4th International Joint Conference on Natural Language Processing (ACL-IJCNLP 2009)*, Singapore, 809–817.
Hiraiwa, Ken, George Akanlig-Pare, Samuel Atintono, Adams Bodomo, Komlan Essizewa & Fusheini Hjudu. 2017. A comparative syntax of internally-headed relative clauses in Gur. *Glossa: a journal of general linguistics* 2 (1), 27. 1–30, DOI: https://doi.org/10.5334/gjgl.40
Horvath, Julia & Alexander Grosu. 1987. On the notion "head": evidence from free relatives and interrogatives. *Theoretical Linguistics* 14 (1). 35–64.
Huang, C.-T. James. 1999. Chinese passive in comparative perspective. *Tsing Hua Journal of Chinese Studies* 29. 423–509.
Huang, C.-T. James, Y.-H. Audrey Li & Yafei Li. 2008. *The syntax of Chinese*. Cambridge et al.: Cambridge University Press.
Iomdin, Leonid. 2005. A hypothesis of two syntactic starts. In Jurij Apresjan & Leonid Iomdin (eds.), *Vostok – Zapad: Vtoraja meždunarodnaja konferencija po modeli Smysl – Text*, 165–175. Moskva: Jazyki slavjanskoj kul'tury.
Iomdin, Leonid. 2007. Russian idioms formed with interrogative pronouns and their properties. In Kim Gerdes, Tilmann Reuther & Leo Wanner (eds.), *Proceedings of the Third International Conference on Meaning-Text Theory*, 179–189. München/Wien: Wiener Slawistischer Almanach [Sonderband 69].
Iomdin, Leonid. 2010a. Gipoteza o dvux sintaksičeskix načalax [The hypothesis of two syntactic starts]. In Jurij Apresjan, Igor' Boguslavskij, Leonid Iomdin & Vladimir Sannikov. 2010. *Teoretičeskie problemy russkogo sintaksisa. Vzaimodejstvie grammatiki i slovarja* [Theoretical problems of Russian syntax. Interaction between grammar and lexicon], 129–140. Moskva: Jazyki slavjanskix kul'tur.
Iomdin, Leonid. 2010b. Sintaksičeskie frazemy: meždu leksikoj i sintaksisom [Syntactic phrasemes: between lexicon and syntax]. In Jurij Apresjan, Igor' Boguslavskij, Leonid Iomdin & Vladimir Sannikov. 2010. *Teoretičeskie problemy russkogo sintaksisa. Vzaimodejstvie grammatiki i slovarja* [Theoretical problems of Russian syntax. Interaction between grammar and lexicon], 141–190. Moskva: Jazyki slavjanskix kul'tur.
Iomdin, Leonid. 2010c. Sintaksičeskie otnošenija [Syntactic relations]. In Jurij Apresjan, Igor' Boguslavskij, Leonid Iomdin & Vladimir Sannikov. 2010. *Teoretičeskie problemy russkogo sintaksisa. Vzaimodejstvie grammatiki i slovarja* [Theoretical problems of Russian syntax. Interaction between grammar and lexicon], 21–43. Moskva: Jazyki slavjanskix kul'tur.
Iordanskaja, Lidija. 1986. Propriétés sémantiques des verbes promoteurs de la négation en français. *Lingvisticæ Investigationes* 10 (2). 345–380.
Iordanskaja, Lidija. 2000. Sopodčinenie prilagatel'nyx v russkom jazyke (po sledam Vendlera) [Cosubordination of adjectives in Russian (following in Vendler's footsteps)]. In Leonid

Iomdin & Leonid Krysin (eds.), *Slovo v tekste i v slovare. Sbornik statej k 70-letiju akademika Ju. D. Apresjana*, 379–390. Moskva: Jazyki russkoj kul'tury.

Iordanskaja, Lidija. 2003. L'ordonnancement des adjectifs co-dépendants en russe. In Sylvain Kahane & Alexis Nasr (eds.), *Proceedings of the First International conference on Meaning-Text theory*, 159–169. Paris: École Normale Supérieure.

Iordanskaja, Lidija. 2007. Lexicographic definition and lexical cooccurrence: presuppositions as a 'No-Go' zone for the meaning of modifiers. In Kim Gerdes, Tilmann Reuther & Leo Wanner (eds.), *Meaning-Text Theory 2007 [MTT'07]*, 209–218. München/Wien: Wiener Slawistischer Almanach.

Iordanskaja, Lidija & Igor Mel'čuk. 1981. On a class of Russian verbs which can introduce Direct Speech. In Per Jakobsen and Helen Krag (eds.), *The Slavic Verb*, 51–66. Copenhague: Rosenkilde & Bagger.

Iordanskaja, Lidija & Igor Mel'čuk. 1995. Traitement lexicographique de deux connecteurs textuels du français contemporain ⌜EN FAIT⌝ vs ⌜EN RÉALITÉ⌝. In Hava Bat-Zeev Shyldkrot & Lucien Kupferman (eds.), *Tendances récentes en linguistique française et générale (volume dédié à David Gaatone)*, 211–236. Amsterdam/Philadelphia: John Benjamins.

Iordanskaja, Lidija & Igor Mel'čuk. 2009a. Establishing an inventory of surface-syntactic relations: valence-controlled surface dependents of the verb in French. In Alain Polguère & Igor Mel'čuk (eds.), *Dependency in linguistic description*, 151–234. Amsterdam/Philadelphia: John Benjamins.

Iordanskaja, Lidija & Igor Mel'čuk. 2009b. Semantics of the Russian conjunction POKA 'while, before, until'. In Tilman Berger, Markus Giger, Sibylle Kurt & Imke Mendoza (eds.), *Von grammatischen Kategorien und sprachlichen Weltbildern – Die Slavia von der Sprachgeschichte bis zur Politsprache. Festschrift für Daniel Weiss zum 60. Geburtstag*, 233–262. München/Wien: Wiener Slawistischer Almanach.

Iordanskaja, Lidija & Igor Mel'čuk. 2015. Ordering of simple clauses in an English complex sentence. *Rhema/Rema* 4. 17–59.

Iordanskaja, Lidija & Igor Mel'čuk. 2017. *Le mot français dans le lexique et dans la phrase*. Paris: Hermann.

Iordanskaja, Lidija & Igor Mel'čuk. 2019. Semantics in syntax: linear ordering of genitive adnominal dependents cosubordinated to a noun in Russian. *Vopropsy jazykoznanija* № 4. 33–46.

Iordanskaja, Lidija & Alain Polguère. 1988. Semantic processing for text generation. In *Proceedings of the First International Computer Science Conference '88. Artificial Intelligence: Theory and Applications*, 310–318. Hong Kong.

Iordanskaja, Lidija & Alain Polguère. 2005. Hooking up syntagmatic lexical functions to lexicographic definitions. In Jurij Apresjan and Leonid Iomdin (eds.), *East-West Encounter, Second International Conference on Meaning-Text Theory [MTT'05]*, 170–186. Moskva: Jazyki slavjanskoj kul'tury.

Jackendoff, Ray. 1984. On the phrase *the phrase 'the phrase'*. *Natural Language and Linguistic Theory* 2. 25–37. [A more recent corrected version: Jackendoff, Ray. 2010. *Meaning and the Lexicon. The Parallel Architecture. 1975–2010*, 327–341. Oxford: Oxford University Press.]

Jackendoff, Ray. 2002. English particle constructions, the lexicon, and the autonomy of syntax. In Nicole Dehé, Ray Jackendoff, Andrew McIntyre & Silke Urban, V*erb-Particle Explorations*, 67–94. Berlin: Mouton de Gruyter. [A more recent corrected version: Jackendoff, Ray. 2010. *Meaning and the Lexicon. The Parallel Architecture. 1975–2010*, 226–249. Oxford: Oxford University Press.]

Jang, Youngjun. 1997. Multiple subject construction in Korean: a functional explanation. *Kansas Working Papers in Linguistics* 22 (1). 25–40.
Jaxontov, Sergej. 1965. *Drevnekitajskij jazyk* [Ancient Chinese]. Moskva: Nauka.
Jaxontov, Sergej. 1974. Nekotorye passivnye konstrukcii v kitajskom jazyke [Some passive constructions in Chinese]. In Aleksandr Xolodovič (ed.), *Tipologija passivnyx konstrukcij. Diatezy i zalogi*, 195–202. Leningrad: Nauka.
Jones, Michael. 1993. *Sardinian Syntax*. London, New York: Routledge.
Kachru, Yamuna. 2006. *Hindi*. Amsterdam/Philadelphia: John Benjamins.
Kahane, Sylvain 1997. Bubble trees and syntactic representations. In Ti mann Becker & Hans-Ulrich Krieger (eds.), *Proceedings of the 5th Meeting of the mathematics of language* (MOL 5), 70–76. Saarbrücken.
Kahane, Sylvain. 2001. A fully lexicalized grammar for French based on Meaning-Text theory. In Alexander Gelbukh (ed.), *Computational linguistics and intelligent text processing, Second International conference, CICLing 2001, Mexico-City, Mexico, February 18–24, 2001, Proceedings* [Lecture notes in computer science 2004], 18–31. Berlin/Heidelberg: Springer.
Keenan, Edward. 1976. Towards a universal definition of "subject." In Charles Li (ed.), *Subject and topic*, 305–333. New York et al.: Academic Press.
Keenan, Edward. 1985. Relative clauses. In Timothy Shopen (ed.), *Language typology and syntactic description. II. Complex constructions*, 141–170. Cambridge et al.: Cambridge University Press.
Keenan, Edward & Bernard Comrie. 1977. Noun phrase accessibility and Universal Grammar. *Linguistic Inquiry* 8 (1). 63–99.
Kholodilova, Maria. 2013. Inverse attraction in Ingrian Finnish relative clauses. *Linguistica Uralica* 49 (2). 96–116.
Kibrik, Aleksandr. 1975. Nominat vnaja/ėrgativnaja konstrukcii i logičeskoe udarenie v arčinskom jazyke [Nominative/ergative construction and logical accent in Archi]. In *Issledovanija po strukturnoj i prikladnoj lingvistike*, 54–62. Moskva: Izdatel'stvo Moskovskogo universiteta.
Kibrik, Aleksandr. 1977. *Opyt strukturnogo opisanija arčinskogo jazyka. III. Dinamičeskaja grammatika* [Towards a structural description of Archi. III. A dynamic grammar]. Moskva: Izdatel'stvo Moskovskogo universiteta.
Kibrik, Aleksandr. 1997. Beyond subject and object: towards a comprehensive relational typology. *Linguistic Typology* 1. 279–346.
Kibrik, Aleksandr. 2001. Grammatical relations. In Neil Smelser & Paul Baltes (eds.), *International encyclopedia of the social and behavioral sciences*, 6342–6348. Amsterdam: Pergamon Press.
Kibrik, Aleksandr. 2003. *Konstanty i peremennye jazyka* [Constants and variables in language]. Sankt-Peterburg: Aletejia.
Kim, Hong-Bok & Peter Sells 2010. Oblique case marking on core arguments in Korean. *Studies in Language* 34 (3). 602–635.
Kimenyi, Alexandre. 1980. *Relational grammar of Kinyarwanda*. Berkeley, CA: UCLA Press.
Koul, Omkar. 2008. *Modern Hindi grammar*. Springfield, VA: Dunwoody Press.
Kovtunova, Irina. 1976. *Sovremennyj russkij jazyk. Porjadok slov i aktual'noe členenie predloženija* [Modern Russian. Word order and "actual division" of a sentence]. Moskva: Prosveščenie.
Kovtunova, Irina. 1980. Porjadok slov [Word order]. In Natal'ja Švedova (ed.), *Russkaja grammatika II*. Moskva: Nauka.

Kozinskij, Icxak. 1983. *O kategorii "podležaščee" v russkom jazyke* ["Syntactic subject" category in Russian], *Predvaritel'nye publikacii Problemnoj gruppy po èksperimental'noj i prikladnoj lingvistike*, vypusk 156. Moskva: Institut russkogo jazyka AN SSSR.

Kroeger, Paul. 1993. *Phrase structure and grammatical relations in Tagalog*. Stanford, CA: CSLI Publications.

Kroeger, Paul. 2007. McKaughan's analysis of Philippine voice. In Loren Billings & Nelleke Goudswaard (eds.), *Piakandatu ami Dr. Howard P. McKaughan*, Manila: Linguistic Society of the Philippines and SIL Philippines, 41–46. See http://gamma.sil.org/acpub/repository/Kroeger-McK-voice-final.pdf

Kručinina, Irina. 1968. Konstrukcija s mestoimeniem KOTORYJ v sovremennom russkom jazyke [Construction with the pronoun KOTORYJ 'which' in Modern Russian]. *Voprosy jazykoznanija* № 2. 82–88.

Kuno, Susumu. 1973. *The structure of the Japanese language*. Cambridge, MA/London: The MIT Press.

Kuroda, Sige-Yuki. 1968. English relativization and certain related problems. *Language* 48 (2). 244–266.

Lakoff, George. 1974. Syntactic amalgams. In *Chicago Linguistic Society: Papers from the 10th Regional Meeting*, 321–344.

Lazard, Gilbert. 1994. *L'actance*. Paris: Presses Universitaires de France.

Lee, Iksop & S. Robert Ramsey. 2000. *The Korean Language*. Albany, NY: SUNY Press.

Lehmann, Christian. 1984. *Der Relativsatz*. Tübingen: Gunter Narr.

Lehmann, Christian. 1986. On typology of relative clause. *Linguistics* 24 (4). 663–680.

Lepschy, Giulio. 1994. The status of subject in linguistic theory. Closing remarks. In Marina Yaguello (ed.), *Subjecthood and subjectivity*, 275–279. Paris: Ophrys/Institut français du Royaume-Uni.

Levi, Judith. 1978. *The syntax of complex nominals*. New York: Academic Press.

Li, Charles & Sandra Thompson. 1981. *Mandarin Chinese. A functional reference grammar*. Berkeley, CA et al.: University of California Press.

Li, Charles (ed.). 1976. *Subject and topic*. New York et al.: Academic Press.

Lister-Turner, Robert & J. B. Clark. 1931. *A grammar of the Motu language of Papua*. Sydney: Pettifer.

Liu, Na. 2016. The structures of Chinese long and short *bei* passives revisited. *Language and Linguistics* 17 (6). 857–889.

MacDonald, Danica & Nicholas Welch. 2009. Topic, focus and double subjects in Korean. In *Proceedings of the 2009 Annual Conference of the Canadian Linguistic Association*, 1–14.

Mahajan, Anoop. 2000. Relative asymmetries and Hindi correlatives. In Artemis Alexiadou, Paul Law, André Meinunger & Chris Wilder (eds.), *The syntax of relative clauses*, 201–229. Amsterdam/Philadelphia: John Benjamins.

Maling, Joan & Soowon Kim. 1992. Case assignment in the inalienable possession construction in Korean. *Journal of East Asian Linguistics* 1. 37–68.

Marlett, Stephen. 2012. Relative clauses in Seri. In Bernard Comrie & Zarina Estrada-Fernández (eds.), *Relative clauses in languages of the Americas. A typological overview*, 213–241. Amsterdam/Philadelphia: John Benjamins.

Marneffe, Marie-Catherine de, Timothy Dozat, Natalia Silveira, Katri Haverinen, Filip Ginter, Joakim Nivre & Christopher Manning. 2014. Universal Stanford Dependencies: a crosslinguistic typology. In *Proceedings of the Ninth International Conference on Language resources and Evaluation*, 4585–4592. European Languages Resources Association (ELRA).

Marneffe, Marie-Catherine de & Christopher Mann ng. 2008/2015. *Stanford typed dependencies manual*. See http://nlp.stanford.edu/software/dependencies_manual.pdf

Maslova, Ekaterina. 2003. *A grammar of Kolyma Yukagir*. Berlin: Mouton de Gruyter.

Matsumoto, Yoshiko, Bernard Comrie & Peter Sells (eds.). 2017. *Noun-modifying clause constructions in languages of Eurasia. Rethinking theoretical and geographical boundaries*. Amsterdam/Philadelphia: John Benjamins.

Mel'čuk, Igor. 1964. Obobščenie ponjatija frazeologizma (morfologičeskie frazeologizmy) [A generalization of the concept "phraseologism" (morphological phraseologisms)]. In Leonid Rojzenzon (ed.), *Materialy konferencii "Aktual'nye voprosy saovremennogo jazykoznanija i lingvističeskoe nasledie E. D. Polivanova", tom I*, 89–90. Samarkand: Samarkandskij Gosudartsvennyj Universitet.

Mel'čuk, Igor. 1965. Porjadok slov pri avtomatičeskom sinteze russkogo teksta (predvaritel'noe soobščenie) [Word order in automatic synthesis of Russian texts (preliminary communication)]. *Naučno-texničeskaja informacija* № 12. 36–44. [A French translation: I. Mel'čuk, 1967: *T.A. Informations* 2. 65–84.]

Mel'čuk, Igor. 1974. *Opyt teorii lingvističeskix modelej «Smysl ⇔ Tekst». Semantika, sintaksis* [Outline of a theory of linguistic Meaning-Text models. Semantics, syntax]. Moskva: Nauka. [Reprint: 1995.]

Mel'čuk, Igor. 1982. Lexical functions in lexicographic description. *Proceedings of the VIIIth Annual Meeting of the Berkeley Linguistics Society* [BLS 8], 427–444.

Mel'čuk, Igor. 1987. Un affixe dérivationnel et un phrasème syntaxique du russe moderne. Essai de description formelle. *Revue des études slaves* 53 (3). 631–648.

Mel'čuk, Igor. 1988. *Dependency syntax: theory and practice*. Albany, NY: State University of New York Press.

Mel'čuk, Igor. 1992–2000. *Cours de morphologie générale, vol. 1–5*. Montréal: Les Presses de l'Université de Montréal/Paris: C.N.R.S.

Mel'čuk, Igor. 2001. *Communicative organization in natural language. The semantic-communicative structure of sentences*. Amsterdam/Philadelphia: John Benjamins.

Mel'čuk, Igor. 2004. Actants in semantics and syntax. I/II: Actants in semantics/in syntax. *Linguistics* 42 (1). 1–66; 42 (2). 247–291.

Mel'čuk, Igor. 2006a. *Aspects of a theory of morphology*. Berlin/New York: Mouton de Gruyter.

Mel'čuk, Igor. 2006b. Calculus of possibilities as a technique in linguistic typology. In Felix Ameka, Alan Dench & Nicolas Evans (eds.), *Catching language. The standing challenge of grammar writing*, 171–205. Berlin/New York: Mouton de Gruyter.

Mel'čuk, Igor. 2007. Lexical functions. In Harald Burger, Dmitry Dobrovol'skij, Peter Kühn & Neal Norrick (eds.), *Phraseology. An international handbook of contemporary research*, 119–131. Berlin/New York: Mouton de Gruyter.

Mel'čuk, Igor. 2009a. Dependency in natural language. In Alain Polguère & Igor Mel'čuk (eds.), *Dependency in linguistic description*, 1–110. Amsterdam/Philadelphia: John Benjamins.

Mel'čuk, Igor. 2009b. Functional linguistic models a step forward in the study of Man. BULAG [= *Bulletin de la linguistique appliquée et générale*] 33 [= International symposium on data and sense mining, machine translation and controlled languages, and their application to emergencies and safety critical domains], 1–10. Besançon: Presses Universitaires de Franche-Comté.

Mel'čuk, Igor. 2011. Word order in Russian. In Igor' Boguslavskij, Leonid Iomdin & Leonid Krysin (eds.), *Slovo i jazyk (Sbornik statej k vos'midesjatiletiju akademika Ju. D. Apresjana)*, 499–525. Moskva: Jazyki slavjanskix kul'tur.

Mel'čuk, Igor. 2012a. Bi-nominative sentences in Russian. In Veronika Makarova (ed.), *Russian Language Studies in North America. New Perspectives from Theoretical and Applied Linguistics*, 85–105. London: Arthem.

Mel'čuk, Igor. 2012b. *Jazyk: ot smysla k tekstu* [Language: from meaning to text]. Moscow: Jazyki slavjanskoj kul'tury.

Mel'čuk, Igor. 2012c. Mestoimennye vyraženija s imenem čertyxatel'nym tipa [*Ona uexala*] *čërt znaet kuda* i im podobnye v russkom jazyke [Pronominal expressions with a blasphemous noun of the type [*Ona uexala*] *čërt znaet kuda* 'She left Devil knows where' and similar ones in Russian]. *Russkij jazyk v naučnom osveščenii* 2 (24). 5–22.

Mel'čuk, Igor. 2012d. Phraseology in the language, in the dictionary, and in the computer. *Yearbook of Phraseology* 3. 31–56.

Mel'čuk, Igor. 2012–2015. *Semantics: from meaning to text.* Vols 1–3. Amsterdam/Philadelphia: John Benjamins.

Mel'čuk, Igor. 2014a. Dependency in language. In Kim Gerdes, Eva Hajičová & Leo Wanner (eds.), *Dependency linguistics. Recent advances in linguistic theory using dependency structures*, 1–33. Amsterdam/Philadelphia: John Benjamins.

Mel'čuk, Igor. 2014b. Syntactic subject: syntactic relations, once again. In Vladimir Plungjan with Mixail Daniėl', Ekaterina Ljutikova, Sergej Tatevosov & Ol'ga Fëdorova (eds.), *Jazyk. Konstanty. Peremennye. Pamjati Aleksandra Evgen'eviča Kibrika* [Language. Constants. Variables. To the memory of Alexander Kibrik], 169–216. Sankt-Peterburg: Aletejja.

Mel'čuk, Igor. 2014c. The East/South-East Asian answer to the European passive. In Sergej Dmitrenko & Natal'ja Zaika (eds.), *Acta Linguistica Petropolitana*, 2014/10 (3) [= Festschrift Xrakovskij], 451–472. Sankt-Peterburg: Nauka.

Mel'čuk, Igor. 2015a. Clichés, an understudied subclass of phrasemes. *Yearbook of Phraseology* 6. 55–86.

Mel'čuk, Igor. 2015b. Multiple "subjects" and multiple "objects" in Korean. *Language Research* 51(3). 485–516.

Mel'čuk, Igor. 2015–2016. A general inventory of surface-syntactic relations in world languages. Part one. *Moscow Journal of Linguistics* 17(2). 75–103; Part two, *Moscow Journal of Linguistics* 18 (1). 94–120.

Mel'čuk, Igor. 2016. *Language: from meaning to text.* Moskva/Boston, MA: Academic Studies Press.

Mel'čuk, Igor'. 2017. KAK..., TAK I...: čto ėto za? [KAK..., TAK I... 'as..., so also...': what kind of stuff is this?]. *Russkij jazyk v naučnom osveščenii* 1 (33). 67–85.

Mel'čuk, Igor. 2018a. Genitive adnominal dependents in Russian: surface-syntactic relations in the N→N$_{GEN}$ phrase. *Voprosy jazykoznanija* № 4. 25–46.

Mel'čuk, Igor. 2018b. Les prépositions zéro en français. *Lingvisticæ Investigationes* 41 (2). 269–283.

Mel'čuk, Igor. 2018c. "Wordlets": One of Zholkovsky's major contributions to the notion of deep-syntactic structure. In Dennis Ioffe, Marcus Levitt, Joe Peschio & Igor Pilshchikov (eds.), *A/Z: Essays in Honor of Alexander Zholkovsky*, 350–360. Boston: Academic Studies Press.

Mel'čuk, Igor & Nikolaj Pertsov. 1987. *Surface syntax of English. A formal model within the Meaning-Text framework.* Amsterdam: John Benjamins.

Mel'čuk, Igor & Alain Polguère. 2007. *Lexique actif du français. L'apprentissage du vocabulaire fondé sur 20 000 dérivations sémantiques et collocations du français.* Brussels: De Boeck.

Mel'čuk, Igor & Alexander Zholkovsky. 1984. *Explanatory Combinatorial Dictionary of Modern Russian*, Wien: Wiener Slawistischer Almanach.

Mel'čuk, Igor & Aleksandr Žolkovskij. 2016. *Tolkovo-kombnatornyj slovar' russkogo jazyka. 2-oe izdanie, ispravlennoe* [Explanatory and combinatorial dictionary of Russian. 2nd edition, corrected]. Moskva: Jazyki slavjanskix kul'tur.
Mel'čuk, Igor et al. 1984–1999. *Dictionnaire explicatif et combinatoire du français contemporain : Recherches lexico-sémantiques I–IV*, Montréal: Les Presses de l'Université de Montréal.
Melis, Ludo. 2000. L'infinitif de narration comme prédication seconde. *Langages* 127. 36–48.
Milićević, Jasmina. 2007. *La paraphrase. Modélisation de la paraphrase langagière*. Bern: Peter Lang.
Milićević, Jasmina. 2009. Linear placement of Serbian clitics in a syntactic dependency framework. In Alain Polguère & Igor Mel'čuk (eds.), *Dependency in linguistic description*, 235–276. Amsterdam/Philadelphia: John Benjamins.
Mille, Simon & Leo Wanner. 2008. Making text resources accessible to the reader: the case of patent claims. In *Proceedings of the 6th Intern. Conference on Language Resources and Evaluation* [LREC'08], 1394–1400. Marrakesh. See also http://www.lrec-conf.org/proceedings/lrec2008/
Mixeev, Mixail. 2000. Žizni myš'ja begotnja ili toska tščetnosti? (O metaforičeskoj konstrukcii s roditel'nym padežom) [Mouse scurrying of life or pining of vanity? The metaphorical construction with the genitive]. *Voprosy jazykoznanija* № 2. 47–69.
Nagel, Ernest, Patrick Suppes & Alfred Tarski (eds.). 1962. *Logic, methodology and philosophy of science*. Stanford, CA: Stanford University Press.
Nichols, Johanna, Gilbert Rappaport & Alan Timberlake. 1980. Subject, topic, and control in Russian. In Bruce Caron et al. (eds.), *Proceedings of the Sixth Annual Meeting of the Berkeley Linguistics Society* [BLS 6], 372–386.
Niu, Ruochen & Timothy Osborne. 2019. Chunks are components: A dependency grammar approach to the syntactic structure of Mandarin. *Lingua* 224. 60–83.
O'Grady, William. 1991. *Categories and case. The sentence structure of Korean*. Amsterdam/Philadelphia: John Benjamins.
O'Grady, William. 1992. On the status of *ha-ta* in the multiple complement structures. In *1992 Seoul International Conference on Linguistics* [SICOL'92], 238–247. Seoul: The Linguistic Society of Korea.
Otsuka, Yuko. 2000. *Ergativity in Tongan*. PhD Thesis. Oxford: University of Oxford. See http://www2.hawaii.edu/~yotsuka
Otsuka, Yuko. 2010. DP ellipsis in Tongan: is syntactic ergativity real? *Natural Language and Linguistic Theory* 28. 315–342.
Padučeva, Elena. 1974. *O semantike sintaksisa* [On semantics of syntax]. Moskva Nauka.
Palmer, Frank. 1994. *Grammatical roles and relations*. Cambridge: Cambridge University Press.
Paris, Marie-Claude. 1998. Syntaxe et sémantique de quatre marqueurs de transitivité en chinois standard: BA, BEI, JIAO et RANG. In André Rousseau (ed.), *La transitivité*, 357–370. Villeneuve d'Ascq: Presses Universitaires de Septentrion.
Partee, Barbara & Vladimir Borschev. 2000. Possessives, *favorite*, and coercion. In Rebecca Daly & Anastasia Riehl (eds), *Proceedings of ESCOL 99*, 173–190. Ithaca, NY: Cornell University.
Patejuk, Agnieszka & Adam Przepiórkowski. 2019. Coordination of unlike grammatical functions. In https://syntaxfest.github.io/syntaxfest19/proceedings/papers/paper_3.pdf
Peranteau, Paul, Judith Levi & Gloria Phares (eds.). 1972. *The Chicago Which Hunt. Papers from the Realtive Clause Festival*. Chicago: Chicago Linguistic Society.
Plank, Frans (ed.). 1984. *Objects. Towards a theory of grammatical relations*. London et al.: Academic Press

Platzak, Christer. 2000. A Complement-of-Nº account of restrictive and non-restrictive relatives. In Artemis Alexiadou, Paul Law, André Meinunger & Chris Wilder (eds.), *The syntax of relative clauses*, 265–308. Amsterdam/Philadelphia: John Benjamins.

Poiret, Rafaël & Haitao Liu. 2019. Les dépendants adnominaux prépositionnels en français : Relations syntaxiques de surface dans le syntagme N→SP. *Français Moderne* 2. 259–280.

Polguère, Alain. 2014. Rection nominale : retour sur les constructions évaluatives. *Travaux de linguistique* 68. 83–102.

Polguère, Alain & Igor Mel'čuk (eds.). 2009. *Dependency in linguistic description*. Amsterdam/Philadelphia: John Benjamins.

Pollard, Carl & Ivan Sag. 1992. Anaphors in English and the scope of binding theory. *Linguistic Inquiry* 23 (2). 261–303.

Pouplier, Marianne. 2003. Referential subject and object gaps in Modern Icelandic. *Nordlyd* 31 (2). 356–371.

Quirk, Randolph, Sydney Greenbaum, Geoffrey Leech & Jan Svartvik. 1991. *A comprehensive grammar of the English language*. London/New York: Longman.

Raxilina Ekaterina. 2010. Konstrukcija s russkim roditel'nym i eë formal'naja interpretacija [The construction with the Russian genitive and its formal interpretation]. In Ekaterina Raxilina (ed.), *Lingvistika konstrukcij* [Construction linguistics], 247–285. Moskva: Azbukovnik.

Rebuschi, Georges. 1978. Cas et fonction sujet en basque. *Verbum* 1 (1). 69–98.

Rebuschi, Georges. 1981. Quelques problèmes de syntaxe anglaise pour la grammaire dite "relationnelle". *Verbum* 4 (1). 85–119.

Rebuschi, Georges. 1982. *Structure de l'énoncé en basque*. [Collection ERA 642, numéro spécial.] Paris: Université Paris 7.

Rebuschi, Georges. 1986. Diathèse et (non-)configuralité : l'exemple du basque. *Actance* 2. 175–208.

Ren, Xiaobo. 1993. *Syntaxe des constructions passives en chinois*. Paris: Langages Croisés.

Roberts, John. 1987. *Amele*. London et al.: Crook Helm.

Roberts, John. 1988. Switch-reference in Papuan languages: a syntactic or extrasyntactic device? *Australian Journal of Linguistics* 8 (1). 75–117.

Roberts, John. 2001. Impersonal constructions in Amele. In Alexandra Aikhenvald, Robert M. W. Dixon & Masayuki Onishi (eds.), *Non-canonical marking of subjects and objects*, 201–250. Amsterdam/Philadelphia: John Benjamins.

Samvelian, Polett. 2012. *Grammaire des prédicats complexes*. Paris: Lavoisier.

Sandfeld, Kristian. 1965. *Syntaxe du français contemporain. Les propositions subordonnées*. Genève: Droz.

Sannikov, Vladimir. 1963. Mesto rasprostranënnogo opredelenija po otnošeniju k opredeljaemomu slovu v russkoj fraze [The position of an expanded adjectival modifier with respect to the modified word in a Russian sentence]. *Voprosy jazykoznanija* № 1. 124–130. [Reprinted 2008 in V. Sannikov, *Russkij sintaksis v semantiko-pragmatičeskom prostranstve*, 585–598. Moskva: Jazyki slavjanskix kul'tur.]

Sannikov, Vladimir. 2010a. Proleptičeskie i blizkie k nim konstrukcii [Proleptic and similar constructions]. In Jurij Apresjan, Igor' Boguslavskij, Leonid Iomdin & Vladimir Sannikov. 2010. *Teoretičeskie problemy russkogo sintaksisa. Vzaimodejstvie grammatiki i slovarja* [Theoretical problems of Russian syntax. Interaction between grammar and lexicon], 113–129. Moskva: Jazyki slavjanskix kul'tur.

Sannikov, Vladimir. 2010b. Konstrukcii s toždestvennymi slovoformami [Constructions with identical wordforms]. In Jurij Apresjan, Igor' Boguslavskij, Leonid Iomdin & Vladimir

Sannikov, *Teoretičeskie problemy russkogo sintaksisa. Vzaimodejstvie grammatiki i slovarja* [Theoretical problems of Russian syntax. Interaction between grammar and lexicon], 191–208. Moskva: Jazyki slavjanskix kul'tur.
Schütze, Carson. 2001. On Korean "case stacking": The varied functions of the particles **ka** and **lul**. *The Linguistic Review* 19. 193–292.
Schwartz, Arthur. 1976. On the universality of subjects: the Ilocano case. In Charles Li (ed.), *Subject and topic*, 519–543. New York et al.: Academic Press.
Shibatani, Masayoshi. 2009. Elements of complex structures, where recursion isn't. The case of relativization. In Talmy Givón & Masayoshi Shibatani (eds.), *Syntax complexity. Diachrony, acquisition, neuro-cognition, evolution*, 163–198. Amsterdam/Philadelphia: John Benjamins.
Siewierska, Anna & Dik Bakker. 2012. Three takes on grammatical relations. A view from the languages of Europe and North and Central Asia. In Pirkko Suihkonen, Bernard Comrie & Valery Solovyev (eds.), *Argument structure and grammatical relations. A crosslinguistic typology*, 295–324. Amsterdam/ Philadelphia: John Benjamins.
Sirotinina, Ol'ga. 1965. *Porjadok slov v russkom jazyke* [Word order in Russian]. Saratov: Izdatel'stvo Saratovskogo universiteta.
Sohn, Ho-Min. 1994. *Korean*. London/New York: Routledge.
Solnceva, Nina. 1962. *Stradatel'nyj zalog v kitajskom jazyke (problemy morfologii)* [The passive voice in Chinese (morphological problems)]. Moskva: Izdatel'stvo vostočnoj literatury.
Suihkonen, Pirkko, Bernard Comrie & Valery Solovyev (eds.). 2012. *Argument structure and grammatical relations. A crosslinguistic typology*. Amsterdam/ Philadelphia: John Benjamins.
Suñer, Margarita. 1984. Free relatives and the matching parameter. *The Linguistic Review* 3. 363–387.
Svenonius, Peter. 2008. The position of adjectives and other phrasal modifiers in the decomposition of DP. In Louise McNally and Christopher Kennedy (eds.), *Adjectives and Adverbs: Syntax, Semantics, and Discourse*, 16–42. Oxford University Press: Oxford.
Tam, Duy Le. 1976. Vietnamese passive. *Papers from the 12th Regional Meeting of the Chicago Linguistics Society*, 438–449.
Tchekhoff, Claude. 1979. *La construction ergative en avar et en tonguien*. Paris: Klincksieck.
Tesnière, Lucien. 1959. *Éléments de syntaxe structurale*. Paris: Klincksieck.
Testelec, Jakov. 1979. Ob odnom javlenii diatezy v dagestanskix jazykax [On a diathesis phenomenon in Daghestanian languages]. In *Materialy IX mežvuzovskoj studenčeskoj konferencii po strukturnoj i prikladnoj lingvistike*, 50–53. Moskva: Izdatel'stvo Moskovskogo universiteta.
Testelec, Jakov. 2001. *Vvedenie v obščij sintaksis* [Introduction to general syntax]. Moskva: Izdatel'stvo RGGU.
Testelets, Yakov & Elizaveta Bylinina. 2005. Sluicing-based indefinites in Russian. In Steven Franks, Frank Gladney & Mila Tasseva-Kurkchieva (eds.), *Formal approaches to Slavic linguistics 13: The South Carolina meeting*, 355–364. Ann Arbor, MI: Michigan Slavic Publications.
Tiffou, Étienne & Richard Patry. 1995. La relative en bourouchaski du Yasin. *Bulletin de la Société de linguistique de Paris* 90 (1). 335–390.
Trương Van Chình. 1970. *Structure de la langue vietnamienne*. Paris: Paul Geuthner.
Vajs, Daniël' [= Weiss, Daniel]. 2000. Russkie dvojnye glagoly: kto xozjain, a kto sluga? [Russian double verbs: who is the governor, and who is the dependent?] In Leonid Iomdin & Leonid Krysin (eds.), *Slovo v tekste i v slovare. Sbornik statej k semidesjatiletiju akademika Ju. D. Apresjana*, 356–378. Moskva: Jazyki russkoj kul'tury.
Van der Auwera, Johan. 1985. The predicative relatives of French perception verbs. In Machelt Bolkenstein, Caper de Groot & Lachlan Mackenzie (eds.), *Predicate and terms in Functional Grammar*, 219–234. Dordrecht, Holland/Cinnaminson, USA: Foris.

Van Valin, Robert. 1981. Grammatical relations in ergative languages. *Studies in Language* 5 (3). 361–394.
Vendler, Zeno. 1968. *Adjectives and nominalizations*. The Hague/Paris: Mouton.
Vincze, Orsolya & Margarita Alonso Ramos. 2011. A proposal for a multilevel linguistic representation of Spanish personal names. In Kim Gerdes, Eva Hajičová & Leo Wanner (eds.), *Depling 2011 proceedings*. Barcelona. 85–93.
Wanner, Leo (ed.). 1996. *Lexical functions in lexicography and natural language processing*. Amsterdam/Philadelphia: John Benjamins.
Wechsler, Stephen. 1995. *The semantic basis of argument structure*. Stanford, CA: CSLI Publications.
Weiskopf, Daniel. 2007. Compound nominals, context, and compositionality. *Synthese* 156 (1). 161–204.
Wierzbicka, Anna. 1971. *Kocha, lubi, szanuje. Medytacje semantyczne* [(S/he) loves, likes, respects (you). Semantic meditations]. Warszawa: Wiedza Powszechna.
Wierzbicka, Anna. 1991. *Cross-cultural pragmatics. The semantics of human interaction*. Berlin/New York: Mouton de Gruyter.
Williamson, Janis. 1987. An indefiniteness restriction for relative clauses in Lakhota. In Eric Reuland & Alice G. B. ter Meulen (eds.), *The representation of (in)definiteness*, 168–190. Cambridge, MA: MIT Press.
Wittgenstein, Ludwig. 1922. *Tractatus logico-philosophicus*. London: Kegan Paul, Trench, Trubner & Co./New York: Harcourt, Brace & Co. See http://gutenberg.org/ebooks/5740
Xolodilova, Marija. 2014. Otnositel'noe pridatočnoe [Relative subordinate clause]. In *Materialy dlja proekta korpusnogo opisanija russkoj grammatiki* (http://rusgram.ru).
Xolodovič, Aleksandr. 1954 [2013]. *Očerk grammatiki korejskogo jazyka* [Outline of Korean grammar]. Moskva: URSS.
Xolodovič, Aleksandr. 1971. Nekotorye voprosy upravlenija v japonskom jazyke [Some problems of government in Japanese]. In Igor' Vardul' (ed.), *Voprosy japonskogo jazyka*, 113–132. Moskva: Nauka.
Xrakovskij, Viktor. 1974. Passivnye konstrukcii [Passive constructions]. In Aleksandr Xolodovič (ed.), *Tipologija passivnyx konstrukcij. Diatezy i zalogi*, 5–45. Leningrad: Nauka.
Xrakovskij, Viktor. 1975. Isčislenie diatez [Diathesis calculus]. In *Diatezy i zalogi*, 34–51. Leningrad: Leningradskoe otdelenie Instituta jazykoznanija AN SSSR.
Xrakovskij, Viktor. 1981. Diateza i referentnost' [Diathesis and referentiality]. In Viktor Xrakovskij (ed.), *Zalogovye konstrukcii v raznostrukturnyx jazykax* [Voice constructions in languages of various structure], 5–38. Leningrad: Nauka.
Xrakovskij, Viktor. 1999. *Teorija jazykoznanija. Russistika. Arabistika* [Linguistic Theory. Russianistics. Arabistics]. Sankt-Peterburg: Nauka.
Xrakovskij, Viktor. 2004. Koncepcija diatez i zalogov (isxodnye gipotezy – ispytanie vremenem) [Concepts of diathesis and grammatical voice (starting hypotheses and the test of time)]. In Viktor Xrakovskij, Andrej Mal'čukov & Sergej Dmitrenko (eds.), *40 let Sankt-Peterburgskoj tipologičeskoj škole*, 505–519. Moskva: Znak.
Xrakovskij, Viktor (ed.). 1981. *Zalogovye konstrukcii v raznostrukturnyx jazykax* [Voice constructions in languages of various structure]. Leningrad: Nauka.
Yaguello, Marina (ed.). 1994. *Subjecthood and subjectivity*. Paris: Ophrys/Institut français du Royaume-Uni.
Yokoyama, Olga. 1985. A diversified approach to Russian word order. In Michael Flier & Richard Brecht (eds.), *Issues in Russian Morphosyntax*, 187–208. Columbus, OH: Slavica.

Yokoyama, Olga. 1986. *Discourse and word order* [= *Pragmatics and Beyond* 6]. Amsterdam/ Philadelphia: John Benjamins.
Zaliznjak, Andrej & Elena Paducheva. 1975. K tipologii otnositel'nogo predloženija [Toward typology of the relative clause]. *Semiotika i informatika* 6. 51–102. [Reprinted in Andrej Zaliznjak, 2002, *"Russkoe imennoe slovoizmenenie" s priloženiem izbrannyx rabot po sovremennomu russkomu jazyku i obščemu jazykoznaniju*, 648–698. Moskva: Jazyki slavjanskoj kul'tury.]
Zangenfeind, Robert. 2012. Towards a system of syntactic dependencies of German. *Computational Linguistics and Intellectual Technologies* 11 (18), 706–715. See also http://www.dialog-21.ru/digests/dialog2012/materials/pdf/106.pdf.
Ziff, Paul. 1960. *Semantic analysis*. Ithaca, NY: Cornell University Press.
Zimmerling, Anton. 2008. Lokal'nye i global'nye pravila v sintaksise [Local and global rules in syntax]. In Aleksandr Kibrik et al. (eds.), *Computational linguistics and intellectual technologies* 7 (14), 551–562.
Zimmerling, Anton. 2012. Nekanoničeskie podležaščie v russkom jazyke [Non-canonical subjects in Russian]. In Maria Voejkova (ed.), *Ot značenija k forme, ot formy k značeniju: sbornik statej v čest' 80-letija A.V. Bondarko*, 568–590. Moskva: Jazyki slavjanskix kul'tur.
Žolkovskij, Aleksandr & Igor Mel'čuk. 1967. O semantičeskom sinteze [On semantic synthesis], *Problemy kibernetiki* 19 177–238.

Index of definitions

Definition 1.1 – functional model (p. 8)

> A system of symbolic expressions **M(E)** created by the researcher to describe the functioning of **E** is a functional model of **E** if and only if it associates with the given inputs the same outputs as **E** does.

Definition 3.1 – syntactic subject (p. 135)

> The syntactic subject in a clause of **L** is the most privileged SSynt-actant of this clause's Main Verb.

Definition 3.2 – direct object (p. 174)

> The direct object is the second most privileged SSynt-actant of a transitive verb in a non-ergative **L**.

Definition 4.1 – prolepsis (p. 184)

> A lexical unit L (with its syntactic dependents) appearing in a clause is a prolepsis if and only if L satisfies simultaneously the following four conditions:
> 1. Syntactically, L is only loosely linked to the rest of the clause: it is neither a syntactic actant of the Main Verb nor one of its circumstantials.
> 2. Linearly, L is positioned clause-initially.
> 3. Prosodically, L is "insulated" from the clause by a pause, a stress and a special intonation contour.
> 4. Morphologically (in a language with cases), L is most often—but not exclusively!—in the nominative, the least marked case.

Definition 4.2 – nominative case (p. 186)

> The nominative is the case of the form of the noun used for nomination.

Definition 4.3 – subjective case (p. 187)

> The subjective is the case used first and foremost for marking the syntactic subject of any type, but which cannot serve for nomination.

Definition 4.4 – syntactic subject (p. 190), cf. Definition 3.1

> The syntactic subject [SyntSubj] is the most privileged surface-syntactic actant in language **L**.

Definition 4.5 – direct object (p. 193), cf. Definition 3.2

> The direct object is the second most privileged surface-syntactic actant in a non-ergative language **L**.

Definition 4.6 – pseudo-conjunct (p. 196)

> L_2 is a **pseudo-coordinate dependent**, or a **pseudo-conjunct**, of L_1, iff L_2 follows L_1 immediately and can play the same surface-syntactic role as L_1, but does not allow for a coordinating conjunction that would link L_2 to L_1.

Definition 6.1 – modifier (p. 237)

$\tilde{L}$ stands for a lexical expression (= a phrase).

> $\tilde{L}$ is a **modifier** of L in utterance **U** if and only if, in **U**, L depends on $\tilde{L}$ semantically (= 'L' is a semantic actant of '$\tilde{L}$'), and $\tilde{L}$ directly depends on L syntactically:
> $$\tilde{L} \xrightarrow[\leftarrow\text{synt}-]{-\text{sem}\rightarrow} L$$

Definition 6.2 – relative clause (p. 240)

C is a subordinate full-fledged (= finite-verb) clause, C' is its superordinate (= matrix) clause, and L is a lexeme in C'.

> A subordinate clause C is called **relative** iff C is a modifier of an LU L.

Definition 8.1 – ergative construction (p. 293)

> Ergative construction is a verbal predicative construction whose SSynt-subject is marked by a case different from the nominative.

Definition 8.2 – diathesis (p. 295)

> The **diathesis** of a lexeme L is the correspondence between L's SemAs and DSyntAs.

Definition 8.3 – grammatical voice (p. 296)

> Grammatical voice is an inflectional verbal category whose grammemes (= particular voices) mark the modification of the basic diathesis of the verb and are themselves formally marked on the verb.

Definition 9.1 – phraseme (p. 328)

A phraseme is a complex linguistic sign (= a configuration of no less than two linguistic signs) that is not free—that is, it is such that at least one sign in it cannot be freely selected by the Speaker
1) according to this sign's meaning and particular combinatorial properties,
2) following general rules of the language, and
3) independently of all other individual signs being part of the complex sign under consideration.

Definition 9.2 – lexemic phraseme (p. 329)

A lexemic phraseme is a phraseme consisting of no less than two lexemes.

Definition 9.3 – morphemic phraseme (p. 330)

A morphemic phraseme is a phraseme consisting of morphemes inside one wordform—that is, either a phraseologized complex stem, or a phraseologized complex affix, or else a phraseologized combination of a stem with an affix.

Definition 9.4 – syntactic phraseme (p. 330)

A syntactic phraseme is a phraseologized complex linguistic sign that consists of at least two minimal syntactic trees such that its signifier is non-segmental, that is, contains prosody or a bound lexemic variable, e.g., L(X), symbolizing the operation of duplication of the phraseme's actant X.

Definition 10.1 – the surface-syntactic structure of a sentence (p. 339)

The SSyntS of sentence S is an unordered dependency tree where each lexeme of S is represented by a node (of which this lexeme is the label) and whose branches represent language-specific surface-syntactic relations [SSyntRels] that link these lexemes; the names of the SSyntRels are labels on the branches.

Definition 10.2 – the surface-syntactic-communicative structure of a sentence (p. 340)

The SSynt-CommS of sentence S is a division of S's SSyntS into communicative areas (= subtrees) such that each has its Comm-dominant node specified and is labeled with a value of a Synt-Comm-opposition.

Definition 10.3 – the deep-morphological structure of a sentence (p. 340)

The DMorphS of sentence S is the linear sequence of all S's lexemes supplied with all relevant grammemes.

Index of notions and terms, supplied with a glossary

The glossary contains brief explanations of linguistic notions appearing in this book. However, the formulations found therein are not necessarily precise and/ or complete.

Boldfaced page numbers refer to spots where the definition or a substantive discussion of the term in question is found.

Ablativus absolutus

> Absolute construction that consists of a noun in the ablative case and a participle dependent on it and fulfills the SSynt-role of a circumstantial; e.g.:
>
>> Lat. ***Cen**+ā→**parat**+ā cuncti triclinium intrant*
>> '[The] supper prepared, all dining-room enter'.
>
> See pp. 71, 85, 272

absolute construction

> Adverbial expression without a finite verb, semantically bearing on the whole clause, but syntactically linked to it loosely; e.g.:
>
>> ***Once home**, he met Mary.* | *John was working, **the child asleep at his side**.*
>
> See pp. 71, 104, 105

absolutive

> Case used to mark the Synt-subject of an intransitive verb and the DirO of a transitive verb (but not used for nomination).
>
> See pp. **141**, 145, 147

accusativus cum infinitivo

> Syntactic construction of a transitive verb where the DirO expresses the Agent of the infinitival object; e.g.:
>
>> *Mary knows **him to be** treacherous* ('he is treacherous'). |
>> *We saw **John enter** the café* ('John entered the café').
>
> See p. 61

accusativus cum participio

> Syntactic construction of a transitive verb where the DirO expresses the Agent of the participial complement of the verb; e.g.:
>
>> *We saw **John entering** the café* ('John was entering the café').
>
> See pp. 61, 65

actant (of an LU L)

— (of L), deep-syntactic

Lexical unit L′ whose presence in the utterance is predicted (= implied) by the signified of the lexical unit L and which depends on L semantically and syntactically:
$$L \overset{-\text{sem}}{\underset{-\text{synt}}{\longleftarrow}} L'$$

E.g.: ***John*** $\overset{-\text{sem}}{\underset{-\text{synt}}{\longleftarrow}}$ *adores* $\overset{-\text{sem}}{\underset{-\text{synt}}{\longrightarrow}}$ ***Mary***.

Cf. modifier/circumstantial (of an LU L).

See pp. 33, 47, 66, 135, 140, 182, 205, 237, 240, 253, 286, 295, 359

— (of 'σ'/L('σ')), semantic

- Either the semanteme 'σ″' that depends on the semanteme 'σ' and corresponds to a semantic actant slot in 'L'; e.g.:

'John←1–love–2→Mary', where 'John' and 'Mary' are, respectively, SemA 1 and 2 of 'love'

- Or the lexical unit L('σ″') that semantically depends on the lexical unit L('σ').

See pp. 33, 106, 182, 205, 221, 237, 323, 402

— (of L), surface-syntactic

Lexical unit L′ that syntactically depends on the lexical unit L and either is L's syntactic subject/direct object or shares several relevant syntactic properties with these clause elements; e.g., indirect object:

GIVE–**indir-objectival**→JOHN [*the permission to leave*]

See pp. 39, 47, 66, 83, 111, 122, 135, 174, 190, 191, 193

adjunct, free (of an LU L)

Modifier/Circumstantial of the lexical unit L.

See p. 352

adjunct, verbal: see *verb, phrasal*

affix

Morph that is not a radical; e.g.: **-s** in *finger+s*, **-ing** in *formulat+ing*, **re-** in *re+formulate*, etc. Cf. radical.

See pp. 27, 159, 169, 262, 296, 330

agreement

One of the two types of morphological dependency (the other one being government): the wordform w_1 is said to agree with the wordform w_2 if and only if some grammemes of w_1 are determined by:

1) Some grammemes of w_2:
       this$_{w_1}$ *stick*$_{w_2}$ ~ *these*$_{w_1}$ *sticks*$_{w_2}$

2) The agreement class of w_2:
       Fr. **beau**$_{\text{MASC-}w_1}$ *palais*$_{(\text{masc})w_2}$ 'beautiful palace' ~
           belle$_{\text{FEM-}w_1}$ *maison*$_{(\text{fem})w_2}$ 'beautiful house'

3) Some semantemes in the signified of w_2:
       Rus. *Vrač*$_{(\text{masc})w_2}$ **prišël**$_{\text{MASC-}w_1}$ 'The doctor [male] arrived'. ~
            Vrač$_{(\text{masc})w_2}$ **prišla**$_{\text{FEM-}w_1}$ 'The doctor [female] arrived'.

See pp. 12, 18, 120, 126–128, 132, 137, 140–173, 349, 350

analysis, linguistic (= speech understanding)

Operation whereby the Addressee of a speech act goes from the text received to the linguistic meaning expressed by it: Text ⟹ Meaning; cf. **synthesis, linguistic**.

See pp. 10, 19, 26, 337

analytical form (of a lexical unit L)

Complex linguistic expression in which a grammeme of the lexeme L is realized by a separate lexeme L'; e.g.: *will*$_{L'}$ *stay*, where the FUTURE grammeme is expressed by an auxiliary verb; cf. **synthetic form**.

See pp. 96, 97, 297, 354

apophony

Meaningful alternation; e.g.: $A_{\text{PAST}}^{/\text{I}/\Rightarrow/\text{æ}/}$, as in *sing* ~ *sang*.

See p. 19

approximate-quantitative syntactic construction (in Russian)

Construction "N + NUM", in which the anteposition of the noun with respect to the numeral expresses the meaning 'the Speaker is uncertain about the number' (the neutral order is NUM + N) ; e.g., *tonn desjat'* lit. 'tons ten' = 'maybe ten tons' (*desjat' tonn* means 'ten tons'). In the deep-syntactic structure, this construction is encoded by the fictitious lexeme «PRIMERNO» (lit. 'approximately') = «MAYBE».

See pp. 87, 88, 177, 351

arborization

> Semantic operation whereby the branches of a deep-syntactic structure are constructed under synthesis. Cf. **lexicalization** and **morphologization**.
>
> See p. 15

asyndetic

> Without conjunction; e.g.: the sentence *John entered, Mary left* features an asyndetic coordination of two clauses.
>
> See p. 115

attribute

> Noun, prepositional phrase or adverb characterizing a noun: e.g.: *days of **happiness**, a man of **integrity**, the formula **above**.*
>
> See pp. 86, 93, 140, 143, 187, 199, 201, 203, 208, 222, 353

Base (of a collocation)

> Component of a collocation that is selected by the Speaker freely and that controls the selection of the **collocate** (see); e.g.: in *pay attention*, ATTENTION is the base; in *black coffee*, COFFEE is the base.
>
> See pp. 23, 55, 199, 234–286, 310, 329

basic structure (of a linguistic representation)

> Structure on which other structures of a linguistic representation (= the **peripheral** ones) are superimposed.
>
> See p. 11

Characterization (= modification)

> Syntactic phenomenon whereby a lexical unit L′ depends on a lexical unit L syntactically, but is its semantic governor:
>
> $$L \underset{\text{synt}\rightarrow}{\overset{\leftarrow\text{sem}-}{}} L'$$
>
> E.g.: *long*$_{L'}$ *stick*$_L$, *girl*$_L$ *with*$_{L'}$ *umbrella*, *running*$_L$ *fast*$_{L'}$. Cf. **complementation**.

clause (simple)

> Phrase that contains a V_{FIN} and all its direct and indirect dependents—except for another phrase of the same type; e.g.:
>
> *John told Mary the news.* | *that I know the truth* | *which we found yesterday*
>
> See pp. 238, 253

clause element

Lexical expression (= a lexeme with its dependents) that can be a direct syntactic dependent of the head of a full-fledged clause; e.g.: the Synt-subject, the DirO and other objects, a circumstantial, etc.

See pp. 52, 57–59, 93, 122*ff*, 327, 347, 365

clausative

Part of speech an element of which is syntactically equivalent to a **clause**; e.g.: *Down [with terrorists!]* | *Wow!* | *Not at all.*

See pp. 54, 311

cleft

Syntactic construction used to express **Focalization**:

IT←BE→(PREP→)N THAT/WHO-CLAUSE

E.g.: ***It was*** *from John*$_{\text{FOCALIZED}}$ *that Mary* ***learnt*** *the news.*

See pp. 52, 252

cliché

Compositional conceptual-lexemic phraseme; e.g.:
Rome was not built in one day. | *Everybody makes mistakes.* | *No parking.*

See pp. 206, 329, 330

clitic

Lexeme L that carries no stress (nor tone) and in the text phonetically "leans" on a normal wordform, called L's **host**.

See pp. 77, 84, 146, 171–173, 265, 344

——, resumptive

Pronominal clitic that repeats (= "resumes") a clause element according to the rules of language; e.g.: Sp. ***Le*** *creo a Juán* 'Him I believe to Juan', where the clitic *le* repeats, or "doubles," the IndirO *a Juan*.

See pp. 49, 50, 58, 67

——, second position

Clitic that must be linearly positioned after the first phrase of the clause; e.g.: Serb. *Supu **sam** pojeo* 'Soup am having.eaten' = 'As for soup, I ate it up' or *Pojeo **sam** supu* 'Having.eaten am soup', where the form *sam* (1.SG present of BITI 'be') is a second-position clitic.

See pp. 171, 344

cognate object

Surface-syntactic object N of a verb V such that N's meaning is the same as that of V, which otherwise cannot have an object; e.g.: *die a heroic **death*** or Rus. *umeret′ gerojskoj **smert′ju**$_{\text{INSTR}}$* [idem].

See pp. 54, 72

collocate

Component of a collocation that is selected by the Speaker as a function of the collocation's base; e.g.: in *pay attention*, PAY is the collocate.

See pp. 23, 25, 55, 199, 284, 286, 310, 324

collocation

Compositional lexemic phraseme one component of which—the base—is selected by the Speaker freely (according to its meaning and combinatorial properties), while the second component—the collocate—is chosen as a function of the base; e.g.: *pay ATTENTION, heavy INVOLVEMENT, under CONSTRUCTION, black COFFEE, leap YEAR*.

See pp. 23, 55, 88, 170, 193, 199, 223, 224, 229, 284–286, 310, 311, 316–321, 324, 329, 330

communicate

Express meanings by clauses that implement propositions describing situations the Speaker targets and that have such a form that they can be negated or questioned. Cf. **signal**$_{(V)}$.

communicatively dominant semanteme (in a configuration of semantemes)

In a configuration of semantemes 'σ_1–σ_2' the semanteme 'σ_1' is communicatively dominant if and only if the configuration 'σ_1–σ_2' can be reduced to 'σ_1' such that the meaning conveyed is simply impoverished, but not distorted (Iordanskaja & Polguère 1988); the communicative dominance of 'σ_1' is shown by underscoring. E.g.: in 'A bird is.singing' the semanteme 'sing' is communicatively dominant, since the utterance is about singing; in 'a singing bird', the semanteme 'bird' is communicatively dominant, since this utterance is about a bird. For a rigorous definition, see Mel'čuk 2012–2015: vol. 1, Ch. 6, 315*ff*.

See pp. 226, 237, 242, 243

comparand (in a comparative construction)

Element to which the **comparate** is compared; e.g.: in *X is heavier than Y* the element Y is the comparand.

See pp. 66, 103

comparate (in a comparative construction)
: Element which is compared to the **comparand**; e.g.: in *X is heavier than Y* the element X is the comparate.

    See p. 103

complement
: Element L′ in a **complementation** construction.

    See pp. 17, 62, 63, 65, 68, 77, 78, 107, 130, 143, 174, 186–188, 195, 196, 202, 208, 226, 299, 332, 350–353, 365

complementation (of L)
: Syntactic phenomenon whereby a lexical unit L′ depends on a lexical unit L syntactically and semantically: $L \xrightarrow[\text{synt}]{\text{sem}} L'$; e.g.: cut_L [a] $log_{L'}$, $John's_{L'}$ $arrival_L$, $over_L$ the $city_{L'}$. Cf. **characterization**.

    See pp. 33, 46

complementizer
: Semantically empty subordinating conjunction that introduces a subordinate clause; e.g.: THAT in *I saw that John was sick*.

    See pp. 102, 261, 280

complex verb: see *periphrastic verb*

compositional (complex linguistic sign **s**)
: Complex **linguistic sign s** that can be represented as a regular "sum" of signs $\mathbf{s_1}$ and $\mathbf{s_2}$: $\mathbf{s} = \mathbf{s_1} \oplus \mathbf{s_2}$.

    See pp. 206, 207, 217, 224, 283, 284, 312, 329, 331

conceptual representation: see *representation, conceptual*

conceptics
: Logical device (= set of rules) responsible for the correspondence between conceptual representations and semantic representations:

    $$\{ConceptR_i\} \Longleftarrow conceptics \Longrightarrow \{SemR_i\}$$

    Conceptics is part of a general model of human linguistic behavior.

    See p. 19

conjunction (in logic and semantics)
: Logical operator "∧": $A \wedge B$ is true if and only if both A and B are true.

    See p. 12

Index of notions and terms, supplied with a glossary — 413

conjunction (in syntax), binary

Conjunction that consists of two components that are not syntactically linked between themselves.

See pp. 76, 275ff

context (of a linguistic rule)

Part of a rule that is not manipulated by the rule, but whose presence (in the rule's input) is necessary for the rule to apply.

See pp. 15, 349

conversion, morphological

Morphological operation of replacing a feature of syntactics of a wordform; e.g. $OIL_{(N)} \Rightarrow OIL_{(V)}$.

See p. 27

coordination

One of the two major types of semantic/syntactic dependency (the other one being subordination), which unites several semantemes/lexical elements playing the same semantic/syntactic role; e.g.: *The dresses were **red, blue, yellow**.* | ***John and Mary*** *travel together.* | *John **awoke, but stayed** in bed.*

See pp. 34, 110, 300, 301

coreference

Relation that holds between two LUs L_1 and L_2 in an utterance if and only if L_1 and L_2 have the same **referent**, i.e. they are coreferential. Coreference is an equivalence relation and is represented by a dashed double-headed arrow: $L_1 \dashleftarrow\dashrightarrow L_2$.

See pp. 119, 138, 139, 168

criteria for SSynt-relations: consult Ch. 2

See pp. 40–44, 50, 58, 67, 209–212, 276, 314, 315

Deep- (sublevel of a linguistic representation)

Sublevel that is closer to meaning.

See p. 11

deep-syntactic relation [DSyntRel]

One of 13 cross-linguistically universal dependency relations introduced for the description of deep-syntactic structures of sentences in any language. Cf. **surface-syntactic relation**.

See pp. 32ff, 176

deep-syntactic representation: see *representation, deep-syntactic*

definition, lexicographic (of an LU L)

Formal description of L's meaning by an expression (of the same language) that is an exact paraphrase of L satisfying five special rules (Mel'čuk 2012–2015: vol. 2, 283–293).

See pp. 25

denotation (of a linguistic sign)

Set of all facts or entities of the extralinguistic world that the sign can describe (= all potential **referents** of this sign).

See pp. 34, 35, 42, 213, 220

dependency relation (semantic or syntactic)

Binary relation between two **semantemes** or two **lexical units** in an utterance: '$\sigma_1 \rightarrow \sigma_2$' or L('$\sigma_1$')$\rightarrow$L('$\sigma_2$'); this relation is antireflexive and antisymmetric, and can be non-transitive (semantic dependencies) or antitransitive (syntactic dependencies).

See pp. 120, 209, 339

dependency tree

Formalism for representing the syntactic structure of a sentence; a network satisfying the following two conditions:

1. Each node receives no more than one entering arc.
2. There is one and only one node that does not receive any arc; this node is the **top node** of the tree.

See pp. 12, 13, 38, 226, 242, 275, 321, 328, 331, 339, 345, 350

derivational means

Expressive means (affix, reduplication, conversion or auxiliary lexeme) that expresses a derivateme; e.g.: the suffix **-er** ('one who...': *swimmer*), the reduplication **R** $\Rightarrow$ **R, shmR** ($\approx$ 'R which is ludicrous': *data, shmata!*), the morphological conversion N $\Rightarrow$ V ('apply N to ...': [*to*] *hammer*), etc.

See pp. 37, 166

descriptive expression

Expression used to communicate a meaning. Cf. signalative expression.

See p. 318

descriptive modifier: see *modifier, restrictive*

diathesis (of an LU L)

correspondence between L's Sem-actants and its DSynt-actants (specified in L's government pattern).

See pp. 118, 129, 143, 158, 295, 296, 298, 303

dictionary article (of an LU L) = lexical entry (of L)

Systematically presented full information about L.

See pp. 25, 229, 284, 285, 321

disjunction

Logical operator "∨": A ∨ B is true if and only if at least A or B is true.

distinctive number: see *lexicographic number*

dominance, communicative: see *communicatively dominant semanteme*

double verbs

Particular type of a verb series: two verbs of which the second is a pseudo-conjunct of the first; e.g.:

Rus. *Ivan sidit smeëtsja* 'Ivan is.seated. is.laughing'. | *Pojdi kupi xleba!* 'Go buy some.bread!'

See p. 113

Ellipsis

Syntactic operation whereby some repeated occurrences of a phrase in the SSyntS are deleted in the DMorphS of the sentence; e.g.: *John travelled to England, and Mary [travelled] to Spain.* | *John can play the guitar, and Mary [can play the guitar] too.*

See pp. 103, 125, 242, 265, 300, 302, 323

'entity'

Class of semantemes denoting objects, living beings, substances, places, etc.; e.g.: 'Sun', 'sand', 'boy', 'water', 'ravine', 'city'. All these are semantic names. Cf. 'fact'.

See pp. 75, 182, 201, 375

equivalence relation

Binary relation that is reflexive, symmetric and transitive.

See pp. 9, 119

equivalent (semantic representations)

$SemR_1$ and $SemR_2$ are equivalent if and only if one can be transformed into the other (without affecting the meaning represented) by some rules of the language.

See pp. 22, 105, 176, 314, 319

ergarive case

Case used to mark the Synt-subject of a transitive verb (but not used for nomination).

See pp. **134**, 141–143, 145, 149, 157, 158, 162

ergarive construction

Syntactic predicative construction where the syntactic subject is not marked by the nominative case.

See pp. 134, 147, 149, 150, 154, 157, 158, 163, 211, 291, **293**

ergative language

Language in which verbs that correspond semantically to transitive verbs of European languages have as the central component of their meaning the semanteme 'undergo' (rather than then semanteme 'cause1/2').

See pp. **134**, 143, 154, 177

evaluative construction

Syntactic construction of the type *your fool$_{N1}$ of a boss$_{N2}$*, where an evaluative noun N_1 that semantically qualifies N_2 is used as its syntactic governor.

See p. 80

explanatory combinatorial dictionary [ECD]

Dictionary proposed by the Meaning-Text theory.

See pp. 25–27, 284

'**F**act'

Class of semantemes denoting states, processes, properties, actions, events, etc.; e.g.: 'grief', 'be.located [somewhere]', 'sick', 'expensive', 'write', 'explode', 'five'. All these semantemes are **semantic predicates**. Cf. 'entity'.

See pp. 254, 255

factive verb

> Verb that accepts the complement clause *that P* and whose meaning includes a presupposed component '[[P being true]]'; e.g.: REGRET$_{(V)}$ being a factive verb, the sentences *He regrets John's having left* and *He does not regret John's having left* both imply that John has left.
>
> See p. 20

fictitious lexeme

> Lexeme that does not exist in the language but is introduced by the linguist in order to represent a meaningful syntactic construction in the DSyntS; e.g.: Rus. «PRIMERNO» (lit. 'approximately') = «MAYBE», which represents the approximate-quantitative construction.
>
> See pp. 12, 32, **36**, 37, 47, 50, 51, 56, 57, 66, 67–72, 80*ff*, 108, 176, 218, 222, 227, 228, 229, 230

filter rule: see *rule, filter*

finite (verbal form): see *verbal form, finite*

flexible (word order): see *word order, flexible*

Focalization

> One of communicative values: *Focalized* is the semantic configuration 'σ̃' that the Speaker presents as logically prominent; e.g.: *It is **a pen** that I need* ~ *What I need is **a pen***.
>
> See pp. 210, 340, 358, 363

functional model: see *model, linguistic functional*

Government

> One of the two types of morphological dependency (the other one being agreement): the wordform w_1 is said to be governed by the wordform w_2 if and only if some grammemes of w_1 are determined by some features of the syntactics of w_2; e.g.:
>
> Fr. **le**$_{ACC-w_1}$ *remercier*$_{w_2}$ lit. 'him thank' or
> Ger. **ihm**$_{DAT-w_1}$ *danken*$_{w_2}$ lit. 'to.him thank',
>
> where the verb determines the case of the object.
>
> See pp. 12, 118, 120, 121, 130, 174, 280

government pattern [GP] (of lexical unit L)

Table that describes the actants of the headword L in a lexical entry: L's dia-thesis, the surface form of L's SSynt-actants, their combinability, etc.

See pp. 46, 59–61, 83, 231, 284, 285, 321, 326, 328

governor, syntactic (of an LU L)

LU L' on which the LU L depends syntactically; e.g.:

some←-synt-***grammemes***; ***Chapter***-synt→*11*; *John*←-synt-***is***-synt→*working*.

See pp. 41–46, 73, 85, 97, 123, 135, 206, 210–212, 232, 241ff, 259ff, 280, 314, 315, 346–348, 354, 359, 360, 372, 374

grammeme

Value of an inflectional category, e.g.:

PAST is a grammeme of the category "verbal tense";
PL(ural) is a grammeme of the category "nominal number";
PL_{ADJ}(ural) is a grammeme of the category "adjectival number".

See pp. 12, 14, 38, 43, 96, 97, 122, 126, 142, 146, 158, 159, 161, 169–171, 209, 296, 338, 340, 345, 353

——, deep (= semantic)

Semantically full grammeme, which has a source in the semantic structure; a deep grammeme appears in the deep- and surface-syntactic structures.

See pp. 13, 87, 345

——, surface (= syntactic)

Semantically empty grammeme, which has no source in the semantic structure; it is imposed by government or agreement and appears in the deep-morphological structure.

See pp. 12, 13, 338

Head, syntactic (of a phrase P)

LU L which is part of phrase P and on which all other LUs of P depend syntactically—directly or indirectly; e.g.:

*South Korean warships **conducted** live-fire exercises.* | ***Hold** Infinity in the palm of your hand* [W. Blake]. | *what wives and children **say**.*

See pp. 34, 41, 42, 49, 53, 56, 63, 73, 74, 89, 125, 136–138, 176, 237, **239**, 243, 245, 247, 261, 274, 277, 280, 286, 314, 315, 322, 347, 350, 370

Index of notions and terms, supplied with a glossary — **419**

homonymy (of linguistic expressions **E₁** and **E₂**)

Relation of homonymy holds between linguistic expressions **E₁** and **E₂** whose signifiers are identical and signifieds do not share a semantic bridge; e.g.: BOX$_{(N)}$¹ 'container that ...' ~ BOX$_{(N)}$² 'sport that...'. Homonymy is indicated by superscripts.

See p. 260

Idiom

One of the two types of lexical units (the other being a lexeme)—a multiword expression. An idiom is a non-compositional phraseme; e.g.:

⌜ALL THUMBS⌝ 'very awkward' or ⌜HIT THE ROAD⌝ '[to] leave'.

See pp. 12, 89, 152, 206, 207, 216, 224, 225, 229, 273, 280, 282, 283, 284, 286, 309ff

—, lexemic

Idiom that consists of at least two full lexemes; e.g.:

⌜ALL THUMBS⌝ 'very awkward' or ⌜HIT THE ROAD⌝ '[to] leave'.

See pp. 96, 99, 100, 107

—, morphemic

Idiom that consists of morphemes inside one wordform; e.g.:

{FOR} + {GET} ⟺ FORGET

See p. 330

—, syntactic

Idiom that is a constrained complex sign **s** if and only if its signifier /s/ is non-segmental, that is, /s/ contains prosody or a bound lexemic variable, e.g., L(X), symbolizing the operation of duplication of the phraseme's actant X; e.g.: [X] ⌜OR NO L(X)⌝ 'no matter whether there is X or not' (*Rain or no rain, we are going.*) | [Xs] ⌜WILL BE L(Xs)⌝ 'Xs have a typical feature, and that's what you have to expect from a particular X' (*Girls will be girls.*).

See pp. 70, 110, 331, 332

inflectional category

Set of mutually opposed grammemes; e.g.:

nominal number = {SG, PL}; verbal tense = {PRES, PAST, FUT}.

See pp. 126, 147, 158, 161, 353

Keenan-Comrie Accessibility Hierarchy

Hierarchy of clause element types from the viewpoint of their ability to undergo different syntactic operations (such as relativization, etc.)

See pp. 123, 135, 258

Lexeme

One of the two types of **lexical unit** (the other one being an **idiom**)—a one-word expression. A lexeme is a set of **wordforms** and **analytical-form** phrases that differ only by inflectional significations; e.g.:

I ={*I*, *me*}; SEE = {*see, sees, saw, seeing, have seen, am seen, will see, ...* }.

For a rigorous definition of lexeme, see Mel'čuk 2012–2015: vol. 1, p. 59, Definition 1.21.

See pp. 13, 14, 15–18, 20, 26, 33, 49, 96, 97, 142, 176, 191, 295, 311, 328

lexical function

Function **f** which is associated to a meaning 'σ' and which, when applied to a lexical unit L, returns the lexical unit L′ that expresses 'σ' in the context of L: $f_{\sigma'}(L) = L'$; e.g.:

'do attention' ⟺ PAY ATTENTION, 'do a step' ⟺ TAKE [a] STEP, 'do a favor' ⟺ DO [a] FAVOR.

See pp. 12, 16, 17, 22, **23**, 24, 55, 223, 247, 285, 286, 317

lexical unit [LU]

A **lexeme** or an **idiom**.

See pp. 11, 12, 15, 20, 23, 25, 182, 312, 335, 348

——, full

Lexical unit that has its source in the semantic structure.

See pp. 12, 96, 97, 248, 352

——, structural (= grammatical, or auxiliary)

Lexical unit that either has no source in the semantic structure (is semantically empty) and is introduced into the syntactic structure by a syntactic rule (*compare John* ***to*** *Mary*; *ask* ***whether*** *John is there*), or expresses a grammeme (*We* ***will*** *follow you.*).

See pp. 12, 13, 46, 130, 270, 297, 332

Index of notions and terms, supplied with a glossary — 421

lexicalization
> Semantic operation whereby the lexical nodes of a deep-syntactic structure are constructed under synthesis. Cf. arborization and morphologization.
>
> See p. 15

lexicographic number
> Code used to identify a particular sense of a polysemous lexical item and to indicate the semantic distance between senses; e.g.: BACK$_{(N)}$I.1 'body part ...' (*My back hurts.*) vs. BACK$_{(N)}$I.2 'part of clothing covering the backI.1' (*back of a vest*) vs. BACK$_{(N)}$I.3 'part of a seat designated to support the back I.1 of the sitting person' (*back of a chair*), etc.

light verb: see *verb, light*

linguistic dependency: see *dependency relation*

linguistic model: see *model, linguistic*

linguistic sign: see *sign, linguistic*

linker
> Part of speech whose elements are semantically empty and fulfill a purely syntactic role—they mark the syntactic dependency between a noun and its characterizer.
>
> See pp. 93, 94, 143, 270

Meaning, linguistic (of an expression **E**)
> Invariant of all paraphrases of **E**.
>
> See pp. 1, 9, 10, 11, 20, 23, 27, 184, 243

meaning-bearing syntactic construction: see *syntactic construction, meaningful*

metaphor (of 'σ_1')
> Relation of metaphor holds between two meanings 'σ_1' and 'σ_2' such that 'σ_2' contains 'σ_1' and the denotation of 'σ_2' is similar to the denotation of 'σ_1'; within 'σ_2', the meaning 'σ_1' is introduced by a semanteme that indicates its role—such as ⌐as if¬. E.g.: 'heartII.1' (*of the problem*) is a metaphor of 'heartI.1' (*of John*), since 'heartII.1 of X' = 'central point of X —⌐as if¬ it were the heartI.1 of X'. Cf. metonymy.
>
> See pp. 80, 207, 218, 222, 223, 230, 371

metonymy (of 'σ_1')

Relation of metonymy holds between two meanings 'σ_1' and 'σ_2' such that 'σ_2' contains 'σ_1' and the denotation of 'σ_2' is contiguous to the denotation of 'σ_1'; e.g.: 'heartI.2' (*He pressed his hands to his heart.*) is a metonymy of 'heartI.1' (*of John*), since 'heartI.2 of X' = 'part of X's chest were X's heartI.1 is'. Cf. **metaphor**.

See pp. 16, 194

model, linguistic functional (of language **L**)

A logical device—that is, a set of rules—that simulates the linguistic activity of speakers of **L** (i.e., speech production and speech understanding). A linguistic model is necessarily functional, in the following two senses: 1) it represents the **functioning**, rather than the structure, of **L**; 2) it models **L** as a mathematical **function**, i.e., a mapping from **L**'s meanings to **L**'s texts, and vice versa.

See pp. 7–9, 19, 27, 28

modification: see *characterization*

See pp. 33, 46, 81, 88

modifier/circumstantial (of an LU L)

Lexical unit L' that syntactically depends on L, but semantically bears on L:

$L \underset{\text{synt}}{\overset{\text{sem}}{\leftrightarrows}} L'$

E.g.: ***red*** $\underset{\text{synt}}{\overset{\text{sem}}{\leftrightarrows}}$ *apple*; *run* $\underset{\text{synt}}{\overset{\text{sem}}{\leftrightarrows}}$ ***fast***

Cf. **actant** (of an LU L).

See pp. 73, 81, 93, 143, 200, 215, 225, 237, 240, 243, 245, 257, 270, 280, 346, 352, 353, 373, 375, 385

——, descriptive

Modifier of an LU L that does not define a subset of entities specified by L, but only adds a non-definitional characterization to 'L'; e.g.:

These books$_L$ [, *sold in our bookstore,*]$_{L's\ Descr.Modif.}$ *are affordable.*

See pp. 34, 35, 86, 87, 88, 89, 90, 92, 210, 243, 244, 245, 258

——, restrictive

Modifier of an LU L that defines a subset of entities specified by L; e.g.:

Books$_L$ [*sold in our bookstore*]$_{L's\ Restrict.Modif.}$ *are affordable.*

See pp. 34, 76, 87, 88, 90, 210, 242, 243, 244, 256–258, 263, 373 module (of a linguistic model)

Component of a linguistic model: a set of rules ensuring the transition between two adjacent levels of representation of utterances (foreseen by the linguistic model).

See pp. 11, 27

—, deep-syntactic

Module ensuring the transition between the deep-syntactic and surface-syntactic representations of utterances.

—, morphological

Module ensuring the transition between the morphological and phonological representations of utterances.

See p. 14

—, phonological

Module of a linguistic model ensuring the transition between the phonological and phonetic representations of utterances.

—, semantic

Module ensuring the transition between the semantic and deep-syntactic representations of utterances.

—, surface-syntactic

Module ensuring the transition between the surface-syntactic and deep-morphological representations of utterances.

See pp. 2, 341

mood

Inflectional category of the verb whose grammemes indicate the way the designated fact is viewed/reported by the Speaker: as objective and real (the indicative mood), as hypothetical (the conditional mood), as possible or wished for (the subjunctive mood), as an injunction (the imperative mood), and so on.

See pp. 12, 98, 156

morphological module: see *module (of a linguistic model), morphological*

morphological representation: see *representation, morphological*

morphologization

Semantic operation whereby the inflectional values for lexical units (of the syntactic structure under synthesis) are constructed. Cf. **arborization** and **lexicalization**.

See p. 15

Name (semantic)

Meaning denoting an entity and having no slots for other meanings; e.g.: 'sand', 'Moon', 'girl', 'rhinoceros', 'ravine'.

See p. 217

network, semantic

Graph that is fully connected, fully directed and fully labeled; is used to represent the meaning of linguistic expressions.

See pp. 11, 12, 226

nominative

Case of nomination; e.g.:

Lat. $aquil+a_{\text{SG.NOM}}$ 'eagle'
Rus. $mal'\check{c}ik+i_{\text{PL.NOM}}$ 'boys'
Basque $begi+\emptyset_{\text{SG}}+\emptyset_{\text{NOM}}$ 'eye'

See pp. 38, 128, 133, 134, 138, 141, 142, 143, 145, 152, 154, 155–157, 159, 162, 168, 176, 184, **186**, 187, 202, 211, 254, 273, 291, 292, 293, 294, 325, 326

nomineme

Non-compositional conceptual-lexemic phraseme, that is, a phraseme constrained with respect to its conceptual representation (= a compound proper name); e.g.: *Medicine Hat* (a Canadian city), *Brown shirts* (a paramilitary wing of the Nazi party), *Saint-Bartholomew's Day* (the massacre of Protestants by Catholics in Paris in 1572).

See pp. 206, 207, 224, 225, 230

non-finite (verbal form): see *verbal form, non-finite*

Object, direct

Second most privileged element of the clause.

See pp. 18, 39, 44, 52, 58, 118, 130, **174**, 190, 193, 200, 201, 211, 241, 291, 305, 343

—, indirect

Third most privileged element of the clause.

See pp. 36, 57, 58, 197

oblique case

Case either opposed to the nominative in a two-case system, or marking cumulatively several heterogeneous syntactic roles.

See pp. 143, 176

Paraphrase (of sentence S)

Sentence S' that is synonymous with sentence S; e.g.:

(1) S: 'Two brothers of Egyptian origin were arrested in France while preparing to commit an attack'. =

(2) S': 'The French police captured two brothers, originally from Egypt, who were getting ready to perpetrate an attack'.

See pp. 10, 226

peripheral structure: see *structure, peripheral (of a linguistic representation)*

periphrastic verb

Verbal phrase of the form V→N where the verb V is semantically empty and the essential meaning of the phrase is expressed by the noun N; e.g.: *pay attention* or *fall in love*. Such a phrase is a verbal collocation.

See pp. 170, 199

phoneme (of **L**)

The set of all phones of **L** whose articulatory/acoustical differences are never used in **L** to distinguish signs; e.g.:

Eng. /t/ = {[t] (*stick*), [tʰ] (*tick*)

/d/ = {[d] (*seed*), [ɾ] (*seeded*)}

See p. 38

phonemic representation: see *representation, phonemic*

phonetic representation: see *representation, phonetic*

phonological module: see *module, phonological*

phrasal verb: see *verb, phrasal*

phrase

Utterance that consists of syntactically linked wordforms, features a prosodic unity, but is not necessarily a unit of communication; e.g.: *the report of the arrival of new shipment of trucks, the report of the arrival, the report, the arrival of the new shipment*, etc. A phrase can be pronounced and understood outside of a particular context; it is perceived by speakers as existing in their language.

See pp. 1, 18, 40–44, 120, 237, 276, 277, 314, 315, 343, 347–349

phraseme

Phrase that is not free: the selection of its components by the Speaker is constrained; four major classes of phrasemes are idioms, nominemes, collocations and clichés.

See pp. 206, 224–226, 283, 309, 310, 319, 324, **328**

——, conceptual-lexemic

Phraseme constrained with respect to its conceptual representation; conceptual-lexemic phrasemes come in two varieties: nominemes and clichés.

——, discontinuous

Phraseme that forms a phrase only taken together with its actants; e.g.: ⌜NOTHING IF NOT⌝ [X].

See p. 286

——, lexemic

Phraseme consisting of lexemes.

——, morphemic

Phraseme consisting of morphemes that appear within one wordform.

See p. **330**

——, semantic-lexemic

Phraseme constrained with respect to its meaning (= its semantic representation); semantic-lexemic phrasemes come in two varieties: idioms and collocations.

See pp. **329**, 331

——, syntactic: see *idiom, syntactic*

See pp. **330–332**

predicate (semantic)

Meaning denoting a fact and having "slots" for other meanings without which it is incomplete; e.g.:

'intelligent(X)' [*X is intelligent*], 'love(X,Y)' [*X loves Y*], 'under(X, Y)' [*X is under Y*], 'order(X, Y, Z)' [*X orders Y to do Z*], 'buy(X, Y, Z, W)' [*X buys Y from Z for W*], etc.

See pp. 11, 182, 205–207, 217, 218, 220–222, 370

prefix

Affix that precedes the radical; e.g.: ***re***+*consider* or ***un***+*constitutional*.

See pp. 37, 96, 99, 100, 132, 140, 159, 162, 164–166, 247, 262

presupposition

Part '⟦σ'⟧' of the meaning 'σ' that is not negated or questioned when the whole 'σ' is negated or questioned; in other words, '⟦σ'⟧' is not accessible to negation or interrogation. E.g.: the sentence *John knows that Mary is in town* presupposes '*Mary is in town*'; this presupposed meaning remains not affected when the sentence is negated or questioned: both sentences *John does not know that Mary is in town* and *Does John know that Mary is in town?* presuppose that Mary is in town.

See pp. 21, 22

Pro-Drop language (= pronoun-dropping language)

Language in which a personal pronoun in a particular syntactic role is normally elided; e.g.:

1) Sp. *¿Cómo estás?* 'How are **you**?'
   or *No tiene sentido* '**It** does not make sense'.
2) Jap. *Kono hon, watasiga yonda* 'This book, I read **it**'.

See pp. 125, 126, 145, 155, 196

prolepsis: see Definition 4.1, p. 184

See pp. 148, 183, **184**, 185, 187, 189, 192, 194–197, 268

pronominalization

Syntactic operation whereby some repeated occurrences of nouns in the DSyntS are replaced by substitute pronouns in the SSyntS. E.g.:

JOHN←SEE→FATHER→**JOHN** ⇔ JOHN←SEE→FATHER→**HIS**

See pp. 124, 126, 131, 133, 140, 143, 144, 242, 263, 344

pronoun, empty

Pronoun that is semantically empty and is introduced by syntactic rules in order to insure syntactic well-formedness of the clause; e.g.: ***It*** *is known that John has left*.

See pp. 49, 128, 136, 167–168, 181, 253, 260, 261

—, indefinite

Pronoun referring to a non-specified entity or fact of a particular type: a person, e.g., ANYBODY, SOMEBODY, NOBODY; a thing: ANYTHING, SOMETHING, NOTHING; a place: ANYWHERE, SOMEWHERE, NOWHERE; etc.

See pp. 49, 91, 109, 315–319, 327

—, substitute

Pronoun used instead of a noun, which is its **source**; e.g.: HE, SHE, THEY, IT, WHICH, etc.

See pp. 67, 239

prosody

Suprasegmental expressive means of language: stresses, tones. intonation contours, pauses.

See pp. 43, 111, 175, 210, 262, 338, 363

pseudo-conjunct

Element of the clause that is linked to its syntactic governor as a conjunct, but does not allow for a coordinating conjunction and semantically represents an elaboration of the governor.

See pp. 55, 112, 194, 196, 201, 203

pseudo-relative clause

Subordinate clause that has the structure of a **relative clause** (contains a WH-word), but is not a modifier of a noun (as a genuine relative is): a pseudo-relative is syntactically equivalent to a noun phrase and functions as a syntactic actant; e.g.: *We will eat **what you brought***.

See pp. 49, 53, 108, 249ff, 268, 325, 326

pseudo-X

Element X′ that is similar to X, but not enough to be confounded with X in a linguistic description. Cf. **quasi-X**.

See p. 33

Quasi-predicate

Meaning denoting entities (as a semantic name), but having "slots" for other meanings (as a semantic predicate); e.g.: 'brother OF $_{\text{person}}$Y', 'head OF $_{\text{person}}$X', 'roof OF $_{\text{building}}$X', etc.

See p. 205

Index of notions and terms, supplied with a glossary — 429

quasi-X

Element X' that is similar enough to X so that it is possible to confound it with X. Cf. **pseudo-X**.

See p. 33

Radical

Morph that is obligatorily contained in any wordform[1] and whose syntactics 1) is similar to the syntactics of the majority of morphs of the language and 2) contributes the majority of features to the syntactics of the wordform to which it belongs; e.g.: **finger-** in *finger+Ø* and *finger+s*, **fast** in *fast*, **formulat(e)-** in *formulat+ing*, etc. Cf. **affix**.

raised possessor

Adnominal complement of the noun N syntactically depending on the verb V becomes an object of V; e.g.: Fr. *Ce livre lui a gâché sa carrière* lit. 'This book to.him has destroyed his carrier', where **lui**, the dative form of ELLE/IL 's/he', is introduced into the clause as a SSynt-actant—the IndirO—of the Main Verb, although the verb GÂCHER does not have a corresponding Sem-actant.

See pp. 47, 57

referent (of a linguistic sign **s**)

Fact or entity in the extralinguistic world (real or imaginary) to which the linguistic sign **s** refers in the given utterance. Cf. **denotation**.

See pp. 37, 57, 87, 128, 130, 133, 305, 318, 373

reflexivity (of a binary relation)

Property of a binary relation **R**:

R(*a*, *b*) ⇒ **R**(*a*, *a*); e.g.: **R** = 'be of the same size'.

relation, syntactic

Relation of syntactic dependency between two lexical units; e.g.:

two←**synt**–*units* or *love*–**synt**→*John*

representation (linguistic)

Formal object designed to represent a particular aspect of linguistic entities; consists of several structures whose character depends on the level of representation.

See pp. 10, 11, 27

---

1 This formulation leaves out **megamorphs**—amalgamated realizations of strings of morphemes, such as: **me** ⇔ {I}⊕{OBL} or **am** ⇔{BE}⊕{IND.PRES}⊕{1.SG}.

—, conceptual

Representation of the informational content of a sentence at a prelinguistic level: a network composed of discrete **concepts** (designations of elements of extra-linguistic reality by means of lexical units of natural language, "freed" as much as possible from their linguistic peculiarities) and the relations between them.

See p. 19

—, deep-syntactic

Representation of the formal organization of sentences at the deep-syntactic level.

See p. 232

—, morphological (of sentences)

Representation of the linear organization of sentences in terms of fully inflected lexemes.

See pp. 232, 269

—, phonemic

Representation of texts in terms of phonemes and prosodemes.

—, phonetic

Representation of texts in terms of allophones and alloprosodies.

See p. 9

—, semantic

Representation of the meaning of a set of synonymous sentences.

See pp. 9, 27, 232

—, surface-syntactic

Representation of the formal organization of sentences at the surface-syntactic level.

See pp. 232, 341

restrictive (modifier)

Modifier L of L′ is restrictive if and only if it semantically specifies a subclass of L′'s denotation; e.g.: in *a **French** book* the restrictive modifier *French* reduces the denotation of 'book' to only 'French book'.

See pp. 34, 87, 90, 210, 243, 244, 257, 258, 373

resumptive clitic: see *clitic, resumptive*

rule (linguistic)

> Formal expression specifying a correspondence between linguistic objects. Consult Chapter 1, 1.2.3.
>
> See pp. 1, 2, 15*ff*, 27, 36–38

——: equivalence rule

> Rule specifying the equivalence between two linguistic objects of the same level of representation: X ≡ Y | C.

——: filter rule

> Rule specifying the ill-formedness of a linguistic object on a given level of representation: *XY* ["the configuration XY is ill-formed"].
>
> See pp. 241, 258, 344, 364

——: transition rule

> Rule specifying the transition between two linguistic objects of two adjacent levels of representation: X ⟺ Y | C.
>
> See pp. 15, 39, 45, 139, 344

Semanteme

> Meaning (≈ signified) of a lexical unit of the language; e.g.: 'fence1' (*a wooden fence*), 'ugly1' (*an ugly face*), 'ugly2' (*an ugly incident*), 'hesitate', '*sit on the fence*', etc.
>
> See pp. 11, 20, 63, 218, 220

semantic component (of a lexicographic definiens)

> Configuration of semantemes in a definiens that plays a particular structural role in this definiens.

——, central

> Component (of the definiens) that expresses the generic part of the meaning of the LU under description.
>
> See pp. 134, 151

——, generic see *component, central*

semantic decomposition

Representation of a linguistic meaning in terms of simpler linguistic meanings.

See pp. 20–22

semantic derivation

Semantic relation between LUs L and L' such that their semantic difference 'σ' = 'L' - 'L'' is regular in the language in question (that is, it is found in many lexical pairs), but there is no regular formal difference between L and L'; e.g., LION ~ DEN, MOVIE ~ (MOVIE) THEATER, SURGERY ~ OPERATION ROOM, etc., 'σ' = 'place where L'.

See p. 22

semantic primitive/prime

Simple meaning (= semanteme) of language L that cannot be decomposed in terms of other meanings of L; e.g.: 'no', 'time', 'speak', 'feel1', 'good', 'this', etc.

See p. 20

semantic representation: see *representation, semantic*

sentence

Maximal utterance that typically consists of clauses (one or more) and is a complete unit of communication.

sign, linguistic

Triplet ⟨X; Y; Z⟩, where X is the signified, Y the signifier, and Z the syntactics; e.g.:

page$_{(N)}$^{1} = ⟨'one side of a piece of paper in ...'; /peʲʒ/; Σ = noun, countable, ...⟩

signification, linguistic

Any type of information carried by a linguistic sign: a genuine meaning, a syntactic feature, a semantically empty grammeme, a stylistic characteristic, etc.

signal$_{(V)}$

Express meanings without using clauses which implement logical propositions describing the situations the Speaker targets and which have such a form that they can be negated or questioned; signaling expressions cannot be negated or questioned. Cf. **communicate**.

Consult Mel'čuk 2001: Ch. 3.

See pp. 148, 286, 317

signalative expression

> Expression that serves to signal a meaning.
>
> See p. 318

simpler, semantically

> Meaning 'σ_1' is simpler than the meaning 'σ_2' if and only if 'σ_2' can be decomposed using 'σ_1', but not vice versa.
>
> See p. 20

source (of a pronoun L)

> LU in the DSyntS that is replaced by the pronoun L in the SSyntS.
>
> See pp. 125, 241, 250

Speaker, the

> The initiator of the given speech act; the person who says *I* in this speech act.
>
> See pp. 20, 22, 23, 37, 126, 184, 222, 304, 313, 317, 373

split ergativity

> Property of a language in which one set of the MV forms requires the ergative construction and the other set of the MV forms is used with the nominative construction.
>
> See pp. 151, 157

stem

> Radical taken together with derivational affixes; e.g.:
>
> **swimmer-** is the stem of the wordforms *swimmer*, *swimmers* and *swimmer's*; **unlucky-** is the stem of the wordforms *unlucky*, *unluckier* and *unluckiest*.
>
> See pp. 99, 330

string

> A linear sequence of elements.
>
> See pp. 14, 19, 38, 190, 215, 269, 318, 345, 355, 370, 429

structural lexical unit: see *lexical unit, structural*

structure

> Component of a linguistic representation.

—, basic

Autonomous structure of a linguistic representation upon which all peripheral structures are superimposed.

See p. 11

—, deep-morphological

Basic structure of a deep-morphological representation.

See pp. 14, 124

—, deep-syntactic

Basic structure of a deep-syntactic representation.

See pp. 12, 13, 32, 33, 45, 176, 222

—, peripheral

Non-autonomous structure of a linguistic representation that is superposed on the **basic** structure and specifies some of its essential properties.

See pp. 11, 13

—, semantic

Basic structure of a semantic representation.

See pp. 11, 12

—, surface-syntactic

Basic structure of a surface-syntactic representation. Cf. Definition 10.1.

See pp. 13, 14, 38, 39, 45, 124–126, 145, 225

—, surface-syntactic anaphoric

One of the peripheral structures of a surface-syntactic representation: a system of coreferentiality links between lexemes of the sentence; it is shown by bidirectional dashed arrow ◄┄┄►.

See p. 39

—, surface-syntactic communicatve

One of the peripheral structures of a surface-syntactic representation. Cf. Definition 10.2, p. 340.

subject, syntactic

The most privileged element of the clause.

See pp. 39, 117*ff*, **135**, 186, 187, **190**, 191, 192, 194–197, 241, 254, 266, 293, 298, 300, 304, 312, 219, 350

subjective

Case used to mark the Synt-subject (but not used for nomination). Cf. Definition 4.3, p. 187.

See pp. 55, 112, 184*ff*

subordination

One of the two major types of syntactic dependency (the other one being coordination), which unites two lexical units L_1 and L_2 to build a phrase that, as a whole, has the passive syntactic valence of one of these LUs—the governor (in **bold**); e.g.: the **dresses**; **were** red; John **travels** a lot.

substitutability test

Test that allows the researcher to see whether two signs/expressions can be included into the same unit of a higher level or be described by a common representation at some level: these signs/expressions must be mutually substitutable at least in some contexts.

See pp. 44, 209

suffix

Affix that follows the radical; e.g.: ch*air*+**s**, read+**ing**, read+**er**.

See pp. 19, 128, 129, 132, 146, 156, 162, 164–166, 169, 170, 180, 189, 192, 202, 204, 247, 254, 262, 266, 273, 295, 303

superentry, lexical (in a dictionary)

Set of lexical entries that describes a *vocable*.

See p. 26

surface- (sublevel of a linguistic representation)

Sublevel that is closer to text. Cf. **deep-**.

See pp. 2, 11

surface-syntactic relation [SSyntRel]

One of several dozen language-specific dependency relations introduced for the description of surface-syntactic structures of sentences in a particular language. Cf. **deep-syntactic relation**.

See pp. 36, 38, 45*ff*, 175, 193, 205, 208, 241, 276, 305, 330, 339, 369, 374

symmetry (of a binary relation)

Property of a binary relation **R**: **R**(a, b) $\Rightarrow$ **R**(b, a); e.g.: **R** = 'be close to'.

synonymous (linguistic expressions E_1 and E_2)

Two linguistic expressions E_1 and E_2 are synonymous iff their meanings are identical; e.g.:

- Sentences
(1) *We are short of booze.* and (2) *We don't have enough alcohol.* are synonymous.
- Sentence (3) and phrase (4)
(3) *John has been absent for three years.* and (4) *John's three-year absence* are synonymous.
- Lexemes MINISTER and MINISTERIAL are synonymous (but by no means synonyms).

See pp. 1, 10, 20, 59, 240, 248, 270, 313

synonyms, exact (= full)

Lexical units 1) that have identical signifieds and different signifiers, 2) whose syntactic actants (if any) correspond one-to-one and 3) that belong to the same deep part of speech; e.g.:

SOFA ~ COUCH, BEHEAD ~ DECAPITATE, CRAZY ~ NUTS.

See p. 284

synonymy (of linguistic expressions E_1 and E_2)
1) Identity of the meanings of two linguistic expressions E_1 and E_2: 'E_1' = 'E_2'.
2) Relation between two lexical units L_1 and L_2 that are synonyms (e.g., FILM ~ MOVIE).

See p. 10

syntactic construction, meaningful

Syntactic construction that carries meaning of lexical type; in the surface-syntactic structure such a construction is described by a special surface-syntactic dependency relation, and in the deep-syntactic structure, by a fictitious lexeme. E.g.: Rus. approximate-quantitative construction, where the anteposition of the quantified noun expresses the meaning 'maybe' (*pjat' metrov* 'five meters' ~ *metrov pjat'* 'maybe five meters').

See pp. 27, 36

syntactic feature (of a lexical unit)

Indication of a cooccurrence property of an LU; e.g.: «postposed» is a syntactic feature of the adjectives that can follow the modified noun (*notary public*, *secretary general*, [in] *matters military*, *times immemorial*). The same as feature of the syntactics of the LU.

See pp. 66, 68, 69, 73, 77, 93, 109, 216, 221, 225, 232, 242, 250

syntactic idiom: see *idiom, syntactic*

syntactics

One of the three components of a linguistic sign (along with the signified and the signifier) that contains information on the sign's cooccurrence with other signs in the form of a set of features; e.g.: the syntactics of the noun SCISSORS contains the following features:

"noun", "plural only", "quantification by *Num pair(s) of*".

See pp. 18, 38, 100, 136, 349

synthesis, linguistic (= speech production)

Operation whereby the Speaker goes from a meaning he wants to convey to the text that expresses this meaning: Text ⇒ Meaning; cf. analysis, linguistic.

See pp. 10, 15, 26, 216, 260, 337

synthetic form

Expression in which a grammeme of the lexical unit L is realized by a morphological means; e.g.: Fr. *pardonne+r+a* [s/he] 'will pardon', where the FUTURE grammeme is expressed by the suffix -*r*. Cf. analytical form (phrase).

See pp. 156, 298

Termeme

Conceptual-lexemic phraseme that is an established term.

See p. 224

text (in the technical sense)

Physical (= superficial) expression of a meaning, in terms of speech sounds or graphic symbols.

See pp. 1, 9, 10, 19, 26

transition rule (= correspondence rule): see *rule, transition*

transitivity (of a binary relation)

Property of a binary relation **R**: **R**(a, b) ∧ **R**(b, c) ⇒ **R**(a, c); e.g.: **R** = 'be bigger than'.

tree, syntactic: see *dependency tree*

Underlying question

Question **Q** formulated by the linguist in order to elicit the semantic-communicative structure of sentence *S*; this is a question to which *S* can be an appropriate answer. E.g.:

Q = "What about John?" allows for identification of the semantic Theme;
Q = "What did John do?" identifies the semantic Rheme:
[*John*]$_{\text{TSem}}$ [*left for the South Pole*]$_{\text{RSem}}$.

See p. 341

Valence, syntactic (of a lexical unit L)

——, active

Set of syntactic elements whose presence in the clause and the surface form controlled by L; e.g.: the active syntactic valence of the noun SECRETARY is the phrase "to N" (*secretary to the company's president*) alternating with a possessive phrase (*John's secretary, his secretary*).

See pp. 33, 46–47, 130, 146, 191, 277

——, passive

Set of syntactic constructions in which L can appear as a dependent element; e.g.: the passive syntactic valence of an English adjective is 1) being a modifier to a noun, 2) being the attribute of a copula verb, etc.

See pp. 42, 115, 314

verb, light

Collocational verb that is semantically empty in the context of its base; e.g.: PAY in *pay attention* or LIE in *the responsibility lies with N*. Light verbs are elements of the value of the lexical functional verbs Oper_i, Func_i and Labor_{ij}.

See pp. 55, 169, 195, 197, 204

——, phrasal

Verbal phrase that is an idiom and consists of a verb and an adverb of a particular kind (= verbal adjunct); e.g.: ⌜BRING UP⌝, ⌜DROP IN⌝, ⌜SHOW OFF⌝.

See pp. 96, 99

verbal form, finite

Verbal form that expresses mood and, as a result, can constitute the syntactic head of a clause; e.g.: *reads, am, read!*

See pp. 39, 47, 138, 191, 238, 245, 265, 348, 352, 354

——, non-finite

Verbal form that does not express mood and, as a result, cannot constitute the syntactic head of a clause; e.g.: *reading, [to] be, written.*

See pp. 186, 194–197, 200, 238, 246, 359

verbal interjection

Russian interjection that denotes a punctual event and can be used as the Main Verb of a clause (with all corresponding actants); e.g.: *A Ivan **vžik** emu po ruke* 'And Ivan quickly.cut to.him on hand', where the interjection vžik refers to the sound produced by quickly cutting something with a sharp tool. In many cases, although not always, a verbal interjection corresponds to the stem of a verb, such as PRYG! from PRYGNUT' 'jump', and is considered as the form of "ultramomentaneous aspect."

See pp. 48, 136

version

Inflectional category whose grammemes mark on a verb for whose benefit the action in question is performed (e.g., 'for oneself' ~ 'for the other' ~ — [neutral]).

See p. **158**–159

vocable

Set of lexical units (= lexemes or idioms) related by polysemy. In the dictionary, a vocable is described by a superentry.

See pp. 26, 148, 239, 332

voice

Verbal inflectional category whose grammemes (= particular voices) mark the modifications of the basic diathesis of the verb and are themselves formally marked on the verb.

See pp. 129, 130, 141, 143, 147, 148, 154, 161, 164, 283*ff*, 296, 298

Weight (of a phrase)

The phrase's length calculated in terms of the number of syllables.

See pp. **210**, 214, 215, 372, 383

WH-word

> Pronoun belonging to one of the four subclasses:
> - interrogative (***Who*** *is this boy?* | ***Where*** *is meat?*)
> - indirect-interrogative (*I know* ***who*** *is this boy.* | *I know* ***where*** *is meat.*)
> - relative (*The hill* ***that*** *we see there is called Sugarloaf.* | *The boy* ***who*** *is reading the book is John.*)
> - pseudo-relative (***Who*** *wants can come.* | *I like* ***what*** *you have bought.*)
>
> See pp. 238, 309, 344, 362, 363

word order: see Chapter 10

——, flexible

> Word order that is more or less independent of the communicative structure and allows for various permutations of wordforms and phrases.
>
> See pp. 124, 145, 147, 164, **337**, 347

wordform

> Segmental sign that is more or less autonomous and not representable in terms of other (previously established) wordforms.
>
> See pp. 10, 36, 43, 48, 64, 108, 126, 325, 330, 344–346

Index of languages

For each language we indicate: family, branch/sub-branch; geographic location.

Acehnese [Austronesian, Malayo-Polynesian; Indonesia, Sumatra] 132, 164, 166, 167

Albanian [Indo-European, Albanian; Albania] 94, 261, 297

Amele [Trans-New Guinea; Papua-New Guinea] 167, 169–171

Ancient Chinese (dead) [Sino-Tibetan, Sinitic; China] 297

Ancient Greek (dead) [Indo-European, Hellenic; Ancient Greece] 65, 71, 181, 272, 273

Arabic [Afro-Asiatic, Semitic; several Arabic-speaking countries] 31, 54, 72, 126, 265, 267, 338

Archi [Nakh-Daghestanian; Russia, Caucasus] 134, 147, 152–155, 173, 174

Armenian [Indo-European, Armenian; Armenia] 294, 296, 305

Awa Pit [Barbacoan; Columbia and Ecuador] 127

Bambara (= Bamana) [Mandé; Mali] 270

Basque [language isolate; Spain and France] 38, 134, 147, 155, 159, 160, 162, 163, 266, 424

Biblical Hebrew (dead) [Afro-Asiatic, Semitic; Ancient Palestine] 128, 181

Bulgarian [Indo-European, Slavic; Bulgaria] 58, 67, 84, 98

Burushaski [language isolate; Pakistan] 266

Catalan [Indo-European, Italic/Romance; Spain] 92, 101

Chichewa [Niger-Congo, Benue-Congo/Bantu; Malawi] 262

Chinese (Mandarin) [Sino-Tibetan, Sinitic; China] 3, 38, 56, 147–149, 181, 201, 289, 290, 297, 298, 300, 302–307, 337, 348

Chukchi [Chukotko-Kamchatkan; Russia, North-Eastern Siberia] 134, 161, 162

Dyirbal [Pama-Nyungan; Australia] 128–130, 134, 154

Enga [Trans-New-Guinea; Papua-New Guinea] 149

English [Indo-European, Germanic; United Kingdom, USA, Canada, Australia, New Zealand] 22, 25, 31, 32, 35–38, 51, 52, 56, 62, 74, 77, 78, 83, 85, 89, 93, 96, 99, 120, 121, 126, 128, 132, 143, 148, 158, 166, 167, 173, 176, 177, 180, 184, 190, 191, 193, 198, 200, 215, 218–221, 244–247, 249, 257, 259, 262, 275, 287, 297, 298, 304, 314, 322, 332, 336, 337, 346, 348, 375

Ewe [Niger-Congo; Ghana] 113

Finnish [Uralic, Finnic; Finland] 65, 102, 103, 133

French [Indo-European, Italic/Romance; France, Switzerland, Belgium, Canada] 31, 32, 34, 50–53, 57, 59–61, 63–66, 70, 71, 74, 75, 77–82, 85, 86, 88, 89, 95, 99, 104, 107, 108, 122, 132, 159, 176, 183, 184, 190, 215, 248, 258, 297, 360, 365

Georgian [Kartvelian; Georgia] 134, 147, 149, 155–159, 176

German [Indo-European, Germanic; Germany, Austria, Switzerland] 31, 32, 49, 52, 54, 66, 81, 83, 96, 99, 103, 105, 108, 159, 176, 198, 259, 297, 325, 343

Hebrew [Afro-Asiatic, Semitic; Israel] 128, 130, 181, 243, 262, 305

Hindi [Indo-European, Indo-Iranian/Indo-Aryan; India] 109, 128, 134, 143, 147, 149–152, 157, 176, 263, 271

Hittite (dead) [Indo-European, Anatolian; Ancient Hittite Empire (Modern Turkey)] 270

Hungarian [Uralic, Ugric; Hungary] 59, 60, 96, 99, 100, 103, 120, 121, 176

Icelandic [Indo-European, Germanic/Scandinavian; Iceland] 167, 168

Ilocano [Austronesian, Malayo-Polynesian; Philippines] 130, 132

Ingrian (= Izhorian) [Uralic, Finnic; Russia] 274
Italian [Indo-European, Italic/Romance; Italy] 66
Kabiyé [Niger-Congo, Atlantic-Congo/Gur; Togo] 270
Kazakh [Turkic; Kazakhstan] 63
Khanty, Western (= Ostyak) [Uralic, Ugric; Russia] 246
Khmer [Austroasiatic; Cambodia] 306, 307
Kinyarwanda [Niger-Congo, Benue-Congo/Bantu; Rwanda] 127, 181
Korean [Koreanic; South Korea, North Korea] 2, 55, 57, 63, 75, 76, 112, 126, 179–194, 196–199, 202–204, 253–255
Lakhota [Siouan; USA] 253–255
Lao [Tai-Kadai; Laos] 306, 307
Latin (dead) [Indo-European, Italic; Ancient Rome] 61, 65, 71, 85, 186, 198, 206, 252, 266, 267, 269, 272, 273, 294, 296
Lezgian [Nakh-Daghestanian; Russia, Caucasus] 38, 128, 134, 135, 141–143, 147, 154, 155
Lushootseed [Salishan; Canada, West Coast] 117, 171–173
Malagasy [Austronesian, Malayo-Polynesian; Madagascar] 126, 130–132, 136, 147, 241
Maori [Austronesian, Malayo-Polynesian; New Zealand] 97
Mohave [Yuman; USA, Arizona] 265
Motu [Austronesian, Malayo-Polynesian; Papua-New Guinea] 292
Navajo [Na-Dené (= Athabaskan); USA] 125
Paamese [Austronesian; Papua-New Guinea] 113
Persian [Indo-European, Indo-Iranian/Iranian; Iran] 55, 143, 170, 193, 199, 256, 266, 273, 320
Polish [Indo-European, Slavic; Poland] 92, 260
Portuguese [Indo-European, Italic/Romance; Portugal and Brazil] 62, 188
Quechua [Quechuan; Perú, Ecuador, Bolivia] 265

Romanian [Indo-European, Italic/Romance; Romania] 54, 67, 130, 294, 305
Russian [Indo-European, Slavic; Russia] 3, 31, 32, 38, 43, 44, 48–51, 53, 54, 56–58, 60, 63, 64, 66–69, 71, 72, 74–80, 82, 84–93, 98, 101, 103, 106–113, 121, 125, 126, 128, 132, 133, 136–140, 159, 166–170, 175–177, 205, 206–212, 215, 216, 220, 226, 230–232, 241, 246, 251, 252, 256–260, 265, 267, 268, 275, 278, 280–284, 309–312, 315, 316, 321, 325, 331, 335–340, 342, 343, 345, 348, 349, 351, 353, 355, 356, 363, 365, 366, 369, 370, 374, 381–385
Russian, Old (dead) [Indo-European, Slavic; Old Russia] 268, 311
Sanskrit (dead) [Indo-European, Indo-Aryan; Ancient India] 181
Sardinian [Indo-European, Italic/Romance; Italy, Sardinia] 82
Serbian [Indo-European, Slavic; Serbia] 53, 57, 97, 101, 198, 344
Seri [language isolate; Mexico, South California] 247, 248
Spanish [Indo-European, Italic/Romance; Spain and Latin America with the exception of Brazil] 31, 49, 54, 57, 58, 62, 79, 90, 95, 97, 101, 106, 125, 130, 168, 188, 305, 326
Swahili [Niger-Congo, Benue-Congo/Bantu; Tanzania, Kenya and several other countries of Eastern Africa] 101, 262, 294, 296
Tagalog [Austronesian, Malayo-Polynesian; Philippines] 100, 132, 143–147, 270
Thai [Tai-Kadai; Thailand] 306, 307
Tongan [Austronesian, Malayo-Polynesian; Tonga] 131, 141, 143, 145–147, 161
Turkish [Turkic; Turkey] 35, 62, 63, 176, 246
Vietnamese [Austroasiatic, Vietic; Vietnam] 147, 148, 264, 306, 307, 348
Warlpiri [Pama-Nyungan; Australia] 134, 162
Yaqui [Uto-Aztecan; Mexico] 247, 248
Yimas [Sepik; Papua-New Guinea] 155
Yukaghir, Kolyma [Yukaghiric; Russia, Eastern Siberia] 190, 246

Index of semantic and lexical units

APPLAUD₍ᵥ₎ — p. 25

BĂ ≈ 'as for', Mandarin Chinese — a preposition that introduces a fronted affected direct object — pp. 302, 305, 306

BÈI 'undergo', Mandarin Chinese — a structural (= auxiliary) verb that introduces a clause — pp. 298–303

'cause1' — the semanteme of involuntary causation ('be the cause') — p. 16

'cause2' — the semanteme of voluntary causation ('be the causer') — p. 16

COMME 'as — like', French — p. 248

⌜ČEM – TEM⌝ 'the – the', Russian — pp. 281–284

⌜ČËRT ZNAET GDE⌝ — 'devil knows where', Russian — pp. 311, 313, 315–318

⌜ČËRT ZNAET KTO⌝ — 'devil knows who', Russian — pp. 312, 314, 316, 318, 328

⌜ČËRT ZNAET SKOL'KO⌝, Russian — 'devil knows how much/many' — pp. 313, 314

ČTO¹ 'that⁵', Russian — an unvariable semantically empty complementizer (subordinating conjunction) that introduces a completive clause — pp. 102, 138, 241, 280, 350

ČTO² ≈ 'which', Russian — nominal relative pronoun — pp. 278, 280

DER¹, DER², German — p. 260

«DERISION», English — p. 37

DOUBT₍ᵥ₎ — p. 20

ESLI – TO 'if – then', Russian — pp. 275–280, 285, 286

ÈTO 'this', Russian — presentative particle — pp. 75, 116

FLOW₍ₙ₎ — pp. 15–17

IT⁶ — empty (= dummy) IT, as in *It is John who left early.* — p. 253

LJUBIMYJ 'favorite', Russian — pp. 221, 228

NE STOL'KO – SKOL'KO — 'not so.much, but.rather', Russian — pp. 279, 282, 284

NO 'but', Russian — pp. 283, 256

'set_and' — semanteme representing logical conjunction — p. 12

SUCH ... THAT ... — p. 248

SURE — pp. 20–22

-TE (in čërt-te), Russian — particle, an abbreviation of *tebe* 'to.you', used as a Dativus Eticus — pp. 319, 321

THAT¹ — demonstrative adjectival pronoun, as in *that decision*, *those decisions* — p. 239

THAT² — demonstrative substitute nominal pronoun, as in *Those who want to go must sign up tomorrow* — p. 239

THAT³ — relative nominal pronoun, as in *a decision that was made in a hurry* — pp. 239, 244, 248, 249

THAT⁴ — degree adverb, as in *not that intelligent*

THAT⁵ — empty subordinating conjunction, i.e. complementizer, as in *It meant that the interest in me was aroused.* — pp. 239, 248

'«they»' — semanteme of the indefinite personal pronoun, equivalent to Fr. ON and Ger. MAN — pp. 49, 57, 137, 191, 256, 309, 316, 324, 329, 352

TO¹, Russian — component of several Russian repeated conjunctions — pp. 275, 279

TO², Russian — empty particle that is the second (optional) component of several binary conjunctions: ESLI ..., TO² ... 'if ..., then ...', KOGDA ..., TO² ... 'when ..., then ...', etc. — pp. 275–277, 279–283, 286

TOT1 'that [*tree*]', Russian — adjectival demonstrative pronoun, as in *tot dom, gde on rotilsja* 'that house where he was.born'

TOT11.1 ≈ 'that.one', Russian — nominal correlative pronoun, as in *Tot, kto ustal, možet otdoxnut'* lit. 'That.one who is.tired can take.a.rest', which has all morphological forms and governs a relative clause — pp. 90, 108, 179, 180

TOT11.2 ≈ 'the.fact', Russian — nominal correlative pronoun—a nominalizer, as in *To, čto on ušël, udivilo menja* lit. 'That that he left amazed me'. TOT11.2 has only neuter singular forms and governs a completive clause — pp. 90, 107, 108, 252, 280

U 'at', Russian — preposition widely used to introduce oblique objects and circumstantials of a very general meaning, as in *U Ivana slučilos' nesčast'e* lit. 'At Ivan happened accident' — p. 84

Ø$_{(3, pl)}^{PEOPLE}$ — zero lexeme that expresses the meaning 'indeterminate people' (≈ '«they»') — p. 49

Ø$_{(3, sg, neu)}^{METEO}$ — zero lexeme that expresses the meaning 'elements/forces of nature' — p. 49

www.ingramcontent.com/pod-product-compliance
Lightning Source LLC
Chambersburg PA
CBHW030515230426
43665CB00010B/623